ROUTLEDGE HANDBOOK ON INFORMATION TECHNOLOGY IN GOVERNMENT

The explosive growth in information technology has ushered in unparalleled new opportunities for advancing public service. Featuring 24 chapters from foremost experts in the field of digital government, this Handbook provides an authoritative survey of key emerging technologies, their current state of development and use in government, and insightful discussions on how they are reshaping and influencing the future of public administration. This Handbook explores:

- Key emerging technologies (i.e., big data, social media, Internet of Things (IOT), GIS, smartphones, and mobile technologies) and their impacts on public administration
- The impacts of the new technologies on the relationships between citizens and their governments with the focus on collaborative governance
- Key theories of IT innovations in government on the interplay between technological innovations and public administration
- The relationship between technology and democratic accountability and the various ways of harnessing the new technologies to advance public value
- Key strategies and conditions for fostering success in leveraging technological innovations for public service

This Handbook will prove to be an invaluable guide and resource for students, scholars, and practitioners interested in this growing field of technological innovations in government.

Yu-Che Chen is the director of the Global Digital Governance Lab and associate professor of digital governance in the School of Public Administration at the University of Nebraska at Omaha. His current research interests are collaborative digital governance, big data analytics, cyberinfrastructure, smart city, and digital government performance.

Michael J. Ahn is an assistant professor of public policy and public affairs in UMass Boston's McCormack Graduate School of Policy and Global Studies. His research interests include digital government, technological innovations in government, public policy communication, and public affairs education. Michael's current research projects on digital government focus on topics such as civic technology, smart city, technology-enabled government call centers, social media use in government, and the effectiveness of IT training in public administration programs.

'IT remains underemphasized in government. Finally, an invaluable source taking a comprehensive view on this topic. Governments are information intensive by nature. This book contains amazing insights from theory, stories and cases. IT is at the very heart of government functioning. Advancing this requires combining theoretical and practical insights which are covered in this book.'

—**Marijn Janssen,** *Delft University of Technology*

ROUTLEDGE HANDBOOK ON INFORMATION TECHNOLOGY IN GOVERNMENT

Edited by Yu-Che Chen and Michael J. Ahn

NEW YORK AND LONDON

First published 2017
by Routledge
711 Third Avenue, New York, NY 10017

and by Routledge
2 Park Square, Milton Park, Abingdon, Oxon, OX14 4RN

Routledge is an imprint of the Taylor & Francis Group, an informa business

© 2017 Taylor & Francis

The right of Yu-Che Chen and Michael J. Ahn to be identified as the author[/s] of the editorial material, and of the authors for their individual chapters, has been asserted in accordance with sections 77 and 78 of the Copyright, Designs and Patents Act 1988.

All rights reserved. No part of this book may be reprinted or reproduced or utilised in any form or by any electronic, mechanical, or other means, now known or hereafter invented, including photocopying and recording, or in any information storage or retrieval system, without permission in writing from the publishers.

Trademark notice: Product or corporate names may be trademarks or registered trademarks, and are used only for identification and explanation without intent to infringe.

Library of Congress Cataloging-in-Publication Data
A catalog record for this book has been requested

ISBN: 978-1-138-92567-0 (hbk)
ISBN: 978-1-315-68364-5 (ebk)

Typeset in Bembo
by Apex CoVantage, LLC

CONTENTS

List of Tables   *viii*
List of Figures   *x*
Contributors   *xii*
Acknowledgments   *xix*

Introduction   1

1. The Promises and Opportunities of Information Technology in Government   3
   Yu-Che Chen and Michael J. Ahn

SECTION I
Theories of Information Technology (IT) Innovations in Government   9

2. Transforming Government Services over Time: Meanings, Impacts, and Implications for Citizen-Government Relationships   11
   Miriam B. Lips

3. Information Policies: Value-Oriented, Instrumental, and Managerial Choices for Governing an Information Society   27
   Sharon S. Dawes

4. An Integrative Framework for Effective Use of Information and Communication Technologies (ICTs) for Collaborative Public Service Networks   49
   Yu-Che Chen

5. Using System Dynamics for the Analysis of Complex Social Problems and Public Policy Alternatives: Fundamentals and Recommendations   71
   Luis F. Luna-Reyes, J. Ramon Gil-Garcia, Eliot Rich, and David F. Andersen

SECTION II
## Emerging Technologies and Their Applications for Government	93

6 Big Data and Local Performance Management: The Experience of Kansas City, Missouri	95
Alfred Tat-Kei Ho, Kate Bender, Julie Steenson, and Eric Roche

7 Mobile Location-Based Service (LBS) Apps for the Public Sector: Prospects and Challenges	108
Sukumar Ganapati

8 Internet of Things for Public Service: Innovative Practice in China	124
Jian-Chuan Zhang, Xiao Zhang, and Zhicheng Wang

9 Big Data Analysis on Public Opinion: A Case Study on the Policy Formation of Free Economic Pilot Zones in Taiwan	137
Hsien-Lee Tseng, Pin-Yu Chu, and Tong-Yi Huang

SECTION III
## Technology-Enabled Cross-Boundary Collaboration and Governance	151

10 E-Government and Citizen Trust in Government: The Role of Citizen Characteristics in the Relationship between E-Government Use and Citizen Trust in Government	153
Seung-Hwan Myeong and Michael J. Ahn

11 Social Media Communication Modes in Government	168
Ines Mergel

12 Resident-Government Engagement via New Technologies	180
Georgette Dumont

13 Civic Hacking: Citizens Creating New Digital Government Interfaces	196
Lora Frecks

SECTION IV
## Advancement of Democratic Accountability and Public Values	217

14 Catching On and Catching Up: Developments and Challenges in E-Participation in Major U.S. Cities	219
Karen Mossberger, Yonghong Wu, and Benedict S. Jimenez

15 Navigating the Open Government Comfort Zone for the Effective Use of Open Data	239
Younhee Kim

16	Technology, Transparency, and Local Government: Assessing the Opportunities and Challenges *Gregory A. Porumbescu, Peter Schaak, and Erica Ceka*	252
17	Protection of Personally Identifiable Information in Government: A Survey of U.S. Regulatory Framework and Emerging Technological Challenges *Anna Ya Ni*	266
18	An Exploratory Study of E-Participation Technology Adoption by Citizens *Jooho Lee*	284

SECTION V
Advancement of Public Service through Technological Innovations — 301

19	Providing Critical Emergency Communications via Social Media Platforms: Multiple Case Study *DeeDee Bennett*	303
20	An Analysis of Main Attributes for Governance in Smart Cities *Manuel Pedro Rodríguez Bolívar*	326
21	Cyberinfrastructure for Collaborative Scientific Networks: Institutional Design and Management Strategies *Yu-Che Chen and Rich Knepper*	341
22	E-Government in China *Nan Zhang and Xuejiao Zhao*	362
23	Critical Factors Behind Korean E-Government Success: A Conversation with the Chairman of Korea's Presidential Special Committee of E-Government *Michael J. Ahn*	380
24	Conclusion: The Future of Information Technology and Government *Michael J. Ahn and Yu-Che Chen*	391

Index — *394*

TABLES

2.1	Impact of Government Service Transformation Concepts	23
3.1	Selected U.S. Information Policy Statutes and Related Actions	30
3.2	Selected Executive Directives and OMB Guidance on Information Policy Topics	32
3.3	Basic Privacy Principles (adapted from OECD 2013)	41
5.1	Definition of Causal Relationships (adapted from Luna-Reyes 2008)	75
5.2	Definition of Causal Relationships (adapted from Luna-Reyes 2008)	75
5.3	Representative System Dynamics Work in Policy Domains (based on Andersen, Rich, and Macdonald 2009)	79
5.4	Steps for Analyzing Public Policies and System Dynamics (Gil-Garcia 2014)	81
6.1	Distribution of "Broken Window" Nuisance Complaints, Semi-annually and by Percentiles	102
8.1	Unique Features of IoT	127
8.2	IoT Cases and the Relevant Public Value	129
9.1	Keywords of the Big Data Analysis on Free Economic Pilot Zones in Taiwan	142
9.2	Example of Content Analysis from News	144
9.3	Reply Distribution of Frames and Channels	145
10.1	Measurement Instruments for Variables	159
10.2	Results of Analysis	160
10.3	Modes of Information Search	161
10.4	Correlation between Familiarity with E-Government and Productive Info Search	162
10.5	Correlations between Medium of Communication	163
12.1	Accessing 630-CITY	186
12.2	630-CITY 2015 Eight-Month Breakdown with MyJax App Data	187
12.3	630-CITY Telephone Requests Summary	187
12.4	630-CITY Call Volume	188
14.1	Comparison by Category between 2009 and 2011	223
14.2	Interactive Tools Utilized in Websites of 75 Largest U.S. Cities—Comparison between 2009 and 2011	223
14.3	Interactive Tools Utilized in Websites of 75 Largest U.S. Cities—Comparison between 2009 and 2011	224
14.4	Change in Weighted Interactivity Score in 2009–2011	227

14.5	Pearson Correlation	229
14.6	Descriptive Statistics	233
14.7	Statistical Results	234
15.1	Open Government Paths	241
15.2	Principles of Open Government Directive with Examples	243
15.3	Open Data Initiatives Projects in Federal Agencies	247
17.1	Mapping of Privacy Issues to E-Government Services	273
18.1	Demographics of Survey Respondents and Adopters of E-Participation Technologies	289
18.2	Types of E-Government Service, Survey Items, Percentage of Adoption, and Variance	291
18.3	Probit Models of E-Participation Technology Adoption	293
19.1	Select Research On Social Media Sites For Emergency Communications	307
19.2	Types of Information Distributed on Twitter and YouTube from Case II	312
19.3	Types of Information Distributed on Twitter and Facebook from Case III	314
19.4	Types of Information Distributed on Twitter, Facebook, and YouTube from Case IV	315
19.5	The Different Employees Responsible for Sending Out Messages during Emergencies and Non-emergencies	318
19.6	The Different Uses of Social Media Platforms per Case across the Life Cycle of Disasters	319
19.7	Overview of Each Case	320
20.1	Dimensions, Codes, and Categories of Governance Models	328
20.2	Questionnaire Design	330
22.1	The Three Components of the E-Government Development Index (EGDI), China, 2003–2014	364
22.2	Leading Indicators of 2015 Evaluation Report of Chinese Government Websites	365
22.3	2015 Rankings of Provincial Government Websites in China	366
22.4	2015 Rankings of Government Websites at the City Level in China	366
22.5	Top Ten E-Government Issues in China	370

FIGURES

3.1	Records and Information Life Cycle, Library and Archives Canada	35
3.2	Information Policy Purposes	38
4.1	An Integrative Conceptual Framework for Managing an ICT-Enabled Collaborative Public Management Network	52
5.1	The System Dynamics Modeling Process (adapted from Luna-Reyes and Andersen 2003)	73
5.2	Common Patterns of Problem Behavior (adapted from Luna-Reyes 2008)	74
5.3	Stock-and-Flow Diagram (adapted from Luna-Reyes 2008)	76
5.4	Feedback Loops in a Stock-and-Flow Diagram (adapted from Luna-Reyes 2008)	76
5.5	Managers Clustering Dynamic Behaviors of Key Variables	81
5.6	Major Stocks and Feedback Loops in the CoastalProtectSim Simulator (adapted from Najaf Abadi et al. 2015)	83
5.7	Total Job-Finding Flows from TANF (Base vs. Middle vs. Edges Policy Packages). Adapted from Richardson, Andersen, and Luna-Reyes (2015)	84
5.8	Total Recidivism Flows Back to TANF (Base vs. Middle vs. Edges Policy Packages). Adapted from Richardson, Andersen, and Luna-Reyes (2015)	84
6.1	Mapping Citizen Satisfaction and Service Complaint Data Spatially	100
6.2	Distribution of Broken Window Cases over Time, by Caseload Percentiles in the First Six Months of 2010	102
9.1	A Framework for Using Big Data to Extract Intelligence Online	139
9.2	Examples of Content Analysis from News	144
9.3	Trends of Positive and Negative Sentiment Discussion about the Free Economic Pilot Zones Online	146
10.1	Theoretical Framework	156
11.1	Volume and Frequency of Social Media Interactions by Type of Government Function	173
11.2	Social Media Modes between Government and Citizens	175
11.3	Screenshot http://analytics.usa.gov taken on July 14, 2015	177
12.1	630-CITY Request Process	191
13.1	A Timeline of Events Enabling Civic Hacking	197
18.1	Conceptual Model of E-Participation Technology Adoption	286
19.1	Other Methods FEMA Alert Authorities Used to Disseminate Public Alerts	304

19.2	Shift in the Model for Disseminating Public Alerts and Warnings. Traditional model adapted from Rodríguez et al. (2007)	305
19.3	Social Media Daily Post Frequency for Case I	312
19.4	Social Media Daily Post Frequency for Case II	313
19.5	Social Media Daily Post Frequency for Case III	315
19.6	Daily Social Media Posts for EMA12 on Both Facebook and Twitter	317
20.1	Relevance of Dimensions According to Their Presence into Prior Research (Theoretical Studies, Empirical Studies, and Total Prior Research)	332
20.2	Relevance of Categories in Each Analyzed Dimensions in Prior Research	334
20.3	Relevance of Categories in Each Analyzed Dimensions in Practitioners' Perceptions versus Prior Research	336
21.1	A Conceptual Framework for a Distributed Public Management Network for Cyberinfrastructure	345
22.1	E-Government Development Index (EGDI), 2003–2014	363
22.2	China's Rankings on E-Government Development Index (EGDI), 2003–2014	364
22.3	Diffusion Status Framework	368

CONTRIBUTORS

Michael J. Ahn is an assistant professor of public policy and public affairs in UMass Boston's McCormack Graduate School of Policy and Global Studies. His research interests include digital government, technological innovations in government, public policy communication, and public affairs education. Michael's current research projects on digital government focus on topics such as civic technology, smart city, technology-enabled government call centers, social media use in government, and the effectiveness of IT training in public administration programs. His articles have appeared in journals, such as *Public Administration Review*, *American Review of Public Administration*, and *Government Information Quarterly*, and he has published internationally in the U.S., Korea, and Japan. Ahn has served as the president of American Society for Public Administration-Massachusetts Chapter and the Northeast Conference on Public Administration (NECoPA) and currently serves as a District 1 Representative for ASPA's national council representing NY, CT, and the New England states.

David F. Andersen is an O'Leary and Distinguished Service Professor of Public Administration, Public Policy, and Information Science at Rockefeller College, University at Albany. His work centers on applying system dynamics, systems thinking, and information technology approaches to problems in the public, not-for-profit, and private sectors, especially using group modeling approaches. He has served as a technical consultant to public and not-for-profit agencies in the federal, state, and local sectors as well as corporate clients in North America and Europe. Most recently, he has been working on information standards for bringing sustainable, fair labor, and environmentally friendly products to market in the NAFTA region as part of his Carlos Rico Fulbright Award for 2010–2011.

Kate Bender is the deputy performance officer of the Office of the City Manager, Kansas City, Missouri. In 2016, the Center for Accountability and Performance Management of the American Society for Public Information presented its first Emerging Leaders award to her and Julie Steenson in recognition of their work in implementing performance management systems and innovative new practices, and for efforts to promote the importance of performance and accountability. Kate Bender received her master of urban planning from New York University and was a L.P. Cookingham Management Fellow of Kansas City.

DeeDee Bennett is an assistant professor in the Emergency Services Program within the School of Public Administration at University of Nebraska at Omaha. Her research focuses on the intersection of emergency management, advanced communications, and socially vulnerable populations. She has authored in several places including journals, textbooks, federal research reports, practitioner briefs, and conference proceedings. Dr. Bennett received her B.S. in electrical engineering, her M.S. in public policy from the Georgia Institute of Technology, and her Ph.D. from Oklahoma State University's Political Science Department in Fire and Emergency Management Administration. She is a member of IAEM, IEEE, and ASPA.

Manuel Pedro Rodríguez Bolívar is an associate professor at the University of Granada. His research interest is mainly focused on e-government. He has authored numerous articles in JCR journals, including *Public Money & Management, Government Information Quarterly, Public Administration and Development, Online Information Review, International Review of Administrative Sciences, American Review of Public Administration, ABACUS, Local Government Studies,* and *Administration & Society.* He has also been the author of several book chapters published by Kluwer Academic Publishers, Routledge, Springer, Taylor and Francis, and IGI Global, and he is an international reviewer and an associate editor of SSCI journals and books.

Erica Ceka is a research assistant and a Ph.D. student of public administration at Northern Illinois University. Her main research focus is on fiscal decentralization in developing countries and intergovernmental relationships. Other research interests include public budgeting, transparency, and nonprofit management. Originally from Moldova, Ms. Ceka received her master's degree in public administration at NIU as a fellow of the Muskie Program, funded by the U.S. Department of State. Prior to her studies at NIU, Ms. Ceka worked in international development, serving as a country representative for Caritas Czech Republic, an international nongovernmental organization.

Yu-Che Chen, Ph.D. & MPA, is associate professor of digital governance and director of the Global Digital Governance Lab in the School of Public Administration at University of Nebraska at Omaha. His research and teaching interests are digital governance, e-government, cross-boundary collaboration, smart city, open data, and big data. He has published one co-edited book and more than 30 journal articles, book chapters, and management reports in the areas of e-government and digital governance. He serves in national and international associations with the focus on information technology and digital government. He has received teaching and service awards.

Pin-Yu Chu received her Ph.D. in the Department of Engineering-Economic System, Stanford University. She is currently the director of the Taiwan E-Government Research Center and a distinguished professor of the Department of Public Administration, National Chengchi University. Her recent research includes electronic governance and technology management.

Sharon S. Dawes is senior fellow at the Center for Technology in Government and professor emerita of public administration and policy at the University at Albany/SUNY. Her research focuses on government information strategy and management with emphasis on information quality and use.

Georgette Dumont is currently an assistant professor in the University of North Florida's Department of Political Science and Public Administration, where she teaches public and nonprofit management. She conducts research on how public and nonprofit organizations utilize technology to promote transparency, accountability, and citizen engagement. Dr. Dumont has presented the results of her research nationally and has published in journals such as *American Review of Public Administration, Public Administration Quarterly,* and *Nonprofit and Voluntary Sector Quarterly.*

Contributors

Lora Frecks is a public administration doctoral student at the University of Nebraska at Omaha. Before returning to school, she managed the intellectual property portfolio of a public medical research university. Continuing her work with innovators and inventions, she volunteers with other civic hackers in Nebraska and serves as the treasurer for the American Society of Public Administration's (ASPA) Section for Science & Technology in Government (SSTIG). Her current research focuses on community members' coproduction of services and policy with governments and nonprofits. She can be found online at frecks.info.

Sukumar Ganapati is an associate professor of public administration and the director of the Ph.D. program in public affairs at Florida International University in Miami. His main research interests are in the use of information technology applications in the public sector and the role of institutions in housing and economic development. He has published reports on use of GIS, dashboards, and mobile apps with the IBM Center of Business of Government.

J. Ramon Gil-Garcia is an associate professor of public administration and the research director of the Center for Technology in Government, University at Albany, SUNY. Dr. Gil-Garcia is a member of the Mexican National Research System and the Mexican Academy of Sciences. In 2009, he was considered the most prolific author in the field of digital government research worldwide, and in 2013 he was selected for the Research Award to outstanding young researchers by the Mexican Academy of Sciences. He has published in prestigious international journals in public administration, information systems, and digital government. His research interests include collaborative electronic government, interorganizational information integration, smart cities and smart governments, adoption and implementation of emergent technologies, digital divide policies, new public management, and multi-method research approaches.

Alfred Tat-Kei Ho is a professor in the School of Public Affairs and Administration at the University of Kansas. His research focuses on performance management, public budgeting and finance, e-government, and citizen participation. He has received funding support from various entities, including the Alfred P. Sloan Foundation, the William Kemper Foundation, and the Asian Development Bank, to conduct engaged research. His previous clients include the city governments of Indianapolis (Indiana), Tulsa (Oklahoma), Kansas City (Missouri), and Des Moines (Iowa) and the provincial governments of Guangdong (China) and Henan (China).

Tong-Yi Huang received his Ph.D. in government from the University of Texas at Austin. He is currently the professor and department chair of the Department of Public Administration, National Chengchi University. His recent research includes e-democracy, deliberative democracy, and public policy.

Benedict S. Jimenez is associate professor at Northeastern University in Boston. His research focuses on urban public finance and management. He is the recipient of the 2013 Paul A. Volcker Junior Scholar Award and the 2014 Clarence N. Stone Early Career Scholar Award from the American Political Science Association. His research has been published in *Public Administration Review*, *American Review of Public Administration*, *International Public Management Journal*, *Urban Affairs Review*, and the *Journal of Public Administration Research and Theory*, among others.

Younhee Kim is an associate professor in the School of Public Affairs at Penn State Harrisburg. Her research interests are in the broad areas of public and performance management, focusing on performance measurement, public entrepreneurship, organizational development, and information technology management. Her recent work has appeared in numerous journals, including *International*

Journal of Health Planning and Management, Public Performance & Management Review, Public Money & Management, Journal of Technology Transfer, and *Administration & Society*.

Rich Knepper is a Ph.D. candidate in social informatics at the Indiana University School of Informatics and Computing, studying cyberinfrastructure and science policy. His current research centers on the usage and management of science cyberinfrastructure and the tension between traditional high-performance resources and usage and efforts to broaden computational support of diverse researchers and domains. He also works for Indiana University's Research Technologies division, where he manages a team providing support for researchers using IU's cyberinfrastructure resources.

Jooho Lee is an associate professor at the School of Public Administration and an associate director of Global Digital Governance Lab at University of Nebraska at Omaha. He has been doing research on the antecedents and consequences of information and communication technology adoption by public organizations and citizen/business users. He earned his Ph.D. in public administration from the Maxwell School of Citizenship and Public Affairs at Syracuse University.

Miriam B. Lips is the chair in digital government at Victoria University of Wellington's School of Government, where she leads and undertakes a five-year research program on "Government and Democracy in the Digital Age" in partnership with several New Zealand government agencies. She currently is a member of the New Zealand Data Futures Partnership, an independent working group appointed by the New Zealand Government. Professor Lips has published widely in her field, including nine books and many publications in leading international journals. She is editor-in-chief of the journal *Information Polity: Government and Democracy in the Information Age* (IOS Press).

Luis F. Luna-Reyes is an associate professor of public administration at the University at Albany in Albany, NY. He holds a Ph.D. in information science from the University at Albany, and he is a member of the Mexican National Research System. His research interests are related to areas such as collaborative governance, information sharing, success of government-wide websites, simulation, policy informatics, and information policy. He is the author or co-author of articles published in the *Government Information Quarterly*, *European Journal of Information Systems*, *Information Polity*, *Gestión y Política Pública*, and *System Dynamics Review*, among others.

Ines Mergel is a full professor of public administration at the University of Konstanz, Germany. She teaches and conducts research on digital innovations in the public sector. She is especially interested in nontraditional approaches to innovation management and new technology. Professor Mergel received a doctor of business administration degree from the University of St. Gallen, Switzerland, and spent six years as a visiting researcher at the National Center for Digital Government and the Program on Networked Governance at Harvard's Kennedy School of Government. From 2008 to 2016, Dr. Mergel served as a faculty member at Syracuse University's Maxwell School of Citizenship and Public Affairs.

Karen Mossberger is a professor and director of the School of Public Affairs at Arizona State University. Her research includes digital government, digital inclusion, evaluation of broadband use, local government, and urban policy. Her most recent book is *Digital Cities: The Internet and the Geography of Opportunity* (Mossberger, Tolbert, and Franko 2013, Oxford University Press), and she recently completed an evaluation of Chicago's Smart Communities Program funded by the MacArthur Foundation and an NSF repository with state, county, metro, and city data on Internet use from 1997 to 2014. The repository fills a gap in subnational data prior to the 2013 ACS. Her co-authored article on e-government and citizen trust and confidence in government (Tolbert and Mossberger 2006) was named as one of the 75 most influential articles for the seventy-fifth anniversary of *Public Administration Review*.

Seung-Hwan Myeong is a professor in the Department of Public Administration, Inha University (Incheon, Korea). He received his Ph.D. from Syracuse University in 1996. His research interests are in electronic government and e-governance, information management in public organizations, and information and communication policy. He currently serves as president of the Korean Association for Policy Analysis and Evaluation (KAPAE) as head director of the Global e-Governance Institute (GeGRI), and is a member of board of directors in Korea Customs UNI-PASS Association. His publications include *Electronic Government* (2006), *Information Society and Modern Organization* (2004), *Effects of IT on Policy Decision-Making Processes: Some Evidences Beyond Rhetoric* (2009), *An Exploratory Study on the Relationship among Talent Characteristics, Information Capability, and Social Network* (2011), *Factors Influencing on Information Use Behavior of Different Generations* (2012), *Smart E-Governance* (2015), and *Which Type of Social Capital Matters for Building Trust in Government?* (2016). His work appeared in *Administration and Society*, *Korean Journal of Information Policy*, *Government Information Quarterly*, *Sustainability*, and others.

Anna Ya Ni is an associate professor of public administration at California State University, San Bernardino. She was a visiting scholar of the Institute of Governance at KU Leuven in 2015. She received an LL.B. from the University of International Relations in China, an M.S. and an M.P.A. from Iowa State University, and a Ph.D. of public administration from Syracuse University. Her research interests center on information assurance, innovation adoption, outsourcing, public–private partnerships, and organizational effectiveness.

Gregory A. Porumbescu is an assistant professor and received his Ph.D. from the Graduate School of Public Administration at Seoul National University in 2013. His research interests primarily relate to public sector applications of information and communications technology, transparency and accountability, and citizens' perceptions of public service provision. Dr. Porumbescu's work has appeared in *The Journal of Public Administration Research and Theory*, *Public Administration Review*, *American Review of Public Administration*, and *Public Performance and Management Review*.

Eliot Rich is an associate professor in the Department of Information Technology and Management, School of Business, University at Albany, State University of New York. His research includes applications of modeling and simulation to problems of sustainability, information security, critical infrastructures, organizational change, innovation, and knowledge management. He holds an M.P.P. from Harvard University, and he earned his Ph.D. in information science from the University at Albany.

Eric Roche is the chief data officer and performance management analyst of the Office of the City Manager, Kansas City, Missouri. He is responsible for the Open Data platform of Kansas City and uses data to uncover relationships, communicate ideas, and improve public program performance. He received his master of public administration from the University of Kansas and was an L.P. Cookingham-Noll Management Fellow of Kansas City.

Peter Schaak is the director of information technology for the Village of Schaumburg (Illinois). He holds a bachelor's degree in finance from Northeastern Illinois University and a master's degree in business administration from DePaul University. Originally from Chicago, Illinois, Peter has over 15 years of information technology experience, with the last 8 years in the public sector.

Contributors

Julie Steenson is the deputy performance officer of the Office of the City Manager, Kansas City, Missouri. In 2016, she and Kate Bender jointly received the first Emerging Leaders award by the Center for Accountability and Performance Management of the American Society of Public Administration for their innovative work in performance management and citizen engagement. Julie Steenson received her master of public administration from Indiana University (Bloomington) and was an L.P. Cookingham Management Fellow of Kansas City.

Hsien-Lee Tseng received his Ph.D. from the Institute of Public Affairs Management at National Sun Yat-Sen University. He is currently the project manager of the Taiwan E-Government Research Center. His recent research includes electronic governance and public policy.

Zhicheng Wang is a senior engineer in the Electronic Technology Information Research Institute, Ministry of Industry and Information Technology of the People's Republic of China. Dr. Wang received his Ph.D. in microelectronics from the Institute of Semiconductors, Chinese Academy of Sciences. His current research projects focus on information technology policies such big data and the Internet of Things. He has published more than 10 journal articles, book chapters, and management reports. His research can be found in scholarly journals such as *Chinese Physics Letters* and *Physical Review*.

Yonghong Wu is an associate professor in the Department of Public Administration at the University of Illinois at Chicago. He received a Ph.D. in public administration from the Maxwell School of Syracuse University. His fields of specialization include state and local public finance, and technology policy. Much of his recent research focuses on e-government issues, particularly on how the Internet and Web 2.0 technologies facilitate civic engagement through more effective information dissemination and interactive communication. He has worked with Dr. Mossberger on several projects on local e-civic engagement. Dr. Wu co-authored with Dr. Mossberger a recent report, *Civic Engagement and Local E-Government: Social Networking Comes of Age*, which has received a great deal of publicity and media attention in the U.S. He also co-authored a book chapter, "Municipal Government and the Interactive Web: Trends and Issues for Civic Engagement" in *E-Governance and Civic Engagement: Factors and Determinants of E-Democracy* published by IGI Global in 2011, and an article "Connecting Citizens and Local Governments? Social Media and Interactivity in Major U.S. Cities" in *Government Information Quarterly* in 2013.

Jian-Chuan Zhang is research fellow in the Academy of Public Policy at Renmin University of China. Dr. Zhang received his M.A. in Public Management from Renmin University of China and his Ph.D. in public administration from Northern Illinois University. His current research projects focus on international and comparative e-governance, e-government performance management, smart city, and Internet governance. He has published more than 20 journal articles, book chapters, and management reports. His research can be found in scholarly journals such as the *Chinese Journal of Communication*, *International Journal of Public Administration in the Digital Age*, *Electronic Government, an International Journal*, and *China Internet*.

Nan Zhang is an associate professor at the School of Public Policy and Management, Tsinghua University. His research interests focus on electronic government and online governance, theories and practices of smart cities, big data, and policy informatics, among others. Dr. Zhang's works have appeared in several international journals including *Computer in Human Behavior*, *Electronic Commerce Research*, *Electronic Markets*, *Information Processing and Management*, *Information Systems Frontiers*, *International Journal of Mobile Communications*, *Journal of Global Information Management*, and *Online Information Review*.

Contributors

Xiao Zhang is a Ph.D. candidate in public policy in Beijing Normal University. She received her M.A. in public policy from Renmin University of China. She has served in the State Council Informatization Office and the Ministry of Industry and Information Technology of the People's Republic of China. Xiao has been assigned to the World Bank and OECD as Chinese informatization policies expert. She has long engaged in digital policy making and digital development promotion and is actively involved in cooperating with international organizations in the digital economy.

Xuejiao Zhao is a post doctor in the School of Public Policy and Management at Tsinghua University, China. Her research interests include e-government, comparative politics and policy, and corruption.

ACKNOWLEDGMENTS

The editors are grateful for the generous assistance and support of their publisher, colleagues, and families. Natalja Mortensen, senior editor at Routledge, has been a champion of our book project while providing assistance and guidance throughout our Handbook preparation. We would also like to recognize Lillian Rand and other team members at Routledge for their timely and quality assistance.

The editors would like to recognize the members of the Editorial Advisory Board for their support of the Handbook. These members include Miriam Lips, Chris Reddick, Lei Zheng, Marijn Janssen, Sharon Dawes, Tong-Yi Huang, Jane Fountain, Stefaan Verhulst, Greta Nasi, Taewoo Nam, Younhee Kim, and Seung-Hwan Myeong. All board members have provided insights into relevant topics, as well as manuscript review services. They have our gratitude. Among the board members, we would like to express our particular thanks to Sharon Dawes for seeing the potential and promise of the Handbook and encouraging us along the way.

We acknowledge the contributions of our colleagues in the field of information technology for public service. These colleagues are mostly contributors of Handbook chapters, and whose expertise and dedication have been instrumental to its quality. They volunteered their time to provide review comments on the works of their colleagues, and this service has helped improve the quality of chapters in the Handbook. In addition, our colleagues at the Section on Science and Technology in Government in the American Society for Public Administration are a source of inspiration and support.

Moreover, Chen would like to express his gratitude for Michael Ahn's efforts as co-editor. Michael has been a source of insight, inspiration, and fellowship. Chen would also like to thank his colleagues at the School of Public Administration and the College of Public Affairs and Community Service for providing such a nurturing work environment. Likewise, Ahn would like to express his sincere gratitude to his co-editor Yu-Che Chen, who has guided him through this project with vision, persistence, and unmatched kindness that is distinctively Yu-Che Chen. Ahn also would like to thank his friends and colleagues at the McCormack Graduate School of Policy and Global Studies and the Massachusetts Chapter of the American Society for Public Administration for their support, encouragement, and fellowship.

Chen would like to express his gratitude for his family. His parents taught him the privilege of being an educator, pursuit of excellence, and kindness to others. Their love and support laid the foundation for his career as an educator/scholar. His elder brother has supported him in his pursuit in academia in the U.S. by encouraging him and shouldering most of the responsibility of caring for their parents. Moreover, he is grateful for his wife, Li-Fen Lu, for seeing his potential and supporting this particular book project. His son, Wesley Chen, has been an incredible source of joy. Wesley also completed a co-edited book project with his friend as a first grader.

Ahn would like to thank his parents for their endless support and love, especially his father, Dr. Moon-Suk Ahn, who, as a public administration scholar himself in Korea, has been a source of inspiration and vision of what e-government should be and how it can improve the lives of many. Ahn would like to thank his wife, Hyunseok (Cori) Lee, for her loving support and encouragement throughout the book project and his three young children, Francesca, Elizabeth, and William, who are his endless source of joy and gratitude.

Introduction

1
THE PROMISES AND OPPORTUNITIES OF INFORMATION TECHNOLOGY IN GOVERNMENT

Yu-Che Chen and Michael J. Ahn

This introductory chapter aims to depict the state of our knowledge in the field of technological innovation in government by providing an overview of the chapters included in the Handbook. This introduction will also highlight the contributions of the chapters to the five main themes of this Handbook, namely, (i) theories of IT innovations in government, (ii) emerging technologies and their applications in government, (iii) technology-enabled cross-boundary collaboration and governance, (iv) advancement of democratic accountability and public values, and (v) advancement of public service through technological innovation. These themes mirror the organization of chapters in the Table of Contents.

The first theme examines the role of information and information technology in government, as well as the theories and methods that provide useful insights in our understanding. The second theme presents emerging technologies and tools that have significant implications for governments in improving their services. The third theme addresses the emerging trends of interactive and collaborative relationships between citizens and government in production of public services and information. The fourth theme focuses on the issues and opportunities associated with the use of technology to advance public values—including citizen participation, transparency, and privacy. The final theme discusses the broad management and governance potentials of information technology in public service.

The following sections are organized around the five thematic areas—previewing the main ideas and contributions of the chapters in each area—as listed in the Table of Contents. We then identify research gaps and opportunities for future study.

Theories of IT Innovations in Government

The development of e-government in the last decade has undergone an evolution from narrowly defined information and technology services available on government websites to a more comprehensive notion of digital governance. Digital governance has two defining features: one is the citizen-centric provision of information and services and the other is the increasing role of citizens in the process of governance enabled by rapid advances in information and communication technologies (ICTs) (Chen and Hsieh 2009). Chapter 2 by Lips traces back over the development of e-government, highlighting this evolution in the changing relationships between government and citizens. If properly implemented, the combination of public administration strategy and information technology has transformational power, as various cases illustrate in this handbook. Lips articulates major developments in e-government, including citizen-centric and evidence-based management, and the rise of mobile government and digital-by-default approaches in government as driving forces behind today's changing e-government.

Strategic use of data and information greatly improve the quality of government services and policy making (Dawes 2010). In the public sector, such strategic use of information is founded in a well-formulated policy framework. Chapter 3 by Dawes provides a comprehensive treatment of the development of information policies as permanent fixtures influencing policymaking and implementation processes—sometimes limiting and sometimes advancing new possibilities in rapidly changing ICTs. The two perspectives on information (information as the object of policy or as an instrument of policy) lend useful lenses to guide the government effort in strategic information use (Dawes 2010). Chapter 6 by Ho et al. and chapter 13 by Frecks reflect policy implications and challenges from two promising areas of emerging technologies—big data and civic hacking.

Theory development is another crucial component for advancing our knowledge in the use of information technology in government. One of the strategies to develop theories in applied and interdisciplinary subject areas, such as e-government and e-governance, is to integrate insights from various streams of theories. Chapter 4 by Chen aims to develop a mid-range theory by integrating theoretical insights on institutionalism by Ostrom (2010), utilizing analytical capabilities and information on public management network management to addresses cross-boundary integration. Explicit modeling of the role of information technology in the management of a service-production system and in actual production of public service is needed to advance e-government and e-governance research.

Moreover, advancing knowledge will require analytical tools that can facilitate the effective use of information and communication technologies to improve public service. Chapter 5 by Luna-Reyes et al. articulates the role of system dynamics in understanding the design, implementation, and impact of e-government initiatives, while providing specific illustrations of tools to study the dynamic of systems. System dynamics are particularly useful for information technology in government because of the need to account for larger systemic-level forces (such as policy and institutions), as well as the time required for technology adoption and implementation. The dynamic nature of ICT implementation lends itself to a system-dynamic model specifically capturing both positive and negative feedback mechanisms.

Emerging Technologies and Their Applications in Government

Technological innovations present opportunities and challenges for improving public services. The chapters on big data, mobile technologies, and the Internet of Things (IoT) provide opportunities to dramatically improve digital government and governance. Moreover, these authors specifically frame these technologies in the context of public service to address public administration challenges. Big data, when used properly, can be a strategic resource for data-driven decision-making to improve services (Chen and Hsieh 2014). Given the rapid advancement of mobile devices and connectivity (Ganapati 2015), governments are afforded various opportunities to provide smart and personalized services. The Internet of Things can potentially provide real-time information and big data for better management and improvement of traffic, emergency response, water, and other public services.

Big data and big data analytics have the potential to transform government service and decision-making by supplying comprehensive and (near) real-time data on service and identifying opportunities for service improvement. Traditionally, most research and evaluation is based on samples and statistical inferences that take months or years for data collection and analysis. Big data offer real-time (or near real-time) comprehensive actual behavioral and activity information (Soares 2012). In chapter 6, Ho et al. offer examples of how to use big data and big data analytics to understand public service performance and identify opportunities for improvement. Moreover, as Tseng et al. have shown in chapter 9, big data and analytics are useful in understanding public opinions as expressed online as a source of information for policy making.

As chapter 7 by Ganapati illustrates, mobile and location-based technologies and applications afford many opportunities for improving public service. The use of mobile apps allows local governments' citizen services to personalize information and transactional services for residents and visitors. Information and service can be rendered by taking into account the location and past service experiences (Ganapati 2015). Public enterprise field operation can benefit significantly from the use of mobile technologies in performing tasks in the areas of public works, transit and traffic management, law enforcement, and land-use planning. Moreover, location-based technologies can advance public values by facilitating "anytime, anywhere citizen engagement." Citizens have the opportunity to actively participate in offering public service to the community or a cause. The "street bump" app in Boston, for instance, allows citizens to help identify potholes on the street for infrastructure maintenance. Citizens can be contributing community members by reporting issues with location information.

The Internet of Things (IoT) offers opportunities to collect and share data in real-time to deal with complex, dynamic, and rapidly changing public service problems. Chapter 8 by Zhang et al. offers examples of using the Internet of Things to collect and share real-time information to improve public services such as making real-time parking spaces available and offering the best route to parking, as well as monitoring water flow and quality for major lakes. The Internet of Things—coupled with supporting information systems for data collection, analytics, and dissemination (i.e., via apps)—has the potential to promote smart urban governance by addressing issues such as traffic, emergency management, air quality, and service management.

Technology-Enabled, Cross-Boundary Collaboration and Governance

The advent of online social networking services and online collaborative platforms, along with the growing trend in collaborative governance, ushers in new opportunities for relationship building between citizens and government. Such interaction and collaboration provide the foundation for service personalization by allowing for a better understanding of user characteristics, needs, and experience. The U.S. federal government has led the effort to focus on users as a way to provide the highest level of e-government services (White House 2012), and the social and collaborative nature of these platforms provide new levels of interactivity and engagement that were cost-prohibitive in the past.

Collectively, this section covers the topics of citizen trust in government, the value of citizen-government communication through new technologies, and these technologies' contributions to promoting good and responsive governance. Chapter 10 by Meyong and Ahn highlights the interactive nature of building relationships between government and citizens with the use of information and communication technologies. The authors find that it is critical to understand the characteristics of citizens to make the communication and service delivery more effective and to engender a sense of trust between government and citizens. Understanding citizen characteristics has begun to receive more attention as an important element of successful e-government outcomes; this emphasis is reflected in the U.S. digital government effort that has engaged behavioral scientists to study the attributes of users in e-government services and the psychological aspects of their behaviors.

Chapter 11 by Mergel offers an analytical lens for the various modes of using social media to improve communication and interaction between governments and citizens. Most of the activities tend to be the traditional one-to-many type of information sharing that is one-way in nature. The second mode is the one-to-one interaction between a citizen and a government office via social media. The third mode that social media can support is many-to-many interactions. Governments can be a listener in these many-to-many interactions and promote dialogue. Knowledge of the communication modes provides governments with the opportunity to utilize them appropriately. In the section on advancement of public service through technological innovations, chapter 19 by Bennett also illustrates how social media can be used to help emergency management by employing a mix of various communication modes.

Chapter 12 by Dumont illustrates the contribution of apps supported by a citizen's customer relationship management (CRM) system to facilitate the production of public service information as well as the personalization of public information and services. With mobile apps, citizens can report community problems via their phones, and the information can be shared and aggregated across these specific reports of community issues. Such use of mobile apps is a way to crowdsource the identification of public service issues and to share the information with other members in the community—providing a new method of collaboration between government and citizens in generating and sharing information on local government services. Such applications allow citizens and residents to track their service requests with government, enabling personalization of government services. Citizen involvement can be leveraged to add great value to government service. Chapter 13 by Frecks provides a survey of the recent developments of such collaboration between governments and civic groups. It emphasizes the importance of open communication between government and civic groups, as well as the need for a partnership model to foster such collaboration. Such collaboration has generated innovative ways of relating government information to citizens, as well as apps on mobile devices, as documented in the chapter.

Advancing Democratic Accountability and Public Values

One focus of IT innovation in the public sector is its defining role in advancing public value. E-government (in its early stages with the dawn of the Internet) provided basic information on websites, which then evolved into online transactions and integrated services. The advent of Web 2.0, anchored by social media, has ushered in a new wave of interactivity between government and citizens as well as peer-to-peer communication and coordination among citizens. All these developments offer unprecedented opportunities to move beyond improving efficiency and effectiveness of government services to focusing on broader notions of citizen participation, transparency, openness, and protection of privacy.

With regard to online citizen participation, chapter 14 by Mossberger et al. and chapter 18 by Lee complement each other by addressing the supply and demand sides respectively. Mossberger et al.'s chapter discusses factors that explain the availability for e-participation on government websites. It suggests that technology and money are not barriers; responsivity to educated segments of the population and the influence of peer CIOs are identified as the main reasons that explain the availability of e-participation. Lee's chapter provides insights into the preferences and interests of online citizen participation, as well as the characteristics of these individuals. Therefore, he cautions against a one-size-fits-all strategy for e-participation and recommends that e-participation applications should reflect the characteristics of specific segments of the population that share similar characteristics and interests.

In advancing information transparency at the local level, chapter 16 by Porumbescu et al. further articulates the need to consider a diversity of capabilities, preferences, and interests. A more productive approach needs to take a user-centric (citizen/business) approach by considering all these factors. More importantly, the online communication of information and data should be done in a way that considers the cognitive capabilities of individuals consuming the information. Such a recommendation is consistent with the push to make data visualization sensible to individuals. As a result, informational transparency can further aid in accountability.

Chapter 15 by Kim details the open government framework by the U.S. federal government. This chapter traces the development of the open-government movement in the United States with three pillars: transparency, participation, and collaboration. The chapter focuses on the role of open data as a core element of open government to promote transparency, increase citizen participation, and foster collaboration between government and citizens in utilizing government data. This chapter offers an assessment of the existing open data initiatives. The challenges lie in the scope and quality of open-government data, as well as in the insufficient understanding of such data by potential citizen users. In addition, the challenge to protect privacy and security is likely to rise with the increasing openness of government data.

The safeguard of individual privacy in an era of tremendous growth in digital personal information presents a significant ongoing challenge. Chapter 17 by Ni surveys the U.S. regulatory framework to provide readers with an understanding of the governance of personal identifiable information for privacy protection. Fragmentation in the establishment and administration of these laws and regulations on privacy protection has created significant challenges in effective protection of privacy. It will be even more challenging with the advent of surveillance technologies, mobile technologies capturing and transmitting location information, and big data. This chapter offers potential policy solutions by integrating some principles and practices from the European Union.

Advancing Public Service through Technological Innovations

This final section includes chapters that take a broad approach to examining the role of information technology in improving and even transforming public service. These chapters provide insights into the challenges and solutions associated with the emerging role of social media in emergency management, integration of cyberinfrastructure and service for innovation, and government-wide approaches to manage information technology.

Emergency management is a prime area where ICTs can be particularly useful for the dissemination and exchange of information. Chapter 19 by Bennett focuses on the role of social media in critical emergency communication. Emergency management communication is cross-boundary in nature with multiple levels of government involved and coordination needed both inside and outside government. This chapter provides lessons for how best to use a variety of social media applications. For instance, Twitter is better for alerts and active emergency information to create situational awareness, while Facebook, as the more popular social media platform, is better suited for the dissemination of emergency-preparedness information. Such differentiation suggests the growing management sophistication in effective utilization of social media applications. Bennett also finds that organizational culture has a strong influence on shaping the extent and ways social media applications are used.

Chapter 20 by Bolívar on the smart city further explores the governance issue in a cross-boundary setting. Issues relating to smart city are more of a challenge to governance than a simple adoption of new ICTs. Smart city can be seen as an integrated system of several subsystems covering areas such as health, economic development, mobility (transportation), utility, and resources. This chapter covers various dimensions of smart city governance, including decision-making structure, goal-setting process, coordination authority, inter-sector collaboration, and collaborative governance. The study of smart city governance highlights the collaborative nature of the next generation of e-government and the need to engage coproducers from the public, private, and nonprofit sectors. Opportunities for advancing our knowledge lie in taking a collaborative and inclusive approach to realize the potential of smart city.

Chapter 21 on cyberinfrastructure for scientific discovery, by Chen and Knepper, further underscores both the positive impact of effective ICT uses and the need for effective governance and management to increase such impact. ICTs can lower the cost and increase the ease for a large number of geographically dispersed organizations to work together. The use of ICTs can help deliver advanced information technology capabilities such as data processing, storage, and application support to facilitate scientific discovery. More importantly, the governance structure needs to meet the complexity of producing and providing technology services with collaboration among organizations across the country. A centralized management structure is needed for matching such complexity.

Understanding past development and future opportunities of e-government in China is critical for the 21st century as China has the largest Internet population—over 600 million in 2015. This number will continue to rise given the Chinese government's push and innovations in Internet-based services. Chapter 22 by Zhang and Zhao provides a research-based treatment on e-government in China, offering a historical overview of the e-government policies and projects in China. In addition, this chapter provides results on the study of key e-government issues in China, including data acquisition and utilization, system integration, information update, and long-term IT planning. The innovative new government initiatives discussed at the end of the chapter offer ideas about the future of applications.

Chapter 23 by Ahn offers important insights into the development and management of e-government initiatives to achieve significant reform and process reengineering in government. This unique first-person account by the chair of the South Korea's special presidential e-government committee effectively captures the essence of South Korea's e-government success. Understanding e-government as an effective instrument of meaningful government reform and process reengineering can result in some remarkable outcomes, as witnessed in the case of South Korea. This chapter confirms that while the general conditions of e-government identified in the literature—such as technological, economic, political, and cultural conditions—matter, these conditions do not necessarily materialize into effective e-government. Only when a government has full leadership support and an effective champion, who can successfully lead an e-government project, do the necessary conditions reach the critical point of combustion that produces highly effective e-government. This chapter also epitomizes many of the future opportunities of digital government as featured in various chapters in this Handbook. These include data government (open and big data), platform government (digital coproduction), and government 3.0 with personalized service.

References

Chen, Yu-Che, and Jun-Yi Hsieh. 2009. 'Advancing E-Governance: Comparing Taiwan and the United States.' *Public Administration Review* 69 (1): S151–S158.

Chen, Yu-Che, and Tsui-Chuan Hsieh. 2014. 'Big Data for Digital Government: Opportunities, Challenges, and Strategies.' *International Journal of Public Administration in the Digital Age* 1 (1):1–14.

Dawes, Sharon S. 2010. 'Stewardship and Usefulness: Policy Principles for Information-Based Transparency.' *Government Information Quarterly* 27 (4):377–383.

Ganapati, Sukumar. 2015. *Using Mobile Apps in Government*. Washington, DC: IBM Center for the Business of Government.

Ostrom, Elinor. 2010. 'Institutional Analysis and Development: Elements of the Framework in Historical Perspective.' In *Historical Developments and Theoretical Approaches in Sociology*, edited by C. Crothers, 261–288. UK: EOLSS (Encyclopedia of Life Support Systems).

Soares, Sunil. 2012. *Big Data Governance: An Emerging Imperative*. Boise, ID: MC Press.

White House. 2012. *Building 21st Century Platform to Better Serve the American People*. Washington, DC: White House.

SECTION I

Theories of Information Technology (IT) Innovations in Government

2

TRANSFORMING GOVERNMENT SERVICES OVER TIME

Meanings, Impacts, and Implications for Citizen-Government Relationships

Miriam B. Lips

Introduction

Government service transformation, with information and communication technology (ICT) as critical enabler, has received a lot of attention since the introduction of the public Internet in the early 1990s. It has been widely acknowledged as a solution not only to deliver better, more effective, and convenient public services to citizens, but also to make government services more efficient and easy to use (e.g., Bellamy and Taylor, 1998; Borins et al., 2007; Danziger and Andersen, 2002; Heeks, 1999; Weerakkody and Reddick, 2012). It may not be surprising therefore that government service transformation concepts, strategies, and initiatives have been a profound item on the agenda of governments around the world, and are still being pursued to date (e.g., the recent UK Central Government's Transformation Programme;[1] the Australian Federal Government's Digital Transformation Office;[2] Lips, 2014; Weerakkody and Reddick, 2012). However, although narratives of technological innovation always have used "transformation" as a major theme, there are a variety of definitions and no clear consensus about what is meant by this term in the context of the impacts of ICT on government (Borins, 2007b).

Consequently, in the last few decades, we can observe the emergence of different government service transformation concepts around the world, such as electronic government, integrated government, citizen-centric government, m-government, digital-by-default government, and data-driven government. These international trends involve different meanings and perspectives not only on the technological capabilities in government service transformation, but also on the impact and implications for citizen–government relationships. However, research into government service transformation has mainly focused on either the technical and organizational aspects of this emerging public sector phenomenon (Lips and Schuppan, 2009) or the inherent capabilities of ICTs to transform public service provision (Dunleavy et al., 2006). While there has been some important empirical work to date on the phenomenon of government service transformation (e.g., Eppel and Lips, 2016; McLoughlin et al., 2013; O'Neill, 2009), there has been little focus thus far on the meanings, impacts, and implications of government service transformation for democratic citizen–government relationships.

This chapter will take a historical perspective on the main international trends in ICT-enabled government service transformation around the world, the role and capabilities of ICT in these government service transformation concepts, the actual impact of these concepts on citizen–government relationships, and the democratic implications. In order to be able to analyze the meanings, impacts, and implications of the different government service transformation concepts for citizen–government relationships over time, this chapter will first provide an overview of existing scholarly thinking on government service transformation.

Existing Theory on Government Service Transformation

Particularly in the 1990s when the public Internet was introduced, many scholars theorized that rapid advances in technological capabilities would profoundly influence not only the organization and structure of government service provision, but also the democratic relationship between citizens and government. Initially, scholarly thinking around ICT-enabled business transformation in the private sector, or business process reengineering (BPR), had an impact on scholars who were considering the influence of new ICTs on government and government service provision to citizens (e.g., Taylor et al., 1997). Advocates claimed that BPR should be used to "obliterate" existing organization, rather than automating it (Hammer, 1990). Although a private sector technique, government organizations could use BPR to fundamentally rethink how to reengineer their business processes through IT, including substantially improving customer service and achieving cost efficiencies (Hammer and Champy, 1993). Critics on the other hand pointed out that BPR was a narrow, technocratic means to dehumanize the workplace, increase managerial control, and reduce the workforce. Consequently, BPR was not considered a suitable tool for the obliteration of (parts of) government organizations or their immanent democratic values, with the technical orientation of ICT-intensive change programs in the public sector being observed as pushing toward apolitical and asocial analysis (Taylor et al., 1997, p.3).

Some form of institutional transformation in public sector organizations however was seen as an inevitable outcome of the rapid technological developments happening in society. Bovens and Zouridis (2002) for example theorized that the use of ICTs would rapidly change the structure of a number of large public sector agencies: from machine bureaucracies in which street-level officials exercised administrative discretion in dealing with individual clients, they pointed to a transformational shift for these organizations to become system-level bureaucracies, in which system analysts and software designers are the key decision makers through their conversion of legislation into software code embedded in decision-making systems. As a result, the new IT-driven decision-making systems used in government service provision would dictate the service outcomes and, with that, limit the discretionary power of service-providing public servants.

Besides acknowledging rapid change in technological developments and the transformation these developments could bring for public sector organizations, many scholars expected to see an equally rapid rate of radical change in citizen–government relationships as a result of the introduction and use of these new ICTs. Two opposite positions emerged from this scholarly debate: several scholars claimed that the "electronic revolution" and in particular the new public Internet would result in a much more democratic society, citizen empowerment, and a drastic renewal of politics, while others believed that the electronic revolution was primarily a technocratic revolution which would automatically lead to an Orwellian surveillance state and enhanced control of citizens by government (see Van de Donk and Tops, 1995 for a useful summary of the literature).

However, some scholars challenged the revolutionary nature and speed at which changes in government and citizen–government relationships might occur because of the use of ICTs, and even questioned whether any major form of change would occur at all. For example, based on empirical research in the U.S., Kraemer and King (2006) had come to the conclusion that the introduction of ICT had reinforced existing organization structures and certainly not caused administrative reform per se. They also observed that in case of substantial change, caused by other factors related to the introduction of ICT, in public sector organizations and their relationships with citizens, senior government officials commonly were the primary beneficiaries. Therefore, this so-called reinforcement thesis assumed that the introduction of digital technology reinforces the status quo with minimal impact on citizen–government relationships: if any, the impact would be to the advantage of senior government managers. Similarly, based on empirical research on over 17,000 government websites in the U.S., West (2005) concludes that, although digital government offers the potential for revolutionary change, social, political, and economic forces constrain the scope of transformation and prevent government officials from realizing the full benefits of available technological capabilities.

Several scholars have argued for more gradual yet transformative change over time. Fountain (2001; 2008) for instance distinguishes between objective technology or available technological capabilities, and enacted technology or "technology-in-use." In her view, the institutional nature of public sector processes explains why the use of new ICTs by governments doesn't follow a predictable technologically determinist pathway, but shows both successes and failures of ICT-based government service transformation reform over longer periods of time (Fountain, 2008). Other scholars argued that several governments were already implementing administrative reform ideas aligned with new public management (NPM) thinking when new ICTs, such as the Internet, were introduced, creating opportunities to reinforce these NPM reforms through the application of digital technology (Bekkers and Homburg, 2005; Cordella, 2007; Homburg, 2004). This situation then usually led to minimal disruption in public sector organizations, using ICTs for example to reinforce NPM ideas on becoming more customer focused (Van Duivenboden and Lips, 2001).

An evolutionary perspective on transformational change has also been acknowledged by scholars who have developed so-called e-government maturity models setting out the pathway from the introduction of ICTs in a public sector organization, to "mature" government ICT use and service transformation. For example, Layne and Lee (2001) developed a four-stage e-government maturity model for public sector organizations, with the first stage, "catalogue," pointing toward the presence of a government agency on the Internet; the second "transaction" stage indicating that citizens can do transactions online with government; the third stage of "vertical integration" involving the integration of a functional area across an hierarchical organization or different administrative levels; and the fourth and final stage of "horizontal integration," pointing to the integration of processes and activities within and across public sector organizations. Another example is a four-stage e-government maturity model developed by the Gartner Group (Baum and Di Maio, 2000), with the first stage involving "web presence" or a government agency having a static website through which basic information is provided to citizens; a second stage of "interaction" involves online interaction tools and features offered by a government agency to citizens; the third stage makes it possible for citizens to complete a "transaction" online; and the fourth and final stage stands for "transformation."

Borins (2007a) however warns against a commonly made mistake in e-government literature that transformational change and its gradual, "maturing" development are similar pathways for government and the private sector—with e-business maturity models being the source of comparison. He points out that government has a special mandate to publish democratic information intended to form the public record, and therefore online information provision can also be a transformational end in itself, of greater significance compared to interaction or transaction, for instance (Borins, 2007a). Also, government transactions are usually much more complex (e.g., social benefits, birth certificates) compared to commercial transactions and are not easily converted into online solutions. Consequently, in the public sector, the unique characteristics of government need to be taken into account when thinking about realistic and institutionally enabled transformational pathways for government information and service provision (Lips, 2011).

Based on an analysis of 49 empirical research publications on the impacts of ICT on public administration, published in peer-reviewed academic journals between 1987 and 2000, Danziger and Andersen (2002) came to the conclusion that ICT did not transform or fundamentally change government within this time frame. For instance, the academic journal articles they studied provide little evidence that ICT has caused a major redistribution of values and power in the public sector, or has dramatically restructured interaction patterns within government or between government and external stakeholders (Danziger and Andersen, 2002, p.617). However, their analysis does provide considerable evidence that impacts of ICT on government are often substantial and result in many significant modifications of behaviors and structures, which could point to a more gradual process of transformation over time. In general, Danziger and Andersen (2002) found that the clearest positive impacts generated by ICT on government are in the areas of efficiency and productivity, both in internal operations of government and in external public service provision. They also found substantial information benefits for both public officials and citizens, such as improved data access and data quality. The most negative impacts of ICT on government and its external relationships were found around citizens' privacy and other legal rights.

However, although many scholars have used "transformation" as a critical concept to theoretically and empirically explore government service transformation developments, the meaning of this concept is usually ill-defined or not defined at all (O'Neill, 2009). According to O'Neill (2009), the concept of transformation has two separate and quite different applications: (1) instrumental transformation, which she defines as a radical change in the existing administration, information management, and service delivery practices of government agencies that may also have a consequential impact on organizational structures and/or management practices. This application of transformation often results in less disruptive changes to operational and management practices that deliver benefits of increased speed, better quality of government service, and lower transaction costs, and can be described as "doing the same things differently"; and (2) systemic transformation, which is a radical, disruptive change in existing governance arrangements in the public sector, including constitutional responsibilities and accountabilities, fiscal management, legislation, regulation, and decision-making rights over public resources. From this perspective, transformation is also about a disruptive, fundamental change in key institutional and democratic relationships (e.g., citizen–government relationships) within a broader systemic order, and therefore is about "doing different things" (O'Neil, 2009).

International Trends in Government Service Transformation

This overview of existing government service transformation theory not only reveals the ambiguity of this concept, but also that most scholars have high expectations around the disruptive nature and impacts of ICT-enabled change in government and its relationship with citizens. In this section, we will look more in-depth into the praxis of ICT-enabled government service transformation thus far: the meanings, impacts, and implications of the different government service transformation concepts enacted by governments around the world since the introduction of the public Internet, also in comparison with available theory. It is important to note that different government service transformation concepts should not be seen as mutually exclusive, separated, or passing trends, but as ongoing developments that co-exist and can even become integrated dimensions of a digital government strategy.

Before we turn to each of these concepts, we should not underestimate the disruptive nature and impact of IT in government in the pre-Internet era. Without these early developments in government computing, many of the web-based service transformation visions proposed by governments could not have been materialized. We briefly will explore this important historical development of the automation of government first before considering later Internet-based government service transformation concepts.

Automated Government

Although governments around the world usually started to present revolutionary ideas about government service transformation after the launch of the public Internet, a "quiet revolution" in government because of the application of IT was already happening for several decades, if not longer. For example, data centers have been used by U.S. federal government agencies for more than 100 years: where early forms of computing were first applied to perform simple mathematical equations and calculations, such as the U.S. Census Bureau's use of a mechanical tabulator to conduct the decennial census in 1890, from 1900 onward U.S. agencies started to centralize administrative processes by introducing punch-card machines and punched cards in batch-processing, operational activities (Daly, 2013).

The military particularly saw a need for building disruptive calculation machines during World War II, when complex wartime calculations were in strong demand and government wartime budgets were available to support innovation in this area. As a result, the first programmable, digital computer, the so-called Electronic Numerical Integrator and Computer or ENIAC, was built between 1943 and 1945 and used by the U.S. Army to run calculations at electronic speed without being slowed by any mechanical parts.[3]

In the 1950s and 1960s, huge mainframe computers carrying out large-scale repetitive administrative tasks were introduced in several governments around the world (Margetts, 1999). This replacement of paper-based government processes mainly concerned those agencies that had to process large volumes of paper-based forms, such as tax departments and social welfare agencies, and led to centralization and increased efficiency within these government organizations. NASA was another U.S. government agency that recognized the incredible power of computers at an early stage: for instance, by the mid-1960s, NASA had already sent a server into space (Daly, 2013).

In the 1980s, personal computers (PCs) became popular not only among the general public but also as personal work stations for individual government employees, who would use PCs as word processing, calculation, data processing and programming tools. Initially this increased the need for mainframe computers, until server-based networked computing solutions were introduced several years later.

Impact and Implications

Under the automated government trend, transformational change especially happened within individual government agencies, where organizational structures in favor of centralization, the public sector workforce, and skills of public servants changed fundamentally, for example. Technocratic elements of new Taylorism, such as the replacement of people by computers and increased managerial control through better calculation power, increased memory, and enhanced speed of decision-making, could be observed under this trend, but also new and additional jobs emerged in the public sector, such as computer and programming experts. The use of new technological capabilities in government agencies led to more decision-making power at the top of the organization. Citizen–government relationships were not so much affected by these fundamental changes, except for a strongly improved speed in government service provision.

Electronic Government

Shortly after the World Wide Web became publicly available in 1991, the Clinton–Gore Administration launched the first ICT-enabled government service transformation vision in a strategy document "Reengineering through Information Technology" under its National Performance Review (NPR) program in September 1993 (Fountain, 2001):

> Today, information technology can create the government of the future, the electronic government. Electronic government overcomes the barriers of time and distance to perform the business of government and give people public information and services when and where

they want them. It can swiftly transfer funds, answer questions, collect and validate data, and keep information flowing smoothly within and outside government.

(Lips and Frissen, 1997, p.117)

According to the Clinton–Gore Administration, the new information super highway would be a critical infrastructure for the government of the future, which would "work better and cost less": in other words, the adoption of new ICTs in government would lead not only to a radically streamlined bureaucracy and substantially less taxes, but also to a government which would be much more responsive to the needs of individual citizens (Bellamy and Taylor, 1997, p.41). According to Fountain (2001, p.19), the NPR differed from most earlier U.S. government reform efforts in resisting the temptation to restructure agencies: instead, it emphasized redesigning process flows, increasing customer service to citizens, and leveraging the potential of IT to enhance the capacity of government in a way that government organizations could patch new ICT solutions onto existing structures and maintain the status quo.

With the White House as one of the lead government organizations in using the new public Internet, manifested by creating their own public website without changing their existing organizational structure, governments all over the world followed this example and set up a public website themselves. Initially, governments used a so-called yellow pages approach by putting the same public information on their website as they offered in paper-based brochures and forms, including their official contact information, such as telephone numbers and staff email addresses. Domain names policy became another important area of additional focus for governments, especially after the experience of a commercial site with illegal content using an almost identical domain name as the White House,[4] to benefit from new Internet users with an interest in visiting the new electronic White House site but not exactly knowing how to navigate the new information super highway.

Impact and Implications

Although the trend of electronic government promised radically different forms of government and democratic governance, in reality ICTs were used by government officials to "plug-and-play" as Fountain (2001, pp.18–19) calls it: new ICTs were used in ways, however innovative, that leave deeper structures and processes, such as authority relationships, democratic relationships, and accountability and oversight processes, undisturbed. Conservative, first attempts were taken to provide existing paper-based government information through an additional, new channel and structured from a government organizational point of view. Government's relationship with the citizen didn't change much, with both citizens and government officials having improved access to government information as a result of the use of new ICTs. Put differently, only instrumental transformation occurred under this trend, with governments doing things differently rather than doing different things (O'Neill, 2009).

Integrated Government

In the second half of the 1990s, another government service transformation trend of integrated government emerged based on newly available technological capabilities: the idea that ICTs offered the opportunity to break down the vertical silos within government and present government information and services to citizens and other stakeholders in a much more integrated way. Technology would enable a more integrated government in several ways and in different transformational stages of development: first, through virtual integration or integrated web portals; second, it would facilitate vertical integration of government service provision via an integrated front office, also called "one-stop shop"; and third, it would enable horizontal integration of the physical front and back offices of government agencies.

For governments around the world, virtual integration or the creation of web portals turned out to be a relatively easy way to achieve government service transformation from a citizen's point of view: without the need to restructure the government agencies involved, network technology enabled the integrated provision of government information and services from various agencies in one virtual location, making it easier for the citizen to navigate government. In the first instance, web portals were used as virtual "doors" to websites owned and maintained by individual government agencies, where they presented their own information and services, leaving the "real-world" organization of government agencies completely intact (e.g., West, 2005). For governments, standardization and interoperability became important policy objectives in order to achieve this situation of virtually integrated government information and service provision via web portals. For citizens, this situation implied clicking on a few hyperlinks in order to find the relevant information or service on a particular government agency's website accessible via the web portal.

After a proliferation of websites within and across government agencies and a raising awareness about the costs involved in designing and maintaining these websites, governments started to introduce website rationalization programs, trying to achieve cost efficiencies by expanding the use of a single government web portal, strongly reducing the number of websites across government, and removing duplication of information provision across government as much as possible. For example, in 2011, the UK central government closed down 74 "redundant" government sites in order to further slim-line its web presence and focus on its remodeled, unified GOV.UK portal, which replaced the central hubs Directgov and Business Link as a single domain for government on the Internet. Governments also started investing into improving website navigation from a citizen's perspective and developing government search functionality, with the latter development leading to public debate about whether government should invest in building its own "independent" search engine or using an existing commercial search engine like Google, with the downside of promoting commercially driven search outcomes.

Second, vertical integration and the creation of one-stop shops for integrated service provision was a development which already was happening in some countries around the world, usually at an administrative level where most of the government service provision to citizens takes place (e.g., local government) or in a particular government sector (e.g., social sector). For example, the clustering and integration of services offered via one physical government service counter was seen by governments in Scandinavian countries as a way to more holistically meet the multiple complex needs of citizens. ICT was seen as a critical infrastructure to connect the integrated front office with multiple back offices of various government departments and to provide access to expert databases and systems, so that relevant customer information from different government organizations was available at the integrated front desk. The establishment of the integrated front office required substantial administrative reform, with integrated service provision having a substantial impact on frontline staff members who needed to be retrained and reskilled in order to serve customers in a more holistic way; however, the various back offices of government departments did not require any major changes and could more or less operate the same, having direct virtual connections with the integrated front office.

The third trend of horizontal integration had a much more profound impact on the organization and processes of government departments: not only the front offices but also the back offices of government agencies and other service delivery partners (e.g., community service providers) needed to be restructured in order to achieve this particular vision. ICT was seen not only as a critical infrastructure to facilitate information exchange and communications between front offices and back offices, but also as a critical enabler for joining up and integrating the back offices. Although some governments experimented with the implementation of this horizontal integration vision, such as The Netherlands through its Government Counter 2000 Program,[5] existing institutional arrangements like accountability, autonomy of government organizations, and legislation (e.g., privacy legislation) turned out to be important barriers for achieving this far-reaching stage of government service transformation. Experience with horizontal integration efforts through government reform programs like Government Counter 2000 learned that governments were forced to completely redesign the front office(s), back office(s), and middleware (i.e., the infrastructure between front office and back office) for providing integrated services.

Impact and Implications

Integrated government was the first government service transformation trend which challenged the organizational structures and institutional processes in government. However, more advanced forms of government service transformation, in accordance with Layne and Lee's e-government maturity model (Layne and Lee, 2001), turned out not to be a necessity in the digital age for presenting government information and services in an integrated way, as governments soon found out through their experience with web portals, for instance. Also, experiments with "deeper institutional change" programs for achieving integrated government, such as in the Netherlands and Scandinavia, demonstrated the inherent complexities of ICT-enabled administrative reform and, with that, constrained the scope of transformation. Although citizen–government relationships in theory could have been negatively impacted in a substantial way as a result of increased cross-government sharing and integration of personal data, the reality was that privacy legislation often stood in the way of reform efforts to achieve more integrated government. Again, government's relationship with the citizen didn't change much under this trend, with the exception perhaps of achieving an improved customer focus through providing integrated government information and services.

Citizen-Centric Government

Citizen-centric government emerged as a government service transformation trend in response to earlier Internet-enabled trends of electronic government and integrated government: where governments had seen these two earlier ICT-enabled service transformation trends as ways to serve individuals better as their customers, which befitted the New Public Management approach embraced by many governments at the time, citizen-centric government became popular as an alternative trend, acknowledging that citizens' rights and obligations are quite different from and unique compared to more narrowly defined customer rights. Another important recognition about the unique nature of government service relationships with citizens was that governments need to balance the distinct interests and needs of different groups of citizens within the broader framework of the public interest. This then implied that governments cannot use a "one-size-fits-all" solution in their service design and therefore need to shift from a uniform, government-centric focus in service provision toward a more differentiated citizen-centric approach.

According to the OECD (2009), one of the major differences between a government-centric and a citizen-centric service design paradigm is that a government-centric approach takes an "inside-out" perspective and focuses on organizational coherence; a citizen-centric approach on the other hand takes an "outside-in" perspective and emphasizes external coherence from a citizen's point of view. A good example of how ICT can enable a citizen-centric solution in government service design is the introduction of the so-called life event model in the online delivery of government services; a model that was first introduced and used by the Singaporean government. A life event model presents, clusters, and integrates government information and services in alignment with major events in the life of the citizen, such as going to school, looking for work, setting up a business, getting married, buying a house, traveling, having a child, and becoming retired. In so doing, citizens do not need to understand the organizational logic of government in order to find relevant government information or services.

More recently, several governments have taken this citizen-centric focus a step further by introducing means and ways to "simplify" government from a citizen's perspective: for example, governments have introduced online "single windows" or "one-entry-only" solutions for particular services, where before citizens needed to go to multiple government service counters and provide the same information over and over again. Good examples are the change of address or dealing with a case of bereavement which, for a UK citizen, implied going to 44 different service counters prior to the "tell us once" administrative simplification initiative. Another citizen-centric government approach has been to offer more customized services to particular groups of citizens through client segmentation or even personalize public services to individual needs of citizens. With the latter approach strongly depending on the sharing of personal information between the citizen and government agencies as well as across government, the implementation of personalized service provision in the public sector is usually limited due to existing privacy legislation. Moreover, human right advocates have argued that a personalized "amazon.com"-type experience in government can create an undemocratic situation, where citizens will no longer receive any government information outside their primary consumer interests and live their lives in "government information cocoons" or "echo chambers"(Sunstein, 2007).

Canada is one of the countries which have adopted a citizen-centered approach to government service transformation. For example, since 1999, the Government of Canada through its Government On-Line (GOL) program has sought to profoundly change the way government deals with the public and related internal administrative practices and culture, involving making government services available to the public in an integrated way and from the perspective of the citizen (Brown, 2007). Building on extensive client consultation and public opinion research, including biennial Citizens First surveys of public preferences in government service provision, the services offered via the Government of Canada's website have been reorganized into three Gateways: for individual citizens and residents (the Canadians Gateway), for the business community (Canadian Business Gateway), and for international clients (Non-Canadians Gateway). Within each Gateway, several portals or Clusters have restructured information found on departmental and program websites to provide more effective access to government information and services by subject (e.g., health), by audience (e.g., seniors), and by life event or activity (e.g., travel abroad) (Brown, 2007, p.43). The Clusters are oriented to reflect the citizen's view of government—from the outside looking in—focusing on demand for services, placing organizational and jurisdictional lines in the background (Brown, 2007, p.47). Each cluster has a full-time management unit and is housed in a "host" department; it has a dedicated project office and numerous collaborative cross-government working groups to develop common standards and working tools for web page design, measurement of client satisfaction, and other steps to increase a consistent and interoperable approach among the clusters (ibid).

Impact and Implications

As the Canadian example demonstrates, citizen-centric government is one of the most far-reaching government service transformation trends, both in terms of administrative reform and of fundamentally changing the relationship with the citizen: based on their logic and preferences, instead of the traditional departmental logic of organizing public service outputs, government information and services are offered to segmented citizen groups in a more integrated, effective, and empowering way. In that sense, it arguably is a good example of systemic transformation: doing different things rather than doing things differently. However, the Canadian experience demonstrates that establishing citizen-centric government is not an easy process. For example, there has been a continuing tension between the government-wide view and the perspective and needs of departmental managers, raising issues around internal governance, cross-government coordination, horizontal vs. vertical accountability, and leadership (Brown, 2007). Although ICT-enabled personalized service provision could take citizen-centric government even further in theory, in practice privacy legislation and other democratic rights turn out to be effective barriers to these developments thus far.

M-Government

Mobile or "m-government" particularly became popular when people started to use mobile devices, such as smartphones or iPads, and wireless access to the Internet. Many governments therefore have introduced m-government as an additional channel for government service provision besides other online and offline channels. However, especially in developing countries where access to mobile technology is much higher compared to much more costly fixed broadband access, governments have realized that the application of m-government enables them to transform government services and engage online with citizens (e.g., OECD, 2011). New digital technologies in these countries are often seen as means to replace nonstandardized and sometimes corrupted human-based government service provision with standardized online government services, which guarantee more democratic treatment of all citizens and, with that, the support of good governance. Moreover, mobile technologies also can provide access to government services where the infrastructure required for Internet or wired phone service is not a viable option, providing governments with the opportunity to reach out to a much greater number of people. For instance, citizens in remote areas can receive m-health assistance and emergency or disaster response, or have educational content delivered when they have limited access to public education.

Besides the fact that governments are increasingly using mobile apps for government service provision, some other practical examples can be found in Malaysia, where citizens can verify their voting information, such as the parliamentary and state constituencies where they are to vote, using Short Message Service (SMS) (Lallana, 2008). Another more recent example is from Indonesia where the Indonesian government has set up an online reporting system "Lapor!" (https://www.lapor.go.id/): citizens can report on the wrongdoings of their government via SMS or mobile app to a public website, and with the government team behind the online reporting system, follow up on these citizen reports. Reports can range from bribery by traffic officers to massive corruption by politicians (Lukman, 2013). Lapor! (which means "report" in Bahasa Indonesia) receives about 1,000 reports every day. In 2013, 78 percent of all reports had been followed up by the government team (ibid).

Impact and Implications

The international trend of m-government shows that the government service transformation implications of the same transformational concept can be different in different contexts or even countries. For example, where m-government in developed countries usually is an additional channel besides existing online and offline channels, in developing countries m-government can contribute to the establishment of more democratic relationships or good governance and, with that, empowering individuals. This fundamental change in transparency and external accountability in government's relationship with the citizen puts pressure on senior government officials to establish fundamental forms of administrative reform internally as well. Put differently, where instrumental transformation is happening around m-government in most developed countries, with minimal disruptions to existing institutional and organizational arrangements, systemic transformation as a result of m-government seems to be taking place in developing countries like Indonesia.

Digital-by-Default Government

Following successful digital business models in the private sector, many governments have recognized the potential offered by digital transformation and have decided to become digital by default. Generally, this means that digitized service provision will become the norm or standard way for government in interacting with citizens, replacing paper-based and face-to-face interactions (Lips, 2014). This digital-by-default development is expected to lead to substantial cost-efficiency savings compared to the delivery of government services via traditional channels. For example, in Denmark, citizens nowadays need to use a personal digital mailbox for all correspondence with government.

In becoming digital-by-default, governments usually aim to be customer-centric and provide digital services to citizens that are of better quality, more convenient, easy-to-use, and less time-consuming (Lips, 2014). Also, they want their customers to be shielded from the internal complexities of government. Some countries, such as the UK and Denmark, use a *service-centric* approach in advancing their digital-by-default strategy, converting paper-based transaction services into web-based equivalents. However, other countries, such as the United States, use a more radical *information-centric* approach. Rather than primarily considering the management of documents, the U.S. federal government decouples information from its presentation by focusing on managing discrete pieces of open data and content, which can be tagged, shared, secured, mashed up, and presented in the way that is most useful for the consumer of that information (The White House, 2012, p.3). By using open standards and web application programming interfaces (APIs), the U.S. federal government is able to make data assets freely available for use by various stakeholders and in a program- and device-agnostic way. Consequently, the same web APIs can be used and reused to present information to customers through multiple channels (e.g., websites, mobile applications) and to release the information to external developers who then can use it to create new information products, services, or applications. For example, the City of San Francisco releases its raw public transportation data on train routes, schedules, and location updates directly to the general public through web services. This has enabled citizen developers to write over 10 different mobile applications to help individuals navigate San Francisco's public transit systems and, with that, to provide more information services than the City of San Francisco could have provided (The White House, 2012, pp.5–6).

To ensure fair access to digital government services for all individuals entitled to them, several governments recognize the importance of actively supporting people who are not online or less capable of accessing digital services (Lips, 2014). For example, acknowledging that the majority of the UK population is online (82 percent) but only 27 percent use online government services (Cabinet Office, 2012b), the UK central government introduced an "assisted digital" program as part of their digital-by-default strategy. Assisted digital aims to develop and apply customer insights about those who use digital services, and those who can't, and to identify the support requirements needed for people who are not online and provide assistance to those who need it. Moreover, both by improving the quality of services offered through digital channels and making people aware of available services, those who are online will be persuaded to use digital services.

In order to make it more attractive for people to use digital services, the UK central government wants to encourage people to move from offline to digital channels through awareness raising, assisting with the use of digital services, and using a positive incentive scheme, including passing on lower costs to digital service users, allowing later deadlines for online process completion, and offering entries into prize draws for digital service users (Cabinet Office 2012a, p.30). However, some groups of the population will not have any choice regarding the uptake of digital-by-default services, such as people highly dependent on government services. Examples are benefit claimants, families with low income, individuals dependent on health services, and senior citizens. With many lower-paid groups in society not having Internet access (Dutton and Blank, 2011), these more vulnerable, government-dependent groups of the population will require assistance in some form or another with digital services, which may add to the costs involved with establishing digital government by default.

Impact and Implications

With digital-by-default government having a fundamental impact on both organizational structures, processes, and staffing within government agencies and government's relationship with the citizen, the latter example about vulnerable groups in society demonstrates that the implications of this government service transformation concept can be negative: digital-by-default government can lead to decreased access to government information and services and more inequitable treatment in government service provision for the most government-dependent groups of the population. Although cost-efficiency savings are driving many governments toward digital transformation, the outcome of decreased effectiveness for the most vulnerable customers of government services could even enhance the costs involved with government's public service obligations to all citizens. For other, less vulnerable groups in society, the information-centric approach of digital-by-default government seems to have more fundamental implications for citizen–government relationships in an empowering sense, compared to the service-centric approach of digital-by-default government.

Data-Driven Government

Another more recent trend in government service transformation is the use of big data and data analytics in order to provide more effective government services to individuals. In general, big data is related to large volumes of data, the speed at which data are generated, accessed, processed, and analyzed, and the capacity to analyze a variety of structured data, but also unstructured datasets from sources including weblogs, social media, mobile communications, sensors, and financial transactions (OECD, 2013). These three main big data characteristics of volume, velocity, and variety are also commonly referred to as the three "Vs," with (increasing socioeconomic) value added by some as a fourth characteristic (ibid).

These new technological capabilities not only have been embraced by private sector companies, but they also are finding their way into the public sector for better evidence-based policy making and more effective and efficient government service delivery. The greater sharing and use of data across the public sector and in collaboration with the private sector and community service providers offers new opportunities for government to segment customers into groups, get more knowledge about each group, such as what government intervention worked or didn't work, and on the basis of this knowledge design more targeted, effective services to individual customers. Another opportunity for governments offered by big data and data analytics is to use behavioral data (e.g., mobile phone data) or social media data (e.g., Twitter data) of individuals to better predict certain situations and offer more effective service interventions. For example, in Indonesia, spontaneous tweets about major floods are being turned into a mapping tool and subsequently analyzed to detect patterns in rising water levels in particular areas and prevent flooding.[6] Another example is the creation of real-time health maps (e.g., HealthMap),[7] where real-time knowledge is gathered, integrated, visualized, disseminated, and monitored on emerging diseases, facilitating early detection of public health threats in certain geographical areas.

The New Zealand Ministry of Social Development (MSD) worked with economic analysts and data specialists to create a "forward liability" data model to estimate the risks of welfare dependency among their most vulnerable client groups (Taylor Fry, 2011). The analysis showed that MSD's strategic emphasis on assisting those on unemployment benefit accounted for only 5 percent of actual welfare payments, whereas those with the highest lifetime costs were those who went on a benefit before the age of 18 and sole parents (Ministry of Social Development, 2012; Taylor Fry, 2013). By matching and analyzing data available across several government agencies, MSD was able to predict the probability of the youth population going on to an adult benefit and, in turn, the cost to New Zealand of future welfare services (SAS, 2013, p.1). These findings and predictive modeling techniques formed the basis for a new "investment approach" to welfare services in New Zealand: the use of a data integration and analytics capability to better understand which social services have the most positive impact on the most vulnerable people over time. With the models set up and through customer segmentation, MSD is able to run real-time trials to determine which policy interventions are making the biggest difference to different cohorts of clients (SAS, 2013). This improved evidence base is used to reshape service provision to particular customer groups or shift funding in response to this greater understanding. With better prioritization in government service delivery, and the capability to collect data and demonstrate results, MSD is able to present stronger evidence to support investment decisions across the New Zealand government around the effective delivery of social outcomes. This may also include investing in programs delivered by other government agencies, where the evidence base shows that those programs can best reach specific customer groups.

Impact and Implications

Data-driven government is another example of a government service transformation trend where we can observe that the same concept can lead to quite different impacts on public service delivery and implications. Where the use of shared open data and predictive modeling leads to more transparency, collaboration, and empowerment of both citizens and public servants, such as flooding prevention and early detection of public health threats in the case of New Zealand's investment approach, the greater cross-government sharing and use of personal data of individual citizens creates improved knowledge and insights for public service providers about the effectiveness of interventions to particular customer groups, which subsequently lead to better targeted and more effective services to individual clients. In the case of the latter, there is no "coproduction" between citizens and service providers to achieve more effective service provision, whereas in the former case there is. Also, the greater cross-government sharing and use of personal data not only potentially raises privacy issues but also leads to more differential treatment of individual (groups of) citizens. However, at the same time, better targeted and more effective service provision to individual clients can also lead to improved access to public service entitlements.

An Overview of Government Service Transformation Concepts

The different government service transformation concepts and their respective impacts, described above, can be summarized in Table 2.1.

Table 2.1 Impact of Government Service Transformation Concepts

Government service transformation concept	Impact
Automated government	Systemic transformation
Electronic government	Instrumental transformation
Integrated government	Restricted systemic transformation
Citizen-centric government	Systemic transformation
M-government	Instrumental transformation in most developed countries; systemic transformation in developing countries
Digital-by-default government	Systemic transformation
Data-driven government	Systemic transformation

Conclusions

This chapter has explored the meanings, impacts, and implications of ICT-enabled government service transformation for governments and citizen–government relationships to date. It has demonstrated that government service transformation has different meanings to different people in different contexts or even countries, and usually is relatively difficult and complex to achieve. In most cases, citizen–government relationships seem to have been rather untouched by government service transformation efforts; however, in some cases, most notably around citizen-centric government, m-government, digital-by-default government, and data-driven government, we can observe more profound positive changes happening in government's relationship with the citizen, such as citizen empowerment, improved access to government information, coproduction, and more effective service provision, or negative changes like privacy breaches and increasing differential treatment in public service provision.

In general, technology will not determine the outcomes of government service transformation, either internally within or across government agencies or externally in citizen–government relationships. Important government service transformation issues, such as leadership, coordination, horizontal collaboration, the complexity of government services, existing institutional arrangements, legislation (e.g., privacy), accountability, authority, skills of government service providers, and last but not least understanding the service demands and needs from the perspective of the citizen, will not and cannot be solved by the technology per se. Instead, the outcomes, including the possibility to transform the power relationships between government and individuals, will be determined by the mutual shaping of technology and a wide range of sociocultural, political, economic, and institutional factors affecting the implementation of government service transformation in each country. Consequently, government service transformation efforts in the end might lead to systemic transformation or equally reinforce government as we know it today, with different outcomes possible in different countries. What has become clear, though, is the critical importance of a robust and in-depth understanding of the varying meanings, impacts, and implications of a seemingly similar government service transformation concept over time.

Notes

1. https://www.gov.uk/transformation
2. https://www.dto.gov.au/
3. http://www.computerhistory.org/revolution/birth-of-the-computer/4/78
4. Whitehouse.com instead of Whitehouse.gov.
5. In Dutch: Overheidsloket 2000 or OL2000. This program was initiated in 1996.
6. https://www.floodtags.com/
7. http://www.healthmap.org/en/

References

Baum, Christopher, and Andrea Di Maio. 2000. *Gartner's Four Phases of E-Government Model*. Stamford, CA: Gartner Group.
Bekkers, Viktor, and Vincent Homburg, eds. 2005. *The Information Ecology of E-Government: E-Government as Institutional and Technological Innovation in Public Administration*. Amsterdam: IOS Press.
Bellamy, Christine, and John A. Taylor. 1997. 'Transformation by Stealth: The Case of the UK Criminal Justice System'. In *Beyond BPR in Public Administration: Institutional Transformation in an Information Age*, edited by John A. Taylor, Ignace Snellen, and Arre Zuurmond, 37–53. Amsterdam: IOS Press.
Bellamy, Christine, and John A. Taylor. 1998. *Governing in the Information Age*. Buckingham: Open University Press.
Borins, Sandford. 2007a. 'Conceptual Framework'. In *Digital State at the Leading Edge*, edited by Sandford Borins, Kenneth Kernaghan, David Brown, Nick Bontis, Perri 6, and Fred Thompson, 14–36. Toronto: University of Toronto Press.

Borins, Sandford. 2007b. 'Is IT Transforming Government? Evidence and Lessons from Canada'. In *Digital State at the Leading Edge*, edited by Sandford Borins, Kenneth Kernaghan, David Brown, Nick Bontis, Perri 6, and Fred Thompson, 355–383. Toronto: University of Toronto Press.

Borins, Sandford, Kenneth Kernaghan, David Brown, Nick Bontis, Perri 6, and Fred Thompson, eds. 2007. *Digital State at the Leading Edge*. Toronto: University of Toronto Press.

Bovens, Mark, and Stavros Zouridis. 2002. 'From Street-Level to System-Level Bureaucracies: How Information and Communication Technology Is Transforming Administrative Discretion and Constitutional Control'. *Public Administration Review* 62 (2): 174–184.

Brown, David. 2007. 'The Government of Canada: Government On-Line and Citizen-Centred Service. In *Digital State at the Leading Edge*, edited by Sandford Borins, Kenneth Kernaghan, David Brown, Nick Bontis, Perri 6, and Fred Thompson, 37–68. Toronto: University of Toronto Press.

Cabinet Office. 2012a. *Government Digital Strategy*. London, UK: Cabinet Office. November.

Cabinet Office. 2012b. *Digital Landscape Research*. London, UK: Cabinet Office. November.

Cordella, Antonio. 2007. 'E-Government: Towards the E-Bureaucratic Form?' *Journal of Information Technology* 22: 265–274. doi:10.1057/palgrave.jit.2000105

Daly, Jimmy. 2013. *The History of Federal Data Centers*. Last updated 16 May 2013. http://www.fedtechmagazine.com/article/2013/05/history-federal-data-centers-infographic

Danziger, James, and Kim Andersen. 2002. 'Impacts of IT on Politics and the Public Sector: Methodological, Epistemological, and Substantive Evidence from the "Golden Age" of Transformation'. *International Journal of Public Administration* 25 (2): 591–627.

Dunleavy, Patrick, Helen Margetts, Simon Bastow, and Jane Tinkler. 2006. *Digital Era Governance: IT Corporations, the State, and E-Government*. Oxford: Oxford University Press.

Dutton, William H., and Grant Blank. 2011. 'Next Generation Users: The Internet in Britain'. *Oxford Internet Survey 2011 Report*. Oxford: Oxford Internet Institute, University of Oxford.

Eppel, Elizabeth, and Miriam Lips. 2016. 'Unpacking the Black Box of Successful ICT-Enabled Service Transformation: How to Join Up the Vertical, the Horizontal and the Technical'. *Public Money and Management*, 36 (1): 39–46.

Fountain, Jane E. 2001. *Building the Virtual State: Information Technology and Institutional Change*. Washington, DC: Brookings Institution Press.

Fountain, Jane E. 2008. 'Bureaucratic Reform and E-Government in the United States: An Institutional Perspective'. In *The Handbook of Internet Politics*, edited by A. Chadwick and P.N. Howard, 99–113. London: Routledge.

Hammer, Michael. 1990. 'Reengineering Work: Don't Automate Obliterate'. *Harvard Business Review*, (July–August): 104–112.

Hammer, Michael, and James Champy. 1993. *Reengineering the Corporation, a Manifesto for Business Revolution*. New York: Harper Collins.

Heeks, Richard, ed. 1999. *Reinventing Government in the Information Age: International Practice in IT-Enabled Public Sector Reform*. London: Routledge.

Homburg, Vincent. 2004. 'E-Government and NPM: A Perfect Marriage?' *Proceedings of the 6th International Conference on Electronic Commerce*, Delft, The Netherlands, October 25–27, ACM: 547–555.

Kraemer, Ken, and John L. King. 2006. 'Information Technology and Administrative Reform: Will E-Government be Different?' *International Journal of Electronic Government Research (IJEGR)* 2 (1): 1–20. doi:10.4018/jegr.2006010101

Lallana, Emmanuel C. 2008. *mGovernment: Mobile/Wireless Applications in Government*. Last updated 19 October 2008. http://www.egov4dev.org/mgovernment/

Layne, Karen, and Jungwoo Lee. 2001. 'Developing Fully Functional E-Government: A Four Stage Model'. *Government Information Quarterly* 18 (2): 122–136.

Lips, Miriam. 2011. 'E-Government Is Dead—Long Live Networked Governance: Fixing System Errors in the New Zealand Public Management System'. In *Future State: Directions for Public Management in New Zealand*, edited by Bill Ryan and Derek Gill, 248–261. Wellington: Victoria University Press.

Lips, Miriam. 2014. 'Transforming Government—by Default?' In *Society and the Internet: How Networks of Information and Communication Are Changing Our Lives*, edited by Mark Graham and William H. Dutton, 179–194. Oxford: Oxford University Press.

Lips, Miriam, and Paul H.A. Frissen. 1997. 'Wiring Government: Integrated Public Service Delivery through ICT in the UK and the USA'. *NWO/ITèR-Series* 8: 67–164. Samsom BedrijfsInformatie bv Alphen aan den Rijn/Diegem.

Lips, Miriam, and Tino Schuppan. 2009. 'Transforming E-Government Knowledge through Public Management Research'. *Public Management Review* 11 (6): 739–749.

Lukman, Enriko. 2013. *Indonesia's Anti-Corruption Website Is Now Getting 1,000 Crowdsourced Reports Every Day*. Last updated 21 October 2013. https://www.techinasia.com/lapor-indonesia-200000-users/

Margetts, Helen. 1999. *Information Technology in Government: Britain and America*. London: Routledge.

McLoughlin, Ian, Rob Wilson, and Mike Martin. 2013. *Digital Government at Work: A Social Informatics Perspective*. Abingdon: Oxford University Press.

Ministry of Social Development. 2012. 'Investment Approach Refocuses Entire Welfare System'. *MSD Media Release 12 September 2012*. Downloaded from www.msd.govt.nz

OECD. 2009. *Citizen-Centric Government*. Paris: OECD.

OECD. 2011. *m-Government: Mobile Technologies for Responsive Governments and Connected Societies*. International Telecommunication Union: OECD. http://www.oecd.org/gov/public-innovation/49300932.pdf

OECD. 2013. 'Exploring Data-Driven Innovation as a New Source of Growth: Mapping the Policy Issues Raised by "Big Data"'. OECD Digital Economy Papers, No. 222, OECD Publishing. http://dx.doi.org/10.1787/5k47zw3fcp43-en

O'Neill, Rose. 2009. 'The Transformative Impact of E-Government on Public Governance in New Zealand'. *Public Management Review* 11 (6): 751–770.

SAS. 2013. 'Transforming Social Welfare with Analytics'. *SAS Customer Story*. Downloaded from www.sas.co.nz. Wellington: SAS.

Sunstein, Cass. 2007. *Republic.com 2.0*. Princeton, NJ: Princeton University Press.

Taylor Fry. 2011. *Ministry of Social Development and the Treasury—Actuarial Advice of Feasibility: A Long-Term Investment Approach to Improving Employment, Social and Financial Outcomes from Welfare Benefits and Services*. Wellington: Ministry of Social Development and The Treasury.

Taylor Fry. 2013. *Ministry of Social Development and the Treasury—Actuarial Valuation of the Benefit System for Working-Age Adults as at 30 June 2013*. Wellington: Ministry of Social Development and The Treasury.

Taylor, John, Ignace Snellen, and Arre Zuurmond, eds. 1997. *Beyond BPR in Public Administration: Institutional Transformation in an Information Age*. Amsterdam: IOS Press.

Van de Donk, Wim, and Pieter Tops. 1995. 'Orwell or Athens? Informatization and the Future of Democracy'. In *Orwell in Athens: A Perspective on Informatization and Democracy*, edited by Wim Van de Donk, Ignace Snellen, and Pieter Tops, 13–32. Amsterdam: IOS Press.

Van Duivenboden, Hein P.M., and Miriam Lips, eds. 2001. *Klantgericht Werken in de Publieke Sector. Inrichting van de Elektronische Overhead*. Utrecht: Boom Lemma.

Weerakkody, Vishanth, and Christopher Reddick, eds. 2012. *Public Sector Transformation through E-Government: Experiences from Europe and North America*. New York: Routledge.

West, Darrell. 2005. *Digital Government: Technology and Public Sector Performance*. Princeton, NJ: Princeton University Press.

The White House. 2012. *Digital Government: Building a 21st Century Platform to Better Service the American People*. Executive Office of the President of the United States, Washington, DC: The White House.

3

INFORMATION POLICIES

Value-Oriented, Instrumental, and Managerial Choices for Governing an Information Society

Sharon S. Dawes

Most police body cam footage would be exempt under bill. Police body camera footage taken in private places would be largely exempt from Freedom of Information Act laws under legislation under consideration Tuesday in the state House of Representatives. Under the rewritten legislation, the footage wouldn't be considered a public record, but would be available to people who are the subject of an audio or video recording, whose property has been seized or damaged by police, or the parent or legal guardian or an attorney representing an individual caught on tape by police. "One of the core functions of body worn cameras is to improve trust with the community," said state Rep. Jim Runestad, R-White Lake, the sponsor of the bill. "But this technology must be guided by a balance between the right of oversight with an individual's right to privacy." Media organizations, however, called the bill bad public policy that isn't protecting police or citizens.

—*Detroit Free Press, June 2, 2015*

Town of Tonawanda's Huntley power plant is biggest polluter in Erie County. Renewable energy advocates said the 440,000 pounds of pollutants that the Huntley electric plant generated in the Town of Tonawanda in 2013 proves it doesn't take much coal to damage the Earth. The plant's operator said the 98-year-old facility has never run cleaner. Both arguments might be true, but it didn't stop Huntley from recapturing its longtime perch atop the U.S. Environmental Protection Agency's annual list as Erie County's biggest polluter. The data, according to EPA's newly published Toxics Release Inventory, shows most of the contaminants from Huntley were collected and transferred off site, but about 56,000 pounds were released into the air, water or land. The federal inventory data shows Huntley released 34,641 pounds of hydrogen fluoride into the environment from its River Road site, along with 20,514 pounds of hydrochloric acid, 884 pounds of barium compounds as well as 83 and 17 pounds of lead and mercury compounds, respectively.

—*Buffalo Evening News, October 22, 2014*

GAO audit: Public records mishandled by federal agencies. An audit prompted in part by the loss of the Wright brothers' original patent and maps for atomic bomb missions in Japan finds some of the nation's prized historical documents are in danger of being lost for good. Nearly 80 percent of U.S. government agencies are at risk of illegally destroying public records and the National Archives is backlogged with hefty volumes of records needing preservation care, the audit by the Government Accountability Office found. The report by the watchdog arm of Congress, completed this month after a year's work and obtained by the Associated Press, also found many U.S. agencies do not follow proper procedures for disposing of public records.

—*The Washington Post, October 28, 2010*

How Much Damage Can Hackers Do With a Million Fingerprints From the OPM Data Breach? The Office of Personnel Management announced last week that the personal data for 21.5 million people had been stolen. But for national security professionals and cybersecurity experts, the more troubling issue is the theft of 1.1 million fingerprints. Much of their concern rests with the permanent nature of fingerprints and the uncertainty about just how the hackers intend to use them . . . Part of the worry, cybersecurity experts say, is that fingerprints are part of an exploding field of biometric data, which the government is increasingly getting in the business of collecting and storing. Fingerprints today are used to run background checks, verify identities at borders, and unlock smartphones, but the technology is expected to boom in the coming decades in both the public and private sectors.

—*National Journal, July 14, 2015*

Introduction

These diverse stories have something important in common. They all illustrate challenges for government information policy. The police video cam story from Detroit shows the potential for information collected in real time via digital technology to improve both the practice and the perception of policing—but at the same time it threatens the privacy of citizens who show up in the video. Erie County is the site of Love Canal, a notorious toxic cleanup site that has become a symbol of environmental justice. In the 1950s and 60s, no one knew how much and what kinds of chemicals were polluting the land and contributing to high rates of cancer in the community. Today, the Toxics Release Inventory, authorized by a federal right-to-know law, requires chemical manufacturers and other industries to report publicly the kinds and amounts of toxic by-products their plants release into the environment. The GAO audit report highlights one of the oldest assurances of government accountability—the Federal Records Act—which prescribes how federal government records in any form must be managed during their active lives and disposed of or preserved for their legal, historical, or cultural value. The last story raises a critical security issue with both managerial and national security implications. The hack of U.S. federal government employee records at the Office of Personnel Management not only threatens the personal identities of more than 20 million current and former federal workers and contractors, it also potentially provides a boon to espionage and terrorism. Each of these stories shows how information is deeply embedded in essential governmental functions and public policy concerns including criminal justice, environmental quality, managerial effectiveness, and national security as well as accountability, privacy, and access to information.

Information policy is relevant to virtually any activity of government and every facet of social and economic life. It frames the way government deals with crucial issues, while it also affects everyday life for ordinary people (McClure and Jaeger 2008). But what is information policy? One often-cited definition holds that information policy is "the set of all public laws, regulations, and policies that encourage, discourage, or regulate the creation, use, storage, and communication of information" (Weingarten 1989). An even broader definition of information policy comprises those "societal mechanisms used to control information, and the societal effects of applying those mechanisms" (Burger 1993). Some would add that information policies are expressed not only by what government does but also by what it chooses not to do with respect to any information issue (Galvin 1992). Others say information policy is a deceivingly unified term that masks a fragmented, overlapping, and sometimes contradictory collection of separate policies that address specific issues like education, consumer protection, or health care (Hernon and Relyea 2009). By any definition, then, information policies comprise a complex web of values, rules, and responsibilities.

This complexity is multiplied by the fact that public information policy is not solely the province of national governments. Policies are also adopted by states and municipalities, and even through international treaties. In addition, advances in information and communication technology cause governments to continually adopt and adapt information policies to better fit the technological environment (Bertot, Jaeger, and Hansen 2012). Further, information policies are often interrelated and the boundaries of policy topics are permeable, making it frequently difficult to see (or agree) where policies about one topic (such as privacy) end and policies about another topic (such as access to information) begin.

This chapter examines information policy from historical and analytical perspectives. It aims to construct a conceptual framework for classifying and examining contemporary information issues that can help both analysts and practitioners reduce ambiguity and manage their inherent complexity. We begin with a historical overview of information policy development in the United States, with particular focus on the period between 1990 and the present. We then review and briefly critique a variety of conceptual frameworks that offer ways to work through the complexity of information policy issues. This is followed by an exploration of the purposes and application of government information policies of three kinds: value-oriented policies that address the flow of information in society, instrumental policies that use information-based activities as part of a strategy to achieve other public policy goals, and managerial policies that shape how government handles its internal information resources and responsibilities. The chapter concludes with discussion of a purpose-driven framework and some thoughts on information policy research, practice, and education.

Historical Development of U.S. Information Policy

The concept of information policy can be traced far back in social and political history into at least the Middle Ages, when independent thought and inquiry were strongly discouraged and even severely punished by the religious establishment (Browne 1997a). However, formal government information policies emerged much later. In the U.S., they began in the 18th century with the U.S. Constitution and the Bill of Rights. Article 1, Section 2 of the Constitution mandates the U.S. Census, the first information collection program, requiring the government to enumerate the population every 10 years. Article 1, Section 5 may be the earliest statement of open government principles: "Each House shall keep a Journal of its Proceedings, and from time to time publish the same, excepting such Parts as may in their Judgment require Secrecy; and the Yeas and Nays of the Members of either House on any question shall, at the Desire of one fifth of those Present, be entered on the Journal." Article 2, Section 3 requires that the president "shall from time to time give to the Congress Information of the State of the Union."

Article 1, Section 8 lays the foundation for intellectual property rights by giving Congress the power to "promote the progress of science and useful arts, by securing for limited times to authors and inventors the exclusive right to their respective writings and discoveries." The same article addresses fundamental information infrastructure by establishing post offices and post roads.

While these articles in the body of the constitution specify the powers of the government, the Bill of Rights embodied in the first 10 amendments enumerates guarantees to the people. The First Amendment, which underpins much of modern information policy formulation and debate, assures freedom of speech, religion, press, and assembly to petition the government. The Fourth Amendment protects people from "unreasonable searches and seizures."

Table 3.1 below lists chronologically many of the key federal statutes and related actions that express U.S. information policies. They range from original provisions of the U.S. Constitution and Bill of Rights to recent statutory amendments to redefine federal records in light of advancing information technologies.

The 19th century brought the earliest internally directed policies resting on the principles of recorded accountability and printed documents (Relyea 2008). In 1813, Congress created the first

Table 3.1 Selected U.S. Information Policy Statutes and Related Actions

Year	Title
1789	U.S. Constitution
1791	First Amendment to the U.S. Constitution
1859	Depository Library Program established
1860	U.S. Government Printing Office established
1873	Congressional Record established
1934	Communications Act, amended by
	1996 Telecommunications Act
1934	National Archives established
1934	Securities and Exchange Commission Act
	2002 Sarbanes-Oxley Act
1935	Federal Register Act
1937	Code of Federal Regulations established
1946	Administrative Procedures Act
1950	Federal Records Act
	2014 Federal Records Act Amendments
1952	National Security Agency established
1966	Freedom of Information Act, amended by
	1986 Freedom of Information Reform Act
	1996 Electronic Freedom of Information Act
1968	Truth in Lending Act (TILA)
1970	Fair Credit Reporting Act
1972	Federal Advisory Committee Act
1974	Privacy Act
1976	Government in the Sunshine Act
1974	Family Educational Rights and Privacy Act (FERPA)
1978	Presidential Records Act of 1978
1980	Paperwork Reduction Act of 1980, amended by
	1996 Clinger-Cohen Act (Information Technology Reform Act)
1986	Computer Fraud and Abuse Act (CFAA)
1986	Emergency Planning and Community Right-to-Know Act (EPCRA)
1988	Computer Security Act (CSA)
1992	Copyright Amendments Act
1993	Government Performance and Results Act (GPRA)
1996	Health Insurance Portability and Accountability Act (HIPAA)
1998	Digital Millennium Copyright Act (DMCA)
1998	§508 of The Americans with Disabilities Act

Year	Title
1998	Children's Online Privacy Protection Act (COPPA)
2001	Data Quality Act
2001	USA PATRIOT Act of 2001, amended 2015
2002	Electronic Government Act of 2002
2002	Federal Information Security Management Act (FISMA)
2003	Homeland Security Act
2003	Do-Not-Call Implementation Act
2009	Health Information Technology for Economic and Clinical Health (HITECH) Act

provisions for the creation and distribution of printed records that were successively improved, culminating with the establishment of the U.S. Government Printing Office in 1859, followed by the Depository Library Program in 1860, which together created both the responsibility and a formal mechanism for routine printing and distribution of government records. The Printing Act of 1895 clarified the roles of the Government Printing Office and Depository Library Program and included the proviso "that no . . . Government publication shall be copyrighted."

No significant new policies emerged again until the New Deal beginning in 1934 with the passage of the Communications Act to regulate "interstate and foreign commerce in communication by wire and radio so as to make available, so far as possible, to all the people of the United States a rapid, efficient, nationwide, and worldwide wire and radio communication service with adequate facilities at reasonable charges . . ." In the same year, the National Archives was created to maintain the historically valuable records of the nation and began to prescribe policies for active records management, as well as disposition and preservation. These were followed in 1935 by the Federal Register Act and the establishment of the Code of Federal Regulations that document the key activities of executive agencies and make documents available for public inspection. The Securities and Exchange Commission Act of 1934, in reaction to the issues that brought about the Great Depression, was the first instance in which the government required private organizations to disclose information about their structure and operations.

In the post–World War II period, several additional significant policy actions emerged. The Administrative Procedures Act of 1946 required executive agencies to follow a uniform procedure for issuing regulations and required methods and places for the public to obtain information or submit comments or requests. The Federal Records Act of 1950 (amended 1964) mandated the "adequate and proper documentation of the organization, functions, policies, decisions, procedures, and essential transactions of the agency," setting a framework for records management in federal agencies. While the foregoing acts represent the maturation of the *administrative state*, the creation of the National Security Agency by Executive Order in 1956 signaled the simultaneous rise of the *national security state* (Relyea 2008). The NSA along with security classification schemes and additional Executive Orders give broad discretion to the president to create official secrets.

While the history presented to this point catalogs essential information policy foundations in the U.S., many scholars agree that modern information policy begins around 1960 and accelerates and expands thereafter (Browne 1997a).

Probably the best known, and arguably the most influential, of these modern policies is the Freedom of Information Act of 1966, enacted in the wake of strong public dissatisfaction with government secrecy and accountability. FOIA established a right of access for any person to unpublished existing departmental records except for those exempted from disclosure by nine specific reasons (including national security, interference with law enforcement, invasion of personal privacy, trade secrets, and internal personnel matters). FOIA also provides for administrative appeal and judicial review of disputes over disclosure requests. The Federal Advisory Committee Act of 1972 and the Government in the Sunshine Act of 1976 had similar goals—to open the policymaking deliberations of federal agencies, boards, and commissions to public scrutiny. The Presidential Records Act of 1978, for the first time, mandated public ownership and management of presidential records.

In further resistance to the power of the administrative state, especially in view of expanding computerized records systems, the Privacy Act of 1974 established a code of fair information practices to govern the collection, maintenance, use, and dissemination of information about individuals maintained in federal government records systems. It prohibits disclosure without written consent of the individual, subject to 12 reasons for exemption. Some of these, such as "routine use," have been the basis for numerous lawsuits. The act also provides for access to and amendment of individual records and judicial review of agency decisions. The vagueness of the language in the Privacy Act has not only led to court cases but also to a number of laws aimed at protecting personal privacy in specific situations, such as health care, education, and consumer transactions.

From the mid-1980s to the present, information policy actions multiplied along several fronts in the form of both laws and executive actions. While Congress has continued to play a substantial role, many of the recent policy decisions have been taken by executive action. Table 3.2 lists significant executive orders, Office of Management and Budget (OMB) guidance, and other presidential instruments that convey and implement information policies. The influence of advancing information and communication technologies is clearly seen in both the number and the topics covered.

Table 3.2 Selected Executive Directives and OMB Guidance on Information Policy Topics

Year	Title
ongoing	OMB Circular A-130 Management of Federal Information Resources
1993	EO 12862 Setting Customer Service Standards
1995	EO 12958 Classified National Security Information
1996	EO 13011 Federal Information Technology
1998	Presidential Decision Directive 63 (Protecting America's Critical Infrastructures)
1998	Presidential Memorandum on Privacy and Personal Information in Federal Records
1999	Presidential Memorandum on Electronic Government
2000	M-01–05 Guidance on Inter-Agency Sharing of Personal Data—Protecting Personal Privacy
2000	EO 13166 (Improving Access to Services for Persons with Limited English Proficiency)
2001	EO Order 13228 (Establishing the Office of Homeland Security and Homeland Security Council)
2001	EO Order 13231 (Critical Infrastructure Protection in the Information Age)
2001	EO Order 13233 (Further Implementation of the Presidential Records Act)
2002	E-Government Strategy
2003	President's Management Agenda
2004	M-05–04 Policies for Federal Agency Websites
2004	Homeland Security Presidential Directive (HSPD—7 Critical Infrastructure Protection Plans to Protect Federal Critical Infrastructures and Key Resources
2004	EO 13356 (Strengthening the Sharing of Terrorism Information to Protect Americans)
2005	M-05–08 Designation of Senior Agency Officials for Privacy
2005	EO 13392 Improving Agency Disclosure of Information
2007	M-07–24 Updated Principles for Risk Analysis
2007	M-07–16 Safeguarding Against and Responding to the Breach of Personally Identifiable Information

Year	Title
2009	Presidential Memorandum, Freedom of Information Act
2009	M-10-06 Open Government Directive
2010	Presidential Memorandum, Social Media, Web-Based Interactive Technologies, and the Paperwork Reduction Act
2010	M-10-22 Guidance for Online Use of Web Measurement and Customization Technologies
2011	EO 13563 Improving Regulation and Regulatory Review
2011	EO 13576 Delivering an Efficient, Effective, and Accountable Government
2013	EO 13642 Making Open and Machine Readable the New Default for Government Information
2013	M-13-13 Open Data Policy—Managing Information as an Asset
2013	Joint Memo to Heads of Executive Departments and Agencies on Principles for Federal Engagement in Standards Activities to Address National Priorities
2013	EO 13636 Improving Critical Infrastructure Cybersecurity

Information and technology management within the government began to receive concentrated attention via a number of laws and executive orders, both encouraging the use of modern technologies and establishing new requirements for management and accountability. The Paperwork Reduction Act of 1980 (amended 1995), the Clinger-Cohen Act of 1996, and the Government Performance and Results Act of 1993 all focus on the management and use of information and technology to achieve better performance and greater transparency. OMB Circular A-130 has become the administrative bible for implementing these and a variety of other information management principles and requirements.

Security of government information and systems has also received significantly increased attention, especially since the terrorist attacks of September 2001. The Computer Security Act of 1987, the Government Information Security Reform Act of 2000 (GISRA), the USA PATRIOT Act of 2001, the Homeland Security Act of 2002, the Federal Information Security Management Act (FISMA) of 2002, and a variety of executive actions have addressed critical infrastructure protection, sharing of terrorist information, risk analysis, surveillance, and related security concerns.

At the same time, policies have been created or updated to increase access to and usability of government information by addressing the needs of people with disabilities, the quality of federal data and federal government websites, use of social media, promotion of open data, and better FOIA performance. Significant updates to records laws and intellectual property rights have also been driven by changes in digital information formats. Nearly all of these topics have become the subject of court cases to sort out competing interests and priorities among stakeholders and principles.

Conceptual Frameworks for Understanding Information Policy

Information policy as a domain of study and action is challenging in several respects. To begin, we lack consensus on any broad conceptual framework that could rationalize and integrate our understanding of the wide range of information issues in society. This state of affairs is all the more problematic because both the variety and the importance of societal issues related to information continue to grow. In addition, no organization inside or outside government is the obvious forum to raise and debate information issues. Instead, information-related questions are treated piecemeal within different policy areas, involving different stakeholders, at every level of government (Browne 1997a). This approach means information policies are often uncoordinated and even conflict with one another. For example, in New York State, real property information is collected by municipalities that may set their own policies for information access and fees. Some post the data online for free access, some require a written request, still others require a fee for reproduction or an ongoing subscription to the data. While the state government provides real property information to requesters without charge, it has only a subset of the detailed information maintained at the local level. Therefore, someone who wants detailed information for the entire state can get it only by requesting and complying with the access policies of each local jurisdiction (Dawes and Helbig 2010). Privacy policies are another example. While there are national and state-level privacy laws that require governments to comply with certain standards for handling personal information, very few industries in the private sector are subject to specific legal requirements. Instead, these policy choices are often left to the market or to individual companies. For multinational firms, the differences in data privacy protections between the U.S. and Europe pose costly and sometimes contentious situations as companies attempt to comply with different sets of rules (Reidenberg 2000).

Several factors help explain this environment of diversity and fragmentation. First, information is relevant across the full range of public administration and policy topics. Information itself has seldom been the main focus of government policy, despite the fact that no governmental program or public decision-making process can exist without an essential information component. Instead, information policies have most often developed as ancillary to policies and practices in other domains. Unlike healthcare policy or education policy, or urban policy, information policy has traditionally been seen as a supporting consideration rather than the primary policy subject (Duff 2004).

Second, information itself is an ambiguous concept with both objective and subjective characteristics with social and economic implications (Orna 2008). In addition, the term "information" is often used as a rough synonym for data, knowledge, or know-how and can be both implicit and explicit (Nonaka 1994). Information resides in databases, records, documents, and publications, but it is also embedded in conversations, debates, expertise, products, and culture. It is often conflated with communication, and information content is increasingly confused with information technology. To address this difficulty, scholars have attempted to define information for purposes of both research and practice. Sandra Braman suggests information can be categorized in four main ways: as a *resource* unattached to any particular body of knowledge, as a *commodity* which can be bought and sold for its economic value, as *perception* represented by human recognition of patterns and context, and as a *constitutive force* in society that has its own power to shape context (Braman 2011). These different characterizations imply inevitable ambiguity and confusion across actors concerned with any particular information policy issue as they adopt, but often do not express, different meanings and interpretations of "information."

Third, as a consequence of its ambiguousness, information policy has no clear disciplinary home (Duff 2004). It has been variously addressed by such diverse fields as computer science, information science, economics, political science, sociology, library and archival studies, public administration, and law (Galperin 2004). Scholarship has emerged mainly from the communication, information studies, and library communities. As such, the topics of interest have been predominantly those that relate to information management and access. However, experts argue that to advance the field beyond these particular topics, "information policy needs to be more integrated within the broader field of mainstream policy studies and become more interdisciplinary in its approaches"(Browne 1997b). Accordingly, several types of integrative approaches are described below.

Categorization Approaches

Categorization approaches (e.g., Chartrand 1986) identify and organize information policy issues according to certain topics or policy goals, such as information resource management; information technology, telecommunications, and broadcasting; information disclosure, confidentiality, and privacy; and intellectual property. Categorization approaches can also rest on a specific purpose. For

Information Policies

example, the National Institute of Standards and Technology issued categorization standards regarding the risks associated with federal government information and information systems for assuring confidentiality, integrity, and availability (National Institute of Standards and Technology 2009). A different categorization approach considers information policies along hierarchical dimensions including infrastructural policies that apply across society, horizontal information policies that apply across the entire information sector, such as providing for public libraries, and vertical policies that apply to specific segments or activities within the information sector, such as the geographic information community (Rowlands 1996).

Life Cycle View

Hernon and Relyea (2009) state that information policy guides oversight and management of the information life cycle. Life cycle components include production, collection, distribution or dissemination, retrieval, and retirement of information as well as information access and use. Figure 3.1, from Library and Archives Canada, depicts one typical presentation of the information life cycle at the national level. This and similar life cycle approaches take an internal government view and focus mainly on the management of information resources within a government organization. Different guidelines or rules are pertinent at different stages of the life cycle. Policies for Stage 2, for instance, emphasize that an information asset is being created with the need for documentation, authentication, and version control. In Stage 4, for example, policies focus on internal and external sharing of complete, accurate, and timely information.

At the operational level, the Western Australia Department of Health provides a good example of the life cycle approach. It specifies policies for data collection (e.g., information is collected only for a legitimate business purpose, collected in an ethical manner, and data requirements and metadata are clearly documented); storage (storage media, records management, security measures, and classification procedures); access and disclosure (focus on data integrity and confidentiality and on providing

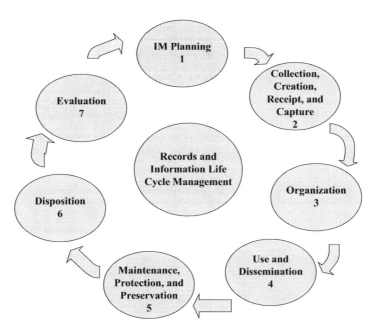

Figure 3.1   Records and Information Life Cycle, Library and Archives Canada

different levels of access for different kinds of users); use (policies to assure information is used in a responsible, ethical, and lawful manner according to business, operational, or legislative requirements); and disposal (covering records retention, transfer, disposal, and archival requirements). The overarching purpose of this life cycle management policy is to assure that data and information handled by the department meets high standards for accuracy and validity and supports the operational needs of its programs. The policy addresses not only ways to handle information but also specifies roles and responsibilities for data stewards, data custodians, and authorized users at various stages of the life cycle (Western Australia Department of Health 2014).

Information Transfer Perspective

A different approach is to consider policies that are germane to different phases of the information transfer process, which is conceptualized as a chain of processes that move information from a source to a user. This perspective emphasizes the *processes* and *actors* involved in the movement of information. It accommodates the roles played by information producers, professional intermediaries, institutions, and individual, organizational, and societal information users. It includes information management processes such as recording, collection, searching, and retrieval. In addition, it provides a means to identify and understand value-adding processes throughout the chain, such as analysis, interpretation, evaluation, and synthesis. In this view, the government is one of many stakeholders in the full process (Browne 1997a).

Rights in Conflict Typology

Galvin describes the domain of information policy as the full range of actions "taken or not taken by any branch of government . . . at any level . . . that affect the character or the quality of the information transfer process" (Galvin 1992, 1997). He offers a typology drawn from Coates's definition of a public policy issue as a "fundamental enduring conflict" that is unlikely to be fully or permanently resolved among competing interests (Coates 1979). This emphasis on conflict underlies a three-part typology for identifying and assessing information policy issues. This "rights in conflict" view is based on three information rights and their potential to conflict with other rights and values as well as with each other. These information rights are access rights, privacy rights, and proprietary or ownership rights.

Type 1 information policy problems represent information issues about which there is broad agreement in principle but conflict over boundaries or method of implementation. In other words, the conflict is not about the principle itself but the means to achieve it. One example is the debate over how to achieve universal access to telecommunications. Among the possible means are government subsidies to certain individuals, government regulation of telecomm providers, and market-based pricing schemes. Another example is the ability of online companies to reuse customers' personally identifiable information. One approach is to prohibit reuse unless consumers "opt-in," putting the main responsibility on the company, the other is to require consumers to "opt-out" of such uses, thus putting the responsibility for privacy protection on the individual.

Type 2 problems represent conflicts between an information right and some other social, political, or economic value or goal. These are very common problems that show up in many different domains. Laws that ban federal funding to clinics that offer abortion counseling represent a conflict between access (an information right) and the state's interest in protecting the unborn (a social value). Similarly, policies embedded in the USA PATRIOT Act following the terrorist acts of 9/11 represent a choice to favor national security interests over certain rights to privacy in personal communications.

In Type 3 problems, the conflict occurs between two or even all three information rights. Ongoing legal battles over music streaming on the Internet, for example, represent a fundamental conflict between the access rights of listeners and the ownership rights of artists and music producers.

In all cases, these policy choices represent a balancing act that takes place within a particular social and political context. They settle the issues temporarily, but because they do not remove the fundamental value conflicts, they are subject to continued advocacy, interpretation, and change. Thus, for example, we see the balance between personal privacy and national security tipping back toward privacy protection in the revised provisions of the USA PATRIOT Act when it was reauthorized in 2015.

Socio-Technical View

A fifth perspective places information policy within a socio-technical context that highlights the interaction between social and technical systems (Trist 1981). This view acknowledges the complexity inherent in the information policy domain from the different types of problems to the various forms of policy instruments (laws, regulations, executive actions, etc.), to traditional and emerging technologies that are used to gather, organize, and convey information. It also takes into account the multiplicity of stakeholders in information policy with their divergent views, needs, resources, and preferences. Further, it highlights the dynamic interplay between social and instrumental concerns. Social concerns encompass culture, norms, and values. Instrumental concerns focus on the work and the technologies used to gather, manage, and disseminate information. In other words, the socio-technical view considers information policy as the result of interaction among humans and various kinds of technology in a given social context (Maxwell 2003).

This view also encompasses the idea of social informatics, which addresses the consequences of the design, implementation, and use of information and communication technologies in social and organizational settings. Social informatics takes the view that social and technical factors are constantly influencing and shaping one another. In the policy arena, this mutual shaping gives rise not only to policy choices but also to new policy problems (Sawyer and Rosenbaum 2000).

Each perspective above offers useful but partial insight into the nature of the information policy domain and the ways in which different professions and disciplines understand it. The topical view underscores the variety of major topics of concern but does not assist either policy makers or implementers to understand how these topics might interact or compete in perception or in practice. The life cycle view focuses on how policies guide government professionals to handle responsibility for the different life cycle stages of information within their control, but it does not acknowledge or advise about the important aspects of information collection and use within the larger society. The information transfer view reveals the importance of dynamics, processes, and actors as information flows through a chain of processes that add value by drawing on different kinds of knowledge and expertise both within and outside the government, but again it stops short of looking at the implications of information use once it reaches the hands of external users. By emphasizing values, stakeholders, and enduring tensions, the rights in conflict typology puts a spotlight on information rights and the ways in which they present policy problems for implementation, balance, and response to changing social, political, and economic conditions. It provides a more complete way to assess and understand information issues from both internal and external perspectives. However, it gives little guidance for managerial or administrative action by government professionals. Finally, in the socio-technical view, attention focuses on the tools and technologies that embody, store, and transmit information in social and organizational settings and how technology and social factors shape one another in the context of information and technology use. This view takes full consideration of how information technologies and social trends are mutually shaping one another and thus giving rise to new kinds of policy challenges. But, like the conflict model, it offers more insight to analysts than to managers.

Policies represent choices and values, but they are also meant to guide action. Laws and executive orders are the best-known forms of policy, but they are not the only form. For government agencies, policy-related responsibilities include policy analysis and formulation to accomplish their missions or to carry out specific laws. Agencies develop rules and regulations that implement policies through a process of notice, public comment, and consultation with stakeholders. Agencies also monitor and evaluate the performance of policies to achieve their intended purposes and make recommendations for policy adjustments to improve performance. In the remainder of this chapter, we draw on these perspectives to explore information policy within the interdisciplinary field of public administration, with particular attention to the roles and practices of government professionals in developing, implementing, and assessing information policies to achieve important public purposes.

A Purpose-Driven Framework

All of the foregoing frameworks offer ways to intellectually simplify the complexity of the information environment so that key dimensions come into better focus. Moving from the categorization view through to the socio-technical view, these frameworks take increasingly broader perspectives on these dimensions. In this section, we take aspects from these ideas to create a practice-oriented framework. By practice-oriented, we mean a conceptual view that offers government professionals, managers, and policy makers a perspective that is useful in government administration and decision-making. The preceding frameworks consider information policy concerns as topics, points in a life cycle, segments of the information transfer process, conflicts among rights, and interactions between the social and technical domains. The practice-oriented view makes use of all of these ideas in considering information policy choices and their impacts according to a set of three main purposes (Figure 3.2):

- Regulating the flow of information in society
- Using information as an instrument to achieve other policy purposes
- Managing information as a governmental and societal asset

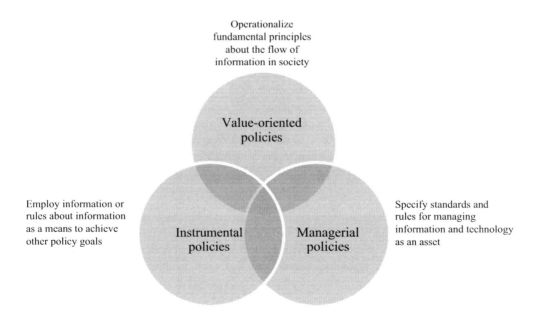

Figure 3.2 Information Policy Purposes

Below, we consider the purposes and performance of government information policies of three kinds: value-oriented policies that regulate the flow of information in society, instrumental policies that use information-based activities as part of a strategy to achieve other policy goals, and managerial policies that shape the way in which government handles its internal information resources and responsibilities for information assets. The sections below briefly discuss these policy types and offer three examples for each.

Value-Driven Information Policies

Public policies pertaining to information flow are among the most fundamental aspects of democracy. Information policies reflect societal choices regarding how information should be produced, processed, stored, exchanged, and regulated (Benkler 1998). For example, the First Amendment to the U.S. Constitution embodies democratic principles of free expression, an independent press, and free exchange of information among citizens. It reflects strong value preference for diversity in information sources and content, as well as universal access to and participation in the marketplace of ideas. In expressions of this kind, government treats information as the *object* of policy, that is, information itself is the subject of policy making. These broad philosophically anchored laws and principles shape the creation, use, expression, and dissemination of information and knowledge by everyone in society. They place government in the position of regulator of societal information flow. Examples of these kinds of policies are laws that ensure access to information, protect personal privacy, support libraries, and provide for patents and copyrights over intellectual property (Dawes 2010).

Overman and Cahill (1990) describe several values served by U.S. information policies: access to information, freedom of expression, personal rights to privacy, openness and right to know, usefulness, cost and benefit tradeoffs, secrecy and security, and ownership of intellectual property. Different statutes address these different kinds of values. Three of them, freedom of expression, access to government information, and protection of personal privacy, are discussed below.

Freedom of Expression

Free expression is probably the most fundamental value served by information policies in a democracy. Freedom of speech, assembly, and press are guaranteed by the First Amendment to the U.S. Constitution as keystone rights of democratic societies. The First Amendment reads in part, "Congress shall make no law . . . abridging the freedom of speech, or of the press; or the right of the people peaceably to assemble, and to petition the government for a redress of grievances."

Much of the policy pertaining to free speech is embodied in case law resulting from a long list of court decisions about such topics as freedom of expression, prior restraint, and freedom of the press.[1] For example, in *Texas v. Johnson* (1989), the Supreme Court held that laws banning flag burning violated the First Amendment right to free speech. *New York Times v. United States* (1971), a landmark case in which the government sought to prevent publication of the Pentagon Papers during the Vietnam War, established that pre-publication censorship is unconstitutional in almost all cases. In *Miami Herald Publishing Co. v. Tornillo* (1974), the Supreme Court unanimously invalidated a state law requiring newspapers criticizing political candidates to publish the candidates' responses. In *Reno v. American Civil Liberties Union* (1997), its first major case on information distributed via the Internet, the Court struck down anti-indecency provisions of the Communications Decency Act of 1996, because while the law sought to protect children from indecent material, it also violated the free speech rights of adults.

Access to Information

The Freedom of Information Act (FOIA) enacted in 1966 and significantly amended in 1986 (Freedom of Information Reform Act) and 1996 (Electronic Freedom of Information Act) is a leading example of information policy driven by the value of openness and access to information. It provides a guaranteed right of access to existing government records unless the records are exempted by one of nine specific reasons, such as unwarranted invasion of personal privacy or national security. FOIA was enacted in the aftermath of the Pentagon Papers controversy as a reaction against the secrecy surrounding the government's pursuit of the Vietnam War. It requires agencies to disclose records upon request unless one of the exemption criteria applies to the records being sought. FOIA is a foundational statement of the right of public access to government information, but it is limited in its application both by the stated exemptions and by the inclination of executive agencies to err on the side of withholding information from disclosure. During the Bush 43 administration, agencies were instructed to deny access to records whenever there was doubt as to the application of any of the exemptions. The Obama administration reversed that instruction, but despite the administration's emphasis on open government, FOIA disclosure rates and the time it takes to comply with requests continue to garner criticism by open government advocates.

FOIA is the subject of numerous appeals and lawsuits. Cases that come before the Supreme Court typically involve disputes over agency application of one of the statutory exemptions used to deny FOIA requests, with many cases involving the personal privacy exemption. For example, in *National Archives and Records Administration vs. Favish* (2004), the court held that family members of a deceased person have a privacy interest that outweighs a third-party request for death scene photos. In *FCC v. AT&T* (2011), the Court ruled that AT&T could not claim a personal privacy exemption to prevent the Federal Communications Commission from releasing records in a law enforcement action against the company because corporations do not have a right to personal privacy.

Personal Privacy

While FOIA addresses one core democratic value, public access to government information, another set of policies respond to a different fundamental value—protection of personal privacy. The U.S. Constitution does not contain an explicit right to privacy, but the Third, Fourth, Fifth, and Fourteenth Amendments have been read by the courts to offer this protection in the context of individual liberties. The first statute to directly address personal privacy was not enacted until the Privacy Act of 1974, which came at the end of a long effort by the Privacy Protection Study Commission and the U.S. Department of Health, Education, and Welfare to formulate "fair information practices" for an environment in which more and more personal information was being collected, stored, and used within automated data systems. The original set of fair practices included prohibition of secret systems; requirements for government organizations to assure reliability of their systems and prevent misuse of personal data; and provisions for individuals to know what data is in their records and how it is used, to correct or amend their records, and to prevent data collected for one purpose from being used for other purposes without their consent.

Today, fair information practices continue to evolve in response to the enormous changes in the scale and penetration of electronic data systems in modern life. Within the U.S., different federal agencies have adopted specific fair information principles for such topics as trusted identity (National Institutes for Standards and Technology) and consumer affairs (Federal Trade Commission). The European Commission, OECD, and other nongovernmental organizations have developed fair information principles (summarized in Table 3.3) that go beyond the U.S. concepts and are designed for international (or universal) application (Gellman 2015).

In the U.S., personal privacy protections have been embodied in a variety of domain-specific laws since the passage of the Privacy Act. For example, the Family Educational Rights and Privacy Act (FERPA) strictly limits access to student records in schools and universities that receive federal funding. It confers most rights to control release of student information to parents or to students over

Table 3.3 Basic Privacy Principles (adapted from OECD 2013)

Principle	Content
Collection limitation	Personal data should be obtained by lawful and fair means and, where appropriate, with the knowledge or consent of the data subject.
Data quality	Personal data should be relevant to the purposes for which they are to be used, and, to the extent necessary for those purposes, should be accurate, complete and up-to-date.
Purpose specification	The purposes for which personal data are collected should be specified and limited to the fulfillment of those purposes.
Use limitation	Personal data should not be disclosed or used for other purposes without the consent of the data subject or by the authority of law.
Security safeguards	Personal data should be protected by reasonable security safeguards against such risks as loss or unauthorized access, destruction, use, modification or disclosure.
Openness	Under a general policy of openness about developments, practices and policies, means should be readily available to establish the existence and nature of personal data, and the main purposes of their use, as well as the identity and location of the data controller.
Individual participation	An individual should have the right to reasonably obtain or confirm the existence of personal data, be given reasons if a request is denied, be able to challenge such denial and challenge data relating to him and, if the challenge is successful, to have the data erased, rectified, completed or amended.
Accountability	A data controller should be accountable for complying with measures which give effect to the principles stated above.

age 18. The Health Information Portability and Accountability Act (HIPPA) lays out strict national standards for protecting medical records and other personal health data held by insurance companies, healthcare providers, and others who conduct healthcare transactions electronically. HIPPA gives patients the right to examine and obtain copies of their healthcare records and to request corrections.

The courts have also influenced privacy policies through decisions such as *Griswold v. Connecticut* (1965), which was the first case to establish a constitutional right to privacy by striking down a state law prohibiting contraception as an unwarranted intrusion of government in private affairs. Information privacy is a more recent subject for the courts and presents new issues arising from the ubiquity and pervasiveness of information technology. In a 2014 decision, *Wiley v. California*, the Court unanimously voted to prohibit police from searching cell phones without a warrant, giving digital information the same protections from search and seizure as other forms of information. Other cases are working their way through the courts on the subject of government surveillance via citizen's telephone records. The plaintiffs in *ACLU v. Klapper* and *Klayman v. Obama* both claim that bulk collection of metadata about private phone records by the National Security Agency is unconstitutional. Court rulings have been made at the District and Appeals Court levels both for and against the government. Further appeals (and more cases on this and other electronic data privacy topics) are likely.

Instrumental Information Policies

Beyond its role as regulator of information flow in society, government plays a second significant role with respect to information. As an information collector, producer, provider, and user, government treats information as an *instrument* of policy. When government plays this role, it decides whether and how to collect, develop, disseminate, analyze, and preserve information in the service of some other policy principle (such as transparency, accountability, or social equity), or to achieve certain goals in domains such as public health, environmental quality, or economic development. These instrumental information policies are generally carried out in three ways: by directly collecting data for the express purpose of publication or public access, by requiring private entities to report or publish certain kinds of information for public consumption, and by the release of information collected in the course of government programs and regulatory activities.

Environmental Quality

One of the news stories that opened this chapter highlighted the Environmental Protection Agency's Toxics Release Inventory (US Environmental Protection Agency 2015). The TRI is a government database that comprises mandated annual reports from thousands of companies that manufacture or produce any of 650 chemicals that can pollute water, air, and ground. Created by the Emergency Preparedness and Community Right to Know Act of 1986, the TRI is partly a policy response to chemical disasters in other parts of the world, such as the Union Carbide explosion in Bhopal, India in 1984. It is also a way to address growing concerns of public health and provide environmental advocates with information about local conditions that can cause adverse community health effects, such as high rates of childhood cancer. The TRI is an instrumental information policy whose goal is not information collection or dissemination for general good government purposes—its aim is to require polluting industries to report the release of specific toxic chemicals in specific locations so that local communities can know and act on the health threats they may face as a result. Its second aim is to use the public reporting requirement to encourage and incentivize companies to improve their processes and reduce pollution at its source (Khanna, Quimio, and Bojilova 1998).

Health Care

Information and technology have become centerpieces of government efforts to improve health care in the United States. A leading example is the Health Information Technology for Economic and Clinical Health (HITECH) Act enacted in 2009 to promote the adoption and "meaningful use" of health information technology (National Coordinator for Health Information Technology 2015). This policy establishes requirements for the design, adoption, and use of electronic health records and health information exchange systems as a condition of federal funding for hospitals, clinics, and other healthcare providers. The ultimate goal of this policy is better-informed health care and better health outcomes for Americans. The electronic records and information exchange requirements, along with incentives and penalties for adoption and performance, are highly detailed instruments for achieving those ends.

Consumer Protection

Information policies that serve the goal of consumer protection generally rest on the concept of information disclosure. For consumers and borrowers, the Fair Credit Reporting Act of 1970 (amended by the Consumer Credit Reporting Reform Act of 1996) allows consumers to obtain free credit reports once a year from each of the three main credit-reporting agencies. It also addresses processes for correcting credit reports and for protecting against identity theft (US Federal Trade Commission 2013). For investors, the Securities and Exchange Act of 1934 and its amendments mandate that publicly traded companies file required disclosure statements about their structures, governance, financial management practices, and other required topics. The disclosures, with some exceptions, are made available to the public through the SEC's Electronic Data Gathering, Analysis, and Retrieval system (EDGAR). This collection of information policies is intended to increase the efficiency and fairness of the securities market (US Securities and Exchange Commission 2015).

Managerial Information Policies

A third category of information policies is directed toward the government itself. These internal policies address the management and performance of government's own information resources as assets of value to both government and society. They focus on such topics as IT procurement, information and records management, system and data security, and data dissemination. These policies also specify the key internal managerial roles and responsibilities vested in positions like chief information officers. Technological developments have spurred many of these policies in the past three decades as government organizations seek to stay abreast of changes in the way technologies are influencing the economy, society, and political activities, such as advocacy and voting. Managerial policies are often linked to value-oriented or instrumental policies in that they prescribe certain operational standards or internal requirements that are necessary for compliance or implementation of those policies.

Transparency and Accountability

The rulemaking authority of federal agencies is a potent form of executive power. Long-standing policies stemming from the Administrative Procedures Act and the Federal Register Act mandate a notice and comment process for issuing rules. However, access to the full rulemaking docket (the entire record of proposals and comments) has been a continuing point of controversy regarding transparency and accountability for agency decisions. Executive Order 13563, "Improving Regulation and Regulatory Review," adds new requirements to ensure these processes are more open and accessible to the public and the decision-making process is subject to public scrutiny (Executive Office of the President 2011). The Order requires agencies to afford commenters the opportunity to participate in the regulatory process through the Internet and to have access to "all pertinent parts of the rulemaking docket, including relevant scientific and technical findings" in a format that is easily searchable on the central federal rulemaking website, Regulations.gov. Transparency and accountability also lie at the heart of the Open Government Directive (M-10–06; Office of Management and Budget 2009), which directs agencies to publish government information online (thus launching Data.gov and the open data movement in the U.S.) and to improve the quality of federal government data to enhance its usability and usefulness both inside and beyond the government.

Security

The Information Security Management Act of 2002 directs all federal agencies to develop and deploy agency-wide programs to secure information and information systems, whether those systems are operated by that agency, by another agency, or by contractors. The Federal Information Security Management Act (FISMA) of 2002 requires an inventory of information systems, assignment of systems to risk categories, compliance with minimum mandatory security controls, ongoing risk assessment, and continuous monitoring. As cybersecurity has grown in importance with the emergence of worldwide networks and cybercrime, additional policies have been adopted, including a 2004 Presidential Homeland Security Directive on protecting critical infrastructure and, in 2015, Executive Order 13636 ("Improving Critical Infrastructure Cybersecurity") that directed the National Institute of Standards and Technology to create a cybersecurity framework with guidelines and recommendations for voluntary adoption by private sector critical infrastructure organizations.

Management and Performance

Together, the Paperwork Reduction Act of 1980 (amended by the Paperwork Reduction Act of 1995) and the Clinger-Cohen Act of 1996 lay out the information resource management objectives and requirements of the federal government. The PRA created the Office of Information and Regulatory

Affairs (OIRA) within OMB to develop comprehensive policies to implement these laws, and the polices are spelled out in OMB Circular A-130, Management of Federal Information Resources (Office of Management and Budget 2000). This set of policies promotes responsible acquisition and use of IT by requiring information resource planning, redesigned business processes, and creation of information architectures to guide system development designs and decisions. Later, in 2001, the White House issued the President's Management Agenda (Executive Office of the President 2001), which included expansion of e-government among five managerial goals. The Agenda directed agencies to create more customer-centered systems and internally automated processes and promised to create a single government e-procurement portal, Public Key Infrastructure, for online identity management and other technology-supported performance improvements. The management agenda also included annual reviews and public reporting of progress on each management goal. Although the detailed review and reporting process has since been eliminated, technology continues to be featured in subsequent presidential management agendas.

The Framework in Action

While each example above pertains to one of the three main purposes of information policy, in practice these policies intersect in both planned and unplanned ways. The transparency and performance examples in the managerial policy type follow a relatively straightforward progression from statute to executive implementation measures to tools for compliance. These policies have also experienced improvement and reform cycles that play out in relatively clear steps and relationships. However, because value-driven and instrumental policies are fundamentally choices about how to balance competing interests, other situations occur in which a policy adopted for one purpose (such as the failed Computer Decency Act's attempt at protecting children from inappropriate online content) conflicts with a policy adopted for another (such as protecting the free speech rights of adults and the commercial interests of Internet providers). In addition, over time policies can swing back and forth between different dominant values, as has happened with instructions for presumptions about handling requests under the Freedom of Information Act. The purpose-driven framework does not solve these problems, but it makes it easier to identify and understand them and perhaps to devise strategies or better policies to address them.

The purpose-driven information policy framework has several benefits. It can be used to diagnose a policy problem or a policy alternative to identify the information-related purpose or purposes it is intended to serve. With a clear understanding of purpose, government professionals are more likely to identify all the salient stakeholders and to consider a wider range of actions to achieve the purpose. For example, a policy to protect the privacy rights of students (a value-oriented policy) needs to take into account the positions, resources, and capabilities of not only students, but also different kinds of educational institutions, parents, teachers, administrators, and so on. Thus, it also requires instrumental and managerial policies for its full implementation. A policy on this topic might comprise rules to restrict who can access student records, prohibit the collection of certain kinds of information, or prescribe rules for managing student records.

Second, the purpose-driven framework can help those involved in designing or implementing domain-specific policies—such as improving health care—to understand the ways in which related instrumental or managerial information policies could assist or detract from achieving those policies. A current example involves requirements for the content and "meaningful use" of electronic health records, which mandate certain kinds of data collection, management, and sharing in order for physicians, clinics, and hospitals to receive enhanced federal funds to improve the processes and outcomes of health care. These instrumental information policies are intended to standardize information in ways that improve clinical practice and information sharing among medical personnel, so that patients experience better health outcomes.

The framework can also help identify mismatches between policy expectations and performance. Open data policies, for example, are generally implemented only as managerial policies that pertain to requirements to publish government data. However, the stated aim of these policies often emphasizes enhancements to democracy, but little progress has been made toward that goal—to do so, complementary value-oriented policies are also needed to further open government's deliberation and decision-making processes.

While a purpose-driven framework offers benefits to practitioners, it is limited by the extent to which government practice actually allows for or encourages analysis of the information dimension of the policies and programs of other domains. It is also limited by the training and awareness of government professionals about information as both a policy focus of its own and as a lever to assist or impose barriers in other policy domains. In addition, today's strong emphasis on technology in the public sector has increased the importance of these issues, but it has also tended to divert attention away from the importance of information content and flow and more toward information technology management. Thus, the problem of having no obvious home for addressing information policy issues continues to limit thinking and action.

Going Forward

Information policies are essential to governing an information society. These policies can be approached in a variety of ways, including by categorizing them into topics or dimensions, or by associating them with information life cycle stages or segments of the information transfer process. Information policies can also be understood as efforts to balance conflicting rights or to accommodate social and technical factors of modern society. This chapter has offered a purpose-driven framework to help government professionals sort and understand information policy goals and methods for achieving them. Most of the material is drawn from the U.S. federal government in order be both comprehensive and coherent within a given context. However, the kinds of policy problems discussed here occur in every society with its own examples and models for consideration.

Drawing from American experience, several conclusions seem evident:

- Information-related values are deeply embedded in social and political culture. Consequently, they are enduring concerns which can be subject to disagreement as to scale, scope, application, and priority. The value-oriented policies discussed here are the ones most likely to be contested in everyday life and in the courts.
- Information is a powerful instrument for pursuing policy goals of all kinds. For this reason, information is frequently a component of policies that aim to achieve a wide variety of social, economic, and political goals. Thus, instrumental information policies are likely to be a permanent fixture of the policymaking and policy implementation processes.
- Good operational performance and public accountability for government decisions are universal concerns that benefit from information policies that address the managerial and fiduciary responsibilities of government organizations. Better data quality, information and technology management, and openness and transparency all depend on sound managerial information policies.

Everywhere in the world, information policies are being tested, stretched, and challenged by advances in information and communication technologies. Ubiquitous devices, local and global networks, social media, wearable devices, and sensors are just a few of the technological innovations that are joining more traditional records management programs, information systems, and databases in shaping the public information context. Government policies typically lag behind this kind of change and innovation, generally responding when these changes disrupt conventional processes and relationships. For these reasons, investments are need in policy research and in professional and public education to improve our ability to identify, analyze, and understand information policy problems and to make reasonable policy choices in the years ahead.

In terms of policy analysis and policy research, a variety of scholars have suggested ways to approach information policy as a topic in its own right worthy of concentrated development. Among these are calls for better understanding of the interrelatedness of information policies (McClure and Jaeger 2008) and for studies of historical development, original intent, implementation and impact, reaction, criticism, and explicit attention to the role of values (Relyea 2008). Case studies, process-oriented studies, and other methods can all be appropriate (Rowlands 1996). The purpose-driven framework offered here should be tested and explored with further research. Case studies would be especially useful ways to understand how information policies of each kind affect the achievement of specific public policy goals. In addition, comparative studies of different policy developments or of similar developments in different contexts could explore and identify the factors in government practice that are associated with better policy outcomes.

Finally public management education needs to more fully recognize information policy as an integral part of government management and administration, policy development, and program implementation. Education programs for government professionals should cover information policy issues, challenges, and analytical tools as a routine part of degree programs to assure awareness and understanding of the important role that information plays in all aspects of government and governance.

Note

1. There are scores of relevant Supreme Court decisions pertaining to the First Amendment and other topics covered in this chapter. Only a few of the more important ones are cited in the text to illustrate the issues discussed. Readers who are interested in a more complete understanding of the role of the Court in information policy can find a great deal of information, references, and source material in several online resources listed at the end of this chapter.

Additional Recommended Reading

Browne, Mairead. 1997. "The Field of Information Policy: 1. Fundamental Concepts." *Journal of Information Science* 23 (4): 261–75. doi:10.1177/016555159702300401.

Galperin, Hernan. 2004. "Beyond Interests, Ideas, and Technology: An Institutional Approach to Communication and Information Policy." *Information Society* 20 (3): 159–68.

McClure, Charles R., and Paul T. Jaeger. 2008. "Government Information Policy Research: Importance, Approaches, and Realities." *Library & Information Science Research* 30 (4): 257–64. doi:10.1016/j.lisr.2008.05.004.

Relyea, Harold C. 2008. "Federal Government Information Policy and Public Policy Analysis: A Brief Overview." *Library & Information Science Research* 30 (1): 2–21. doi:10.1016/j.lisr.2007.11.004.

Resources

Congressional Record (https://www.congress.gov/congressional-record)
Federal Register (https://www.federalregister.gov/)
Legal Information Institute, Cornell University (https://www.law.cornell.edu/)
Stanford Libraries Freedom of Information Act Archive (https://archive-it.org/collections/924)
THOMAS, Library of Congress (http://thomas.loc.gov/home/thomas.php)

References

Benkler, Yochai. 1998. 'The Commons as a Neglected Factor of Information Policy'. In *26th Annual Telecommunications Research Conference*. http://dlc.dlib.indiana.edu/dlc/handle/10535/414

Bertot, John Carlo, Paul T. Jaeger, and Derek Hansen. 2012. 'The Impact of Polices on Government Social Media Usage: Issues, Challenges, and Recommendations'. *Government Information Quarterly* 29 (1): 30–40. doi:10.1016/j.giq.2011.04.004

Braman, Sandra. 2011. 'Defining Information Policy'. *Journal of Information Policy* 1 (January): 1–5. doi:10.5325/jinfopoli.1.2011.0001

Browne, Mairead. 1997a. 'The Field of Information Policy: 1. Fundamental Concepts'. *Journal of Information Science* 23 (4): 261–75. doi:10.1177/016555159702300401

———. 1997b. 'The Field of Information Policy: 2. Redefining the Boundaries and Methodologies'. *Journal of Information Science* 23 (5): 339–51. doi:10.1177/016555159702300501

Burger, R.H. 1993. *Information Policy: A Framework for Evaluation and Policy Research*. Norwood, NJ: Ablex Publishing Corporation.

Chartrand, Robert. 1986. 'Legislating Information Policy'. *Bulletin of the American Society for Information Science* 12 (5): 10.

Coates, Joseph F. 1979. 'What Is a Public Policy Issue? An Advisory Essay'. *Interdisciplinary Science Reviews* 4 (1): 27–44. doi:10.1179/030801879789801759

Dawes, Sharon S. 2010. 'Stewardship and Usefulness: Policy Principles for Information-Based Transparency'. *Government Information Quarterly* 27 (4): 377–83. doi:10.1016/j.giq.2010.07.001

Dawes, Sharon S., and Natalie Helbig. 2010. 'Information Strategies for Open Government: Challenges and Prospects for Deriving Public Value from Government Transparency'. In *Proceedings of the 9th IFIP WG 8.5 International Conference on Electronic Government*, 50–60. EGOV'10. Berlin, Heidelberg: Springer-Verlag. http://dl.acm.org/citation.cfm?id=1887132.1887138

Duff, Alistair S. 2004. 'The Past, Present, and Future of Information Policy: Towards a Normative Theory of the Information Society'. *Information, Communication & Society* 7 (1): 69–87. doi:10.1080/1369118042000208906

Executive Office of the President. 2011. 'Executive Order 13563, Improving Regulation and Regulatory Review'. https://www.whitehouse.gov/sites/default/files/omb/inforeg/eo12866/eo13563_01182011.pdf

Executive Office of the President, Office of Management and Budget. 2001. 'The President's Management Agenda, Fiscal Year 2002'. https://www.whitehouse.gov/sites/default/files/omb/assets/omb/budget/fy2002/mgmt.pdf

Galperin, Hernan. 2004. 'Beyond Interests, Ideas, and Technology: An Institutional Approach to Communication and Information Policy'. *Information Society* 20 (3): 159–68.

Galvin, Thomas J. 1992. 'Rights in Conflict: Public Policy in an Information Age'. In *Proceedings of the 46th FID Conference and Congress*. The Hague, Netherlands.

———. 1997. 'Rights in Conflict: An Introduction to Public Information Policy'.

Gellman, Robert. 2015. 'Fair Information Practices: A Basic History'. http://bobgellman.com/rg-docs/rg-FIPShistory.pdf

Hernon, Paul T., and Harold C. Relyea. 2009. "Information Policy: United States." In *Encyclopedia of Library and Information Sciences*, Third ed, edited by Marcia J. Bates and Mary Niles Maack. New York: Dekker.

Khanna, Madhu, Wilma Rose H. Quimio, and Dora Bojilova. 1998. 'Toxics Release Information: A Policy Tool for Environmental Protection'. *Journal of Environmental Economics and Management* 36 (3): 243–66. doi:10.1006/jeem.1998.1048

Maxwell, Terry. 2003. 'Toward a Model of Information Policy Analysis: Speech as an Illustrative Example'. *First Monday* 8 (6). doi:10.5210/fm.v8i6.1060

McClure, Charles R., and Paul T. Jaeger. 2008. 'Government Information Policy Research: Importance, Approaches, and Realities'. *Library & Information Science Research* 30 (4): 257–64. doi:10.1016/j.lisr.2008.05.004

National Coordinator for Health Information Technology. 2015. 'Select Portions of the HITECH Act and Relationship to ONC Work'. Accessed July 27. http://healthit.gov/policy-researchers-implementers/select-portions-hitech-act-and-relationship-onc-work

National Institute of Standards and Technology. 2009. 'Standards for Security Categorization of Federal Information and Information Systems, FIPS PUB 199'. http://csrc.nist.gov/publications/fips/fips199/FIPS-PUB-199-final.pdf

Nonaka, I. 1994. 'A Dynamic Theory of Organizational Knowledge Creation'. *Organization Science* 5 (1): 14–37. doi:10.1287/orsc.5.1.14

Office of Management and Budget. 2000. 'CIRCULAR NO. A-130 Revised, Management of Federal Information Resources'. https://www.whitehouse.gov/omb/circulars_a130_a130trans4/

Office of Management and Budget, Patrice. 2009. 'Open Government Directive'. https://www.whitehouse.gov/sites/default/files/omb/assets/memoranda_2010/m10-06.pdf

Orna, E. 2008. 'Information Policies: Yesterday, Today, Tomorrow'. *Journal of Information Science* 34 (4): 547–65. doi:10.1177/0165551508092256

Overman, E. Sam, and Anthony G. Cahill. 1990. 'Information Policy: A Study of Values in the Policy Process'. *Policy Studies Review* 9 (4): 803–18.

Reidenberg, Joel R. 2000. 'Resolving Conflicting International Data Privacy Rules in Cyberspace'. *Stanford Law Review* 52 (5): 1315. doi:10.2307/1229516

Relyea, Harold C. 2008. 'Federal Government Information Policy and Public Policy Analysis: A Brief Overview'. *Library & Information Science Research* 30 (1): 2–21. doi:10.1016/j.lisr.2007.11.004

Rowlands, I. 1996. 'Understanding Information Policy: Concepts, Frameworks and Research Tools'. *Journal of Information Science* 22 (1): 13–25. doi:10.1177/016555159602200102

Sawyer, Steve, and Howard Rosenbaum. 2000. 'Social Informatics in the Information Sciences: Current Activities and Emerging Directions'. *Informing Science* 3 (2): 89–89.

Trist, Eric L. 1981. 'The Sociotechnical Perspective'. In *Perspectives in Organizational Design and Behavior*, edited by Andrew H. Van de Ven and William F. Joyce. New York: Wiley.

US Environmental Protection Agency. 2015. 'Toxics Release Inventory (TRI) Program'. Accessed July 27. http://www2.epa.gov/toxics-release-inventory-tri-program

US Federal Trade Commission. 2013. 'Credit and Your Consumer Rights'. https://bulkorder.ftc.gov/system/files/publications/pdf-0070-credit-and-your-consumer-rights.pdf

US Securities and Exchange Commission. 2015. 'Researching Public Companies Through EDGAR: A Guide for Investors'. Accessed July 27. http://www.sec.gov/investor/pubs/edgarguide.htm

Weingarten, Fred W. 1989. 'Federal Information Policy Development: The Congressional Perspective'. In *United States Government Information Policies: Views and Perspectives*, edited by Charles R. McClure, Peter C. Hernon, and Harold C. Relyea, 77–99. Norwood, NJ: Ablex Publishing.

Western Australia Department of Health. 2014. 'Information Lifecycle Management Policy'. http://www.health.wa.gov.au/circularsnew/attachments/944.pdf

4
AN INTEGRATIVE FRAMEWORK FOR EFFECTIVE USE OF INFORMATION AND COMMUNICATION TECHNOLOGIES (ICTS) FOR COLLABORATIVE PUBLIC SERVICE NETWORKS

Yu-Che Chen

Introduction

The public administration and management literature is important for understanding the context in which adoption and implementation decisions on information and communication technologies (hereafter, ICTs) are made and their impact on public service. Key factors identified in the literature—political motivation, bureaucratic politics, policy implementation in an intergovernmental context, and contract management—can all affect decisions about which technology to adopt and whether implementation of new technologies will be successful (i.e., Ahn and Bretschneider 2011; Fountain 2001; Ni 2006; Norris and Reddick 2013). For instance, the need for political and bureaucratic control appeared to be a primary consideration for ICT adoption (Ahn and Bretschneider 2011; Im, Porumbescu, and Lee 2013).

The rich and diverse intellectual traditions that public administration and management literature has drawn from (Frederickson and Smith 2003) can offer specific insights into the challenges and opportunities of employing ICTs to improve public service. For instance, the long-standing tradition of studying bureaucracy as a form of organization for the production and delivery of public service, the politics surrounding bureaucracy, and the danger of bureaucratic inertia can all inform the interplay between government structure and ICTs. Another intellectual tradition studies institutions in terms of how the rules affect the behaviors of individuals and organizations and vice versa. Institutionalism assists in the understanding of the role of public institutions in shaping the outcome of public service. Moreover, the theories and practice of public management—from early scientific management and new public management to performance management—provide general lessons for managing public organizations and service. The above-mentioned intellectual tradition goes beyond a single theoretical perspective or area of research interest to embody insights from various disciplines such as political science, business administration, sociology, and psychology.

However, the majority of the e-government studies falls short of benefiting from the scholarship of public administration and management (Yildiz 2007). Although technologies are new, the basic structure and challenges of public administration remain relatively consistent. More importantly, the effectiveness of information technologies depends on whether they are able to address structural and process characteristics in the context of public service. For the studies grounded in information system literature, an in-depth discussion about the public service context seems to be missing. E-government studies tend to miss the opportunity to integrate the key theoretical and practical insights of public administration and management in the formation of conceptual frameworks and research hypotheses (Yildiz 2007). Policy is usually a key aspect of empirical investigation in these e-government studies, but for the most part, they lack a direct connection to the public policy, administration, and management literature.

At the same time, the public administration and management literature could benefit from a more in-depth understanding of the roles information technologies play in improving public service and advancing public values. Digital information and information technology have become integral to government operations (Reddick 2012). Technological advances, such as location-based technologies (sensors), apps, social media, open data, and big data, have continuously offered governments opportunities to improve services (Chen and Hsieh 2014; Ganapati and Reddick 2014; Grimmelikhuijsen and Meijer 2015; Mergel 2013). However, the scholarship and practice of public administration have not kept up with the rapid development of ICTs nor fully realized the potential of employing these technologies for a citizen-centric 21st-century government.

This chapter focuses on the use of ICTs to improve cross-boundary collaboration for the production and delivery of public information as an area that creates cross-fertilization between e-government literature and public administration and management literature. The selection of cross-boundary collaboration for public service is the salient feature of ICTs in facilitating coordination and collaboration. Moreover, such citizen/service-oriented collaboration corresponds to a high level of maturity associated with e-government. This chapter will develop a conceptual framework that serves as an example of infusing public administration and management research into the study of electronic government. Such integration not only provides the governmental context in which these ICTs become adopted for e-government scholars, but also offers insights into the potential impact of ICTs on performance for public administration and management scholars.

The next section will briefly outline the relevant bodies of literature for the proposed integrative framework. Then, the main section of the chapter will present various core components of the framework and the interactions between them, including governance structure, characteristics of interorganizational collaboration, the capabilities of ICTs, and performance. Next is a discussion of network leadership and management activities that can affect the role of ICTs in shaping performance. This chapter will conclude with unique contributions of this framework and opportunities for future research.

The Role of ICTs in Cross-Boundary Collaboration for Public Service: Relevant Literature

The relevance of various bodies of the literature is determined by the overarching research question: What is the role of information and communication technologies (ICTs) in shaping the performance of public service in an interorganizational context? Several bodies of literature in the study of public administration and management can inform an answer to this question. First is institutionalism, particularly in the vein of collective action across organizational boundaries, as articulated in Ostrom's work, and the research on interlocal collaboration. Ostrom and her colleagues' works have provided a framework for analyzing institutions by unpacking them into seven types of rules (Ostrom 1998; Ostrom, Gardner, and Walker 1994; Schweik and Kitsing 2010). Such distinctions are helpful in analyzing the specific aspect of the institutions affecting a technology decision. For instance, the specifics of payoff rules can help explain why certain technology has been adopted. The perspective of institutional collective action also provides valuable insights into the challenge of governments working together. One of the key organizing concepts is the transaction cost involved in overcoming institutional collective action (Feiock, Steinacker, and Park 2008; Kwon and Feiock 2010). The policy prescription would advise implementing institutional mechanisms to lower such transaction costs, such as establishing informal networks (Kwon and Feiock 2010; LeRoux 2005). Such prescription also implies the potential role that ICTs can play in reducing transaction costs to overcome collective action problems.

Second is the stream of studies focusing on collaborative and network governance (i.e., Ansell and Gash 2008; Emerson, Nabatchi, and Balogh 2012; Isett et al. 2011; Provan and Lemaire 2012). Collaborative governance helps explain how various organizations work together to achieve shared goals across organizational boundaries and sectors. A meta-analysis of studies by Ansell and Gash (2008) identifies several key factors affecting the outcome of collaborative governance, such as the history of cooperation/conflict, participation incentives, and institutional design. This meta-analysis delineates the conditions under which such collaboration would be effective. Drawing from these conditions, ICTs can play a role in providing incentives or information about incentives to solicit collaboration. In terms of institutional design, the studies of network governance have developed hypothesized relationships on fitting network administrative mechanisms to specific structural characteristics (Provan and Kenis 2008). The studies of network governance have also informed scholars and practitioners on the potential dynamics in collaborative governance. Emerson and her colleagues have identified important constructive efforts for collaborative governance, such as engaging according to principle, cultivating shared motivation, and developing capacity for joint actions (Emerson, Nabatchi, and Balogh 2012).

Third, the literature on network/collaborative management and performance is also relevant in understanding how ICTs can play a role in an interorganizational context. The studies of network management have provided support for the need for active management of a network of organizations providing public service (Agranoff 2007; McGuire 2002; Thomson and Perry 2006). In addition, these studies identify the activities that network managers need to engage in (Agranoff 2007; McGuire 2006). What is particularly useful is the role that a collaborative public manager needs to play (O'Leary and Bingham 2009; O'Leary, Choi, and Gerard 2012; Thomson and Perry 2006). The list of network management activities offers a starting point to identify how ICTs can help make these activities more efficient and effective. For instance, information technology has the potential to aid in knowledge management that provides the network manager critical information on more effective management of a complex network (Agranoff 2007) and on which organization needs to be mobilized to increase network effectiveness (McGuire 2002). Performance of networks can be measured at various levels of aggregation, spanning from individuals and program to community (Provan and Milward 2001). Performance should not be treated as homogeneous across various levels. Tensions can exist between performance results between levels (Provan and Milward 2001).

The last body of literature introduced here is the collection of e-government studies focusing on e-government projects across organizational boundaries (Dawes, Cresswell, and Pardo 2009; Pardo et al. 2009; Scholl and Klischewski 2007; Scholl et al. 2012), as well as the role of ICTs in providing citizen-oriented public service (Bekkers 2009; Chen 2010; Goldsmith and Crawford 2014). Although there is limited cross-reference to the bodies of public administration and management literature mentioned above, the studies of cross-boundary e-government projects tend to point to similar conditions for success and effective mechanisms for collaboration. Shared goals and values among participating organizations are important for cross-boundary e-government projects (Hellberg and Grönlund 2013). Political support in the form of mandates is critical for the integration of systems across governmental agencies (Bekkers 2007; Roy 2009) and cross-boundary information sharing (Dawes, Cresswell, and

Pardo 2009). Supporting institutions are also critical for cross-boundary e-government projects, especially those projects that require supporting rules and regulations (Dawes, Cresswell, and Pardo 2009; Luna-Reyes, Gil-Garcia, and Cruz 2007). Effective management requires addressing potential conflicts (Hellberg and Grönlund 2013), fostering interorganizational trust (Gil-Garcia et al. 2010), and providing incentives (Yang and Maxwell 2011). Performance of these cross-boundary projects has traditionally been measured by output. However, there is a growing recognition of the importance of measuring outcomes as defined by core public values such as transparency and accountability.

An Integrative Framework of the Role of ICTs in Cross-Boundary Collaboration for Public Service

This integrative framework for the role of ICTs in cross-boundary collaboration for public service, drawing from the groups of studies mentioned above, has five main components, as seen in Figure 4.1: governance structure, conditions for interorganizational collaboration, adoption and use of information and communication technologies, performance (ICTs), and leadership and management activities. One unique feature of this framework is the explicit identification of the role of ICTs in shaping governance structure, modifying the characteristics of the collaborative, and ultimately improving service performance. The component of leadership and management activities directly interact with the other components for successful network management.

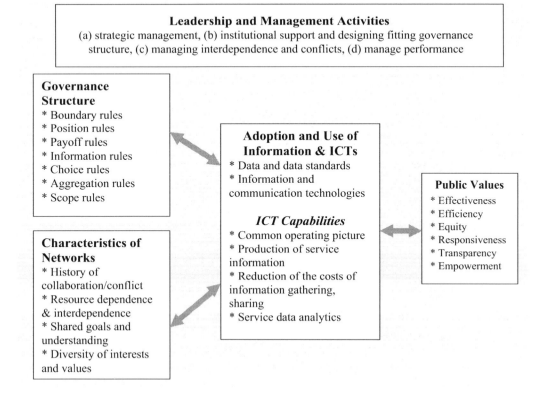

Figure 4.1 An Integrative Conceptual Framework for Managing an ICT-Enabled Collaborative Public Management Network

Governance Structure

The first component introduced here is governance structure. The collaborative governance literature underscores the importance of institutional design (Ansell and Gash 2008). There are various ways to conceptualize governance structure, such as degree of centralization and control. This framework utilizes categories of rules as developed by Ostrom and her colleagues (Ostrom 2010; Ostrom, Gardner, and Walker 1994) because of their analytical strength and empirical validity. An example of such application is the use of this categorization for understanding the Open Source movement (Schweik and Kitsing 2010). For the purpose of developing the proposed framework, these categories have been adapted to the network context.

Position rules define the specific official roles that participating organizations can take. These rules delineate specific titles and responsibilities associated with the governance and management of an interorganizational network. For instance, this type of position could be a member of the governing board, an executive director, or a network member. Boundary rules regulate the boundaries of these positions and include rules on which organizations, and individuals representing these organizations, can assume these positions. Such network boundary rules specify the eligibility of participating organizations. The boundary rule about emergency response programs, for example, dictates which governmental units can participate. In addition, boundary rules can address the main governing body of the network to specify which organizations are eligible to serve on the governing board and which only qualify to be member organizations receiving services.

Choice rules outline the set of choices associated with various positions that are legitimate in the interorganizational setting.[1] For instance, the participating organizations can choose the level of participation as a set of permissible choices. However, these organizations may not have the choice to leave a network if network participation is mandated by the state or federal government to deliver public information and service. Aggregation rules specify how individual choices/decisions are aggregated. For example, such rules can specify whether a single organization has veto power. Some common aggregation rules include majority rule, weighted voting, or consensus rules. These rules help clarify the relative power and positions that various participating organizations have in shaping decisions and outcomes.

Payoff rules dictate the incentive structure for participating organizations. For instance, the payoff for participating local governments in a cross-boundary government information-sharing service is access to central government information to provide citizen-centric services and to reduce the amount of time and energy in routing paperwork for approval. The specific amount of payoff and investment is likely to vary across participating organizations. Information rules are broadly defined to include the kind of information being generated and shared as well as the channels of communication (Schweik 2006). For cross-boundary governance, information rules can govern what kind of information needs to be produced, such as meeting minutes of the governance board and performance information on participating organizations. Such rules also govern who has access to what information. For instance, some information can be shared among participating organizations, but with no one outside the network. These rules can also dictate the frequency and channels of communication, as when meeting minutes are made available 24/7 via an online network portal.

Scope rules stipulate the scope of outcomes as opposed to choice rules, which focus on actions. These scope rules can specify the mission and goals of a collaborative network. These rules articulate the purposes of a network and what is considered inside the scope of what this network does. For instance, a network of organizations delivering mental health services would limit their scope of service to mental health and not get involved in financial services. Scope rules can be articulated in the goals of a network. For example, since outreach is a major goal of an NSF-funded scientific collaborative network, it falls within the scope of this network.

An understanding of the rules should be focused on rules-in-use rather than those rules in the book (Ostrom 2010). Codified rules may not be the rules actually being used by participating organizations. A network may have bylaws, for example, that characterize the decision-making process as following consensus rule for aggregation of choices, but in reality such decisions are usually made by majority rule of several core member organizations. Moreover, it is the configuration of rules, rather than individual rules, that ultimately makes the difference (Ostrom, Gardner, and Walker 1994). The effectiveness of a governance structure needs to take into account the combination of multiple rules. For instance, the combination of boundary rules for stakeholder inclusion with payoff rules to bring sanctions for noncompliance could be effective in managing a loosely structured common pool resource management regime without a central government authority.

Such categorization of rules is particularly useful when linking them to the adoption and use of ICTs. The use of ICTs can directly alter information rules, especially since the old mode of production and dissemination of information is paper based and cost prohibitive. If the cost of distributing information becomes minimal, it is possible for each participating organization, and even participant, to gain access to planning documents, meeting minutes, and technical materials. The use of ICTs can also affect boundary rules by lowering the cost of an organization assuming a position and serving its role. For instance, ICTs can help contracted service providers serve on an advisory board to help identify the most effective way of delivering service. ICTs can also affect the payoff (incentives) for individual organizations. If the central mission of the network is information sharing, the use of integrated information significantly increases the benefits of citizen-centric integrated information and reduces the cost of obtaining such information.

Moreover, the use of ICTs can alter the governance structure as a whole by reinforcing political control of the central office (Garson 2006; Im, Porumbescu, and Lee 2013). When a central management office requires that all the participating organizations use the same information system and data formats, it has generated the benefits of harmonizing data standards and increasing data quality. However, such a centralized information system and process can be used to strengthen the power of the network administrative organization. Participating organizations are dependent on the information service provided by the central management office, and such dependence is a source of power for the central office. Additionally, a central management office collecting all performance information on participating organizations can further strengthen central control.

On the other hand, the use of ICTs can make the governance structure more democratic and flatter. The democratization of information access as the result of lowering information cost can empower individuals and participating organizations to hold each other and the central administration accountable. For instance, each participating organization can find out more about how resources are allocated across the network and whether such allocation is done according to the rules. ICT use can also allow for low-cost coordination and collaboration for individuals and/or participating organizations to self-organize and form teams to solve problems together.

Characteristics of Collaborative Governance Networks

History of Collaboration/Conflict

One important characteristic of collaborative governance networks is their history of collaboration and/or conflict (Ansell and Gash 2008; Bryson, Crosby, and Stone 2006; Daley 2008). This characteristic should be treated as the initial condition for the establishment of a collaborative network, and should be understood as a continuum from a high level of conflict to a high level of cooperation. This condition is recognized in various studies of interorganizational collaboration with diverse terms used to capture it (Hellberg and Grönlund 2013; O'Leary and Bingham 2009; Yang and Maxwell 2011). A history of collaboration is highly related to the level of social capital and trust that exists among the potential participating organizations prior to the establishment of a network (Bryson, Crosby, and Stone 2006). As a result, the formation of the network is likely to be a natural outgrowth of existing relationships with constructive discussions about appropriate governance structure. In contrast, if there has been a long history of conflicts and distrust, building a collaborative network can be quite challenging.

The relevance of initial conditions is also articulated in the institutionalist literature, especially the discussion about path dependency (North 1990; Parkhe, Wasserman, and Ralston 2006). The workable and acceptable arrangements for a network are dependent on the initial level of collaboration and conflicts as well as the beginning institutional design. Studies of system dynamics have also highlighted the importance of initial conditions that affect the possible outcomes (end states) (Sterman 2000). The greater the amount of change involved from the initial to the end state, the more challenging it is to build networks.

Resource Dependence and Interdependence

Resource dependence is central in understanding why organizations join networks and maintain their network membership (Pfeffer and Salancik 2003; Rethemeyer and Hatmaker 2008; Wood and Gray 1991). The essence of network implies that the goals of the network cannot be performed by a single organization. Organizations participate in a network to secure the cooperation and support of other members that are otherwise unavailable to them. For instance, a local nonprofit organization that provides mental health services might need to join a network of mental health service providers to secure government funding as well as for referral of clients.

The resources go beyond funding and staff to include social structural resources (Rethemeyer and Hatmaker 2008). Such social structural resources could take the form of persistent communication and relationships between several actors before the formulation of a particular network. Resources can be informational, in that participation in a network provides the participating organizations information on regional planning (Agranoff 2007). Another useful categorization of resources is based on the distinction between tangible and intangible resources. Tangible resources tend to promote tight coupling, while intangible resources tend to be associated with more diffused sub-network groupings (Provan and Huang 2012).

The nature and pattern of resource interdependency is likely to determine the power structure of the network. The source of power comes from the ownership and control of resources by the network as a whole and the network's ability to make allocation decisions. The more a participating organization depends on the resource allocation from a network center, the more power that network has over it. Such dependence also shapes the motivation for individual organizations to participate. If an individual organization depends heavily on the resources from the network, it has a strong motivation to remain in the network.

On one hand, a network administrative organization can utilize ICTs to increase the level of dependence of participating organizations on the network for informational service. A centralized information system for all the services rendered via the network can further strengthen the position of central offices. On the other hand, the use of ICTs can gather relevant information to create a high level of interdependency that binds all the participating organizations together. For instance, the same centralized information system that could be used to strengthen a central office's position can also reveal the need for coordination to reduce waste in resources as the result of service duplication. With data available on resource flow and service production, participating organizations may be able to understand levels of interdependence that could have been ambiguous in the past.

Shared Goals and Understanding

Shared goals and understanding is an important condition for effective cross-boundary collaboration (Ansell and Gash 2008; Bekkers 2007; Bryson, Crosby, and Stone 2006; Wood and Gray 1991). The alignment of the goals of participating organizations with those of the network can provide important incentives to bring these organizations together. For instance, the shared goal of efficient and effective provision of human services can motivate city governments, county governments, nonprofit organizations, and businesses to form an alliance. The higher the level of alignment between the goal of a participating organization and that of the collaborative network, the higher the level of commitment that can be seen from individual organizations.

Shared understanding is critical for the effectiveness of a network (Bekkers 2007). A shared understanding of the severity of problems helps secure commitment of time and resources that are not otherwise available. A shared understanding of interdependence can provide the necessary glue to keep various participating organizations together (Bryson, Crosby, and Stone 2006; Gray 1985). For instance, a shared understanding of the various organizations that need to be involved in emergency response helps keep these organizations together. Moreover, a shared belief of positive outcomes is necessary to help propel organizations in implementation (Gray 1985).

ICTs, when used properly, can help facilitate the creation of shared goals and understanding (Comfort and Haase 2006). Collaborative ICTs can facilitate the creation of mission statements and network goals. Such technologies can augment a face-to-face meeting by providing efficient means of collecting key ideas and voting on them. Another potential use of ICTs, such as video conferencing tools, is to provide low-cost ways of meeting for coordination and enable discussions for developing shared goals. Moreover, information technology can aid in the creation of shared understanding. Such a shared understanding could involve the roles and responsibilities of participating organizations. In addition, ICTs are particularly powerful in collecting, managing, and presenting information for public service production and delivery. An illustrative example is the employment of ICTs by an incident command center at a time of crisis to create and modify a shared understanding of the nature of the crisis as it evolved (Ansell and Keller 2014).

Diversity of Interests and Values

One of the fundamental challenges associated with collaboration across organizational boundaries is the diversity of interests and organizational cultures. Tension could exist between the interests of the collective (network as a whole) and the interests of participating organizations. Diversity of interests can make such tension between the self-interest of individual organizations and the interest of the collective more complicated. Moreover, such diverse interests tend to instigate bargaining among the participating organizations.

Diversity of organizational values can be a barrier to interorganizational collaboration, and differences in values among participating organizations can be a main source of conflict. In cross-sector collaboration, there is typically a tension between for-profit organizations' focus on the bottom line and the government's focus on equity, transparency, and other values. In the realm of information sharing, there is tension between the privacy that governments wish to protect and the business interest in getting unfettered personal information from government (Hellberg and Grönlund 2013). Such conflict of values can also be seen between the network as a whole and individual participating organizations. For instance, while the overarching value of a cybersecurity network organization is about protecting cybersecurity for all by sharing information across the network, individual businesses and organizations participating in this network are leery about sharing their incidents of security breach because of their concerns about liability and the loss of customer trust in their operation.

The diversity and potential conflicts among various organizational interests and values can impede the adoption of data standards and/or ICTs. Value conflicts can manifest themselves in the debate over which technology to adopt for the network as a whole. On the other hand, the discussion about technology can create a neutral space that allows people to sit down and discuss the technical aspects of a collaboration without getting into direct confrontation. The use of ICTs can facilitate the bargaining process to reach a workable agreement that accommodates diverse interests and values. Moreover, the use of ICTs can provide the monitoring and sanctioning needed for the parties to agree to the collaboration in the first place. A collective action situation can be managed with the use of information technology to facilitate division of labor, exchange of information, and enforcement as critical transaction activities.

Data, Data Standards, ICTs, and ICT Capabilities

Data, Data Standards, and ICTs

Both data and ICTs are important in understanding the effectiveness of public management networks. Data play an important role in collaborative networks for public service. For some networks, the primary function is informational, one of the main types of public management network at the local level as classified by Agranoff (2007). Such a network could be a geographic information consortium for a state whose main responsibility is to develop information standards for geographic information and to serve as the main organization for the repository and dissemination of such information. Another example is a multi-state cybersecurity information center whose primary function is the collection and dissemination of cybersecurity information.

Data standards are crucial for information interoperability, allowing meaningful aggregation, comparison, and interpretation of data. Data standards can be as specific as definition, format, and quality assurance. For a single information system for a public management network, participating organizations may need to follow exact data standards to be in compliance. For instance, the reporting of regulatory compliance with toxic waste needs to follow a single data standard. Another example is that the National Health Service in Britain requires all participating hospitals, clinics, and other healthcare facilities to adopt the same electronic patient record standards for data entry. Such data standards can also been in the reporting of financial data. The XBRL consortium has a standard way of adding contextual information to all the financial numbers (taxonomy). As a result, financial data become machine readable and directly comparable (Mousa and Chen 2013). Such standards significantly increase the transparency of financial data and enable the use of software/applications for the analysis of a large amount of financial data.

The adoption and use of ICTs have several elements in addition to data (Laudon and Laudon 2010). One element of ICTs deals with telecommunication and includes a backbone infrastructure, such as a private network or Internet for data transmission. Another element is the devices that allow individual users to access data—these devices can be computers or mobile devices running with various operating systems. Another element, data storage and access, can be accomplished by having a database that stores business information. The next element is the business applications that provide interface and analytical power for analytics. Individual users typically interact with the business applications to access data and perform analysis. It should be noted that there is an increasing integration of these elements into one application suite, with the support of a telecommunication infrastructure in the cloud for delivering ICT services over the Internet.

ICT Capabilities

For public management networks, a productive perspective to organize a variety of ICTs is by their capabilities. Doing so will allow a stronger connection with the governance structures and the characteristics of the collaborative network. Moreover, such categorization allows the adaptation to fast-advancing technologies with different names and enhanced features by focusing on what functionalities these technologies can deliver to aid with managing a public service network. For communication and scholarly exchange, the focus on capabilities will also allow for better connection between ICTs and key arguments made in the public administration and public management literature.

CREATION OF A COMMON OPERATING PICTURE

In a public management network for emergency response, the capability to provide a common operating picture is critical (Comfort and Haase 2006; Jenkins 2006; Moynihan 2005). This includes a slew of technologies supporting an incident command center in a natural and/or mandate emergency. These technologies can include radios, an integrated information system, a geographic information system, and visualization technologies. The effective use of such technologies would require supporting rules. For instance, boundary rules are critical in the inclusion of important actors in a collaborative network, and position rules are important for delineating their responsibility in the governance. The lack of participation by some telecommunication and utility companies in the wake of the September 11 terrorist attack hampered the effectiveness of emergency response (Kapucu 2006). Another important set of rules shaping the effectiveness of ICT use in emergency response includes information rules governing information sharing, dissemination, and use. Which organization is the official syndication of information and what kind of information participating nonprofits can access about the emergency response effort are all important questions that information rules need to address. If a nonprofit disaster relief organization such as the Red Cross does not receive information from other collaborative organizations in responding to an earthquake, there could be duplication of efforts or a lack of targeted effort on the most affected area.

The proper use of ICTs can create a common operating picture, which is critical in emergency response situations and even long-term disaster relief (Comfort 2007). Such a common operating picture addresses the need of a collaborative network to have a shared understanding of the extent and nature of the problem and data-driven decisions, especially in a time of crisis. Moreover, utilizing ICTs for creating a common operating picture helps articulate resource interdependency. Seeing the common operating picture, participating organizations and individuals tend to realize that, since no single organization can provide the complete operating picture alone, they must rely on each other for operating information, staff, and resources for disaster relief.

PRODUCTION OF SERVICE INFORMATION

For a public management network, one of the key capabilities of ICTs is the production and dissemination of service information in electronic format for the ease of analysis and dissemination. An integrated citizen service information system (such as 311) providing citizen-centric information would require the collaboration of various city departments and, sometimes, independent commissions (Fleming 2008). The key capability of ICTs is to provide citizen-centric service information that is the aspiration of advanced e-government services (Chen and Hsieh 2009; United Nations 2012). The proliferation of smartphones and social networking services further provides opportunities for users (citizens) to participate in the coproduction of public service information (Linders 2012). Some citizen service information systems offer applications for citizens to download on their phones to report service issues, such as "Citizen Connect" in the City of Boston.

Dissemination of service information among the participating organizations as well as to service recipients is enhanced by the use of ICTs. A collaborative network needs to have information on what type, amount, and time of service is being provided to the targeted recipients. For instance, a network management organization that is responsible for childcare service for an entire region or state needs to have an account of who is in the system and what kind of service is delivered to whom. In the case of 311, such integrated and detailed information can aid with the management of a citywide network of organizations for service improvement (Goldsmith and Crawford 2014). Participating organizations and individuals can also access information about their service production and performance via a central information system or portal. Moreover, frontline service providers (such as social workers) can obtain integrated client information.

Choice and information rules are likely to govern the use of ICTs for production and dissemination of service information. Choice rules determine the choices that an organization/individual assuming a particular position in the network can make. Such choices include the production and dissemination of service information. One choice could be to migrate from a single-department service information system to the network-as-a-whole information system. Such decisions could also be about allowing access to information collected by individual police departments to be shared among them.[2] Moreover, information rules can affect the specific information and communication technologies deployed. For example, information rules that focus on providing an integrated view of customers are likely to favor a single system that brings in service information from various sources, but integrates such information to an individual or organization.

The deployment of ICTs to generate and disseminate service information can provide information on both interdependence and diversity of interests. Interdependence can be seen in the requirements for all relevant participating organizations to use the same data standards and information system in order to generate citizen-centric information. Diversity of interests can also be seen in such an integrated information system when a private contractor for health service provision is more focused on profit maximization and the collective is more concerned about cost containment. Also, the availability of resource allocation information, and that there exists major inequality of such allocation, may prompt bargaining of collective service agreements.

REDUCTION OF TRANSACTION COSTS

Another major capability of ICTs in an interorganizational setting is a reduction of the cost of information sharing and searching. A paper-based process of information sharing across organizational boundaries is not only costly, but also slow. One example is the delivery of paper documents from one organization to another, requiring these documents to be manually entered into the receiving organization's information system. The studies of cross-boundary information sharing systems have shown the effectiveness and efficiency of integrated information systems when properly implemented. Most government processes are information-intensive, and a proper deployment of relevant ICTs can improve both efficiency and effectiveness of the business process. For instance, a permitting process that automates the exchange of information and provides a central repository of information can significantly reduce the number of days involved in issuing the permit.

Moreover, the cost of information search can be significantly reduced with the appropriate ICT use, such as a service information portal. Information search cost is recognized as one of the main cost items by institutionalists. In providing citizen-oriented service, the cost of information search could be prohibitive if each participating organization has its own system with various identification methods. With an integrated system, a caseworker can search the entire database for any service rendered to his/her client as a basis to formulate a coordinated plan.

Publishing information on government websites and/or social media sites has greatly reduced the burden on individual citizens or civic organizations in search of public information (Chen 2013;

Mergel 2013). The long tradition of making government information available online via websites has made council meeting information available on the Internet for 24/7 citizen access (Norris and Reddick 2013). For a public management service network, ICTs furnish the ability to provide information service to its members in a low-cost manner. An example of an information service network is a geographic information consortium that coordinates geographic information standards and systems across various local governments and state agencies to increase the interoperability of geographic information. As a result, the cost of information sharing between the consortium and all other entities can be lowered significantly. Moreover, the use of GIS data portals and online tools (i.e., open data portal for Kansas City, MO) can allow governmental agencies, civic organizations, and individuals to pick and choose relevant layers of information for dynamic customization. Such information compilation and customization was costly before the introduction of such a dynamic GIS data portal.

The reduction of the cost of information sharing can have implications for modifying information rules. Without ICTs, some of the broad and open information rules can simply be too costly to implement. The use of ICTs enables organizations to have more open information rules that allow information sharing across organizational boundaries, as well as to empower civic organizations and citizens to gain access to information. Moreover, a good use of ICTs can alter the payoff structure by significantly reducing the cost of information search. At the same time, the potential of ICTs is bound by existing governance structure. That is why studies of cross-boundary information-sharing efforts have highlighted the importance of institutional support to allow for information sharing across organizational boundaries (Yang and Maxwell 2011).

SERVICE DATA ANALYTICS

Another area in which ICTs can be impactful is data analytics. This capability has long been recognized in the area of business intelligence, and it is also consistent with the push in the public sector on performance. Data analytics can be applicable in three functional areas in public management networks. First is the analysis of resource input information. This area involves the analytics of how much resource each participating organization contributes. In the case of a collaborative scientific network providing supercomputing power, it could be about how much resource each participating supercomputing center contributes to the network in terms of staff time, equipment, and supercomputing power. Such analytics are able to help the network manager, as well as the governance board, understand the investment of each participating organization.

The second area is performance. Data analytics can provide an analytical view of public service provided to the entire network. This view can be customized to fit any analytical unit of interest—such as clients, network, type of service, delivery time, or participating organization—given that such information is tracked by the information system. The third functional area is analytics on service demand. The analysis of 311 data across departments can be useful for local governments to understand the kind of services that citizens tend to request from a particular department (Goldsmith and Crawford 2014). Such 311 data analysis will help with decisions on resource allocation across departments.

One of the most significant advances in data analytics is the employment of big data analytics (Chen, Chiang, and Storey 2012; Chen and Hsieh 2014). For instance, CMS (Centers for Medicare and Medicaid Services) can utilize such tools of big data analytics to understand the resource input, cost, and benefits of coordinated care among a network of service providers. Big data is also about the capability of handling data in variety of formats. The growth of social media prompts the development of data analytical tools that are geared toward social media data, such as natural language data mining and social network analysis. For emerging health crises and mapping disease contraction incidents, the use of big data analytics can provide respondents and decision makers more lead time for response and better information in making decisions.

Moreover, the use of data analytics can help uncover the link between governance structure and performance if formulated properly. Discovering such links could be done via traditional research methods with experimental design, case study, statistical analysis, and/or mixed methods using resource input, rule configuration, and performance data. For instance, with such data, a network of organizations providing service to homeless people can gauge the extent to which a move from a treatment model to a prevention one can save government money. In addition, data analytics can provide intelligence on service need and effective service delivery mechanisms. Whatever new insights are generated, they can be disseminated rather quickly electronically via any ICT-enabled communication channels.

Public Values as Performance Measures

The focus here is to articulate how public values can be used by public management networks as measures of performance. Public values include, but are not limited to, public interests, meeting public expectations, equity, and treating citizens both as customers and citizens (Jørgensen and Bozeman 2007; Moore 1995). A comprehensive review of public values adopted mainly a relationship-based approach to identify the value chain based on the actors and their relationships (Jørgensen and Bozeman 2007). For instance, in the relationship between the public sector and civil society, the key public values include, but are not limited to, public interest, social cohesiveness, and sustainability. In the relationship between public administration and citizens, the relevant public values include, but are not limited to, legality, equity, and dialogue. This review presents an inventory of public values to draw from.

Cresswell and his colleagues offer a public value framework for understanding the public values in the adoption and use of ICTs for public service (Cresswell, Burke, and Pardo 2006). This framework takes a broad perspective by focusing on the public rather than on government. The values created are outcome oriented, such as efficiency and effectiveness, as well as process oriented, such as citizen enablement. One of the unique contributions of this public value framework is its attention to return on investment, by articulating the cost and risks associated with public service IT projects, as well as to return for government specifically and the public as a whole.

The integrated framework proposed in this chapter first takes the position that public values should be central for adoption and use of ICTs for public purposes. This position is consistent with those taken by scholars studying information technology for public service (Cresswell, Burke, and Pardo 2006; Kearns 2004), as well as the articulation of publicness for the use of information and technology in the public sector (Bozeman and Bretschneider 1986; Bretschneider and Wittmer 1993). This proposed framework takes a broad perspective of public values, which connects to the discussion about public values in the public administration and management literature.

The first three main public values identified in the broad public administration and management literature are efficiency, effectiveness, and equity. Efficiency is about the reduction of time and cost to provide the same level of service via a network organization. Effectiveness has two possible aspects. First is the effectiveness of providing integrated service information in response to emergency and citizen-centric service information, as in the case of 311. The other aspect is the cost-effectiveness in providing the same service by the network as opposed to by multiple service providers independently. Equity is about the process and treatment of service recipients.

In addition, this framework adds responsiveness, transparency, and empowerment to the list of public values. Responsiveness is about a public service network's ability to be responsive to the changing environment as well as service demands of citizens/residents. Transparency is a core public value of democratic governance for addressing potential informational asymmetry and advancing democratic governance (Bertot, Jaeger, and Grimes 2010). Empowerment is about enabling citizens to participate in coproduction of public information and service.

Leadership and Management Activities for Creation of Public Values

Engage in Strategic Management Activities

Strategic management is salient for a network of organizations and individuals in the creation of public values. Moore (1995) has articulated the need for strategic actions to achieve public values by treating them strategically as overarching objectives. Bryson and his colleagues (Bryson, Crosby, and Stone 2006) also highlight the importance of strategic management in achieving the goals and objectives of a public service network, particularly in the context of cross-sector collaboration. The studies of information technology in government have also underscored the need for a strategic IT plan to bring various departments and governmental agencies together (Dufner, Holley, and Reed 2003; Rocheleau 2006).

In the context of public service networks for the creation of public values, strategic management can be effective in the following ways. First, it is an important first step in addressing the history of cooperation and conflict for interorganizational collaboration. Conducting some version of strategic planning sessions for key stakeholders can help enlist key sponsors as a facilitating condition for initial success (Bryson, Crosby, and Stone 2006). To gain the involvement of key stakeholders, a network manager can engage in activation and mobilization activities as suggested by McGuire (2006).

Second, strategic management could also serve as an opportunity to create a shared understanding of the goals, as well as the challenges, associated with a public service management network. Agreement on key public values as overarching goals and the development of sub-goals can be especially helpful in managing a collection of organizations and individuals. A shared understanding of goals and specific performance measures helps guide the actions of individuals and individual organizations to work toward the agreed-upon goals (Lundin 2007).

Third, strategic management sessions can be an important forum to deal with high-level institutional design issues. Position, boundary, choice, and information rules can all be designed to support the strategic objectives of a public service network. Strategic management forums can focus on creating these facilitating rules. For instance, for a large-scale distributed network, the position and information rules should allow for a network administrative office with supporting information rules for collective governance (Provan and Kenis 2008).

Lastly, strategic management can aid in shaping the direction of information technology for the interest of the network as a whole. One of the biggest technology-related challenges for a public management service network is to ensure information interoperability. Strategic management sessions can make decisions on adopting ICTs to achieve public values such as efficiency and effectiveness of producing and delivering public information and services.

Secure Institutional Support and Design Fitting Institutional Arrangements

In contrast to intraorganizational initiatives, cross-boundary initiatives are particularly in need of institutional support to gain the cooperation of the participating organizations (Bryson, Crosby, and Stone 2006; Dawes, Cresswell, and Pardo 2009). For public service, legitimacy of the collaborative structure is one of the main facilitating conditions (Provan and Lemaire 2012). Governmental agencies and nonprofit organizations need to be assured that the network formed has some legitimacy to justify their participation. Such institutional support can be a legal mandate requiring service providers to participate in a state-created network (Ryu and Rainey 2009). The examination of multiple cross-boundary information-sharing efforts also underscores the importance of having a legal mandate as an important facilitating condition (Eglene, Dawes, and Schneider 2007; Willem and Buelens 2007). Another central institutional support mechanism is to designate a federal agency as the main funder for the creation of and resource support for the collaborative. For instance, NSF has provided more than 100 million U.S. dollars for the creation and support of the cyberinfrastructure program called XSEDE.

Alternatively, institutional support can be in the form of agreements among governmental and nonprofit entities. At the local level, interlocal agreements for various public services, ranging from information service to emergency service, are the institutional foundation for collaboration across organizational boundaries. Such agreements can specify the positions that participating organizations can play and their respective resource commitments and implementation responsibilities.

Designing fitting institutional arrangements is a critical leadership and management activity to ensure the success of public service delivery networks (Provan and Lemaire 2012). Provan and Kenis (2008) have argued that the institutional arrangement should favor a network administrative organization when the number of participating organizations increases, trust and goal agreement decrease, and the need for network-level competency elevates. In contrast, when there is a strong goal agreement and a low-level task complexity associated with coordinating and managing network-level activities, the network does not need a strong and centralized administrative structure as seen in some interlocal collaborations.

Such institutional support should assist in connecting governance structure and performance with appropriate use of ICTs. When the primary design structure of the network is more centralized with a network administrative organization, the adoption of ICTs should gear toward improving the efficiency and effectiveness of network administrative functions. The key ICT capabilities should include the creation of a common operating picture for the network, as well as technology that reduces the cost of information gathering. For a less centralized way of managing a network, the focus could be on the production of service and performance information for the entire network to access in order to promote the peer monitoring and accountability that are central to the success of a network.

Another productive use of ICT is to promote learning. A successful network needs to be able to adapt to new circumstances (Provan and Lemaire 2012). Adaptability is one of the advantages of a network structure over the traditional pyramid organizational structure. In a network of organizations, learning can be enhanced by the adoption of ICTs to facilitate interactions. Such learning can be accomplished by a knowledge management system that is deemed as the primary function of some public management networks (Agranoff 2007). Moreover, learning can be done with information gathered from staff members working on a service provided by the network. For instance, a public service network (XSEDE) providing computing resources conducted a staff climate survey to understand the opportunities and challenges associated with working for the collaborative.

Manage Interdependence and Conflicts

Resource interdependence brings the network participating organizations together. Collaborative governance is premised on the tasks that cannot be done or are difficult to accomplish by a single organization. Interdependence should be managed to provide the needed incentives for participation. Most of the network-participating organizations join the network to gain access to resources that are not otherwise available, since these resources are collectively produced and only then available to members of the network. Lundin (2007) has argued for the importance of resource dependence as one of the prime motivations for authorities to work together, even without a high level of mutual trust.

The use of ICTs can modulate the level of interdependence when the network service operation depends heavily on information technology. The level of interdependence can be shaped by adopting a centralized information system and specifying access control to information. When participating organizations' operation is heavily dependent on access to information produced by the central information system, it creates a high level of resource dependence. If the network administrative organization is responsible for paying for the information technology equipment, maintenance, and upgrade, it creates a high level of dependence of participating organizations on the central administrative organization for operational purposes.

The use of ICTs can also shape the perception of resource dependence. ICTs can keep track of the resource commitment from individual organizations, as well as the resources that they draw from the network as a whole. Such information can be communicated to participating organizations at quarterly meetings or other forums. Alternatively, such information can be related online in a user-friendly format, such as dashboard, to grant instant access.

Conflicts are an inevitable aspect of collaborative governance (O'Leary and Bingham 2009). One of the main sources of such conflict is the challenge of dual loyalty that individual participating organizations (and individuals) face (Bardach 1996). The conflicts could be fundamental ones such as values (Bryson, Crosby, and Stone 2006; Van Bueren, Klijn, and Koppenjan 2003) or about the distributions of costs and benefits. Tension develops between time committed to the network and time allocated to activities for the home organization.

Leaders and managers of public service networks can resolve some conflicts with an appropriate design of the governance structure. To deal with dual loyalty, a network manager can create positions that are fully funded by the network for the staff to secure his/her exclusive loyalty to the network. To a large extent, doing so will alleviate the tension due to an individual's dual loyalty. Another strategy is to manage the payoff associated with devoting time and energy to the network as opposed to someone's home organizations. One of the advantages of working for the network is the career opportunities for an individual to work on a larger scale and at a higher level than is available in his/her home organization. Working for the network can open up career opportunities that are crucial for long-term career development for individuals working across organizational boundaries. Such management strategy alters payoff rules to incentivize individuals to commit more time and energy to the network.

Some ICT capabilities enable the resolution of conflicts. One of the process requirements for resolving conflicts is to allow participating organizations to bargain. ICTs can reduce the transaction costs for these bargaining activities by offering low-cost video conferencing opportunities to supplement in-person bargaining and negotiation. Group decision-making applications can aid in multilateral negotiations that are potentially complex (Laudon and Laudon 2010). Moreover, ICTs can help significantly reduce the cost of information search as well as that of data analytics. Participating organizations can get an accounting of the resource allocation to various organizations as well as analytics on payoff for the network funder, participating organizations, and service recipients.

Achieve Performance and Manage Tradeoffs

There are two salient challenges in managing network performance, especially for networks that produce and deliver public services. The first one is the potential tradeoffs between multiple goals set by the network. A procedural and process requirement may come at the cost of speed. For instance, an inclusive stakeholder involvement may take months to plan and accommodate. Moreover, there could be a competition for resources between the goal of providing more service and the goal of providing service to a diverse group of potential clients/users. As an example, the cyberinfrastructure program (XSEDE) devotes a significant number of resources to serve social scientists as well as researchers in minority institutions, which competes with the resources allocated to serving well-established groups of heavy users (scientists).

The other challenge is the tradeoff between various levels of the network. Provan and Milward (2001) have made a compelling argument on the existence of tension between performance at the community level and that at the program level. What is good for the entire ecosystem, such as creating multiple similar programs for competition and redundancy as well as long-term sustainability, may not be good for the performance of a single program facing the challenge of survival or severe competition. What is good for the program as a whole, such as some cost-cutting measures, may be detrimental to individual participating organizations that aim to maximize their return on investment.

The use of ICTs can aid in providing timely service performance data for service improvement and an enhanced understanding of the tradeoffs. For instance, instead of waiting for an annual report for a multi-year program to come in before planning the activity for the next year, a monthly or even weekly update of the service provided to the clients, as well as some notion of quality, can be useful for the public service management network to continuously improve service in adapting to the changing environment. Moreover, the use of ICTs can improve the data analytics needed for organizing performance information in any desirable units such as goals, participating organizations, and/or even individuals. Such information, at minimum, can shed light on the potential tradeoffs between goals when there is a cap on the overall budget/resources to be allocated across multiple areas. Such information can also help in understanding the theory of change underlying the program by combining with the use of a logic model and resource input as well as service performance information.

The use of ICTs can further provide both information and analytics to address the potential tradeoffs between performance results at the levels of participating organizations, program (network), and community (ecosystem). For instance, a centralized project management information system can track key performance indicators, and then such performance information can be aggregated to the organizational level or the program (network) level. Recognizing that it is more challenging to get community (ecosystem) level information, the use of ICTs has become more imperative to gather information from a broad group of stakeholders. Using ICTs allows the generation of information that could inform the nature and type of tradeoffs between various levels. Moreover, analytics can be performed to understand the potential sources of tradeoffs at various levels. It could be that the network (program) manager needs to implement stringent cost control measures for the survival of the network, but at the expense of significantly reducing the resource allocation to individual participating organizations. Overall, the use of ICTs can greatly enhance the potential of incorporating data to inform decision-making.

Adjusting governance structure in terms of rules can also be a useful device for managing the potential tensions between performance results at various levels. One of the institutional designs is to enlist the participation of major actors (organizations and individuals) at all three levels to understand the potential implications on these respective levels. In order to facilitate participation across these levels, various rules can be utilized. Position rules can be modified (i.e., the creation of positions for members from other levels to serve on an advisory board). Information rules can be more open for the exchange of information between individuals and organizations at all three levels. Another major type of rule is the payoff rule. If the goal is to maximize performance at the program/network level, the payoff rules should be designed to help advance that goal.

Conclusion

This chapter proposes an integrative framework that articulates the role of information and communication technologies (ICTs) in the production and delivery of public service. It aims to exemplify a potential synthesis of public management research and e-government scholarship with the focus on collaborative public management networks. Such a framework seeks to advance the scholarship of e-government by developing research hypotheses on how ICTs can make a difference in the performance of public information and service. Moreover, this framework adds to the scholarship of public management and collaborative governance by depicting various ways of utilizing ICTs to enhance the performance of the governance and implementation of collaborative public service networks.

The proposed framework has several unique features with the intent to advance the theory and practice of utilizing information technology for improving public service. First, it explicitly models the role of ICTs by delineating their capabilities in solving the challenges of cross-boundary collaboration for public service. Previous studies tend to touch on a broad concept of technology (i.e., Internet) at the expense of understanding the impact of specific capabilities of ICTs on service performance. Therefore, this framework, as indicated in Figure 4.1, positions ICTs at the center for explicit modeling. For instance, the capability of ICTs to create a common operating picture is considered a capability that will link to a high level of efficiency and effectiveness in a network of organizations for emergency response.

Second, this framework addresses the relationship between institutional design and the utilization of ICTs. Such modeling of relationships details the specific categories of rules that could reinforce or dampen the impact of ICTs or vice versa. Most of the earlier discussions about institutionalism provides a broad stroke of the role of institutions by arguing the need for institutional support. Nonetheless, much less is known about how specific rules can affect the adoption of ICTs and vice versa. For instance, this framework allows for the examination of how ICTs can enable a more open information rule and also how information rules shape the access control that ICTs have to reinforce.

Third, this framework further integrates the research and practice of collaborative governance by identifying the key factors affecting the structure and process of public management networks and attempting to discover the relationship between ICT use and these factors. The existing studies of public management networks and collaborative governance tend not to make these specific connections that can be productive to understanding the roles of ICTs. For instance, the use of ICTs can further strengthen interdependence when all participating organizations need to access the same pool of technological resources and rely on common data standards for their operation. Alternatively, use of ICTs can increase such a shared understanding of interdependence to induce desirable behavior for the benefits of the network.

Moreover, this framework further informs the scholarship of both collaborative governance and cross-boundary e-government, integrating the perspective of collaborative public managers. It has identified research propositions on specific leadership and management activities that are conducive to smart use of ICTs to promote public value: (a) having a strategic planning session with an explicit discussion and inclusion of information technology will be helpful in leveraging ICTs to deliver public value; (b) leadership and management efforts can focus on articulating the interdependence of network participating organizations and individuals to provide more incentives for their contribution to network effectiveness; (c) management needs to dynamically enhance goal congruence among network participants because conflicts will inevitably arise, and bargaining is an integral part of the network management; and (d) network management activities need to be directed to address the potential tradeoffs of multiple goals, as well as the tensions between effectiveness at various levels of network (individuals, network, and community).

Notes

1. In the initial formation of the terms, Ostrom, Gardner, and Walker (1994) called this "authority rule." This chapter adopts the adaptation by Schweik and Kitsing (2010) to call it "choice" rule, as that term that better captures the meaning of these type of rules.
2.. There is an informational sharing arrangement called LEADS that allows various law enforcement agencies at various levels of government to share law enforcement information.

References

Agranoff, Robert. 2007. *Managing within Networks: Adding Value to Public Organizations*. Washington, DC: Georgetown University Press.
Ahn, Michael J., and Stuart Bretschneider. 2011. 'Politics of E-Government: E-Government and the Political Control of Bureaucracy'. *Public Administration Review* 71 (3): 414–424.

Ansell, Chris, and Alison Gash. 2008. 'Collaborative Governance in Theory and Practice'. *Journal of Public Administration Research and Theory* 18 (4): 543–572.

Ansell, Chris, and Ann Keller. 2014. *Adapting the Incident Command Model for Knowledge-Based Crises: The Case of the Centers for Disease Control and Prevention*. Washington, DC: IBM Center for the Business of Government.

Bardach, Eugene. 1996. 'Turf Barriers to Interagency Collaboration'. In *The State of Public Management*, edited by Donald Kettl and Brinton Milward, 168–192. Baltimore, MD: Johns Hopkins University Press.

Bekkers, Victor. 2007. 'The Governance of Back-Office Integration'. *Public Management Review* 9 (3): 377–400.

Bekkers, Victor. 2009. 'Flexible Information Infrastructures in Dutch E-Government Collaboration Arrangements: Experiences and Policy Implications'. *Government Information Quarterly* 26 (1): 60–68.

Bertot, John C., Paul T. Jaeger, and Justin M. Grimes. 2010. 'Using ICTs to Create a Culture of Transparency: E-Government and Social Media as Openness and Anti-Corruption Tools for Societies'. *Government Information Quarterly* 27 (3): 264–271.

Bozeman, Barry, and Stuart Bretschneider. 1986. 'Public Management Information Systems: Theory and Prescription'. *Public Administration Review* 46 (Special Issue): 475–487.

Bretschneider, Stuart, and Dennis Wittmer. 1993. 'Organizational Adoption of Microcomputer Technology: The Role of Sector'. *Information Systems Research* 4 (1): 88–108.

Bryson, John, Barbra Crosby, and Melissa Middleton Stone. 2006. 'The Design and Implementation of Cross-Sector Collaborations: Propositions from the Literature'. *Public Administration Review* 66 (Supplement to Issue 6 (Special Issue)): 44–55.

Chen, Hsinchun, Roger H. Chiang, and Veda Storey. 2012. 'Business Intelligence and Analytics: From Big Data to Big Impact'. *MIS Quarterly* 36 (4): 1165–1188.

Chen, Yu-Che. 2010. 'Citizen-Centric E-Government Services: Understanding Integrated Citizen Service Information Systems'. *Social Science Computer Review* 28 (4): 427–442.

Chen, Yu-Che. 2013. 'Improving Transparency in the Financial Sector: E-Government XBRL Implementation in the United States'. *Public Performance and Management Review* 37 (2): 241–262.

Chen, Yu-Che, and Jun-Yi Hsieh. 2009. 'Advancing E-Governance: Comparing Taiwan and the United States'. *Public Administration Review* 69 (Supplement 1): S151–S158.

Chen, Yu-Che, and Tsui-Chuan Hsieh. 2014. 'Big Data for Digital Government: Opportunities, Challenges, and Strategies'. *International Journal of Public Administration in the Digital Age* 1 (1): 1–14.

Comfort, Louise. 2007. 'Crisis Management in Hindsight: Cognition, Communication, Coordination, and Control'. *Public Administration Review* 67 (Supplement): 189–197.

Comfort, Louise, and Thomas Haase. 2006. 'Communication, Coherence, and Collective Action: The Impact of Hurricane Katrina on Communications Infrastructure'. *Public Works Management and Policy* 10 (4): 328–343.

Cresswell, Anthony M., G. Brian Burke, and Theresa A. Pardo. 2006. *Advancing Return on Investment Analysis for Government IT: A Public Value Framework*. Albany, NY: Center for Technology in Government.

Daley, Dorothy M. 2008. 'Interdisciplinary Problems and Agency Boundaries: Exploring Effective Cross-Agency Collaboration'. *Journal of Public Administration Research and Theory* 19 (3): 477–493. doi: 10.1093/jopart/mun020

Dawes, Sharon, Anthony Cresswell, and Theresa Pardo. 2009. 'From 'Need to Know' to 'Need to Share': Tangled Problems, Information Boundaries, and the Building of Public Sector Knowledge Networks'. *Public Administration Review* 69 (3): 392–402.

Dufner, Donna, Lyn M. Holley, and B. J. Reed. 2003. 'Strategic Information Systems Planning and U.S. County Government'. *Communications of the Association for Information Systems* 11: 219–244.

Eglene, Ophelia, Sharon Dawes, and Carrie Schneider. 2007. 'Authority and Leadership Patterns in Public Sector Knowledge Networks'. *American Review of Public Administration* 37 (1): 91–113.

Emerson, Kirk, Tina Nabatchi, and Stephen Balogh. 2012. 'An Integrative Framework for Collaborative Governance'. *Journal of Public Administration Research & Theory* 22 (1): 1–29.

Feiock, Richard C., Annette Steinacker, and Hyung Jun Park. 2008. 'Institutional Collective Action and Economic Development Joint Ventures'. *Public Administration Review* 69 (2): 256–270.

Fleming, Cory. 2008. *Call 311: Connecting Citizens to Local Government Case Study Series: Minneapolis 311 System*. Washington, DC: ICMA.

Fountain, Jane. 2001. *Building the Virtual State: Information Technology and Institutional Change*. Washington, DC: Brookings Institution Press.

Frederickson, George H., and Kevin Smith. 2003. *Public Administration Theory Primer*. Boulder, CO: Westview Press.

Ganapati, Sukumar, and Chris Reddick. 2014. 'The Use of ICT for Open Government in U.S. Municipalities: Perceptions of Chief Administrative Officers'. *Public Performance & Management Review* 37 (3): 365–287.

Garson, David. 2006. *Public Information Technology and E-Governance: Managing the Virtual State*. Sudbury, MA: Jones and Barlett Publishers, Inc.

Gil-Garcia, J. Ramon, Ahmet Guler, Theresa A. Pardo, and G. Brian Burke. 2010. 'Trust in Government Cross-Boundary Information Sharing Initiatives: Identifying the Determinants'. Paper read at 43rd Hawaii International Conference on System Sciences (HICSS-43), 5–8 January 2010, at Koloa, Kauai, HI.

Goldsmith, Stephen, and Susan Crawford. 2014. *The Responsive City: Engaging Communities through Data-Smart Governance.* Hoboken, NJ: Wiley.

Gray, Barbara. 1985. 'Conditions Facilitating Interorganizational Collaboration'. *Human Relations* 38 (10): 911–936.

Grimmelikhuijsen, Stephan, and Albert Jacob Meijer. 2015. 'Does Twitter Increase Perceived Police Legitimacy'. *Public Administration Review* 75 (4): 598–606.

Hellberg, Ann-Sofie, and Åke Grönlund. 2013. 'Conflicts in Implementing Interoperability: Re-Operationalizing Basic Values'. *Government Information Quarterly* 30 (2): 154–162.

Im, Tobin, Greg Porumbescu, and Hyunkuk Lee. 2013. 'ICT as a Buffer to Change: A Case Study of the Seoul Metropolitan Government's Dasan Call Center'. *Public Performance & Management Review* 36 (3): 436–455.

Isett, Kimberley R., Ines A. Mergel, Kelly LeRoux, Pamela A. Mischen, and R. Karl Rethemeyer. 2011. 'Networks in Public Administration Scholarship: Understanding Where We Are and Where We Need to Go'. *Journal of Public Administration Research and Theory* 21 (Supplement 1): i157–i173.

Jenkins, William. 2006. 'Collaboration Over Adaptation: The Case for Interoperable Communications in Homeland Security'. *Public Administration Review* 66 (3): 319–321.

Jørgensen, Torben Beck, and Barry Bozeman. 2007. 'Public Values: An Inventory'. *Administration & Society* 39 (3): 354–381.

Kapucu, Naim. 2006. 'Interagency Communication Networks During Emergencies: Boundary Spanners in Multiagency Coordination'. *American Review of Public Administration* 36 (2): 207–225.

Kearns, Iain. 2004. *Public Value and E-Government.* London: Institute for Public Policy Research.

Kwon, Sung-Wook, and Richard C. Feiock. 2010. 'Overcoming the Barriers to Cooperation: Intergovernmental Service Agreements'. *Public Administration Review* 70 (6): 876–884.

Laudon, Kenneth C., and Jane P. Laudon. 2010. *Management Information Systems: Managing the Digital Firm.* 11th ed. Upper Saddle River, NJ: Pearson Education.

LeRoux, Kelly. 2005. 'Networks of Local Governments: Examining Community Conferences as Mechanisms for Achieving Interlocal Cooperation'. Paper read at Creating Collaborative Communities: Management Networks, Services Cooperation, and Metropolitan Governance at Wayne State University, 31 October 2005.

Linders, Dennis. 2012. 'From E-Government to We-Government: Defining a Typology for Citizen Coproduction in the Age of Social Media'. *Government Information Quarterly* 29 (4): 446–454.

Luna-Reyes, F., J. Ramon Gil-Garcia, and Cinthia Betiny Cruz. 2007. 'Collaborative Digital Government in Mexico: Some Lessons from Federal Web-Based Interorganizational Information Integration Initiatives'. *Government Information Quarterly* 24: 808–826.

Lundin, Martin. 2007. 'Explaining Cooperation: How Resource Interdependence, Goal Congruence, and Trust Affect Joint Actions in Policy Implementation'. *Journal of Public Administration Research and Theory* 17 (4): 651–672.

McGuire, Michael. 2002. 'Managing Networks: Propositions on What Managers Do and Why They Do It'. *Public Administration Review* 62 (5): 599–609.

McGuire, Michael. 2006. 'Collaborative Public Management: Assessing What We Know and How We Know It'. *Public Administration Review* 66 (6(Supplement)): 33–43.

Mergel, Ines. 2013. *Social Media in the Public Sector: A Guide to Participation, Collaboration and Transparency in the Networked World.* San Francisco, CA: John Wiley & Sons.

Moore, Mark H. 1995. *Creating Public Value: Strategic Management in Government.* Cambridge, MA & London: Harvard University Press.

Mousa, Rania, and Yu-Che Chen. 2013. 'E-Government Adoption of XBRL: A U.K./U.S. Comparison'. In *Public Sector Transformation through E-Government: Experiences from Europe and North America,* edited by Vishanth Weerakkody and Christopher G. Reddick, 198–210. New York and London: Routledge.

Moynihan, Donald. 2005. *Leveraging Collaborative Networks in Infrequent Emergency Situations.* Washington, DC: IBM Center for the Business of Government.

Ni, Anna Ya. 2006. *What Drives the Development of E-Government? An Analysis of U.S. County Government's Adoption of E-Government Services.* Madison, WI: APPAM 2006 Fall Conference.

Norris, Donald, and Christopher Reddick. 2013. 'Local E-Government in the United States: Transformation or Incremental Change?' *Public Administration Review* 73 (1): 165–175.

North, Douglass C. 1990. *Institutions, Institutional Change, and Economic Performance.* Cambridge: Cambridge University Press.

O'Leary, Rosemary, and Lisa Blomgren Bingham, eds. 2009. *The Collaborative Public Manager: New Ideas for the Twenty-First Century.* Washington, DC: Georgetown University Press.

O'Leary, Rosemary, Yujin Choi, and Catherine M. Gerard. 2012. 'The Skill Set of the Successful Collaborator'. *Public Administration Review* 72 (Supplement): S70–S78.

Ostrom, Elinor. 1998. 'A Behavioral Approach to the Rational Choice Theory of Collective Action'. *American Political Science Review* 92 (1): 1–22.

Ostrom, Elinor. 2010. 'Institutional Analysis and Development: Elements of the Framework in Historical Perspective'. In *Historical Developments and Theoretical Approaches in Sociology*, edited by C. Crothers, 261–288. UK: EOLSS (Encyclopedia of Life Support Systems).

Ostrom, Elinor, Roy Gardner, and James Walker. 1994. *Rules, Games and Common-Pool Resources*. Ann Arbor, MI: University of Michigan Press.

Pardo, Theresa, J. Ramon Gil-Garcia, G. Brian Burke, and Ahmet Guler. 2009. *Factors Influencing Government Cross-Boundary Information Sharing: Preliminary Analysis of a National Survey*. Albany, NY: Center for Technology in Government, University at Albany, SUNY.

Parkhe, Arvind, Stanley Wasserman, and David A. Ralston. 2006. 'Introduction to Special Topic Forum: New Frontiers in Network Theory Development'. *Academy of Management Review* 31 (3): 560–568.

Pfeffer, Jeffrey, and Gerald Salancik. 2003. *The External Control of Organizations: A Resource Dependence Perspective*. Stanford, CA (originally New York): Stanford University Press (Originally Harper and Row in 1978).

Provan, Keith G., and Kun Huang. 2012. 'Resource Tangibility and the Evolution of a Publicly Funded Health and Human Services Network'. *Public Administration Review* 72 (3): 366–375. doi: 10.1111/j.1540-6210.2011.02504.x

Provan, Keith G., and Patrick Kenis. 2008. 'Modes of Network Governance: Structure, Management, and Effectiveness'. *Journal of Public Administration Research and Theory* 18 (2): 229–252.

Provan, Keith G., and Robin H. Lemaire. 2012. 'Core Concepts and Key Ideas for Understanding Public Sector Organizational Networks: Using Research to Inform Scholarship and Practice'. *Public Administration Review* 72 (5): 638–648.

Provan, Keith G., and Brinton Milward. 2001. 'Do Networks Really Work? A Framework for Evaluating Public-Sector Organizational Networks'. *Public Administration Review* 61 (4): 414–423.

Reddick, Christopher. 2012. *Public Administration and Information Technology*. Burlington, MA: Jones & Barlett Learning.

Rethemeyer, Karl, and Deneen Hatmaker. 2008. 'Network Management Reconsidered: An Inquiry Into Management of Network Structures in Public Sector Service Provision'. *Journal of Public Administration Research and Theory* 18 (4): 617–646.

Rocheleau, Bruce. 2006. *Public Management Information Systems*. Hershey, PA: Idea Group Publishing.

Roy, Jeffrey. 2009. 'E-Government and Integrated Service Delivery in Canada: The Province of Nova Scotia as a Case Study'. *International Journal of Electronic Governance* 2 (2/3): 223–238. doi: 10.1504/IJEG.2009.029131

Ryu, Jay Eungha, and Hal G. Rainey. 2009. 'Collaborative Public Management and Organizational Design: One-Stop Shopping Structures in Employment and Training Program'. In *The Collaborative Public Manager: New Ideas for the Twenty-First Century*, edited by Rosemary O'Leary and Lisa Blomgren Bingham, 177–194. Washington, DC: Georgetown University Press.

Scholl, Hans Jochen, and Ralf Klischewski. 2007. 'E-Government Integration and Interoperability: Framing the Research Agenda'. *International Journal of Public Administration* 30 (8/9): 889–920.

Scholl, Hans Jochen, Herbert Kubicek, Ralf Cimander, and Ralf Klischewski. 2012. 'Process Integration, Information Sharing, and System Interoperation in Government: A Comparative Case Analysis'. *Government Information Quarterly* 29: 313–323.

Schweik, Charles, and Robert English. 2006. *Uncovering Design Principles of Open Source Software Collaborations: Implications for Government Agencies*. Madison, WI: APPAM Paper (Nov. 4, 2006).

Schweik, Charles, and Meelis Kitsing. 2010. 'Applying Elinor Ostrom's Rule Classification Framework to the Analysis of Open Source Software Commons'. *Transnational Corporations Review* 2 (1): 13–16.

Sterman, John D. 2000. *Business Dynamics: System Thinking and Modeling for a Complex World*. Boston: Irwin McGraw-Hill.

Thomson, Ann Marie, and James Perry. 2006. 'Collaboration Processes: Inside the Black Box'. *Public Administration Review* 66 (6 (Supplement)): 20–32.

United Nations. 2012. *United Nations E-Government Survey 2012: E-Government for the People*. New York: United Nations.

Van Bueren, Ellen M., Erik-Hans Klijn, and Joop F.M. Koppenjan. 2003. 'Dealing with Wicked Problems in Networks: Analyzing an Environmental Debate from a Network Perspective'. *Journal of Public Administration Research & Theory* 13 (2): 193–212.

Willem, Annick, and Marc Buelens. 2007. 'Knowledge Sharing in Public Sector Organizations: The Effect of Organizational Characteristics on Interdepartmental Knowledge Sharing'. *Journal of Public Administration Research and Theory* 17 (4): 581–606.

Wood, Donna, and Barbara Gray. 1991. 'Toward a Comprehensive Theory of Collaboration'. *Journal of Applied Behavioral Science* 27 (2): 139–162.

Yang, Tung-Mou, and Terrence A. Maxwell. 2011. 'Information-Sharing in Public Organizations: A Literature Review of Interpersonal, Intra-Organizational and Inter-Organizational Success Factors'. *Government Information Quarterly* 28: 164–175.

Yildiz, Mete. 2007. 'E-Government Research: Reviewing the Literature, Limitations, and Ways Forward'. *Government Information Quarterly* 24: 646–665.

5
USING SYSTEM DYNAMICS FOR THE ANALYSIS OF COMPLEX SOCIAL PROBLEMS AND PUBLIC POLICY ALTERNATIVES

Fundamentals and Recommendations

*Luis F. Luna-Reyes, J. Ramon Gil-Garcia,
Eliot Rich, and David F. Andersen*

1 Introduction

On February 28, 2015, the Network of Schools of Public Policy, Affairs, and Administration (NASPAA), in a partnership with the Rippel Foundation, held the first National Student Simulation Competition. During the competition, 181 students from 93 schools of public administration and public policy in the United States gathered at six host sites to work on the challenge of redesigning a regional healthcare system (McFarland et al. 2015). The day of the competition, student teams worked with a simulator to experiment with different policy combinations, getting immediate feedback about their impact on healthcare costs, death rate, quality of the care, inequity, and employee productivity, all compared to the current conditions in the region. Moreover, participants in the competition could also explore the main pitfalls of their policies and other variables affecting key stakeholders in the system, such as doctors and hospital managers. Such information allowed participants not only to improve the impact of their policies, but also to observe stakeholders' interests in a way that allowed them to better understand the feasibility of each policy package. Toward the end of the day, each team prepared a presentation, and one winner per site was selected.

A key component of the event was the use of System Dynamics computer simulation. Health policy making and analysis like the scenarios students experienced in the competition require not only data, but also an understanding of the system that provides policy makers with a framework for planning the future by exploring potential scenarios. Whether that future is five or fifty years out, the process requires informed projections based on history and an understanding of the problem's underlying causes, often outside the scope of patient records and health outcome datasets. These predictions are not simple linear extrapolations. They require a deep understanding of the interactions and effects that drive system behavior over time. Such an understanding of the system was provided to participants in the competition by the Rippel Foundation's ReThink Health simulation (http://www.rethinkhealth.org/), a System Dynamics model that projects the effects of socioeconomic and government interventions, as well as health models to estimate the long-term costs of action and inaction on our health futures. The goal of this simulation is the development of "an aligned vision, system-wide strategy and a long-term plan" (Fannie E. Rippel Foundation 2015).

The model itself is the result of years of research and development with the involvement of policy makers and other stakeholders in the health system. The ReThink Health Model can be traced back to efforts by the Rippel Foundation in 2007, which adapted simulation and modeling developed at the Center for Disease Prevention and Control (CDC), using a specific approach to systems thinking and policy making called System Dynamics (McFarland et al. 2015, Milstein, Homer, and Hirsch 2009, 2010). Subsequently, the Rippel Foundation decided to use the ReThink Health Model as a key element of a toolset to help local policy makers to better understand reform efforts. Just as with students in the competition, the model has been used effectively by policy makers to envision and build policy to improve their health systems (Milstein, Hirsch, and Minyard 2013). From the very beginning, model development involved collaboration with a group in Pueblo, Colorado, which was facing real challenges for local health reform. The model provided results that became the basis for a strategic plan (McFarland et al. 2015). After working with model refinements in several other cities such as Atlanta, Georgia, and Cincinnati, Ohio, the foundation funded the effort to create an "Anytown" version, which has been used by local communities to better understand health policy and health reform (Milstein, Hirsch, and Minyard 2013). ReThink Health is just one example of a modeling and simulation effort that uses System Dynamics simulation and systems thinking in understanding health policy (Homer and Hirsch 2006, Homer, Hirsch, and Milstein 2007, Homer et al. 2004).

The purpose of this chapter is to introduce System Dynamics modeling and simulation as a powerful tool to promote systems thinking in the process of policy making and analysis. To accomplish this purpose, the chapter is organized in five sections, including this introduction. The second section defines System Dynamics as a systems approach, its purpose and origins, and also constitutes a primer of the System Dynamics methods. The third section discusses previous examples of the use of System Dynamics in the public policy area, and the fourth section proposes an integration of the method with the policymaking process, providing examples of such integration. Finally, the last section of the chapter concludes with a summary, as well as some strengths and limitations of the approach.

2 System Dynamics: Definition, Fundamentals, and Group Model Building

This section presents definitions of System Dynamics as a systems approach and method. It also includes a brief history of System Dynamics, its fundamentals and approach to building models through the interaction with decision and policy makers, called group model building.

2.1 What Is System Dynamics?

System Dynamics (SD) is a systems approach that has been highly influenced by the development of technology, exact sciences, and the application of computer simulation methods to the analysis of complex social science and economic problems (Wolstenholme 1999). Its purpose is to gain a better understanding of certain problems and behaviors in order to be able to design strategies and policies that improve the performance of the system over time (Grizzle and Pettijohn 2002, Kopainsky and Luna-Reyes 2008). SD is linked to a strong computational component for modeling and analyzing problems given that simulation is an essential tool for visualizing systems and relationships between elements (Luna-Reyes and Gil-Garcia 2011). Involving clients and stakeholder groups in the model-building process has been a common strategy to improve model validity and its usefulness for policy making (Forrester 1961, Zagonel 2002).

System Dynamics was developed in the 1950s by Jay W. Forrester at the Massachusetts Institute of Technology (MIT). Forrester distinguished SD from other variants of the systems approach by its

System Dynamics and Public Policy

intensive use of feedback cycles and greater emphasis on structure as the main cause of the behavior of a system (Forrester 1973). System dynamics uses models to represent abstractions or simplifications of mental models with the purpose of learning about complexity (Wolstenholme 1982). Since its early beginnings, System Dynamics has been characterized by the use of formal models in order to support policy making and problem solving (Aracil 1983, Richardson and Pugh III 1981, Roberts et al. 1994, Sterman 2000). The processes of modeling and simulation are mainly intended to learn about how the world works, helping policy makers to improve their way of thinking about a problem or challenge (de Geus 1992, Senge 1990, Sharp 1977). A computer model is needed because of human limitations to predict and manage the behavior of these complex structures (Forrester 1975). The modeling process forces policy analysts to explicitly and clearly express their mental models about the relationships in the system (Black 2002, Jackson 1991, 2000). A dynamic model is best viewed as a support tool for understanding social problems and formulating possible public policy solutions (Sherwood 2011) (Van Gigch 1990).

2.2 The System Dynamics Language and Method

As we describe in the previous section, System Dynamics is a method for studying and managing complex feedback systems (Forrester 1961, Luna-Reyes 2008, Richardson and Pugh III 1981, Roberts et al. 1994, Sterman 2000). One of its basic principles is that a system's performance over time is closely linked to an underlying structure of endogenous feedback processes. That is to say, patterns of behavior in the system are explained mainly by endogenous processes, not by exogenous factors.

2.2.1 The Modeling Process

System Dynamics practitioners have described the modeling process as an iterative process, going from problem understanding to model validation and use, as represented in Figure 5.1 (Randers 1980, Richardson and Pugh III 1981, Roberts et al. 1994, Sterman 2000, Wolstenholme 1990). The modeling process involves analysis of problem dynamics (expressed in graphs of behavior over time) and problem structure (expressed graphically in causal-loop diagrams or stock-and-flow diagrams, and mathematically in systems of differential equations). A System Dynamics computer model is the result of an iterative process of comparing and contrasting a set of assumptions about the system structure and its known behaviors. In this way, defining problems in terms of behavior over time (graphs over time) and developing feedback-rich diagrams (causal-loop and stock-and-flow diagrams) are two basic skills necessary to model problems (Luna-Reyes 2008).

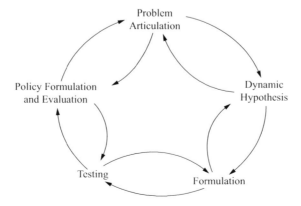

Figure 5.1 The System Dynamics Modeling Process (adapted from Luna-Reyes and Andersen 2003)

2.2.2 Defining Policy Problems in Terms of Behavior over Time

In System Dynamics, defining policy problems means to express them in terms of their behavior over time (Richardson and Pugh III 1981), moving from static pictures of the problem's symptoms to a dynamic definition of it (Mashayekhi 1992, Senge 1990).

The term *reference mode* refers to patterns of behavior over time. These patterns represent the dynamic behavior of important problem-related variables. The reference mode is an abstract concept to guide the modeling process, which is built by using multiple sources of historical evidence, such as verbal descriptions, time series, or key events (Saeed 1998a). In terms of the data available, a modeler can draw graphs of either historical data series (information available from records in the organization) or idealized reference modes (information available from actors' judgments and mental models). In terms of the project scope, modelers create sketches of historical data, forecasted dynamics (what we can expect to happen), or preferred dynamics (what we desire to have happen).

Historical data series are complex patterns that represent the effects of multiple problem components on system behavior (Saeed 1992). Therefore, historical data series can be used as the starting point to create a reference mode, but using that pattern as the reference mode itself can be misleading to the modeling effort in early stages; historical data series are more useful in later stages of the model with a greater focus on testing and evaluation. Although historical data series can show many different behaviors, most of those rich behaviors are combinations or instances of a limited set of behavioral patterns like the ones shown in Figure 5.2. Moreover, it is common to find out in public sector applications that relevant variables are not recorded in any information system. Thus, many reference modes are based upon actors' judgments and mental models.

System Dynamics is best suited for problems that show dynamic behaviors like the ones presented in Figure 5.2, particularly when the pattern can be explained by actors' decisions and actions (endogenous explanation).

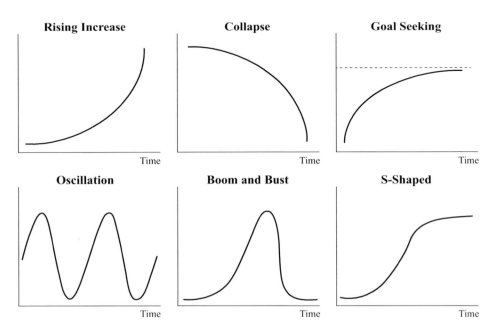

Figure 5.2 Common Patterns of Problem Behavior (adapted from Luna-Reyes 2008)

2.2.3 Feedback-Rich Diagrams

Researchers in the field have developed a series of "mapping tools" to represent endogenous explanations of observed problematic behaviors (Lane 2008, Morecroft 1982, 2007). A study of best practices in the field suggests that the preferred mapping tools among highly recognized experts are the stock-and-flow and causal-loop diagrams (Lane 2008, Martinez-Moyano and Richardson 2013).

2.2.3.1 CAUSAL-LOOP DIAGRAMS

The building blocks of causal-loop diagrams are variable names and causal links, which can be either positive or negative. Table 5.1 shows the conceptual and mathematical definition of the direction of causal relationships. A closed path of causal links constitutes a *feedback loop*. "A feedback loop exists when decisions change the state of the system, changing the conditions and information that influence future decisions" (Richardson 2010). A *reinforcing loop* (or positive loop) represents a changing process where the characteristic is growing, decaying, destabilizing, or accelerating. A reinforcing loop contains only positive links or an even number of negative links. A *balancing loop* (or negative) represents a process implying resistance to change, goal seeking, or stabilizing behavior. A balancing loop contains an odd number of negative links.

Table 5.2 shows three balancing loops representing processes associated with technical support requests to a helpdesk that were used to represent problems migrating a system to a client-server

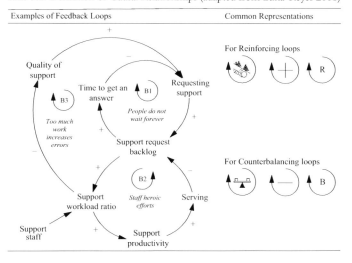

Table 5.1 Definition of Causal Relationships (adapted from Luna-Reyes 2008)

Graphic representation	Conceptual Definition	Math Definition
X $\xrightarrow{+}$ Y	X adds to Y, or changes in X lead to changes in Y in the same direction	$Y = \int_{t_0}^{t}(X + \ldots)ds + Y_{t_0}$ or $\frac{\partial Y}{\partial X} > 0$
X $\xrightarrow{-}$ Y	X subtracts from Y, or changes in X lead to changes in Y in the opposite direction	$Y = \int_{t_0}^{t}(-X + \ldots)ds + Y_{t_0}$ or $\frac{\partial Y}{\partial X} < 0$

Table 5.2 Definition of Causal Relationships (adapted from Luna-Reyes 2008)

architecture in a state agency (the example will be described in the next section). As shown in the table, it is common to name the loops with words that describe the main dynamic process.

2.2.3.2 STOCK-AND-FLOW DIAGRAMS

Other common structural representations are stock-and-flow diagrams. Stocks (also called state variables) represent accumulations in the system, and are increased or decreased only by inflows or outflows, which represent activities in the system. We can identify one accumulation and two activities in the feedback loops in Table 5.2 (see Figure 5.3). The "clouds" at the origin of the inflow and the end of the outflow represent the conceptual boundaries of the system. That is to say, things flow from and to somewhere outside the representation of the problem. Challenging these conceptual boundaries is an important activity during the modeling process.

Stocks and flows are analogous to a bathtub. Inflows and outflows represent the pipes (faucet and drain) and the stock is analogous to the bathtub itself. Actor's decisions and actions in the system are influenced by accumulations in it. Figure 5.4 shows the same feedback loops from Table 5.2, associated with the accumulation and activities presented in Figure 5.3.

Causal-loop diagrams are considered better tools to communicate feedback processes to people; stock-and-flow diagrams, meanwhile, enable simulations of the problem. One caveat of causal-loop diagrams is that there are subtraction or addition links that can be misinterpreted as proportional links (Richardson 1997). These links are clearer in the stock-and-flow representation, because they are associated with inflows or outflows such as *Requesting support* and *Serving*.

Figure 5.3 Stock-and-Flow Diagram (adapted from Luna-Reyes 2008)

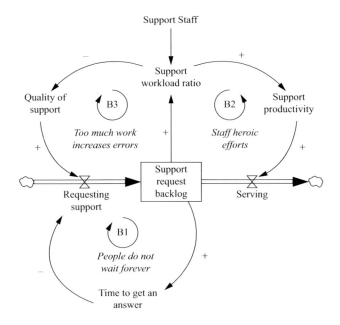

Figure 5.4 Feedback Loops in a Stock-and-Flow Diagram (adapted from Luna-Reyes 2008)

2.2.4 Model Formulation and Validation

Once a modeler has hypothesized a relationship between a problem structure and a problematic behavior, the next task involves the translation of the assumptions into mathematical formulations and the validation of those assumptions. Validation in System Dynamics is intimately tied to the process of building confidence in the model, as Forrester and Senge (1980) demonstrate. The validation process not only improves confidence in the final model, it also helps to improve how the model functions. Once a model is mature enough to be used for practical policy work, decision makers need to make sense out of its behavior and policy implications in order to know what needs to be done next (Andersen et al. 2012). This process of sense-making involves some form of model assessment and is related to the process of model implementation (Roberts 1978).

Validation is a complex issue, given that the iterative nature of the model-building process suggests that building confidence in a System Dynamics model is not the last step in the modeling process, but intertwined along the whole process (Richardson and Pugh III 1981). In fact, from the System Dynamics point of view, validating a model is impossible, given that "all models are wrong" (Sterman 2000). This is why the process of "building confidence" in the model is seen as relative to some specific purpose (Richardson and Pugh III 1981, Sterman 2000). As posed by Forrester and Senge (1980), the validation of a model has as its main purpose to attain "transferred confidence in a model's soundness and usefulness as a policy tool." Tying the validation process to the main purpose for which the model was created promotes a validation method that uses a series of semi-formal processes involving a "social conversation, rather than objective confrontation [with reality]" (Barlas and Carpenter 1990, 163).

This view on model validation has created several debates about the formality of System Dynamics as a scientific method of inquiry. Barlas and Carpenter (1990) discussed this controversy in terms of the philosophy of science, concluding that "the views of system dynamicists on validation parallel the relativist philosophy of science." That is to say, from the traditional logical empiricist point of view, the System Dynamics method does not fulfill the criteria of "good science," but it adheres to the practices of theory confirmation followed by the contemporary relativist point of view.

Consistent with the relativist philosophy of science, the validation process in System Dynamics considers the use of many different tests to promote the conversation about the adequacy of and confidence in the model in terms of its structure and behavior (Forrester and Senge 1980, Richardson and Pugh III 1981, Sterman 2000). These tests are a combination of formal, mathematical tools and qualitative assessments of the appropriateness of model structure and behavior (Balci 1994, Barlas 1989, Barlas and Carpenter 1990, Kleijnen 1995, Oliva 2003, Sterman 1984) and its applicability to diverse audiences (Howick et al. 2008).

2.3 Group Model Building

An interesting feature of several modeling and simulation techniques such as System Dynamics consists of their emphasis on policy making and problem solving with clients (Kim, MacDonald, and Andersen 2013). In the specific case of System Dynamics, there is a clear research interest in working with groups, managers, and policy makers to facilitate strategy and policy development. This literature can be traced back to 1987, when New York State was facing a crisis in its medical malpractice system (Richardson, Andersen, and Luna-Reyes 2015). Doctor- and hospital-paid premiums into the state-sanctioned system were skyrocketing. Physicians, especially obstetricians, were refusing to treat new patients and some were moving out of the state to practice elsewhere. The governor and the legislature were caught in crossfire between hospital associations, medical associations, trial lawyer associations, and insurance carriers. Pressing for dramatic hikes in doctors' premiums, actuarial calculations predicted that the malpractice insurers' reserve funds were statistically insolvent to the tune of $2 billion. A problem of this magnitude, based on complex legal and technical arguments and involving the core interests of competing powerful stakeholders, would now be characterized in the literature as a "messy" or "wicked"[1] problem.

As part of a solution to this crisis, the Commissioner of the New York State Insurance Department convened a group of expert political, financial, and actuarial stakeholders internal to his agency to contemplate and design possible solutions to this connected set of issues. As previously reported in the management science literature (Reagan-Cirincione et al. 1991), with the support of the Decision Techtronics Group (DTG),[2] the collected group designed and implemented a series of computer-based simulation models and multi-criteria decision-making models that helped to guide the state toward a resolution of the crisis.

These meetings became the first published example of what System Dynamics modelers later came to call group model building (GMB). Four developments had come together right around 1988 to make the first case of GMB possible. First, the field of computer simulation and modeling was maturing and moving toward working directly with multiple competing stakeholder groups, a common characteristic of the public sector. Second, microcomputing and early computer projection technology had made it possible for the first time to bring live computer support into group meetings. Third, methods of group facilitation, long a subject of study for small-group experts, had formed the basis for the newly emerging field of group decision support systems (GDSS).[3] Fourth and finally, the recent development of icon-oriented System Dynamics simulation software (initially STELLA, later Vensim and Powersim Studio) enabled modelers to develop high-level simulation models in real time with live client groups in the room. While many of the formulation and calibration tasks of the modeler remained "in the back room," key system conceptualization and problem-defining tasks could now be accomplished in front of, and with the active involvement of, client groups representing diverse stakeholder interests.

Since 1987, the field of GMB has made considerable progress. It has diffused out from its origins in public sector work (where it was uniquely suited to support complex and conflicting stakeholder groups of clients) to become a consulting practice used in private, public, and not-for-profit organizations. In a meta-analytic survey, Rouwette, Vennix, and van Mullekom (2002) reported on over 100 cases appearing in the recent published literature. A literature documenting systematic methods of carrying out GMB has emerged, giving practice guidelines to consultants and practitioners new to the field. Building on the larger body of literature in GMB (Ackermann et al. 2010, Rouwette et al. 2011, Vennix 1996), the System Dynamics Group at the University at Albany has developed a series of tools and methods to facilitate team work (Andersen and Richardson 1997, Reagan-Cirincione et al. 1991, Richardson and Andersen 1995, Zagonel et al. 2004). We emphasize three pillars: First, the approach is based on the definition of specific roles in facilitating the model-building process (Richardson and Andersen 1995). The second pillar consists of a series of structured activities called scripts (Andersen and Richardson 1997, Luna-Reyes et al. 2006, Luna-Reyes et al. 2013). The last pillar involves improvised facilitation (Andersen and Richardson 2010).

Other examples of using GMB include analyzing the impact of the 1996 welfare reform on New York's state and county welfare systems (Zagonel et al. 2004), understanding foster care caseload dynamics (Wulczyn et al. 1990), understanding rises in Vermont Medicaid costs (Andersen, Richardson, and Ratanawijitrasin 1992), studying failed efforts to integrate vocational services for mental health clients (Huz et al. 1997, Richardson and Andersen 1995), transforming the role of the NYS Office of Real Property Services into a consulting model with localities (Griffen et al. 2000), understanding the dynamics of tobacco prevalence and control (Best et al. 2007), and understanding collaboration processes in public information technology implementations (Luna-Reyes and Gil-Garcia 2011, Luna-Reyes and Gil-Garcia 2014, Luna-Reyes et al. 2004).

3 System Dynamics and Public Policy Analysis

This section describes how System Dynamics has been used and could be used in the future to analyze complex public problems and assess multiple policy alternatives. It presents some of the policy domains in which this computer simulation approach has been used, including a few representative examples. It also explains how System Dynamics could be used to analyze public policies by showing the parallels between the modeling process and the policy analysis process.

3.1 Policy Domains

According to a review of previous literature (Andersen, Rich, and MacDonald 2009), the System Dynamics field first addressed the issue of public policy with Forrester's *Urban Dynamics* (1969) and the follow-up work contained in *Readings in Urban Dynamics* (Mass 1974). The field then introduced itself into sustainability policies with the work in *World Dynamics* (Forrester 1973). Since then, System Dynamics has been applied to areas as diverse as drug policy (Levin, Hirsch, and Roberts 1975), mental health (Levin et al. 1976), and the development of emerging economies (Saeed 1994, 1998b, 2003). Some policy areas that may deserve special attention are health, education, defense, and the environment (Andersen, Rich, and MacDonald 2009). In the area of health policy, for example, System Dynamics has been extensively applied, which was briefly described in the introduction of this chapter. However, as it has been described in the literature, work on health policy in System Dynamics can be categorized in three main categories: patient flow management, general health policy, and specific health problems (Andersen, Rich, and MacDonald 2009). The first category focuses on issues and policies associated with patient flows in hospitals in countries where healthcare service is universal. The more general applications involve policy and decision-making at both the micro and macro levels. Finally, there are several specific applications in the areas such as AIDS, malaria, and tobacco control.

In the area of education, there are two different types of application: pedagogy and policy. The former consists of the description of tools for public management education, while the latter looks at resource allocation in higher education and the creation of educational policies in developing countries. In the area of defense, System Dynamics has been used to explore strategies and to better understand the management of resources in the military. In terms of environmental issues, the application of System Dynamics can be traced back to Forrester's (1973) work, as well as the research

Table 5.3 Representative System Dynamics Work in Policy Domains (based on Andersen, Rich, and Macdonald 2009)

Policy Area	Category	Authors
Health	Patient Flow	(Lane, Monefeldt, and Rosenhead 1998, van Ackere and Smith 1999, Wolstenholme 1999a)
	General Health Policy	(Cavana et al. 1999, Senge and Asay 1988, Taylor and Lane 1998)
	Specific Health Problems	(Flessa 1999, Homer et al. 1982, Homer and St. Clair 1991, C. A. Roberts and Dangerfield 1990)
Education	Management Education	(Graham et al. 1992)
	Education Policy	(Forsyth, Hirsch, and Bergan 1976, Galbraith 1988, Mashayekhi 1977, Saeed 1996)
Defense	Strategy	(Coyle 1992, Wils, Kamiya, and Choucri, 1998)
	Resource Management	(D. F. Andersen and Emmerichs 1982, Bakken and Gilljam 2003, Cavana, Boyd, and Taylor 2007, Clark 1987, 1993)
Environment		(Cavana and Ford 2004, Forrester 1973, Meadows and Meadows 1974)

collected in Meadows and Meadows (1974) about promoting sustainable industries. By 2004, Cavana and Ford (2004) found 635 citations to environmental studies that used System Dynamics in 11 areas, including energy, water, climate, wildlife, forestry, and more. However, maybe one of the most relevant applications of System Dynamics in this area is the C-Roads simulation model (https://www.climateinteractive.org/tools/c-roads/), which consists of an interactive simulation model that governments, corporations, and NGOs have used to better understand long-term impacts of policies to reduce greenhouse gas emissions.

3.2 System Dynamics Analysis of Public Policies

This section links the methods of System Dynamics described in previous sections of the chapter with the literature on the analysis of public policies (Gil-Garcia 2014). A public policy is a deliberate course of action undertaken by different levels of government to achieve a specific objective (Allen et al. 1995), which is not only limited to legislation and regulation, but to the different actions a legitimate authority or government power decides to take (or not take) (Meny and Thoenig 1992, Theodoulou and Cahn 1995). According to Theodoulou and Cahn (1995) there are two approaches to the study of public policies. The first approach is mainly based on the actors, controls, and benefits of the policy. The analyst studies public policy through the group that dominates the political process, using group theory, elite theory, corporatism, and sub-governments, among other approaches. The second approach focuses on analyzing the behavior of system elements through phases (or a cycle-process approach) through perspectives such as systems theory, structural functionalism, and political cycle theory.

The application of systems theory to the social and political field can be seen through the work of Easton (2001). He considers public policy as a political system in which petitions are made to resolve problems in a specific environment. The political system is one in which the demands of citizens are introduced and processed to create a public policy that assures the stability of the system (Easton 2001). Public policy, viewed as an output of the system, produces new demands in turn, which may be a new input into another system or feedback from the same one. The usefulness of viewing a public policy as a system rests in analyzing it as a set of elements that interact and exhibit certain behavior over time to achieve a goal. Complementarily, the application of SD allows public policy scenarios and their implications to be analyzed over time according to the problem of interest (Coyle 1997).

According to Bardach (1996), the complexity of analyzing a public policy lies, among other things, in the fact that many actors are involved: interest groups, public officials, popularly elected public officials, citizens, and civil organizations, among others. In addition, institutional and legal frameworks govern all public policy, which includes laws, standards, regulations, and important cultural aspects. The interaction between multiple social actors and the context means that the analysis of public policy is considered more of an art than a science (Bardach 1996). However, using a consistent methodology can help us understand the complexity, since it allows one to identify the elements or parts of a problem and analyze their exchanges. He proposes eight steps for the systematic analysis of public policies: (1) define the problem; (2) obtain data and information; (3) prepare alternative solutions; (4) select criteria; (5) project the effects of results; (6) review costs and benefits; (7) choose a solution that addresses the specific problem; and (8) reveal the solution's history. Analogically, as we have shown in Figure 5.1, the System Dynamics modeling process can be represented by stages: (1) state the problem dynamically; (2) create a hypothesis explaining the dynamic behavior; (3) formulate the model; (4) evaluate the model created; and (5) formulate and evaluate policy options.

Taking into account the similarities and differences between these two processes, Table 5.4 gives a brief description of the steps to follow when analyzing a public policy using System Dynamics specifically and the systems approach in general.

Table 5.4 Steps for Analyzing Public Policies and System Dynamics (Gil-Garcia 2014)

Public Policies (Bardach 1996)	System Dynamics (Sterman 2000)	Application of System Dynamics to Public Policy
1. Define the problem	1. State the problem	1. Define a dynamic problem
2. Obtain data and information	2. Dynamic hypothesis	2. Develop a simulation model
	3. Formulate the model	
	4. Validate the model	3. Evaluate the model with real data
3. Prepare alternative solutions	5. Formulate and evaluate the policy	4. Explore public policy scenarios
4. Select criteria		
5. Project effects or results		
6. Review costs and benefits		5. Develop policies or strategies
7. Choose a solution that addresses the specific problem		
8. Reveal its history		

3.2.1 Define a Dynamic Problem

The first step is to define a dynamic problem, which refers to defining a problem in terms of its behavior over time and not a one-time situation that does not consider the evolution or behavior of the variables (Richardson and Pugh III 1981, Sterman 2000). Defining the problem is one of the most critical steps of the entire process and depends in large part on the experience and knowledge of the researcher or analyst (Randers 1980, Van Gigch 1991). For example, a dynamic problem would be "the number of families in extreme poverty has increased over the last few years," compared to the more traditional way of defining a social problem as "there are a large number of families in extreme poverty." This way of defining the problem to be studied is important since it attempts to understand the structural sources of the problem over time.

Figure 5.5 Managers Clustering Dynamic Behaviors of Key Variables

As we discussed in previous sections, one powerful way of representing a dynamic problem is through graphs of behavior over time, which show the different values of a key variable related to a policy problem. When a group of policy makers engages in a modeling exercise to better understand public policy, drawing and discussing behaviors over time for different variables contributes to a better understanding of the policy problem and its boundaries. Figure 5.5, for example, shows a group of managers discussing and clustering behaviors over time as part of a group exercise.

3.2.2 Develop a Simulation Model

Once the dynamic problem has been defined, the next step is to create mathematical representations for all variables that affect the problem behavior. More precisely, as a result of the initial discussions around behaviors over time, managers get to clarify and agree on alternative understandings of a policy problem, also triggering a conversation related to the causal relationships among variables. Discussing such relationships leads to the identification of key mechanisms or feedback loops that explain the main problem (dynamic hypothesis), which are then represented in a simulation model according to the tenets of System Dynamics. This simulation model usually represents a set of frequently competing goals related to a public problem, as well as the main processes that cause the problem and its effects on an interconnected system. The relationships between variables, and particularly the feedback cycles represented in the model, produce dynamic behaviors that can then be explored by policy makers to better understand the policy domain and the policy options. Of course, policy analysis and simulation also play a role in validating the model, not only through the intense and rigorous process of sensitivity analysis, but also by including all available qualitative knowledge and quantitative data as they relate to the policy problem. In a sense, simulation models may work as boundary objects to help managers and policy makers to understand key interdependencies between their areas of influence in the policy domain (Black 2013, Black and Andersen 2012), helping them to develop potentially more effective policy.

As a result of the process, it is common that public managers and policy makers identify main feedback processes and leverage points. Figure 5.6, for example, includes the main feedback mechanisms in CoastalProtectSim, a model designed to develop community policy making for protection against storm damage (Deegan et al. 2014, Najaf Abadi et al. 2015). CoastalProtectSim represents the coastal town of Pointe Claire, which is a fictitious town set on the U.S. Gulf Coast. The model is based on an actual planning project undertaken by the U.S. Army Corps of Engineers on the Mississippi Coast, but is not calibrated to any specific place. It captures the essential elements of coastal storm planning though five model sectors: (1) structural mitigation; (2) land development and natural barriers; (3) storm intensity and climate change; (4) costs associated with damages and mitigation measures; and (5) benefits from cumulative tax revenue.

3.2.3 Evaluate the Model with Real Data

Evaluating a System Dynamics model is a task that starts from the beginning of the modeling process (Richardson and Pugh III 1981, Sterman 2000). Discussions about model boundaries and behaviors over time, for example, contribute to the validity of the model's boundaries, as well as the validity of the policy goals and main indicators. Experimenting with the model, incorporating data, and running a wide variety of policy scenarios contributes to the evaluation of model-generated behavior as it compares to known trends (Sharp 1977, Sterman 2000). The development of the ReThink Health model introduced at the beginning of the chapter, for example, involved qualitative knowledge of policy makers in Pueblo, CO, knowledge of policy makers in other model

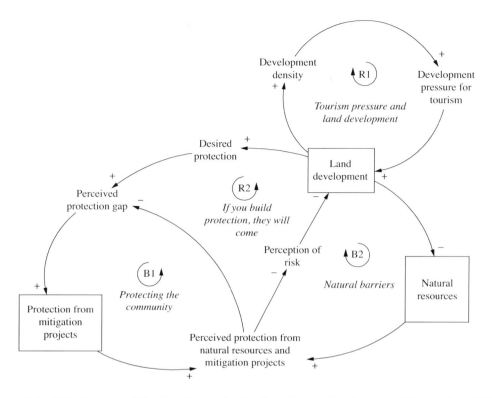

Figure 5.6 Major Stocks and Feedback Loops in the CoastalProtectSim Simulator (adapted from Najaf Abadi et al. 2015)

implementations, clinical knowledge of chronic diseases as it is published in the health literature, and statistical information from many different sources such as the U.S. census. The quantitative data test, although very important in the process of building confidence in a model, is not the only test that a model needs to go through.

3.2.4   Explore Public Policy Scenarios

Once the model has been calibrated and evaluated with real data, the next step is to explore alternative policy interventions. For example, in the case of the increase in the number of families in extreme poverty, different programs and policies that could be used to counteract the problem, such as the distribution of food assistance, the awarding of scholarships, and the inclusion of families in low-cost insurance schemes, or combinations of these alternatives, can be incorporated into the model.

Each of these alternatives would have an effect on the different variables in the system, and the simulation model will reveal their overall effect on the target variable (in this example, the number of families in extreme poverty). The systems approach and simulation allow a large number of variables to be considered simultaneously and help us to understand their interrelationships and the feedback cycles that exist between the different processes.

Figures 5.7 and 5.8 are examples of the application of System Dynamics to the analysis of welfare reform at the county level in New York State for the Temporary Assistance for Needy Families

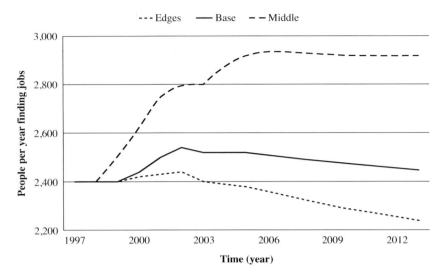

Figure 5.7 Total Job-Finding Flows from TANF (Base vs. Middle vs. Edges Policy Packages). Adapted from Richardson, Andersen, and Luna-Reyes (2015).

Copyright 2015 by Georgetown University Press. George Richardson, David Anderson, and Luis F. Luna-Reyes, "Joining Minds: System Dynamics Group Model Building to Create Public Value." From *Public Value and Public Administration*, John M. Bryson, Barbara C. Crosby, and Laura Bloomberg, Editors, pp. 53–67. Reprinted with permission. www.press.georgetown.edu

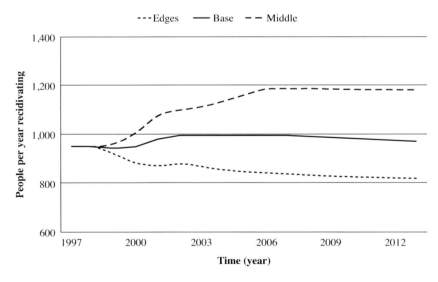

Figure 5.8 Total Recidivism Flows Back to TANF (Base vs. Middle vs. Edges Policy Packages). Adapted from Richardson, Andersen, and Luna-Reyes (2015).

Copyright 2015 by Georgetown University Press. George Richardson, David Anderson, and Luis F. Luna-Reyes, "Joining Minds: System Dynamics Group Model Building to Create Public Value." From *Public Value and Public Administration*, John M. Bryson, Barbara C. Crosby, and Laura Bloomberg, Editors, pp. 53–67. Reprinted with permission. www.press.georgetown.edu

program. An important policy insight produced by tests during the modeling process involved the comparison of two investment policies labeled "Edges" and "Middle." The "Base" run (or "reference" run) shows the model's projection of what would happen to the county's welfare system if no policy changes were made and if there were no external scenario changes. The "Middle" policy simulated a high investment in assessment, monitoring, and job-finding functions traditionally associated with a social services unit. The "Edges" policy contained a mixture of resource investments that concentrated on the "front" and "back" ends of the system (i.e., prevention, child support enforcement, and self-sufficiency promotion) (Richardson, Andersen, and Luna-Reyes 2015).

Figure 5.7 compares the Base run to the Middle and Edges policy packages for one key performance indicator—total job finding flows from TANF. The graphs suggest that investments in the Middle policy package increase the number of people finding jobs. However, as it occurs in many complex systems, the conclusions from this figure are misleading, because focusing on a less commonly articulated performance measure—total recidivism into the welfare program—Figure 5.8 reveals an important structural insight. The Edges policy has the effect of significantly reducing recidivism in the system. Richardson, Andersen, and Wu (2002) have demonstrated that in the simulation model, the high influx of families on TANF into the post-TANF employment support system had the effect of "swamping" these downstream resources, leading to long-term increases in recidivism. Since federal legislation does not require that recidivism be tracked and it is hard to document, the increased TANF caseload could easily be misinterpreted as the result of some external influence, such as rising unemployment, rather than as a natural, endogenous consequence of the Middle policy intended to reduce caseloads. Whatever the final policy choice, the simulation model provides a "level playing field" for evaluating the implications of multiple policy and scenario changes, always using precisely the same agreed-upon set of assumptions and numbers (Richardson, Andersen, and Luna-Reyes 2015).

3.2.5 Develop Policies or Strategies

Although models can be useful to explore different public policy alternatives and scenarios, people and not models make policy. In this sense, policy makers need to develop a strategy based on their newly acquired understanding of the system, their current resources, and contextual and institutional limitations. The majority of computer packages for System Dynamics allow for the comparison of effects from multiple alternatives (Van Gigch 1991). Moreover, it can be used with different stakeholder groups to extend learning and develop awareness of the problem and solutions to increase policy effectiveness. In other words, the analysis of public policies through System Dynamics allows for a more comprehensive view of a public problem and its possible solutions, as well as the involvement of key stakeholders prior to making a decision and implementing a governmental program.

4 Final Comments

It has been shown throughout this chapter that System Dynamics represents a useful systems approach for the analysis of complex social problems and public policies (Sherwood 2011). According to Simon (1949), it is very difficult for human beings to calculate all the possible consequences of their actions. Their decision-making capacity is based on the context surrounding them and the way they perceive it. However, "human beings strive to achieve rationality and although they are bounded by the limits of their knowledge, they have developed certain work procedures to help them partially overcome this difficulty" (Simon 1949, 79). However, tools that help to comprehend the complexity of reality could improve the current state of affairs. Consequently, the use of models to represent social problems is very useful, since it allows us to understand a finite number of possible solutions, the relationships between variables, and the way they are immersed in a specific problem (Sherwood 2011). Systems approaches such as System Dynamics are used in science to test hypotheses, improving our understanding of social problems in order to achieve change in the status quo through the intervention of governmental authorities (Olsson and Sjöstedt 2004). Similarly, simulation models can be used as laboratories for policy and decision makers to explore policy scenarios and options (Zagonel et al. 2004). Compared to other analytical tools, such as optimization techniques or econometrics, simulation models allow for the inclusion of more of the complexity of problems in the exploration of policy options.

According to Flood and Jackson (1991a, b), the use of System Dynamics in the analysis of public policies has received three main criticisms. The first refers to the *ideology*. In their view, designers using System Dynamics to analyze problems have become technical elites who decide how a policy is to be developed and use the technique to justify their decisions as neutral and objective. Furthermore, these elites do not always generate spaces for other actors to participate in the construction of the models, which is why the policy they develop is clearly biased toward the values of the designers themselves. This second point refers to *usefulness*. System dynamics must always be based on a rich source of empirical data or on known and accepted theories and principles, which is why it is necessary that analysts express the main sources that validate and legitimate the results of the system and its respective simulation. Last, the third criticism is related to *methodology*. According to its creator, System Dynamics was developed to build models that accurately represent reality. However, the development of a model is strongly influenced by the data collection and data availability, which is not always explicitly described.

Because of such criticisms, system dynamicists have learned over time that involving stakeholders and policy makers in discussions and debate about policy problems increases the probability of truly understanding the problems and developing useful and legitimate policies and strategies. Group approaches generate spaces for communication between participants to jointly develop models and explore solutions (Olsson and Sjöstedt 2004). As we described in the chapter, group model building is the System Dynamics approach to promoting dialogue to create a shared understanding of the policy problem and the interdependencies of policy packages (Luna-Reyes 2008). Another way of increasing the usefulness of the models has been to develop games such as ReThink Health to promote conversations, learning, and knowledge sharing in specific policy domains. Other notable examples are the models developed by Climate Interactive (https://www.climateinteractive.org/) to explore climate change and energy policies to reduce carbon emissions. The models have been used during the United Nations Climate Talks, most recently in Paris during December 2015.

Additional criticisms involve common practices in building models (Wolstenholme 1999): (1) data is required for all variables in order to conduct computer simulations, which may result, for some variables, in the inclusion of theoretical assumptions or opinions based only on the experience of the researcher; (2) by being able to use many variables and elements from a system, highly complex problems have to be designed clearly and accurately, which can often lead models to have such a high degree of detail that it is very difficult to understand them; (3) it requires a certain level of experience and skill to manage feedback diagrams and a knowledge of systems thinking; and (4) System Dynamics is a specialized variant for the management of information flows and many computer software packages have been developed by experts in the field, but there is no guide for which one to use in a specific situation, and sometimes these programs are not compatible with one another or with other general applications.

Just as in any other modeling technique, the value of the conclusions of a System Dynamics model are only as good as the model itself (Spector and Davidsen 2002). Potential causes of this inadequate definition are theoretical directives, the researcher's capacity or field of study, time or factors related to financial resources, etc. Properly delimiting the object of study is very important in order to obtain reliable results. Therefore, both modelers and policy makers need to pay constant attention to the objectivity and legitimacy of the modeling process (Van Gigch 1991). This information helps to perform an appropriate evaluation of the model as a policy tool (Olsson and Sjöstedt 2004). Moreover, the weakness presented in the previous paragraph suggests that parsimony is important in the model development process, but also that good models are those that are clearly documented. These are basic requirements in any model.

On the other hand, an important contribution of system approaches such as System Dynamics is the growing use of diagrams to represent the endogenous nature of complex systems through feedback cycles (Richardson 1999). Such diagrams have the potential of becoming effective tools for learning and knowledge sharing. Diagrams and models involve both qualitative and quantitative strengths (Wolstenholme 1999). First, diagrams are important analytic tools that allow modelers and policy makers to trace the main causes of problematic behaviors and the reasons why certain policy options might be effective. Second, computer simulation allows systems to be represented more completely and comprehensively because it combines hard data with qualitative elements of the system, which are quite often intangible (Forrester 1992).

Although the use of System Dynamics and computer simulation requires specialized knowledge and abilities, this approach is a valuable alternative for researchers and public policy analysts. There are clear advantages in the use of the systems approach and System Dynamics in the analysis of public policies. Perhaps the most important is that it allows different public policy alternatives to be analyzed systematically and without the need for pilot projects or full implementation, which could be costly not only in a financial sense. Moreover, as we proposed in the chapter, we believe that the modeling process is very much consistent with the policymaking process (see Table 5.4). Following this process has the potential of yielding better results in the analysis of different stages of the policy process, particularly when facing complex social problems for which the causes are multiple and difficult to isolate.

Notes

1. The terms "wicked" (Rittel and Webber 1973) and "messy" (Eden, Jones, and Sims 1983) refer to problems lacking a clear definition, the goals to pursue, or feasible solutions. Problems are "messy" partially because of a diversity of stakeholders with different—sometimes conflicting—points of view about a given situation. Dawes, Cresswell, and Pardo (2009) had coined the term "tangled" problems for those problems whose main source of complexity is such diversity of interests.
2. The Decision Techtronics Group has a long tradition of developing computer-based models with groups of managers to analyze policy and strategy (Rohrbaugh 1992). DTG's approach has been used to understand and tackle problems in a diversity of areas using many kinds of models (Milter and Rohrbaugh 1985, Schuman and Rohrbaugh 1991), and particularly using System Dynamics models (Andersen and Richardson 1997, Reagan-Cirincione et al. 1991, Richardson and Andersen 1995, Rohrbaugh 2000).
3. GDSS are computer-based systems and techniques developed for group decision support (Desanctis and Gallupe 1987, Quinn, Rohrbaugh, and McGrath 1985).

References

Ackermann, Fran, David F. Andersen, Colin Eden, and George P. Richardson. 2010. 'Using a group decision support system to add value to group model building'. *System Dynamics Review* 26 (4): 335–346. doi: 10.1002/sdr.444

Allen, David T., Frank J. Consoli, Gary A. Davis, James A. Fava, and John L. Warren. 1995. 'Public policy applications of life-cycle assessment'. Pellston Workshop on Application of Life-Cycle Assessment to Public Policy, Wintergreen, VA, August 14–19.

Andersen, Deborah Lines, Luis Felipe Luna-Reyes, Vedat G. Diker, Laura Black, Eliot Rich, and David F. Andersen. 2012. 'The disconfirmatory interview as a strategy for the assessment of system dynamics models'. *System Dynamics Review* 28 (3): 255–275. doi: 10.1002/sdr.1479

Andersen, D.F., E. Rich, and R. MacDonald. 2009. 'System dynamics applications to public policy'. In *Encyclopedia of Complexity and Systems Science*, edited by Robert A. Meyers, 7051–7061. Berlin: Springer.

Andersen, D.F., and G.P. Richardson. 1997. 'Scripts for group model building'. *System Dynamics Review* 13 (2): 107–129.

Andersen, D.F., and G.P. Richardson. 2010. 'Improvised facilitation: A third leg on the Group Model Building stool'. International System Dynamics Research Conference, Seoul, Korea.

Andersen, D.F., G.P. Richardson, and Sauwakon Ratanawijitrasin. 1992. *Vermont Medicaid interim report*. Albany, NY: Rockefeller College of Public Affairs and Policy.

Andersen, D.F., and R.M. Emmerichs. 1982. 'Analyzing US military retirement policies'. *Simulation* 39 (5): 151–158.

Aracil, Javier. 1983. *Introducción a la dinámica de sistemas*. Madrid: Alianza.

Bakken, B.T., and M. Gilljam. 2003. 'Dynamic intuition in military command and control: Why it is important, and how it should be developed'. *Cognition, Technology and Work* 5: 197–205.

Balci, O. 1994. 'Validation, verification and testing techniques throughout the life cycle of a simulation study'. *Annals of Operations Research* 53: 121–173.

Bardach, Eugene. 1996. *The eight-step path of policy analysis: A handbook for practice*. Berkeley, CA: Berkeley Academic Press.

Barlas, Yaman. 1989. 'Multiple tests for validation of system dynamics type of simulation models'. *European Journal of Operational Research* 42 (1): 59–87.

Barlas, Yaman, and Stanley Carpenter. 1990. 'Philosophical roots of model validation: Two paradigms'. *System Dynamics Review* 6 (2): 148–166.

Best, Allan, Pamela I. Clark, Scott J. Leischow, and William M.K. Trochim. 2007. 'Greater than the sum: Systems thinking in tobacco control'. Smoking and Tobacco Control Monograph Series No. 18. NIH Pub. No. 06-6085, April 2007. Bethesda, MD: National Cancer Institute.

Black, Laura J. 2002. 'Collaborating across boundaries: Theoretical, empirical, and simulated explorations'. Doctoral Dissertation, Sloan School of Management, Massachusetts Institute of Technology, Cambridge, MA.

Black, Laura J. 2013. 'When visuals are boundary objects in system dynamics work'. *System Dynamics Review* 29 (2): 70–86. doi: 10.1002/sdr.1496

Black, Laura J., and David F. Andersen. 2012. 'Using visual representations as boundary objects to resolve conflict in collaborative model-building approaches'. *Systems Research & Behavioral Science* 29 (2): 194–208. doi: 10.1002/sres.2106

Cavana, Robert Y., and Andrew Ford. 2004. 'Environmental and resource systems: Editor's introduction'. *System Dynamics Review* 20 (2): 89–98.

Cavana, Robert Y., D.M. Boyd, and R.J. Taylor. 2007. 'A systems thinking study of retention and recruitment issues for the New Zealand army electronic technician trade group'. *Systems Research and Behavioral Science* 24 (2): 201–216.

Cavana, Robert Y., P.K. Davies, R.M. Robson, and K.J. Wilson. 1999. 'Drivers of quality in health services: Different worldviews of clinicians and policy managers revealed'. *System Dynamics Review* 15 (3): 331–340.

Clark, R.H. 1987. 'Defense budget instability and weapon system acquisition'. *Public Budgeting and Finance* 7 (2): 24–36.

Clark, R.H. 1993. 'The dynamics of [US] force reduction and reconstitution'. *Defense Analysis* 9 (1): 51–68.

Coyle, R. Geoffrey. 1992. 'A system dynamics model of aircraft carrier survivability'. *System Dynamics Review* 8 (3): 193–213.

Coyle, R. Geoffrey. 1997. 'System dynamics at Bradford University: A Silver Jubilee review'. *System Dynamics Review* 13 (4): 311–321.

Dawes, Sharon S., Anthony M. Cresswell, and Theresa A. Pardo. 2009. 'From 'need to know' to 'need to share': Tangled problems, information boundaries, and the building of public sector knowledge networks'. *Public Administration Review* 69 (3): 392–402.

Deegan, Michael, Krystyna Stave, Rod MacDonald, David Andersen, Minyoung Ku, and Eliot Rich. 2014. 'Simulation-based learning environments to teach complexity: The missing link in teaching sustainable public management'. *Systems* 2 (2): 217–236.

de Geus, A.P. 1992. 'Modelling to predict or to learn?' *European Journal of Operational Research* 59 (1): 1–5. doi: http://dx.doi.org/10.1016/0377-2217(92)90002-Q

Desanctis, Gerardine, and R. Brent Gallupe. 1987. 'A foundation for the study of group decision support systems'. *Management Science* 33 (5): 589–609.

Easton, David. 2001. 'Categoriás para el análisis sistémico de la politica'. In *Diez textos básicos de ciencia politica*, edited by Albert Batlle, 221–230. Barcelona: Editorial Ariel, S.A.

Eden, Colin, Sue Jones, and David Sims. 1983. *Messing about in problems: An informal structured approach to their identification and management*. Headington Hill Hall: Pergamon Press.

Fannie E. Rippel Foundation. 2015. 'Our vision'. Accessed June 30. http://www.rethinkhealth.org/about-us/vision/

Flessa, S. 1999. 'Decision support for malaria-control programmes--a System Dynamics model'. *Health Care Management Science* 2 (3): 181–191.

Flood, R.L., and M.C. Jackson. 1991a. *Creative problem solving—Total systems intervention*. Chichester, UK: Wiley.
Flood, R.L., and M.C. Jackson. 1991b. *Critical systems thinking*. Berlin: Springer.
Forrester, Jay W. 1961. *Industrial dynamics*. Cambridge, MA: MIT Press.
Forrester, Jay W. 1969. *Urban dynamics*. Cambridge MA: Productivity Press. Original edition, MIT Press. Reprint, Pegasus Communications.
Forrester, Jay W. 1973. *World dynamics*, 2nd ed. Cambridge, MA: Wright-Allen Press.
Forrester, Jay W. 1975. 'Counterintuitive behavior of social systems'. In *Collected papers of Jay W. Forrester*, 211–244. Waltham, MA: Productivity Press.
Forrester, Jay W. 1992. 'Policies, decisions and information sources for modeling'. *European Journal of Operational Research* 59 (1): 42–63. doi: http://dx.doi.org/10.1016/0377-2217(92)90006-U
Forrester, Jay W., and Peter M. Senge. 1980. 'Tests for building confidence in system dynamics models'. In *System Dynamics*, edited by Augusto A. Legasto, Jr., et al., 209–228. New York: North-Holland.
Forsyth, B.R., G.B. Hirsch, and T.A. Bergan. 1976. 'Projecting a teaching hospital's future utilization: A dynamic simulation approach'. *Journal of Medical Education* 51 (11): 937–939.
Galbraith, P. 1988. 'Mathematics education and the future: A long wave view of change'. *For the Learning of Mathematics* 8 (3): 27–33.
Gil-Garcia, J.R. 2014. *Systemic thinking and system dynamics for the analysis of public policies: Fundamentals and recommendations*. Mexico City: Centro de Investigacion y Docencia Economicas.
Graham, A.K., J.D.W. Morecroft, P.M. Senge, and J.D. Sterman. 1992. 'Model-supported case studies for management education'. *European Journal of Operational Research* 59 (1): 151–166.
Griffen, T.D., D.F. Andersen, G.P. Richardson, and C. Finn. 2000. 'Using group model building to support strategic reform of the real property tax system in New York State: A case study'. Proceedings of the 18th International Conference of the System Dynamics Society, Bergen, Norway.
Grizzle, Gloria A., and Carole D. Pettijohn. 2002. 'Implementing performance-based program budgeting: A system-dynamics perspective'. *Public Administration Review* 62 (1): 51–62.
Homer, J.B., and C.L. St. Clair. 1991. 'A model of HIV transmission through needle sharing. A model useful in analyzing public policies, such as a needle cleaning campaign'. *Interfaces* 21 (3): 26–29.
Homer, J.B., E.B. Roberts, A. Kasabian, and M. Varrel. 1982. 'A systems view of the smoking problem'. *International Journal of Biomedical Computing* 13: 69–86.
Homer, J.B., and Gary Hirsch. 2006. 'System dynamics modeling for public health: Background and opportunities'. *American Journal of Public Health* 96 (3): 452–458.
Homer, J.B., Gary Hirsch, and Bobby Milstein. 2007. 'Chronic illness in a complex health economy: The perils and promises of downstream and upstream reforms'. *System Dynamics Review* 23 (2–3): 313–343. doi: 10.1002/sdr.379
Homer, J.B., Gary Hirsch, Mary Minniti, and Marc Pierson. 2004. 'Models for collaboration: How system dynamics helped a community organize cost-effective care for chronic illness'. *System Dynamics Review* 20 (3): 199–222. doi: 10.1002/sdr.295
Howick, Susan, Colin Eden, Fran Ackermann, and Terry Williams. 2008. 'Building confidence in models for multiple audiences: The modelling cascade'. *European Journal of Operational Research* 186 (3): 1068–1083.
Huz, Steven, David F. Andersen, George P. Richardson, and Roger Boothroyd. 1997. 'A framework for evaluating systems thinking interventions: An experimental approach to mental health system change'. *System Dynamics Review* 13 (2): 149–169.
Jackson, Michael C. 1991. *Systems methodology for the management sciences*. New York: Springer Science & Business Media.
Jackson, Michael C. 2000. *Systems approaches to management*. New York: Springer Science & Business Media.
Kim, Hyunjung, Roderick H. MacDonald, and David F. Andersen. 2013. 'Simulation and managerial decision making: A double-loop learning framework'. *Public Administration Review* 73 (2): 291–300. doi: 10.1111/j.1540-6210.2012.02656.x
Kleijnen, Jack P. C. 1995. 'Verification and validation of simulation models'. *European Journal of Operational Research* 82 (1): 145–162.
Kopainsky, B., and L.F. Luna-Reyes. 2008. 'Closing the loop: Promoting synergies with other theory building approaches to improve system dynamics practice'. *Systems Research and Behavioral Science* 25: 471–486.
Lane, David C. 2008. 'The emergence and use of diagramming in system dynamics: A critical account'. *Systems Research and Behavioral Science* 25: 3–23.
Lane, David C., C. Monefeldt, and J. Rosenhead. 1998. 'Emergency—but no accident'. *OR Insight* 11 (4): 2–10.
Levin, Gilbert, Gary B. Hirsch, and Edward B. Roberts. 1975. *The persistent poppy: A computer aided search for heroin policy*. Cambridge, MA: Ballinger.
Levin, Gilbert, Edward B. Roberts, Gary B. Hirsch, Deborah S. Kligler, Nancy H. Roberts, and Jack F. Wilder. 1976. *The dynamics of human service delivery*. Cambridge, MA: Ballinger.

Luna-Reyes, L.F. 2008. 'System dynamics to understand public information technology'. In *Handbook of Research on Public Information Technology*, edited by G.D. Garson and M. Khosrow-Pour, 476–492. Hershey, PA: Information Science Reference.

Luna-Reyes, L.F., and J.R. Gil-Garcia. 2011. 'Using institutional theory and dynamic simulation to understand complex e-government phenomena'. *Government Information Quarterly* 28 (3): 329–345.

Luna-Reyes, L.F., and J.R. Gil-Garcia. 2014. 'Digital government transformation and Internet portals: The co-evolution of technology, organizations, and institutions'. *Government Information Quarterly* 31 (4): 545–555. doi: http://dx.doi.org/10.1016/j.giq.2014.08.001

Luna-Reyes, L.F., Ignacio J. Martinez-Moyano, Theresa A. Pardo, Anthony M. Cresswell, David F. Andersen, and George P. Richardson. 2006. 'Anatomy of a group model-building intervention: Building dynamic theory from case study research'. *System Dynamics Review* 22 (4): 291–320. doi: 10.1002/sdr.349

Luna-Reyes, L.F., M. Mojtahedzadeh, D.F. Andersen, G.P. Richardson, T. Bodor, B. Burke, D. Canestraro, A.M. Cresswell, S. Dawes, F. Demircivi, T.A. Pardo, F. Thompson, and Y.J. Wu. 2004. 'Scripts for interrupted Group Model Building: Lessons from modeling the emergence of governance for information integration across government agencies'. 23rd International Conference of the System Dynamics Society, Oxford, UK.

Luna-Reyes, L.F., Weijia Ran, Holly Jarman, Jing Zhang, Deborah Andersen, Giri Tayi, Djoko Sayogo, Joanne Luciano, and David Andersen. 2013. 'Group Model Building to support interdisciplinary theory building'. Proceedings of the 31st International Conference of the System Dynamics Society, Cambridge, MA, USA.

Martinez-Moyano, Ignacio J., and George P. Richardson. 2013. 'Best practices in system dynamics modeling'. *System Dynamics Review* 29 (2): 102–123. doi: 10.1002/sdr.1495

Mashayekhi, Ali N. 1977. 'Economic planning and growth of education in developing countries'. *Simulation* 29 (6): 189–197.

Mashayekhi, Ali N. 1992. 'From a static picture to a dynamic problem definition'. Proceedings of the 1992 International System Dynamics Conference Utrecht, the Netherlands.

Mass, Nathaniel J., ed. 1974. *Readings in Urban Dynamics*. 2 vols. Vol. 1. Cambridge, MA: Productivity Press. Original edition, Wright-Allen Press and MIT Press.

McFarland, Laurel, Emily Reineke, Bobby Milstein, Rebecca Niles, Gary Hirsch, Ernest Cawvey, Jack Homer, Anand Desai, David Andersen, and Rod MacDonald. 2015. 'Systems thinking and simulations in the US public policy community: NASPAA's student simulation competition'. Proceedings of the 33rd International Conference of the System Dynamics Society, Cambridge, MA.

Meadows, Dennis L., and Donella H. Meadows, eds. 1974. *Toward global equilibrium: Collected papers*. Cambridge, MA: Productivity Press. Original edition, Wright-Allen Press and MIT Press.

Meny, Ives, and Jean Claude Thoenig. 1992. *Làs políticas públicas*. Barcelona: Ariel SA.

Milstein, Bobby, Gary Hirsch, and Karen Minyard. 2013. 'County officials embark on new, collective endeavors to ReThink their local health systems'. *NACA The Journal of County Administration* (March/April 2013): 5–10.

Milstein, Bobby, Jack Homer, and Gary Hirsch. 2009. 'The Health Bound policy simulation game: An adventure in US health reform'. Proceedings of the 27th International Conference of the System Dynamics Society, Albuquerque, NM.

Milstein, Bobby, Jack Homer, and Gary Hirsch. 2010. 'Analyzing national health reform strategies with a dynamic simulation model'. *American Journal of Public Health* 100 (5): 811–819. doi: 10.2105/AJPH.2009.174490

Milter, Richard G., and John Rohrbaugh. 1985. 'Microcomputers and strategic decision making'. *Public Productivity Review* 9 (2/3): 175–189.

Morecroft, John D.W. 1982. 'A critical review of diagraming tools for conceptualizing feedback system models'. *Dynamica* 8 (1): 20–29.

Morecroft, John D.W. 2007. *Strategic modelling and business dynamics*. West Sussex, UK: Wiley.

Najaf Abadi, M., B. Bahaddin, R. Behnagh Shah, M. Deegan, David Andersen, L.F. Luna-Reyes, R. MacDonald, and E. Rich. 2015. 'A learning science protocol for evaluation of a learning science environment'. 33rd International Conference of the System Dynamics Society, Cambridge, MA.

Oliva, Rogelio. 2003. 'Model calibration as a testing strategy for system dynamics models'. *European Journal of Operational Research* 151 (3): 525–568.

Olsson, Mats-Olov, and Gunnar Sjöstedt, eds. 2004. *System approaches and their application: Examples from Sweden*. Dordrecht, The Netherlands: Springer Netherlands.

Quinn, Robert E., John Rohrbaugh, and Michael R. McGrath. 1985. 'Automated decision conferencing: How it works'. *Personnel* 62 (6): 49–55.

Randers, Jørgen. 1980. 'Guidelines for model conceptualization'. In *Elements of the system dynamics method*, edited by Jørgen Randers, 117–139. Cambridge, MA: Productivity Press.

Reagan-Cirincione, Patricia, Sandor Schuman, George P. Richardson, and Stanley A. Dorf. 1991. 'Decision modeling: Tools for strategic thinking'. *Interfaces* 21 (6): 52–65.

Richardson, George P. 1997. 'Problems in causal loop diagrams revisited'. *System Dynamics Review* 13 (3): 247–252.

Richardson, George P. 1999. 'Reflections for the future of system dynamics'. *Journal of the Operational Research Society* 50 (4): 440–449.

Richardson, George P. 2010. 'Tools for systems thinking and modeling'. Accessed January 14. http://www.albany.edu/faculty/gpr/PAD624/Conceptualization.pdf

Richardson, George P., and David F. Andersen. 1995. 'Teamwork in group model building'. *System Dynamics Review* 11 (2): 113–137.

Richardson, George P., David F. Andersen, and Luis Luna-Reyes. 2015. 'Joining minds: System Dynamics Group Model Building to create public value'. In *Public value and public administration*, edited by John M. Bryson, Barbara C. Crosby, and Laura Bloomberg, 53–67. Washington, DC: Georgetown University Press.

Richardson, George P., David F. Andersen, and Yi Jung Wu. 2002. 'Misattribution in welfare dynamics: The puzzling dynamics of recidivism'. Proceedings of the 20th International Conference of the System Dynamics Society, Palermo, Italy, July 28–August 1.

Richardson, George P., and Alexander J. Pugh III. 1981. *Introduction to system dynamics modeling with DYNAMO*. Cambridge, MA: MIT Press.

Rittel, Horst W. J., and Melvin M. Webber. 1973. 'Dilemmas in a general theory of planning'. *Policy Sciences* 4 (2): 155–169.

Roberts, C.A., and B.C. Dangerfield. 1990. 'Modelling the epidemiological consequences of HIV infection and AIDS: A contribution from operational research'. *Journal of the Operational Research Society (UK)* 41 (4): 273–289.

Roberts, Edward B. 1978. 'A simple model of R & D project dynamics'. In *Managerial applications of system dynamics*, edited by Edward B. Roberts, 293–314. Cambridge, MA: Productivity Press.

Roberts, Nancy, David Andersen, Ralph Deal, Michael Garet, and William Shaffer. 1994. *Introduction to computer simulation: A system dynamics modeling approach*. Waltham, MA: Productivity Press.

Rohrbaugh, John. 1992. 'Cognitive challenges and collective accomplishments'. In *Computer augmented teamwork: A guided tour*, edited by R. Bostrom and S.T. Kinney, 299–324. New York: Van Nostrand Reinhold.

Rohrbaugh, John. 2000. 'The use of system dynamics in decision conferencing'. In *Handbook of public information systems*, edited by G. David Garson, 521–534. New York: Marcek Dekker.

Rouwette, Etiënne A.J.A., Hubert Korzilius, Jac A.M. Vennix, and Eric Jacobs. 2011. 'Modeling as persuasion: The impact of Group Model Building on attitudes and behavior'. *System Dynamics Review* 27 (1): 1–21.

Rouwette, Etiënne A.J.A., Jac A.M. Vennix, and Theo van Mullekom. 2002. 'Group model building effectiveness: A review of assessment studies'. *System Dynamics Review* 18 (1): 4–45.

Saeed, Khalid. 1992. 'Slicing a complex problem for systems dynamics modeling'. *System Dynamics Review* 8 (3): 251–262.

Saeed, Khalid. 1994. *Development planning and policy design: A system dynamics approach*. Aldershot, UK: Avebury Books.

Saeed, Khalid. 1996. 'The dynamics of collegial systems in the developing countries'. *Higher Education Policy* 9 (1): 75–86.

Saeed, Khalid. 1998a. 'Constructing reference modes'. 16th International Conference of the System Dynamics Society, Quebec City, Canada.

Saeed, Khalid. 1998b. *Towards sustainable development: Essays on system analysis of national policy*, 2nd ed. Aldershot, UK: Ashgate Publishing Company.

Saeed, Khalid. 2003. 'Articulating developmental problems for policy intervention: A system dynamics modelling approach'. *Simulation and Gaming* 34 (3): 409–436.

Schuman, S., and J. Rohrbaugh. 1991. 'Decision conferencing for systems planning'. *Information and Management* 21: 147–159.

Senge, Peter M. 1990. *The fifth discipline: The art & practice of the learning organization*. New York: Doubleday.

Senge, P.M., and D. Asay. 1988. 'Rethinking the healthcare system'. *Healthcare Forum Journal* 31 (3): 32–34, 44–45.

Sharp, John A. 1977. 'System dynamics applications to industrial and other systems'. *Operations Research Quarterly* 28 (3): 489–504.

Sherwood, Dennis. 2011. *Seeing the forest for the trees: A manager's guide to applying systems thinking*. London: Nicholas Brealey Publishing.

Simon, Herbert A. 1949. *Administrative behavior*. New York: Free Press.

Spector, J.M., and P.I. Davidsen. 2002. 'Cognitive complexity in decision making and policy formulation: A system dynamics perspective'. In *Systems perspectives on resources, capabilities, and management processes*, edited by John Morecroft, Ron Sanchez and Aimé Heene, 155–171. Kidlington, UK: Pergamon.

Sterman, John D. 1984. 'Appropriate summary statistics for evaluating the historical fit of system dynamics models'. *Dynamica* 10 (2): 51–66.

Sterman, John D. 2000. *Business dynamics: Systems thinking and modeling for a complex world*. Boston: Irwin/McGraw-Hill.

Taylor, K.S., and D.C. Lane. 1998. 'Simulation applied to health services: Opportunities for applying the System Dynamics approach'. *Journal of Health Services Reseach and Policy* 3 (4): 226–232.

Theodoulou, Stella Z., and Matthew A. Cahn. 1995. 'The contemporary language of public policy: A starting point'. In *Public policy: The essential readings*, edited by Stella Z. Theodoulou and Matthew A Cahn, 1–9. Upper Saddle River, NJ: Prentice Hall.

van Ackere, A., and Smith, P.C. 1999. 'Towards a macro model of National Health Service waiting lists'. *System Dynamics Review* 15 (3): 225–252.

Van Gigch, John P. 1990. *Teoría general de sistemas, Editorial Trillas*. Mexico City: Trillas.

Van Gigch, John P. 1991. *System design modeling and metamodeling*. New York: Springer Science & Business Media.

Vennix, Jac A.M. 1996. *Group model building: Facilitating team learning using system dynamics*. Chicester: John Wiley & Sons.

Wils, A., M. Kamiya, and N.D. Choucri. 1998. 'Threats to sustainability: Simulating conflict within and between nations'. *System Dynamics Review* 14 (2-3): 129–162.

Wolstenholme, Eric F. 1982. 'System dynamics in perspective'. *Journal of the Operational Research Society* 33 (6): 547–556.

Wolstenholme, Eric F. 1990. *System enquiry: A system dynamics approach*. Chichester, UK: John Wiley.

Wolstenholme, Eric F. 1999. 'Qualitative vs quantitative modelling: The evolving balance'. *Journal of Operational Research* 50 (4): 422–428.

Wulczyn, F.H., D.F. Andersen, E.A. Wuestman, and G.P. Richardson. 1990. *Caseload and fiscal implications of the foster care baby boom*. Albany, NY: New York State Department of Social Services.

Zagonel, A. A. 2002. 'Model conceptualization in Group Model Building: A review of the literature exploring the tension between representing reality and negotiating a social order'. 20th International Conference of the System Dynamics Society, Palermo, Italy, July 28–August 1.

Zagonel, A.A., J. Rohrbaugh, G.P. Richardson, and D.F. Andersen. 2004. 'Using simulation models to address 'what if' questions about welfare reform'. *Journal of Policy Analysis and Management* 23 (4): 890–901. doi: 10.1002/pam.20054

SECTION II

Emerging Technologies and Their Applications for Government

6
BIG DATA AND LOCAL PERFORMANCE MANAGEMENT
The Experience of Kansas City, Missouri

*Alfred Tat-Kei Ho, Kate Bender,
Julie Steenson, and Eric Roche*

Introduction

For the past few years, there has been more public discussion about the use of "big data" analytics in policymaking and management. Some observers are positive, looking at the possibility of more evidence-based policymaking and "smarter" governing to deliver what citizens want (Goldsmith and Crawford 2014; O'Malley 2014; Yin et al. 2015). Others, however, are more reserved about the promise of big data and the potential harm it may cause to privacy and the protection of individual rights, especially after the revelation by Edward Snowden about how different governments in the world are using big data tools to monitor citizens and their communication. The potential and the challenges of big data should not be ignored by researchers and practitioners of public management, because these tools may not only impact the cost efficiency and effectiveness of service delivery, but also fundamental governance issues, such as the government–citizen relationship, the upholding of public service values, and the roles of the government in a world of rapidly changing technology.

The purpose of this chapter is to explore some of these issues and their implications for public management, especially at the local level. In the following, we first define the definition and scope of big data and discuss some of the benefits of big data tools and the ways they are being used at the local level. We then use Kansas City, Missouri, as a case study to illustrate how a mid-sized city in the U.S. uses different data strategies and analytics tools to gain a better understanding of public expectations and service delivery results. This case study also illustrates the need for local managers and policy makers to recognize the organizational and governance challenges raised by the big data movement. Based on the experience of Kansas City and observations of other local governments' reform experiences, we conclude by discussing how local officials should respond to these challenges and the changing technological and governance environment.

What Is Big Data About?

As computer technologies and statistical tools that are needed to process, analyze, and store large datasets become more accessible and powerful, the notion of using big data analytics to rethink management, decision-making, and service delivery has become increasingly popular among business leaders, policy makers, and academics. Some academics, governmental leaders, and policy observers see it as a revolution that will transform fundamentally how organizational resources are planned and managed and how service providers can relate to users, the larger community of stakeholders, and the general public. For example, the World Economic Forum (2012) argues that user-centric data analytics can lead to more efficient tracking and timely responses to policy problems, improve our understanding of behavioral change, and offer new possibilities to predict and meet public demands for governmental services, especially in health, education, financial management, and agriculture. In 2012, President Obama also launched a new Big Data Research and Development initiative in the U.S., encouraging the use of big data analytics not only in scientific research, but also in every day decision-making by resource managers at all levels of government, engineers, first responders, and citizens, so that constantly flowing data streams from many sources can be used to make more optimal decisions, monitor and identify risk, inform more accurate predictions, and advance national policy goals (U.S. White House 2013). Goldsmith and Crawford (2014) go even further and argue that social media and data science will not only make the basic managerial functions of the government "smarter," but will also transform local governance by spurring a sense of renewed civic engagement and unleashing the now-untapped resources of collaborative community action.

So what is big data about and why does it have such a great potential impact? By its name, it is natural to associate big data with the volume of data used in analysis (Laney 2001). Because of the advancement in computing technologies and statistical tools to quantify, digitize, and analyze all kinds of behaviors and activities, we are in the petabyte era, and the unprecedented volume of data opens up new possibilities for managers and policy analysts to rethink many managerial and policy questions. However, just having large quantities of data is not sufficient to guarantee good intelligence. If the available data are biased, inaccurate, or irrelevant to the research question or policymaking purpose, having a lot of data is still unhelpful (Boyd and Crawford 2012). Also, focusing too much on the "bigness" of data is problematic because it is a relative concept and varies over time and by contexts and purposes. For example, in some policy areas or at certain levels of government, hundreds of thousands of records and gigabytes of data may be regarded as "big" data, whereas in other policy areas or at the national level, even millions of records and terabytes of data may not impress people as "big."

Therefore, instead of focusing on the volume of data as the defining characteristic of big data, we suggest to measure the "bigness" of data in terms of complexity and variety. Big data analytics often need to integrate data from multiple sources. Also, the complexity of data increases significantly when some of the data are unstructured and are not collected in a scientifically designed and structured approach to guarantee validity, representativeness, and reliability. In traditional statistical analysis, this type of data are often regarded as useless or unmanageable. In big data analytics, unstructured data are embraced as legitimate sources of information and advanced analytical tools are used to try to extract useful intelligence, despite the messiness of the data.

In addition, big data analytics is about the velocity of analytical tasks (Chen and Hsieh 2014; Laney 2001). Traditional data analysis takes time, and the results are often not available to decision makers until weeks or months later. Big data analytics, on the other hand, emphasizes the time sensitivity of analysis. Because of the advancement of computing technologies and the growing speed of the Internet, data feeds and computational analysis can now happen in real time so that data patterns, deviation detection, and predictions can be updated instantly. The power of real-time predictive analytics creates many new possibilities for decision-making, especially in policing, public health monitoring and hospital management, emergency response, and disaster management.

Desouza (2014) also suggests other important "V"s that characterize big data analytics. For example, big data work embraces data with high variability and veracity in data flow that traditional analysis may regard as "noise." It also looks at the freshness or volatility of data differently, since data feeding can be more immediate and the use life of data drops tremendously in real-time analysis.

Finally, big data analytics is about micro customization and personalization (Chen and Hsieh 2014). Because of the volume and complexity of data, analysts can drill down more deeply to understand data patterns at a micro level, such as addresses or a small geographical area. This type of understanding allows customization of services or even anticipatory policy responses to potential issues faced by individuals. Traditional analysis, on the other hand, is more likely to focus on aggregate patterns and the average trend of data and ignore individual specificity and micro information relevancy.

Big Data and Local Management

Local governments are certainly well positioned to take advantage of these characteristics of big data analytics. First, the local government sector touches on many social and economic aspects of a community, including public safety, infrastructure, economic development, human development, cultural development, and social services, that are essential to individual residents. Many of these activities are highly related to each other and their impact may cut across policy spheres. For example, the effectiveness of crime prevention and public safety protection is strongly embedded in the larger socioeconomic context of a community and can be influenced strongly by the effectiveness of human development, social services, and development of economic opportunities for different social classes and demographic groups. Similarly, the effectiveness of education, which can be measured in different ways beyond standardized tests, is dependent on many socioeconomic factors over which city and county agencies may have some degree of influence through law enforcement and crime prevention activities, provision of essential social services to support families and children, and provision of community health and nutritional support programs for needy families. These linkages among local services and policies provide ample opportunities for managers and policy makers to use big data methodologies and tools to understand how different community conditions, policies, and service results are related to each other and to break down the silo effects of departmental planning and thinking.

In addition, local governments today are data-rich. After decades of e-government initiatives and development, the information technology capacity of many local governments in the U.S. has been enhanced tremendously, and many local services have extensive digital records that can be used for data analytics purposes. Here are some examples of local data that should be readily available in most communities:

- Local property records, including housing characteristics, value, and, possibly, conditions
- Crime activities and records of police activities
- Community health records
- Social service utilization and programming records
- Student academic records and attendance records
- Library patron records
- Utility consumption records
- Service requests, including emergency services and non-emergency services
- Registration records of businesses
- Tax records of businesses and individuals or households
- Permit applications and license records of regulated activities
- Records of public works projects
- Traffic patterns in major street interactions
- Locations of traffic accidents
- City website usage and search history
- Social media text records

The above list includes many structured, administrative records that can be integrated and analyzed to answer a lot of important and interesting policy and programming questions faced by local managers today, such as what programs and services are most needed by whom, and when, where, and how these programs should be delivered. The rising popularity of social media, such as Facebook and Twitter, has also led to new possibilities for understanding public concerns and sentiments that traditional tools, such as citizen surveys and neighborhood meetings, cannot provide because of administrative costs and the time constraints faced by citizens and public agencies.

Finally, local governments also collect a lot of unstructured data in different formats at different locations. For example, many cities have put video cameras in strategic locations to monitor traffic flows of key interactions and the public safety condition of certain neighborhoods. Censors are also used to detect movement and capture human traffic or the usage of certain facilities or equipment. Many local governments today also solicit help from citizens and allow them to take digital pictures and upload geographically coded data through smartphone apps, so that citizens can help local departments understand different neighborhood conditions and take responsive actions to address public concerns.

All these data collected by local governments present many opportunities for local officials to harness useful information about community conditions and the impact of individual actions and to evaluate what policy actions and services should be used to achieve desired policy goals. Some communities have already taken such initiatives. For example, the City of Chicago has launched a SmartData platform to analyze citizen complaints from its 311 center and has used data analytics to understand service delivery challenges in different neighborhoods, so that departments can take proactive action (Goldsmith and Crawford 2014, pp. 87–91). One of their initiatives is the deployment of data analytics to control rat problems. Using resident complaint data over 12 years, city officials analyzed the geographical pattern of rodent problems and developed predictive analytics of the pattern using different variables, such as trash overflow complaints and cases of food poisoning in restaurants. Based on the results, the city's sanitation team was deployed more strategically to control the problem in rat-infested areas, and the results led to 20 percent efficiency gains (Jeelani 2015).

Other cities, such as Los Angeles, Memphis, Richmond, VA, and Arlington, TX, have also used data analytics to examine crime trends and pursue "predictive policing," so that policing activities can be more strategically deployed in high-risk areas and at certain time periods (Mayer-Schönberger and Cukier 2013, p. 158; Pearsall 2010; Perry et al. 2013). For example, by analyzing the spatial patterns of crime incidents over time, the police department of Richmond was able to increase weapons seizure and reduce random gunfire and personnel costs significantly on New Year's Eve in 2003 (Pearsall 2010). Within six months of introducing predictive policing, the Foothill area in Los Angeles experienced a 12 percent drop in property crimes, while neighboring areas experienced a 0.5 percent gain in similar crimes (Economist 2013).

Other local services are also impacted by the big data trend. For example, New York City used data analytics to evaluate homeless problems and after examining the relationships among different variables, including overcrowdedness in housing, domestic violence, and hazardous living conditions, analysts found that the largest contributing factor was eviction. Based on these results, New York City has developed an alert system to help social workers and nonprofit organizations to better serve those families who are at the risk of becoming homeless early in the eviction process (Shueh 2015; Sumall.org 2015). The City of Boston and New Urban Mechanics under the Mayor's Office has developed a smartphone app that allows citizens to collect data on street smoothness automatically while riding. The app results help the city become more proactive and cost-effective in addressing pothole problems (City of Boston 2015).

These are just a few examples showing how big data analytics have the potential to contribute to "smart governing" and help local managers and citizens use information to make public policies more cost-effective and responsive (Goldsmith and Crawford 2014). In general, the potential functions of big data analytics include the following:

- To present and visualize trends and patterns so that policy makers, managers, and citizens can understand an issue through the perspective of evidence-based reasoning;

- To detect deviations and abnormal events early so that responsive corrective actions can be taken promptly to mitigate risk and potential harm;
- To predict the occurrence of certain events and allow public agencies, community organizations, and individual residents to take proactive actions to reduce the risk of having those events and their associated social and individual harms;
- To evaluate the impact of certain policies or programs from a systemic perspective, rather than from a single departmental perspective and understanding;
- To allow a wider dialogue across departments and sectors about policy challenges and possible solutions and to foster greater interdepartmental and intersectoral collaboration;
- To tailor the delivery of services and programs to individual needs and preferences.

In the following, we use Kansas City, Missouri, as a case study to demonstrate some of these potential benefits and the challenges in pursuing these functions.

Case Study: The Performance Management Initiative of Kansas City, Missouri

Kansas City, Missouri, is a midwestern city in the U.S., with a diverse population of about 450,000, including about 40 percent African Americans and Hispanics. The median housing value is about $135,000, and about 19.1 percent of the population is below the federal poverty level, which is about the same as the national urban poverty rate in the 2011–2012 period (Nichols 2013).

Kansas City approaches the big data trend through several strategies. First, it emphasizes the importance of open data and gives the public and interested parties open access to many administrative data owned by the city, and sometimes by the state, so that they can make their own inquiries and analysis. The city's open data portal (https://data.kcmo.org/) is a depository of more than 180 datasets and several thousand visualizations tied to these data. Popular data available at the portal include the incidence of crime, citizen service requests, property violations and nuisance problems, traffic flow counts, business licenses and permit data, building permits and demolition data, and data on public works and development projects. Many of these data are also available as map data, so that interested citizens and analysts can examine the data spatially. On the open data portal, the city also solicits public input on what other data should be provided and what types of mobile apps should be developed to facilitate the public use of the city data.

Second, Kansas City understands that it cannot pursue big data by relying only on city resources and staff time. As a result, it has launched partnerships with different organizations. For example, it works with students and researchers of different universities to analyze data to inform decision-making. It also engages civic hackers, such as the Kansas City Code for America Brigade (codeforkc.org), so that the city can leverage the skills and community assets of these members to use the data to inform policy making, meet the needs of citizens, and improve the quality of life of local communities. One of the important Brigade projects is the "Neighborhood Dashboard," which aims to bring together high-value datasets like 311 service requests, crime data, and property violations within the framework of a neighborhood, in order to allow residents to be aware of the issues in their neighborhood and how they compare to other neighborhoods.

Within the city, the Office of Performance Management under the City Manager's Office is responsible for taking the lead in using data and performance indicators to improve services and local policy making. Each month, the mayor and the city manager moderate "KCStat" meetings with departments to review the city's progress in one of the following areas: customer service; finance and governance; infrastructure and transportation; neighborhoods and healthy communities; planning, zoning, and economic development; and public safety. Citizen satisfaction survey data and program outputs and outcomes are used to evaluate and monitor departmental performance.

To facilitate the KCStat effort, the Office of Performance Management worked with a team of university researchers in 2014–2015 to analyze data from more than 12,000 citizen surveys in 2010–2014, more than 90,000 cases of citizen service requests annually, and about 60,000 reported crime incidents annually to understand better what influence resident perceptions of city services and how service delivery and managerial practices should be changed to enhance the city's quality of life and public satisfaction. Because the data were integrated spatially by neighborhoods and census block groups (see Figure 6.1), local officials and researchers could control for various factors, identify which were relatively more important, and focus on specific neighborhoods that were at a higher risk of deterioration and needed more policy intervention.

For example, one of the major public concerns in Kansas City was about public safety. By integrating perception-based survey data with various service result data and demographic and housing data at the neighborhood level, data analysts and local managers found that the most important factor influencing local residents' perception of public safety was the effectiveness of city communication. Many demographic and socioeconomic factors, such as race and the percentage of single-parent households in a neighborhood, were also very important. While the level and change of crime rate in neighborhoods were statistically significant, they did not shape public perception substantially (Ho and Cho 2015).

These results were somewhat surprising and provided additional insights about public safety management—even if the police are very effective in combating crime and reducing the crime rate in certain neighborhoods of the city, the public may still perceive certain areas as unsafe unless they are more informed about

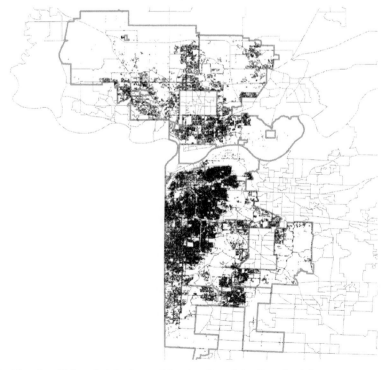

Figure 6.1 Mapping Citizen Satisfaction and Service Complaint Data Spatially

Note: Light gray lines indicate the census block group boundary, thick gray lines indicate neighborhood boundaries.

what the city has done and what results have been accomplished. Also, the results confirm the findings of many previous criminal justice and sociological studies and suggest that effective policing and crime prevention efforts are linked significantly to the social environment of neighborhoods (Dunham and Alpert 1988; Sampson 2012; Wu, Sun, and Triplett 2009).

Findings like these encourage the city to pursue a more holistic approach to policing and crime prevention. In order to combat crime and improve the public's perception of public safety, Kansas City's policy makers and managers understand that they cannot rely solely on the efforts and performance of the police department. For example, Kansas City launched a collaborative initiative known as "KC No Violence Alliance" (KC NoVA) with the police department, the Jackson County Prosecutor's Office, the U.S. Attorney's Office, the Missouri Department of Corrections, and the University of Missouri–Kansas City. This initiative aims at reducing violent crime by encouraging more public reporting of criminal activities and creating a network of social service providers in education, job training, and drug treatment to help criminals leave a life of crime (Office of Mayor Sly James 2013). In November 2015, Mayor Sly James also established a new citizen task force to examine the causes of violence and provide policy recommendations for the city. The initial meeting of the task force already recognized the need to address structural problems in society, including poverty, unemployment, and blight that affect the urban core (Cummings 2016). Within the city government, a cross-departmental working group has also been meeting to share data and discuss strategies with regard to vacant and abandoned property, which have a blighting influence on neighborhoods that impact feelings of safety. Another task force has been developing a suggested approach to addressing "problem businesses," which is informed by combining public safety data with data from other city departments. While big data analysis might not be the sole or most important driver for these initiatives, the results of big data analysis have certainly contributed to and reinforced the thinking behind the initiatives.

Because the results of data analysis about public safety perception have shown that certain types of neighborhood nuisance problems, such as graffiti, illegal dumping, vacant property complaints, and property nuisance complaints, tend to cluster together and are significantly associated with a more negative view of public safety by local residents (Ho and Cho 2015), city officials were particularly interested in seeing the data trends of these types of cases. These cases, generally known as "broken window" cases (Keizer and Steg 2008; Wilson and Kelling 1982), were analyzed by month and by neighborhood. The results show that the majority of 240 neighborhoods in Kansas City had very few problems, and a large share of the broken window cases were concentrated in a small cluster of neighborhoods. Over time, the number of cases in these high-risk neighborhoods that were in the seventy-fifth percentile or above declined gradually, showing a sign of general improvement (see Table 6.1). Despite the trend, these high-risk neighborhoods remained the most vulnerable. This pattern of neighborhood vulnerability is illustrated by Figure 6.2—those neighborhoods in the top ninetieth percentile in the first six months of 2010 (indicated by ○) remained mostly in the top range of the caseload distribution in 2015 and had relatively more cases per month. This result implies that there are structural causes for these neighborhoods being more vulnerable to property nuisance problems, and persistent focus on these neighborhoods and more comprehensive solutions, such as anti-poverty programs, crime control, assistance to broken families, and more youth programming and activities, may be needed to deal with the root causes of the property nuisance problems in these neighborhoods.

The above are just some of the data analytics initiatives undertaken by the Office of Performance Management and various city departments in recent years, and more have been planned to expand the use of data analytics. For example, knowing the data patterns and trends is certainly helpful, but it will be even more helpful if predictive analytics can be used to analyze when and where certain problems tend to occur, so that more strategic actions can be pursued to prevent them from happening or to

Table 6.1 Distribution of "Broken Window" Nuisance Complaints, Semi-annually and by Percentiles

	95th percentile	90th percentile	75th percentile	median	25th percentile	10th percentile
2010, January–June	62	41	17	7	3	1
2010, July–December	30	19	9	4	2	1
2011, January–June	40	25	12	5	2	1
2011, July–December	28	19	10	4	2	1
2012, January–June	37	23	12	5	2	1
2012, July–December	28	18	9	4	2	1
2013, January–June	33	23	11	5	2	1
2013, July–December	26	17	10	4	2	1
2014, January–June	33	21	11	5	2	1
2014, July–December	32	22	11	5	2	1
2015, January–June	32	22	12	5	2	1

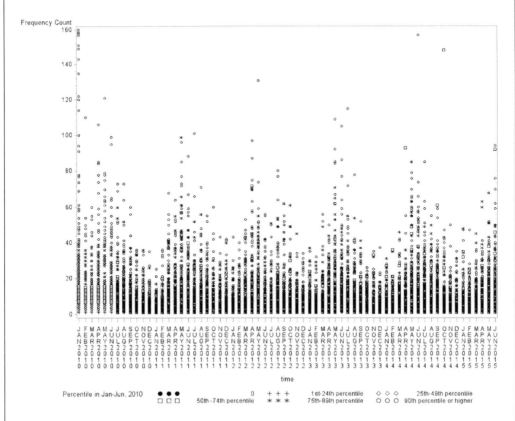

Figure 6.2 Distribution of Broken Window Cases over Time, by Caseload Percentiles in the First Six Months of 2010

allow city departments to become more prepared in anticipation of the problems. The Office of Performance Management is currently pursuing this direction and has been gradually building internal capacity to conduct big data analytics. The office's oversight of the city's open data portal has provided a natural connection point to the sources of data available in the city, as well as a mechanism to increase the quality and number of these datasets. From an analytical perspective, the office has been developing expertise in coding language such as R in order to run more sophisticated and automated analytical models. Going forward, the office is also considering adding staff resources in the area of information technology and computer programming to further build this capacity.

The work of the Office of Performance Management has also been bolstered through communication with officials in other major U.S. cities that are pursuing similar data analytics efforts. For example, Kansas City was one of the first cities selected for the What Works Cities Initiative, a technical assistance program funded by Bloomberg Philanthropies that focuses on improving the use of data-driven decision-making by cities. What Works Cities has provided a platform for Kansas City to compare its efforts to nationwide efforts, develop a scope of work for improving its data-driven management systems, and access a community of peer cities for ideas and best practices. Another effort supported by the National League of Cities as well as the MacArthur Foundation has been a series of conferences involving data-oriented staff from major U.S. cities, including New York, Boston, Philadelphia, Pittsburgh, Dallas, Fort Lauderdale, New Orleans, Chicago, Los Angeles, San Francisco, and Kansas City. These conferences have focused on identifying shared opportunities and barriers in data-driven decision-making at the local level that could represent collaboration points with universities and philanthropic communities.

Lessons Learned

Through the case study of Kansas City and the experiences of many other U.S. cities, several lessons can be drawn about big data development in the local public sector. First, big data is certainly getting a lot of attention among local officials, and many cities are willing to invest money and staff time to pursue it. Because the development is still new and the technical skills and data infrastructure requirements are significant, many cities tend to pursue big data initiatives incrementally to make sure that public investment in this area is spent most cost-effectively and to avoid serious mistakes.

Hiring competent staff and providing continuous training and development in this rapidly changing area is fundamental to any big data efforts. Besides acquiring technical skills in statistical analysis, machine learning, spatial mapping and visualization, and database management, city staff should also develop greater legal and managerial understanding associated with the big data development. For example, how to coordinate and motivate different departments to share data, how to work with volunteers such as civic hackers, community organizations, and local businesses in supporting a city's big data initiatives, and how to rely on contractors to handle some of the work are all important challenges faced by managers of big data initiatives. In response to these challenges, Desouza (2014) suggests that government agencies should create a working group(s) consisting of departmental representatives and key stakeholders to oversee big data projects. This collaborative process can start with a white paper or policy brief to frame the goals and strategies of the working group. Then the group should focus on the development of a clearinghouse for data governance standards and processes and on leveraging resources to pursue its goals. Ideally, such a working group should be chaired by a senior executive of the government to foster political support and interagency coordination.

Preparedness to handle the legal and ethical challenges of the big data movement is also important (Boyd and Crawford 2012; Chen and Hsieh 2014). Because the government is often the only legal authority who may collect some of the local data, and citizens and businesses have no choice but to file the required information to the government, local officials have a special obligation to the public to protect their privacy. How to balance the need for privacy and the desire to provide open access to government-held data to foster business development, crowdsource analytics tasks, encourage new apps development, and facilitate information flows to enhance public benefits and convenience is a critical issue. Privacy, citizens' constitutional rights, and governmental surveillance have become an even more sensitive subject since the whistleblowing by Edward Snowden about the U.S. federal government's mass surveillance program. This event has political spillover effects on local governments, and as a result, how local officials handle data privacy appropriately given a community's political atmosphere is an important subject in local big data development.

In response to the legal and ethical challenges, city officials need to have explicit policies to define data ownership and use rights. They also need to have clear guidelines to protect individual privacy, especially when many governments are pursuing open data aggressively to encourage crowdsourcing of data analytics and app development. Some cities, including Kansas City, are highly conscious of their legal and ethical responsibilities and are sensitive to the public's concern about the government's potential overreach in collecting and mining data. For example, Kansas City's data governance practices involve the Law Department in determining whether privacy issues are a legal concern. Also, some sensitive data, such as data on the incidence of crime, are processed carefully so that identifiable personal information are stripped in any open data records and only approximate addresses, such as the addresses of the nearby street interactions, are used instead of the exact address or location.

In addition to privacy concerns, local governments should pay close attention to data security concerns. As more data are collected and stored centrally for analysis purposes, there is greater vulnerability for data breach. This concern is especially serious when sensitive individual information is involved, such as tax records, health records, criminal and victim information, nonpublic business records, and information of critical infrastructure facility. Also, if real-time data analytics is involved to manage certain critical public services, such as traffic signal control, police patrol activity management, and the maintenance and monitoring of infrastructure conditions, how to guarantee the integrity of the computer systems involved, the security of communication flows between systems, and the accuracy and reliability of computer programming are critically important, because failures to do so may cause significant economic loss and social chaos. Hence, as big data becomes more and more prevalent in our daily life and is used more widely in many governmental operations, more attention to security issues and investment in the critical information technology infrastructure should become a high priority of local governments.

Besides privacy and security concerns, local officials should also be conscious about the limitations of big data tools. For example, one of the promises of big data is that it can go beyond traditional sampling methodologies that only provide "snapshots" of the reality and can provide a more comprehensive understanding of the "whole truth" by using powerful computing tools and methods to collect and analyze as much data as possible, even if the data are unstructured and messy. However, in reality, data collection is always constrained by resources, legal constraints, technological barriers, and social norms. Also, unlike private businesses that can target and tailor their client base, because the "clients" of local services are the whole community and all of its residents, local departments cannot and should not select and discriminate against certain population groups. With the principles of equity and public service values in mind, local officials have to be conscious about how they use big data to understand public needs and expectations, anticipate who may be excluded from the data collection process, and consider whose voice and standing may be missing in the analysis.

For example, in business research, text mining of social media is commonly used to understand public sentiment and consumer preferences. For local governments, social media are also becoming more widely used, and so text mining of social media content can be helpful by adding another layer of information about public preferences and concerns. However, despite the new possibilities and excitement about social media analytics, local officials need to understand that a significant portion of the U.S. population do not use social media such as Twitter as their primary means of communication, and certain segments of the population still favor traditional modes of communication, such as TV, printed newsletters, telephone calls, and face-to-face meetings, to receive information or express their views of certain policy issues and community affairs. According to a recent study by the Pew Research Center (Duggan et al. 2015), only 58 percent of all American adults ages 18 and above use Facebook, 23 percent use LinkedIn, 22 percent use Pinterest, 21 percent use Instagram, and 19 percent use Twitter. While social media usage is more prevalent among the younger population, only 56 percent of Internet users ages 65 and older use Facebook, and the percentages are even lower for other social media tools. These results suggest that local officials cannot rely solely on text mining of social media tools to understand public opinions and preferences. Traditional tools, such as representative random surveys of local residents, phone contacts, and neighborhood meetings, are still necessary to reach out to all segments of the population in the policymaking and program planning process.

Another limitation that local officials should understand is that while big data and predictive analytics can be very powerful and may provide new insights on the relationships between factors, jumping from understanding these associational relationships to hypothesizing causal relationships between them and acting upon the results can sometimes be dangerous. Big data analytics may only provide initial insights on these relationships. More systematic, in-depth examination of the data, or even experimental pilot studies, may be necessary to test some of the hypothetical causal relationships.

For example, clustering analysis of nuisance complaint data, citizen satisfaction data, and usage of fire and emergency medical services may reveal that citizen satisfaction with quality of life is negatively associated with satisfaction with the fire department's response time and with the frequency of fire and emergency medical services. However, it would be a significant policy error to jump to the conclusion that more frequent and rapid deployment of fire and emergency medical services lowers quality-of-life perception, and so the local fire department should perhaps provide less responsive services to certain neighborhoods to increase their public satisfaction with quality of life! Because so many intervening factors, such as a neighborhood's public safety conditions and socioeconomic challenges, may be involved, the associational relationship may merely be spurious and not causal. Without more careful statistical analysis or experimental design, local officials should be careful in assuming that an association is causal and in using big data analytics to jump to any policy recommendation.

Furthermore, even if a relationship is found to be valid and causal, whether local departments should take proactive action based on the analytical results can be a difficult question, as it sometimes requires considerations that are beyond what statistics and computing analytics should handle. Local managers should understand that policy and programming decisions are based not solely on efficiency or cost-effectiveness concerns, and what is "appropriate" and politically and social acceptable is defined by social norms, culture, and community values, not just by economics and effectiveness calculation.

A good example of this challenge is the use of predictive policing (Perry et al. 2013). As suggested earlier, many large cities have begun to explore the possibilities of using big data analytics to understand the public safety vulnerability of certain areas and the risk profile of specific individuals so that more strategic and proactive policing activities can be used to reduce crime. However, there are many controversies about predictive policing and using the results of big data analytics to target specific individuals, racial groups, or neighborhoods through "stop and frisk" tactics. Critics of these types of policing strategies argue that they violate the civil rights of individuals because if no laws have been violated by an individual, he or she should not be subject to any discriminative targeting and harassment. Some also point out that stop and frisk tactics may lead to an erosion of public trust and may harm the police–citizen relationship, which may lead to more public safety problems and difficulties in crime prevention and investigation in the long run.

Hence, the question of how to use the results of big data analytics effectively, ethically, and legally to improve policymaking and public service programming is an important one that is beyond the technical capacity concerns of local management. Local officials have to consider the governance issues related to big data carefully, and public representatives and key stakeholders should be involved to discuss what data should be collected and analyzed, how data should be used to inform decision-making, and what ethical boundaries should be imposed on data analytics tasks. One example of this type of governance in Kansas City is the Smart Cities Advisory Board that has been convened to involve multiple stakeholders in making decisions about the city's smart city infrastructure development and program deployment. Internally, the city has also developed an Open Data Governance Committee consisting of representatives from different departments.

Conclusion

This chapter examines big data trends and its possibilities for local governments. It also discusses some of the challenges resulting from these developments and what local policy makers and managers should think about in response to the rising digitalization of society and daily life. While many tools and opportunities of big data are technical, driven often by the advancement in technologies and statistics, many of the challenges and concerns are beyond what computer programming and statistical analysis can handle. Some of the policy challenges, governance concerns, and ethical dilemmas are related to the fundamental questions about individual rights, the relationship between the government and the citizenry, the roles and boundaries of the public sector, and the political acceptability and social behavior norms. For example, what types of data government agencies and private entities are allowed to collect on individual citizens, how data can be collected and used, what and how individual records held by government can be shared with nongovernmental entities, and the extent to which the public should have a voice in determining the privacy guidelines and data use policies are all among the digital governance issues local policy makers should consider carefully today. Also, questions about who has access to what technologies and platforms, who may have more influence in the digital decision-making process, and what are the implications of data-driven policymaking for individuals and social groups raise new concerns of digital divide in society. Given these challenges, policy makers and managers should be mindful of data limitations and understand that what can be done technically or computationally may not be the right or appropriate action to pursue.

This is why public managers in the big data era not only need good technical training and solid quantitative skills, but also solid training and understanding of organizational collaboration, interdepartmental communication, ethical reasoning, and public accountability. These fundamental building blocks of public management have remained the same, or have perhaps become even more important, as a result of technological advancement in computing power and analytical capacity.

References

Boyd, Danah, and Kate Crawford. 2012. 'Critical questions for big data: Provocations for a cultural, technological, and scholarly phenomenon'. *Information, Communication & Society* 15 (5): 662–679.

Chen, Yu-Che, and Tsui-Chuan Hsieh. 2014. 'Big data for digital government: Opportunities, challenges, and strategies'. *International Journal of Public Administration in the Digital Age* 1 (1): 1–14.

City of Boston. 2015. 'Street bump: Help improve your streets'. Accessed October 15. http://www.cityofboston.gov/DoIT/apps/streetbump.asp

Cummings, Ian. 2016. 'Kansas City task force on violence confronts complex issues in first meeting'. *Kansas City Star*, January 12. Accessed January 13, 2016. http://www.kansascity.com/news/local/article54402150.html

Desouza, Kevin C. 2014. *Realizing the promise of big data: Implementing big data projects*. Washington, DC: The IBM Center for the Business of Government.

Duggan, Maeve, Nicole B. Ellison, Cliff Lampe, Amanda Lenhart, and Mary Madden. 2015. *Social Media Update 2014*. Washington, DC: Pew Research Center.

Dunham, Roger G., and Geoffrey P. Alpert. 1988. 'Neighborhood differences in attitudes toward policing: Evidence for a mixed-strategy model of policing in a multi-ethnic setting'. *Journal of Criminal Law and Criminology* 79 (2): 504–523.

Economist. 2013. 'Predictive policing: Don't even think about it'. July 20. Accessed September 15, 2015. http://www.economist.com/news/briefing/21582042-it-getting-easier-foresee-wrongdoing-and-spot-likely-wrongdoers-dont-even-think-about-it

Goldsmith, Stephen, and Susan Crawford. 2014. *The responsive city: Engaging communities through data-smart governance*. San Francisco: Jossey-Bass.

Ho, Alfred Tat-Kei, and Wonhyuk Cho. 2015. 'Government communication effectiveness and satisfaction with the police: A large-scale survey study'. Working Paper. University of Kansas.

Jeelani, Mehboob. 2015. 'Chicago uses new technology to solve this very old urban problem'. *Fortune.com*, April 29. Accessed September 15, 2015. http://fortune.com/2015/04/29/chicago-big-data/

Keizer, Kees, Siegwart Lindenberg, and Linda Steg. 2008. 'The spreading of disorder'. *Science* 322 (5908): 1681–1685.

Laney, Doug. 2001. *3D data management: Controlling data volume, velocity, and variety*. Meta Group Application Delivery Strategies, February 6. https://blogs.gartner.com/doug-laney/files/2012/01/ad949-3D-Data-Management-Controlling-Data-Volume-Velocity-and-Variety.pdf

Mayer-Schönberger, Viktor, and Kenneth Cukier. 2013. *Big data: A revolution that will transform how we live, work and think*. London: John Murray.

Nichols, Austin. 2013. *Fact sheet: Poverty in the United States*. Washington, DC: Urban Institute.

Office of Mayor Sly James. 2013. 'Mayor James, KC NoVA remain unified and focused on its community-based, multi-dimensional approach to crime reduction'. Press release on June 27, 2013. Accessed January 10, 2016. http://kcmayor.org/newsreleases/mayor-james-kc-nova-remain-unified-and-focused-on-its-community-based-multidimensional-approach-to-crime-reduction

O'Malley, Martin. 2014. 'Doing what works: Governing in the age of big data'. *Public Administration Review* 74 (5): 555–556.

Pearsall, Beth. 2010. 'Predictive policing: The future of law enforcement?' *National Institute of Justice Journal*, 266. Accessed September 15, 2015. http://www.nij.gov/journals/266/Pages/predictive.aspx

Perry, Walter L., Brian McInnis, Carter C. Price, Susan C. Smith, and John S. Hollywood. 2013. *Predictive policing: The role of crime forecasting in law enforcement operations*. Santa Monica, CA: Rand.

Sampson, Robert J. 2012. *Great American city: Chicago and the enduring neighborhood effect*. Chicago: University of Chicago Press.

Shueh, Jason. 2015. 'Data innovation day 2015: Methodologies behind analytics success stories'. *Government Technology*, January 25. http://www.govtech.com/data/Data-Innovation-Day-2015-Assessing-Methodologies-Behind-Analytics-Success-Stories.html

Sumall.org. 2015. 'Homeless by the numbers'. Accessed September 15, 2015. http://www.sumall.org/homelessness

U.S. White House. 2013. 'Unleashing the power of big data'. Press release on April 18. Accessed November 1, 2015. https://www.whitehouse.gov/blog/2013/04/18/unleashing-power-big-data

Wilson, James Q., and George L. Kelling. 1982. 'Broken windows'. *Atlantic Monthly* 249 (3): 29–38.

World Economic Forum. 2012. *Big data, big impact: New possibilities for international development*. Geneva, Switzerland: World Economic Forum.

Wu, Yuning, Ivan Y. Sun, and Ruth A. Triplett. 2009. 'Race, class or neighborhood context: Which matters more in measuring satisfaction with police?' *Justice Quarterly* 26 (1): 125–156.

Yin, Chuan-Tao, Zhang Xiong, Hui Chen, Jingyuan Wang, and Daven Cooper. 2015. 'A literature survey on smart cities'. *Science China: Information Sciences* 58 (10): 1–18.

7

MOBILE LOCATION-BASED SERVICE (LBS) APPS FOR THE PUBLIC SECTOR

Prospects and Challenges

Sukumar Ganapati

The mobile environment provides an exciting frontier for geographic information systems (GIS) development, especially in the evolution of location-based services (LBS) for the public sector. The mobile environment could be described as a convergence of mobile devices and wireless infrastructure. Mobile devices generally refer to smartphones and tablets (and intermediate-size devices such as phablets). Wearables (body-worn devices, such as smart watches) are also poised to grow significantly in the near future. Mobile devices fundamentally depend on the wireless infrastructure for communications. While 4G networks have become increasingly common, the devices often come equipped with Wi-Fi, Bluetooth, and near field communications (NFC) capabilities. The devices commonly include several hardware features, such as the geographical positioning system (GPS) (allows real time location), camera (to take geocoded still life and motion pictures), and sensors (such as accelerometers that sense motion, including shake and tilt of the device), all of which aid in location-based services.

Location-based services harness the real-time location information to give customized personal and neighborhood-level services to the user. A popular location-based service is the turn-by-turn navigation in a car. According to a Pew survey, nearly three out of four adult smartphone owners use the phone to get directions or other information (Zickuhr, 2013). A visitor in an unfamiliar neighborhood can locate a nearby amenity (e.g., the nearest gas station for fueling) using a mobile app. In this vein, FourSquare and Yelp have become popular apps to locate businesses of interest (e.g., restaurants, bars, etc.) in the neighborhood. These apps crowdsource the reviews about quality and other aspects of the business through a community of users (rather than by an expert community). The wayfinding is not only important for outdoor pursuits, but also required for many indoor activities (e.g., finding the way in a large airport or mall, navigating the floors, etc.). Location-based services are essential features of the sharing economy, whereby the mobile apps have facilitated new modes of peer-to-peer shared services (such as Uber and Lyft for ride sharing). The apps could overlay advanced technologies such as augmented reality to provide additional location-specific information about the physical environment. For example, a visitor walking in an unfamiliar neighborhood can point the camera along the street and identify the buildings using the augmented reality app.

In this chapter, I examine the prospects and challenges of location-based services for the public sector. Location-based services have proliferated across the private sector in several industries (e.g., automobile, hospitality, tourism, etc.). Public agencies could similarly benefit from location-based services. These benefits are oriented toward both citizens and public enterprises. There are two dimensions of citizen-oriented benefits. First, location-based services can enhance citizen engagement with public agencies, whereby each citizen can provide ambient intelligence in real time. Public agencies can usefully tap on such active citizen engagement. Second, public agencies can use the location-based services to provide new services or enhance existing services. In this respect, location-based services have been particularly adapted to the 311 non-emergency services provided by county and city governments. From the public enterprise perspective, location-based services could potentially transform internal organizational management, blurring the lines between back-office management and field activities. Location-based services are not, however, without their challenges. Locational privacy and security is a major concern. They also raise new challenges attendant with the new sharing economy.

The chapter is structured as follows. The next section provides a background of the enabling technologies behind location-based services. Then, the evolution of mobile location-based services is outlined. After this, prospects of the location-based services for public sector agencies are examined, followed by their challenges for these agencies. The chapter concludes with the future and significance of location-based services for the public sector.

Enablers of Location-Based Services: GIS and Mobile Technologies

Geographic information systems is the core component of location-based services. Classically, GIS has been described as "a system of hardware, software, and procedures that capture, store, edit, manipulate, manage, analyze, share, and display georeferenced data" (Fu, 2015, p. 4). GIS is a powerful method of producing maps, integrating spatial (e.g., addresses, streets, city/state, etc.) and attribute data. GIS maps are dynamic, conducive for user interactivity (e.g., search, pan, and zoom) and for spatial analysis (e.g., point patterns, clustering, path analysis). GIS itself has evolved from being stand-alone desktop software to an Internet-based *geospatial web* platform (Ganapati, 2011; Scharl, 2007). Lake and Farley (2007, p. 15) define the geospatial web platform as "the global collection of general services and data that support the use of geographic data in a range of domain applications." The Internet accessibility of the geospatial platform is crucial to location-based services—users can avail themselves of location-based services through location-based search.

The advantage of the geospatial platform is that the public sector agency does not need to host and maintain expensive GIS software in-house on its servers. Rather, the GIS mapping services are availed over the Internet through an independent geospatial platform provider. Common examples of the commercial platforms include ArcGIS online, Microsoft's Bing Maps, Google Maps, Nokia's Here, MapQuest, and Yahoo Maps. The Open Street Map (OSM) is an open source platform for mapping, and the NASA World Wind was an early entrant in the public sector. A key feature of these platforms is the mashup, whereby data from external sources could be overlaid on the platform using application programming interfaces (APIs). API is a structured way of accessing data online from an external source, allowing third-party software developers to provide value-added location-based services. For example, a transit agency could make its transit data publicly available. A software developer (or the agency itself) could then use APIs to mashup the transit data with a geospatial platform and create a mobile app that provides real-time location of a bus or train.

Modern mobile devices (especially smartphones and tablets) offer four core advantages for location-based services. First, mobile devices are Internet connected with high-speed wireless broadband networks. The devices and the communications speeds of the wireless networks have advanced rapidly over this century. The smart devices are at least 3G (with speeds between 384 kilobits per second and 2.0 megabits per second), which comply with the International Mobile Telecommunications (IMT-2000) umbrella standards specified by the International Telecommunications Union (ITU) (Korhonen, 2003). Whereas 3G combines circuit switching for voice and packet switching for data, 4G is a fully Internet protocol-based packet switching system with a communication speed between 10 Mbps and 100 Mbps (Dahlman, Parkvall, and Skold, 2014). It is commercially referred to as LTE

(Long Term Evolution), a version of which is recognized to meet the IMT-Advanced specification adopted by the ITU in 2012. The emerging 5G networks would further propagate the growth of the mobile communications, with speed up to 10 gigabits per second (Federal Communications Commission, FCC, 2014). The high-speed networks and the emerging devices provide good prospects for growth of mobile-based computation and increased capacity for location-based services.

Second, the devices can be geolocated through various means. The GPS gives the real-time location of the mobile device, which could be used by the apps to tailor services to the vicinity of the location. Pictures and videos taken with the devices are automatically geotagged. Mobile devices can also be located through cellular phone towers or Wi-Fi networks (the device's Internet protocol address also gives the location) at different levels of granularity. The devices have inbuilt functions that third-party apps could use to obtain the location. For example, Apple's "Visit Monitoring" monitors an Iphone's (running iOS version 8.0 or later) destination and allows for opportunistic location-based use of the apps.

Third, mobile devices are an instantaneous means of crowdsourcing—an individual can upload information about an event (e.g., traffic accident or building fire) that happens in the vicinity. People are intelligent sensors who can report on the events in their surroundings, including physical evidence of geotagged pictures and videos taken with the mobile device's camera. Goodchild (2007, p. 211) coined the phenomenon as Volunteered Geographic Information, which refers to "the explosion of interest in using the Web to create, assemble, and disseminate geographic information provided voluntarily by individuals."

Fourth, mobile technologies have the potential for synergistic integration with other parallel technologies, such as augmented reality and sensors, which bode well for location-based services. Augmented reality is the combination of virtual reality and the real world (e.g., overlaying a picture or video with virtual information in real time); platforms for such mobile apps include Layar, Wikitude, and Metaio (acquired by Apple in 2015). Although still evolving, augmented reality techniques could be useful for tourists (e.g., getting information about points of interest), infrastructure maintenance, public works, zoning, and other activities (Graham, Zook, and Boulton, 2013; Liao and Humphreys, 2015; Lin et al., 2014). Sensor technologies such as radio frequency identification (RFID) and near field communications enable a wide range of activities when they are linked to mobile devices. RFID can identify each object uniquely. It is used in the public sector for electronic toll collection, driving licenses, passports, keyless secure access, and other uses. NFC is used for very close distance (less than 10 centimeters) communication between devices. It is commonly used for contactless transactions (e.g., secure mobile payments in retail stores), access control (e.g., ticketed access to transport or an event), and connecting devices (e.g., to access digital content from another device). Some of the new generation smartphones have integrated NFC into the device.

In addition to the evolution of mobile technology, the deep penetration of mobile devices provides the demand side of location-based services. Mobile devices (numbering 7.4 billion) exceeded the world population (of 7.2 billion) in 2014 (CISCO, 2015). The share of "smart" mobile devices (i.e., connected to the Internet) is projected to increase from 26 percent to over 50 percent between 2014 and 2019. Wearable devices are expected to grow fivefold (from 109 million to 578 million) during the same period. The wearables include smart watches, smart glasses, heads-up displays, health monitors, scanners, and navigation devices. Although wearables have limited embedded cellular connectivity, they could connect to mobile networks through other devices (e.g., smartphones).

Within the United States, there is a dramatic growth of mobile phones (and wearables) in general and smartphones in particular. The share of the American population owning cell phones went up from 53 percent to 90 percent between 2000 and 2014, and smartphone ownership went up from 35 percent to 58 percent between 2011 and 2014 (Smith, 2015). Over 85 percent of millennials (those born between 1977 and 1995) owned a smartphone in 2014 (Nielsen, 2014a). Wireless-only households increased from 34 percent to over 45 percent from 2011 to 2014 (Blumberg and Luke, 2015).

Mobile social media use also went up, from 8 percent in 2005 to 74 percent in 2014 (Duggan et al., 2014). These are significant changes in such short time periods.

Various reports show that the mobile environment has been closing the digital divide between minority groups, or even turning it around on its head. According to Pew Internet (Lopez, Gonzalez-Barrera, and Patten, 2013), about 86 percent of Hispanics and 90 percent of African Americans owned a cell phone in 2012, compared to 84 percent for Whites; smartphone penetration was 49 percent, 50 percent, and 46 percent respectively among the three groups. African Americans and Hispanic adults spent about 53 and 49 hours respectively on apps in 2014, more than the average app user (Nielsen, 2014b). Of these, 12 percent of African Americans and 13 percent of Latinos use a smartphone for accessing online services, compared with 4 percent of whites.

Mobile has reduced the digital divide across income categories too. Nearly 60 percent of the poor households were wireless-only in 2014, compared to 41 percent for non-poor households, suggesting the deeper reliance on wireless among poor households (Blumberg and Luke, 2015). The low-income groups depend greatly on smartphone for online access—about 13 percent of Americans from low-income households (earning less than $30,000 per year) are smartphone dependent for Internet access, compared to only 1 percent of those in the high-income bracket (earning more than $75,000 per year) (Smith, 2015). In 2014, households that rented were twice as likely than those who owned a home to be wireless-only households (66 percent vs. 33 percent respectively) (Blumberg and Luke, 2015). The greater accessibility of wireless and smartphones among low-income households raises the prospects of delivering the public location-based services through apps more broadly. Of course, the digital divide still exists in terms of age: cell phone ownership is 77 percent for seniors (of which only 18 percent own a smartphone). Tablet penetration is relatively higher among seniors (27 percent). About 27 percent of seniors use social networking sites, but these users socialize more frequently with others (Smith, 2014). The trends suggest that the accessibility of the location-based services is not restricted to an elite prosperous group.

Evolution of Location-Based Services

Location-based services have evolved rapidly over the last decade. Partly deriving from their Web 2.0 conceptualization, the O'Reilly Radar group began hosting an annual Where 2.0 conference in 2005. The conference brought together some of the major initiatives in the growth of the location-based services. The initial set of location services (until about 2007 when iPhones came on the market) were interactive online GIS maps on the computer, often accompanied with routing options for making trips (e.g., Google Maps was introduced in 2005; Google acquired Keyhole to create Google Earth in 2004). An early mashup of two distinctive services was Housing Maps (housingmaps.com), which overlaid Craigslist apartment and real estate listings onto Google Maps (Dalton, 2013). Map providers also began to allow external developers to access their geospatial platform through APIs. The spurt in social networking gave opportunities for spatial representations of the online networks through places (e.g., geotagged tweets). Although many new initiatives of mashups emerged, several of them had short life spans. For example, O'Reilly Radar's Forrest and Torkington (2008) hailed Frappr (a community mapping service) as an innovative mapping equivalent of MySpace, the leading social networking site. However, Frappr was acquired by Platial, a competitor in 2007; Platial itself ceased operations in 2010 (ironically, MySpace also has since become quite tertiary as a social networking platform).

The initial years of smartphone growth (until about 2012) were accompanied by a euphoric growth of innovative location-based services. Many startups gained quick acclaim as innovative location-based services. Such startups included Brightkite (a location-based social network using text messages or mobile app, begun in 2007), Gowalla (social network service that allowed users to check in at "spots," begun in 2007), Loopt (social-mapping service to connect with friends, started in 2005), and Yobongo (a chat service, begun in 2010). Even though they gained much fanfare, these startups also had short life spans: Brightkite merged with Limbo (another social networking site) and closed doors in 2012; Facebook acquired Gowalla in 2011; Green Dot (a financial services firm) acquired Loopt in 2012; and Mixbook, a photosharing service, acquired Yobongo in 2012. Even Google, which initiated Google Latitude in 2009 as a location-aware feature in Google Maps to allow Google users to share their location with friends, retired the feature in 2013.

Despite the initial fuzziness, a few key location-based services did survive the next phase of adolescence. A key such independent startup is Foursquare, which was launched in 2009. Foursquare popularized the concept of users to "check-in" in various locations (e.g., bars, coffee shops, grocery shops, restaurants,), which also had competitive playful features (e.g., becoming the "mayor" of the local hangout place based on the most number of check-ins). In 2014, Foursquare transformed to become a business and restaurant discovery service, giving recommendations based on users' tastes and ratings for similar places. (It spun off Swarm as a mobile app for users to check-in and meet up with friends.) Indeed, many location-based services for travel and tourism have become popular. For example, Yelp, TripAdvisor, and CitySearch provide location-specific suggestions for services based on crowdsourced ratings of the businesses (e.g., restaurants, hotels, etc.). San Francisco and New York began collaborating with Yelp in 2013 to put the health ratings of the restaurants on the mobile service; Los Angeles, Evanston, and Raleigh have also followed up to post health scores on the Yelp app (Hickey, 2015). Users can review the restaurants' health grades on the app to aid in selecting an eating place.

Location is significant for social media platforms (like Facebook, Google Plus, LinkedIn, Pinterest, Twitter, and others) too, although they are primarily oriented toward social connections and sharing information. Indeed, many popular social media platforms have elements of location-based services. Wilken (2014, pp. 1087–88) argues that the "global significance of Facebook is amplified significantly when it is conceived of as a location platform." Facebook began the Facebook Places feature as a means to discover local amenities in 2010. Twitter launched the Nearby feature in 2014 for users to see other tweets from the same area, which enables geographic-based community interest groups. Some social networking groups are geographically organized (e.g., Yik Yak, Nearby Live), focusing on the local area of the user.

The intersection of social media and location-based services offers interesting new opportunities for the individual user, commercial groups, and public agencies. Social media users gain from the place-based recommendations and services. Groupon, a discount savings coupons service, offers location-based comparative shopping in real time through the Groupon Now feature. Location information is also an important aspect of multimedia sharing sites like Yahoo's Flickr, Facebook's Instagram, Google's Panoramio, Twitter's Vine, and Pinterest's Placepins (although the last is somewhat distinctive in being a photosharing site for third-party pictures). Private businesses can provide targeted place-based advertising and marketing. Public agencies can respond to common needs for providing local services generated through social media (e.g., from Facebook comments and tweets). The location-based social media intelligence has become especially useful for public safety purposes (Crump, 2011; Grimmelikhuijsen and Meijer, 2015). Transportation agencies can also harvest social media reports in real time to give traffic conditions. The Waze app, since 2010, is such a community-based traffic and navigation app that is popular in over 100 countries (it merged with Google in 2013). Users can passively contribute traffic and other road data by driving with the app open or take a more active role by sharing incident reports (e.g., accidents, road closures, etc.) along the way. The reports are updated to report traffic conditions for other Waze users in real time.

Location-based services have enabled new means of organizing social and economic activities. The new *sharing* economy (Gansky, 2010) is essentially premised on location-based services. People living in the same geographical community can share various services, such as rides (e.g., Uber), shopping, and to obtain domestic help. The services are quite hyperlocal, often targeting at the neighborhood level. The local focus also benefits community residents to collaborate and organize events—the virtual networking enables physical community interaction. Event-based social networks such as

Eventbrite and Plancast bring together people for specific events. Hyperlocation is especially appealing for the news media, which could make the news specific to the community. For example, hyperlocal media outlets such as Patch gather and disseminate news relevant to local communities. Major newspapers also often deliver hyperlocal news tailored to the community. The explicit hyperlocal focus benefits businesses to target their advertisements to their local clientele.

Prospects of Location-Based Services for the Public Sector

As mobile location-based services have grown, they have become significant for the public sector. Citizens capitalize on them for various on-demand services, which benefit both citizens and public enterprises. From an external citizen perspective, location-based services have enabled the *anywhere, anytime* citizen engagement with public sector agencies. Public agencies can also tap on location-based services to enhance their non-emergency services to citizens. From an enterprise perspective, location-based services could potentially transform the field operations of public agencies, blurring the space between the field and back-office work. These three prospects of location-based services for public agencies are summarized below.

Anywhere, Anytime Citizen Engagement

Whereas electronic government entailed anytime access to public e-services, mobile government implies "anytime, anywhere" government services on demand at the location. Although online mechanisms through non-mobile means also allow for 24/7 Internet connections across space, the mobile difference lies in the spatial sensitivity of the context. A mobile user can engage with the immediate built surroundings (and other people in the vicinity) in new ways. The mobile device has transformed consumer behavior into a series of *intent-rich micro moments*, when "we reflexively turn to a device to act on a need we have in that moment, to learn, discover, find, or buy something" (Forrester Research, 2015). Location-based services harness real-time location information of the device to give customized personal services in the immediate vicinity. Such apps increase the scope of its use for citizens to engage with the public sector. Citizens can use the geotagged photos and social media to influence delivery of public services.

Mobile-enabled location-based services are hyperlocal, often targeting the immediate vicinity of the person. Schadler, Bernoff, and Ask (2014, p. 6) argue that there is a *mobile mind shift* in the mobile environment, in which a person expects that "I can get what I want in my immediate context and moments of need." Government services are also required on demand from public agencies, highly contextualized to the person and the location. Citizens need information on the go, affecting how public agencies deliver the information. Travelers, for example, expect transit information that is customized to the specific location in real time. Mobile transit apps need to provide accurate and timely information about the next bus or train. Unlike smartphones' *mobile* moments, wearables like watches are characterized by even briefer *glanceable* moments (Schadler, 2015). Smaller devices allow greater portability, but have limited screen space for presentation and user interaction. Wearables are used for personalized location-based activities in real time. Utah created the first app for Google Glass to send transit notification on the spot (Newcombe, 2014). Arkansas launched the first government app for the Apple Watch, epitomizing the personalized delivery of government services. Called Gov2Go, the app provides customized digital government information, allowing the user to set reminders for government transactions, such as property tax payments and vehicle registration renewals (Williams, 2015).

Mobile location-based services enable citizen engagement that is contextual to space and time. People can use the power of immediate geography to engage both *passively* and *actively*. In the passive mode, people can harness the collective intelligence available about the immediate location to make intelligent decisions. Public agencies could play an important role in channeling spatial information contextually. In the active mode, people can be proactive in reporting on events as they occur and in organizing collective action. While hyperlocal reports can assist public sector agencies in channeling their services, the collective action could also influence the public service processes.

Passive engagement is often exhibited in spatial exploration. At a simple level, the exploration is to find nearby public facilities of interest, quite similar to finding the points of interest in commercial location-based services. Users can decide on which facility to use based on the location and real-time information about the facility's other properties. The National Health Services (NHS) in the United Kingdom established a TripAdvisor-styled user feedback mechanism (NHS Choices) for patient feedback; users can review the information in their decision to choose a facility (Ramesh, 2013). Tourists can get information about local public facilities, such as parks and recreational facilities. Almost every state has an app focused on providing such information on state parks (the ParksByNature Network has developed official park guides for several states). Similar apps are also provided by local governments for guiding tourists (e.g., San Antonio Official Travel Guide), active recreation (e.g., Utah County's *Trail Guide*, Summit County's *To the Trails*), and providing information on public art and spaces (e.g., Portland's Public Art PDX).

National parks and museums in the United States often use quick response (QR) codes that can be read by mobile devices for interpretive site information, wayfinding, and audio tours. Exceptional apps combine QR codes and/or augmented reality for park visitors to enhance their park experience (Ghadirian and Bishop, 2008). The app for Camp Lawton, Georgia, is a good illustration. Visitors can scan QR codes of exhibits using a smartphone or tablet and get additional information, which include multimedia presentations, interactive tables, and external links. The QR code can also be used as a waypoint system for park navigation and to make a game out of the sites to improve the user experience (Martínez-Graña, Goy, and Cimarra, 2013). Augmented reality is a technique by which virtual reality can be overlaid on the smartphone's visual display through the camera. Thus, using the smartphone camera, visitors can get a 3D reconstruction of a view of Camp Lawton prison stockade situated in the real world (Georgia Department of Natural Resources, 2014). Lorenzi et al. (2014) illustrate how the use of mobile devices and QR codes could yield new means of government interactions with the public, including incentivizing park use by gamifying site attractions. Liao and Humphreys (2014) observe that deploying mobile augmented reality apps in the real-time location can potentially change how people interact and experience public spaces.

Active citizen engagement implies that people take on voluntary roles in engaging with the community and influence the public decision-making process. The voluntary geographic information is a form of community engagement that benefits public agencies. For example, the Federal Communications Commission's (FCC) Speed Test app automatically measures the broadband speed of the communications network at a given location, and uploads the information to the FCC for evaluating the country's broadband performance. Similarly, the NOAA's (National GeoPhysical Data Center) CrowdMag app records the magnetic field data in the background and uploads the information, so that NOAA can track the earth's changing magnetic fields. NOAA's apps empower citizens to become scientists: the Meteorological Phenomena Identification Near the Ground (mPING) allows people to submit a weather observation to the National Severe Storms Laboratory database; the Dolphin and Whale 911 app allows one to report the location of dead or stranded sea creatures. Crowdsourcing assists in generating information that the agencies could not have been able to gather by themselves. Street Bump is an innovative project of Boston's Mayor's Office of New Urban Mechanics for infrastructure maintenance. The mobile app works in the background on a smartphone to collect data about the smoothness of the car rise, using the device's accelerometer and GPS. Street bumps due to potholes or other bad road conditions are automatically recorded and uploaded to the city's server. Potholes could thus be automatically identified without the city staff having to survey the streets.

Some social networking groups are geographically organized, which could benefit the local community and public agencies. Nextdoor, for example, is an online platform that organizes neighborhoods geographically (there are over 54,000 such neighborhoods). Only verified residents within the specified neighborhood boundaries can view the Nextdoor postings. Over 750 local government agencies, such as police, public works, and utilities, provide community specific information with the online neighborhoods. Police officers can monitor spatially circumscribed social media postings to undertake proactive public safety intervention (Brunty and Helenek, 2015; Trottier and Fuchs, 2015).

Although useful, we should recognize the limits of volunteered geographic information (VGI) and geographically centered social networks. Sieber and Haklay (2015) provide a compelling critique of VGI. They argue that VGI could have problematic implications for GIScience and participatory GIS. VGI could crowd out the expert information entailed by GIScience and users would not be able to differentiate between authoritative experts and anonymous volunteers. VGI should also not be conflated with participatory GIS, as the voluntarism is distinctive from the democratic ideals of participation. The VGI apps illustrated above expand the space for citizens to be engaged with public agencies, but are carried out within the bounds of extant power relations between the agencies and citizens. Geographically centered social networking sites compete with a range of other popular social media and communications mechanisms. Privacy concerns loom large with these sites, especially due to spatial proximity. Masden et al. (2014) highlight such privacy concerns relating to Nextdoor and how the site is mainly used for doing business rather than for civic participation. We need to be cautious about making grand claims of democratization due to apps. Themistocleous et al. (2012) argue, however, that location-based services could be useful means of e-participation in public policy decision-making, especially with the active engagement enabled through the dynamic and interactive applications.

Local Government Non-Emergency Services

Location-based services have become a useful means of enhancing non-emergency services for local governments. Non-emergency services are typically organized through 311 centers, which are customer contact centers within local governments. Enabled by a 1997 Federal Communications Commission policy to reduce the volume of non-emergency calls to 911 centers, 311 centers have emerged as central organizations in several local governments in the late 1990s. Since then, 311 centers have expanded to become a hub for local services, fielding both information and service requests from residents. The requests can be made via mobile apps, social media, online chats, emails, text messages, in-person visits, and phone calls. Typically, the 311 center routes the service requests to the relevant department through a 311 customer relationship management (311/CRM) system. The 311/CRM is the central technological core of the 311 center, enabling coordination of services between different departments. It is staffed by personnel who respond to the service requests. The working hours vary across cities—from 24/7 to limited periods each day during the week. Over 300 local governments have such 311 centers. They are crucial one-stop service centers in large cities—New York City had over 28 million customer contacts through 311 in 2014.

Mobile apps have grown particularly with Open 311, which is a standardized protocol for customer service request data (Ganapati and Scutelnicu, 2015). The Open 311 protocol conforms to the Open 311 Geo Report API specification, which sets the standard for how service requests are managed and coordinated (the latest version is the Geo Report v2 specification, hosted on the Open311.org Wiki). The standard specification allows government agencies and third-party developers to interface new applications with back-end CRM systems seamlessly. A customer enters a service request using an Open 311 app, which captures the data about the service and the location. Location is the key element—since smartphones are typically equipped with GPS, the apps capture the latitude and longitude. The app then uses a geolocation service (e.g., GeoWebDNS) to obtain the API of the appropriate municipality based on the location. If the municipality's API is identified, the service request and accompanying data are sent to the municipality. Since the Open 311 API is standardized, the data forwarded to the municipality are in a consistent format. The municipal government then uses CRM at the back end to automatically route the service request to the appropriate department and to track the service request. If no municipal government supporting the Open 311 API is found, the app forwards the service request to an ad hoc site that acts as a default 311 jurisdiction. Information about the same service request could also be crowdsourced through other apps (e.g., social media) and other persons, who could be someone other than the original person making the service request.

The standard protocol allows external actors to connect online with the 311 center for submitting or retrieving service requests. Over 30 cities have adopted Open 311. Most of these local governments had call centers or CRM systems that handled service requests. Open 311 was initially begun by a consortium of seven cities—Boston, Chicago, Los Angeles, New York City, San Francisco, Seattle, and Washington, DC. Since then, Open 311 also has also been adopted by smaller cities such as Bloomington (Indiana), Grand Rapids (Michigan), Hillsborough (California), Manor (Texas), and others. Open 311 allowed the addition of another layer of communication through web or mobile apps. Some of the cities developed their own apps for obtaining 311 service requests and interfacing with 311 data. Bloomington, for example, even released the source code for their GeoReporter App (for obtaining service requests) and uReport App (a lightweight CRM tool with the Open 311 API) for use by other municipalities (Dietz, 2012).

Nonprofit organizations and private-sector vendors have assisted in the proliferation of non-emergency location-based apps. Citizen coproduction with nonprofits and private sector participation has spurred innovative ways in which the local governments, as well as other actors, engage in dealing with specific problems (Clark, Brudney, and Jang, 2013; Eggers and Macmillan, 2013; Fountain, 2015). Nonprofits have been instrumental for the cities to overcome technical barriers. Code for America assisted municipalities—such as New York, San Francisco, Baltimore, Chicago, Boston, Albuquerque, New Mexico, and Asheville—in implementing the Open 311 standard and the tools. The Code for America formed the 311 Labs to encourage collaboration and experimentation with Open 311 applications. Open Plans, another New York–based nonprofit, supported the creation of the open311 website, and hosted the final Open Geo Report v2 specification.

Many private firms have also emerged to provide 311 services through their web and mobile apps. In 2009, SeeClickFix was the first entrant into the field in the United States (based in New Haven, Connecticut), which was also instrumental in shaping the Open 311 API. It contracts with over 290 cities for using the mobile app to submit service requests. The requests are routed to appropriate local government officials who receive the alerts and can track the service requests through a tool called "Watch Area." The SeeClickFix service is integrated with social media (Twitter and Facebook) and is also used by many hyperlocal nonprofits and newspapers.

Besides SeeClickFix, several other firms provide similar real-time mobile civic engagement platforms; they include CitySourced, Connected Bits, Fix311, and Accela's PublicStuff. Private vendors have contractual arrangements with cities that do not necessarily have 311 centers to make the online service requests. In this manner, Accela's PublicStuff serves about 200 cities; CitySourced about 100 cities. These platforms allow citizens to report civic issues and track them in real time. While most of the software platforms allow submitting photographs, some also allow submitting multimedia (e.g., video recordings) with the service requests. They also offer opportunities for local governments to integrate the service request reports with the city's back-end CRM systems to route the requests to the appropriate department or official. Several vendors provide hosted CRM solutions that support Open 311 (e.g., Kana's Lagan), which means that the local government does not need to host the back-end CRM system internally. The spurt in private firms providing civic engagement services is illustrative of the great potential for location-based services in transforming non-emergency public services.

Public Enterprise Field Operations

Location-based services hold good potential for transforming internal enterprise operations, particularly with respect to field activities that are distributed across many locations. Mobile apps give a means of spatial coordination and collaboration among the organization's employees. Although in their nascent stages of growth, mobile enterprise apps promise to be the next frontier for organizational process and productivity improvements. The enterprise apps act as an interface to access the organization's proprietary (and secure) data and content information from disparate locations, allowing employees in the field to access data on the go from their mobile devices and to report information from the site on the fly. The apps could thus lead to productivity improvements in field operations. They can have a transformative impact on public agencies that require time-sensitive field interventions, such as disaster management, code enforcement, transit and traffic management, public works, and law enforcement (Malhotra et al., 2013; Pritchard et al., 2014; Quercia and Saez, 2014; Ricker, Daniel, and Hedley, 2014; Turner and Forrest, 2008). Enterprise apps are lucrative growth industries in the private sector as well, as businesses are adopting them for productivity gains, especially among the salesforce (Columbus, 2015; Kerschberg, 2015).

Enterprise apps are task oriented, for solving specific issues. They are often native apps installed on the mobile device, since employees would use them often to conduct their chores. Native apps also allow employees to work offline. While generic commercial off-the-shelf solutions may be available for addressing the task, native apps assist in addressing tasks that are organization specific. Often, internal hackathons and agile teams of software developers and operational teams assist in creating enterprise apps that are customized to the organizational tasks. The organizational leaders can provide a supportive environment for the collaborative approach. The hackathons are also supported by social enterprises such as Code for America, MindMixer (now mySidewalk), Open Knowedge Foundation, and so on.

Enterprise apps building on location-based services could enhance organizational productivity in several ways. First, the apps can aid in managing mobile assets. In transit agencies, the apps can assist in managing the vehicular fleet, deploying and routing them in real time with greater flexibility. Remote sensor technologies to evaluate the conditions of the vehicle would provide cost savings for repair and maintenance of the fleet. Mobile apps benefit vehicle fleet management, assisting both drivers and fleet managers (Ziadeh, 2014). The U.S. Department of State as well as the General Services Administration (GSA) have developed apps that allow flexible use of the vehicles. The State Department's Integrated Logistics Management System (ILMS) tracks the department's fleet of 14,000 vehicles spread over 176 countries. Employees can use the Mobile Driver app to record trip information, review assigned trips, and manage reassignments and transfers in real time. They do not have to carry a clipboard or do additional paperwork. The app also improves fleet management data quality. The GSA's FMS2GO app extends the agency's Fleet Management System (FMS) capacity, which manages over 200,000 vehicles in real time. FMS2GO connects with the FMS database using an application programming interface. The app facilitates drivers to manage and record their inventory on site and at delivery locations, thus improving the supply chain management.

Second, enterprise apps assist in increasing the productivity of employees, allowing employees to work from anywhere, anytime behind secure firewalls. Routine and simple human resource tasks that require cursory examination (e.g., some of the approval processes in payroll and benefits transactions) are amenable to being performed on the mobile devices on the go. The Food and Drug Administration's (FDA) Field Investigator Tool with Mapping (FITMAP) pilot app, for example, allows FDA inspectors to report directly from the farm through Personal Identification Verification (PIV)–enabled Windows mobile devices, with photos, site documents, and geocoded data about the location of the product (Otto, 2014). It is aimed toward reducing the occurrence of foodborne illnesses warranted under the Food Safety Modernization Act (FSMA) enacted in 2011 (Cheeseman and Trujillo, 2014).

The FSMA prescribed a proactive early warning system for preventing foodborne outbreaks, such as the 2006 *E. coli* outbreak due to spinach contamination and the 2011 *Listeria monocytogenes* outbreak due to cantaloupes. The tool can be utilized for survey, inspection, and/or tracking of any FDA regulatory investigation information. The data enable FDA to monitor food products from across the country in real time. The app can support predictive analytics for proactive interventions across the agency. The app received the Best Business Investment Award in the 2015 Mobile Application Fair hosted by the American Council for Technology and Industry Advisory Council (ACT-IAC) (https://actiac.org/custom-links/14853/69677/70998).

Third, the transformational use of location-based services is in reengineering field processes, such that there is greater degree of integration between line workers in the field and back-office workers. These enterprise apps provide opportunities for collaboration and networking between the field offices of a public agency. Employees working on the same issue at different branches use the same enterprise app—the app can assist the employees in getting the information in real time on the field, which can be helpful especially in emergency management and law enforcement. Enterprise apps are crucial for field workers to reduce their administrative onus. Typically, employees would need to return to their home office to file field reports on their activities (e.g., case management workers, law enforcement officers, and surveyors). Enterprise apps allow the employees to file their data and reports directly from the field, reducing the additional time spent on back-office work. Even if a broadband network connection is not available in the field to enable such direct filings, native apps can synchronize the data once the connection is available. Such direct filing does not only increase efficiency, but also increases data integrity and quality. Field case management, road and rail infrastructure maintenance, and supply chain management are all areas that have potential efficiency gains with the mobile location-based services. The Pennsylvania Department of Transportation's (PennDOT) Posted and Bonded Road (PBR) mobile application provides an illustration. Timely survey and audits of the posted and bonded roads are required for their timely repair and maintenance. The mobile process replaced manual paper-based reports, reducing the field workers' administrative duties. The PBR app allows workers to record road conditions with pictures and upload them. The electronic process also reduced intervening human errors, increasing survey data quality. The data are uploaded and available in real time over wireless broadband (if not available, the data are synchronized with the PennDOT database later when a connection is available).

Challenges of Location-Based Services

Although location-based service apps hold several prospects, they also pose several challenges for public agencies. The principal challenge is that of privacy and security in the mobile environment. Individual privacy is a major concern. For example, map and navigation apps on mobile devices collect location data to provide consumers with location-based services (e.g., car companies collect location data to provide turn-by-turn directions, which could also be shared with traffic information providers). While the consumers benefit from the services, the information sharing could also compromise individual privacy (Cheung, 2014). Consumer tracking, identity theft, threats to personal safety, and surveillance are potential problems. Adequate safeguards need to be in place for protecting privacy (Government Accountability Office, 2012, 2014). The Geolocational Privacy and Surveillance Act (GPS Act), which is under consideration with the U.S. Congress, prohibits intercepting geolocation information pertaining to another person, disclosing such location information without the knowledge of the person, and using such geolocation information in courts of law. The Location Privacy Protection Act is another bill under consideration that would prohibit firms from collecting or disclosing geolocation information from an electronic device without the user's consent (with exceptions for emergency services, law enforcement, and parents to track their children). The bill would also prohibit stalking apps in order to prevent geolocation-enabled violence against women.

Moreover, wireless devices and communications face additional security vulnerabilities that are not inherent to wired communications. As public agencies are repositories of sensitive public data, any security breach poses high risks. Mobile apps are subject to the same set of security concerns as those of other online connections. Vulnerable coding of mobile apps, accessing sensitive data over insecure wireless connections, and lost mobile devices could compromise enterprise security. Mobile apps need to be vetted and the devices need to be subject to enterprise security measures. Mobile devices manufactured by different vendors also pose interoperability challenges, both from technical and organizational perspectives. Mobile device and app management (MDAM) becomes a priority for implementing the "bring your own devices" (byod) schemes in order to accommodate the different devices, their software platforms, and the mobile apps.

Moreover, on-demand location-based services are enabling a new form of sharing economy. Such an economy creates new opportunities, but is also disruptive. Public agencies need to contend with the organizational impact of the sharing economy, and how similar apps could be leveraged for delivery of public services. Consumers engage with each other in the neighborhood directly (Botsman and Rogers, 2010; Fowler, 2015; Gansky, 2010). Prime examples of such a sharing economy are Uber and Lyft, which are platforms that allow riders and drivers to connect. A person requiring a ride makes the request through an app; the request is routed to a nearby willing Uber or Lyft driver, who then provides the ride. Similar types of location-specific on-demand services have arisen across a range of other economic activities: for ordering food delivery from local restaurants (e.g., DoorDash, GrubHub, Sidecar, SpoonRocket); for getting assistance with daily chores such as cleaning, handyman jobs, shopping, and delivery (e.g., Clutter, Instacart, Postmates, TaskRabbit); for peer-to-peer car rental (e.g., Getaround); for tourists to book accommodations (e.g., homes or apartments) from independent hosts (e.g., Airbnb, Couchsurfing, Homeaway); and for experiencing the local culture through independent insiders (e.g., Vayable) at the destination.

The sharing economy opens new economic arrangements, but is also disruptive in affecting existing arrangements. Many localities have restricted Uber and Lyft from participating in their jurisdictions, mainly under pressure from taxi driver unions. Legitimate concerns also exist regarding private surveillance, insurance of life and property, and whether or not the drivers are to be considered as employees (Hill, 2014; Michael and Clarke, 2013). Local communities have also rallied against Airbnb bookings in their neighborhood. Regulations over the sharing economy are still emerging and are quite controversial. Yet, a few transit agencies have also accommodated the sharing economy. The GoPass mobile app used by Dallas-area transit agencies is an illustration. Commuters pay for the transit fare using the app. In addition to the ticketing, the app also offers additional location-based services for planning trips using Google Transit for checking real-time bus and train arrivals. Recently, GoPass also integrated Uber with the app, so that travelers can arrange motorized transport for the first or the last mile on demand (Wilonsky, 2015). The mobile transit ticketing is an interesting illustration of a public app used in conjunction with the sharing economy, which benefits both the customer and the public agency.

Conclusion

With the exponential growth of mobile devices (phones as well as wearables), location-based services are quite significant for the public sector, both for external citizen engagement and internal organizational management. From an external citizen engagement perspective, mobile apps provide the space for citizens to be proactively engaged in the provision of services. In local governments, 311 apps allow citizens to report non-emergency physical problems in the vicinity. The information is relayed to the relevant public agency directly, without the need for the citizen having to know which agency to contact.

From an internal organizational management perspective, location-based services could potentially transform the field operations of public agencies that provide services on demand. Agencies can deploy their field workers efficiently based on real-time neighborhood need, improving their speed and response time. At the base level, mobile apps significantly reduce paperwork and back-office time that employees otherwise need for reporting their field operations. At a more advanced level, these mobile apps blur the space between field operations and back-office work.

Location-based services are, however, not without their challenges. Location awareness comes with security issues and snooping through unauthorized access. It could infringe on a citizen's rightful expectation of privacy. Stalking is a potential threat that could put citizens in harm's way. Location-based services are also a disruptive phenomenon—the technology has contributed to a new sharing economy that has been quite controversial across cities. Regulations overseeing locational privacy and work in the new sharing economy are emerging as a result.

Despite the challenges, public sector agencies will need to contend with the rapid evolution of location-based services, as smart mobile technologies are not only getting more popular, but also more sophisticated, with greater demands for instantaneous services on location. Overall, location-based services could be argued to be a significant element of the "smart" city, bridging the public sector and citizens. In this respect, mobile apps signify a coproduction of citizen services with distinctive roles of public agencies and citizen groups. Public agencies are extensive data repositories, as they routinely collect data, which are generally in the public domain. The data should be openly and reliably available through APIs to the public. Private citizen groups can access the data (perhaps in conjunction with social media) to jumpstart a range of value-added local services required by a mobile user at the hyperlocation in real time. The need for such on-demand, on-location services is already being exhibited in several areas, such as tourism, traffic and transportation, geographical social networking, parks and recreation, and so on. Location-based services also hold good promise for enterprise apps that are oriented toward increasing organizational productivity, coordination, and collaboration between employees who are placed in different locations and need to be in the field. Such enterprise apps allow field workers to carry out their field tasks with the mobile devices, without the need to duplicate their reports in the back office. Public agencies with field operations could take advantage of location-based services for increasing their efficiency.

References

Blumberg, S.J., and J.V. Luke. (2015). 'Wireless substitution: Early release of estimates from the National Health Interview Survey'. July–December 2014. National Center for Health Statistics. June 2015. Retrieved from http://www.cdc.gov/nchs/nhis.htm

Botsman, R., and R. Rogers. (2010). *What's mine is yours: The rise of collaborative consumption*. New York: HarperCollins.

Brunty, J., and K. Helenek. (2015). *Social media investigation for law enforcement*. New York: Routledge.

Cheeseman, K., and S. Trujillo. (2014). 'Developing FDA's field investigator tool with mapping (FIT-Map) prototype'. ESRI User Conference Proceedings, San Diego. Retrieved from http://proceedings.esri.com/library/userconf/proc14/papers/181_17.pdf

Cheung, A.S.Y. (2014). 'Location privacy: The challenges of mobile service devices'. *Computer Law & Security Review* 30 (1): 41–54.

CISCO. (2015). 'Cisco visual networking index: Global mobile data traffic forecast update, 2014–2019'. CISCO White Paper. Retrieved from http://www.cisco.com/c/en/us/solutions/collateral/service-provider/visual-networking-index-vni/white_paper_c11–520862.html

Clark, B.Y., J.L. Brudney, and S.G. Jang. (2013). 'Coproduction of government services and the new information technology: Investigating the distributional biases'. *Public Administration Review* 73 (5): 687–701.

Columbus, L. (2015, February 22). 'Why enterprise mobile apps are most lucrative to build in 2015'. *Forbes*. Retrieved from http://www.forbes.com/sites/louiscolumbus/2015/02/22/why-enterprise-mobile-apps-are-most-lucrative-to-build-in-2015

Crump, J. (2011). 'What are the police doing on Twitter? Social media, the police and the public'. *Policy & Internet* 3 (4): 1–27.

Dahlman, E., S. Parkvall, and J. Skold. (2014). *4G: LTE/LTE-Advanced for mobile broadband*, 2nd ed. Waltham, MA and Oxford: Academic Press.

Dalton, C.M. (2013). 'Sovereigns, spooks, and hackers: An early history of google geo services and map mashups'. *Cartographica: The International Journal for Geographic Information and Geovisualization* 48 (4): 261–274.

Dietz, R. (2012). 'City of Bloomington releases open source GeoReporter and uReport tools for open311'. City of Bloomington Press Release. Retrieved from http://bloomington.in.gov/documents/viewDocument.php?document_id=6515

Duggan, M. et al. (2014). 'Social media update 2014'. Pew Research Center. Retrieved from http://www.pewInternet.org/2015/01/09/social-media-update-2014/

Eggers, B., and P. MacMillan (2013). *The solution revolution: How business, government, and social enterprises are teaming up to solve society's toughest problems*. Cambridge, MA: Harvard Business Review Press.

FCC (Federal Communications Commission). (2014). 'Use of spectrum bands above 24 GHz for mobile radio services'. GN Docket No. 14–177. Retrieved from https://www.fcc.gov/document/noi-examine-use-bands-above-24-ghz-mobile-broadband

Forrest, B., and N. Torkington. (2008). 'The state of where 2.0'. O'Reilly Media Inc. Retrieved from http://whereconf.com/where2008/public/content/about

Forrester Research, Inc. (2015). 'Moments that matter: Intent-rich moments are critical to winning today's consumer journey'. Retrieved from https://storage.googleapis.com/think/docs/forrester-moments-that-matter-research-study.pdf

Fountain, J.E. (2015). 'Connecting technologies to citizenship', In *Technology and the resilience of metropolitan regions*, edited by M. Pagano, 25–50. Chicago: University of Illinois Press.

Fowler, G.A. (2015, May). 'There's an Uber for everything now'. *The Wall Street Journal*. Retrieved from http://www.wsj.com/articles/theres-an-uber-for-everything-now-1430845789

Fu, P. (2015). 'Getting to know Web GIS'. ESRI Press, Redlands.

Ganapati, S. (2011). 'Uses of public participation geographic information systems applications in e-government'. *Public Administration Review* 71 (3): 425–434.

Ganapati, S., and G. Scutelnicu. (2015). 'Open innovation in the public sector: The case of open 311', In *Innovation in the Public and Nonprofit Sectors: A Public Solutions Handbook*, edited by P. Lancer and E. Gibson, 74–90. New York: Routledge.

Gansky, L. (2010). *The mesh: Why the future of business is sharing*. New York: Portfolio Penguin.

Georgia Department of Natural Resources. (2014). 'Camp Lawton augmented reality'. NASCIO 2015 State IT Recognition Awards. Retrieved from http://www.nascio.org/awards/nominations2015/2015/2015GA3-NASCIO Submission, Georgia Department of Natural Resources, Camp Lawton Augmented Reality.pdf

Ghadirian, P., and I.D. Bishop. (2008). 'Integration of augmented reality and GIS: A new approach to realistic landscape visualization'. *Landscape and Urban Planning* 86 (3–4): 226–232.

Goodchild, M.F. (2007). 'Citizens as sensors: The world of volunteered geography'. *GeoJournal* 69 (4): 211–221.

Government Accountability Office (2014). 'Consumers' location data: Companies take steps to protect privacy, but practices are inconsistent, and risks may not be clear to consumers'. GAO report no. GAO- GAO-14-649T. Retrieved from http://www.gao.gov/products/GAO-14-649T

Government Accountability Office (2012). 'Mobile device location data: Additional federal actions could help protect consumer privacy'. GAO report no. GAO-12-903. Retrieved from http://www.gao.gov/products/GAO-12-903

Graham, M., M. Zook, and A. Boulton. (2013). 'Augmented reality in urban places: Contested content and the duplicity of code'. *Transactions of the Institute of British Geographers* 38 (3): 464–479.

Grimmelikhuijsen, S.G., and A. J. Meijer. (2015). 'Does Twitter increase perceived police legitimacy?' *Public Administration Review* 75 (4): 598–607.

Hickey, K. (2015, March). Cities tap Yelp to improve health inspection process. *GCN*. Retrieved from http://gcn.com/articles/2015/03/02/yelp-city-restaurant-inspections.aspx

Hill, K. (2014, November). 'God view: Uber allegedly stalked users for party-goers viewing pleasure'. (Updated). Retrieved from http://www.forbes.com/sites/kashmirhill/2014/10/03/god-view-uber-allegedly-stalked-users-for-party-goers-viewing-pleasure/

Kerschberg, B. (2015, January 15). 'Four critical reasons to build enterprise apps'. *Forbes*. Retrieved from http://www.forbes.com/sites/benkerschberg/2015/01/15/four-critical-reasons-to-build-enterprise-apps/

Korhonen, J. (2003). *Introduction to 3G mobile communications*. Norwood, MA: Artech House Inc.

Lake, R., and J. Farley. (2007). 'Infrastructure for the geospatial web'. In *The geospatial web: How geobrowsers, social software and the web 2.0 are shaping the network society*, edited by Scharl and Arno, 15–26. London: Springer-Verlag.

Liao, T., and L. Humphreys. (2015). 'Layar-ed places: Using mobile augmented reality to tactically reengage, reproduce, and reappropriate public space'. *New Media & Society* 17 (9): 1418–1435.

Lin, P.J., S.C. Chen, Y.H. Li, M.S. Wu, and S.Y. Chen. (2014). 'An implementation of augmented reality and location awareness services in mobile devices'. In *Mobile, ubiquitous, and intelligent computing*, edited by J. Park, H. Adeli, N. Park, and I. Woungang, 509–514. Lecture Notes in Electrical Engineering, Volume 274. Heidelberg: Springer:.

Lopez, M.H., A. Gonzalez-Barrera, and E. Patten. (2013). 'Closing the digital divide: Latinos and technology adoption'. Pew Hispanic Research Center. Retrieved from http://www.pewhispanic.org/2013/03/07/closing-the-digital-divide-latinos-and-technology-adoption/

Lorenzi, D., J. Vaidya, S. Chun, B. Shafiq, and V. Atluri. (2014). 'Enhancing the government service experience through QR codes on mobile platforms'. *Government Information Quarterly* 31 (1): 6–16.

Malhotra, R., G. Virk, F. Nwoko, and A. Klepper. (2013). 'Web-based geospatial technology tools for metropolitan planning organizations'. *Southeastern Geographer* 53 (3): 296–309.

Martínez-Graña, A.M., J.L. Goy, and C.A. Cimarra. (2013). 'A virtual tour of geological heritage: Valourising geodiversity using Google Earth and QR code'. *Computers & Geosciences* 61: 83–93.

Masden, C., C. Grevet, R. Grinter, E. Gilbert, and W.K. Edwards. (2014). 'Tensions in scaling-up community social media: A multi-neighborhood study of nextdoor'. Proceedings of the SIGCHI Conference on Human Factors in Computing Systems, 3239–3248. ACM, New York.

Michael, K., and R. Clarke. (2013). 'Location and tracking of mobile devices: Überveillance stalks the streets'. *Computer Law & Security Review* 29 (3): 216–228.

Nielsen. (2014a, September). 'Mobile millennials: Over 85% of generation Y owns smartphones'. Nielsen Newswire. Retrieved from http://www.nielsen.com/us/en/insights/news/2014/mobile-millennials-over-85-percent-of-generation-y-owns-smartphones.html

Nielsen. (2014b, October). 'Tech-ortreat: Consumers are sweet on mobile apps'. Nielsen Newswire. Retrieved from http://www.nielsen.com/us/en/insights/news/2014/tech-or-treat-consumers-are-sweet-on-mobile-apps.html

Newcombe, T. (2014). 'Utah leading the mobile-friendly government movement'. *Government Technology*. Retrieved from http://www.govtech.com/state/Utah-Leading-the-Mobile-Friendly-Government-Movement.html

Otto, G. (2014). '3 innovative ways agencies are leveraging mobile apps'. Fedscoop. Retrieved from http://fedscoop.com/great-government-mobile-apps/

Pritchard, G., J. Vines, P. Briggs, L. Thomas, and P. Olivier. (2014). 'Digitally driven: How location based services impact on the work practices of London bus drivers'. CHI '14 Proceedings of the SIGCHI Conference on Human Factors in Computing Systems, pp. 3617–3626. Retrieved from http://dl.acm.org/citation.cfm?id=2557156

Quercia, D., and D. Saez. (2014). 'Mining urban deprivation from foursquare: Implicit crowdsourcing of city land use'. *Pervasive Computing, IEEE* 13 (2): 30–36.

Ramesh, R. (2013, November 27). 'NHS to launch Tripadvisor-style website'. *The Guardian*. Retrieved from http://www.theguardian.com/society/2013/nov/28/nhs-launch-tripadvisor-style-website.

Ricker, B., S. Daniel, and N. Hedley. (2014). 'Fuzzy boundaries: Hybridizing location-based services, volunteered geographic information and geovisualization literature'. *Geography Compass* 8: 490–504. doi: 10.1111/gec3.12138

Schadler, T. (2015). 'Apple watch—bliss or bling? Glanceable moments will decide'. Ted Schadler's Blog, Forrester. Retrieved from http://blogs.forrester.com/ted_schadler/15-04-24-apple_watch_bliss_or_bling_glanceable_moments_will_decide

Schadler, T., J. Bernoff, and J. Ask. (2014). *The mobile mind shift: Engineer your business to win in the mobile moment*. Cambridge: Groundswell Press.

Scharl, A., ed. (2007). *The geospatial web: How geobrowsers, social software and the web 2.0 are shaping the network society*. London: Springer-Verlag.

Sieber, R., and M. Haklay. (2015). 'The epistemology(s) of volunteered geographic information: A critique'. *Geo: Geography and Environment* 2: 122–136. doi: 10.1002/geo2.10

Smith, A. (2014). 'Older adults and technology use'. Pew Research Center. Retrieved from http://www.pewInternet.org/2014/04/03/older-adults-and-technology-use/

Smith, A. (2015). 'U.S. smartphone use in 2015'. Pew Research Center. Retrieved from http://www.pewInternet.org/files/2015/03/PI_Smartphones_0401151.pdf

Themistocleous, M., N.A. Azab, M.M. Kamal, M. Ali, and V. Morabito. (2012). 'Location-based services for public policy making: The direct and indirect way to e-participation'. *Information Systems Management* 29 (4): 269–283. doi: 10.1080/10580530.2012.716743

Trottier, D., and C. Fuchs. (2015). *Social media, politics and the state: Protests, revolutions, riots, crime and policing in the age of Facebook, Twitter, and Youtube.* New York: Routledge.

Turner, A., and B. Forrest. (2008). *Where 2.0: The state of the geospatial web.* O'Reilly Sebastopol, CA: Radar Report.

Wilken, R. (2014). 'Places nearby: Facebook as a location-based social media platform'. *New Media & Society* 16 (7): 1087–1103.

Williams, J. (2015, May 14). 'Arkansas launches first state government apple watch app'. *Statescoop.* Retrieved from http://statescoop.com/arkansas-launches-first-state-government-apple-watch-app/

Wilonsky, R. (2015, April 14). 'Dallas area rapid transit, uber partner in an effort to fill in riders' 'first mile-last mile' gap'. *The Dallas Morning News (Transportation Blog).* Retrieved from http://transportationblog.dallasnews.com/2015/04/dallas-area-rapid-transit-uber-partner-in-an-effort-to-fill-in-riders-first-mile-last-mile-gap.html/

Ziadeh, A. (2014). 'Mobile apps drive fleet management'. *GCN.* Retrieved from http://gcn.com/articles/2015/07/06/fleet-management-apps.aspx

Zickuhr, K. (2013). 'Location-based services'. Pew Research Center. Retrieved from http://pewInternet.org/Reports/2013/Location.aspx

8

INTERNET OF THINGS FOR PUBLIC SERVICE

Innovative Practices in China

Jian-Chuan Zhang, Xiao Zhang, and Zhicheng Wang

Introduction

As a result of the fast-growing urbanization process, city governments around the world have been faced with a series of critical governance challenges in such areas as traffic, healthcare, public security, and environment protection. Information and communication technologies (ICT) have long been playing a crucial role in enabling government to resolve urban problems. For instance, a new ICT-enabled initiative called "smart city" has become increasingly prominent due to the expectation of its capacity in addressing urban governance challenges. However, the concept of smart city features a very broad scope. From a technical infrastructure point of view, the goals of smart city initiatives can be achieved by a variety of platforms. For instance, web technologies, including interactive Web 2.0, could serve as such a platform. Currently, people might have become more accustomed to applications (apps). Apps and many other new technical components entail the latest technical platform—Internet of Things (IoT).

IoT represents one of a set of evolutionary advances in information and communication technologies: mobile/wireless communication, big data, cloud computing, and instant collaboration with anyone, anywhere. It is one of the emerging technology trends measured by Gartner's IT Hype Cycle (Gartner 2014). Like many other emerging phenomena, there is no widely accepted definition of IoT. However, it is generally agreed that IoT envisions a near future in which a huge number of different and heterogeneous end systems are connected transparently and seamlessly (Zanella et al. 2014; Shark 2015). The interconnected "things" have enormous potential to transform the current static Internet into a fully integrated dynamic Internet (Gubbia et al. 2013).

When an increasing number of things is connected, governments at all levels will eventually find themselves confronted with great challenges in reaching out to and serving citizens. For instance, public managers might be bombarded with information and/or data overload from both citizens and various sensors. The private sector faces the same challenge, but it was reported that the private sector was leading the way in IoT deployment, while the public sector fell behind (Gartner 2015). Leading IT companies such as AT&T, Cisco, IBM, Intel, and General Electric created the Industrial Internet Consortium in early 2014, a collaborative IoT initiative to further development, adoption, and widespread use of "interconnected machines, intelligent analytics, and people at work" (Industrial Internet Consortium 2014).

In the meantime, experts believe that IoT holds considerable promise for the public sector, in that IoT will significantly impact the way government provides public services and engages citizens (Cisco

2013; Pew Research Center 2014; FTC 2015). Unfortunately, the impact of IoT on public service delivery has not been studied sufficiently in the literature of public administration. This study aims to fill the gap by examining how city governments utilize IoT to address urban governance challenges. Since IoT-enabled public service delivery is still in its early stage of development, this study is by nature a preliminary case study. Four real-world cases are all drawn from Chinese practice.

The remainder of this chapter is organized as follows. In the first section, we briefly review previous studies to form a better understanding of the concept of IoT in general and public sector IoT in particular. In the second section, we propose a typology of IoT-enabled public service delivery from a public-value perspective. The typology delineates a framework for conceptualizing the impact of IoT on the innovative practice of urban problem solving. In the third section, we provide four Chinese cases that match each type as proposed in the second section. Finally, we present the concluding remarks in the last section.

Defining Internet of Things

Around 2009, for the first time in history, the number of "things" connected to the Internet surpassed the number of people (FTC 2015). It was estimated that over 25 billion devices would be connected to the Internet by 2015 and 50–75 billion by 2020 (Evans 2011; Proffitt 2013). IoT was believed to represent a paradigm shift of communication from human-to-human and human-to-machine communication to machine-to-machine communication without human intervention. Although IoT has been increasingly deployed in the public sector to address public problems (Cisco 2013, 2014; Pew Research Center 2014), there was little discussion on this topic in the literature of public administration. The IoT studies were more commonly found in such research fields as telecommunication and electronic engineering, where IoT was primarily discussed as a concept driven by technological advances rather than by applications or user needs (Perera et al. 2014).

Semantically, "Internet of Things" is composed of two words and concepts: "Internet" and "Things." Internet generally refers to the worldwide network of interconnected computer networks, based on a standard communication protocol, the Internet suite (TCP/IP), while the definition of "Things" has changed as technologies evolve. "Thing" could be an RFID tag, a sensor, an actuator, any device ranging from embedded devices to cloud computing devices (Pew Research Center 2014), and even "everything," like Cisco (2013) has proposed. Therefore, IoT could be literally understood as a worldwide network of interconnected objects that are uniquely addressable with standard communication protocols.

However, back to 1999 when the term IoT was originally coined by Kevin Ashton in the context of supply chain management (Ashton 2009), it essentially referred to a network of Electronic Product Code (EPC), by which the Internet was connected to the physical world via the RFID tags attached to products. In 2005, the International Telecommunication Union (ITU) published a report on IoT, in which IoT was defined as a vision "to connect everyday objects and devices to large databases and networks . . . [using] a simple, unobtrusive and cost-effective system of item identification" (ITU 2005, 9). From ITU's perspective, IoT goes far beyond RFID technologies that simply tag things, but instead includes sensor technologies feeling things, smart technologies thinking things, and nanotechnologies minimizing things. In addition, besides the EPC network, IoT was considered more closely associated with wireless sensor network (WSN) technologies.

In a joint research report about IoT in 2020, the Information Society and Media Directorate-General of the European Commission (DG INFSO) and the European Technology Platform on Smart Systems Integration (EPoSS) considered IoT from two different perspectives. If functionality and identity are made central, IoT indicates "things having identities and virtual personalities operating in smart spaces using intelligent interfaces to connect and communicate within social, environmental, and user contexts" (DG INFSO and EPoSS 2008, 6). By contrast, if the focus is placed on seamless integration, it stands for "interconnected objects having an active role in what might be called the Future Internet" (DG INFSO and EPoSS 2008, 6). There were two points worth noting in these two definitions. First, they emphasized the smartness of IoT by introducing intelligent interfaces and smart spaces. This understanding is critical in that sensors can only collect data from the environment, while intelligent interfaces are capable of generating information and awareness about their context. Second, they moved forward from identification to real-time communication (sense and response) in the social context.

Responsible for outlining EU's IoT strategic research and innovation agenda, the European Research Cluster on the Internet of Things (IERC) defined IoT as a "dynamic global network infrastructure with self-configuring capabilities based on standard and interoperable communication protocols where physical and virtual 'things' have identities, physical attribute, and virtual personalities and use intelligent interfaces, and are seamlessly integrated into the information network" (Vermesan et al. 2014, 16). This definition underscored two features of IoT. One was "dynamic," meaning that the quantity and places of the things change constantly. Another was "seamless integration." The fully integrated physical and virtual things with the information network might provide public managers with a fuller picture of the events to which they respond.

When the scope of "things" kept expanding, Cisco replaced "things" with "everything," and thus formulated a term—"Internet of Everything" or IoE. With this slightly different term, IoT was conceived as "the networked connection of people, process, data, and things" (Cisco 2013, 1), which has the ability to extract and analyze growing amounts of data, and then to use that analysis in automated and people-based processes. As a whole, Cisco's definition posited an environment of ubiquitous sensing and connecting. In addition, it identified the gap between the sensory data and meaningful information or actionable knowledge. As illustrated by Rowley (2007) in the well-known "wisdom hierarchy," only knowledge can provide people with a better understanding of the physical world surrounding them and create more value-added services. Therefore, connection is simply the first step. The subsequent data collection and information processing are more important for actions.

Previous discussions indicate that the definition of the term IoT is still somehow fuzzy, depending on the perspectives taken. For instance, a popular technology-centric perspective will focus on hardware, middleware, visualization tools, and various technologies with respect to identifier, network standards, and protocols (Gubbia et al. 2013). By contrast, a public service-oriented perspective will be more concerned about the people and processes that IoT projects are applied to. In addition, it focuses on the differences that IoT will make in public service delivery from other traditional ICTs. Therefore, this study adopts the definition of IoT by Cisco (2013). In addition to a concise definition, we believe that a summary of the unique features of IoT might be more helpful for a better understanding of how public administrators could utilize IoT in an innovative way. After all, all governments today face a similar dilemma: provide more and better public services with more severe budget constraints.

Table 8.1 summaries the four critical features that matter for public managers from a public service point of view. First, from a time point of view, IoT is able to provide real-time information on a 7×24×365 basis. Second, from a space point of view, IoT can produce information from both the physical and virtual world, as well as from both the natural and social environment. Third, quantitatively, information generated by IoT is in unprecedented high volume. Fourth, qualitatively, IoT enables seamlessly integrated information. These features lead to an understanding that IoT is synonymous with a wide range of "smart" systems: smart homes, smart traffic, smart police, smart health care, smart cities, and so on (Thierer 2014). Moreover, these unique features offer greater opportunities for public managers to solve the problems that seem impossible to be solved in the traditional way. For example, effective cross-department integration means that IoT could serve as a catalyst for breaking down organizational silos—a long-standing problem among public sector organizations.

Table 8.1 Unique Features of IoT

Perspective	Critical Features
Time	Real-time and 7x24x365
Space	Data come from both physical and virtual world; from both natural and social environment
Quantity	Massive data
Quality	Seamlessly integrated information

Typology of IoT-Driven Public Values

IoT advocates believe that utilization of IoT could produce various benefits at different levels. At the global level, ITU (2005) claimed that the converging platform of IoT could serve as effective and efficient tools for developing countries in ensuring their inclusion on the international stage. In addition, new technologies of IoT meant better health, greater opportunities, extended access, and improved possibilities for international trade. At the national level, analysts and consultancies have predicted the overall growth and economic impacts of the IoT applications on a nation or the major industries in this nation (Manyika et al. 2013). Take the United States as an example. IoT has the largest economic impact on health care and manufacturing industries (Thierer 2014). At the city level, the prospected benefits of IoT were more closely related to the concept of the smart city (Schaffers et al. 2011; Mulligan and Olsson 2013; Vlacheas et al. 2013; Perera et al. 2014; Zanella et al. 2014). In these discussions, IoT was generally thought as a technical solution to unleash the potential of the smart city vision, including the delivery of public services. It is worth mentioning, however, that the current IoT-based public sector programs were characterized by a high degree of sponsorship and encouragement by national or international governments (IDC Government Insights 2013).

Despite the national or international backup, cities will be the primary beneficiaries of IoT's total public-sector benefits over the next 10 years (Cisco 2013). A popular theme in the discussions on IoT at the city level was to identify the broad spectrum of public service in which IoT was or should be utilized. Based on that, some tangible benefits such as cost saving were calculated or estimated. For instance, Cisco's (2013) report delineated the following domains that IoT could facilitate: workplace conditions, traffic congestion, recreation-area management, environmental impact, and citizen experiences. A report (Perez and Rushing 2007) on the CitiStat system run in the City of Baltimore described how the system efficiently and effectively managed the city programs and services, such as pothole abatement, trash collection, snow removal, sewage overflows, and the like.

Although it is valuable to identify the domains that IoT could apply to solve urban problems, there might be an endless list of the domains when new cases emerge along with the fast advance in technologies. Moreover, a set of different use cases possibly point to the same goal, e.g., increased efficiency. From a citizen perspective, people are more concerned about what effects or benefits information technologies could bring about to their life rather than how the technologies have been applied. In this regard, the concept of public value provides a useful way of thinking about the goals and performance of ICT-enabled public services (Cordella and Bonina 2012). In fact, government's investments in ICT for public issues have generally been justified by such democratic values as enhanced efficiency, policy effectiveness, trust, and so on (Heeks 1999; Fountain 2001; Gil-Garcia and Pardo 2005; Kamarck 2007). In a survey report by Cisco (2014), worldwide government leaders and department heads claimed that the excellent IoT solutions must address people and process, not just data and things. Therefore, a public value perspective might be more important in understanding the benefits and performance of various IoT applications in the public sector.

Unfortunately, despite the widespread recognition of the importance of public values in public administration and policy, there is a dearth of consensus on the understanding of a public values set (Jørgensen and Bozeman 2007; Cordella and Bonina 2012). Previous studies tend to divide public value into different categories and then identify a set of public values falling into each category (Kelly, Mulgan, and Muers 2002; Jørgensen and Bozeman 2007). Limited by the scope and purpose of this chapter, we cannot hope to discuss a variety of public values with a limited number of cases. On the contrary, we resort to more general or fundamental values that are critical to public administration. There are four values named as pillars of public administration by the National Academy of Public Administration in 2005, including efficiency, effectiveness, social equity, and economy. Note, however, that we replace economy with smart decision-making, as we found little evidence supporting the idea of economy in the IoT cases.

Efficiency

Efficiency has long played a central role in the contested terrain of public administration values (Frederickson and Smith 2003; Denhardt and Denhardt 2007). Weimer and Vining (2009, 1) define efficiency as "maximizing the total value to the members of society obtained from the use of scarce resources." Put simply, the notion of efficiency envisions managers pursuing given ends by means of the least costs or spending given costs to achieve the maximum ends. One of the key aspects of IoT is its capacity to use sensors and location data to pinpoint problems, which will help reduce cost. For instance, network-connected water meters would generate data on residential water usage and the vulnerability of water mains. Sensors on roads and in cars could monitor traffic and improve the timing of stoplights to ease congestion. Some cities have already developed apps to provide citizens and the government with real-time data, for example, showing the progress of filling potholes and trash collection. In the City of Baltimore, the IoT-based system called CitiStat could track all sorts of data on response times for public services and on civil servants' overtime and sick leave. It was reported that the system significantly increased the efficiency of city government by saving Baltimore an estimated $350 million during five years (Perez and Rushing 2007).

Effectiveness

As an almost equally important concept to efficiency, effectiveness represents the degree to which objectives are achieved and the extent to which targeted problems are solved. In contrast to efficiency, effectiveness is determined without reference to costs. Although government is often expected to operate in an economical and efficient manner, it is also critical to ensure it is doing what it is supposed to do in the first place. In the practice of public administration, effectiveness is reflected in such things as improved water quality, reduced pollution, increased employment rates, lower crime rates, better roads, and the like (Norman-Major 2011). Reaching effectiveness is often hindered by some factors that fall out of government control. For instance, a city government may lack enough human resources to do the 7×24 surveillance on a river. In general, government could only deploy personnel to do on-site inspection during working hours, but pollution might happen anytime. As a result, government can only find it after a river has been polluted. This is where IoT comes in. Sensors or surveillance cameras can be installed to replace human inspection, and they are operational all the time in all weather conditions. Fighting crime is another case. Crimes are hard to anticipate and prevent due to the lack of the latest pattern of criminal activities, which can be solved by the introduction of IoT-enabled systems. For instance, in the aftermath of the introduction of the IoT-based system called CityStat, Baltimore's murders rate dropped around 67% and robberies declined 54%, far ahead of the national average (Perez and Rushing 2007).

Social Equity

Social equity was named the fourth pillar of public administration by the National Academy of Public Administration in 2005, although it still struggles to find an equal place with other traditional public administration values, such as efficiency and effectiveness (Frederickson 2005; Norman-Major 2011). As a key component of the New Public Administration movement led by H. George Frederickson, social equity means different people are entitled to be served equally or public service should be fairly delivered. However, part of the challenge in realizing equity is the normative nature of the concept. Unlike the relatively objective nature of efficiency and effectiveness, it is more difficult to reach agreement on what it exactly means and how it is incorporated in practice (Norman-Major 2011). Despite the conceptual ambiguity, in practice there were people who received less fairly delivered public services due to the problems of spatial distance, environmental disadvantages, and socioeconomic development status. A typical example is that the people living in the metropolitan areas have easier access to higher quality health care than do their counterparts on the periphery. IoT is capable of achieving equity and fairness by overcoming these disparities. For instance, with the help of IoT-based medical systems, highly ranked doctors will become available to diagnose the sick in far-away places who cannot afford to travel to the doctors' home hospital. IoT might enhance social equity by serving those traditionally underserved people.

Smart Decision-Making

Data-based decision-making, which means that government should base its decisions on data, evidence, and rational analysis, is not a new idea. However, decision-making is often limited by serious information constraints. One primary constraint is the limited capacity of individuals and organizations to sort and process information, especially in today's information-abundant environment. In addition, even the properly sorted information must be further interpreted (Bendor, Taylor, and Gaalen 1987). With the growing volume of data from interconnected people, objects, and devices, high-quality decision-making has to rely heavily on the advances in analytic capability technologies to bring out the intelligence/knowledge in data. Traditional analytics is performed as a back-end resource and is done by pre-creation of metadata before the actual analytics processes take place. On the contrary, new forms of analytics based on IoT have emerged to remove the need to pre-model metadata, resulting in faster queries and more dynamic data processing. As a whole, IoT creates opportunities for government not only to collect and analyze data to spotlight problem areas and present potential solutions, but also to develop quantifiable measures to assess policy performance and draw comparisons across similar circumstances. All these new capacities result in smarter decisions: public managers are empowered to focus on the biggest problems, efficiently and equitably allocate resources, and design policies that are appropriately targeted and produce desired results (Cisco 2014).

IoT Cases in China

In this section, we discuss four IoT-enabled public service cases that match each public value as described in the previous section. Table 8.2 provides a quick overview of these cases and the corresponding value respectively.

Table 8.2 IoT Cases and the Relevant Public Value

Case #	Names of the Cases	Relevant Values
1	Intelligent Parking Guidance System, City of Wuhan	Increased efficiency
2	Taihu Lake Water Environment Monitoring System, City of Wuxi	Enhanced effectiveness
3	Telemedicine Service Platform, County of Tonglu	Improved social equity
4	Integrated Transport Information Management System, City of Shanghai	Smarter decision-making

Case #1: Intelligent Parking Guidance System in Wuhan, Hubei Province

As one of the metropolises with a population of over 10 million, the City of Wuhan, located in central China, has experienced great challenges with traffic jams. The average speed of inner-city traffic was as low as about 20 km per hour, and further reduced to 10 km per hour in bad weather. The problem was caused not only by the fast-growing number of vehicles, but also by the unbalanced distribution of parking lots and the lack of a parking guidance system, which led to a large portion of the lanes being used by car owners as temporary parking space. The occupancy of the normal lanes resulted in worse congestion. According to statistics, it took a driver an average of 25 minutes to find a parking place. However, they failed to find one most of the time. Meanwhile, the utilization ratio of some less-visible places, such as indoor underground parking lots and parking lots in shopping malls, was lower than 60%. It was estimated that the overall economic loss caused by traffic jams reached an average of 20 billion yuan each year, and traffic jams cost each commuter an extra 16 working days per year.

To solve this problem, the city's traffic administration developed and deployed the Intelligent Parking Guidance System in 2011, in cooperation with business corporations. The system includes three layers: sensing layer, transmission layer, and processing layer. The sensing layer consists of RFID tags attached to vehicles and traffic facilities, surface magnetic field sensors installed on the road, high-definition imaging sensors installed in arterial road and intersections, in-car GPS navigation terminals, and apps. This layer is used to collect real-time information of the occupancy of all parking lots distributed in different areas. In addition, it could collect the location information of all the vehicles that were using GPS terminals and the smartphone app.

The transmission layer uses short-range wireless communication technologies, such as Zigbee and Wi-Fi, to transmit real-time information to area data centers, which further transmit the information to the city's big data center by means of 3G, 4G, or LAN. The processing layer is composed of such platforms as road parking management platform, parking lots management platform, parking fee clearance platform, and parking guidance platform.

The system is able to disseminate the information regarding the available parking spaces to car owners through mobile communication, social media, broadcasting, and TV. In addition, car owners are able to check the availability of parking spaces around them through the app. The app will locate the car and the nearest parking space and suggest the best route to the place. The app also has an anti-collision function, which could remind one of the two car owners to select another place when both owners are approaching the same place. The app could remember the parking time and calculate the parking fee automatically, so that car owners are able to pay the parking fee immediately by third-party online payment platforms installed in their smartphones.

The system has significantly decreased the searching time and increased the usage rate of available parking lots by combining demand-side information and supply-side information. By the end of 2014, the system has covered the vast majority area of the city, including 50% of ground parking lots, 80% of inner-building parking, 90% of business-area parking, 60% of residential-area parking, and 70% of scenic region parking. Fifty-six percent of Wuhan's car owners have become registered users of the system, and so do the nearly 200,000 car owners of the neighboring areas. Since its introduction, the system has provided guidance service for about 6 million vehicles, and saved an average of 20 minutes per day for each vehicle owner. Moreover, traffic jams have been reduced by 20%, without considering the jams caused by the increased number of cars. According to a third-party poll, citizen satisfaction with the overall traffic status has increased from 33% in 2011 to 56% in 2014. More specifically, satisfaction with the parking service increased from 21% to 76% in the same period. Wuhan's ranking of traffic jams also dropped 11 places among the national metropolises.

Case #2: Taihu Lake Water Environment Monitoring System in Wuxi, Jiangsu Province

Taihu Lake, located in the most economically advanced and most populated Yangtze River Delta, has long been the main source of industry water and residential water consumption in this region. However, Taihu's water quality has undergone dramatic deterioration in the first decade of the 21st century due to unlimited industry wastewater and sanitary sewage draining off into the lake. In 2007 and 2009, the lake experienced massive blue algae outbreaks two times, causing massive fish death and a widespread worry about the drinking water shortage among the local residents in Wuxi, Jiangsu Province. At first, the city government started to monitor water quality by manual data collection. The collection was conducted once each month, and only a small number of critical perimeters were included each time. The manual data collection only lasted two years and failed to reach the expected outcomes due to the high percentage of errors, high cost, inefficiency, and low frequency.

The crisis led to an IoT-based Water Environment Monitoring System initiated by the city government in 2012. Sensors were installed in all critical points of the basin to monitor quantity of flow, the five conventional parameters of water quality, and other chemical elements such as ammonia, nitrogen, total phosphorus, total nitrogen, and so on. All the sensory data were transmitted to the data center in buoy stations or early warning stations in a real-time manner. Meanwhile, tour gauging vehicles and gauging boats were equipped with advanced monitoring devices to supplement the installed sensors. The tour vehicles and boats also did quality control to ensure accuracy of the data and reliability of the data transmission process.

A communication network was in charge of transmitting the data collected by the sensors and other equipment to the city's water environment monitoring center. Once the city-level monitoring center received the data, it would automatically analyze the quality of the water and compare the results with historical data and the data based on a mathematic model. If the comprehensive index of the water quality went over the threshold set in advance, the system would raise the alarm and indicate which area had been polluted and what the primary pollutants were.

Based on the detected area and the pollutants, the system was able to determine the source of pollution and even determine the enterprise(s) that might have discharged the pollutant. The information would be sent immediately to all the relevant regulation agencies and the frontline staff working in the monitoring stations so that they could respond right away to stop the pollution or reduce the pollution to the minimum level. So far, the system has included more than 1,000 different types of sensors installed in all of the critical points, 112 water quality monitoring stations, 3 water source early waring stations, 11 buoy stations, 3 emergency response boats, and 12 tour gauging vehicles. All these devices and equipment formed an automatic monitoring and early warning network covering the whole lake basin all year around and in all weather.

The system has mitigated the pollution effectively. Enterprises' pollution in the lake area has been curbed effectively—secret waste discharges decreased from 150 times to 5 times each year, and all of them were detected and handled successfully. In addition, the full-time personnel who used to do the on-site examination have been reduced from 250 to 100, while patrol frequency increased from one time per month to three times per day. The error rate in data collection was reduced to 2% from the original 10%. Currently, it takes only 30 minutes to get the analysis result out of the collected data, while traditionally it took about three days. Since 2013, the system has automatically captured 88 water quality abnormal fluctuations in the 39 cross-sections of rivers, and sent automatic alarms to environmental protection and flood protection agencies. The information proved to be critical for the agencies to respond in a timely and effective manner. Consequently, the pollution level has undergone significant reduction.

Case #3: Telemedicine Service Platform in Tonglu, Zhejiang Province

Despite the remarkable achievements in economic and social development over the last three decades, China still faces the problem of a rural–urban development divide, especially with regard to health care and medical treatment. According to the statistics of the Chinese Academy of Social Sciences in 2012, the number of average medical resources available to urban residents was 2.5 times greater than that of rural residents. The number increased to five times when it came to Midwest China. Other statistics indicated that about 25% of the elderly in rural areas had long been suffering from high blood pressure, and around one-third of them suffered from diabetes at the same time. Other chronicles such as asthma and high cholesterol were also common among this group of people. However, the vast majority of the elderly never received any treatment. One of the primary reasons is the low-level household income. The poor healthcare conditions often led to death or disability due to the lack of timely treatment when emergencies happened. Also because of insufficient resources, a large portion of the aged in rural areas passed away at home rather than in hospitals.

To make it easier for rural residents to be treated when they are sick, the County of Tonglu in Zhejiang Province established the IoT-enabled Telemedicine Service Platform in 2011. The platform connected all 163 township and village hospitals/clinics with the county hospital and the remote diagnosis center in the PLA General Hospital, a high-profile national hospital located in Beijing. The platform was composed of three systems: the front-end diagnosis system, the middle-end data sharing system, and the back-end data analysis system. The diagnosis system included a variety of mobile and portable human physiological parameters monitoring devices, remote video equipment, and various information terminals. The human physiological parameters monitoring devices installed in suburban and rural areas were used to collect patients' data, such as heart rate, pulse, respiration, and blood pressure, and transmit them to Beijing. The remote video equipment was used to facilitate face-to-face communication between doctors and patients. Various information terminals provided patients with diagnostic reports and medical records inquiries.

Based on the mobile communication network and fixed broadband network, the middle-end data sharing system connected the following records or subsystems into one interoperable network: hospital information system (HIS), electronic medical record (EMR), health archives management system, and picture archiving and communication system (PACS), etc. To ensure interoperability, all systems were required to follow the international standard format for health data transmission and storage. The back-end data analysis system was an automatic diagnosis system based on patients' massive data, including patients' clinical history and medical records.

The real-time physiological parameters assist the doctors in Beijing in forming a primary diagnosis. The doctors could choose to have video/audio conversations with the patients in Tonglu if necessary. According to the data transferred from the front-end sensors and the patient's clinical history and medical records stored on the back-end analysis system, the doctors in Beijing can make an accurate diagnosis. In some cases, if a patient had a rare illness, local doctors and Beijing doctors can hold a joint teleconference to determine the optimal treatment options. If a patient had to have an operation, the local doctors could obtain live remote assistance through the video equipment.

Since its inception in 2011, the system has received more than 200,000 copies of electrocardiograms and 600,000 copies of blood pressure readings, among which there were 6,620 cases of cardiac arrhythmia, 5,280 cases of abnormal ST-T change, and 152 cases of myocardial infarction. Over 100 patients with myocardial infarction obtained prompt medical treatment. Overall, the mean time to diagnostic decreased by 90%, and medical expenditure decreased by 85%. More importantly, about 76% of patients avoided death or disability due to timely and high-quality treatment. In the presence of the remote medical system, a vast majority of the rural residents ends up seeking treatment locally rather than traveling to big cities such as Beijing or Shanghai, which was beneficial for both the residents and the cities' hospitals.

Case #4: Integrated Transport Information Management System in Shanghai

Like many other big cities, Shanghai, China's business and financial center, has been struggling to deal with serious traffic congestion. The city's downtown area features 0.3 kilometers in per capita road length and 5.59 square meters in per capita road area. Although these two factors reflecting the general road network density is very close to the international standard, the actual traffic situation used to be seriously troublesome due to the uneven distribution of the population, improper urban planning, and the mismatch between land use and transport facilities. Statistics indicated that the mean velocity in the downtown area was only 15 km per hour in 2012, far behind that of developed countries. During peak hours, the average unblocked reliability of the major corridors was 65.4% and only 42.1% in some special road segments. Traffic congestion had become a hindering factor in the rapid development of the city.

In 2011, the Shanghai municipal government established the Integrated Transport Information Management System. The system consisted of three layers: perception layer, transmission layer, and processing layer. The perception layer was responsible for collecting various static and dynamic traffic-related data. It was composed of the following sensing equipment: 22,000 sets of inductive coils, 25,000 GPS floating vehicles, 334 license plate recognition cross-sections, and more than 3,000 SCATS-based intersection traffic signal control equipment. This layer covered 1,042 bus routes, 11 rail transit routes, 732 public parking garages/lots, 2 international airports, and 3 railway stations and was able to collect around 240 categories of static and dynamic transportation data.

The transmission layer was composed of a gigabit Ethernet redundant self-healing network, which focused on interconnection and interoperability of the data by enforcing the same data interface and communication norms among different departments and districts. Therefore, all the traffic-related data coming from road administration, traffic police, public transport, railway department, aviation administration, and Pudong New Area (port administration) could converge in the city's central data center. The processing layer, located in Shanghai's traffic management and command center, was composed of dozens of high-performance computers, high-availability and high-capacity network-attached storage equipment, traffic flow simulation and early warning system, and traffic emergency communication system.

Currently, the system connects both governmental agencies and enterprises that are relevant to public transport, including airport, railway, port, taxi, subway, and the like. The data collected by a variety of sensors were sent to the traffic management and command center by the transmission layer. The processing layer helped visualize and display the real-time traffic status on the large screens of the center. Whenever a traffic jam happened, the traffic administration would take necessary measures to control traffic flow and ease congestion, which included disseminating traffic information, adjusting traffic lights, and opening the tidal lanes. It is the first comprehensive system in China that is able to bring together traffic flow information in the same platform for real-time online sharing. The information was collected from inner-city road transportation, public transportation, and inter-city transportation. Through this integrated information management system, road administration, public security administration, and hospitals realized timely discovery of traffic accidents, quick dispatch, and coordinated handling. Besides, variable traffic information sign specification and planning were researched and drafted by multi-department efforts, and the information from the cross-river transportation facilities and urban and suburban roads were publicized jointly. In addition, information sharing with regard to entrance control and traffic of the elevated roads was conducted in a collaborative manner. Finally, the self-adaptive traffic lights based on traffic flow in the intersections provided decision makers a sound basis to make and fine tune the city's transportation policies.

> Since the deployment of the system, the city's traffic congestion has been in a slight decline, compared with the relatively slow growth in road mileage and rapid growth in the number of vehicles. From 2010 to 2014, road mileage of the downtown area was about 4,865 kilometers, an increase of only 3%, and the road area was about 105 square kilometers, an increase of 8%. By contrast, the number of vehicles grew from 2.29 million to 3.04 million during the same period of time, an increase of 33%. The mean velocity in the downtown area rose to 18 km per hour, close to that of the developed countries. The average unblocked reliability of the major corridors during the peak hours was 64.4% and 41.5% in the special sections, respectively.

As a whole, these practical cases demonstrated tangible outcomes, such as increased efficiency, enhanced effectiveness, improved equity, and smart decision-making. The outcomes not only benefited local residents, but also those from neighboring areas. These cases have also demonstrated that the IoT-enabled public service delivery could serve as a catalyst for interdepartmental, intersectoral, and even interjurisdictional collaboration. In the meantime, we realize that the factors shaping the outcomes remain unclear. For instance, what motivated urban doctors to telemetrically treat remote patients? How were organizational silos removed to make interdepartmental collaboration happen? More broadly, there are three main challenges that may hinder further development of IoT in the area of public service delivery.

First, the vast majority of the IoT projects involve heavy initial investment on infrastructure and systems, and continuous funding will be needed to maintain normal operating conditions. Without a proper business model, the risk of failure of IoT projects is relatively high. Local governments are exploring the possibilities of attracting private investment through the public-private-partnership model. Second, IoT technologies are not yet mature enough to meet the practical requirements in a few aspects. For instance, at the sensing layer, some terminals cannot meet the requirements in accuracy and volume. At the transmission layer, near-distance wireless communication technologies fail to live up to the actual needs of the transmission rate. To this end, the central government has created an IoT Special Fund that provides CNY 500 million annually to support the research and development of key technologies. Third, a big portion of people have not been fully aware of or really perceived the benefits of the IoT projects, and thus hold passive attitudes toward IoT implementation. Moreover, concerns over privacy and personal information protection might lead to reluctance to share information and even resistance to the IoT projects. For example, technologies improving parking enforcement could also enhance daily life surveillance. Local governments are making efforts to increase awareness and sell the benefits of IoT to people by pilot projects and various exhibitions.

Conclusion

We have explored the innovative characteristics of IoT and examined its impact on public service delivery. The cases demonstrate the great potentials and advantages that IoT could bring to the public. Meanwhile, we realize that IoT is still one of the emerging technologies according to Gartner's (2014) IT Hype Cycle. Therefore, our observation and discussions should be understood as exploratory and preliminary ones.

In addition to the opportunities, it is worth noting that IoT initiatives have introduced challenges to public managers as well. Among others, the three primary challenges reported involve sustainable development, technical advances, and citizen perception or attitudes. Although these challenges are not unusual for IT projects in the public sector (Streib and Willoughby 2005; Cullen and Reilly 2008; Jain and Kesar 2011), the novel features and the unprecedented coverage and penetration of IoT in social life might magnify the impact of these challenges. For the success of IoT projects, governments need to do more to ensure availability of the projects to citizens and alleviate citizens' concerns at the same time.

One limitation of this chapter is the lack of discussion on the institutional and organizational changes that play a critical role in implementing IT projects successfully in the public sector (e.g., Fountain 2001; Garson 2006). From the perspective of institutionalism, technologies themselves do not automatically evolve toward desired outcomes. Rather, technologies, institutions, and organizations must coevolve. We discussed four successful cases, but as Esty and Rushing (2007) argued, even if we had all the necessary data, public managers may still lack the expertise, decision-making processes, and commitment from top leadership to make the right decisions. Therefore, proper mechanisms are needed to ensure that data are used to guide policy priorities and solutions. In its IoT survey report, Cisco (2014) also emphasized the importance of senior leadership, effective cross-department data sharing, and focusing on people and process in successful IoT projects. In our case study, one may question what motivations the urban doctors have to remotely treat the patients in underdeveloped areas. Another question arising from the Shanghai case might be the reasons underlying the collaboration among road administration, railway department, and aviation administration. Future studies could pay more attention to supportive institutional arrangements and organizational structures that ensure the success of IoT projects.

References

Ashton, Kevin. 2009. 'That 'Internet of Things' Thing'. *RFID Journal* June 22. www.rfidjournal.com/articles/view?4986

Bendor, Jonathan, Serge Taylor, and Roland Van Gaalen. 1987. 'Politicians, Bureaucrats, and Asymmetric Information'. *American Journal of Political Science* 31 (4): 796–828.

Cisco. 2013. *Internet of Everything: A $4.6 Trillion Public-Sector Opportunity*. San Jose: Cisco.

Cisco. 2014. *Internet of Everything (IoE): Top 10 Insights from Cisco's IoE Value at Stake Analysis for the Public Sector*. San Jose: Cisco.

Cordella, Antonio, and Carla M. Bonina. 2012. 'A Public Value Perspective for ICT Enabled Public Sector Reforms: A Theoretical Reflection'. *Government Information Quarterly* 29 (4): 512–520.

Cullen, Rowena, and Patrick Reilly. 2008. 'Information Privacy and Trust in Government: A Citizen-Based Perspective from New Zealand'. *Journal of Information Technology & Politics* 4 (3): 61–80.

Denhardt, Janet, and Robert Denhardt. 2007. *The New Public Service: Serving, Not Steering (Expanded Edition)*. Armonk, NY: M.E. Sharpe.

DG INFSO, and EPoSS. 2008. *Interent of Things 2020: A Roadmap for the Future*. Brusells: DG INFSO, and EPoSS.

Esty, Daniel C., and Reece Rushing. 2007. *Governing by the Numbers: The Promise of Data-Driven Policymaking in the Information Age*. Washington, DC: Center for American Progress.

Evans, Dave. 2011. 'The Internet of Things [INFOGRAPHIC]'. *Cisco Blogs*, July 15. http://blogs.cisco.com/diversity/the-Internet-of-things-infographic

Fountain, Jane E. 2001. *Building the Virtual State: Information Technology and Institutional Change*. Washington, DC: Brookings Institution.

Frederickson, George H. 2005. 'The State of Social Equity in American Public Administration'. *National Civic Review* 94: 31–38.

Frederickson, George H., and Kevin Smith. 2003. *Public Administration Theory Primer*. Boulder, CO: Westview Press.

FTC. 2015. *Internet of Things: Privacy & Security in a Connected World*. Washington, DC: FTC (Federal Trade Commission).

Garson, David G. 2006. *Public Information Technology and E-Governance: Managing the Virtual State*. Sudbury, MA: Jones and Barlett.

Gartner. 2014. *Hype Cycle for Emerging Technologies*. Stamford, CT: Gartner.

Gartner. 2015. *The Internet of Things Enables Digital Business*. Stamford, CT: Gartner.

Gil-Garcia, J. Ramon, and Theresa A. Pardo. 2005. 'E-Government Success Factors: Mapping Practical Tools to Theoretical Foundations'. *Government Information Quarterly* 22 (2): 187–216.

Gubbia, Jayavardhana, Rajkumar Buyyab, Slaven Marusic, and Marimuthu Palaniswami. 2013. 'Internet of Things (IoT): A Vision, Architectural Elements, and Future Directions'. *Future Generation Computer Systems* 29: 1645–1660.

Heeks, Richard. 1999. *Reinventing Government in the Information Age*. New York: Routledge.
IDC Government Insights. 2013. *Worldwide Smart City 2013 Top 10 Predictions*. Framingham, MA: IDC.
Industrial Internet Consortium. 2014. *The Industrial Internet Consortium: A Global Nonprofit Partnership of Industry, Government and Academia*. http://www.iiconsortium.org/about-us.htm
ITU. 2005. *ITU Internet Report 2005: Internet of Things*. Geneva: ITU (International Telecommunication Union).
Jain, Vikas, and Shalini Kesar. 2011. 'E-Government Implementation Challenges at Local Level: A Comparative Study of Government and Citizens' Perspectives'. *Electronic Government, an International Journal* 8 (2/3): 208–225.
Jørgensen, Torben Beck, and Barry Bozeman. 2007. 'Public Values: An Inventory'. *Administration & Society* 39 (3): 354–381.
Kamarck, Elaine C. 2007. *The End of Government . . . As We Know It: Making Public Policy Work*. New York: Routledge.
Kelly, Gavin, Geoff Mulgan, and Stephen Muers. 2002. *Creating Public Value: An Analytical Framework for Public Service Reform*. London: Strategy Unit, Cabinet Office.
Manyika, James, Michael Chui, Jacques Bughin, Richard Dobbs, Peter Bisson, and Alex Marrs. 2013. *Disruptive Technologies: Advances That Will Transform Life, Business, and the Global Economy*. Boston: McKinsey Global Institute.
Mulligan, Catherine E.A., and Magnus Olsson. 2013. 'Architectural Implications of Smart City Business Models: An Evolutionary Perspective'. *IEEE Communications Magazine* 51 (6): 80–85.
Norman-Major, Kristen. 2011. 'Balancing the Four Es; or Can We Achieve Equity for Social Equity in Public Administration?' *Journal of Public Affairs Education* 17 (2): 233–252.
Perera, Charith, Arkady Zaslavsky, Peter Christen, and Dimitrios Georgakopoulos. 2014. 'Sensing as a Service Model for Smart Cities Supported by Internet of Things'. *Transactions On Emerging Telecommunications Technologies* 25 (1): 81–93.
Perez, Teresita, and Reece Rushing. 2007. *The CitiStat Model: How Data-Driven Government Can Increase Efficiency and Effectiveness*. Washington, DC: Center for American Progress.
Pew Research Center. 2014. *The Internet of Things Will Thrive by 2025*. Washington, DC: Pew Research Center.
Proffitt, Brian. 2013. 'How Big the Internet of Things Could Become'. *ReadWrite*, September 30. http://readwrite.com/2013/09/30/how-big-the-Internet-of-things-could-become
Rowley, Jennifer. 2007. ;The Wisdom Hierarchy: Representations of the DIKW Hierarchy'. *Journal of Information Science* 33 (2): 163–180.
Schaffers, Hans, Nicos Komninos, Marc Pallot, Brigitte Trousse, Michael Nilsson, and Alvaro Oliveira. 2011. 'Smart Cities and the Future Internet: Towards Cooperation Frameworks for Open Innovation'. *The Future Internet, Lecture Notes in Computer Science* 6656: 431–446.
Shark, Alan R. 2015. *Technology and Public Management*. New York: Routledge.
Streib, Gregory D., and Katherine G. Willoughby. 2005. 'Local Governments as E-Governments: Meeting the Implementation Challenge'. *Public Administration Quarterly* 29 (1/2): 77–109.
Thierer, Adam. 2014. 'The Internet of Things and Wearable Technology: Addressing Privacy and Security Concerns without Derailing Innovation'. *Mercatus Working Paper*.
Vermesan, Ovidiu, Peter Friess, Patrick Guillemin, Harald Sundmaeker, Markus Eisenhauer, Klaus Moessner, Marilyn Arndt, Maurizio Spirito, Paolo Medagliani, Raffaele Giaffreda, Sergio Gusmeroli, Latif Ladid, Martin Serrano, Manfred Hauswirth, and Gianmarco Baldini. 2014. 'Internet of Things Strategic Research and Innovation Agenda'. In *Internet of Things-From Research and Innovation to Market Deployment*, edited by Ovidiu Vermesan and Peter Friess, 7–142. Aalborg, Denmark: River Publishers.
Vlacheas, Panagiotis, Raffaele Giaffreda, Vera Stavroulaki, Dimitris Kelaidonis, Vassilis Foteinos, George Poulios, Panagiotis Demestichas, Andrey Somov, Abdur Rahim Biswas, and Klaus Moessner. 2013. 'Enabling Smart Cities through a Cognitive Management Framework for the Internet of Things'. *IEEE Communications Magazine* 51 (6): 102–111.
Weimer, David L., and Aidan Vining. 2009. *Investing in the Disadvantaged: Assessing the Benefits and Costs of Social Policies*. Washington, DC: Georgetown University Press.
Zanella, Andrea, Nicola Bui, Angelo Castellani, Lorenzo Vangelista, and Michele Zorzi. 2014. 'Internet of Things for Smart Cities'. *IEEE Internet of Things Journal* 1 (1): 22–32.

9

BIG DATA ANALYSIS ON PUBLIC OPINION

A Case Study on the Policy Formation of Free Economic Pilot Zones in Taiwan

Hsien-Lee Tseng, Pin-Yu Chu, and Tong-Yi Huang

The Trend of Public Opinion Survey

Political scientists using various research techniques have documented a robust congruence between aggregated public opinion and public policies (Eriksom, MacKuen and Stinson 2002; Monroe 1998; Page and Shapiro 1983; Patrick 2012). Page and Shapiro (1983) even suggest that public opinion is often a proximate cause of policy, affecting policy more than policy influences opinion. In addition, responsiveness is now a central concern of various normative and empirical theories of democracy. In response to citizens' need to have a more responsive and democratic public administration, it is important for public policy makers to obtain public opinions during the policymaking process.

Since public opinions play a huge role in the development of political strategies, researchers adopt both qualitative and quantitative techniques for a rich understanding of public opinions, such as telephone surveys, focus groups, face-to-face interviews, etc. (Anstead 2014). Face-to-face interview, for example, the Current Population Survey (CPS) sponsored jointly by the U.S. Census Bureau and the U.S. Bureau of Labor Statistics (BLS), is the primary source of labor force statistics for the population of the United States. Focus groups are underused in social research, although they have a long history in market research (Morgan 1988). Focus groups usually consist of experts gathered to discuss a particular issue or idea to measure the potential impact of a particular issue or a new policy. Among these methodologies, telephone survey is one of the most common ways to collect public opinions, because it enables data to be collected from a large geographic scale not only more cheaply and quickly than by field interviewing, but it also avoids the well-known limitations of postal surveys (Thomas and Purdon 1994).

However, the rise of the Internet, various information and communication technologies (ICTs), and social media has brought fundamental changes in the way society works. ICT applications such as Skype, Line, and WeChat all have changed the way people communicate. Social media such as Facebook and Twitter provide citizens with many options to express their political opinions and even become a critical tool for social movements for the past few years (Khan, Yoon, Kim and Park 2014; Tufekci and Freelon 2013). Consequently, traditional public opinion survey is facing tremendous challenges, such as low response rate and the difficulty in reaching younger generations. A report by The Pew Research Center shows that survey research using traditional methods, such as telephone survey, is getting increasingly expensive because of the low response rate, only 9%, on public opinion surveys (The Pew Research Centre 2012). Lee, Huang and Chen's (2012) survey results show that traditional telephone survey is getting harder and harder to reach younger generations because they use cell phones instead of telephones at home. Citizen involvement in public governance is changing and thus the prevailing paradigm of public opinion and survey research is shifting. Therefore, researchers are seeking new methodologies to observe public opinions. Specifically, there is a significant effort underway to use big data for the purpose of collecting public opinions and to use big data analyses for politics and public policy.

In the following sections, we first review the literature of big data and its applications to public policy and public opinion survey. We then introduce the policy of the Free Economic Pilot Zones in Taiwan in the third section, and present our big data research design to gather public opinions on the issue of the Free Economic Pilot Zones from social media in the fourth section. The empirical results are then introduced, followed by policy implications and concluding remarks.

Big Data and Public Policy

Characteristics of Big Data

Data burst from applications of information and communication technology, when using a cell phone, shopping online, and in countless other everyday acts, with characteristics of volume, velocity, variety, and veracity, is so-called big data. The four Vs characterize what big data is all about: (1) volume—the massive scale and growth of unstructured data; (2) velocity—data is generated in real time with demands for usable information to be served up as needed; (3) variety—data is collected from new sources, including email, social media, video, images, blogs, and sensor data, as well as "shadow data" such as access journals and web search histories, that have not been mined for insight in the past; and (4) veracity—data, being stored and mined, is meaningful to the problem being analyzed (Intel IT center 2012; Normandeau 2013).

Big data analysis, one of the social media research techniques, nowadays has become a prevalent focus for governments and research institutions worldwide, because it allows researchers to obtain public opinion online in an unobtrusive, more conversational, and more accessible way. Anstead (2014) mentions that field experiments are costly and time-consuming, but the online world is an opportunity for real-time, inexpensive, and large-scale testing of the effectiveness of persuasion and political communication.

Big Data Methodologies

Big data analysis allows us to filter the entire large dataset based on time and issues. According to Ingram Micro Technology Solutions (2015), there are four types of big data analyses: (1) Prescriptive analysis reveals what actions should be taken; (2) predictive analysis uses big data to identify past patterns and then provide likely scenarios of what might happen in the future; (3) diagnostic analysis looks at past performance to determine what happened and why; and (4) descriptive analysis shows what is happening now based on incoming data. Where big data analytics, in general, sheds light on a subject, prescriptive analytics provides a laser-like focus to answer specific questions; however, it is largely not used. According to Robb (2012), 13% of organizations are using predictive analytics, but only 3% are using prescriptive analytics. Ingram Micro Technology Solutions (2015) suggests: "descriptive analytics or data mining are at the bottom of the big data value chain, but they can be valuable for uncovering patterns that offer insight."

While social media data collection can rely on standardized API services, the analysis of such collected data becomes challenging because the data are less structured (e.g., texts, informal expressions) and more

Big Data Analysis on Public Opinion

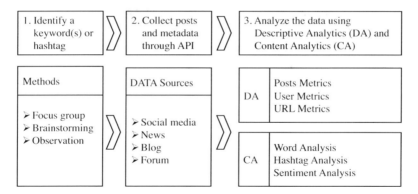

Figure 9.1 A Framework for Using Big Data to Extract Intelligence Online (revised from Chae 2015)

enriched (e.g., user profiles, follower, hashtags, URL) (Zeng, Chen, Lusch and Li 2010) than traditional data (e.g., sales data), and the analytical framework or methodology is not readily available. The use of diverse research methods and metrics is necessary to extract intelligence from the highly enriched and unstructured social media data (Chau and Xu 2012; Fan and Gordon 2014; Zeng et al. 2010).

Figure 9.1 shows an analytical framework encompassing such research methods and metrics for extracting intelligence online. Three major steps are identified in the framework. (1) Identify a keyword(s) and hashtag. Big data contain a large amount of information, including transcript and metadata (e.g., user information). Massive unstructured data and unlimited information can be classified efficiently by the adequate use of keywords. We can employ methods such as focus group, brainstorming, and observation to identify proper keywords to improve the quality of big data analysis. (2) Collect posts and metadata through API. Public opinion online can be categorized into four channels, social media, news, blog, and forum, and each channel has their own metadata (Hsiao, Chen, and Liao 2015). Researchers need to categorize metadata information from difference sources for analytical purposes. (3) Analyze the data. Chae (2015) suggests two methodologies from different intellectual backgrounds that could be used for big data analysis: descriptive analytics and content analytics. Descriptive analytics focuses on descriptive statistics, such as the number of replies, distribution of different types of reply, and the number of hashtags. While a small number of metrics (e.g., sample size, response rate, responder profile) are used for the survey data, the enriched nature of big data enables intelligence extraction, using a large set of metrics regarding posts, users, hashtags, URLs, etc. Content analytics refers to a broad set of natural language processing and text-mining methods for extracting intelligence from Web 2.0 (Chau and Xu 2012). Content analysis is often used to analyze social media data, which are primarily texts and thus "unstructured" in nature. A text is informal and composed of a short list of words, hashtags, URLs, and other information. A careful consideration of text cleaning and processing is a prerequisite for intelligence gathering. Thus, advanced text-mining techniques, such as sentiment analysis, are the key for extracting such opinions.

In addition to these analyses and metrics, Chae (2015) suggests that there is a myriad of network concepts, analyses, and metrics. For example, Facebook data enables the layout of different networks (e.g., personal, group, fan page, timeline). Thus, a well-framed research question can be helpful for selecting a manageable list of analyses and metrics when using descriptive analytics.

Big Data Analysis, Public Policy, and Public Opinions

Ranging from technical to legal and regulatory challenges, Maaroof (2015) illustrates three different dimensions of big data and policies, including evidence-informed policymaking, data for policy, and policy for data. While the issues of policy for data such as standardization, open data, etc., are important, the focus of public administration is in the inner circle, i.e., data-driven approaches to support policy making. Two approaches are commonly distinguished (Maaroof 2015):

The first approach is the use of public datasets (administrative open data and statistics about populations, economic indicators, education, etc.) that typically contain descriptive statistics, which are now used on a larger scale, used more intensively, and linked (Maaroof 2015). For example, dealing with massive amounts of data, Desouza (2014) indicates that public agencies now are operating in data-intensive environments. IBM suggests that big data can improve efficiency and effectiveness across the broad range of government responsibilities, including threat prediction and prevention, social program fraud (waste and errors), tax compliance (fraud and abuse), and crime prediction and prevention (IBM 2014a). In 2012, the Obama administration first spent more than $200 million to launch the Big Data Research and Development Initiative. Since then, governments worldwide have embraced big data and used it for a diverse range of applications, such as accelerating scientific discovery, improving national security, enhancing teaching and learning, and increasing innovation. The City of Baltimore launched a new performance measurement system enterprise-wide, named CitiStat, using mapping, adding geographic information systems (GIS) for a birds-eye view of each independent action, such as monitoring crime activities in the neighborhood (O'Malley 2014).

The second approach is data from social media, such as Facebook or Twitter, sensors, and mobile phones, which are typically new sources of public opinion for policy making. The use of big data now holds great promise for increasing citizen engagement and public value in the public sector (Desouza 2014). Government agencies adopt big data analysis to monitor social media for public opinion detection or hints of illegal activity. For example, the FBI and the Defense Advanced Research Projects Agency, part of the Department of Defense, is exploring how to "forecast dynamic group behavior in social media" (Schulz 2012). During the 2012 Republication National Convention, The Florida Department of Law Enforcement monitored social media to predict and prevent where and when crimes and other disruptive events may occur; the City of Tampa Police Department, the Hillsborough County Sheriff's Office, the FBI, the U.S. Secret Service, the Division of Alcoholic Beverages and Tobacco, and the State Fire Marshall were also involved (IBM 2014b). In Italy, Siracusa, recognized as a World Heritage Site by the United Nations Educational, Scientific and Cultural Organization in 2005, took a two-pronged approach to gathering public sentiment: they used the "Love City Index" interactive mobile application, which gathers visitors' feedback directly, and a social media analytics solution that helps uncover the candid opinions of past and present visitors. Since the "Love City Index" application was announced, the number of Twitter comments posted about the city each day increased by 25%, from 800 to 1,000 on average (IBM 2014c).

Besides surveillance and threat prediction and prevention, a significant effort is underway to use big data for purposes of collecting public opinions and analyzing politics and public policy. For example, the Urban Attitudes Lab at Tufts University has conducted research on accessing big data on Twitter for civic purposes of accessing how people think about the places they live, work, and play (Hughes 2014). The Urban Attitudes Lab uses IBM's SPSS Modeler software to leverage a sentiment dictionary of nearly 3,000 words, assigning a sentiment score to each phrase. After a six-week period, about 11,000 messages containing sentiments were analyzed. In this project, researchers acknowledged and pointed out that big data analysis is one way to glean public opinion, but may not have a valid statistical representation of the population. Corbett and Durfee (2004) tried to capture the issue of climate change frames expressed in public discourse through social media conversations on Twitter in the U.S., the UK, Canada, and Australia for over two years. The results show that hoax frames are more frequent in the U.S. than in the UK, Canada, and Australia, and are particularly prevalent in traditionally Republican-leaning states. In other words, when users discuss global climate change in terms of hoax frames, they prefer "global warming" to "climate change." Big data analysis has been demonstrated to be an effective method to enhance the understanding of public opinions, compared with traditional telephone surveys, especially concerning the younger generation respondents (Anstead 2014; Hsiao, Chen and Liao 2015; Hughes 2014; Lee, Huang and Chen 2012).

While there are opportunities for full-scale implementation of data-driven approaches across all stages of the policy cycle (Dunn 2012), including agenda setting, formulation, evaluation, and impact assessment, our discussions focus on the application of big data on public opinions at the stage of policy formulation, in particular, data from social media. The particular case "the Free Economic Pilot Zones in Taiwan" is presented in the following section.

The Free Economic Pilot Zones and Sunflower Movement

At the end of World War II in 1945, the Republic of China (ROC) government declared Taiwan a province of the Republic. Four years later, after fighting a civil war with Chinese Communist Party (CCP) rebels, the ROC government led by the Chinese Nationalist Party, or Kuomintang (KMT), relocated to the island. The CCP regime, meanwhile, declared the establishment of the People's Republic of China (PRC). Since then, the ROC government's effective jurisdiction has been limited to Taiwan and the Penghu, Kinmen, and Matsu archipelagos, in addition to a number of smaller islands. Estrangement and military tension marked relations between the two sides of the Taiwan Strait until the early 1990s, when cross-strait talks were launched and later became institutionalized in mid-2008, moving on to a relationship of extensive economic and people-to-people exchanges (Executive Yuan 2011).

Since President Ma was elected in 2008, the government of Taiwan has tried to improve cross-strait investment and trade relationship with China. The main ideas of the Free Economic Pilot Zones are liberalization, globalization, and innovation on the flows of goods, people, capital, and market opening. With two strategic stages, the Free Economic Pilot Zones in Taiwan is expected to prepare Taiwan for joining the Trans-Pacific Partnership (TPP) and the Regional Comprehensive Economic Partnership (RCEP). The first stage, focusing on the amendment of administrative regulations, is designed to integrate and network with neighboring industry zones. On December 26, 2013, the Executive Yuan approved the draft of a special bill for the Free Economic Pilot Zones. The second stage of the policy will begin right after the proclamation of the special bill. Under the special bill, the Free Economic Pilot Zones can be set up as designated by the central government or under application by local governments. Private land can also be subject to the establishment of the Free Economic Pilot Zones through co-development with the government (China go aboard n.d.). According to the main policy-planning agency of the Executive Yuan, the National Development Council (NDC), which is charged with the tasks of planning, designing, coordinating, reviewing, and evaluating the nation's overall development, the Free Economic Pilot Zones will employ new business models such as "Inside the Border but Outside of Customs" and "Store in the Front, Factory in the Back" to link with nearby industrial parks and local businesses and then to facilitate economic growth.

However, those in opposition of the pact insist that there is a lack of transparency during negotiations, leaving many to believe China will have the upper hand over Taiwan as the two economies converge, and Taiwan eventually will suffer forthcoming political pressure from Beijing. In addition, they believe that the new agreement will show favoritism to large conglomerate companies, while small to medium-sized businesses are left to suffer and struggle (Martin 2014). On March 18, crowds of students, academics, civic organizations, and other protesters climbed over the fence of the Legislative Yuan and occupied the legislative chamber. More than 210,000 protesters gathered around the front of the Legislative Yuan for a sit-in, and the crowd continued to grow in size as hundreds more joined in. The symbol of this act is a sunflower, as a symbol of hope as the flower is heliotropic (Sunflower Movement 2014). The Sunflower movement continued the unprecedented month-long occupation of Taiwan's legislature to protest against the Cross-Strait Service Trade Agreement and the import of Chinese agricultural products for processing in the Free Economic Pilot Zones, from March 18 to

April 10, 2014. It is worth noting that the protest was launched by younger generations, aged 16 to 29, and that most of them were college students. Moreover, the success of the Sunflower movement was due to heavy social media use, such as Facebook, the bulletin board system (BBS), and Google Hangout, which quickly turned the protest into a much larger political movement (Chen, Liao, Wu and Hwan 2014; Hioe 2014).

This observation raises an important question: Is the government losing their understanding of the younger generation? Or, does the public opinion survey system fail to reflect civic opinion? Commissioned by the National Development Council and the Taiwan E-Government Research Center, this research aims to gather public opinions on the issue of the Free Economic Pilot Zones online. A quasi-experimental design is employed to examine the effects of a sequence of online policy summits. In the following section, we present our methodology in details.

Research Design

Data Sources

The current study employs descriptive analysis of big data to analyze transcripts from four different channels: news, blog, forum, and Facebook, from July 8 to August 11, 2014. The data on Facebook used for this study represent active accounts run by real people. We elected to use these channels in our analysis because prior literature indicates that they are effective indicators for the extent to which messages are perceived as important in the network (Graham and Avery 2013).

Data Characteristics

To answer our research questions about public opinion on the Free Economic Pilot Zones, we filtered transcripts based on the title, content, and reply. We include messages that mention the Free Economic Pilot Zones and Sunflower movement by utilizing 130 keywords in 7 related frames, i.e., trade, education, service industry, logistics, agriculture, medical care, and finance (see Table 9.1). As for the keywords, we adopt, for example, keywords such as the TPP, RCEP, and demonstration industries in the trade issue. In the logistics issue, we adopt keywords such as inside the border but outside of customs, store in the front, factory in the back, Made in Taiwan (MIT), etc.

Table 9.1 Keywords of the Big Data Analysis on Free Economic Pilot Zones in Taiwan

Frame	*Keywords*
Trade	Demonstration Industries, Physical Industry Park, designated pilot, TPP, RCEP, deregulation, institutional innovation, carte blanche, one-stop shop, tax incentives, market liberalization, foreign talent, break off the chains, reversal of stuffy economy, global air hub, land expropriation, section expropriation, environmental impact assessment, enclosure, land speculation, back door to trade service agreement, one china trilogy, online, web*forum, national development council, ministry of education
Logistics	smart logistics, international logistics, front shop—back factory, free trade port area, free trade port, bonded area, express shipping, smart cloud, cloud platform, e-account smart card, customs innovation, remote auditing, night time approval service, weekend approval service, automobile assembly, 6 sea port and 1 airport, Port of Taipei, Port of Keelung, Port of Taichung, Port of Kaohsiung, Anping Port, Port of Suao, *Aviation free*trade*port area, multiple-country consolidation, processing outsourcing, customs, Custom, Ministry of Finance, Ministry of Transportation and Communications

Frame	Keywords
Agriculture	value-added agriculture, agriculture industrial park, ornamental fish, conservation, wild animals, animal vaccination, MIT, 830 agriculture items, Chinese agricultural products, food processing, agro-processing, peanut, tea, pineapple cake, agricultural annihilation, sensitive agricultural industries, smuggling paradise, Council of Agriculture, Chen Bao-ji
Medical care	International health, international healthcare, international medical service center, international healthcare industry park, medical examinations and cosmetics, medical manpower, license fee, front shop—back factory, commercialization of medical care, all is empty, social stratification, blood and sweat medical care, Ministry of Health and Welfare, Lin Tzou-yien
Education	Education innovation, higher education deregulation, branch school, branch, college, EMBA, professional curriculum, Designated Pilot, run a school, foreign student, *higher education internationalization*, the publicity of education, for-profit school, elite school, class division, carte blanche, Ministry of Education, Chen, Der-hwa
Finance	virtual consumption, deregulation, bank, stock, Offshore Banking Unit (OBU), Offshore Securities Unit (OSU), wealth management, Designated Pilot, business classification, non-resident, class division, Financial Supervisory Commission (FSC)
Service	Lawyer, accountant, architect service industry deregulation, market deregulation, business office, Ministry of Justice, Financial Supervisory Commission (FSC), Ministry of the Interior

Coding Frames

The respective frames in the four different channels are identified by running a Boolean search that contains keywords and phrases unique to the frame. Previous research suggests that big data analysis based on keyword search results offers special promise for framing analysis (Neuman, Guggenheim, Jang and Bae 2014); moreover, with appropriate prudence in execution of research designs and judiciousness in drawing conclusions, big data offer special promise for issue framing analysis. The key may be in identifying rarer elements of public rhetoric that clearly link to single frames of a more complex issue[1] (Neuman et al. 2014). For example, real frames could be identified using a Boolean search that paired "climate change" or "global warming" with real or fact. For example, a reference to one or more of these search terms anywhere in an individual posting meant that the posts online was identified as having a real frame. In other words, we assumed that any messages that mentioned "climate change" (or "global warming") and real (or fact) at the same time in a single post were understanding and discussing climate change in terms of its legitimacy. The key of this approach may be to identify unique components of public rhetoric that clearly represent single frames of a more complex issue (Jang and Hart 2015).

To collect data and metadata discussing the Free Economic Pilot Zones, the Sunflower movement, and related events from the Internet, we initially conducted a series of keyword searches, including "the Free Economic Pilot Zones," "Sunflower movement," "logistics," and so on. This led us to find out the most prevalent and related keywords about the Free Economic Pilot Zones issue. Finally, we are able to compile the number of transcripts for the Free Economic Pilot Zones for a month. To detect both positive and negative opinions, we use sentiment keywords such as support, against, good, and bad.

Table 9.2 and Figure 9.2 illustrate how we analyze the transcripts online. We devise four types of transcript: title, content, reply to transcript with keywords, and reply to transcript without keywords. Table 9.2 is an excerpt of a news report and the keyword is "foreign trade," which appeared in the title. As for reply to transcript, some people reply with keywords, but in most circumstances, people tend to use short sentence to express their thought on the Internet, in this case, is "I support this."

Table 9.2 Example of Content Analysis from News

Transcript types	Title / Article / Post
Title of transcript	Protests in Taiwan: A Long-Term Threat to Foreign Trade?
Content of transcript	"Mass protests and police clashes in Taiwan have indefinitely postponed ratification of a trade deal between the island's expansion-starved service sector and its larger counterpart China. . ."
Reply to transcript with keywords	Protesters overall are mostly upset about due process, wanting more review/transparency for the *trade pact*.
Reply to transcript without keywords	I support this.

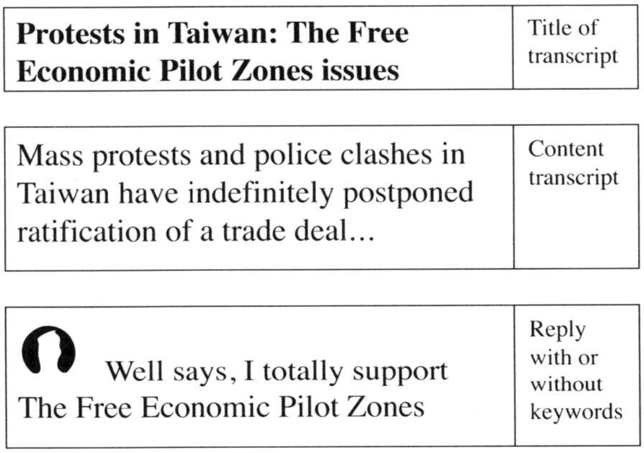

Figure 9.2 Examples of Content Analysis from News

Quasi-Experimental Design

During the period of our big data analysis, an experimental research design was particularly employed to examine the effects of a sequence of online policy summits. The summits were held by the National Development Council on July 21, 24, 31, and August 4, 2014. Each summit focused on a special issue of the Free Economic Pilot Zones issues. The first summit illustrated the vision and strategy of the Free Economic Pilot Zones. The rest of the three summits described strategic plans for medical care, agriculture export, and education innovation separately. Government officers from eight different agencies attended the summits and answered questions from civic groups and mass media for 120 minutes, including the minister of the National Development Council, Dr. Guan; the Secretary-General of the Industrial Development Bureau, Ministry of Economic Affairs, Mr. Yu; and the senior technical specialist of the Ministry of Transportation and Communications, Mr. Lu. All summits were posted live on YouTube,[2] Hackpad, and the website of the National Development Council. After the summits, we monitored for are any comments about the summit online and any changes of public opinion difference on the Free Economic Pilot Zones issues.

Online Survey—Big Data and Survey Data

Despite the theoretical and practical advantages of Big Data analysis described above, a preferred strategy is to use a combination of new and traditional data sources to support research, analytics, and decision-making, with the precise combination depending on the demands of public opinion detection.

Researchers recently have formulated ideas for blending Big Data with traditional research in the area of market research, which has traditionally been heavily reliant on data collected through surveys. For example, Porter and Lazaro (2014) described a series of business case studies to illustrate how survey data can be blended with data from other sources to enhance the overall analysis. One of their cases, consumer behavior data from website activity and transactions, is combined with survey data capturing perceptions, attitudes, life events, and offsite behavior. By using respondent-level models to relate customer perceptions (from survey data) to behaviors for the same customers (from data on website activity), they were better able to understand the whys behind online behavior and prioritize areas for improvement based on an understanding the needs of different individuals. Similarly, the U.S. Census Bureau is identifying ways in which big data can be used to improve surveys and census operations to increase the timeliness of data, increase the explanatory power of Census Bureau data, and reduce operational costs of data collection (Bostic 2013). However, combining big data and survey data on public opinion detection is a missing piece of the puzzle. Therefore, this research developed an online questionnaire to reveal the mystery of the combination. The first part of our questionnaire was composed of three questions measuring policy awareness, policy support, and policy discussion. The second part was designed to obtain background information, such as sex, age, and living location.

Results

This research aimed to gather public opinions on the issue of the Free Economic Pilot Zones online, employing content analysis and automated text analysis techniques to analyze articles by utilizing keywords to detect both positive and negative opinions online. The positive and negative opinion analyses were based on the source of online information and attitudinal semantics. The online search was conducted by a third-party licensed firm eLand Technologies.

Volume Analysis

Table 9.3 shows the reply distribution of frames and channels from the Internet. During the observation period, we uncovered 2,198 main transcripts talking about the Free Economic Pilot Zones from

Table 9.3 Reply Distribution of Frames and Channels

	Channels				Total
	News	Blogs	Forums	Social Media	
Transcript	1,742	70	100	286	2,198
Frames					
Trade	707	34	53	132	926
Logistics	463	13	19	54	549
Agriculture	586	9	20	91	706
Medical care	370	23	9	72	474
Education	577	23	18	73	691
Finance	458	13	21	34	526
Service	308	10	8	31	357
Sum up	3469	125	148	487	4229
Reply					
with keywords	5,698	150	242	825	6,915
without keywords	17,377	82	601	21,104	39,164

news, blogs, forums, and Facebook. Some articles contain more than one issue in their contents; therefore, the total number of transcripts (3,469) is larger than the transcript number (1,742) we analyzed.

Among these channels, the news channel had the largest volume at main transcript and reply with keywords, with 1,742 reported on main transcripts, 5,698 replies with keywords. We believe that mass media in Taiwan still dominates the agenda-setting process and leads the discussion of the Free Economic Pilot Zones. The second largest volume channel was Facebook, with 286 reported on main transcripts, 825 replies with keywords, and 21,104 posts of replies without keywords. The minimum volume channel was blogs, with only 70 transcript posts during the survey. Since the Free Economic Pilot Zones is mainly about trade negotiations, trade issue has the largest volume, followed by the agriculture issue. Some stakeholders against import agriculture from China caused the high volume.

Sentiment Analysis

Figure 9.3 shows the results of sentiment analysis with positive and negative sentiment during the research period. Analyses based on the source of online information and attitudinal semantics demonstrate that positive sentiment was lower than negative sentiment during the whole period, though sometimes the gap is not clear, as illustrated by the period from July 12 to 14, and from July 20 to 22. In addition, each wavelength lasted only two to four days if no other event or opinion leader was involved. We also found out that the most positive attitudes were derived from news channels, and the most negative attitudes from discussions by netizens on a bulletin board system named Professional Technology Temple (PTT). Some posts from forums and social media show no clear attitude.

In Figure 9.3, the sentiment analysis shows two pinpoints—July 28 and August 7. We suspect the first pinpoint was caused by a mayoral candidate's advocacy of "a small island in the northwest of Taipei"—the Shezidao (社子島) peninsula—into the Free Economic Pilot Zones. The second cause could be when the Minister of Economic Affairs submitted his resignation over a gas blast in Kaohsiung. Netizens worry about the aftershock of resignation may have caused uncertainty of the Free Economic Pilot Zones policy. Clearly, the two pinpoints were not directly correlated with the Free Economic Pilot Zones itself, but were a key informer related to the issue. Thus, the research suggests

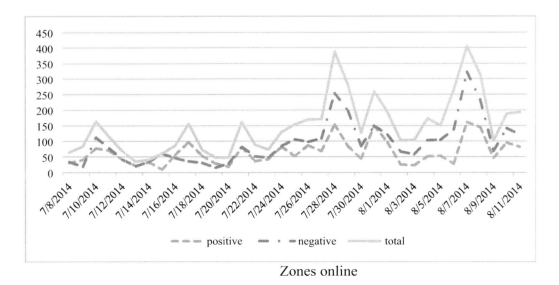

Figure 9.3 Trends of Positive and Negative Sentiment Discussion about the Free Economic Pilot Zones Online

that any use of big data analysis to monitor Internet public opinion requires a long period of observation to obtain more precise analysis.

During the period, an experimental research design was employed to examine the effects of a sequence of online policy summits. The summit was broadcast live on YouTube, with 937 views, with the total volume higher than July 21, a day before the summit. But we do not have significant evidence to ascribe this increase to online policy summits, because the volume before and after the summit is similar.

Online Survey

The online survey was conducted from July 21 to August 3, 2014. From a total of 1,663 respondents, 735 (44.2%) of our respondents were male. For policy awareness, 961 (57.8%) respondents answered that they were aware of the Free Economic Pilot Zones Policy, 702 (42.2%) respondents answered that they were not. According to our survey, 50% of the respondents supported the policy, 28% opposed it, and 21% were undecided. As for those people who were not aware of the Free Economic Pilot Zones policy, in the survey we provided a short explanation statement, as follows: "the FEPZs are trial zones for a free economy, with liberalization, internationalization and forward vision as their defining concepts. In FEPZs, all restrictions on the flow of goods, people, capital, information, and knowledge are greatly loosened, and market opening is carried out." Unexpectedly, 35% of respondents supported the policy after the statement, 25% were against it, and 36% of respondents were undecided. Finally, we asked, "Have you ever discussed the policy of the Free Economic Pilot Zones with others online?" Of the respondents, 77% declared that they did not discuss the policy online.

Conclusion

Responsiveness is a central concern of democracy, and it is important for public policy makers and government to obtain public opinion during the policymaking process. Due to the wide penetration of the Internet and other ICT applications, the traditional public opinion survey is facing tremendous challenges, such as a low response rate and the difficulty in reaching younger generations. Methodological challenges have led to a scarcity of empirical research on framing public opinion online. Responding to this gap in the literature, this research adopted big data analysis for framing public opinion online in an unobtrusive, more conversational, and more accessible way. To do so, we gathered public opinions on the issue of the Free Economic Pilot Zones online. The research utilized 130 keywords to detect both positive and negative online opinions, from July 8 to August 11, 2014. In addition, an experimental research design was employed to examine the effects of a sequence of online policy summits on July 21, 2014.

There are four key research findings in this study. First, the result of big data analysis demonstrated that most people had negative sentiment regarding the Free Economic Pilot Zones policy, due to suspicion of trade with China. In contrast, public opinion obtained from online surveys tended to support the policy. Second, our research findings also show that the ratio of news reported on mass media was much greater than on social media. Although public opinion on social media had much higher volume of discussions, the discussions were less organized and less structured than those demonstrated in the news. Third, most online discussions lasted only two to four days if no other events or opinion leaders were involved. In fact, the application of big data analysis of the observation of online opinions could easily be affected by events which were not taken into account in the original research. And last, the online policy summit did not have a significant effect on public opinion online. In other words, online public policy summits, awareness, or explanatory campaigns have limited positive impact on policy marketing. The policy publicity event used in the analysis did not significantly raise citizen awareness and support for the Free Economic Pilot Zones. The findings of this study help to answer important questions about how to observe and analyze online public opinions in practice.

Data mined from social media or administrative operations in this way provide a range of new data that can enable government agencies to monitor—and improve—their own performance. With empirical data from both big data analysis and online survey, the research team suggests that NDC could adopt big data analysis regularly and hold more public hearings and online forums to improve policy understanding, since teenagers are the main component in the protest. In fact, NDC did hold at least four public hearings in various universities. Moreover, NDC used data from social media for self-improvement, by understanding what public policies, services, or providers were attracting negative opinions and complaints.

Despite all the care given to this study, several limitations of the present study should be noted and addressed in any future research. First, because automated keyword inquiries do not identify all the posts that are relevant to specified frames, the actual distribution of each frame may remain unclear. For example, although we identified posts about the Free Economic Pilot Zones frames by using carefully selected keywords, the searched results do not necessarily include the entire volume of the Free Economic Pilot Zones–related posts. Thus, the current analysis is not designed to provide full descriptive statistics of issue frames represented in all of four channels. Such analysis may require a human-coding approach with random samples of posts. Second, it is with great concern that collecting public opinion using big data analysis might involve with other issues: unequal policy representation and the digital divide. People surfing on the Internet usually are younger and well educated, but policy makers have to respond to every citizen, not just netizens. Government agencies must design and administer their data collection instruments and methods for public opinions in a manner that achieves the best balance between maximizing data quality and representation and controlling measurement error.

Notes

1. Issue framing is important in understanding the potential dynamics of attention because the broadly defined issues of the day, such as unemployment, immigration, abortion, and global warming, have been around, and are likely to continue to be prominent in one form or another, in public debate for decades.
2. This video is available at https://www.youtube.com/watch?v=adFNN0dgsEY (in Chinese).

References

Anstead, Nick. 2014. 'ICA Presentation: Big Data and Public Opinion'. Accessed July 5, 2015. http://nickanstead.com/blog/2014/6/2/ica-presentation-big-data-and-public-opinion

Bostic, William G. 2013. 'Big Data Projects at the Census Bureau'. *Presentation to the Council of Professional Associations on Federal Statistics (COPAFS)*, March 1. Washington, DC.

Chae, Bongsug. 2015. 'Insights from Hashtag #supplychain and Twitter Analytics: Considering Twitter and Twitter Data for Supply Chain Practice and Research'. *International Journal of Production Economics* 165: 247–259.

Chau, Michael, and Jennifer Xu. 2012. 'Business Intelligence in Blogs: Understanding Consumer interactions and Communities." *MIS Quarterly* 36 (4): 1189–1216.

Chen, Boyu, Da-Chi Liao, Hsin-Che Wu, and San-Yih Hwan. 2014. 'The Logic of Communitive1 Action: A Case Study of Taiwan's Sunflower Movement'. Accessed July 5, 2015. http://ipp.oii.ox.ac.uk/sites/ipp/files/documents/IPP2014_Chen.pdf

China Go Aboard. n.d. 'Introductions of the Free Economic Pilot Zones in Taiwan.' Accessed July 5, 2015. http://www.chinagoabroad.com/en/node/10768

Corbett, Julia B., and Jessica L. Durfee. 2004. 'Testing Public (Un)certainty of Science: Media Representations of Global Warming'. *Science Communication* 26 (2): 129–151.

Desouza, Kevin C. 2014. 'Realizing the Promise of Big Data-Implementing Big Data Projects'. Accessed December 10, 2015. http://www.businessofgovernment.org/report/realizing-promise-big-data

Dunn, William N. 2012. *Public Policy Analysis* (5th ed). New York: Routledge Press.

Eriksom, Robert S., Michael B. Mackuen, and James A. Stinson. 2002. *The Macro Polity*. New York: Cambridge University Press.

Executive Yuan. 2011. 'Cross-Strait Relations'. Accessed July 15, 2015. http://www.ey.gov.tw/pda_en/cp.aspx?n=FC5BD9B3D7E30CBD
Fan, Weiguo, and Michael D. Gordon. 2014. 'The Power of Social Media Analytics'. *Communications of the ACM* 57 (6): 74–81.
Graham, Missy, and Elizabeth J. Avery. 2013. 'Government Public Relations and Social Media'. *Public Relations Journal* 7 (3): 1–21.
Hioe, Brian. 2014. 'Beyond the Sunflower Movement: Present Issues for Future Taiwanese Activism'. Accessed July 15, 2015. http://thinking-taiwan.com/beyond-the-sunflower-movement/
Hsiao, Naiyi, Don-Yun Chen, and Zhou-Peng Liao. 2015. *A Feasibility Study on Improving Public Service Quality and Public Policy Analysis by Big Data Analysis*. Taiwan: National Development Council Press.
Hughes, Jessica. 2014. 'Can Government Mine Tweets to Assess Public Opinion?' Accessed July 15, 2015. http://www.govtech.com/data/Can-Government-Mine-Tweets-to-Assess-Public-Opinion.html
IBM. 2014a. 'Produce Actionable Information with Big Data Analytics for Government'. Accessed July 15, 2015. http://www-03.ibm.com/software/businesscasestudies/us/en/corp?synkey=V277236H42361R94
IBM. 2014b. 'Social Media Helps FDLE Secure Republican National Convention'. Accessed July 15, 2015. http://www-03.ibm.com/software/businesscasestudies/us/en/corp?synkey=P873207L42958S87
IBM. 2014c. 'Mobile App and Social Media Content Analysis Leads to the Development of a Plan to Increase Tourism'. Accessed July 15, 2015. http://www-03.ibm.com/software/businesscasestudies/us/en/corp?synkey=V277236H42361R94
Ingram Micro Technology Solutions. 2015. 'Four Types of Big Data Analytics and Examples of Their Use'. Accessed July 15, 2015. http://www.ingrammicroadvisor.com/big-data/four-types-of-big-data-analytics-and-examples-of-their-use
Intel IT center. 2012. 'Big Data 101: Unstructured Data Analytics'. Accessed July 5, 2015. http://www.intel.com/content/www/us/en/big-data/unstructured-data-analytics-paper.html
Jang, S. Mo., and P. Sol Hart. 2015. 'Polarized Frames on 'Climate Change' and 'Global Warming' across Countries and States: Evidence from Twitter Big Data'. *Global Environmental Change* 32: 11–17.
Khan, Gohar F., Ho Y. Yoon, Jiyoung Kim, and Han W. Park. 2014. 'From E-Government to Social Government: Twitter use by Korea's Central Government." *Online Information Review* 38 (1): 95–113.
Lee, Chung-Pin, Tong-Yi Huang, and Chun-Ming Chen. 2012. 'Forecasting the Trends of Internet Society: World Internet Project Survey in Taiwan and International Comparison'. Accessed July 15, 2015. http://www.teg.org.tw/web_en/research/view.do?id=1334130032469&language=en
Maaroof Abbas. 2015. 'Big Data and the 2030 Agenda for Sustainable Development'. Accessed December 10, 2015. http://www.unescap.org/sites/default/files/Final%20Draft_%20stock-taking%20report_For%20Comment_301115.pdf
Martin, Donna. 2014. 'Taiwan Trade Pact with China Heavily Protested'. Accessed July 15, 2015. http://guardianlv.com/2014/03/taiwan-trade-pact-with-china-heavily-protested/
Monroe, Alan D. 1998. 'Public Opinion and Public Policy, 1980–1993'. *Public Opinion Quarterly* 62 (1): 6–28.
Morgan, David L. 1988. *Focus Groups as Qualitative Research*. London: Sage.
Neuman, W. Russell, Lauren Guggenheim, S. Mo Jang, and Soo Young Bae. 2014. 'The Dynamics of Public Attention: Agenda-Setting Theory Meets Big Data." *Journal of Communication* 64 (2): 193–214.
Normandeau, Kevin. 2013. 'Beyond Volume, Variety and Velocity Is the Issue of Big Data Veracity'. Accessed July 15, 2015. http://insidebigdata.com/2013/09/12/beyond-volume-variety-velocity-issue-big-data-veracity/
O'Malley, Martin. 2014. 'Doing What Works: Governing in the Age of Big Data'. *Public Administration Review* 74 (5): 555–556.
Page, Benjamin, and Robert Shapiro. 1983. 'Effects of Public Opinion on Policy'. *American Political Science Review* 77 (1): 175–190.
Patrick, Flavin. 2012. 'Income Inequality and Policy Representation in the American States'. *American Politics Research* 40 (1): 29–59.
The Pew Research Centre. 2012. 'Assessing the Representativeness of Public Opinion Surveys'. Accessed July 5, 2015. http://www.people-press.org/files/legacy-pdf/Assessing%20the%20Representativeness%20of%20Public%20Opinion%20Surveys.pdf
Porter, Scott, and Carlos G. Lazaro. 2014. 'Adding Big Data Booster Packs to Survey Data'. *Presented at the CASRO Digital Research Conference 2014*, March 12. San Antonio, TX.
Robb, Drew. 2012. 'Gartner Taps Predictive Analytics as Next Big Business Intelligence Trend'. Accessed July 5, 2015. http://www.enterpriseappstoday.com/business-intelligence/gartner-taps-predictive-analytics-as-next-big-business-intelligence-trend.htm
Schulz, G. W. 2012. 'Homeland Security Office OKs Efforts to Monitor Threats Via Social Media'. Accessed July 5, 2015. https://www.revealnews.org/article/homeland-security-office-oks-efforts-to-monitor-threats-via-social-media/

Sunflower Movement. 2014. Accessed July 5, 2015. https://www.facebook.com/sunflowermovement
Thomas, R., and S. Purdon. 1994. 'Telephone Methods for Social Surveys'. Accessed July 5, 2015. http://sru.soc.surrey.ac.uk/SRU8.html
Tufekci, Z., and D. Freelon. 2013. ;Introduction to the Special Issue on New Media and Social Unrest'. *American Behavioral Scientist* 57 (7): 843–847.
Zeng, Daniel, Hsinchun Chen, Robert Lusch, and Shu-Hsing Li. 2010. 'Social media analytic sand intelligence'. *Intelligent Systems IEEE* 25 (6): 13–16.

SECTION III

Technology-Enabled Cross-Boundary Collaboration and Governance

10

E-GOVERNMENT AND CITIZEN TRUST IN GOVERNMENT

The Role of Citizen Characteristics in the Relationship between E-Government Use and Citizen Trust in Government

Seung-Hwan Myeong and Michael J. Ahn

Introduction

With the level of public trust in government at its historic low (Saad 2011), much research in public administration has been devoted to studying factors that influence citizen trust in government. Among these, e-government has received much attention as a potential remedy to improve citizen trust by providing citizens with the convenience of online services available 24/7 and enabling citizens to communicate directly with the government and its officials through online channels of communication. As a public sector innovation, e-government was expected to have a positive impact on citizen trust in government, and numerous studies have found such a relationship between e-government use and citizen trust in government (Bart et al. 2005; Beldad et al. 2012; Carter and Bélanger 2005; Parent, Vandebeek, and Gemino 2005; Tolbert and Mossberger 2006; West 2004).

However, the main emphasis on e-government research has been how e-government influences the level of citizen trust or how citizen trust influences the adoption of e-government, without much consideration for the variation in the individual characteristics of citizens. This chapter takes the position that citizen trust in government is a two-way process, in which e-government use does not automatically translate into a high level of trust but interacts with various attributes of citizens. This chapter explores the relationship between dynamic characteristics of citizens, their e-government use, and trust in government using multiple measures of citizen characteristics, such as citizen's information processing behaviors, attitude (positive or negative) toward information technology in general, and value orientation (public service commitment).

In the following section, some key literature on information processing behavior and citizen trust in government are discussed, followed by elaboration on the methodology and findings. Theoretical and practical implications of the findings are discussed in the conclusion.

Literature Review

Information Processing Behavior and Trust

Sociopsychological theories of behavior assume that attitudes precede behaviors (Ajzen and Fishbein 1980). In the information systems (IS) context, Melone (1990) suggested that users' attitudes refer to "a predisposition to respond favorably or unfavorably to a computer system, application, system staff member, or a process related to the use of that system or application" (p. 81) and proposed that attitudes toward a certain behavior (e.g., use) are affected by complex beliefs and intentions of the users. Similarly, Ajzen and Fishbein (1980) posited that attitudes are an important predictor of behavioral intentions. Here, the effects of attitudes on behaviors are thought to be, in turn, "contingent upon other factors such as the circumstances surrounding the behavior and the conditions under which the attitude was formed" (Melone 1990). Zajonc and Markus (1982) pointed out that attitudes may be a function not only of the object attitude, such as output accuracy, but also of individuals' characteristics, roles, and tasks in a given situation. Pratkanis (1988) identified the circumstances influencing attitudes as IS attributes related to reasons for certain actions, events related to IS implementation, and technological expectations.

This empirical evidence shows that the effectiveness and outcomes of IS are influenced by the characteristics and preexisting perceptions of the users. This attitude–behavior perspective is useful in explaining the level of citizen trust in government as an outcome of citizens' information processing behaviors and their attitude and perception toward information technology in general. These characteristics are expected to influence the kind of information citizens receive or choose to receive (including information about government) and their experience with e-government services, which ultimately influence citizens' perception and trust in government.

Citizen Trust in Government

From an individual's perspective, trust can be defined as the extent to which an individual is willing to ascribe to the good intentions of and has confidence in others' words and actions (Cook and Wall 1980; Rotter 1967). Mayer, Davis, and Schoorman (1995) defined that trust in government as an individual's willingness to be vulnerable to government actions based on his or her expectation that the government would make certain efforts that are important to him or her, regardless of his or her ability to monitor or control the government. More specifically, Zucker (1986) identified three sources of trust: (1) process-based trust that is produced through the process of past or expected exchange; (2) characteristic-based trust, which is influenced by various social and individual characteristics and attributes; and (3) institutional-based trust, tied to formal societal structures, based on individual or firm-specific attributes or on intermediary mechanisms. While citizen trust in government is a fairly well-researched subject in public administration and political science traditions, more focus is placed on the process-based and institutional-based trust in this study than on characteristic-based trust.

Some studies explored the relationship between public service performance and citizen trust in government. The idea is that citizens interact with the government through their transactions with government, and therefore the quality of the services provided by the government and satisfaction with the transactions primarily influence the level of citizen trust in government (Van Ryzin 2007). Here, high-quality public service serves as a precondition to trust in government (Vigoda-Gadot and Yuval 2003).

Outside the public service performance and trust argument, broader political and social factors are examined. The perception of Congress, negative economic performance, and citizen concerns for crime contribute negatively to citizen trust in government (Chanley, Rudolph, and Rahn 2000). Political corruption and government openness to citizen inputs significantly influence the level of citizen trust in government (Kim 2010). Social capital in our society is considered to have a decisive role in influencing public trust in government and in society in general (Keele 2007; Rothstein and Uslaner 2005). Additionally, trust in one social institution is found to be linked to trust in other institution, and general satisfaction with democracy had a strong influence on people's trust in government (Christensen and Lægrei 2005).

With the emergence of e-government, scholars began exploring the link between e-government performance and citizen trust where high-quality e-government services and online service transactions were expected to have positive impact on the level of citizen trust in government (Bart et al. 2005; Beldad et al. 2012; Carter and Bélanger 2005; Parent, Vandebeek, and Gemino 2005; Tolbert and Mossberger 2006; West 2004). Tolbert and Mossberger (2006) suggested that "e-government can increase process-based trust by improving interactions with citizens and perceptions of responsiveness" and "improve citizen evaluations of government," and (Welch, Hinnant, and Moon 2005) confirmed that citizens who are more satisfied with e-government and government websites trust the government more, as trust is produced in a reciprocal service transactions between citizens and the government.

However, there is some disagreement, as some authors did not find significant linkage between e-government performance and trust (Morgeson, VanAmburg, and Mithas 2011), and the causal direction between government performance and trust is questioned where an individual's characteristic, such as a preexisting level of trust in government, is thought to affect how government performance is perceived, which, in turn, influences the level of trust in government (Van de Walle and Bouckaert 2003). As Welch, Hinnant, and Moon (2005) have pointed out, most research focuses on institution-based and process-based trust[1] and individuals' personal characteristics are hidden, making it difficult to examine characteristic-based trust. This can be the source of disagreement in the literature, because when we don't know individual attributes, it is difficult to draw a full picture of the dynamics of citizen trust in government—what internal characteristics and attributes of citizens influence the level of citizen trust in government. While demographic characteristics such as age, education, and occupation matter in trust (Akman et al. 2005; Christensen and Lægrei 2005), this falls short of taking into account of a wide range of attitudinal and expectation characteristics of individual citizens in the function of citizen trust in government. Therefore, this study utilizes a survey of 1,520 randomly sampled citizens that measures various aspects of individual characteristics, attitudes, and perceptions to examine how they actually influence the level of citizen trust in government.

Data and Propositions

The data used for this study were collected from a national survey conducted on 1,520 randomly sampled citizens in South Korea between ages 20 and 70 from March 14 to May 31, 2011. The survey was conducted by mail or by visiting individual citizens. These individuals are selected randomly but stratified by the locations of the sample population to make the sample more representative to the general Korean population. Of 1,520 surveys sent out, we collected 1,211 survey answers, resulting in an overall response rate of 79.7%.

The survey collected information on various perceptional, attitudinal, and information processing characteristics of individual citizens, such as the medium of communication they use in an information search, the kind of information they seek in general, their perceptions about the increasing informatization of our society, their familiarity with e-government sites, their perception of government performance and the level of each citizen's public service motivation, and their willingness to contribute to the public good. Building on the previous work by the author, which focused on the political–ideological tendencies of citizens and perceptions on the role of information technology in society and their influence on trust (Myeong et al. 2012), this paper explains citizen trust as an outcome of e-government use, various citizen value characteristics, information processing behavior, and perception of general government service performance and quality. Figure 10.1 illustrates this relationship.

The dependent variable, the level of citizen trust in government, was measured in three dimensions—the extent to which public policy information is trustful (information trust), the extent to which government is trustful compared to nongovernmental organizations (NGOs) and other civic groups (institutional trust), and whether the public officials are perceived to be effective and prompt (competency trust).

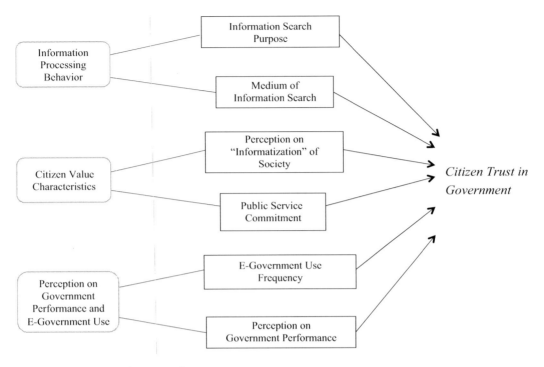

Figure 10.1 Theoretical Framework

For information processing behavior, a number of dimensions were measured. First, the survey asked which mediums of communication citizens use in an information search from a choice of the Internet, cell phones, newspaper, TV/radio, or face-to-face contact to examine whether the choice of communication medium for information search has any significant impact on the perception of trust in government. Second, we collected information on the frequency of citizens' visits to e-government sites to examine the extent to which citizens are using e-government (e-government use). Third, we measured what kind of information search activities citizens are engaged in, including searches for educational, economic, and political information, obtaining skills and knowledge in specific fields of interest, and obtaining information for entertainment purposes.

To measure the perception about the effects of information technology on our society in general (*informatization*), we asked our survey respondents how they perceived informatization would affect various aspects of their lives, such as improving the convenience of daily activities, developing local communities, creating economic opportunities and employment opportunities, and how it affects privacy and whether it improves/deteriorates social order.

Third, in order to examine how a citizen's perception of government performance affects their level of trust in government, the survey included a question on how citizens perceive the government performance improved over time.

The survey also measured the level of public service commitment by asking if citizens are engaged in local voluntary services for philanthropic purposes. Some key demographic information is also collected, such as level of education, gender, age, and income, as control variables. Based on the survey data and proposed theoretical framework above, the following propositions are examined.

H1: Information Processing Behavior and Trust in Government

H1–1: Medium of Communication and Citizen Trust in Government

Citizens who use online mediums such as the Internet (using personal computers) and cell phones are expected to have a significantly different level of trust in government than citizens who use traditional offline mediums of communication. From an individual citizen's point of view, an online medium of communication and information provides far more information on a real-time basis, as it is open to not only the traditional media outlets that dominate offline channels but also to all others who have access to the Internet. Exposure to different informational environments is expected to influence the level of trust in government, as citizens will be subjected to different kinds of information and opinions (in terms of amount and sources) about the government: Namely, as mentioned above, information from traditional media outlets in offline environments and information from online media of which there are a far greater number of information contributors and a greater variety of opinions. However, the direction of the influence on trust is not anticipated, as a greater number of information contributors and wider variety of opinions do not necessarily mean positive information about the government—just as it may include positive information about the government, it may include negative information and opinions about the government and it is difficult to anticipate where the pendulum of opinion on government is hovering at an aggregate level. However, in one study, Im et al. (2014) have found a negative relationship between the time spent on the Internet and the level of citizen trust in government and compliance.

H1–2: Citizens Who Use E-Government More Frequently Are Likely to Have Higher Level of Trust in Government

We expect that citizens who visit e-government sites more frequently and therefore engage in more online contact with the government will have developed greater trust in government—whether it is using e-government services, obtaining public information from a government website, or communicating with government officials online. The greater exposure to and familiarity with e-government is expected to translate into greater trust in government, consistent with the research on this relationship (Tolbert and Mossberger 2006; Welch, Hinnant, and Moon 2005).

H1–3: Information Search Purposes and Citizen Trust in Government

We speculate that there will be a difference in the level of trust of government depending on the kinds of information sought by citizens on the Internet. Just as different mediums of information search and use in hypothesis 1–1 are expected to expose citizens to different kinds of information, we anticipate that different intentions and reasons for using the Internet by citizens will also expose them to different information, knowledge, and opinions, which consequently influence the level of trust in government. Of the kinds of reasons the survey collected on why citizens use the Internet, we expect that citizens who are primarily engaged in information search for political and social issues will have distinctively different level of trust of government than will citizens who use the Internet for other purposes—online search for economic activities, education and employment opportunities, obtaining skills and knowledge in the fields of citizens' interests, entertainment materials, or Internet browsing with no particular purposes. It is expected that citizens who actively search for political and social issues will be exposed to a greater amount of information and opinions about government on the Internet, and they may display different levels of trust in government. In addition, these citizens may have different levels of expectation from the government, which in turn influence their level of trust. Similar to hypothesis 1, the direction of the difference in trust is hard to speculate as they may be exposed to more favorable or unfavorable information about government in their political and social issue-related searches.

H2: General Attitude toward Information Technology

This looks at citizen's general predisposition toward information technology and its influence on their trust in government. We anticipate that citizens who perceive the informatization of our society and transition into an information society in a favorable light are more likely to have a greater level of trust in government with e-government use than are citizens with negative views. It is expected that citizens with a positive outlook are expected to perceive e-government more favorably and that this will have a positive impact on their trust in government with e-government use. Conversely, citizens who have a negative perception on information technology in general and its impact on society are not likely to view e-government positively, and here e-government use will have little impact on their trust in government. The survey measured the perception of citizens on increasing informatization of our society on a number of dimensions, including improving the convenience on daily lives, local community development, economic development, employment opportunity, personal privacy, and general social order.

H3: Perception of Government Performance and Trust

We expect there will be a positive correlation where citizens who perceive government is performing well will have higher level of trust in government. Here, a high level of government performance will translate into a high level of competency in government, which in turn leads to a greater level of trust in government (Christensen and Lægrei 2005; Kim 2010; Vigoda-Gadot and Yuval 2003). Conversely, if citizens perceive government performing at a low level, this perceived incompetency is expected to have a negative consequence on their trust in government. This has been a point of continued academic discussion, as this seemingly intuitive relationship between performance and trust is not always supported in the literature due to the difficulty in defining and measuring performance (Yang and Holzer 2006). We measured perception of performance in a general fashion by asking citizens if they believe government performance has improved over time.

H4: Public Service Commitment and Trust

If hypothesis 2 examined the role of citizen's general disposition toward technology and its influence on trust, this examines the role of citizen's general disposition toward public service on trust. Similar to hypothesis 2, controlling for the level of e-government use or perception of government performance, inherent value orientation of individual citizens is expected to influence their trust in government. We measured citizens' value orientation by asking them about the extent to which they are involved in voluntary community services, and it is our expectation that citizens with a greater sense of public service value will display a higher level of trust in government. Citizens whose value orientation is aligned with public service value are likely to view government more positively than those not.

For all these variables as detailed in Table 10.1 below, Myeong and Lee's (2010) instruments were adopted and measured based on a seven-point Likert-type scale ranging from 1, "strongly disagree," to 7, "strongly agree." Table 10.1 shows the measurement instruments.

Table 10.1 Measurement Instruments for Variables

Variable	Measurement		Mean	Std. Deviation
E-Government Use	E-government Use. Range: 1 (low) – 7 (high)	Frequency of visiting government websites	3.77	1.73
Information Processing Behavior	Medium of Communication and Information Use. Response range 1 (low) – 7 (high use)	Computer and the Internet	5.70	1.54
		Cell phone (accessing the Internet and using apps)	3.48	2.09
		Print media—newspaper and magazine	3.93	1.66
		TV or Radio	4.87	1.51
		Face-to-face contact and communication	4.56	1.38
	Purposes of information search. Range: 1 (unlikely) – 7 (very much so)	Education/job information	4.34	1.61
		Health information	4.35	1.52
		Entertainment	4.73	1.85
		Information on economic activities	3.05	1.70
		Information on political and social changes	4.12	1.66
		Information on community activities	3.31	1.67
		Information on obtaining specialized knowledge	3.95	1.76
		No particular purpose in information search	3.83	1.74
		General interest in politics	3.51	1.73
Perception on Informatization of Our Society	Range: 1 (strongly disagree) – 7 (strongly agree)	Offering convenience in daily activities and transactions	5.48	1.39
		Facilitate regional development and reduce regional economic disparities	4.50	1.59
		Improving international relations	4.78	1.49
		Facilitate economic development	4.97	1.42
		Expanding employment opportunities	4.58	1.61
		Cause loss of self-control	4.61	1.48
		Violate privacy of citizens	5.53	1.47
		Cause general social disorder	5.22	1.52
Perception of Government Service Performance	Range: 1 (strongly disagree) – 7 (strongly agree)	Do you think the promptness of government services and transactions have improved over time?	4.64	1.60
Public Service Commitment	Range: 1 (not at all) – 7 (very much so)	Are you actively involved in local events and volunteer activities?	2.99	1.56
Trust in Government	Range: 1 (not at all) – 7 (very much so)	Policy information from the government is trustworthy.	3.13	1.41
		Government officials are prompt and effective in addressing citizen requests.	3.58	1.38
		Government is trustful (compared to NGOs).	3.35	1.48

Findings

Table 10.2 shows the results from the ordinary least squares (OLS) analysis. The results show that Hypotheses 1–2 (e-government use), 3 (government performance), and 4 (public service commitment) are supported, while hypotheses 1–3 (information search intentions) and 2 (perception on informatization) are partially supported. Hypothesis 1–1 (medium of communication) was not supported. The model explained approximately 40% of the variance in citizen trust in government with an R^2 score of 0.399, and the overall regression model was a good fit for the data with

Table 10.2 Results of Analysis

Model		Unstandardized Coefficients B	Std. Error	t	Sig.
	(Constant)	6.012	0.919	6.541	0.000
Medium of communication and information use	The Internet	0.001	0.07	0.018	0.985
	Cell Phone	0.032	0.048	0.66	0.510
	Print Media	0.073	0.066	1.106	0.269
	TV/Radio	−0.007	0.07	−0.094	0.925
	Face-to-Face Contact	−0.11	0.072	−1.53	0.126
E-government Use	**Do you visit government websites frequently?***	**0.122***	**0.063**	**1.931**	**0.054**
Purpose of Information Search	Education, employment information	−0.005	0.066	−0.077	0.938
	Health information	−0.069	0.071	−0.962	0.336
	Entertainment purpose	0.039	0.052	0.753	0.452
	Information on economic activities	−0.043	0.063	−0.69	0.491
	Information on political and social changes*	**0.123***	**0.071**	**1.722**	**0.085**
	Information on community activities	0.038	0.065	0.585	0.559
	Obtaining skills and knowledge**	**0.138****	**0.063**	**2.202**	**0.028**
	No particular purpose in information search	−0.025	0.055	−0.445	0.656
	Interested in politics in general	0.024	0.065	0.364	0.716
Perception on Informatization of Our Society	Increasing convenience for daily life	−0.091	0.085	−1.067	0.286
	Regional development**	**0.16****	**0.072**	**2.229**	**0.026**
	Improve international relationships**	**0.158****	**0.079**	**2.004**	**0.045**
	Facilitate economic development	−0.014	0.085	−0.16	0.873
	Improve employment opportunities**	**0.14****	**0.069**	**2.04**	**0.042**
	Informatization will cause loss of self-control	−0.066	0.072	−0.907	0.364
	Informatization will increasingly violate privacy of citizens**	**−0.19****	**0.088**	**−2.159**	**0.031**
	Informatization will facilitate spread of rumors and cause general social chaos	0.119	0.084	1.418	0.156

Model		Unstandardized Coefficients		t	Sig.
		B	Std. Error		
Perception of Government Service Performance	Do you think the promptness of administrative services have improved over time?	0.223***	0.066	3.355	0.001
Public Service Commitment	Are you actively involved in local community and volunteer services?	0.245***	0.071	3.45	0.001
Control Variables	Gender	−0.272	0.192	−1.422	0.155
	Age	**0.35***	**0.073**	**4.782**	**0.000**
	Education	0.013	0.047	0.288	0.773
	Household Income	−0.105	0.075	−1.404	0.161

*$p < .10$. **$p < .05$. ***$p < .01$.

$F (29, 1243) = 8.108$, $p < .01$. However, the adjusted R^2 score is .159, indicating potential inclusion of variables with little explanatory power.

First, as anticipated, citizens who were familiar with e-government sites and use them frequently showed a statistically significant and higher level of trust in government than those with low e-government use, confirming the findings in the literature that e-government use has a positive impact on citizen trust. However, our analysis showed that the medium of communication did not have any independent influence on the level of citizen trust on government. This is contrary to our initial expectation, in which we anticipated that different mediums of communication and information, especially the online medium as opposed to traditional offline medium, would expose citizens to different kinds of information about government and influence their perception of trust in government—either positively or negatively. Of the five mediums of communication used in the survey, no medium had any statistically significant impact on trust in government. As shown by the means in the table below, among the citizens who were surveyed for this study, citizens used the Internet most extensively, followed by TV/radio, face-to-face communication, newspaper/magazine, and cell phones. It was surprising to see relatively high reliance on face-to-face communication for information searches and low reliance on cell phones.

While the medium did not matter, intentions and purposes of information search mattered. Out of nine items measuring various purposes of information search and use—education, health, entertainment, economic activities, political and social change, community activities, obtaining skills and knowledge, general interest in politics, or no particular purposes in information search—we found that citizens engaged actively in information search for political and social changes and for obtaining new skills and knowledge in the fields of citizen interest. The positive effects of information searches

Table 10.3 Modes of Information Search

	N	Mean	Std. Deviation
Internet	1469	5.7	1.537
Cell phone	1450	3.48	2.089
Newspaper/Magazine	1455	3.93	1.66
TV/Radio	1457	4.87	1.507
Face-to-face	1453	4.56	1.381

for political and social purposes on trust were consistent with our expectation, as citizens who actively pursue information on political and social issues will be exposed to a greater amount and more diverse information and opinions about government and subsequently display different levels of trust in government. However, another kind of information search—to obtain new skills and knowledge in the fields of citizens' interest—and its impact on trust is difficult to explain. Compared to some other search intentions, such as entertainment or no particular purpose (just browsing the web), this is a more focused and "productive" use of the Internet. Therefore, one possible explanation is that citizens who use the Internet for productive purposes may be more familiar with e-government sites, which we found to have positive impacts on trust. Correlation between the two variables seem to be significant, as shown in the correlation matrix below.

Out of the eight items we used in the survey to assess the general perception of citizens on informatization of our society, citizens who perceive positive effects of informatization of our society displayed greater level of trust in government. Citizens who perceived that informatization lead to greater regional development, better international relations, and greater employment opportunities had a significantly higher level of trust in government. Relatedly, citizens who had a negative perception of informatization on personal privacy showed a lower level of trust in government.

Perception of government performance, e-government, and public service commitment all had positive impact on trust. Citizens who thought highly of government service in general had a higher level of trust in government. Last, citizens who had a high level of public service commitment showed a high level of trust in government. A similar study by Dimitrova and Chen (2006) has found a relationship between civic-mindedness and e-government adoption, and it is interesting to note that civic-mindedness (or public service commitment in this research context) has a positive impact on citizen trust in government. Looking at the coefficients, while most factors used in our analysis had a relatively small magnitude of impact on trust, the perception of government performance and public service commitment had the greatest impact on trust. Of the control variables, only age had a statistically significant impact on the level of trust—older citizens had more trust in government than younger ones had.

Discussions

As illustrated above, we find that while e-government use and perception of general government performance matter in improving citizen trust in government, various information processing behaviors, attitudes, and perceptions of citizens also have a significant impact on trust.

First, consistent with the literature, this chapter confirmed that e-government use had a positive impact on the level of trust, as citizens who are more familiar with e-government sites and visit

Table 10.4 Correlation between Familiarity with E-Government and Productive Info Search

		Productive Search Intention	E-Gov't Familiarity
Productive search intention	Pearson Correlation	1	.307**
Sig. (2-tailed)			.000
N		1461	1458
E-Gov't familiarity	Pearson Correlation	.307**	1
Sig. (2-tailed)		.000	
N		1458	1471

*$p < .10$. **$p < .05$. ***$p < .01$.

government websites more frequently displayed a higher level of trust in government (Tolbert and Mossberger 2006; West 2004). In addition, citizens who thought highly of government service performance had a significantly higher level of trust on government, endorsing the link between government performance and citizen trust (Bozeman and Straussman 1991; Van Ryzin and Gregg 2007).

Second, however, we found no relationship between the medium of communication and trust in government. We anticipated that different mediums of communication would expose citizens to a different pool of information and opinions, causing a different level of trust in government. As shown in Table 10.4, there were some variations in the medium that citizens use for information searches, with Internet being the most extensively used medium of information search. Furthermore, the correlation matrix in Table 10.5 shows that the Internet tends to replace newspaper/magazine and TV/radio use, as greater use of the Internet is negatively correlated to the use of those mediums.

Interestingly, the use of the Internet was positively related to face-to-face communication and to more cell phone use. Again, however, the variation in the medium did not have any effect on the level of trust in government, indicating that there is no distinctive difference in the kind of information about government whether it is transmitted through online mediums or traditional mediums. Relatively high reliance on face-to-face communication and TV/radio may play a mediating role between online and offline information. The relatively high correlations among variables point to a potential multicollinearity issue in the model. However, additional analysis indicates that variables show VIF (variance inflation factor) values between 1.0 and 2.0 (except for a variable that measured

Table 10.5 Correlations between Medium of Communication

		Internet	Cell Phone	Newspaper/Magazine	TV/Radio	Face-to-face communication
Internet	Pearson Correlation	1	.176**	−.083**	−.063*	.088**
	Sig. (2-tailed)		0	0.001	0.017	0.001
	N	1469	1448	1450	1453	1449
Cell Phone	Pearson Correlation	.176**	1	−.092**	−.158**	.052*
	Sig. (2-tailed)	0		0	0	0.047
	N	1448	1450	1442	1443	1441
Newspaper/Magazine	Pearson Correlation	−.083**	−.092**	1	.377**	.191**
	Sig. (2-tailed)	0.001	0		0	0
	N	1450	1442	1455	1447	1444
TV/Radio	Pearson Correlation	−.063*	−.158**	.377**	1	.265**
	Sig. (2-tailed)	0.017	0	0		0
	N	1453	1443	1447	1457	1447
Face-to-face Communication	Pearson Correlation	.088**	.052*	.191**	.265**	1
	Sig. (2-tailed)	0.001	0.047	0	0	
	N	1449	1441	1444	1447	1453

$*p < .10.$ $**p < .05.$ $***p < .01.$

the perception of information technology in society with a VIF value of 2.062—"informatization will facilitate spread of rumors and cause general social chaos"), indicating that the possibility of severe multicollinearity is relatively low.

Third, unlike the medium of information search, the purpose of an information search had a significant impact on citizen trust in government. Intentions and purposes of an information search were thought to expose citizens to different kinds of information. Our analysis shows that citizens who are primarily engaged in information searches for political and social issues and those who used the Internet to obtain new skills and knowledge showed a higher level of trust than those who searched for economic activities, employment opportunities, entertainment, or had no particular information search purposes. The reason for this is somewhat difficult to speculate on, other than that they may have a more positive and productive disposition that positively influence their perception toward government. There is some support for this argument in our findings, where citizens who possess a high level of public service commitment show a much higher level of trust in government. Putting these together, we can characterize that citizens with a high level of interest in political and social issues in their information searches, with a high level of public service commitment, and who are actively engaged in productive information searches for personal development (by obtaining skills and knowledge) are most likely to have a high level of trust in government.

Fourth, and relatedly, the general outlook toward the informatization of our society had a significant effect on the level of trust in government. Citizens who had a positive view about informatization—that informatization promotes regional development, aids international relations, and improves employment opportunities—scored a significantly higher level of trust in government, while those who viewed informatization negatively, believing that it increasingly violates the privacy of citizens, had lower levels of trust in government. This finding further supports our findings in which citizens' broad attitudes, tendencies, and outlooks have a considerable impact on their trust in government, controlling for their e-government use and the perception of the quality of government performance.

Last, our analysis shows that age mattered the most, as older citizens have a significantly higher level of trust in government than younger citizens have, while gender, education, and income had no effect when other characteristics of citizens, as tested in this chapter, were controlled for.

Conclusion

This chapter set out to examine the role of citizen characteristics in the relationship between e-government use and citizen trust in government. The basic assumption in this chapter was that e-government use does not necessarily increase citizen's trust in government but "interacts" with various characteristics, predispositions, and tendencies of citizens. In particular, we posited that it interacts with citizens' characteristics, such as their information processing behavior, attitude (positive or negative) toward information technology in general, value orientation (public service commitment), and perception of government service quality and performance. We confirmed that these individual attributes have considerable impact on the level of citizen trust in government. It revealed different types of citizens with varying degrees of trust in government. In particular, citizens who are actively engaged in information searches for political and social issues and productive information and citizens with high level of public service commitment had considerably higher level of trust in government. Similarly, citizens with a positive perception on information technology in general possessed a high level of trust in government, while those with negative outlooks tended to have a low level of trust in government, controlling for their e-government use and their perception of government service quality and performance. As anticipated and consistent with the literature, the presence and familiarity with e-government and a general perception of government service performance were also positively related to trust in government.

Understanding the impact of citizen characteristics on their trust in government is an increasingly important aspect of e-government with the rise of Web 2.0 and social networking services (SNS), which signaled the beginning of a new model of e-government where the limitations of traditional e-government are overcome by the involvement of citizens (including NGOs and businesses) in the development of e-government services. Arguably, this prompts the beginning of a new chapter in e-government history, where there is a shift in the role of government from that of a developer of e-government applications to a provider of public data, upon which various innovative e-government applications are "coproduced" with citizens (Ahn 2012; Chun et al. 2010; Ganapati 2011; Nam 2012; Roberts 2011). With its novel emphasis on the role of citizens in the e-government development process, the outcome of e-government is increasingly influenced by the dynamic and diverse characteristics of citizens. The shifting e-government paradigm will change many previously held understandings of the effects of e-government on the relationship between citizens and the government, including their trust in government and factors that influence it. This chapter showed that dynamic characteristics of citizens all had considerable influence on trust, independent of citizens' e-government use and perception of government service quality and performance, and identified different types of citizens who display varying degrees of trust in government. Our findings paint an encouraging picture of increasing collaboration and coproduction of e-government applications, as they will accommodate a wider range of citizens with varying degree of needs, expectations, and trust in government. That is, if traditional e-government applications with a one-size-fits-all approach produced different reactions and results (such as trust), the new approach can potentially address the variability of citizen types, needs, and characteristics, leading to a greater leap in enhancing citizens' trust in government.

Note

1. According to Welch, Hinnant, and Moon (2005), "Process-based trust is garnered through expectations of reciprocity in which the giver essentially obligates the receiver to return goods or services of equivalent 'intrinsic or economic value'" (Thomas 1998, 180). Institutions engender trust either directly through adoption of professional standards or codes of ethics or indirectly through the observance or administration of laws and regulations.

References

Ahn, Michael J. "Whither e-government? Web 2.0 and the future of e-government." In Christopher G. Reddick and Stephen K. Aikins (eds.), *Web 2.0 Technologies and Democratic Governance*, pp. 169–182. New York: Springer, 2012.

Ajzen, Icek, and Martin Fishbein. *Understanding Attitudes and Predicting Social Behavior*. Englewood Cliffs, NJ: Prentice Hall, 1980.

Akman, Ibrahim, Ali Yazici, Alok Mishra, and Ali Arifoglu. "E-government: A global view and an empirical evaluation of some attributes of citizens." *Government Information Quarterly* 22, no. 2 (2005): 239–257.

Bart, Yakov, Venkatesh Shankar, Fareena Sultan, and Glen L. Urban. "Are the drivers and role of online trust the same for all web sites and consumers? A large-scale exploratory empirical study." *Journal of Marketing* 69, no. 4 (2005): 133–152.

Beldad, A., T. Van der Geest, M. de Jong, and M. Steehouder. "A cue or two and I'll trust you: Determinants of trust in government organizations in terms of their processing and usage of citizens' personal information disclosed online." *Government Information Quarterly* 29 (2012): 41–49.

Bozeman, B., and J.D. Straussman. *Managing Information Strategically: Public Management Strategies*. San Francisco: Jossey-Bass Publishers, 1991.

Carter, Lemuria, and France Bélanger. "The utilization of e-government services: Citizen trust, innovation and acceptance factors." *Information Systems Journal* 15, no. 1 (2005): 5–25.

Chanley, Virginia A., Thomas J. Rudolph, and Wendy M. Rahn. "The origins and consequences of public trust in government: A time series analysis." *Public Opinion Quarterly* 64, no. 3 (2000): 239–256.

Christensen, Tom, and Per Lægreid. "Trust in government: The relative importance of service satisfaction, political factors, and demography." *Public Performance & Management Review* 28, no. 4 (2005): 487–511.

Chun, Soon Ae, Stuart Shulman, Rodrigo Sandoval, and Eduard Hovy. "Government 2.0: Making connections between citizens, data and government." *Information Polity* 15, no. 1 (2010): 1.

Cook, John, and Toby Wall. "New work attitude measures of trust, organizational commitment and personal need non-fulfilment." *Journal of Occupational Psychology* 53, no. 1 (1980): 39–52.

Dimitrova, Daniela V., and Yu-Che Chen. "Profiling the adopters of e-government information and services—the influence of psychological characteristics, civic mindedness, and information channels." *Social Science Computer Review* 24, no. 2 (2006): 172–188.

Ganapati, Sukumar. "Uses of public participation geographic information systems applications in e-government." *Public Administration Review* 71, no. 3 (2011): 425–434.

Im, Tobin, Wonhyuk Cho, Greg Porumbescu, and Jungho Park. "Internet, trust in government, and citizen compliance." *Journal of Public Administration Research and Theory* 24, no. 3 (2014): 741–763.

Keele, Luke. "Social capital and the dynamics of trust in government." *American Journal of Political Science* 51, no. 2 (2007): 241–254.

Kim, Soonhee. "Public trust in government in Japan and South Korea: Does the rise of critical citizens matter?" *Public Administration Review* 70, no. 5 (2010): 801–810.

Mayer, Roger C., James H. Davis, and F. David Schoorman. "An integrative model of organizational trust." *Academy of Management Review* 20, no. 3 (1995): 709–734.

Melone, Nancy Paule. "A theoretical assessment of the user-satisfaction construct in information systems research." *Management Science* 36, no. 1 (1990): 76–91.

Morgeson, Forrest V., David VanAmburg, and Sunil Mithas. "Misplaced trust? Exploring the structure of the e-government-citizen trust relationship." *Journal of Public Administration Research and Theory* 21, no. 2 (2011): 257–283.

Myeong, S.H., M. Kwon, J. Park, and B. Lee. "Research on the role of the perception of informatization, and information use purpose on citizen trust." *Informatization Policy* 19, no. 1 (2012): 25–44. (in Korean).

Myeong, S.H., and Bok-Ja Lee. "A study on elderly people's behavior for information use: Focusing on the elderly people's perception on information technologies." *Journal of Korean Association for Regional Information Society* 13 (2010): 23–47.

Nam, Taewoo. "Suggesting frameworks of citizen-sourcing via Government 2.0." *Government Information Quarterly* 29, no. 1 (2012): 12–20.

Parent, Michael, Christine A. Vandebeek, and Andrew C. Gemino. "Building citizen trust through e-government." *Government Information Quarterly* 22, no. 4 (2005): 720–736.

Pratkanis, A.R. "The cognitive representation of attitudes." In A.R. Pratkanis, S.T. Breckler, and A.G. Greenwald (eds.), *Attitude Structure and Function*, pp. 71–89. Hillsdale, NJ: Erlbaum.

Roberts, Nancy C. "Beyond smokestacks and silos: Open-source, web-enabled coordination in organizations and networks." *Public Administration Review* 71, no. 5 (2011): 677–693.

Rothstein, Bo, and Eric M. Uslaner. "All for all: Equality, corruption, and social trust." *World Politics* 58, no. 1 (2005): 41–72.

Rotter, Julian B. "A new scale for the measurement of interpersonal trust1." *Journal of Personality* 35, no. 4 (1967): 651–665.

Saad, Lydia. "Americans express historic negativity toward US government." *Gallup.com*, September 26 (2011), accessed April 8, 2016.

Thomas, Craig W. "Maintaining and restoring public trust in government agencies and their employees." *Administration & Society* 30, no. 2 (1998): 166–193.

Tolbert, Caroline J., and Karen Mossberger. "The effects of e-government on trust and confidence in government." *Public Administration Review* 66, no. 3 (2006): 354–369.

Van de Walle, Steven, and Geert Bouckaert. "Public service performance and trust in government: The problem of causality." *International Journal of Public Administration* 26, no. 8–9 (2003): 891–913.

Van Ryzin, Gregg G. "Pieces of a puzzle: Linking government performance, citizen satisfaction, and trust." *Public Performance & Management Review* 30, no. 4 (2007): 521–535.

Vigoda-Gadot, Eran, and Fany Yuval. "Managerial quality, administrative performance and trust in governance revisited: A follow-up study of causality." *International Journal of Public Sector Management* 16, no. 7 (2003): 502–522.

Welch, Eric W., Charles C. Hinnant, and M. Jae Moon. "Linking citizen satisfaction with e-government and trust in government." *Journal of Public Administration Research and Theory* 15, no. 3 (2005): 371–391.

West, Darrell M. "E-government and the transformation of service delivery and citizen attitudes." *Public Administration Review* 64, no. 1 (2004): 15–27.

Yang, Kaifeng, and Marc Holzer. "The performance—trust link: Implications for performance measurement." *Public Administration Review* 66, no. 1 (2006): 114–126.

Zajonc, Robert B., and Hazel Markus. "Affective and cognitive factors in preferences." *Journal of Consumer Research* (1982): 123–131.

Zucker, Lynne G. "Production of trust: Institutional sources of economic structure, 1840–1920." *Research in Organizational Behavior* (1986).

11
SOCIAL MEDIA COMMUNICATION MODES IN GOVERNMENT

Ines Mergel

Who
Says What
In Which Channel
To Whom
With What Effect?

(Lasswell, 1948:216)

1 Introduction

Social media technologies are an important communication channel that many government organizations have added to their public affairs toolkit. Social technologies, including weblogs such as WordPress, microblogging services such as Twitter, instant messengers such as Yammer, photosharing sites such as Instagram, or social networking sites such as Facebook, are used for intra- as well as extra-organizational purposes. What these tools have in common is usually a networking component: Users can create their own profile page with individual information about themselves, follow each other's updates, or create a newsfeed with their own updates. Boyd and Ellison define social media tools as

> web-based services that allow individuals to (1) construct a public or semi-public profile within a bounded system, (2) articulate a list of other users with whom they share a connection, and (3) view and traverse their list of connections and those made by others within the system.

(2007:210)

Many of the previously mentioned sites allow organizations, such as government agencies, to create pages that indicate their organizational status, geographic location, opening hours, and advanced analytic capabilities beyond those functionalities provided to individual users. An important characteristic of social networking sites and other social media tools is the publicness character of the updates: users can follow public updates, without visiting the organizations' oftentimes relatively static (e-government) websites.

For government organizations, the use of social media has posed different challenges. Mergel and Bretschneider highlight that government organizations go through three different stages to make sense of social media tools to understand how they might help support the mission of an organization (2013). They showed that initial experimentation is needed to understand the changes in interactive practices, acceptance from citizens, usefulness for outreach, or how online interaction can lead to offline changes in behavior (such as recalls of medications or food, calls for votes, etc.). After the initial experimentation, a consolidation phase usually occurs that leads to the adaptation of existing rules and regulations: social media policies emerge that guide both employee as well as citizen behavior. At the same time, a process of sense making happens during which the alignment with existing rules and policies occurs (see, for example, the EPA's social media policy at http://www.epa.gov/epahome/commentpolicy.html). Meijer and Thaens called this phase Alignment 2.0 (2010). In the last stage, social media technologies and new practices are implemented and institutionalized. Routines, such as posting schedules, emerge and the once innovative practices are included in the standard operating procedures (Mergel, 2016). The stages or phases of the diffusion and ultimately the adoption of new technologies follow similar pathways as other types of technological innovations in the public sector.

What is new is who the initiator of the online communication is and what the resulting modes of online interactions are. The public character of social media practices in government highlights both noncommunication (not responding to citizens) and dramatic mistakes in communicating with the public. Government organizations' practices are always publicly observable on social media, oftentimes leading to scrutiny and change in practices as soon as errors are made.

It is therefore important to distinguish the different types of communication modes that different types of government organizations are selecting. Even though citizens might have the expectation that with the availability of social media tools government organizations need to be available to their needs 24/7, the reality is that social media oftentimes does not fit the 9–5 work schedule of government organizations. Organizations schedule updates at certain times of the day to provide maximum coverage to educate and inform the public, but they usually don't respond after hours.

In addition, different levels of government (federal, state, local) have different audiences. Citizens are more likely to directly communicate with local governments about issues that affect them individually, while state and federal agencies are likely to attract an audience on larger-scale issues that are broader than the micro level of a neighborhood or city. Many social media interactions are driven by the specific tasks an organization has to fulfill as part of its mission. This can result in specific issue-related campaigns or incident-related online interactions. We also need to distinguish communication for political purposes or when candidates are running for government (office) positions. For example, candidates for Congress have to distinguish their campaign accounts from their office accounts with separate staff, billing for software, etc. (Mergel, 2012a). Once in office, political appointees, such as the Secretary of State, will have his or her individual social media accounts, speaking in the first person, which needs to be distinguished from the department as a whole.

Oftentimes researchers are conflating these task-related and position-related social media interactions and call for more meaningful, frequent online interaction without taking the context and standard operating procedures of the organization or the intentions of individual office holders into account. Take for example social media interactions of emergency management (EM) organizations. The standard operating procedures to interact with the public can be divided into two modes: (1) 911 calls from citizens, and (2) after-action reports usually in press release form from the EM organization to inform the public after the event. Tweeting an emergency beat-by-beat would add to the spreading of rumors, because the emergency management organization can only update the public using incomplete information. The standard operating procedure is still to first collect all information, respond and deploy resources to the scene, and after lives are saved, compile a report that includes complete and authoritative information without confusing the public or causing a panic (see, for example, Hughes & Palen, 2012).

In addition, social technologies are used for two different purposes in the public sector: (1) External use focuses on advocacy and public awareness, but also to increase transparency of government actions and decisions to create trust and higher degrees of accountability. Besides social media, government organizations usually use a combination of technologies, such as email, their website, or face-to-face interactions. (2) Internal use includes intranet tools to create connections, awareness for existing knowledge and expertise in the organization (Corridor at the State department, A-(i)-Space in the intelligence community, NASA's Space Book, direct interactions on instant messengers such as Yammer, in-house Wikis based on MediaWiki or similar platforms to collaborative create an organizational knowledge base.

The evidence for this chapter is based on qualitative interviews with social media directors in the 15 executive departments of the U.S. federal government, an additional 19 interviews with emergency managers volunteering their time to help with social media monitoring during incidences, and a long-term digital ethnography. The findings presented here are extracted from these different data sources, and a summary of the findings that the author has accumulated over the last five years are presented in narrative form.

This chapter therefore sets out to review the barriers and drivers for social media use in government, distinguishes different types of social media communication modes based on the different types of missions of government organizations, and provides examples for different types of audience focus and the intended outcomes of the social media communications.

2   Barriers and Drivers for Social Media Use in Government

The traditional press release paradigm in the public sector includes information collection, the verification of the received information, several iterations in the writing and editing process of the final release, and then the publication to specific stakeholders, such as journalists and the general public. The voice used in press releases is a neutral tone, and the content is focused on objectivity to gain trust and integrity. Otherwise, government organizations especially can lose their established reputation as trusted and formal information sources. In the following sections, the factors that serve as barriers to government communication on social media, as well as the drivers that incentivize organizations to participate in these new forms of online interactions with citizens, are derived.

Barriers to the Innovative Use of Social Media

For the adoption of social media technologies, the context of government is important and differs from the private sector. Existing rules and regulations, which govern the use of technologies and direct the behavior of public managers, are very strict and are oftentimes labeled as red tape because they tend to prevent innovation use outside the existing bureaucratic context (see Bertot, Jaeger, & Hansen, 2012 for an overview of laws, acts, and regulations governing the use of social media in government).

Red tape, such as bureaucratic norms in the public sector, oftentimes leads to slow adoption and inconsistencies across jurisdictions or government organizations when it comes to new technologies. Many government organizations block social networking sites for their employees or do not even provide Internet access at all. Even if they do, only dedicated staff members are allowed to use social technologies on behalf of the organization to mitigate privacy and security, as well as public records–keeping concerns. Guidance and policies are adjusted after every major event, such as a media frenzy or an online firestorm (Picazo-Vela, Gutierrez-Martinez, & Luna-Reyes, 2012).

At the same time, existing system support focuses mostly on in-house tools, which come with costs for maintenance of the equipment or necessary upgrades. Oftentimes, government organizations are far behind industry standards and have not yet upgraded their websites to mobile-responsive designs. At the same time, the training and professional development of staff is focused on the existing systems but does not follow industry standards, for example, for mobile computing.

Other barriers include digital divide aspects that have to do with technical skills but also the trustworthiness of the channels (technical breakdowns and changes in functionalities), manipulation of algorithms (who sees what on Facebook?), inclusion, accessibility, and information overload issues. The volume of information produced on social media exceeds human capacity: Social media information needs to be located (who talks about an event or the agency online) and organized and then interpreted by human beings, so that the agency can act on the information. These vetting and filtering procedures of trusted sources have become especially challenging, given the velocity and sometimes doubtful veracity of social media data. Government organizations are oftentimes blamed for their slow uptake when they try to do "damage control" before they spread rumors or false information (Oboler, Welsh, & Cruz, 2012).

Drivers for the Use of Social Media in the Public Sector

Social media use has the potential for better and more effective communication, audience engagement, and innovative forms of online collaboration with the public (Mergel, 2012c). It allows government organizations an enhanced ability to meet community expectations to have the right conversation in the right place with the right content. While the setup takes time to vet the use with legal and IT staff in-house first, the ease with which social media messages can be shared presents opportunities for real-time access to information in a very cost-effective way. Government organizations do not have to build and maintain the technological platforms and usually will not be locked into multi-year service contracts; instead, most social media platforms are free and hosted outside of government by third parties.

Done well, government organizations can ask their audience for quick responses on a range of issues, initiatives, and policies, learning from citizens about the potential support for or the impact of a new policy on their lives. Social media therefore provides a new channel for receiving feedback from the public without setting up a formal participatory governance process or inviting citizens to town hall meetings. One of the most challenging tasks of government is to develop and maintain a trusted voice, but also to change the oftentimes negative external perceptions of government (see for example Crump, 2012, for a review of online police practices on Twitter). While social media is oftentimes seen as a casual information communication tool, it also helps to spread the word, especially in crisis situations or at times when governments need citizens to pay attention (see, for example, the FDA's use of social media during the peanut butter recall: Ostrove, 2011).

When citizens go online, they seek immediate and in-depth information and feedback. If government organizations are not part of the search results or official and trusted information is not available in real time, citizens tend to trust their friends and family members more. Social media can help to establish a trusted voice. Especially, government organizations have access to unique information, and while citizens are "milling" online information, government can interact with them to provide formal information (Fraustino, Daisy, & Jin, 2012).

3 Social Media Modes of Different Types of Government Entities

The actual observable social media communication modes differ based on the type of government organization, its strategic and operational goals, and expected outcomes of its social media use.

Oftentimes, the public as well as existing research create the expectation that social media interactions can be modeled in similar fashion as successful presidential campaigns, such as President Obama's 2004 and 2008 social media campaigns (see, for example, Wortham, 2012). The reality is, however, that as soon as a political candidate moves into office, day-to-day social media interactions (see mode (1) in Figure 11.1) are regulated by the existing information technology and public affairs paradigm of each government organization (see, for example, Bertot et al., 2012; Cogburn & Espinoza-Vasquez, 2011). In office, the focus is to create a steady and trusted communication stream that is characterized by low volume and low frequency of updates, and information is provided whenever government is legally obligated to inform the public. Most government agencies specifically state in their mission statements that they have an obligation to *inform* and *educate* the public. As soon as government has created authoritative information, which went through a rigorous internal vetting and editing process, it is published on social media and picked up by traditional media or the general public. One social media director describes the resulting online attention the information receives as follows:

> We do have information: the trend seems to be big pick up for two or three days on social media for a particular piece, and then a fade off. Unless it is something that stays in the public consciousness. So you can look over time what's being shared of our content.

Similarly, another social media manager observes:

> Right when [a piece of content] comes out, sharing is low, and then a day later it peaks, and then it is still being talked about, and then it's after two or three days it seems to drop off on the social media discussion radar.

In contrast, political campaigns (5) are focused on propagating the opinions or actions of a single candidate running for office and are aimed to change or modify behavior of voters (example: get off the couch or go offline to vote). As opposed to day-to-day governance, political campaigning is never neutral and oftentimes does not even provide trusted and formal information.

Organizational campaigns (2) are similar to political campaigns and are designed to create attention for an issue for a short period. They will end when the online campaign has reached a certain goal. Campaigns are designed to raise attention and awareness for issues such as a new policy, for a deadline, or for a specific event. An example is the very effective Food and Drug Administration's campaign to alert to the risks of peanuts at a time when people were dying from foodborne *Salmonella* outbreaks (Ostrove, 2011). The frequency of targeted campaign updates is much higher and content is specifically designed for a certain event or a specific expected outcome (such as the recall of food, the return of the food to a supermarket, the change in behavior of citizens who stop consuming peanut butter). Citizens are asked to participate in sharing news, content, or opinions. Oftentimes, setting a duration, for example, with a begin and end date of campaign activities, increases the urgency and motivation for citizens to participate. After a campaign ends (a deadline is reached or a specific event occurred, such as a conference or an event like Earth Day), the organization will return to day-to-day governance mode (1). Examples for these types of campaigns can be revolving or even evolving based on seasonal events, such as the Centers for Disease Control and Prevention's flu preparedness campaigns in the fall flu season. Other issue campaigns are of a more continuous nature, such as the Federal Emergency Management Agency's (FEMA) Ready.gov campaign to prepare for emergencies on an ongoing basis, or the White House's Let's Move campaign.

The last type of social media interaction focuses on crisis situations or emergencies (4). The Ready.gov campaign by FEMA is an ongoing preemptive campaign to create an audience and trust, so that the agency can activate its followers on social media as soon as a man-made or natural disaster happens. This type of social media use will move back and forth between day-to-day messaging at times when there is no incident and high-frequency interactions with alerts and calls for action as soon as a crisis situation develops. Similarly, organizational crisis situations occur when a lot of media attention or publicity is created that moves the organization out of its day-to-day governance mode into high alert. An example is the General Services Administration's (GSA) conference spending scandal, which unfolded on social media when not only GSA employees made fun of their own organization, but the media also picked up excessive expenses for mind readers, clowns, bike assemblies, and a fake award that justified dinner expenses at a GSA conference in Las Vegas (Gay Stolberg & Schmidt, 2012).

Figure 11.1 depicts the different types of social media tactics with their volume and frequency of updates:

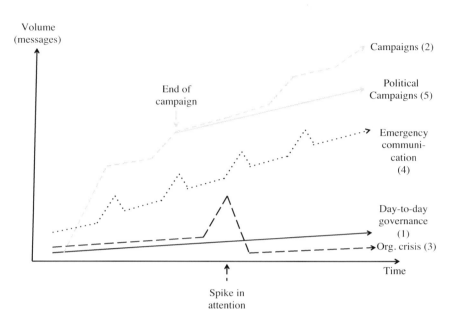

Figure 11.1 Volume and Frequency of Social Media Interactions by Type of Government Function

4 Communication Modes on Social Media

Depending on the task, the strategic and operational goals of a government agency's social media communication modes will vary (Mergel, 2010, 2013). Either the following three communication modes are used at the same time by a single agency or the agency might take a conservative approach and use social media in the traditional press release style only.

1 *One-to-many information sharing:* Most government agencies are committed to educating and informing the public as part of their core mission. This standard operating procedure is observable from the majority of agencies who are used to communicating only when they are obligated by law to inform the public; for example, about a new policy or changes in existing policies. This communication mode is usually characterized by a one-directional push tactic: Information that the government perceives as important is shared to the public without any additional call for action or request for input from the public. Usually, back-and-forth answers to questions that are posed are ignored and updates are automated: Press releases that are pushed out through the website or directly to news outlets are also automatically "recycled" to all social media accounts without an accompanying statement, requests for action, or possibilities to ask questions. Government limits the social media channels to simple distribution channels and ignores the social networking functionalities of social media sites that allow for interactive and bidirectional interactions. Content that is also available through all other channels—and might not be specifically curated for social media use—is pushed through the social media channels.

Examples of agencies that use this mechanism include emergency management organizations who post their after-action reports when all information is collected and the incident has already passed (Wukich & Mergel, 2015). Their main mission is to respond to an emergency on the ground in the moment an incident occurs, and currently most emergency management organizations do not provide beat-by-beat updates about their ongoing operations, either for intelligence purposes or because they themselves do not have complete information and prefer not to add to the rumor mill.

This traditional information distribution is oftentimes met with criticism based on expectations of omnipresence: Citizens expect their government to be available 24/7 (Zavattaro & Sementelli, 2013), and government agencies are oftentimes misinterpreted when they post updates outside the 9–5 core office hours. Similarly, regulatory agencies are oftentimes prohibited by law to conduct direct interactions with citizens or only have the need to communicate with the public when important deadlines are coming up, updates and changes to policies have to be communicated by law, or alerts have to be sent out to the public. Two examples are food or medicine recalls published by the FDA or upcoming tax day deadlines by the IRS.

The one-to-many communication mode is useful as a standard operating procedure for a selected group of agencies to support their information and education mission (Bertot, Jaeger, Munson, & Glaisyer, 2010). For other agencies that need to gain followership and trust or create transparency, this mode might be one among several different activities in their public affairs tool box.

2 *One-to-one interactions:* The second communication mode is characterized by direct interactions between an individual citizen and a government organization. It occurs at two different incidences: either in response to a one-to-many push campaign of information out through social media channels, or self-initiated by a citizen who asks a question or requests information and support. Very few government organizations are willing to directly respond to citizens. Usually government organizations evaluate whether a response can also help other citizens and are not a unique one-on-one service. Is there a broader audience? Instead, they weigh the advantage of spending time on a single citizen or taking the time to craft a general response available to all citizens (Mergel, 2012b).

However, the U.S. federal government's recent Digital Government Agenda highlights the necessity for increased customer service (The White House, 2012). These are not just interactions, such as responses to rumors or setting the record straight when government information is misinterpreted. Instead, government organizations are actively creating targeted campaigns to pull information in from citizens, encouraging them, for example, to send their favorite pictures, conduct microtasks in citizen science projects, or submit incidence and event-related information to government. This pull tactic creates a degree of citizen satisfaction that a mere push tactic cannot create (see, for example, Sashi, 2012).

An example is the Department of Interior's Twitter and Instagram accounts that actively encourage citizens to provide their favorite pictures of public lands, which are then reshared through government social media. The DOI also answers questions about opening hours and creates campaigns, for example, in preparation for national holidays or encourages educators and students to get engaged.

3 *Many-to-many interactions*: In the last social media communication mode, government sees itself as part of a network of peers and acknowledges that many different actors in the network have valuable information to contribute. The role an organization then takes on social media is the one of the "listening bureaucrat" (Stivers, 1994). Stivers found that bureaucrats who are listening to citizens need to have higher degrees of openness, respect for differences, and reflexivity. She argued that especially responsiveness to citizens and reciprocal communication contributes to increased democratic accountability and administrative effectiveness. In addition, Heise suggests that this

Social Media Communication Modes

type of communication model might also lead to the closing of the confidence gap between the public and government (1985), and Vigoda points out that higher degrees of responsiveness will lead to more collaboration between government and citizens (2002).

In this third mode, government carefully scans its environment and conducts sentiment analyses (understanding what the current perceptions of its stakeholders are) and jumps in when needed to diffuse rumors, provides correct information, or tries to be part of the larger network of citizens who are concerned with a specific issue (Crawford, 2009). This networking tactic will likely lead to novel insights and an increased understanding of how stakeholders perceive government's effectiveness. Mossberger, Wu, and Crawford also argue that the adoption of social media technologies, especially in local government, has the potential to improve interactions with citizens through dialogue (2013). This networking mode, however, requires that government does not see itself as the sole authority for the right information and values interactions with its stakeholders instead of viewing citizens as a burden. Here the networking activities can be interpreted either as community-building or as intelligence-gathering activities that might lead to crime prevention and reconnaissance.

The graphic in Figure 11.2 summarizes the three social media communication modes in government with their direct or indirect interactions with citizens:

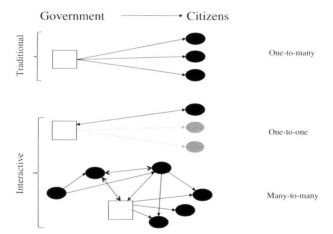

Figure 11.2 Social Media Modes between Government and Citizens

A potential fourth interaction mode includes actual e-government *transactions*, such as bill payments through Facebook's new payment feature, submission of information through forms created in a Google document, or individualized information sharing through direct messages on Twitter. All of these functions are technically possible, but there is no empirical evidence yet that these services are provided through social media and they won't necessarily be publicly observable for a researcher. Barriers to this level of online transaction include the scalability of the service, concerns about personally identifiable information that include privacy, and security concerns.

5 Audience Focus and Access to Content in Social Media Communication

Many government organizations have the need to constantly scan their environment to understand what the needs of their stakeholders are (see the examples mentioned earlier in the text of the regulatory agencies EPA and FDA); stay up to date on news and developments, for example, for public diplomacy purposes (Department of State or Department of Defense); or understand the most recent industry developments. Some agencies have naturally developed segments of their audiences, such as the Internal Revenue Service that serves different stakeholders, including individual taxpayers and small businesses. They can easily segment their social media content and accounts based on these stakeholders or their stakeholders' representatives (such as professional tax preparers, lawyers, etc.), who need much more technical information than regular citizens do. Other agencies serve "the whole public" and only because of social media have discovered that the public has different segments, even though they are all interested in a similar topic. The IRS has, for most citizens, one—designed by law—interaction need: tax day in the U.S. on April 15 when income tax returns have to be filed. According to these segments of their audience and certain seasonal deadlines, social media campaigns and interactions are designed to inform the public about deadlines or to create educational YouTube videos about the process.

Another audience-driven social media strategy is NASA's mission-driven segmentation. With over 11 million followers on Twitter and one of the most prominent Instagram accounts with over 3.6 million followers, NASA is an agency that has a so-called *fan base*, similar to sports teams interacting with their fans on social media (Mergel, 2016). However, different types of followers have divergent informational and educational needs. They can be segmented into citizens who are generally interested in the scientific aspects of space and space travel, fans of TV shows and movies about space (such as Star Trek), but also people who believe in UFOs and extraterrestrial life. Mixing information or levels of technical detail will likely throw off some of the fans. NASA's mission includes educational activities, but also campaigns around missions, such as the 2015 Pluto discovery for which continuous interactions throughout the whole year attracted a lot of publicity. As a result, as NASA's social media director explains, every mission receives its own accounts on social media sites and attracts followers who are specifically interested in it. Accounts for the New Horizons team were created just in time for the Pluto flyby on July 14, 2015. Other prominent missions include Mars Curiosity, NASA JPL, or Asteroid Watch. The NASA social media director explained the difference between the Mars Rover account and the Asteroid Watch account and how the organization discovered the need to segment its audiences based on their different types of interests in the organization:

> I tweeted, oh, there's an asteroid that'll pass between the distance of earth and moon, and total panic ensued. I realized that these were not space fans covering the account, they were people who were terrified of asteroids destroying earth. So I had to completely change the way I handle that account. Now the word "safe" goes into every single tweet, at least once, if not twice. That one is like the one where I'm walking on eggshells with people and trying to reassure them that the world is not ending. But it was amazing, because here we had a million new followers that probably had no interest in space, and I look at that as an audience that I'm going to introduce the missions to them through this asteroid watch account, and maybe I'll get some people who want to come over and learn more about what we are doing on Mars or what we are doing at the space station.

The quality of content for online interactions in government depends on many different aspects: the mission of each agency, the chosen social media strategy (reuse and recycling vs. curation of content specifically for social media use), but also the ability to have access or produce content that no other agency or entity produces on its own. Recently, visuals from government organizations have started to trump text, such as from the Department of Interior, which posts pictures of landscapes of publicly owned land, or from NASA, which is the only agency in the U.S. that has access to pictures created on the Space Station, the Hubble telescope, the Mars Rover, or the New Horizons Spacecraft. As an example, in preparation for the flyby event in July 2015, NASA's New Horizons mission teamed

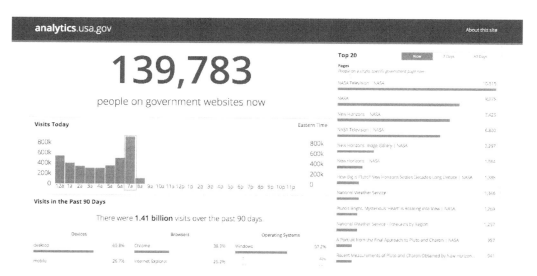

Figure 11.3 Screenshot http://analytics.usa.gov taken on July 14, 2015

up with Instagram to exclusively post the first pictures online (see Instagram at https://instagram.com/p/5HTXKMoaFL/).

The recent Pluto flyby mission created immense attention around the world. Fifty-six percent of all click-throughs (from social media to NASA's website) were generated from outside the U.S. The screenshot in Figure 11.3 taken from GSA's analytics.gsa.gov website shows the impact that NASA's Pluto picture had on the visits to NASA's New Horizon and general NASA websites. Right after the Instagram picture release on July 14, 2015, at 7 am EST, the hits to NASA's websites are visible at the 7 am mark on the chart. After that, attention dramatically drops back to what we can assume to be the regular numbers of visitors.

6 Summary

Government use of social media tools always needs to be discussed in the specific context of the public sector itself and each individual agency with its unique mission. Rules, regulations, and existing administrative and bureaucratic standard operating procedures guide the adoption and use of new technologies. Social media is in many ways comparable to previous waves of e-government innovations; however, the publicness of the medium and visibility of every error that an organization might make restricts and guides what communication modes government organizations choose to utilize. The barriers are therefore much more prevalent than in other sectors, where experimentation is more common and innovative practices are emerging at a faster speed. However, social media tools are adopted from drivers that are both top-down, by a presidential mandate to harness new technologies, and also bottom-up, by pressure from a citizenry demanding improved customer service and higher degrees of responsiveness from government.

This chapter provided a communication model that includes three different modes of government social media communication: one-to-many, one-to-one, and many-to-many. Depending on the organizations' missions and tasks, all of these modes might be preferred communication tactics, or organizations might move back and forth between the different modes. Additional research is needed to provide large-scale empirical evidence for each of the communication modes derived in this chapter. In addition, research is needed that focuses on the outcomes of social media interactions: Are citizens changing their perceptions about an agency as a result of their social media interactions? Or, do citizens change their behavior as a result of calls for actions from a government organizations transmitted through social media? This chapter can serve as a theoretical research framework to investigate some of the aspects mentioned here in more detail.

References

Bertot, J. C., Jaeger, P. T., & Hansen, D. (2012). The impact of polices on government social media usage: Issues, challenges, and recommendations. *Government Information Quarterly*, *29*(1), 30–40.

Bertot, J. C., Jaeger, P. T., Munson, S., & Glaisyer, T. (2010). Social media technology and government transparency. *Computer*, *11*, 53–59.

Boyd, D. M., & Ellison, N. B. (2007). Social network sites: Definition, history, and scholarship. *Journal of Computer-Mediated Communication*, *13*(7), 210–230.

Cogburn, D. L., & Espinoza-Vasquez, F. K. (2011). From networked nominee to networked nation: Examining the impact of Web 2.0 and social media on political participation and civic engagement in the 2008 Obama campaign. *Journal of Political Marketing*, *10*(1–2), 189–213.

Crawford, K. (2009). Following you: Disciplines of listening in social media. *Continuum: Journal of Media & Cultural Studies*, *23*(4), 525–535.

Crump, J. (2012). What are the police doing on Twitter? Social media, the police and the public. *Policy & Internet*, *3*(4), 1–27.

Fraustino, J., Daisy, B. L., & Jin, Y. (2012). Social Media Use During Disasters: A Review of the Knowledge Base and Gaps. Retrieved from http://www.start.umd.edu/publication/social-media-use-during-disasters-0

Gay Stolberg, S., & Schmidt, M. S. (2012). Agency trip to Las Vegas is the talk of Washington. *New York Times*. Retrieved from http://www.nytimes.com/2012/04/04/us/politics/gsa-las-vegas-trip-is-the-talk-of-washington.html

Heise, J. A. (1985). Toward closing the confidence gap: An alternative approach to communication between public and government. *Public Administration Quarterly*, *9*(2), 196–217.

Hughes, A. L., & Palen, L. (2012). The evolving role of the public information officer: An examination of social media in emergency management. *Journal of Homeland Security and Emergency Management*, *9*(1), 1–20. doi:10.1515/1547-7355.1976

Lasswell, Harold D. (1948). The prospects of cooperation in a bipolar world. *The University of Chicago Law Review*, *15*(4): 877–901.

Meijer, A., & Thaens, M. (2010). Alignment 2.0: Strategic use of new Internet technologies in government. *Government Information Quarterly*, *27*(3), 113–121.

Meijer, A., & Thaens, M. (2014). Social media strategies: Understanding the differences between North American police departments. *Government Information Quarterly*, *30*(4), 343–350.

Mergel, I. (2010). Government 2.0 revisited: Social media strategies in the public sector. *PA Times*, *33*(3), 7 & 10.

Mergel, I. (2012a). Connecting to congress: Twitter use by members of congress. *Journal of Policy Advice and Political Consulting*, *3*, 108–114.

Mergel, I. (2012b). A manager's guide to designing social media strategies in the public sector. *Using Technology—Special Report*. Washington, DC: IBM.

Mergel, I. (2012c). *Social Media in the Public Sector: A Guide to Participation, Collaboration and Transparency in the Networked World*. San Francisco: Jossey-Bass/Wiley.

Mergel, I. (2013). Social media adoption and resulting tactics in the US federal government. *Government Information Quarterly*, *30*(2), 123–130.

Mergel, I. (2016). Social media institutionalization in the U.S. federal government. *Government Information Quarterly*. doi:10.1016/j.giq.2015.09.002

Mergel, I., & Bretschneider, S. I. (2013). A three-stage adoption process for social media use in government. *Public Administration Review*, *73*, 390–400.

Mossberger, K., Wu, Y., & Crawford, J. (2013). Connecting citizens and local governments? Social media and interactivity in major US cities. *Government Information Quarterly*, *30*(3), 351–358.

Oboler, A., Welsh, K., & Cruz, L. (2012). The danger of big data: Social media as computational social science. *First Monday*, *17*(7). doi:http://dx.doi.org/10.5210/fm.v17i7.3993

Ostrove, N. (2011). Using Social Media Feedback to Improve FDA Risk Communication. Retrieved from http://www.fda.gov/downloads/AdvisoryCommittees/CommitteesMeetingMaterials/RiskCommunicationAdvisoryCommittee/UCM254288.pdf

Picazo-Vela, S., Gutierrez-Martinez, I., & Luna-Reyes, L. F. (2012). Understanding risks, benefits, and strategic alternatives of social media applications in the public sector. *Government Information Quarterly, 29*(4), 504–511.

Sashi, C. M. (2012). Customer engagement, buyer-seller relationships, and social media. *Management Decision, 50*(2), 253–272.

Stivers, C. (1994). The listening bureaucrat: Responsiveness in public administration. *Public Administration Review, 54*(4), 364–369.

Vigoda, E. (2002). From responsiveness to collaboration: Governance, citizens, and the next generation of public administration. *Public Administration Review, 62*(5), 527–540.

The White House. (2012). Digital Government: Building a 21st Century Platform to Better Serve the American People. Retrieved from https://www.whitehouse.gov/sites/default/files/omb/egov/digital-government/digital-government.html

Wortham, J. (2012). The presidential campaign on social media. *New York Times*. Retrieved from http://www.nytimes.com/interactive/2012/10/08/technology/campaign-social-media.html

Wukich, C., & Mergel, I. (2015). Closing the citizen-government communication gap: Content, audience, and network analysis of government tweets. *Journal of Homeland Security and Emergency Management, 12*(3), 707–735.

Zavattaro, S. M., & Sementelli, A. J. (2013). A critical examination of social media adoption in government: Introducing omnipresence. *Government Information Quarterly, 31*(2), 257–264.

12
RESIDENT-GOVERNMENT ENGAGEMENT VIA NEW TECHNOLOGIES

Georgette Dumont

People are increasingly connected to the Internet, either via a computer or their smartphone. Moreover, these connections have led individuals to expect an immediate response when contacting others or to quickly find the information to a question. While the quality of some of the information found may be dubious at best, what has resulted is an expectation of responses or information 24 hours a day, seven days a week. The implication of this shift is that citizens expect all-day, everyday service from private companies like Amazon.com or immediate "likes" and comments on social media platforms, but they have also come to expect interactions at similar levels and frequencies from government as well.

As technology has become more ubiquitous, arguments have been continually made about all the potential benefits these technologies can have for the government–citizen relationship: From providing information at low costs to having citizens engage with their governments, both asynchronously by making requests and synchronously by virtually asking questions to elected representatives while they are conducting meetings that the citizen is watching online or on his or her television. This engagement has also begun to shift from stationary to mobile technologies. Where e-government's inception was the discussion of data management and e-governance was government–citizen interaction online, m-government (mobile government) takes this a step further to utilize mobile technology for citizens to gain access to information and interact with government in a place of an individual's choosing.

In administrative terms, citizen interaction with government happens through requests for public information and documents, requests for services, and complaints. For as long as there have been communities and neighborhoods, residents have had problems. These problems became more acute over time as cities grew and aged and density increased. What has changed is how residents address these problems. Municipalities across the country have been involved in these interactions for generations, with technology now allowing for a more seamless process for both the initial interaction as well as the in-house processes for responding to the individual requests. While conceptually the process should be seamless, in reality, there are many complexities involved, from the initial contact through the closing of a service ticket when the request has been addressed. This paper discusses these complexities, as well as some of the challenges, through a case study of a municipal customer relationship management (CRM) system in the consolidated city of Jacksonville, FL: 630-CITY. In 2013, the city was ranked #3 in the large city category in the U.S. for digital cities by the Center for Digital Government, and was designated a Citizen-Engaged Community for 2014–2016 by the Public Technology Institute. What follows is a brief review of relevant literature, the methods used, the background of the city and its 630-CITY system, and the findings, followed by a discussion on applying the findings from this case to other cities.

Literature Review

New technologies have come with many promises to increase government–citizen engagement. E-government focuses on the use of technology for government to interact with governments, citizens, employees, and businesses to improve efficiency and the effectiveness of the delivery of public services (Jeong 2007). There are four stages to e-government: catalogue, transaction, vertical integration, and horizontal integration (Layne and Lee 2001). The first stage, catalogue, is merely having an online presence. Interaction is completed via forms that can be downloaded. This is the simplest manner in which government can be engaged in e-government, and the integration with internal systems and departments is sparse. The ability to complete forms online and request services takes place in the second, or the transactional, stage. An example would be having the ability to renew a driver's license online or to pay a fine. The third stage includes vertical integration of internal systems, or when the integration extends within a specific function at different units of government. For example, the Department of Motor Vehicles (DMV) databases would be connected across states or between the state and national registration. The fourth stage, or horizontal integration, is the integration of different functions within a government. For example, being able to apply for a demolition permit online while also disconnecting water and sewer services. Each stage represents a different level of adoption and utilization by government.

Many studies have looked at the adoption of technology by attempting to understand why individuals will either accept or reject a new technology (Legris, Ingham, and Collerette 2003; Venkatesh and Davis 2000). The technology acceptance model (TAM) argues that a technology's perceived ease of use and perceived usefulness play a large role in its adoption by the individual (Davis 1989). TAM was extended to include playfulness to apply the model to Internet use (Moon and Kim 2001). While these studies focused on why an individual will adopt a new technology, interest grew in why organizations adopted online technologies, what factors were needed for the adoption, and how well, once adopted, these technologies were being utilized.

The potential that online technologies offer governments has not fully been realized. D'Agostino, Schwester, Carrizales, and Melitski (2011) analyzed the websites of the largest 20 cities in the U.S. and found they were predominately transactional, but not designed for engagement. In order to ensure the website is designed more for engagement, state and local governments need to strategically adopt web services and technology for citizen interactions. Still, governments at all levels have not fully utilized information communication technologies to engage citizens and promote ways for them to have more input into government.

One e-government system that governments are increasingly adopting to make it easier for residents to engage government is 311, or CRM, systems. Through this system, residents can request services, find information, or file non-emergency complaints. E-governance services, such as CRMs, also help to increase the level of trust between citizens and government. Tolbert and Mossberger (2006) argue how effective use of e-government tools can increase the amount of trust people have in government. Similarly, Teo, Srivastava, and Jiang (2008) conclude that trust is an important variable with regard to the success of e-government services, including CRMs. These systems provide an avenue for residents to file a request or complaint, such as a nonworking traffic light, and see that they were heard when the traffic light is fixed. They feel that government is being responsive to their needs, and this increases their political efficacy.

CRM systems have an external and internal purpose. Externally, they provide a means for residents to have input into the government. Internally, once a request has been submitted, they have the potential to not only track the request and progress to its completion, but also to increase the efficiencies of the internal process. The ability to geocode requests with mobile applications has further enhanced these efficiencies. CRM systems have moved beyond being a city's call center, as they were when first developed. Residents want to interact with government through multiple mediums, from physically going to a public office to filing a request through an app on a smartphone.

CRMs have kept pace with the multiple modes through which people are interacting. Ishmatova and Obi (2009) argued that m-government brings added value to government services for citizens. The authors view m-government from the end-user perspective and find that it adds value through use and mobility. In other words, having the ability to request services or information from government at the moment the need arises, regardless of location, adds value and increases the ease of engaging government. It is the perceived usefulness, perceived ease of use, trust, interactivity, external influence, interpersonal influence, self-efficacy, and facilitating conditions that determine whether an individual will adopt and utilize m-government applications (Hung, Chang, and Kuo 2013; also see Shareef, Archer, and Dwivedi 2012). Once adopted, the way to improve the implementation of m-government initiatives is to plan for their use, secure financial resources, garner the support of political leaders, and promote collaboration (Moon 2010). Given the importance of CRM systems to citizen engagement, the first two research questions are,

RQ1: How do residents of Jacksonville, FL, access 630-CITY?
RQ2: How do residents of Jacksonville, FL, utilize 630-CITY?

In addition to knowing how CRMs are being used and how individuals are accessing the system, whether the system is being utilized equally is also telling. Baird, Zelin, and Booker (2012) found the presence of a digital divide when analyzing access to e-government services at the county level. Counties with lower median household incomes were less likely to have e-government services available to them. Similarly, Cavallo, Lynch, and Scull (2014) analyzed citizen–government interaction via CRMs at the census tract level and whether service requests are equal in cities with regard to different social-demographic variables. They found that sociodemographic characteristics are significant when looking at who uses 311 systems. To broadly understand how sociodemographics impact the use of Jacksonville's 630-CITY system, the next research questions is,

RQ3: Is there a sociodemographic divide between those who use 630-CITY?

Transparency in reporting where service requests are occurring and what types of services are being requested add a significant layer of government transparency. Demonstrating the levels of use and the outputs derived through the use of the CRM system allows government to build trust and support for funding the system. In addition to spreadsheets and reports, which are static, dashboards are dynamic tools that provide easily understood information on large amounts of data in a visual context (Smailovic 2012). They have also been used to monitor and measure performance. In other words, dashboards provide individuals, those inside as well as those outside government, the needed information in a user-friendly format to better understand how effectively government functions. The fourth research question is,

RQ4: How does 630-CITY report its data?

Presenting data on how the CRM system is utilized also helps to secure the resources that are needed to maintain the system. This is important because CRM systems can only be utilized if they are functional. Through survey analysis, Schwester, Carrizales, and Holzer (2009) examined 14 municipalities' 311 systems. They found that successful e-government adoption is a function of a combination of financial resources, technical resources, and available human resources. In addition, they also found that political support for IT projects is also important, especially for funding. Similarly, Nam and Pardo (2014) also completed a comparative case study of New York and Philadelphia's 311 systems and found that political support is helpful. Top management's administrative and political support help resolve interagency conflict. This leads to the fifth research question,

RQ5: *How do Jacksonville city council members view the 630-CITY system?*

Nam and Pardo (2014) also analyze the integration of 311 service systems. Through an analysis of case studies in two states, they found that state 311 systems require timely investment. They also found interoperability to be a challenge. To help lessen the hurdles that noninteroperable systems cause, they found that training employees, or the city's customer service agents (CSAs), was critical. Customer service provisions play a key role in noninteroperable systems between front-office systems and back-office systems. Training customer service employees is key. By training employees on both the processes that are outward facing, or those that residents engage with, and the back-end cross-agency processes, they are given the ability to best meet the needs of the resident. This leads to the final research questions,

RQ6: *What is the process for requests entered into the 630-CITY system?*
RQ7: *What is the level of interoperability between 630-CITY and local departments?*

A multi-methods research approach was taken to answer these questions, and this is discussed next.

Methods

To understand the history and the inner processes of 630-CITY, two in-depth interviews were completed. The first was with the CIO in spring 2014 and lasted for approximately 2.5 hours, and the second was conducted in the summer of 2015 with the manager of Jacksonville's 630-CITY division and lasted for 1.5 hours. Both interviews were recorded and transcribed, then analyzed using the qualitative software package NVivo.

In order to learn how the members of the city council view 630-CITY, an electronic survey was distributed to their city email addresses in June 2015. It was open for one month, with four follow-up emails sent to those who had not completed the survey. It should be noted that the survey was sent after the local election and 10 of the 19 council members were either term limited or were not seeking reelection. The month in which the survey was opened was each council member's last term for that administration. It was decided to send the survey out to the seasoned council members, since they had at least four years' worth of experience interacting with city departments and had passed at least four budgets. The survey contained six closed-ended questions inquiring about the 630-CITY system and one open-ended question at the end asking why the respondent supports or opposes the city's 311 system and the dashboard.

Finally, data on how the 630-CITY system was accessed and used in FY2011–2014 was analyzed using SPSS. The data recorded were the monthly totals of the types of calls, length of calls, number of full-time employees, and the number of requests entered into the care system and how they were received. The MyJax app, a mobile application that can be used to file requests into 630-CITY, was not released until July 15, 2015, so the data on the requests received through the app are not included, but the process through which they are entered into the system is, which was obtained in the interviews. In addition, partial information was available for FY2015 on how the system was accessed, and it was used for preliminary findings on whether people were using the app to access the system.

630-CITY: Jacksonville, FL

Jacksonville, FL, is the largest city in the contiguous United States with regard to area (885 square miles), and is the twelfth most populated municipality in the country (2014 population estimate was 853,382). Its size is due to a voter-passed referendum that called for the consolidation of Duval County and the City of Jacksonville. This consolidation took effect on October 1, 1968, with the exception of Atlantic Beach, Jacksonville Beach, Neptune Beach, and Baldwin, which all voted for consolidation, but also to keep their own governments. Each of these entities has its own interlocal agreement with the City of Jacksonville as to the services the county provides to each city and, in some instances, the costs for these services. For example, Atlantic Beach and Neptune Beach each have their own police departments, but their fire and rescue services are provided by Jacksonville. Jacksonville Beach, on the other hand, has its own police department and its own fire department, but Jacksonville Fire and Rescue provide transport to a hospital. Baldwin controls its own development, but the majority of services are provided through the City of Jacksonville. As can be seen, the City of Jacksonville is under different contractual arrangements regarding the services it must provide to the four independent governments within the county.

Prior to the consolidation of Duval County, there were multiple layers of government and numerous elected officials, with little coordination between them, resulting in slow to no services for residents. Moreover, the poor and at times corrupt management of Jacksonville and Duval County had led to the schools being de-accredited and large sections of the city without stable water or sewage services. Consolidation was passed to streamline government; to make it more efficient by eliminating service duplication and providing centralized services for all government agencies; and to make sure equal services were provided for all residents of the newly Consolidated City of Jacksonville. The use of technology seeks to further streamline government processes.

Jacksonville has a strong-mayor form of government with 19 council members: There are 14 district council members and five at-large members. This design allows a resident to seek redress not only with his or her district representative, but also through the five at-large representatives, giving each resident six voices on the council. This also applies to the residents at the Beaches and in Baldwin, with each being part of a county district with its own representative as well as at-large representation for county matters, in addition to their own municipal governments. For new residents, and for some not-so-new residents, the consolidated government can be somewhat confusing, especially for those living in one of the independent municipalities. On Election Day, in addition to voting for their own mayors and council members for their city, residents are also voting on the mayor for the City of Jacksonville and county representation, because the City of Jacksonville is also Duval County.

In 2000, Mayor Delaney's administration was committed to total quality management (TQM). TQM emphasized product improvement in the public sector. Its application to the public sector was clearly laid out by Swiss (1992), in what he referred to as "reform TQM," with a focus on services that emphasized client feedback, performance monitoring, continuous improvement, and worker participation. In order to improve the delivery of government services, a need to centralize services was identified. While consolidation created a unified government through which services would be implemented, there was no clear avenue for residents to know how to submit a request to the appropriate department. Finding the correct department to address a problem was like playing Russian roulette: You would bounce around from slot to slot hoping you landed on the winner. Since consolidation, the population of Jacksonville continued to grow and urban sprawl increased, especially given the size of the physical land area of the city. Between 1970 and 2010, the population grew by 28%. Sprawl in the north, east, and south sides of the city created more strains on government services, with more intensive services having to be provided for a broader geographical area, while older core parts of the city still required maintenance and upkeep.

City leaders saw that a more centralized and standardized system for interacting with the needs of residents was needed. Non-emergency 311 city contact centers were first introduced in Baltimore, MD, in 1996, and Jacksonville was on the leading edge of the curve in its adoption. On July 15, 2000, 630-CITY held its first training. Jacksonville joined Chicago, New York, and Miami-Dade County in adopting customer service centers to help guarantee a resident's issue would be efficiently addressed in a standardized manner. Prior to its development, residents would receive varying responses to their requests and questions depending on the person answering the call. The goals for 630-CITY were to improve access to government; resolve issues at the lowest possible level of government; increase accountability; and ensure residents received accurate, courteous, and consistent service or information. The first Jacksonville location of the 630-CITY division was located in City Hall, along with the mayor's office and city council members' offices.

As with many other cities throughout the country, Jacksonville has been faced with a decline in revenue due to the collapse of the real estate market in 2008. Further complicating matters is that the main funding stream for the state of Florida is sales tax, as the state does not have an income tax. This compounded the decline in revenue streams because with fewer people going on vacation and spending money, there was no way to recoup those lost revenues. The declining economy also meant fewer state revenues flowing into the coffers of municipalities. This, coupled with staunch local resistance to raising the millage rate and growing pension obligations, caused the city to repeatedly reduce funding to all its departments, forcing them to continually do more with less. This is not an issue unique to Jacksonville, but an ongoing issue that continually takes money out of the general fund, which finances services that can be offered to improve the quality of life for the city's residents.

The decline of revenue streams was at the fore when the Brown administration took office in 2011. Holding firm on his campaign promise to not raise taxes and offer better services, Brown sought to streamline the government and find ways to reduce costs. One way he sought to accomplish this was in the Information Technology Division (ITD). He appointed a new chief information officer (CIO) with the expectation that she would find that many services the ITD provided to the city could be done better, and at a reduced cost, through privatization. However, after working with the employees within the division, she saw that there was a lot of talent, and that they had been restrained by previous CIOs, inhibiting the division from being innovative when it sought to solve problems.

The 630-CITY system is one of multiple projects the division was engaged in. Out of the ITD's 138 employees, 35 work on initiative projects, with an ongoing queue of projects. Even though employees had not received raises or bonuses in six years, they were still committed to the division. In order to promote employee morale and to improve the perception of ITD among political leaders, the CIO sought awards for the work it was doing. Jacksonville was named the third best digital city government in the United States in 2013 and 2014 by e.Republic's Center for Digital Government and Digital Communities Program. The receipt of each award was brought to city council's attention, and the ITD was also being awarded external grants to hire contractors to work on specialized projects. The perception of the division started to change, enough so that the FY2014 and FY2015 budget increased, albeit slightly. However, during a time with across-the-board cuts to department budgets, the division was able to demonstrate a return on taxpayer dollars through external validation.

ITD's available resources are directly connected with the 630-CITY division because its role is to manage, update, and integrate the 630-CITY operating system with other systems in the city. In 2014, the city released JaxScore 1.0, which provided static data on the progress of each city department or function through the data captured through 630-CITY. These data were compiled in separate PDFs for each department and made available to the public in a user-friendly format. In January 2015, JaxScore 2.0 went live (http://www.coj.net/jaxscore). The upgrade allows the public to see the number of requests by the type of request for the county as a whole, by the location of the request by zip code, or requests by council district. These data can then be further refined by type of service or department, and the data also shows the number of those requests that have been completed, the percentage completed on time, and the number that are still open. Users of the system can look at the data by fiscal year. These data have always been available to anyone who is using a city computer, including city council members.

While Jacksonville is moving forward with its level of transparency, the data reported are only as good as the data inputted into the system. As of 2015, residents are able to contact the city with requests, complaints, or praise in person or via the telephone, mail/email/fax, the website at www.coj.net, or the city's MyJax app. These data are then relayed to the appropriate department or agency where they can be addressed, and individuals who made the request can track it through the same system and be notified when completed. Because of 630-CITY, Jacksonville was designated a Citizen-Engaged Community 2014–2016 by the Public Technology Institute. The award recognizes "excellence in multi-channel contact centers and best-practices for the use of [CRM] systems" (ICMA 2014).

Findings

To answer the first research question, how residents of Jacksonville were accessing 630-CITY, data from FY2011 through FY2014 were analyzed. As can be seen in Table 12.1, the dominant way that residents engage the city is via the telephone, which comprise over 80% of the contacts made each fiscal year. Interestingly, how people access the system has remained constant for each of the years studied. After the telephone, there is little variance in how people access 630-CITY between in person/mail/fax, email, the website, or filing a request through a representative's office.

Since the data was gathered in the middle of FY2015, they were not complete, but they do include five months when the mobile app was available to access 630-CITY. Because the dataset is small, it cannot be determined if those who use the app are choosing to not use another mode. However, the data show very little use of the app (less than 1%) as can be seen in Table 12.2. Still, it can also be seen that in FY2015, there was a slight increase in using the website and email. These findings align with the city's goal of reaching out to a different customer base: Some individuals are more apt to use an app or send a text than to make a phone call. The city ultimately wants its residents to be able to access city services at a place and time of their choosing and to make interacting with government a pleasurable experience.

Table 12.1 Accessing 630-CITY

Mode of contact				
Walk up/Mail/Fax	14,681	11,863	12,446	15,025
	4%	3%	4%	4%
Emails	6,525	11,148	11,029	11,916
	2%	3%	3%	3%
Calls	293,567	288,722	293,654	315,322
	87%	84%	85%	85%
Website	16,860	23,256	16,992	17,137
	5%	7%	5%	5%
Other*	5,923	8,089	10,620	11,964
	2%	2%	3%	3%
TOTAL RESIDENTS ENGAGED	337,557	343,079	344,742	371,365

* Requests made through the mayor's office, city council, or a city dept.

Table 12.2 630-CITY 2015 Eight-Month Breakdown with MyJax App Data

	FY2015^	OCT	NOV	DEC	JAN	FEB	MAR	APR	MAY
Mode of contact									
Walk up/Mail/Fax	8,511	1,227	869	818	1,108	1,154	1,220	1,112	1,003
Emails	10,361	1,283	863	1,070	1,105	1,045	1,510	1,681	1,804
Calls	205,074	28,616	20,081	24,943	24,345	21,988	29,578	29,747	25,776
Website	15,597	1,786	1,243	1,327	1,693	1,612	2,328	2,760	2,848
Mobile app	552	0	0	8	50	69	151	146	128
Other**	3,882	1,180	928	1,281	1,098	1,298	1,690	1,882	1,832
TOTAL RESIDENTS ENGAGED***	237,222	32,564	22,862	27,785	28,119	25,504	34,263	35,306	30,819

^ Oct. 1, 2014—May 31, 2015
* Human-to-human interaction. Does not include self-service through website.
** Requests made through the mayor's office, city council, or city dept.
*** Sum of modes does not equal 100 due to duplicate entries into the system through different modes.

Fewer individuals may be using the website or the app because of the lack of marketing of the different ways that people can access 630-CITY. When the system was first released, the city marketed 630-CITY as the number for residents to use for non-emergency requests. However, as budgets tightened, the funds available to market how people can file requests faded. Accessing 630-CITY via the telephone is often noted in news reports as the way that people who have experienced a delay in their trash pickup, potholes, or blighted areas get the issue resolved. Of course, since the system's name is the phone number, it is also easier to remember than a URL. Few news reports mention the website or using the app.

The second research question went deeper into understanding how 630-CITY was being utilized. The system allows individuals to file many requests, from letting the city know that trash was not collected to requesting public documents. As can be seen in Table 12.3, in each fiscal year analyzed, most of the contacts with the city via the telephone were inquiries. This includes asking what days trash is picked up in a specific area to where a city department is located. These inquiries require no follow through from a department: They are questions that are answered by the customer service agent. Inquiries are followed by complaints, requests for service, and follow-up calls. Both complaints and requests for service normally result in the issuing of a service ticket to the appropriate department that can address the issue. Follow-up calls check on the progress of an already issued service ticket. These can also be tracked online via the website if an individual has the issue number.

Table 12.3 630-CITY Telephone Requests Summary

	FY2011	FY2012	FY2013	FY2014
Types (by percent)				
Complaints	22%	24%	27%	29%
Requests for Service	14%	15%	18%	24%
Follow-up	11%	10%	13%	14%
Inquiries	50%	49%	39%	33%
Not entered into system	3%	2%	3%	n/a

Given that 630-CITY is mainly accessed through the telephone, it may help to understand the volume of calls that enter the system to better understand the experience of interacting with government from the user end. Table 12.4 shows the volume of calls received by 630-CITY, the percentage of calls that were answered, and the satisfaction level of those who called. Customer satisfaction ratings were only available for FY2011 and FY2012, because the system was upgraded at that time and no longer supported the function needed to survey those who used the system. This feature will be supported in the next system upgrade to allow those who oversee the 630-CITY division to acquire the feedback needed to continually improve the service.

As can be seen in Table 12.4, for the two years where the data were available, customer satisfaction was higher when their calls were answered, and answered quickly (51 seconds, FY2011). FY2012 and FY2013 showed that it took customer service agents more time to answer calls while the average time they spent on the phone remained roughly the same, a little over three minutes per call on average. However, times got better when the average number of customer service agents available to answer calls increased. When comparing this with the money spent by the division in the corresponding fiscal year, drastic cuts were introduced in FY2012. While there was an increase in the budget in FY2013, the increase still totaled less that the FY2011 budget. While the data span only four fiscal years, one can see a trend that a higher cost per engagement results in lower wait times and an increase in the percentage of calls being answered. This is important when an individual is trying to engage his or her city to make an inquiry, request a service, or file a complaint. The less time waiting on the phone, the more pleasurable the experience will be.

Knowing how residents access and use the system, whether this usage is similar based on socioeconomic data is analyzed next. While CRMs are convenient tools that allow residents to interact with government and request services, knowing if the usage is roughly equal across the municipality is important. This can help to identify if all residents of the city are receiving services and allow for better target marketing for those demographics that use the system less. A Pearson's correlation was conducted between a zip code's median household income and the number of public works service requests per population. It showed that those who reside in zip codes with lower median household incomes used the 630-CITY system to request public works services more than did those who live in zip codes with higher median household incomes ($r = -.390$, $p < .05$). This contradicts other studies that find less use of e-governance services among less affluent neighborhoods. However, this study is using the zip code as the unit of analysis, while other studies have used the census tract. So it is possible that this data is not refined enough. Another explanation is that Jacksonville has some old neighborhoods, where those in a lower socioeconomic demographic tend to live, and those neighborhoods tend to have more infrastructure issues.

Table 12.4 630-CITY Call Volume

	FY2011	FY2012	FY2013	FY2014
Calls Answered	293,567	288,722	293,654	315,322
Pct. Calls Answered	92%	81%	79%	89%
Avg. Speed of Answer	0:00:51	0:02:19	0:02:49	0:01:13
Avg. Talk Time	0:03:04	0:03:10	0:03:23	0:03:25
Avg. Positions Staffed	11	10	12	13
Total Customer Contacts*	320,696	319,882	327,749	354,227
Average Daily Customer Contacts*	1,279	1,333	1,372	1,414
Customer Satisfaction (Likert 1–5 scale)	4.49	4.39	n/a	n/a

* Human-to-human interaction. Does not include self-service through website.

Many higher socioeconomic zip codes are in newer neighborhoods that require fewer public works services.

One of the promises of e-governance is increased transparency. In June 2015, Jacksonville released the city's dashboard, JaxScore 2.0. This site is available to the public and allows individuals to look at requests made through 630-CITY by citywide service requests, location, and council member district. The system is GIS-based, and the data are reported in the aggregate. In other words, a resident cannot use the system to determine if his or her neighbor filed a request complaining that the neighbor's lawn is too high. Service type, department, or agency can further refine the aggregate data.

The release of these data to the public was touted as making Jacksonville more transparent: Residents would be able to see what the city was doing with their tax dollars. They are able to see which services are requested the most in their council district or their zip code, and the completion rate. Moreover, they can also see the percentage of requests that are completed on time in relation to other areas. While Jax-Score recently was released to the public, the data that it displays has always been available to anyone on a city computer. In other words, city council members could access the work of the 630-CITY division.

As uncovered in prior research (Nam and Pardo 2014; Schwester 2009), political supports are very important for the success of a CRM system. To better understand how city council members perceived Jacksonville's system, a survey was sent out to all 19 members via email, and nine replied, or 45%. Of the nine who replied, six were district council members while three were at-large. I received an email on June 15, 2015, from Celeste Holland, councilmember Joost's administrative assistant, informing me "as an at-large council member, CM Joost has never used the 630-CITY system and therefore wouldn't need to answer a survey." Still, combined, 70% were somewhat or very supportive of 630-CITY, while only 44% review the data the system tracks. Support for 630-CITY was seen by district members and at-large members, respondents from both groups comprised the 44% who noted that they review 630-CITY data.

Seven of the nine respondents noted that they refer their constituents to 630-CITY, and of these, all refer constituents to access the system via the phone, three refer constituents to the website, and only one refers constituents to the app. Those who referred their constituents to the 630-CITY system were also more likely to support funding a dashboard that would allow them to see the needs of their district. Interestingly, though, this was not seen in the support of a public facing dashboard. All respondents noted they would support better marketing of the system to the public.

The one open-ended question on the survey asked why the respondent supports or does not support 630-CITY. One respondent who was very supportive of 630-CITY noted:

> I also served on the City Council for a period of eight years when 630-CITY did not exist. Back then, all constituent complaints had to be reduced to written correspondence and then sent via inter-office mail to the appropriate city department/division. Neither I, nor the constituent, had access to real time information about the status of the complaint. When the complaint was finally resolved, the appropriate city department/division would send written correspondence back to me summarizing their findings/action taken. Then, I in turn had to notify the constituent. 630-CITY has eliminated most of those steps resulting in a huge savings of time (labor) and printing expenses and now provides Council members and constituents with the current status of their respective inquiries/complaints.

This respondent sees how 630-CITY helped to streamline government services and the cost savings that the system provides the city. On the other hand, another respondent who was not supportive of 630-CITY noted:

> Residents find it difficult to enter many types of requests; no night or weekend responses [to file a request via the phone]; matters are frequently "Closed" when work is not completed;

just noted and a response issued. This totally distorts the dashboard and frustrates those who file again and again for the same issue that is not resolved: it is just closed. The system SHOULD be the main entry point but needs to have a hotline type backup or online monitoring for the noise violations, weekend park issues, etc., and the incentive to close [the request] to reflect performance is misguided unless closing means completed. I now encourage multiple neighbors to file on same issue (despite clogging system and creating unnecessary reports) because more complaints bump up priority of service.

The frustration in this response results from the ease of use of the system more than the CRM system itself. Since the survey sample was small ($n = 9$), a Kendal's Tau correlation was used to test the relationship between a council member's level of support for 630-CITY and the percentage of requests that were completed on time in his or her district, and a positive correlation was found ($t = .649$, $p < .05$). Respondents with higher on-time completion rates of requests submitted in their districts were more likely to support or strongly support 630-CITY.

This was further supported in a series of correspondences between a council member and one of her constituents. The issue at hand was an overgrown undeveloped private lot. A resident in the neighborhood filed a request to have the lot mowed and cleaned up, as it was negatively impacting surrounding properties. The resident submitted the original request on September 24, 2013, and since no city action was taken that was noticeable, the individual contacted 630-CITY. It was noted in this email that the original request was unable to be processed because no street number was provided. The second email sent on November 3, 2013, contained the lot's real estate number, its owners, and the owner's address. The resident also carbon copied her district council member and the mayor's office on the email. Later that day the council member contacted the resident letting her know that there was an active ticket on that property. The next day, an employee with the city's Municipal Code Compliance Division contacted the resident and council member. The email contained both the process that the city must go through each time a complaint such as this is filed on a privately owned parcel or building to explain the delay in addressing the issue.

First, a complaint must be filed that a property owner is not violating municipal code. Then the city confirms this assumption and notifies the property owner of the violation and the timeline in which the property must be brought into compliance. Once that date has passed, the city inspects the property, and if it is still not in compliance, then a work order is sent to the assigned zone contractor to remove the violation(s). After that, the issue is closed. Unfortunately, in this case, a Municipal Code Compliance Division employee caused even more of a delay by mistakenly closing the case. This delay, compounded by similar requests for the city to take the same action on this property in 2012, before the exchange of these emails, and again in 2014, a year after this exchange, was very frustrating for both the resident and the council member who had to continually intervene. As noted by one council member who responded to the survey,

> The main frustration I have heard from constituents over the years and that I have personally experienced when accessing the system is that many issues will show as "Closed" when the issue has not truly been resolved or the system offers little to no specific information on what took place regarding the issue.

This frustration leads to a negative perception of 630-CITY and reduces political support, which in turn can reduce funding.

This exchange is laid out in detail to note the delineation between the CRM and the city departments charged with fulfilling the service requests. Regardless of where the delays lie, the point of contact is the CRM system, and in this case, and in similar cases, the process was not centralized or streamlined.

Jacksonville, FL, presents an interesting case study. Since the county is consolidated, the processes to address requests for services are already centralized. Streamlining services and effectiveness to create efficiencies was the purpose behind the county's consolidation. Similarly, streamlining government's responses to the needs of its residents is also supposed to be more efficient through CRMs. However, the presence of silos in the consolidation of the city's structure also can be seen in the flow of information in 630-CITY, as well as the interoperability between city departments and agencies. In other words, Jacksonville is at the early stages of horizontal integration (Layne and Lee 2001).

As of June 2015, 630-CITY had 12 employees, the vast majority of which are female. The space in which 630-CITY operates is comprised of pods, with two to three customer service agents per pod and a pod lead, who answers questions and addresses problems. While 630-CITY has very little turnover, it does face challenges with employees, such as leave time, motivation in the face of stagnant wages, and keeping employees positive in the light of some very difficult contact with residents. One of the techniques used to help with employee motivation is a gratitude wall, where employees, on their own volition, can add a post-it note to the gratitude wall noting what they are grateful for that day. Each employee also receives a daily attitude adjustment email, which contains positive quotes to help employees start their day off with a smile. The supervisor, as with other CRMs, has the ability to tune into individual calls to ensure quality. The division is open from 8:00 a.m. to 5:00 p.m., Monday through Friday, and during this time, customer service agents are answering calls and entering requests into the system. These requests come not only from the phone, but also from emails, faxes, mail, and the mobile app, MyJax.

As can be seen in Figure 12.1, there are multiple avenues for requests to enter the 630-CITY system. However, some are more direct than others. Requests made via the 630-CITY website are directly entered into the system, which is indicated by the thicker solid arrow. When individuals file a request, the type of request and a specific location is needed. It is up to the individual to decide if he or she wants to be anonymous or not. If the exact street address is not known or is irrelevant to the request being made, then a cross street is needed to identify where the issue is located.

The same information is required for all requests, but the difference is that there is a customer service agent entering the information. While the information the app sends to the city is geocoded and the individual does not need to provide the location information, the app is not interoperable with the system, so all requests made through this medium go to a customer service agent, who then

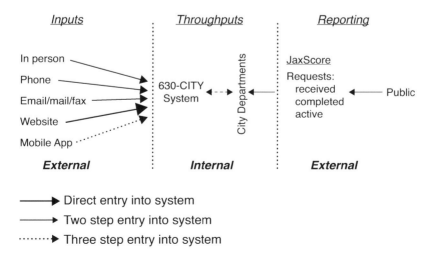

Figure 12.1 630-CITY Request Process

enters the information into the system. To answer the sixth research question, regarding the process of how information flows through the system and its efficiency, at first it is dependent on how the information is introduced to the system, but once it is in the system, all requests go through a similar process. Streamlining of processes, though, is not simple. While CRMs are highly technical, they are still heavily dependent on individuals to both input the work as well as complete the requests.

To address research question seven, the interoperability between 630-CITY and the software the departments use is analyzed. Similar to the interoperability issues seen between the app and the system, there are also interoperability issues between department systems. While the potential is present for a seamless flow of information between the individual making a request and the appropriate department, legacy systems pose barriers. Each department or agency is charged with acquiring the software and technological systems that best meet its needs, but until recently, little attention has been paid to how interoperable a system is with the city's other systems. While this has moved more to the fore, it is costly to change a department's operation system, as well as difficult due to internal resistance to change. This interoperability creates another step between the 630-CITY system and the seamless flow of information into a department's system, which would also allow for tracking the progress on the request as well as the outputs of each department. This aligns with Nam and Pardo's (2014) findings.

Discussion

Technology is not the panacea for perfecting government–citizen engagement. It provides an additional avenue through which individuals can contact their elected representatives and employees: It is an additional tool in the communication tool belt. However, what it can do, and do well, is help to streamline government processes and increase transparency so that individuals can see their government in action, whether it is city action on their own request, or action at-large. Jacksonville's 630-CITY system is a case study of the system itself and how the individual parts of the system need to be balanced for maximum efficiency.

Multiple access points to the CRM system allow for a greater diversity of inputs and requests. As noted, the addition of an additional access point is not to lessen the use of existing points of access, but to encourage participation by those who were not likely to use one of the other access points. This can be seen with the addition of the mobile app. It was not created to lessen the call volume, but to provide another avenue for an individual who would be more likely to file a request to let the city know of an issue that needs to be addressed via a smartphone than to call or visit the website. But to get more people to access the system, it needs to be marketed to targeted groups in ways that inform them on how using the CRM system, whether via phone, Internet, or mobile app, will make their lives better.

Similarly, the app also makes using the system easier, as the location is geocoded and does not require the individual to know the address or exact location. However, this information is not automatically entered into the system. The current process in Jacksonville still requires a city employee to input the request. Each individual who is involved in the process presents another point at which the process can be broken. To increase the efficiency and effectiveness of requests via mobile devices, apps need to be integrated into the CRM system. Further research will be needed on whether additional access points to a CRM are attracting a new customer base, or if it is the same individuals accessing the system through different modes.

In addition to providing multiple access points, government should also be concerned with analyzing the requests being submitted and making sure that all areas of the city are being serviced equally, regardless of which areas are making the most requests. The data inputted into CRMs can be used to proactively predict larger problems within the city. If there are multiple requests to address a caved-in road, city engineers and public works could take that information and cross-check the location with the underground infrastructure to make sure it is not aging too quickly or failing. In this way, CRMs can be used as a crowdsourcing tool: Government cannot know all things that are going on at all times. However, by connecting citizen requests with each other, patterns can emerge and action can be taken. Similarly, CRMs can be used to ensure that all areas of the city are receiving services. The absence of requests for services does not equate to there being no need for services. Departments again can be proactive by driving through areas of the city where few to no requests are made and performing a visual inspection, and submit requests themselves if code violations are seen.

While government has access to the data, it is important for the public to also see the work that the city is engaged in. On an individual level, once requests submitted through the app are completed, a text is sent to all the individuals who filed the issue. For instance, if five people submitted a request through their app to have a pothole filled, once it was filled, the workers who filled the pothole can take a picture of themselves pointing at the filled pothole, and send it to the five individuals who sent the request. This creates a very individualized experience, and as such, helps to increase trust. JaxScore allows the public to see what services the government is providing in the aggregate, and in which locations on a dynamic platform. While the literature notes that transparency helps to build trust in government, more research is needed on the connection between trust and government dashboards from the citizen perspective. Similar research is also needed on how m-government impacts trust.

It can be seen in this study that the transparency created by JaxScore has not necessarily helped with how 630-CITY is perceived: Council members who support 630-CITY see it as a centralized tool for residents to contact their government. However, few noted that they analyze the data on what the city is doing and how well it is doing it, which is what JaxScore reports. Perception of the systems were based more on constituent feedback and the processes involved once a ticket is issued to a department, not the 630-CITY system itself, which inputs, monitors, and reports on progress. Therefore, how CRM outcomes are provided to elected officials is very important: These outcomes need to be reported in a way that clearly shows how the system is helping the individual council member and his or her district. In addition to providing spreadsheets and data, visual dashboards and/or reports not only inform individual council members about the types and location of services that have been performed in their districts, but also the processes involved in completing the requests. This would help council members, as well as those in the executive branch, see where some implementation issues are, and possibly point to ways to resolve these issues.

External validation of the system brings recognition to the city as well as improves the perception that elected officials have of the system. CRM managers and CIOs should actively seek external awards; external validation helps to motivate employees as well as improve council members' perception of the system, which can result in an increase in funding for both technology and employees.

The importance of employees is extended beyond the departments that are charged with addressing the requests; the customer service agents are also critical (Nam and Pardo 2014). Whether a person calls, emails, faxes, or submits their request in person, it is the individual in the CRM department who takes the information, must correctly submit it into the system, and interacts with residents in a friendly manner. More research is needed on how to motivate employees and keep them positive in somewhat stressful situations. In addition, constant training and monitoring are needed to ensure users are getting high-quality service. This is even more important when CRMs are not fully interoperable with software and platforms in other municipal departments.

The process is streamlined through the use of 630-CITY, but there is little interoperability between the 630-CITY system and the departments. While ITD is moving toward increasing interoperability, there are institutional, financial, and work force constraints. Each department has its own system that is designed for the specific function that the department is charged with, and the design of these legacy systems is not focused on interoperability with other systems. Purchasing new systems is costly, and then integrating all the systems together takes both time and money. However, if employees are trained to know what to look for in these issues, they can be resolved in a timely manner. As more governments adopt CRMs and face interoperability issues, more research can be conducted on successful methods on how this problem can effectively be addressed. Once the processes can be streamlined and the municipality's technological infrastructure fully interoperable, then interacting with government can be pleasurable for users of the system, taking some of the pressure off the customer service agents.

Conclusion

Technology has been held up as a tool not only to help citizens engage with their government, but also to make government more accountable to its citizens. The case of Jacksonville's 630-CITY demonstrates that CRM systems do bring about some centralization and streamlining. The addition of different modes of access to government are aimed at additional citizens involved with government. This increase can put more pressure on both elected officials and city employees. However, CRMs alone cannot overcome institutional processes, some legal, some human, that are involved in addressing citizen requests. For CRMs to live up to the lofty outcomes that have been bestowed on them, the technology, institutional processes, and employees working within the system must be balanced. As Chen and Popovich (2003) note, "managing a successful CRM implementation requires an integrated and balanced approach to technology, process, and people" (672).

References

Baird, J., Zelin II, R., and Booker, Q. 2012. "Is There a 'Digital Divide' in the Provision of E-Government Services at the County Level in the United States?" *Journal of Legal, Ethical and Regulatory Issues* 15(1): 93–104.
Cavallo, S., Lynch, J., and Scull, P. 2014. "The Digital Divide in Citizen-Initiated Government Contacts: A GIS Approach." *Journal of Urban Technology* 21(4): 77–93.
Chen, I.J. and Popovich, K. 2003. "Understanding Customer Relationship Management (CRM): People, Process and Technology." *Business Process Management Journal* 9(5): 672–688.
D'Agostino, M., Schwester, R., Carrizales, T., and Melitski, J. 2011. "A Study of E-Government and E-Governance: An Empirical Examination of Municipal Websites." *Public Administration Quarterly* 35(1): 3–25.
Davis, F.D. 1989. "Perceived Usefulness, Perceived Ease of Use, and User Acceptance of Information Technology." *MIS Quarterly* 13(3): 319–340.
Hung, S.Y., Chang, C.M., and Kuo, S.R. 2013. "User Acceptance of Mobile E-Government Services: An Empirical Study." *Government Information Quarterly* 30: 33–44.
ICMA. 2014. "Apply for Designation as 2014–2016 Citizen-Engaged Community." Accessed 7/14/2005 http://icma.org/en/BlogPost/2935/Apply_for_Designation_as_20142016_CitizenEngaged_Community.
Ishmatova, D. and Obi, T. 2009. "M-Government Services: User Needs and Value." *Journal of E-Government Policy and Regulation* 32: 39–46.
Jeong, C.H.I. 2007. *Fundamentals of Development Administration*. Selangor: Scholar Press.
Layne, K. and Lee, J. 2001. "Developing Fully Functional E-Government: A Four Stage Model." *Government Information Quarterly* 18: 122–136.
Legris, P., Ingham, J., and Collerette, P. 2003. "Why Do People Use Information Technology? A Critical Review of the Technology Acceptance Model." *Information & Management* 40(3): 191–204.
Moon, J.W. and Kim, Y.G. 2001. "Extending the TAM for a World-Wide-Web Context." *Information & Management* 38(4): 217–230.
Moon, M.J. 2010. "Shaping M-Government for Emergency Management: Issues and Challenges." *Journal of E-Governance* 33: 100–107.
Nam, T. and Pardo, T. 2014. "Understanding Municipal Service Integration: An Exploratory Study of 311 Contact Centers." *Journal of Urban Technology* 21(1): 57–78.
Schwester, R. 2009. "Examining the Barriers to E-Government Adoption." *Journal of E-Government* 7(1): 113–122.
Schwester, R., Carrizales, T., and Holzer, M. 2009. "An Examination of the Municipal 311 System." *International Journal of Organization Theory and Behavior* 12(2): 218–236.
Shareef, M., Archer, N., and Dwivedi, Y. 2012. "Examining Adoption Behaviour of Mobile Government." *Journal of Computer Information Systems* 53(2): 39–49.
Smailovic, N. 2012. "Data Visualization on Information Tables—Dashboards." *Journal of Information Technology and Applications* 2: 68–74.

Swiss, J. 1992. "Adapting Total Quality Management (TQM) to Government." *Public Administration Review* 52(4): 356–362.

Teo, T., Srivastava, S., and Jiang, L. 2008. "Trust and Electronic Government Success: An Empirical Study." *Journal of Management Information Systems* 25(3): 99–131.

Tolbert, C.J. and Mossberger, K. 2006. "The Effects of E-Government on Trust and Confidence in Government." *Public Administration Review* 66: 354–369.

Venkatesh, V. and Davis, F.D. 2000. "A Theoretical Extension of the Technology Acceptance Model: Four Longitudinal Field Studies." *Management Science* 46(2): 186–204.

13

CIVIC HACKING

Citizens Creating New Digital Government Interfaces

Lora Frecks

In the early 2010s, citizens started banding together and doing something new. They received data from local governments and created new digital interfaces (websites and apps) for their fellow citizens to access that data. The general goal is to make this information more accessible—to move information from difficult-to-find locations or difficult formats and to make it easier for people to find, access, and understand. This chapter explains how this phenomenon known as civic hacking became possible, how it can be fostered, and what it might mean for the future of public administration.

An Example

In 2013, the Boston area experienced an unprecedented outbreak of the flu.[1] Boston's city government reached out to a local citizen group known as civic hackers for assistance after declaring a public health emergency.[2] The Boston civic hackers contacted a similar group in Chicago (Open City), which shared the open source code for a website they had developed.[3] With some modifications to this code and data from Boston's government, the Boston civic hackers launched a website allowing any Bostonian with a smartphone or other online access to easily and quickly locate a flu shot clinic.[4] In addition to the clinic's location, the website told citizens when the clinic was open and how much the flu shot would cost (http://flushot.newurban mechanics.org/). This was all done in just under 36 hours.[5]

To be clear, this event did not require a procurement process. No one negotiated and monitored a service contract. Instead, self-organized Boston civic hackers volunteered their time to respond to a public need. They worked hard those two days to modify the Chicago group's code and integrate Boston's data. Chicago's civic hackers freely shared their earlier work. As a result of all this citizen volunteer work, Boston-area citizens benefited from having an easier way to access information critical to their immediate health. Eventually, Chicago-area citizens also benefited from improvements the Boston civic hackers made to the original code.[6]

This example illustrates the potential civic hacking has for both citizens and their governments. Because civic hacking is a new phenomenon, this introduction to the topic is focused on the basics. First, we explore what advances in technology, government policies, and societal trends enabled civic hacking to evolve at this particular point in time. Next, we explore civic hacking in greater detail. This description includes both details about how individual groups operate and national trends. We conclude with a look toward the future of civic hacking and some best practice recommendations for interactions between civic hacking groups and governments, nonprofits, and academics.

Civic hacking has spread outside the United States, but it originated in the United States and remained a U.S. American phenomenon for several years. At the time that this chapter is written, civic hacking remains largely a U.S. American activity. Given the goal of introducing readers to the topic of civic hacking and its origins within this chapter, the author is therefore focusing solely on U.S. civic hacking. The author respects the work of civic hackers everywhere and plans to publish a comparison of civic hacking activities across countries and global regions elsewhere.

A History of Civic Hacking

The onset of civic hacking was closely accompanied by a nexus of developments. Some of these advances were technology based. Others were societal based and fostered changes in how we think about certain government policies and citizen responsibilities. Figure 13.1 provides a quick chronological overview of some of these technological, policy and societal developments.

Technology Innovations

While there are certain key technological components enabling civic hacking, each of these was enabled by the open source movement.[7] Within the open source movement, programming languages, software, and programs are developed in an open source format either in the creative commons or curated by volunteers appointed by a self-governing community.[8,9] Together, all of these open source innovations generated an environment in which vast amounts of data can be easily and affordably stored and accessed by many people. These innovations have also enabled the same data to then be analyzed using free or affordable programs.[10]

Civic hacking would be difficult without recent technological developments in cloud computing and database capabilities.[11] Advances in these technologies have made this type of volunteer civic work economically feasible and technologically possible. For example, GitHub, a website enabling programmers to share open source code and a core component in civic hacking work, launched in 2008.[12,13] GitHub functions much like a lending library in which each book's various alternative plot twists are written by those checking out the book. Instead, code is posted for others to modify as they

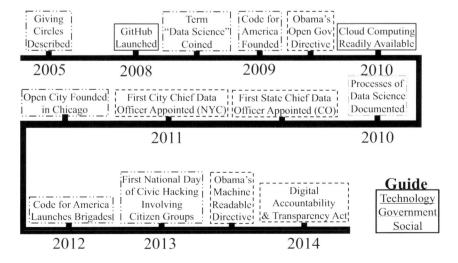

Figure 13.1 A Timeline of Events Enabling Civic Hacking

see fit. For example, Programmer A posts some new code she wrote and finds useful. Programmer B forks this code, modifying it and posting his new modified version. Programmer C also forks Programmer A's code, modifies it and posts her new version. Programmer D forks Programmer B's code and adds the modifications made by Programmer C.

Cloud computing became readily available to the public in 2010.[14] By readily available we mean that it was affordable and easy to access for much of the public by 2010. Civic hacking would not be economically feasible without these advancements in cloud computing. It allows numerous members of civic hacking groups to collaborate online. Civic hacking groups store large amounts of data and code in cloud computing servers.

Figure 13.1 provides a timeline of how these technological innovations became economically feasible for individuals or volunteer groups to access. To be clear, what was once only affordable to large well-funded organizations can now be done by small loosely organized groups or even individuals. This enables civic hacking groups to tackle and complete unprecedented projects independent of any large formal organization. Without the drop-in cost to access these technologies in the 2000s and early 2010s, civic hacking groups depending on their own individual resources and limited donations would not be able to afford to do this work.

Government Policies

At the same time that our technological resources increased to enable the work of civic hacking, governments at all levels began to alter information policies to allow for the sharing of data. Closely related to the open source movement, these policy changes by government are often referred to as open data.[15] The open data policy shift by government makes the work of civic hackers easier by providing access to data. A summary of these policy changes in chronological order can be found in Figure 13.1.

Changes in governmental information policy can be seen in the establishment of new policies and in the appointment of staff to oversee open data initiatives. In 2010, Colorado became the first state to appoint a chief data officer (CDO).[16] New York City led local governments in this policy area with the appointment of the first city CDO in 2011.[17,18] Several federal agencies have had CDOs since at least 2014. In contrast, the White House appointed the nation's first administration CDO in February 2015.[19,20] These appointments by federal entities and state and local governments are important. The creation of a full-time staff position devoted to government information represents both a recognition of the importance of making data available to the public and a resource commitment by governments to an open data policy.

Policies concerning open government are more formalized on the federal level in the United States. This is an area of policy where the federal government has clearly led the way for all other levels of government in the U.S. President Obama issued his Open Government Directive in December 2009, long before any government CDOs.[21,22] The 2009 Open Government Directive states that, with regards to federal data, "the presumption shall be in favor of openness (to the extent permitted by law and subject to valid privacy, confidentiality, security, or other restrictions)."[23] However, there are many ways that data can be made available to the public—and some of these means are easier for the public to work with than others. For many reasons (including various aging legacy software and hardware systems within governmental entities), paper copies or pdf electronic file versions of data are the easiest for federal agencies, departments, or bureaus to make available to citizens.

Unfortunately, both pdfs and paper copies of data are difficult for all citizens, including those working in civic hacking groups, to work with and integrate into their digital systems. The result is that individual civic hackers within a group must enter the government data by hand into a shared database. Basically, the data is retyped into a shared spreadsheet (generally a Google Sheet). This also requires an additional step to verify that the retyping of the data has been done correctly and in a consistent manner among all the data entry civic hacking workers. This entire data entry and verifying process is time consuming, tedious, and prone to error.

This is one of the reasons why President Obama issued an Executive Order in 2013 titled "Making open and machine readable the new default for government information."[24] The 2013 Executive Order builds on the open data directive four years earlier, which requires federal entities to provide citizens with requested data unless there was a strong justification not to do so.[25] The 2013 Executive Order makes it the default of the federal government to provide data to citizens in a machine-readable format unless there is a strong justification not to do so.

Given the burden of outdated legacy systems, there is still ample justification for portions of the federal government to provide data in non-machine-readable formats. However, this justification should diminish over time. Legacy systems will eventually be updated at all levels of government, and new technologies will be developed to aid in accessing data locked away in any remaining outdated systems. In the meantime, civic hacking groups continue to convert government data into machine-readable formats. Steeped in a culture of sharing, each civic hacking group then makes these new machine-readable datasets publicly available.

Congress has supported the Obama Administration's progress in opening government data. In 2014, Congress passed the Digital Accountability and Transparency Act (known as the DATA Act).[26] The DATA Act echoes much of the open data policy established by President Obama. It's significant that Congress took this action for two primary reasons. The first is that it indicates that open data and government transparency are not just a priority of the executive branch of the federal government. The legislative branch also recognizes their value. Secondly, the DATA Act passed at a time of extreme partisanship between Democratic and Republican party members in Congress. Little was accomplished during this session of Congress.[27,28] This indicates that members of both parties in the United States are committed to open data and transparency within the federal government. It also indicates that these policies have such overwhelming popularity in society that they are not viewed as controversial topics for politicians.

Societal Developments

As illustrated in Figure 13.1, the development and rise of civic hacking has also been aided greatly by changes in society. It can be difficult to parse out societal influences on the development of technological innovations and policy changes aiding civic hacking activities. However, to understand how civic hacking groups came to exist, it's important for us to know that these societal influences exist. There are five main categories: Giving Circles, Knowledge Access, Maker Groups, Code for America, and Data Science.

Giving Circles

In the 1990s, larger numbers of U.S. citizens became more comfortable with the idea of taking action in small groups. In the public administration sphere, this was demonstrated in the giving circle movement first described in an academic publication in the early 2000s.[29] In giving circles, individuals self-organize into groups and pool their combined resources into donations.[30] Such groups existed in the past. However, the moniker "giving circles" clearly identified these groups and solidified the concept for both the general public and academics.

These donations are primarily financial but can also take the form of donated clothes, food, and other items. Some giving circles pool resources for a local purpose.[31] Others send their pooled resources longer distances and even overseas.[32] Giving circles effectively function as mini, nonformal, nonofficial nonprofits. Occasionally, people first hearing the term "giving circles" are surprised to discover that they've been members of at least one giving circle in the past.

Giving circles are a critical societal contributor to the development of civic hacking for several reasons. The prevalence of these groups normalized the idea of small groups of individuals working together to benefit society. The success of these groups also bolsters individual participant's confidence that they and others have made a difference in both their own communities and communities farther afield. This confidence in turn influences society's perspective on how likely other similar endeavors are to succeed. Civic hacking groups could be viewed as a specialized form of giving circles focused on donating members' time and skills to make government information more available for all citizens.

Knowledge Access

At the same time that giving circles were rising in prominence in the United States in the 1990s and early 2000s, information was becoming available at an unprecedented rate. The World Wide Web matured and was populated during much of the 1990s.[33,34] Later in the 1990s, search engines began making more of this information easily findable.[35] By the late 2000s and early 2010s, people were accustomed to easily finding answers to all their questions at any time and in almost any location. Not being able to access answers or information became an abnormal state for many people in the United States. This shift in our expectations for how easily and immediately we should be able to access answers and information is both radical and unprecedented. Unfortunately, the ease by which we are able to access information digitally has also become a reliable indicator of our socioeconomic status.[36]

Maker Groups

Like giving circles, maker groups are usually self-organized groups of individuals who band together. But rather than donating resources to another party, maker groups band together to make things.[37] Members of maker groups can make anything they set their minds to: furniture, 3-D printers, security systems, robots, engines, computers, biotech equipment, even diamonds.

Sometimes maker groups form around a business or nonprofit that provides customers or members with access to certain often-specialized tools or other resources useful in the making of things.[38] (Visit http://www.techshop.ws/ for a business example and http://quelab.net/blog/ for a nonprofit example.) However, many maker groups are informal self-organized groups of individuals pooling their resources and knowledge to build a shared dream project.

Maker groups are increasingly being referenced as representative of a new industrial revolution.[39,40] Similar to how advances in open source code, cloud computing, and other technological tools made civic hacking affordable in the 2000s and early 2010s, innovations in manufacturing and software are increasingly making it more affordable for individuals and small groups to generate the parts needed to manufacture nearly anything.[41,42]

The maker movement, which is said to have begun in 2005, is a broader concept than maker groups,[43] much like the concepts of open data and transparent government are much broader than the actions of civic hacking groups. According to Mark Hatch, the CEO of the largest maker group company, the goal of the maker movement is to "collectively use our creativity to attack the world's greatest problems and meet people's most urgent needs."[44]

There is some overlap among the membership of maker groups and civic hacking groups. Certainly members of both groups share an expectation that they can access the information and resources they want when they want to and that they can do and create what they want to when they want to create it. Both types of groups also share an idealistic view described in the maker manifesto that individuals and small groups of individuals can make significant changes in the world. And they're not wrong. Crowdfunding is providing access to financing for nearly anyone who can effectively communicate a good idea.[45] Technological innovations are enabling individuals to prototype and even manufacture goods that only specialized and wealthy corporations could create a short time ago.[46] Individuals and small groups of people can now accomplish what once required the resources of large, wealthy organizations.

Code for America Nonprofit

Among this environment of seismic shifts in possibilities and scales, Jennifer Pahlka created Code for America in 2009. She was inspired by Teach for America, which pairs teachers with communities for a set period of time. Code for America partners programmers with local governments for set periods of time. The programmers in these partnerships are called fellows and spend at least part of their time in their partnering community. The Code for America fellowships provide programmers with opportunities to give back to local communities.[47]

In 2011, some Chicago information technology professionals self-organized into the first civic hacking group, which they named Open City. True to the business environment many of them operated in professionally, they categorized their new venture as a civic startup.[48] It wasn't long before other civic hacking groups began forming around the United States.

Recognizing the value of civic hacking groups to its mission, in 2012 Code for America began to organize and support local self-organized civic hacking groups into brigades.[49,50] Brigades is Code for America's official term for civic hacking groups.[51] All brigades are civic hacking groups. However, not all civic hacking groups are Code for America brigades. Civic hacking groups must apply for brigade status and meet a set of qualifications before attaining brigade status. Most of the civic hacking groups in the U.S. have opted to become or at least attempt to become Code for America brigades.[52] Code for America also supports civic hacking groups outside the U.S.

Code for America's first National Day of Civic Hacking was held in 2012 and involved only Code for America fellows.[53] However, the 2013 National Day of Civic Hacking involved civic hacking groups that had sought status as a brigade and qualified, those that were seeking brigade status, and those that were not seeking Code for America brigade status.[54,55] Code for America's National Day of Civic Hacking is now held annually in June, and it's become a date which individuals seeking to form a new local civic hacking group rally local events and attention around.[56] Contrary to its name, Code for America's National Day of Civic Hacking is often a weekend-long event for civic hacking groups.

Code for America contributes greatly to the civic hacking community. The code created by Code for America fellows working with local governments is made available for all civic hacking groups to access—regardless of their brigade status. The brigade program within Code for America provides structure and resources to the sometimes loosely organized civic hacking groups scattered around the country and the world. Code for America also provides a valuable means for government representatives and the press to access and understand civic hacking that wouldn't be possible without a large nonprofit organization. Code for America's National Day of Civic Hacking is an excellent example of the nonprofit's work in this capacity. Additionally, Code for America's founder and CEO, Jennifer Pahlka, served as a formal advisor to President Obama in the White House.

Data Science

The term data science was first used in 2008 by D. J. Patil (who in 2015 became the first White House Chief Data Officer) and Jeff Hammerbacher to describe the data analytics work they were each doing at LinkedIn and Facebook respectively.[57,58] Later in 2010, a self-organized group of engineers and scientist regularly met in New York City to discuss how the rapid technological advances had and would continue to influence their work.[59] In 2010, these meetings led to the development of a list of characteristics describing the work of the relatively new job of data scientist.[60] The processes of data science documented by this group were obtain, scrub, explore, model, and interpret.[61]

These processes are essentially the same as those collectively conducted by civic hacking groups. More importantly, these data science processes provide a useful framework for structuring the work of civic hacking groups. The processes provide individual civic hackers with a means for understanding how their skillset fits within the work of a civic hacking group.

Even before its recognition as a formal field and job title, data science has been growing.[62] This is important to civic hacking because it increases the odds that the public will encounter and become familiar with the concept and therefore find the work of civic hacking groups recognizable and understandable. This growth rate is also relevant to civic hacking, because it increases the number of individuals skilled at doing the work necessary in a successful civic hacking group.

A Description of Civic Hacking and Civic Hacking Groups

Christopher Whitaker's flu shot–finding example of civic hacking at the beginning of this chapter likely provided you with some understanding of civic hacking.[63,64] Likewise, the historical explanation of how technological, policy, and societal innovations in the 1990s to early 2015 gave you some insight into the context from which civic hacking arose. What follows is some specifics about civic hacking groups, including definitions and purpose, a description of the work done by civic hacking groups, and a national view of civic hacking groups in the United States.

Definitions and Purpose

One of Code for America's fellows, Jake Levitas, provided the first formal definition of civic hacking.[65] He carefully and clearly reviewed related definitions at the time (2013), gathering common themes of (1) local problems, (2) technology, and (3) citizen action.[66] At the end of his assessment, he settles on the following definition: "Civic hacking is the act of *quickly improving* the processes and systems of local *government* with new tools or approaches, conducted with cities, *by citizens*, as an act of citizenship" [emphasis added].[67]

For the purpose of her own research, the author has defined civic hacking groups as "self-organized groups of *citizens* voluntarily *creating new* digital interfaces for *government* data or service information."[68] Key components of both definitions include: new innovations, government and citizens.

But recent exciting innovations in civic hacking groups have rendered both definitions incomplete. Since late 2014, there has been a trend toward civic hacking groups pairing with nonprofits or even loosely organized community organizations. Therefore, a more updated version of these definitions would appropriately read as follows:

> Updated Levitas, 2013, definition: Civic hacking is the act of quickly improving the processes and systems of governments *and nongovernmental organizations (NGOs)* with new tools or approaches, conducted with governments *and NGOs*, by citizens, as an act of citizenship.
>
> Updated Frecks, 2014, definition: Self-organized groups of *citizens* voluntarily creating new digital interfaces for government and *nongovernmental organization (NGO)* data or service information.

Regardless of how civic hacking is defined, it serves as a catalyst for generating increased levels of citizen participation in communities and local governments.[69,70,71,72] Civic hacker groups create apps and websites for the purpose of improving their fellow citizens' access to government data.[73,74] They provide data management tools that enable citizens to become more actively involved in their local governments and communities.[75] They also provide governments with platforms for citizens to interact with local governments and fellow community members.[76] With these activities, civic hackers don't just increase citizen participation. Their work can provide an entirely new method for this participation to occur. Both citizens and governments benefit from the volunteer efforts of civic hackers.[77,78]

Civic hacking's commitment to openness and transparency is demonstrated in the names civic hacking groups select for themselves. Examples of use of the term "open" in civic hacking names include Open City (Chicago), Open Data STL (St. Louis, MO), Open Nebraska, Open Salt Lake (UT), and Open Twin Cities (Minneapolis and St. Paul, MN). Inherent in the goal of openness is the concept that civic hacking groups serve the needs of citizens and governments. This concept is demonstrated even more frequently in the name of civic hacking groups, such as Code 4 SAC (Sacramento, CA), Code for BTV (Burlington, VT), Code for Connecticut (New Haven), Code for Detroit (MI), Code for Hampton Roads (VA), Code for KC (KS), Code for Seattle (WA), and Hack for Western MASS (Massachusetts). While names of organizations do not necessarily communicate true intentions, it is unlikely that so many groups have been intentionally misleading with their choices of names.

The Work of Civic Hacking Groups

Civic hacking groups generally form around hackathon events. Hackathons are useful for grabbing the attention of potential civic hackers and bringing them to an event where they meet other potential civic hackers. Hackathons are also useful for gaining the attention of governments and nongovernmental organizations that might be motivated to provide datasets for the hackathon participants. The work of less established civic hacking groups generally revolves around periodic hackathons.

In contrast, more established civic hacking groups have regular work sessions that are not considered to be hackathons. Frequently these work sessions are referred to as Hack Nights. Since this term is not used universally and because some of these work sessions can occur during the day, the more general term work sessions will be used throughout this discussion.

These work sessions are comprised of subgroups of civic hackers within the group. The sessions focus on sustained work concerning specific projects that the civic hacking group has been working on for some time. It is anticipated that work will be completed during the work session, but, unlike a hackathon, there is no expectation that a project will be completed from start to finish in a work session. Government or nongovernmental organization representatives might attend the work sessions periodically or even regularly to aid in the work and discuss the data.

The most well-established and productive civic hacking groups have weekly work sessions. This is likely because they have a critical number of projects and civic hackers to sustain this level of work. Some civic hacking groups have monthly or biweekly work sessions. Others schedule work sessions as needed. The least established civic hacking groups do not have work sessions and rely on hackathons to generate and work on projects. More commonly, a project begins with a hackathon and members of a subgroup continue working on the project in semi-regular work sessions.

Steps of a Project

Members of a civic hacking group work through the steps of data science together: data gathering (obtain), data tidying (scrub), database/API creation, data analysis (explore), and website/interface creation (model and possibly interpret).[79] Optimally, civic hacking groups like to skip the first two-and-a-half steps by receiving pristine data in a computer readable format compatible with whatever API format the group members wish to work in for that project. However, this is rarely the case.

BEST-CASE SCENARIO

When the best-case scenario does occur, civic hackers with programming skills can start immediately on creating the application program interface (API). An API is like a liaison between the database and the website/app interface (sometimes referred to as a graphical user interface (GUI—pronounced "gooey"). It's the API that knows that a human clicking a certain button on the website wants this specific data from the database. Basically, APIs make websites work.

Other civic hackers skilled in programming and interface design will begin creating the GUI, which may be a website, an app, or some other format. The two groups of programmers (the API and GUI groups) will need to talk to each other a lot to make sure the two components interact together properly. However, a lot of this discussion may happen via instant messaging (IM), email, or even social media. This means that uninitiated attendees at work nights or hackathons may be left with the impression that no communication is occurring and the work isn't well coordinated.

The silences described above are periodically punctuated by collective and seemingly random bursts of joy or frustration, which can startle and bewilder first-time visitors. These outbursts are generally brought about by testing to see how well the API is pulling information from the database or how well the API and GUI are interfacing. These can be some of the happiest times in civic hacking work and some of the most frustrating.

The process of programming at hack nights or hackathons also has frequent pauses in which humans must wait for either computers or other humans to complete some activity before proceeding. During these times, there is often a lot of joking among participants. These periods of play while waiting can appear unproductive to new participants. In summary, the communication methods of civic hackers are not always readily apparent, and the pace of work is erratic due to constraints in the process.

At some point, less technologically skilled civic hackers will need to test whether the GUI makes sense. For this work, having absolutely no technological knowledge is the best possible asset to the civic hacking group. The goal is to determine whether the website or app makes sense to members of the general public. In other words, if you're the tester and can't figure out how to navigate the website or app and make it work, you've provided invaluable information for the programmers. No one wants to create something that no one can use.

Less technologically skilled civic hackers might also be involved in creating language for the GUI. This language might describe how to use the app or website. It might also explain why the GUI was created and where the data originated from.

NOT THE BEST-CASE SCENARIO (AKA THE USUAL PROCESS)

When data isn't received in a pristine format, with clear definitions of what each dataset represents, it's optimal to form a small team to determine how best to proceed. Ideally, this team would include (1) a representative of the data provider knowledgeable about the data, (2) a civic hacker who will be primarily responsible for developing the API, (3) a civic hacker who will be primarily responsible for designing the GUI, (4) a civic hacker who will be primarily responsible for creating the Google spreadsheet and seeing that the data is entered and verified, and (5) possibly a civic hacker skilled in communications—especially in communicating across professional fields and silos of information. This civic hacker may also be responsible for creating the language used in the GUI to communicate with users.

Topics that the little team may need to decide can include (1) What data is complete? (2) What data would we like to include in the project or what would we like to accomplish with the project? (3) What time and other resource constraints does the project face? (4) What data can be included in the project or what can we accomplish? This is includes prioritizing goals if possible.

Once this team ensures that everyone has a shared understanding of the data and the plan, the Google spreadsheet, API, and GUI can be generated. With this approach, the early stages of the project rely heavily on patience and care to ensure that everyone understands the data and plan. Then even more patience and care are needed to enter and confirm the data in a shared spreadsheet. Google Sheets is useful at this stage because multiple people can enter data at the same time. This helps maintain the integrity of the data by preventing the creation of multiple spreadsheets with varying data. An added bonus to using Google Sheets at this stage is that all the team members' email addresses are needed for them to access the spreadsheet. This email information can be extraordinarily useful later as the team continues to work on the project over time.

Individual Civic Hackers

Anyone can be a civic hacker. As individuals, civic hackers are programmers, designers, data management experts, project management experts, and other volunteers with less technological skills. It's important to note that individuals without technological skills make important contributions to the work of civic hacking groups.[80,81] Though not as technologically skilled as a programmer or designer, academics and other citizens can help gather, verify, and organize data; write and proofread language for a website or other digital interface; and test to ensure the digital interface makes sense, functions properly, and is generally usable for the general population. Most of the civic hacking groups the author has interacted with have not indicated that they've experienced a shortage of API or user interface programmers volunteering. Instead, groups have expressed a need for more lay people to volunteer. Nontechnologically skilled civic hackers are extremely valuable to civic hacking groups because they free the technologically skilled members to focus solely on activities requiring their advanced abilities. Excitingly, this means that anyone really can be a civic hacker.

More is known about individual civic hackers than civic hacking groups. Two studies have explored the motivations of individual civic hackers. Both published in academic journals during 2014.[82,83] In contrast, there hasn't yet been a published academic paper concerning civic hacker groups.

Stepasiuk focused specifically on the motivations of individual civic hackers through interviews and observations of members of a single civic hacking group in the U.S. She determined that civic hackers' motivations fall into "one or motivational classifications; activists, volunteers, and 'hackers.'"[84] Activists have a political agenda and tend to drop out if no one in the civic hacking group is interested in their ideas.[85] Volunteers are giving some resource.[86] "Hackers" seek to "repurpos[e] something."[87] What Stepasiuk found is that few civic hackers identified as activists. Instead, those who were technologically skilled identified as hackers, while those who were not technologically skilled identified as volunteers.[88] The civic hackers with advanced programming or design skills perceived volunteering as charity work and their work with the civic hacking group as being "more specialized than doing charity work."[89]

Juell-Skielse and his team used a case study and a survey and interviews of participants within the case study event to examine motivations for both individuals and groups involved. The case study concerned an innovation contest held by a European government agency and was a one-time event.[90] Unlike Stepasiuk's (2014) study, almost half of the individuals and groups participating in this study were affiliated with a business and participating in the event as representative of their organizations.[91] Despite this difference, the Juell-Skielse team had nearly identical findings to Stepasiuk's. The top two motivators Juell-Skielse's team found were "fun and enjoyment" and "intellectual challenge."[92] The intellectual challenge motivation corresponds to Stepasiuk's finding that civic hackers find problem solving enjoyable.

It should be noted that these findings are fairly similar to earlier studies focused on determining what motivates volunteer programmers developing free/open source codes and software.[93,94,95,96]

While civic hackers generally utilize free/open source codes (Levitas, 2013), they use the code to create interfaces that foster citizen participation in communities and local governments.[97,98,99,100,101] In contrast, the previously studied volunteer programmers focus entirely on developing free/open source codes and software to provide these as tools to the wider open source community.[102,103,104] Stated differently, civic hackers use the products developed by free/open source programming volunteers.

Despite the differences in their work, both civic hackers and free/open sources code and software developers are motivated by fun and intellectual challenges.[105,106,107] However, several studies have found that free/open source code and software developers are also highly motivated by self-marketing, networking, altruism, and community identification.[108,109,110]

National Information about Civic Hacking Groups

There are approximately 63 civic hacking groups in the United States.[111] Roughly 20 percent of these groups are not seeking to become Code for America brigades.[112] This doesn't mean that these groups might not someday decide to pursue brigade status.

Only nine of the 51 states and district in the United States do not yet have a civic hacking group. Of these, only two are Democratic-leaning states. Similarly, 78 percent of the civic hacking groups are located in Democratic-leaning states—which also happen to be the more urban states.[113]

Given civic hacking's dependence on skilled information technology (IT) volunteers, one might suspect that areas with IT clusters would have many civic hacking groups. However, 19 percent of IT clusters lack a civic hacking group and 46 percent of civic hacking groups are not located near an IT cluster.[114] In contrast, 100 percent of the communities with a chief data officer have at least one civic hacking group.[115] While preliminary, these findings suggest that the existence of civic hacking groups is more dependent on an environment rich in government support than one heavily populated by IT professionals.

Local versus State or Federal

Civic hacking can occur at any level of government. However, citizen participation is actually more frequent at the local level. There are two likely causes for this. First, local government and the public administrators who make it work are more accessible to citizens than their more remote state and federal colleagues. This remoteness is both physical in terms of the state and federal worker's locations and topical in terms of what matters most in the daily life of citizens. For example, issues concerning citizen's respective local schools, law enforcement, and public health generally matter more to citizens than federal international regulations or dealings. This is less true with state issues, but the premise still applies. The more local a government topic, the more citizens are interested in the topic and the easier it is for them to become involved in citizen participation activities.

The second reason that citizen coproduction is more likely to occur at the local level of government has to do with numbers. There is only one federal government in the United States and 50 state governments. In contrast, there are collectively tens of thousands of local governments in the form of cities, towns, townships, counties, parishes, etc. Some of these local governments even have overlapping physical and topical jurisdictions.

Collaborating with Civic Hacking Groups

There are a wide variety of approaches to improving collaborations between civic hacking groups and government and nongovernmental organization (NGO) representatives. Some of these involve improving communications. Other approaches are focused on specific actions that governments, nongovernmental organizations, and civic hacking groups can take to create partnerships.

Communications

Stepasiuk recommends civic hacking groups emphasize the good being done in communities to attract participants primarily motivated as volunteers. She also recommends ensuring gatherings allow for "problem solving, one of their intrinsic-enjoyment based motivations."[116] Juell-Skielse's team had similar recommendations that "governments need to . . . care for making citizen coproduction in the execution and monitoring phases fun and enjoyable."[117] While small in number and scope, these studies make it resoundingly clear that governments and civic hacker groups can attract more technologically skilled professions by emphasizing the fun associated with events and associated work.

Additionally, Stepasiuk recommends that governments and civic hacking groups communicate with each other regarding what projects each would like to work on. This would avoid redundancies in efforts. She also points out that such communications could help governments lure civic hacking groups into working on specific projects.[118]

Establishing shared language and understanding is crucial to achieving successful collaborations. Therefore, establishing a common language and understanding of what type of work civic hacking groups can do will aid government representatives and civic hackers in creating better collaborations. It is a common anecdote among civic hackers that their offers to volunteer have been frequently misunderstood by local governments. More than one civic hacker has been asked to scan boxes of documents after attempting to offer assistance in fixing government websites.

Creating Partnerships

Civic hacking works best when there are successful collaborations between the civic hacking groups and the entities providing data. Close working relationships between the two organizations provides familiarity and clear communications between the two groups. But how do these groups create these levels of familiarity, communication, and successful collaboration?

Government Representatives

There are many steps governments can take to help create working relationships with civic hacking groups. One of the most important is to provide datasets and descriptions of dream projects on their website along with contact information for asking additional questions about the data or projects. Like other coproduction groups, civic hackers like to know that their labors will be used.[119] Another is to include non-Freedom of Information Act (non-FOIA) request information on the government's website.[120] Lacking any other instructions for requesting data, civic hackers will often pursue this more formal, labor intensive, and time-consuming procedure for requesting data from governments.

Once a governmental entity has received a request for data from a civic hacking group, it should respond as soon as possible.[121] The civic hackers are likely excited about working on this project and will perceive any delays as taking far longer than they actually are. Even if the only response you can send the civic hackers is—We've received your request and appreciate your interest in our data. We're not sure yet whether we can provide you with the data you've requested, but we have begun our internal process to make a formal determination. Please bear with us as we work through this internal procedure. It may take some time and we apologize in advance for any delays—it will still help.

Once a determination has been made that the data can be shared, governments should do their best to provide the data to the civic hackers in the requested format.[122] However, this doesn't mean that governments must go to extreme measures to achieve the requested format. Feel free to describe to the civic hackers what format is feasible with the resources available to your agency or department.

There is likely a reasonable compromise that can be reached. And in the process of reaching that compromise, the government representative and civic hacker will likely have increased their understanding of each other's goals.[123]

Government representatives should also feel free to offer to discuss and explain the data to the civic hackers.[124] Government employees have likely labored greatly over the collection of this data and important to them that the data be used and interpreted appropriately. The civic hackers requesting the data are very interested in it and will undoubtedly be happy to hear whatever additional information you would like to share about it. How often do public administrators have citizens willing to listen to a description of the fruits of their hard labor? This is a prime opportunity for public administrators to shine!

And while they are shining, these public administrators should also try to be as enthusiastic as possible.[125] The energy levels and degrees of excitement vary greatly between government employees and civic hackers. For government workers, this is often just another day in the office. For civic hackers, this can be an exciting new endeavor they feel strongly enough about to invest their free time in for a chance to make a difference in their community.

Nongovernmental Organizations (NGOs)

Civic hacking groups are often pursuing data from government agencies and departments. In contrast, NGOs are becoming increasingly aware of the benefits of working with civic hacking groups and have begun pursuing them. This shift to pursuer requires a corresponding shift in how NGOs attempt to initiate collaborations with civic hacking groups.

In an increasingly competitive market where there are more and more NGOs seeking out civic hacking partners, it's critical for NGOs to have a clear description of the proposed project and pristine data for the civic hacking group to work with.[126] In especially competitive communities, NGOs should strive to have the data available in the civic hacker's preferred mode. NGOs might also prepare a brief but highly compelling description of why the proposed project is important to the community. This information could be displayed on the NGO's website.

Civic Hacking Groups

When seeking data from governments, civic hacking groups should do their best to avoid beginning with a Freedom of Information Action request.[127] A better approach would be to email the chief data officer, chief information officer (CIO), or the chief technology officer (CTO). If none of those individuals can be located or none of them responded to your request after 3–6 weeks, you should contact the head of the department or agency. Please do not begin by tattling on the unresponsive officers you tried to contact. They may have a good reason for not having responded, and it will place their boss in a defensive position before she even knows what you're requesting.

If you have any doubts about your ability to clearly communicate what data you want, what format you'd like to receive it in, and what you intend to do with it, recruit help.[128,129] You're a clever civic hacker volunteering your valuable time to help your community. There is no shame in asking for help to craft the best request for data possible. In fact, it's the smart thing to do.

Once you receive word that the data will be sent to you, be open to receiving it in alternative formats.[130] Even if you receive the data in the worst possible format, be sure to express appreciation for the data.[131] Someone spent time and effort gathering the data for you. If they have an IT background, they may even be embarrassed at their inability to provide the data in a more modern, accessible format. At the very least, expressing appreciation increases your chances that the agency or department will be more open to your or another civic hacker's requests for data in the future.

Feel free to ask your government contact questions about the data.[132] This can happen either before you receive the data or after you've had a chance to look at it and try to understand it. There is always a chance that your request will be turned down and you should be prepared for this. However, it is far more likely that your request will be met with some level of enthusiasm. Public administrators don't often get to discuss their work in detail with citizens and may greatly enjoy your interest in their work.

Above all, always remember that public administrators should be treated with respect. They do difficult work with limited resources. They likely entered the profession to be public servants, not to become rich. At heart, they care greatly about their community and they spend every workday serving that community. They are also experts in how the bureaucracy works and can be great aids as you seek to navigate unknown government systems.

The Future of Civic Hacking within the United States

Citizen participation within the United States is increasing in frequency and occurring in new forms. At the same time, citizens are expecting all levels of government (local, state, and federal) to become more transparent and share information more readily. Fortunately, citizens are increasingly able to help their governments make these changes due to innovations in technologies and policies. Increases in these technology-based forms of citizen participation in turn are acting as force multipliers and enabling additional citizens to become active in citizen participation activities.[133]

A self-perpetuating spiral of increasing citizen participation results. Technologically skilled citizens create new ways for fellow community members to interact with government. The new participants expect more services and information from government, leading more people to become involved in creating additional ways for community members to participate.[134] Given the continued trends toward governments and nonprofits valuing open data and transparency, it's likely that collaborations between civic hacking groups and governments and nongovernmental organizations will increase in the future.

Academics and Civic Hacking

For civic hacking to grow in the future, government and nongovernmental organization (NGO) workers must know they exist and what can be accomplished through collaborations with these citizen groups. Academia could play a critical role in raising government and NGO administrators' awareness of civic hacking. This could be as simple as Information Technology and public administration instructors mentioning occasionally to their students that civic hacking exists. It could involve inviting a local civic hacker to speak about their experiences in the classroom. In its extreme form, university faculty could reach out to local civic hacking groups to establish community engagement opportunities for their students to participate in civic hacking activities or research concerning civic hacking. Any of these activities would increase students' awareness and comfort with interacting with civic hacking groups. Some of these activities might provide students with valuable opportunities to make connections and gain practical experience in the working world. Some of these activities might also provide a means for students to work across fields and gain experience negotiating the accompanying cultural and language barriers associated with such collaborations.

Public administration academics might also consider reaching out to local civic hacking groups to see if they have any interest in a short general civics training session for civic hackers. Civic hacking groups often have teaching sessions where members learn from each other and guest speakers about a variety of topics related to civic hacking. Many civic hackers may have missed learning about civic hacking in school or forgotten what they were taught. This is especially true for the youngest civic hackers, because civics training has been diminished in U.S. public schools due to an emphasis on teaching to topics tested as a result of federal education policies. Less than half of the states now have social studies assessments of any type.[135] Similarly, university academics might consider proposing a short session on data management or assessment strategies.

If university academics become acquainted with members of the civic hacking group in their community, several opportunities might become possible. The academics might enjoy volunteering with a civic hacking group while adding valuable community service activities to their CV. They might learn of new opportunities for research with governmental entities and nonprofits in their local community. They might even have fun while interacting with a new group of talented people interested in helping their local communities.

Forecasting: Government's Reliance on Citizen Volunteers

There is some evidence that government can grow so dependent on the volunteer work of citizens that we fail to recognize the work of these volunteers. One example of this phenomenon is weather predictions in the United States (U.S.). Accurate U.S. weather predictions are dependent on more than weather satellites and modern mapping technologies.[136,137]

As of 2015, a network of more than 10,000 citizen volunteers daily report local weather conditions including temperatures, precipitation, and wind speeds and directions in the U.S.[138,139] While this daily data has only been fully compiled and collectively stored in one database since the 1950s, citizens have been extensively collecting and reporting this data for more than two hundred years.[140] Many branches of government (defense, aviation, agriculture, etc.) rely on this source of weather data. Citizens and businesses also depend on the data collected by these citizens for the accuracy of daily local and national weather reports. The financial impact of this data is incalculable.

This network of citizen volunteers is possibly the first example of crowdsourcing within the U.S. The first volunteers were elites of society. Select colonists voluntarily formed loose networks to compare weather reports and trends among their collective properties.[141] Eventually, these networks became more formal organizations. Now, this nationwide network of citizen volunteers has become such an institutional force and established part of society that most of us take it for granted and fail to acknowledge that it even exists. Additionally, the number of citizens coproducing weather data and weather reports with the federal government has grown over time from several dozen plantation- and farm-owning colonists to thousands of volunteers.[142,143]

Government Costs

Traditionally, politicians, political appointees, and public administrators view citizen participation as a necessary, but expensive, endeavor. Citizen participation is assumed to require vast investments of time, energy, and money that could be invested elsewhere. However, citizen participation in the form of citizen coproduction could save government and taxpayers money while enhancing services.[144,145] When more than 10,000 citizens report weather conditions each day to NOAA, one has to wonder how expensive this citizen participation is to the federal agency. Surely if these coproduction efforts were highly expensive, NOAA would hire people to fill these positions. Could it be possible that these citizen volunteers are saving NOAA money?

Of course, there are other types of expenses to be considered. Citizens may have undisclosed conflicts of interests that could interfere with their coproduction work. Government workers' unions may have great objections to the use of volunteers. Public administrators themselves may feel their job security is threatened. Volunteer citizens may not be as reliable, responsible, or professional as public administrators.[146]

However, there are also benefits to consider. Citizens may have more trust in governments engaged in robust coproduction efforts with citizens. Citizens participating in coproduction work may better understand the goals and constraints of government and share this insight with their fellow citizens.[147] Government may be able to gather insightful ideas and solutions from a broader segment of the population than politicians, political appointees, public administrators, and citizens who have the extensive amount of time, patience, and perseverance currently needed to influence government.[148,149,150,151]

Expertise

The foundation of modern public administration is the public administrator as expert.[152] Expertise is what drove cronyism and corruption out of public administration in the late 1800s and early 1900s. As a result, modern public administrators are secure in their role as expert.

Coproduction, especially coproduction involving citizens with professional knowledge of a field not familiar to the collaborating public administrators, threatens the core of public administrators' identity as expert. Public administration and society as a whole may need to reinterpret what expertise means for public administrators. For example, expertise may no longer be professional knowledge in a field but rather an ability to communicate across fields to guide an interdisciplinary team of volunteer citizens and paid public administrators through a project. This is a large shift, similar in scale to the modernization of public administration at the end of the 19th century, which will not be easy.

As we learned from the Boston flu shot example of digital coproduction, some public administrators are able to set aside their expert personas to collaborate with expert citizens. Consulting civic hackers and asking for their assistance in response to a public health emergency requires a hefty level of respect for the skills and opinions of citizens. Likewise, government crowdsourcing efforts often involve expert public administrators asking citizens for more input that just their opinions.[153,154,155,156] Moderating organizations such as Code for America, New Urban Mechanics, Accela, OpenGov, and Socrata may help ease this transition and enable these collaborations. Likewise, crowdsourcing platforms such as Challenge.gov can provide federal organizations with a controlled environment for structuring community member's participation.[157,158]

Conclusions

Civic hacking may be a new technological phenomenon in citizen participation and coproduction, but its mission and goals are not. In *Reinventing Government or Reinventing Ourselves*, Hindy Lauer Schachter describes how the Bureau for Municipal Research taught early 20th century (1906–1914) community members to collect data on government works and display the data in charts and graphs.[159] Citizens were even encouraged to spend their vacations collecting data.[160] Civic hacking is essentially a high-tech version of these early efforts. One can only imagine how the bureau's champion of these community efforts, William Henry Allen, would delight in the policies, technological advances, and citizen initiative that make civic hacking possible today.

The bureau's efforts to train and support citizens in their data collection and checking efforts ultimately failed.[161] This was largely due to the dominance by those favoring a professional government workforce not requiring assistance or oversight from citizens.[162] However, the current level of bipartisan support for open data at multiple levels of government makes it far more likely this modern form of data-driven citizen participation will thrive, as do the technological advancements that continually make more powerful resources available to community members at increasingly affordable prices. Given the current trajectory, it's not unreasonable to wonder if someday the work of civic hacker groups will be as ubiquitous and valuable as our ten thousand plus daily weather reporters are today.

Notes

1. Seth Cline, "Worst Flu Outbreak in Recent History Strikes United States: A Nasty Flu Strain and the Worst Whooping Cough Outbreak in 60 Years Are Making for a Rough Flu Season," *U.S. News & World Report*, January 10, 2013, http://www.usnews.com/news/articles/2013/01/10/worst-flu-outbreak-in-recent-history-strikes-united-states
2. Christopher Whitaker, "Civic Hacking 101," *YouTube*, March 2, 2014, hppts://www.youtube.com/watch?v=H_on0kXZ07M. This video is the introductory talk Mr. Whitaker gives new civic hackers to Chicago's Open City nearly every Tuesday night at the group's hack night. His example of civic hacking is what the author has utilized to begin this chapter, as it is the best and most understandable explanation of the power of civic hacking she has seen.
3. Christopher Whitaker, "Civic Hacking 101."
4. Ibid.
5. Christopher Whitaker (Open City civic hacker trainer) in discussion with the author July 17, 2014.
6. Christopher Whitaker (Open City civic hacker trainer).
7. Michael Manoochehri, *Data Just Right: Introduction to Large-Scale Data & Analytics* (Upper Saddle River, NJ: Addison-Wesley, 2014).
8. Michael Manoochehri, *Data Just Right*.
9. "Hadoop and Big Data," *Cloudera*, 2015, http://www.cloudera.com/content/en/why-cloudera/Hadoop-and-big-data.html
10. "Hadoop and Big Data," *Cloudera*.
11. Michael Manoochehri, *Data Just Right*.
12. Klint Finley, "What Exactly is GitHub Anyway?" *TechCrunch*, July 14, 2012, http://techcrunch.com/2012/07/14/"techcrunch.com/2012/07/14/what-exactly-is-github-anyway/
13. "We Launched," *GitHub*, April 10, 2008, https://github.com/blog/40-we-launched
14. Raj Jain & Subharthi Paul, "Network Virtualization and Software Defined Networking for Cloud Computing: A Survey," *IEEE Communications Magazine* 51, no. 11 (2013): 24–31.
15. Open Government, 2014, https://www.data.gov/open-gov/
16. Steve Towns, "Which States and Cities Have Chief Data Officers? Ranks of Government CDOs Grow as Agencies Implement Analytics," *Government Technology*, June 13, 2014, http://www.govtech.com/state/Which-States-and-Cities-Have-Chief-Data-Officers.html
17. Steve Towns, "Which States and Cities."
18. Stephen Goldsmith, "Big Data, Chief Data Officers and the Promise of Performance," *Governing: The States and Localities*, October 16, 2013, http://www.governing.com/blogs/bfc/col-city-chief-data-officers-performance-new-york-philadelphia.html
19. Jack Moore, "Here's What the White House's First Chief Data Scientist Will Do," *NextGov*, February 18, 2015, http://www.nextgov.com/big-data/2015/02/heres-what-white-houses-first-chief-data-scientist-will-do/105579/
20. Jack Moore, "Rise of the Data Chiefs: Meet the Federal Officials Aiming to Usher in Government's 'Golden Age' of Data," *NextGov*, March 18, 2015, http://www.nextgov.com/big-data/2015/03/rise-data-geeks-meet-federal-officials-aiming-usher-governments-golden-age-data/107736/
21. Aneesh Chopra & Ethan Skolnick, *Innovative State: How New Technologies Can Transform Government* (New York, NY: Grove/Atlantic Inc., 2014).
22. Peter Orszag, "Memorandum for the Heads of Executive Departments and Agencies: Open Government Directive," December 8, 2009, https://www.whitehouse.gov/open/documents/open-government-directive
23. Peter Orszag, "Memorandum for the Heads."
24. Barak Obama, "Executive Order 13642 of May 9, 2013: Making Open and Machine Readable the New Default for Government Information," 2013, *Federal Register*, 78, no. 93: 28111–28113.
25. Peter Orszag, "Memorandum for the Heads."
26. "Digital Accountability and Transparency Act (DATA Act)," 2014, *113th Congress*, S.994.
27. Philip Bump, "The 113th Congress Is Historically Good at Not Passing Bills," *The Washington Post*, July 9, 2014, http://www.washingtonpost.com/blogs/the-fix/wp/2014/07/09/the-113th-congress-is-historically-good-at-not-passing-bills/
28. Drew Desilver, "Congress Continues Its Streak of Passing Few Significant Laws," *Pew Research Center*, July 31, 2014, http://www.pewresearch.org/fact-tank/2014/07/31/congress-continues-its-streak-of-passing-few-significant-laws/
29. Angela Eikenberry, *Giving Circles and the Democratization of Philanthropy* (Doctoral Dissertation, University of Nebraska Omaha, Omaha, NE), 2005.
30. Angela Eikenberry, *Giving Circles and the Democratization*.

31. Angela Eikenberry, "Giving Circles: Growing Grassroots Philanthropy," *Nonprofit and Voluntary Sector Quarterly* 35, no. 3 (2006): 517–532.
32. Angela Eikenberry, *Giving Circles: Philanthropy, Voluntary Association, and Democracy* (Bloomington: Indiana University Press, 2009).
33. Matthew Gray, "Web Growth Summary," 1996, http://www.mit.edu/people/mkgray/net/web-growth-summary.html
34. "History of the Web," *World Wide Web Foundation (W3 Foundation)*, 2014, http://webfoundation.org/about/vision/history-of-the-web/
35. "Our History in Depth," *Google*, 2015, http://www.google.com/about/company/history/
36. Karen Mossberger, Caroline Tolbert & Ramona McNeal, *Digital Citizenship: The Internet, Society, and Participation* (Cambridge, MA: The MIT Press, 2008).
37. Chris Anderson, *Makers: The New Industrial Revolution* (New York, NY: Crown Business, 2012).
38. Chris Anderson, *Makers: The New Industrial Revolution*.
39. Ibid.
40. Andrea Maietta & Paolo Aliverti, *The Maker's Manual: A Practical Guide to the New Industrial Revolution* (San Francisco, CA: Maker Media, 2015).
41. Andrea Maietta & Paolo Aliverti, *The Maker's Manual*.
42. Chris Anderson, *Makers: The New Industrial Revolution*.
43. Mark Hatch, *The Maker Movement Manifesto: Rules for Innovation in the New World of Crafters, Hackers, and Tinkerers* (New York, NY: McGraw Hill Education, 2014).
44. Mark Hatch, *The Maker Movement Manifesto*, p. 10.
45. Chris Anderson, *Makers: The New Industrial Revolution*.
46. Ibid.
47. Ibid.
48. Marisa Paulson, "Civic Startup Open City Makes Chicago More Transparent," *Medill Reports Chicago*, January 26, 2012, http://news.medill.northwestern.edu/chicago/news.aspx?id=199203
49. Catherine Bracy, "Why Good Hackers Make Good Citizens," *TED*, February 25, 2014, https://www.ted.com/talks/catherine_bracy_why_good_hackers_make_good_citizens?language=en
50. Kevin Curry, "Introducing the Brigade Captains Program," *Code for America*, August 23, 2012, http://www.codeforamerica.org/blog/2012/08/23/introducing-the-brigade-captains-program/
51. Kevin Curry, "Introducing the Brigade Captains Program."
52. Lora Frecks, "Descriptive Information, Statistics and Little Known Facts Derived from a Database of U.S. Civic Hacking Groups" (presentation, Digital Government Society Conference, Aguascalientes City, Mexico, June 18–21, 2014).
53. "About National Day of Civic Hacking," *Code for America*, 2014, http://hackforchange.org/page/about
54. "About National Day of Civic Hacking."
55. Lily Liu, "When Hacking Is Actually a Good Thing: The Civic Hacking Movement," *The Huffington Post*, August 5, 2013, http://www.huffingtonpost.com/lily-liu/when-hacking-is-actually-_b_3697642.html
56. "About National Day of Civic Hacking."
57. Thomas H. Davenport & D. J. Patil, "Data Scientist: The Sexiest Job of the 21st Century," *Harvard Business Review*, October 2012, https://hbr.org/2012/10/data-scientist-the-sexiest-job-of-the-21st-century/
58. Jack Moore, "Here's What the White House's First Chief Data Scientist Will Do?"
59. Hilary Mason, "Dirty Secrets of Data Science by Hilary Mason," *YouTube*, March 6, 2013, https://www.youtube.com/watch?v=fZuDwiM1XBQ
60. Hilary Mason, "Dirty Secrets of Data Science."
61. Ibid.
62. Thomas H. Davenport & D. J. Patil, "Data Scientist: The Sexiest Job."
63. Christopher Whitaker, "Civic Hacking 101."
64. Christopher Whitaker (Open City civic hacker trainer).
65. Jake Levitas, "Defining Civic Hacking: How a Common Framework Can Unite New Forms of Engagement," *Code for America*, June 7, 2013, http://codeforamerica.org/2013/06/07/defining-civic-hacking/
66. Jake Levitas, "Defining Civic Hacking."
67. Ibid.
68. Lora Frecks, "Descriptive Information, Statistics and Little Known Facts."
69. Alissa Black & Rachel Burstein, "Local Scale and Local Data," In *Beyond Transparency: Open Data and the Future of Civic Innovation*, ed. Brett Goldstein & Lauren Dyson (San Francisco, CA: Code for America Press, 2013), 173–181.
70. Tanya Stepasiuk, "Civic Hacking: A Motivation Framework," *New Visions for Public Affairs* 6 (2014): 21–30.

71. Alexis Williams, "Civic Hacking and Ingenuity Ease Election Technology Challenges: As the Nation Prepares for this Year's Elections, the State of Election IT Is Being Shaped by Volunteers," *State Tech*, October 10, 2013, http://www.statetechmagazine.com/article/2013/10/civic-hacking-and-ingenuity-ease-election-technology-challenges
72. Laura Baverman, "Civic Hackers Help Local Governments: Cities Struggling to Keep Up with Modern-Day Technology Benefit," *USA Today*, June 24, 2013: 3b.
73. Laura Baverman, "Civic Hackers Help Local Governments."
74. Jake Levitas, "Defining Civic Hacking."
75. Jennifer Pahlka, "Coding a Better Government," *YouTube*, March 8, 2012, http://www.youtube.com/watch?v=n4EhJ898r-k
76. Jennifer Pahlka, "Coding a Better Government."
77. Lily Liu, "When Hacking Is Actually a Good Thing."
78. Laurel White, "Civic Hackers: 21st Century Community Organizers?" *Medill Reports Chicago*, January 24, 2013, http://news.medill.northwestern.edu/chicago/news.aspx?id=214509
79. Hilary Mason, "Dirty Secrets of Data Science."
80. Jennifer Pahlka, "Coding a Better Government."
81. Christopher Whitaker, "Civic Hacking 101."
82. Gustaff Juell-Skielse, Anders Hjalmarsson, Paul Johannesson & Daniel Rudmark, "Is the Public Motivated to Engage in Open Data Innovation?" (presentation, Electronic Government: 13th IFIP WG 8.5 International Conference, EGOV 2014, Dublin, Ireland, September 1–3, 2014, proceedings. pp. 277–288).
83. Tanya Stepasiuk, "Civic Hacking: A Motivation Framework."
84. Ibid, p. 23.
85. Ibid.
86. Ibid, p. 23.
87. Ibid, p. 24.
88. Ibid.
89. Ibid, p. 27.
90. Gustaff Juell-Skielse, Anders Hjalmarsson, Paul Johannesson & Daniel Rudmark, "Is the Public Motivated."
91. Ibid.
92. Ibid, p. 284.
93. Alexander Hars & Shaosong Ou, "Working for Free? Motivations for Participating in Open-Source Projects," *International Journal of Electronic Commerce* 6, no. 3 (2002): 25–39.
94. Guido Hertel, Sven Niedner & Stefanie Herrmann, "Motivation of Software Developers in Open Source Projects: An Internet-Based Survey of Contributors to the Linux Kernel," *Research Policy* 32, no. 7 (2003): 1159–1177.
95. Karim Lakhani & Robert Wolf, "Why Hackers Do What They Do: Understanding Motivation and Effort in Free/Open Source Software Projects," In *Perspectives on Free and Open Source Software*, ed. Joseph Feller, Brian Fitzgerald, Scott Hissam & Karim Lakhani (Boston, MA: MIT Press, 2005): 3–22.
96. Dongryul Lee & Byung Cho Kim, "Motivations for Open Source Project Participation and Decisions of Software Developers Motivations for Open Source Project Participation and Decisions of Software Developers," *Computational Economics*, February 2012, http://filebox.vt.edu/users/lee78/M.pdf
97. Jake Levitas, "Defining Civic Hacking."
98. Laura Baverman, "Civic Hackers Help Local Governments."
99. Alissa Black & Rachel Burstein, "Local Scale and Local Data."
100. Tanya Stepasiuk, "Civic Hacking: A Motivation Framework."
101. Alexis Williams, "Civic Hacking and Ingenuity."
102. Alexander Hars & Shaosong Ou, "Working for Free."
103. Karim Lakhani & Robert Wolf, "Why Hackers Do What They Do."
104. Dongryul Lee & Byung Cho Kim, "Motivations for Open Source Project."
105. Karim Lakhani & Robert Wolf, "Why Hackers Do What They Do."
106. Gustaff Juell-Skielse, Anders Hjalmarsson, Paul Johannesson & Daniel Rudmark, "Is the Public Motivated."
107. Tanya Stepasiuk, "Civic Hacking: A Motivation Framework."
108. Alexander Hars & Shaosong Ou, "Working for Free."
109. Guido Hertel, Sven Niedner & Stefanie Herrmann, "Motivation of Software Developers."
110. Dongryul Lee & Byung Cho Kim, "Motivations for Open Source Project."
111. Lora Frecks, "Civic Hacking in the US" (presentation, American Society of Public Administrators National Conference, Chicago, IL, March 6–10, 2015).

112. Lora Frecks, "Civic Hacking in the US."
113. Ibid.
114. Ibid.
115. Ibid.
116. Tanya Stepasiuk, "Civic Hacking: A Motivation Framework," p. 28.
117. Gustaff Juell-Skielse, Anders Hjalmarsson, Paul Johannesson & Daniel Rudmark, "Is the Public Motivated," p. 277.
118. Tanya Stepasiuk, "Civic Hacking: A Motivation Framework."
119. Tony Bovaird & Elke Loeffler, "From Engagement to Co-Production: The Contribution of Users and Communities to Outcomes and Public Value," *Voluntas* 23, no. 4 (2012): 1119–1138.
120. Ross Nelson (civic hacker) in discussion with the author, October 29, 2014.
121. Ross Nelson (civic hacker).
122. Ibid.
123. Satish Nambisan & Priya Nambisan, *Engaging Citizens in Co-Creation in Public Services: Lessons Learned and Best Practices* (Washington, DC: IBM Center for the Business of Government, 2013).
124. Ross Nelson (civic hacker).
125. Ibid.
126. Satish Nambisan & Priya Nambisan, *Engaging Citizens in Co-Creation*.
127. Ross Nelson (civic hacker).
128. Ibid.
129. Satish Nambisan & Priya Nambisan, *Engaging Citizens in Co-Creation*.
130. Ross Nelson (civic hacker).
131. Ibid.
132. Ibid.
133. Aneesh Chopra & Ethan Skolnick, *Innovative State*.
134. Tony Bovaird & Elke Loeffler, "From Engagement to Co-Production," p. 139.
135. "Some Standard Reform Proposals Are Based on Misconceptions," *Center for Information & Research on Civic Learning and Engagement (CIRCLE)*, 2015, http://www.civicyouth.org/quick-facts/quick-facts-civic-education/
136. "NOAA History: Cooperative Weather Observers," *National Oceanic and Atmospheric Administration (NOAA)*, June 8, 2006, http://www.history.noaa.gov/legacy/coop.html
137. "Cooperative Observer Network COOP," *National Oceanic and Atmospheric Administration (NOAA)*, 2015, https://www.ncdc.noaa.gov/data-access/land-based-station-data/land-based-datasets/cooperative-observer-network-coop
138. "NOAA History: Cooperative Weather Observers."
139. "Cooperative Observer Network COOP."
140. Ibid.
141. Ibid.
142. Ibid.
143. "NOAA History: Cooperative Weather Observers."
144. Albert Meijer, "Co-Production in an Information Age: Individual and Community Engagement Supported by New Media," *Voluntas* 23 (2012): 1156–1172.
145. Albert Meijer, "New Media and the Coproduction of Safety: An Empirical Analysis of Dutch Practices," *American Review of Public Administration* 44, no. 1 (2014): 17–34.
146. Alison Ledger & Bonnie Slade, "Coproduction without Experts: A Study of People Involved in Community Health and Well-Being Service Delivery," *Studies in Continuing Education* 37, no. 2 (2015): 157–169.
147. Satish Nambisan & Priya Nambisan, *Engaging Citizens in Co-Creation*.
148. Ibid.
149. Ines Mergel & Kevin C. Desouza, "Implementing Open Innovation in the Public Sector: The Case of Challenge.gov," *Public Administration Review* 73, no. 6 (2013): 882–890.
150. Kevin C. Desouza, *Challenge.gov: Using Competitions and Awards to Spur Innovation* (Washington, DC: IBM Center for the Business of Government, 2012).
151. Darin Brabham, *Using Crowdsourcing in Government* (Washington, DC: IBM Center for the Business of Government, 2013).
152. Camilla Stivers, *Bureau Men, Settlement Women: Constructing Public Administration in the Progressive Era* (Lawrence, KS: University Press of Kansas, 2000).
153. Ines Mergel & Kevin C. Desouza, "Implementing Open Innovation."
154 Darin Brabham, *Using Crowdsourcing in Government*.

155. Catherine Needham, "Realising the Potential of Co-Production: Negotiating Improvements in Public Services," *Social Policy and Society* 7, no. 2 (2008): 221–231.
156. Ines Mergel & Kevin C. Desouza, "Implementing Open Innovation."
157. Darin Brabham, *Using Crowdsourcing in Government*.
158. Catherine Needham, "Realising the Potential of Co-Production."
159. Hindy Lauer Schachter, *Reinventing Government or Reinventing Ourselves* (Albany, NY: State University of New York Press, 1997).
160. Hindy Lauer Schachter, *Reinventing Government*.
161. Ibid.
162. Ibid.

SECTION IV

Advancement of Democratic Accountability and Public Values

14

CATCHING ON AND CATCHING UP

Developments and Challenges in E-Participation in Major U.S. Cities

Karen Mossberger, Yonghong Wu, and Benedict S. Jimenez

Introduction

Scholars have long noted what might be described as a democratic deficit in e-government, with greater emphasis on service delivery and efficiency than on transparency or citizen participation (Musso, Weare and Hale 2000; Ho 2002; Chadwick and May 2003; West 2004; Scott 2006; Coursey and Norris 2008; Dawes 2008; Holzer et al. 2008; Ganapati 2011). Yet, a recent Pew survey shows that a third of all American adults now use online methods for engaging with government, including contacting government officials, signing online petitions, or commenting on a policy issue (Fox and Rainie 2014). Social media, like other interactive features of Web 2.0, may facilitate political and economic participation online (see Boulianne 2009 for a meta-analysis). A majority of online American adults (52%) used two or more social media sites as of 2014, with Facebook, at 71%, the most popular (Duggan et al. 2015). While those who use social networking sites to engage in political or civic engagement online are a minority, still 21% of these users joined or started a political or social-issue group in a social networking site in 2012. This was up from 13% of users just four years earlier (Smith 2013).

To what extent have information and participatory opportunities for citizens on government websites changed in recent years, especially at the local level, and through interactive Web 2.0 features such as social networking sites? Civic engagement refers to *involvement in the public sphere*, broadly construed (Bennett 2008), and we measure information and participatory opportunities on local government websites that might facilitate citizen engagement in government, policy issues, and voluntary or neighborhood efforts.

Local governments are a traditional focus of citizen participation, and citizens are often most interested in or most knowledgeable about issues that are (literally) closest to home (Oates 1972; Berry, Portney and Thomson 1993; Peters 2001; Oakerson 1999). Prior research has identified large cities as the leaders in local e-government (Ho 2002; Moon 2002; Jun and Weare 2010; Jimenez, Mossberger and Wu 2012), and so observing change across these cities may indicate how digital government ideas and practices for citizen engagement have evolved.

In this chapter, we examine change in online information and interactivity scores for the websites of the 75 largest U.S. cities between 2009 and 2011—a period that was marked by federal initiatives and the rapid growth of social media use. The Obama administration declared open government a priority in the early days of the president's first term (Obama 2009), emphasizing greater transparency online and the use of interactive platforms such as open data portals, social media, and forms of online participation such as crowdsourcing. The spread of new digital tools and shifting agendas at the federal level might stimulate changes throughout the federal system (Jones and Baumgartner 2005). Additionally, the use of social media more than doubled between 2008 and 2011 to 59% of the population (Hampton, Sessions and Her 2011). So, this was a critical period for examining local government responses to new technologies for civic engagement.

While we examine both information and interactivity on local government websites, here we focus, in particular, on the marked change in interactivity scores, which track features that allow for customization of information, one-way input, and two-way interaction or discussion of policy. This contrasts with more incremental change in information on these same websites during this two-year period.

The largest changes during this two-year period occurred for cities that were furthest behind, narrowing initial gaps between cities. We compare the results to theories of non-incremental diffusion (Jones and Baumgartner 2005; Boushey 2010), discuss subsequent research on the use of social media and other interactive tools, and also examine challenges that remain for effective use of these tools in light of their rapid adoption. In the concluding section, we discuss the future implications of these findings for greater government transparency and involvement of citizens through e-government.

Civic Engagement, Information, and Interactivity Online

Researchers have not found widespread support for democratic participation through digital government at the local level (Musso, Weare and Hale 2000; Ho 2002; West 2004; Coursey and Norris 2008; Dawes 2008; Ganapati 2011). This is particularly true for online discussion of policy issues. For example, based on his 2004 content analysis, Scott (2006) found that only 2 of the 100 cities he studied provided for online discussion, but that 45 offered comment forms for one-way feedback. A study by Holzer et al. (2008) gave municipal governments a poor grade for e-government use to advance online citizen participation. Yet, some studies have found that major city websites in the U.S. host a considerable amount of information, despite limited online participation (Scott 2006). These prior studies did not include the adoption of social media, which potentially enables two-way interactions between citizens and governments and collective dialogue among citizens.

A notable advance within the past years is the emergence of "Web 2.0," or the interactive web. Tim O'Reilly introduced the term Web 2.0 in 2005 to distinguish web-based technologies that facilitate integrated but cost-effective services and allow users to be co-developers, which aim to harness collective intelligence (O'Reilly 2005). Social media technologies are part of Web 2.0 and are described by Kaplan and Haenlein (2010) as a "group of Internet-based applications that build on the ideological and technological foundations of Web 2.0 and that allow the creation and exchange of User Generated Content."

Theories of policy change demonstrate that although they are rare, periods of rapid change may punctuate the incrementalism that tends to characterize public policy (Baumgartner and Jones 1993; Jones and Baumgartner 2005). Policy diffusion is an important mechanism for promoting change across multiple jurisdictions in a decentralized federal system (Walker 1969; Gray 1973; Berry and Berry 1990), and such decentralization can make system-wide change a slow process. Yet, at times, ideas may cascade rapidly across jurisdictions (Baumgartner and Jones 1993). Policies that spread contagiously are relatively salient, simple, noncontroversial and low-cost (Boushey 2010, 63; see also Rose 1993 on policy characteristics and adoption). Public attention to some aspect of e-government, such as social media, might encourage its adoption. Federal example through the open government initiative might also promote "point source diffusion." Advocacy by professional associations or civic groups may raise the salience of some features. Broader changes in how individuals use technology may increase the salience of these tools. We investigate incremental and rapid changes in information and activities online, and factors associated with these developments.

Online Information and Interactivity Scores

This study uses content analysis of the official websites of the 75 largest U.S. cities (as measured by population) to score and rank cities in 2009 and 2011. The first wave of content analysis was conducted from late March through May 2009, assessing cities on 74 or 78 different variables, depending on whether or not they had a city manager. The instrument was developed based on an extensive review of the literature, including analysis of different measures that were used in previous studies that assessed government websites in the U.S. (e.g., West 2004; Holzer et al. 2008; see also Website Attribute Evaluation System of the Cyberspace Policy Research Group, http://www.cyprg.arizona.edu/).

Among scholars concerned with digital government and citizen engagement, there is precedent for examining information as well as participatory opportunities on government websites, as Scott (2006) has for local governments and as the United Nations has for its e-participation index (Chang, Lee and Berry 2011). Here we measure both, and are able to compare both prevalence and change.

Information Index

We measured the following types of information that might contribute to citizen knowledge and engagement, whether online or offline: how to contact public officials; government officials, duties, and organizational structure; government processes, laws, and regulations; city policies and performance information, including budgets and audit reports; neighborhood data and resources; neighborhood and nonprofit organizations; offline events sponsored by the city, such as hearings; and offline events, volunteering, donating, or other activities involving neighborhoods and local nonprofits. Information on government officials, processes, hearings and events, and community organizations can facilitate citizen contacting or intervention on issues, whereas government transparency and citizen knowledge are enhanced by open information on policies, performance, budgets, and neighborhood data.

Interactivity Index

Interactivity on local government websites includes customization of information to suit citizen preferences and mechanisms for online participation. Our online interactivity index integrates the following online features: participatory tools such as blogs, comment forms, electronic town meetings, online surveys, or social network sites; online customization of information search; and tools to facilitate interaction, such as search engines and downloadable forms. Customization through email alerts, RSS feeds, videos, and visualization in open data portals means that citizens can obtain the information that matters to them in ways that are convenient, and such customization is part of the wave of Web 2.0. Participatory opportunities include individual citizen-initiated contact (such as online comment forms), collective feedback (through online surveys), content creation and sharing through social media (such as Facebook or Twitter), or online discussion (through social media or blogs that allow comments, and events such as online town hall meetings). We refer to this as interactivity on local government websites, because the content analysis does not note whether citizens are actually discussing issues or mobilizing others by sharing information on social networks. But we do offer evidence of the presence of interactive mechanisms in local government websites.

Methods

A detailed coding manual with website examples and instructions was used to train multiple coders and to assure reliability. Pre-tests of the website-assessment instrument were conducted, and intercoder reliability ranged between 66 and 75 percent, which parallels the results for other website coding (see Musso, Weare, and Hale 2000). To ensure greater reliability, each website was coded carefully and independently by two coders, and differences were reconciled by a third coder. Measurements that are dichotomous—such as the presence or absence of background information on an issue—are most appropriate for this method, rather than a judgment about the quality of the information.

One issue in website content analysis is how to define the "website," especially for governments that have a variety of departments and multiple links (Weare and Lin 2000). With a few exceptions discussed below, we otherwise restricted our analysis to the main website and avoided examining separate departments. Conceptually, we were most concerned with the policies of the city leadership, especially the mayor, city council, and city manager. Coders did go to the community or neighborhood page (where it existed). For budget or audit information, coders were allowed to go to a separate finance page, if necessary. It is possible that this research understates some participatory opportunities or information located only on department websites. For that reason, we emphasize that we are researching the main city web page, the city leadership, and major citywide policy documents. This is consistent with Musso, Weare and Hale (2000), who concentrated on the main website for the local governments they studied; it contrasts with West (2004), who examined more than 1,800 web pages related to the 70 largest cities, but on a narrower range of variables.

A second wave of analysis was implemented in 2011. The 2011 study included 94 criteria for council-manager governments (90 for governments without a city manager).[1] To ensure comparability of the 2009 and 2011 assessments, *we compare city scores and rankings only on the original 74–78 criteria for 2009 and 2011*. We constructed a weighted information and interactivity index, which is simply the sum of raw scores as a percentage of 78 possible points for council-manager cities, and 74 possible points for others. The information and interactivity criteria used in the content analysis are described below, along with frequencies showing patterns of change across the two years.

Prevalence and Change, 2009–2011

In Table 14.1, we can see that in 2009, interactivity on local government websites (the last category) was less prevalent than information. Most of the items we measured were informational, as shown in the table. Additionally, however, the mean score for several information categories was at least 90% of the criteria in 2009, compared to only 55% of the interactivity category criteria.

Changes in the overall score or the combined information and interactivity indices indicate a slight increase over the two years, using the original 2009 criteria, with the mean score for cities rising 5 percentage points to 83% of the criteria in 2011. For the information measures (in all but the last category), the largest change is a 13 percentage point increase in organizational information. In comparison, however, the interactive category jumped 20 percentage points over the course of the two years.

Table 14.2 includes measures of interactivity, such as customization of information, and mechanisms for input or discussion. There is an increase in most of the categories in this table during 2011, with the exception of comment forms, which dropped a little in 2011. This small decrease may be due to greater use of social media as an alternative. For many of these features, the increase in the percentage of adopters is modest. In contrast, however, social media adoption grew exponentially in this period. Twitter use grew from 25% to nearly 87%, Facebook from 13% to 87%, and YouTube

Table 14.1 Comparison by Category between 2009 and 2011

Category	No. of Items in Category	75 U.S. Cities Mean in 2009	Mean in 2011
Overall Score	74, 78*	78%	83%
Contact Information	12, 16*	95%	93%
Organizational Information	3	63%	76%
Processes and Regulations	11	75%	80%
Neighborhood Information	2	99%	99%
Policy and Performance Information	8	95%	91%
Offline Participation Information	12	86%	86%
Transparency and Accessibility	13	67%	71%
Online Interactivity and Participation	13	55%	75%

* No city manager—74 points possible rather than 78 for overall score, and 12 points possible rather than 16 for contact information score.

Table 14.2 Interactive Tools Utilized in Websites of 75 Largest U.S. Cities—Comparison between 2009 and 2011

Tools	Status	2009 Frequency	Percent	2011 Frequency	Percent
Online newsletter subscriptions or email updates	Yes	59	78.7	68	90.7
Downloadable information materials	Yes	75	100.0	75	100.0
Searchable databases	Yes	73	97.3	73	97.3
Comment or message box	Yes	60	80.0	56	74.7
RSS feed	Yes	42	56.0	55	73.3
Twitter	Yes	19	25.3	65	86.7
Discussion boards	Yes	1	1.3	2	2.7
Virtual town hall meetings	Yes	0	0.0	6	8.0
Facebook link	Yes	10	13.3	65	86.7
YouTube link	Yes	12	16.0	56	74.7
Blog for city in general	Yes	N/A	N/A	8	10.7
Blog for elected official	Yes	N/A	N/A	17	22.7
Flickr link	Yes	N/A	N/A	28	37.3
Open data portals	Yes	N/A	N/A	12	16.0

from 16% to 75%. Interestingly enough, there are some small steps toward other forms of online discussion. Online town hall meetings were totally absent among these cities in 2009, but by 2011, they had been held in six cities. Open data portals were a new category in 2011. While it is not possible to measure change from 2009, it is clear that only a relatively small proportion of cities—16%—had adopted such portals by 2011. Their use clearly pales in comparison with social media. Looking at these descriptive data, we can see small increases (or decreases) in most of the interactivity measures, with the exception of social media.

Changes in the Information Index Scores

We assessed the performance of cities in providing information or interactivity online separately. For the weighted information score, we summed city raw scores for information about contacting, organization, government process, community and neighborhood, policy documents, agency performance, and offline participation opportunities, and converted this score as a percentage of the total possible score. As shown in Table 14.4, the weighted information score, on average, remained virtually constant in 2011 as compared with 2009.

The weighted information score showed some fluctuation, as it increased for 36 cities, remained constant for 8 cities, and declined for 31 cities. The cities with the largest growth in the information score were those with low-ranking scores in 2009. Six of the 10 cities with the fastest-growing information scores were ranked below sixtieth in 2009. On the other hand, some top cities in 2009 such as Seattle, Phoenix, and Louisville show some minor decreases in their information scores over the two-year period. The category for contact information was the most common source of decrease in the information index. Four cities decreased their information scores by 10–14 percentage points, and for three of these it was due to changes in contact information. Table 14.3 confirms the pattern of

Table 14.3 Interactive Tools Utilized in Websites of 75 Largest U.S. Cities—Comparison between 2009 and 2011

City	Population	Change in weighted information score in 2009–2011	Weighted information score in 2009	Ranking of weighted information score in 2009
Portland	583,776	16.67	81.25	59
Newark	277,140	16.67	56.25	75
Honolulu	953,207	15.38	76.92	68
Raleigh	403,892	15.38	71.15	74
Kansas City	459,787	13.46	82.69	53
Denver	600,158	10.42	87.50	35
Indianapolis	820,445	10.42	72.92	73
Tucson	520,116	9.62	76.92	68
Las Vegas	583,756	7.69	82.69	53
Corpus Christi	305,215	7.69	80.77	64
Stockton	291,707	7.69	76.92	68
Lincoln	258,379	6.25	81.25	59
Oklahoma City	579,999	5.77	86.54	39
Sacramento	466,488	5.77	84.62	49
Colorado Springs	416,427	5.77	82.69	53
Bakersfield	347,483	5.77	75.00	71
Lexington-Fayette	295,803	5.29	81.25	59
Houston	2,099,451	4.17	87.50	35
Milwaukee	594,833	4.17	85.42	46
Virginia Beach	437,994	3.85	92.31	15
Arlington	365,438	3.85	86.54	39

City	Population	Change in weighted information score in 2009–2011	Weighted information score in 2009	Ranking of weighted information score in 2009
Fort Worth	741,206	3.85	80.77	64
Fresno	494,665	3.85	82.69	53
Long Beach	462,257	3.85	90.38	23
Mesa	439,041	3.85	90.38	23
Plano	259,841	3.85	82.69	53
Minneapolis	382,578	3.21	88.46	31
Anchorage	291,826	3.04	86.54	39
Albuquerque	953,207	2.08	87.50	35
Cleveland	396,815	2.08	81.25	59
Pittsburgh	305,704	2.08	85.42	46
Buffalo	261,310	2.08	75.00	71
Glendale	226,721	1.92	88.46	31
Philadelphia	1,526,006	0.80	89.58	26
Washington DC	601,723	0.64	91.67	18
Atlanta	420,003	0.64	91.67	18
Dallas	1,197,816	0.00	86.54	39
Jacksonville	821,784	0.00	89.58	26
Detroit	713,777	0.00	83.33	51
Oakland	390,724	0.00	86.54	39
Aurora	325,078	0.00	88.46	31
Cincinnati	296,943	0.00	86.54	39
St. Paul	285,068	0.00	87.50	35
Fort Wayne	253,691	0.00	81.25	59
San Francisco	805,235	−1.92	100.00	1
Greensboro	269,666	−1.92	90.38	23
St. Petersburg	244,769	−1.92	92.31	15
San Jose	945,942	−1.92	96.15	6
San Diego	1,307,402	−2.08	95.83	8
Columbus	787,033	−2.08	89.58	26
Seattle	608,660	−2.08	100.00	1
Tulsa	391,906	−2.08	83.33	51
St. Louis	319,294	−2.08	89.58	26
New York	8,175,133	−2.08	97.92	4
El Paso	649,121	−3.85	94.23	11
Phoenix	1,445,632	−3.85	98.08	3
Anaheim	336,265	−3.85	82.69	53
Santa Ana	324,528	−3.85	80.77	64
Toledo	287,208	−4.17	77.08	67
Memphis	646,889	−4.17	93.75	14
Los Angeles	3,792,621	−5.13	91.67	18
Miami	399,457	−5.77	86.54	39
San Antonio	1,327,407	−5.77	96.15	6

(Continued)

Table 14.3 (Continued)

City	Population	Change in weighted information score in 2009–2011	Weighted information score in 2009	Ranking of weighted information score in 2009
Riverside	303,871	−5.77	84.62	49
Chicago	2,695,598	−6.25	91.67	18
Omaha	408,958	−6.25	85.42	46
Charlotte	731,424	−7.69	92.31	15
Wichita	382,368	−7.69	94.23	11
Baltimore	620,961	−8.33	95.83	8
Boston	617,594	−8.33	95.83	8
Tampa	335,709	−8.33	89.58	26
Nashville-Davidson	601,222	−10.42	91.67	18
Henderson	257,729	−11.54	88.46	31
Louisville	597,337	−12.50	97.92	4
Austin	790,390	−13.46	94.23	11
Mean value		0.70	86.79	

Note: The observations are sorted in descending order by the change in weighted information score.

catching up for the bottom cities in 2009. For instance, the city of Newark and the city of Raleigh were ranked last in the 2009 list for information scores. They increased their information scores by more than 15 percentage points in only two years. Cities with the largest gains included large increases in contact information, but also tended to add more information on organizations and government processes as well.

Changes in the Interactivity Index Scores

We assessed the performance of cities in providing interactivity online. For the weighted interactivity score, we summed city raw scores for 13 web features enabling citizen–government interactions, including provision of online services, online surveys, and tools to facilitate online interactions, and converted this score as a percentage of the total possible score. As shown in Table 14.4, the weighted interactivity score, on average, increased by almost 20 percentage points from 2009 to 2011.

The weighted interactivity score increased for 61 cities, remained constant for 10 cities, and declined only for 4 cities. This is the area where we observe almost universal and large increases in the two-year period. The scores of five cities more than doubled from 2009 to 2011, and one-third of the cities experienced more than a 50% increase in their interactivity scores. The pattern of catching up still exists despite almost universal and across-the-board growth in this category. Among the 10 cities with largest increases in their interactivity scores, seven were ranked below sixtieth in the 2009 list for interactivity scores. Such pronounced change may reflect new priorities with changes in the mayor of chief information officer, but we do not have data about city officials.

Because the adoption of social media was so widespread over this period, we explored the cities that had not adopted all of the three most common platforms—Facebook, Twitter, and YouTube. There were 22 cities that did not have all three by 2011, mostly because 19 of the cities did not use YouTube. Only six cities lacked any of these three platforms: Atlanta, Bakersfield, Stockton, Toledo, Cleveland, and Dallas. One visible pattern is that these cities (other than Toledo) had

Table 14.4 Change in Weighted Interactivity Score in 2009–2011

City	Population	Change in weighted interactivity score in 2009–2011	Weighted interactivity score in 2009	Ranking of weighted interactivity score in 2009
Lincoln	258,379	53.85	30.77	68
Philadelphia	1,526,006	46.15	38.46	61
Omaha	408,958	46.15	46.15	51
Raleigh	403,892	46.15	30.77	68
Miami	399,457	46.15	30.77	68
San Antonio	1,327,407	38.46	38.46	61
San Diego	1,307,402	38.46	46.15	51
Jacksonville	821,784	38.46	46.15	51
Cincinnati	296,943	38.46	38.46	61
Anchorage	291,826	38.46	38.46	61
Houston	2,099,451	30.77	53.85	32
Austin	790,390	30.77	53.85	32
Charlotte	731,424	30.77	46.15	51
Detroit	713,777	30.77	38.46	61
Memphis	646,889	30.77	46.15	51
Washington DC	601,723	30.77	53.85	32
Milwaukee	594,833	30.77	53.85	32
Tucson	520,116	30.77	53.85	32
Colorado Springs	416,427	30.77	53.85	32
Oakland	390,724	30.77	30.77	68
Arlington	365,438	30.77	53.85	32
Tampa	335,709	30.77	53.85	32
Pittsburgh	305,704	30.77	38.46	61
Riverside	303,871	30.77	46.15	51
Fort Wayne	253,691	30.77	53.85	32
Albuquerque	953,207	23.08	61.54	22
San Jose	945,942	23.08	61.54	22
Fort Worth	741,206	23.08	53.85	32
Las Vegas	583,756	23.08	61.54	22
Fresno	494,665	23.08	53.85	32
Sacramento	466,488	23.08	53.85	32
Kansas City	459,787	23.08	53.85	32
Virginia Beach	437,994	23.08	61.54	22
Aurora	325,078	23.08	61.54	22
Lexington-Fayette	295,803	23.08	61.54	22
St. Paul	285,068	23.08	61.54	22
Henderson	257,729	23.08	53.85	32
St. Petersburg	244,769	23.08	53.85	32
New York	8,175,133	15.38	69.23	9

(*Continued*)

Table 14.4 (Continued)

City	Population	Change in weighted interactivity score in 2009–2011	Weighted interactivity score in 2009	Ranking of weighted interactivity score in 2009
Los Angeles	3,792,621	15.38	61.54	22
Chicago	2,695,598	15.38	69.23	9
Indianapolis	820,445	15.38	53.85	32
El Paso	649,121	15.38	46.15	51
Baltimore	620,961	15.38	61.54	22
Seattle	608,660	15.38	84.62	1
Denver	600,158	15.38	69.23	9
Portland	583,776	15.38	69.23	9
Long Beach	462,257	15.38	69.23	9
Atlanta	420,003	15.38	30.77	68
Tulsa	391,906	15.38	69.23	9
Minneapolis	382,578	15.38	69.23	9
Anaheim	336,265	15.38	61.54	22
Santa Ana	324,528	15.38	30.77	68
Newark	277,140	15.38	38.46	61
Greensboro	269,666	15.38	69.23	9
San Francisco	805,235	7.69	76.92	5
Boston	617,594	7.69	76.92	5
Nashville-Davidson	601,222	7.69	53.85	32
Louisville	597,337	7.69	76.92	5
Wichita	382,368	7.69	53.85	32
Buffalo	261,310	7.69	46.15	51
Phoenix	1,445,632	0.00	84.62	1
Dallas	1,197,816	0.00	46.15	51
Honolulu	953,207	0.00	69.23	9
Columbus	787,033	0.00	69.23	9
Mesa	439,041	0.00	84.62	1
Cleveland	396,815	0.00	46.15	51
Bakersfield	347,483	0.00	30.77	68
St. Louis	319,294	0.00	69.23	9
Corpus Christi	305,215	0.00	69.23	9
Plano	259,841	0.00	76.92	5
Oklahoma City	579,999	−7.69	84.62	1
Stockton	291,707	−7.69	53.85	32
Toledo	287,208	−7.69	30.77	68
Glendale	226,721	−7.69	69.23	9
Mean value		19.59	55.49	

Note: The observations are sorted in descending order by the change in weighted interactivity score.

Table 14.5 Pearson Correlation

	Change in weighted overall score 2009–2011	Change in weighted information score 2009–2011	Change in weighted interactivity score 2009–2011
Weighted overall score in 2009	–.539***		
Weighted information score in 2009		–.671***	
Weighted interactivity score in 2009			–.530***

Note: *** denotes significance level < 1%

minority populations of 40% or more. But, other high-minority cities do use all the social media platforms, and there may be other explanations, such as professional capacity. Three of the six are relatively smaller cities as well.

Table 14.4 shows that the increase in overall scores over the two-year period is primarily attributable to the remarkable growth in the interactivity score. It also shows increasing utilization of interactive tools in city websites in 2011 as compared with 2009. Cities with the largest increases in interactivity—of 40 points or more—gained because of the introduction of a number of such online tools, according to our examination of the categories for interactivity.

Correlation Analysis

As shown in Table 14.5 for weighted interactivity scores, many of the cities with lower rankings in 2009 caught up with the cities higher in the rankings. This pattern of catching up is a clear indication of diffusion of online features, particularly the Web 2.0–related tools. Whether practices spread because of awareness of what others are doing or because of similar needs, there are some non-incremental changes for individual cities, as well as large leaps forward for the adoption of social networks.

As a preliminary step in examining the pattern of catching up, we conducted a correlation analysis on the change in the weighted score and the 2009 score. The Pearson correlation estimate is –0.530, which confirms what we found from the descriptive data. The correlation coefficient is highly statistically significant and negative, showing that, on average, a lower initial score for online interactivity is significantly correlated with a larger increase in the interactivity score from 2009 to 2011.

As Table 14.5 shows, the gaps between the top and bottom cities have been shrinking, as the bottom cities advanced at a faster pace than others did. This pattern of catching up may reflect competition or emulation among city officials (Walker 1969). It is also relatively easy for the bottom cities to add some features and move up on the list. However, it is harder for the top cities to advance, taking on more challenging features such as town hall meetings.

Explaining Change in Interactivity and Differences across Cities

Theories of policy change and diffusion can help to explain the factors that account for change, including both rapid and incremental growth. They also provide a basis for theorizing about differences across cities overall—why some changed more than others did over time. Processes of diffusion can be explained by the characteristics of the innovation, the adopters, and the interest groups or professional networks encouraging diffusion (Rose 1993; Boushey 2010). We explore the characteristics of cities and their ties to professional networks in the next section to account for cities with the greatest amount of change between 2009 and 2011. In the final section, we explore the implementation of interactive features, especially social media.

Characteristics of Cities and Involvement in Networks

We are interested not only in what changes, but also in who changes. What cities are most likely to undertake change during this period? Research on the diffusion of local e-government has primarily focused on city characteristics such as professionalization, resources, demand, and professional networks. Political variables are also important in some studies of the adoption of online participatory practices. We discuss these below in relationship to changes in the adoption of interactivity online. The literature on adoption of e-government may provide explanations for changes in the scope of adoption as well, as measured in our scores (Tolbert, Mossberger and McNeal 2008).

H_1: **Measures of Professional Capacity, Including Council-Manager Government and City Size, Should Be Related to Positive Change in the Adoption of Interactivity Features**

Government capacity and professionalism may be important influences in policy change. Cities with council-manager governments (professional city managers) were the first adopters of e-government (Moon, 2002; Jun and Weare 2010). Government size, managerial innovation, and government capacity were significant predictors of e-government adoption in studies conducted by Norris and Moon (2005). City size may well be a proxy for professionalization. Local governments with larger populations are likely to have more developed administrative systems, as well as more specialized staff and greater technical expertise (Musso, Weare and Hale 2000; Ho 2002; Moon 2002). Yet, it is possible that size may at some level decrease information and participatory opportunities online. Scott (2006) found that opportunities for public involvement online were higher in medium-sized cities in his sample, with populations between 120,000 and 459,000. This was primarily for information about council activities and for contact information for public officials rather than for mechanisms for online feedback or discussion.

H_2: **Financial Resources Will Also Be Significant Predictors for Change in Adopting Interactive Features on City's Websites, Because of the Cost of Implementation for Some of the Online Features**

Financial resources may be an important factor, too, although this would be most relevant for costly steps such as open data portals or actively managing social media. Recently, Jimenez, Mossberger and Wu (2012) found that cities with higher fund balances provided greater opportunities for citizen participation through their websites, while Jun and Weare (2010) discovered that early adopters of e-government services had higher per capita expenditures. However, research on changes in the scope of e-government implementation at the state level provided no evidence that financial resources mattered (see West 2005; Tolbert, Mossberger and McNeal 2008).

H_3: **Given the "Digital Divide," Cities with Populations That Are Younger, with Fewer Minorities, and Higher Income and Education Will Have Higher Demand for E-Government and Hence Should Be Related to Positive Change in Interactivity Online**

Population characteristics associated with a higher probability of Internet use have been significant predictors of e-government innovation. Local governments at the forefront of the diffusion of e-government in California had populations that were older, more White, higher income, more educated, and more likely to be employed in managerial occupations (Musso, Weare and Hale 2000; see also Jun and Weare 2010). Older individuals are among the least likely to be online, but otherwise these community characteristics would also predict higher levels of Internet use. Similarly, Ho (2002) found in his study of the 55 largest U.S. cities that those with less user-centered websites were likely to be cities with higher minority populations, which were also the cities with the least experience with e-government.

H$_4$: More Politicized Environments Will Experience Less Change in Interactivity Online

Political variables may be especially prominent when considering the use of e-government for informing and communicating with citizens about community and policy issues. Ahn (2011) examined the factors that influence extensiveness of e-communication services offered by city governments, such as displaying codes or ordinances, streaming video, allowing service requests, and facilitating communication with individual elected and appointed officials. He found that political competition, party sensitivity, and ward elections decreased adoption of e-communication services, while larger council membership had positive effects.

U.S. cities vary in whether their elections are partisan or nonpartisan, and cities that employ partisan ballots may have higher levels of civic engagement because the major parties may work to mobilize voters. Although the evidence is somewhat mixed, a number of scholars have argued that nonpartisan elections depress voter turnout (see Karnig and Walter 1983; Schaffner, Wright and Streb 2001; Caren 2007; but see Wood 2002 for other results). Voter apathy may lead to lower demand for online participatory opportunities. On the other hand, a greater role for political parties at the local level may produce a substitution effect, in which political parties perform their traditional function of communicating citizens' interests to government, reducing the demand for online participatory mechanisms (Ahn 2011). So, whether because of this substitution effect or greater sensitivity of governments in more partisan environments, we expect that interactivity scores will be lower in partisan environments.

H$_5$: Participation in Relevant Professional Networks Will Be Positively Related to Change in the Interactivity Online

Finally, greater rates of change in online interactivity may be related to participation in professional networks of local governments, which have been significant for diffusion and change in e-government across states (McNeal et al. 2003; Mossberger Tolbert and McNeal 2008) and internationally for online information and participation (Lee, Chang and Berry 2011). Professional networks matter for adoption in other policy areas (Balla 2001; Mossberger and Hale 2002; Hale 2011). Diffusion may be facilitated through advice and learning in professional organizations. Cities that participate in professional networks may be more aware of what others are doing, and this could decrease uncertainty about an innovation, or increase competition with other adopters. Jun and Weare (2010) pointed out that there may be external institutional pressure to conform. Professional organizations represent national networks that may be important for promoting change through the diffusion of new e-government practices, whether that is through learning, competition, or both.

Model and Measures

Given the varied pace of change across cities, one important question is why some cities moved faster than others did in recent years as measured by the online interactivity index. To examine this question, we use ordinary least squares (OLS) regression with robust error specification to model the factors associated with the change in the interactivity index in 2009–2011 for the 75 large cities. Although much of the previous work on e-government has measured adoption or technical sophistication (Moon 2002; Jun and Weare 2010), there have been few studies of the change in features that might support civic engagement. This analysis extends our understanding of what city characteristics may determine their progress in adopting the online interactivity features on the websites.

Measures of professional capacity (including council-manager government and city size), demand-side factors (demographics, income, and education), political environment, and participation in relevant professional networks are included in the model. As we learned from descriptive analysis, the initial state is a significant factor affecting the magnitude of change in the index. Thus, we include the weighted interactivity index in 2009 as one of our independent variables.

City Capacity

Similar to prior studies (Moon 2002; Ahn 2011; Jun and Weare 2011), we include a dummy variable for whether or not a city has a council-manager system. We expect that cities with council-manager governments may have more rapid advancement in their scores, as they have tended to be leaders in e-government more generally (Moon 2002). In addition, larger organizations have greater professional and resource capacity for innovation (Rogers 1995, 380; Moon 2002). We use city population as the measure of city professional capacity for innovation in this regard.

Population Demand

The characteristics of the population likely influence the development of online engagement, especially as these may represent citizen demand for better communication with government. The model includes several demographic and socioeconomic variables. Well-educated, White residents are among those who are more likely to be online and to use e-government (Mossberger, Tolbert and Stansbury 2003; West 2005; Mossberger, Tolbert and McNeal 2008; Smith 2010), and so we would predict more attention to civic engagement online in cities with higher percentages of such residents. We use the percent of White population as well as the percent of Latino population of a city. We also include the percent of population below 18 and the percent of population at or over 65, because young people who are not yet adults and seniors are likely those who do not use Internet as much for civic engagement (Mossberger, Tolbert and McNeal 2008).

Education and income are strong predictors of civic engagement and political participation in general (Verba, Schlozman and Brady 1995). We include the percent of population 25 or older who are at least high school graduates as the measure of educational attainment. Median household income is a common measure of community wealth or financial capacity in a jurisdiction. Residents in a wealthier city likely demand better services from its government. We expect the same with demand for resources supporting civic engagement.

Cities with higher proportions of residents whose work involves some use of information technology may have higher citizen expectations for participatory opportunities online. We use the percent of employed civilians in information industries. Such individuals likely have the skills and capacities for online engagement, including Internet skills (Best and Krueger 2005), and hence likely demand a higher level of online interactivity. We also include the percent of employed civilians in public administration as a control. The data for population, race and ethnicity, resident employment, and community wealth are from the U.S. Census Bureau's American Community Survey. The data we use are directly derived from 2005–2009 American Community Survey 5-Year Estimates.

Political Environment for Civic Engagement

We also include a political variable—whether the city has partisan or nonpartisan elections. While e-government websites are of course nonpartisan, there may be a difference in the participatory climate in cities with active parties.

Participation in Professional Networks

One of our hypotheses is that participation in relevant professional networks will be positively related to change in the interactivity online. In order to account for potential emulation or learning effects from peer cities in professional networks, we use a dummy variable—whether the city is a member of the Public Technology Institute (PTI). As the only technology-related organization for local governments, PTI has been closely working with its member jurisdictions to identify and share local practices with regard to use of technologies. The member communities can communicate with and learn from each other through this professional network. We expect this membership dummy variable to have a positive effect.

Table 14.6 presents descriptive statistics for the variables. We estimate the model using OLS with robust error specification. We first run the regression using all independent variables except the political, institutional, or membership variables. Then we include some or all the political, institutional, or membership variables in other regressions. The statistical results are presented in Table 14.7.

Results

As expected, the estimated coefficient of the weighted interactivity score in 2009 is highly significant and negative, showing the influence of catching up for cities ranked lower at the start of the two-year period. Also, as expected, the size of the city's population and the percent of population who are at least high school graduates have positive effects and the estimates are statistically significant. In

Table 14.6 Descriptive Statistics

Variable	Obs.	Median	Mean	Std. Dev.	Min.	Max.
Change in weighted interactivity score 2009–2011	75	23.08	19.59	14.6	−7.69	53.85
Weighted interactivity score in 2009	75	53.85	55.49	14.65	30.77	84.62
Population	75	459,787	734,888	1,035,594	226,721	8,175,133
Percent of population below 18	75	24.57	24.36	3.55	13.5	31.9
Percent of population 65 and over	75	10.5	10.53	1.99	6.39	16.26
Percent of White population	75	65.91	62.31	15.55	11.68	90.35
Percent of Latino population	75	14.94	22.96	18.96	2.3	80.31
Percent of high school graduates or higher	75	84.3	82.73	6.89	51.4	92.9
Median household income	75	$46,662	$47,819	$10,992	$27,349	$81,822
Percent of civilian employed population in information industries	75	2.57	2.7	0.9	1.55	5.79
Percent of civilian employed population in public administration	75	4.29	4.82	2.42	1.84	16.49
Dummy for whether city has a manager or not	75	1	0.53	0.5	0	1
Dummy for whether city has a partisan election or not	75	0	0.13	0.34	0	1
Dummy for whether city is a member of Public Technology Institute	75	0	0.41	0.5	0	1

Table 14.7 Statistical Results

Variable	OLS(1)	OLS(2)	OLS(3)
Weighted interactivity score in 2009	−0.6909***	−0.6914***	−0.7196***
	(0.1259)	(0.1222)	(0.1183)
Population (in logarithm)	4.3504**	4.4457**	3.3665*
	(1.9023)	(2.1491)	(2.0416)
Percent of population below 18	−0.8858*	−0.8693*	−0.5889
	(0.4814)	(0.5263)	(0.5531)
Percent of population 65 and over	−0.5864	−0.6686	−0.3155
	(0.7210)	(0.7709)	(0.7605)
Percent of White population	−0.0071	0.0116	0.0255
	(0.1523)	(0.1436)	(0.1384)
Percent of Latino population	0.2029	0.159	0.1378
	(0.1348)	(0.1372)	(0.1352)
Percent of high school graduates or higher	1.0523***	0.9765**	0.896**
	(0.3680)	(0.3857)	(0.3816)
Median household income (in logarithm)	−1.0499	−2.3973	−1.3721
	(6.4462)	(7.3840)	(7.1922)
Percent of civilian employed population in information industries	−1.0391	−1.0981	−0.331
	(1.5448)	(1.5742)	(1.6281)
Percent of civilian employed population in public administration	−0.2665	−0.3831	−0.2217
	(0.4818)	(0.5136)	(0.5206)
Dummy for whether city has a manager or not		−0.257	−1.3025
		(3.5201)	(3.4282)
Dummy for whether city has a partisan election or not		−5.7458	−6.6675
		(5.8824)	(5.7593)
Dummy for whether city is a member of Public Technology Institute			4.9278*
			(2.5174)
Constant	−47.5725	−26.1189	−29.8154
	(79.727)	(90.493)	(86.675)
N	75	75	75
R-squared	0.4555	0.4712	0.4918

Note: The dependent variable is the change in weighted interactivity score 2009–2011. The model is ordinary least squares (OLS). Robust standard errors are in parentheses. *** denotes significance level < 1%, ** for 5%, and * for 10%.

addition, the estimated coefficient of the percent of population below 18 is negative and significant in two of the models, but not the full model with all variables included. The dummy PTI membership variable shows significant and positive effects on the change in the weighted interactivity score. Other variables do not show statistically significant effects on the change of the score.

In terms of the magnitude of effects, a city ranked 10 percentage points lower in 2009, on average, advanced faster by seven points in two years. In other words, on average, cities that lagged behind in 2009 may have covered 70 percent of their score deficit from 2009 to 2011. This catching-up process happened quite rapidly at the local level, and it is likely a result of emulation and diffusion across large cities. Larger cities, being more managerially and technologically capable for innovation, generally performed better in the catching-up process, all else being equal.

In addition, demand matters, as a one-percentage point increase in the percent of population who are at least high school graduates raises the change in the weighted interactivity score by about a similar amount. This fits with the research on political participation and civic engagement overall (Verba, Schlozman and Brady 1995; Norris 1999).

Finally, cities' participation in relevant professional networks help them advance faster in adopting online interactivity features: being a member of the Public Technology Institute raises the city's change of the interactivity index score by five percentage points.

Conclusion: Adoption, Implementation, and Change

While the overall change in the combined index is clearly incremental, this surface view masks more rapid changes occurring for interactivity online, including the explosive growth of social media. Over this period, major cities that were further behind hurried to catch up with their peers in both information and interactivity, especially in the adoption of social networks. Cities with greater change in interactivity had populations that were larger and more educated, and were active in professional networks for chief information officers. Financial resources did not matter for change in interactivity scores, and neither did the political environment, when controlling for other factors. The marginal cost of adopting social media platforms is small.

The findings also largely fit theories of policy change that predict more rapid diffusion of innovations that are salient, simple, and low cost. For example, open data portals have begun to appear at the local level but are less well known to citizens than are social media, and they are more complex and costly to adopt initially. Growing familiarity with social media in the population and relative simplicity of adoption have clearly helped to spread their presence on local government websites.

Simple and low-cost solutions, combined with salience, symbolism, and flexibility, may mean that social media likely spread during this period like "policy labels" (Mossberger 2000, 116) with varied implementation, including some symbolic adoption. Counting the presence of social media on government websites has its limits for understanding implementation. As Mergel (2013) has argued, social media can be employed for push, pull, and networking relationships with citizens, ranging from one-way broadcasting of information in push strategies to active dialogue in networking strategies. At the federal level, she has found that one-way push strategies are most prevalent (Mergel 2013). While there is some evidence of variation in strategies at the local level, interviews with local government officials indicate that many challenges exist for interactive networking strategies and effective use (Mossberger, Wu and Crawford 2013).

Realizing this potential of social media depends on how cities implement these tools. Rogers (1995) distinguishes between the adoption and implementation of innovations, and it is useful to employ this distinction in considering the costs and complexity of employing social media. Staff are needed to maintain information, and monitoring discussions raises thorny legal issues of censorship (Kavanaugh et al. 2012). Implementing a civic engagement strategy effectively, whether online or offline, requires planning and recruitment, as well as responses from officials (Bryer 2011; Leighninger 2012). Studies of social media in government highlight the absence of a long-term vision on how social media is supposed to help these organizations (Kavanaugh et al. 2012; Campbell, Lambright and Wells 2014).

Finally, there is also a demand issue when it comes to the use of social media for citizen engagement. Recent research indicates that a majority of online American adults use two or more social media sites (Duggan et al. 2015). Yet, one reason why social media have yet to facilitate greater engagement between citizens and their governments is that many citizens may not want a high level of engagement (Grimmelikhuijsen and Meijer 2014). According to a Pew survey, in the era of open government, citizens largely use government websites to find basic information such as office hours or for other transactions such as paying fines (Horrigan and Rainie 2015). This may be a matter of information supply on websites, however, as well as demand.

Developing effective implementation—beyond simple adoption of platforms—requires understanding how best citizens may interact with governments through social media. This goes beyond elected officials or chief executives. In their survey of 500 U.S. cities, Feeney and Welch (2014) report that 85% of responding officials from five departments, including community development, finance, police, mayor's office, and parks and recreation, use social media tools. Kavanaugh et al. (2012) explore the potential of social media for crisis management, noting that social media are a less expensive way to gather data about community concerns, and can provide real-time data on emergencies. Graham, Avery and Park's (2015) survey of more than 300 officials from municipal governments in the U.S. finds that more than a third use social media for crisis communication. The influence of professional networks visible in this study indicates that as cities gain more experience with social media, professional associations are one resource to support effective implementation and further learning through research, advice, and the sharing of ideas across cities (Mossberger 2000; Balla 2001; Hale 2011).

Note

1. The increased number of criteria for 2011 partly reflects new developments, such as open data portals. Additionally, the 2011 study tracked whether local governments allowed comments to be posted on various platforms, and whether the content posted was related to public policy issues (in contrast with service delivery).

References

Ahn, Michael J. 2011. "Adoption of E-Communication Applications in U.S. Municipalities: The Role of Political Environment, Bureaucratic Structure, and the Nature of Applications." *American Review of Public Administration* 41(4): 428–52.

Balla, Steven J. 2001. "Interstate Professional Associations and the Diffusion of Innovations." *American Politics Research* 29: 221–45.

Baumgartner, Frank R., and Bryan D. Jones. 1993. *Agendas and Instability in American Politics*. Chicago: University of Chicago Press.

Bennett, W. Lance, ed. 2008. *Civic Life Online: Learning How Digital Media Can Engage Youth*. Cambridge, MA: MIT Press.

Berry, Frances Stokes, and William D. Berry. 1990. "State Lottery Adoptions as Policy Innovations: An Event History Analysis." *American Political Science Review* 84: 395–416.

Berry, J.M., K.E. Portney, and K. Thomson. 1993. *The Rebirth of Urban Democracy*. Washington, DC: Brookings Institution Press.

Best, Samuel, and Bryan Krueger. 2005. "Analyzing the Representativeness of Internet Political Participation." *Political Behavior* 27(2): 183–216.

Boulianne, Shelley. 2009. "Does Internet Use Affect Engagement? A Meta-Analysis of Research." *Political Communication* 26(2): 193–211.

Boushey, Graeme. 2010. *Policy Diffusion Dynamics in America*. New York: Cambridge University Press.

Bryer, Thomas A. 2011. "The Cost of Democratization: Social Media Adaptation Challenges within Government Agencies." *Administrative Theory and Praxis* 33(3): 341–61.

Campbell, David A., Kristina T. Lambright, and Christopher J. Wells. 2014. "Looking for Friends, Fans, and Followers? Social Media Use in Public and Nonprofit Human Services." *Public Administration Review* 74(5): 655–63.

Caren, Neal. 2007. "Big City, Big Turnout? Electoral Participation in American Cities." *Journal of Urban Affairs* 29(1): 31–46.

Chadwick, Andrew, and Christopher May. 2003. "Interaction between States and Citizens in the Age of the Internet: 'E-Government' in the United States, Britain and the European Union." *Governance* 16(2): 271–300.

Coursey, David, and Donald F. Norris. 2008. "Models of E-Government: Are They Correct? An Empirical Assessment." *Public Administration Review* 68(3): 523–36.

Dawes, Sharon. 2008. "The Evolution and Continuing Challenges of E-Governance." *Public Administration Review* 68(6): 82–102.

Duggan, Maeve, Nicole B. Ellison, Cliff Lampe, Amanda Lenhart, and Mary Madden. 2015. *Social Media Update 2014*. Pew Research Center, January 2015. Washington, DC: Pew Charitable Trusts. Accessed on July 19, 2015 at http://www.pewInternet.org/files/2015/01/PI_SocialMediaUpdate20144.pdf

Feeney, Mary K., and Eric W. Welch. 2014. "Technology–Task Coupling: Exploring Social Media Use and Managerial Perceptions of E-Government." *The American Review of Public Administration* 46(2): 162–79. doi:10.1177/0275074014547413.

Fox, Susannah, and Lee Rainie. 2014. *The Web at 25 in the U.S.* Pew Research Center, February 2014. Washington, DC: Pew Charitable Trusts. Accessed on July 19, 2015 at http://www.pewInternet.org/files/2014/02/PIP_25th-anniversary-of-the-Web_0227141.pdf

Ganapati, Sukumar. 2011. "Uses of Public Participation Geographic Information Systems Applications in E-Government." *Public Administration Review* 71(3): 425–34.

Graham, Melissa W., Elizabeth J. Avery, and Sejin Park. 2015. "The Role of Social Media in Local Government Crisis Communications." *Public Relations Review* 41(3): 386–94.

Gray, Virginia. 1973. "A Diffusion Study." *American Political Science Review* 67(4): 1174–85.

Grimmelikhuijsen, Stephan G., and Albert J. Meijer. 2014. "Does Twitter Increase Perceived Police Legitimacy?" *Public Administration Review* 75(4): 598–607.

Hale, Kathleen. 2011. *How Information Matters: Networks and Public Policy Innovation.* Washington, DC: Georgetown University Press.

Hampton, Keith N., Lauren Sessions, and Eun Ja Her. 2011. "Core Networks, Social Isolation, and New Media: Internet and Mobile Phone Use, Network Size, and Diversity." *Information, Communication & Society* 14(1): 130–55.

Ho, Alfred T.K. 2002. "Reinventing Local Governments and the E-Government Initiative." *Public Administration Review* 62(4): 434–44.

Holzer, Marc, Aroon Manoharan, Robert Shick, and Genie Towers. 2008. *U.S. States E- Governance Report.* Newark, NJ: National Center for Public Performance, Rutgers University, Campus at Newark.

Horrigan, John B., and Lee Rainie. 2015. *Americans' Views on Open Government Data.* Pew Research Center, April 2015. Washington, DC: Pew Charitable Trusts. Accessed on July 19, 2015 at http://www.pewInternet.org/files/2015/04/PI_OpenData_042115.pdf

Jimenez, Benedict S., Karen Mossberger, and Yonghong Wu. 2012. "Municipal Government and the Interactive Web: Trends and Issues for Civic Engagement." In *E-Governance and Civic Engagement: Factors and Determinants of E-Democracy*, edited by M. Holzer and A. Manoharan, 251–71. Hershey, PA: IGI Global.

Jones, Bryan D., and Frank R. Baumgartner. 2005. *The Politics of Attention: How Government Prioritizes Problems.* Chicago: University of Chicago Press.

Jun, Kyu-Nahm, and Christopher Weare. 2010. "Institutional Motivations in the Adoption of Innovations: The Case of E-Government." *Journal of Public Administration Research and Theory* 21(3): 495–519.

Kaplan, A.M., and M. Haenlein. 2010. "Users of the World, Unite! The Challenges and Opportunities of Social Media." *Business Horizons* 53: 59–68.

Karnig, Albert K., and Walter Oliver. 1983. "Decline in Municipal Voter Turnout." *American Politics Quarterly* 11: 491–506.

Kavanaugh, Andrea L., Edward A. Fox, Steven D. Sheetz, Seungwon Yang, Lin Tzy Li, Donald J. Shoemaker, Apostol Natsev, and Lexing Xie. 2012. "Social Media Use by Government: From the Routine to the Critical." *Government Information Quarterly* 29: 480–91.

Lee, C., K. Chang, and F.S. Berry. 2011. "Testing the Development and Diffusion of E-Government and E-Democracy: A Global Perspective." *Public Administration Review* 71(3): 444–454.

Lee, Chung-pin, Kaiju Chang, and Frances Stokes Berry. 2011. "Testing the Development and Diffusion of E-Government and E-Democracy: A Global Perspective." *Public Administration Review* 71(3): 444–54.

Leighninger, Matt. 2012. "Public Hearings   Public Values." *Public Administration Review* 72(5): 708–9.

McNeal, Ramona S., Caroline J. Tolbert, Karen Mossberger, and Lisa Dotterweich. 2003. "Innovating in Digital Government in the American States." *Social Science Quarterly* 84(1): 52–70.

Mergel, Ines. 2013. "A Framework for Interpreting Social Media Interactions in the Public Sector." *Government Information Quarterly* 30: 327–34.

Moon, M. Jae. 2002. "The Evolution of E-Government among Municipalities: Rhetoric or Reality?" *Public Administration Review* 62(4): 424–33.

Mossberger, Karen. 2000. *The Politics of Ideas and the Spread of Enterprise Zones.* Washington, DC: Georgetown University Press.

Mossberger, Karen, and Kathleen Hale. 2002. "Polydiffusion in Intergovernmental Programs: Information Diffusion in the School-to-Work Network." *American Review of Public Administration* 32(4): 398–422.

Mossberger, Karen, Caroline J. Tolbert, and Ramona S. McNeal. 2008. *Digital Citizenship: The Internet, Society and Participation.* Cambridge, MA: MIT Press.

Mossberger, Karen, Caroline J. Tolbert, and Mary Stansbury. 2003. *Virtual Inequality: Beyond the Digital Divide.* Washington, DC: Georgetown University Press.

Mossberger, Karen, Yonghong Wu, and Jared Crawford. 2013. "Connecting Citizens and Local Governments? Social Media and Interactivity in Major U.S. Cities." *Government Information Quarterly* 30: 351–8.

Musso, Janet A., Christopher Weare, and Matt C. Hale. 2000. "Designing Web Technologies for Local Governance Reform: Good Management or Good Democracy?" *Political Communication* 17(1): 1–19.

Norris, Donald F., and M. Jae Moon. 2005. "Advancing E-Government at the Grassroots: Tortoise or Hare?" *Public Administration Review* 65(1): 64–75.

Norris, Pippa, ed. 1999. *Critical Citizens: Global Support for Democratic Governance.* New York: Oxford University Press.

Oakerson, Ronald. 1999. *Governing Local Public Economies: Creating the Civic Metropolis.* Oakland, CA: Institute of Contemporary Studies Press.

Oates, Wallace. 1972. *Fiscal Federalism.* New York: Harcourt, Brace, Jovanovich Inc.

Obama, Barack. 2009. "Appendix: Memo from President Obama on Transparency and Open Government." In *Open Government: Collaboration, Transparency, and Participation in Practice*, 2010, edited by Daniel Lathrop and Laurel Ruma, 389–90. Sebastopol, CA: O'Reilly Media, Inc.

O'Reilly, T. 2005. "What Is Web 2.0? Design Patterns and Business Models for the Next Generation of Software." O'Reilly. Accessed at http://oreilly.com/web2/archive/what-is-web-20.html

Peters, B. Guy. 2001. *The Future of Governing: Four Emerging Models.* 2nd, rev. ed. Lawrence: University Press of Kansas.

Rogers, Everett M. 1995. *Diffusion of Innovations.* 4th ed. New York: The Free Press.

Rose, Richard. 1993. *Lesson Drawing in Public Policy: A Guide to Learning Across Time and Space.* Chatham, NJ: Chatham House.

Schaffner, Brian F., Gerald Wright, and Matthew Streb. 2001. "Teams without Uniforms: The Nonpartisan Ballot in State and Local Elections." *Political Research Quarterly* 54: 7–30.

Scott, Allen J. 2006. "Creative Cities: Conceptual Issues and Policy Questions." *Journal of Urban Affairs* 28(1): 1–17.

Smith, Aaron. 2010. *Government Online: The Internet Gives Citizens New Paths to Government Services and Information.* Pew Research Center, April 2010. Washington, DC: Pew Charitable Trusts. Accessed on August 28, 2010 at http://www.pewInternet.org/2010/04/27/government-online/

———. 2013. *Civic Engagement in the Digital Age.* Pew Research Center, April 2013. Washington, DC: Pew Charitable Trusts. Accessed on July 19, 2015 at http://www.pewInternet.org/files/old-media//Files/Reports/2013/PIP_CivicEngagementintheDigitalAge.pdf

Tolbert, Caroline J., Karen Mossberger, and Ramona McNeal. 2008. "Institutions, Innovation and E-Government in the American States." *Public Administration Review* 68(3): 549–63.

Verba, S., K. Schlozman, and H. Brady. 1995. *Voice and Equality: Civic Voluntarism in American Politics.* Cambridge, MA: Harvard University Press.

Walker, Jack L. 1969. "The Diffusion of Innovations among the American States." *The American Political Science Review* 63(3): 880–99.

Weare, Christopher, and W.Y. Lin. 2000. "Content Analysis of the World Wide Web: Opportunities and Challenges." *Social Science Computer Review* 18(3): 272–92.

West, Darrell M. 2004. *Urban E-Government, 2004.* Center for Public Policy, September 2004. Accessed on October 10, 2009 at http://www.insidepolitics.org/egovt04city.html

———. 2005. *Digital Government: Technology and Public-Sector Performance.* Princeton, NJ: Princeton University Press.

Wood, Curtis. 2002. "Voter Turnout in City Elections." *Urban Affairs Review* 38: 209–31.

15
NAVIGATING THE OPEN GOVERNMENT COMFORT ZONE FOR THE EFFECTIVE USE OF OPEN DATA

Younhee Kim

Introduction

Open government is not a new paradigm; it originated in the Freedom of Information movement in the 1950s. However, its practices have been recently reengineered to extend its open boundary related to new developments of e-governance and information technology (IT). After the Obama administration's proactive actions to open government, its direction prioritizes a collaborative partnership between governments and citizens through massive open data, where the new partnership is expected to solve complex government problems. The commitment to open data policies has been high, so diverse open data have become publicly available to make government more open and transparent. Although releasing data in any form is better than releasing no data at all, open government data still tend to be heavily generated by the government-centric perspective (Janssen, Charalabidis, & Zuiderwijk, 2012).

The exponential growth of data continues in the public sector, corresponding to increased investment in data management and network technologies. The proliferation of data has altered government attention from more data generation to better data usability, so governments have reacted aggressively to move toward more effective use of data that helps government predict trends and target needed public services more precisely. The emergence of extensive data predictive analytics enables government agendas to be more data driven, which have been ambitiously adopted by all levels of governments. The recent case of Chicago's SmartData Project, the first open source predictive analytics platform launched in 2014, helps city managers prevent problems and clarify community needs based on data-driven predictions. SmartData shows how the government application of big data can transform disparate data into useful information even at the local level. Furthermore, the Chicago case could strengthen transparency and participation by changing the communication channels between government and residents (Kassen, 2013).

Manyika et al. (2011) reported that government achieved strong productive growth from the substantial use of big data, which are typically large, heterogeneous datasets that help government identify emerging patterns and create new public values. Many governments have opened their data to the general public and private industries in order to stimulate potential data values in transparency (Robinson et al., 2012), accountability (Janssen, 2012), participation, innovation (Janssen, 2011), and economic growth. In particular, opening government data emphasizes open collaboration that can lead to the creation of innovative solutions to government problems with all stakeholders: An example of this would be the creation of new business growth opportunities like civic startups. Instead of outsourcing government IT projects, civic startups bridge the gaps between government and external stakeholders in the innovative use of open data and increase participation of citizens and communities. Code for America is an example of an organization that has strengthened citizen engagement in the development of civic-minded digital programs.

Data are generated from everywhere due to fast-growth user-generated content platforms like social media and the Internet of Things. Data and information are neither one-way nor static anymore. Although the majority of social computing platforms are still in their preliminary stages, they will offer government new opportunities to expand the ownership of information, including more external stakeholders. In response to citizen-centered initiatives and various needs, open government policies have adopted innovative features of open data status. These efforts have placed recent open government in conflict with matching with the original concept of open government. Different perspectives of open government have been understood differently. To achieve the comprehensive open government presence, dynamic perspectives on open government and open data disclosure should be discussed. This chapter reviews the developments of open government and explores the state of the recent open government data practices to discuss effective open data approaches that promote the values of open government for all citizen groups.

Development of Open Government

The term open government was first referenced in 1953 to offer the ground of public access to government records. However, its core principles were cemented by the passage of the Freedom of Information Act (FOIA) of 1966. Somewhere along the line, Parks (1957) extended the very early concept of open government in order to ensure the status of good government and guarantee the public accessibility of government information without long holding. Availability of government information to the public is expected to allow external stakeholders to take on a watchdog role and monitor government processes in the interest of the public. The public, at first, was not simply designated as general citizens. It originally referred to the broad target population inside and outside government, such as the press, interested parties, nongovernmental specialists, committee members of the Congress, and other government officials. The movement of open government was escalated by the FOIA in 1966 and 1974, which allowed the public to be entitled to the right to access any federal government records, except under any of the nine exempt categories or by one of the three special law enforcement record exclusions. The principle of disclosure of public records was also embodied in the Presidential Records Act in 1978.

Before the mid-1990s, open government was mainly about holding itself accountable to the public by making government information available. Its original idea has been rapidly evolving in accordance with the development of e-government and Internet-based technologies since that time. The Electronic Freedom of Information Act (EFOIA) Amendments of 1996 were at the first step in merging IT into open government territory. The use of government websites to disseminate government information has moved forward to the next phase of open government opportunities, while access to digital records is still limited to reproducing new information for the public. At the federal level, the U.S. Census Bureau made the first effort to release government information by making it available through census.gov in 1994. After that, the widespread creation of e-government sites and the E-Government Act of 2002 opened up new possibilities of open government.

Opening government is not "a sub-dimension of e-government" (Abu-Shanab, 2015, p. 454), but a by-product of e-government practices that improves government transparency and a fundamental idea of open government (Chadwick & May, 2003). The use of e-government platforms and Internet technologies have truly enabled government to disclose a wide range of information in a digitized format (Cuillier & Piotrowski, 2009). Concurrently with newly articulated openness by the Obama administration, open government has also redefined the focus of e-government practices at the federal level over the past few years. For example, prioritizing technological capacities to promote open government principles demands the intensive use of e-government websites, such as incorporating new Internet capacities (Harrison et al., 2012). The scope of the open government tradition has been expanded considerably due to a series of changes. The identity of open government has changed from a static status, which is a synonym for information disclosures, to an active presence that promotes broad participation.

The Obama administration has profoundly reinforced open government initiatives with emphases in government transparency and technology-driven data openness, as a reaction to the Bush administration's limited disclosure practices due to the aftermath of the September 11 attacks. During the Bush administration, government openness and transparency were undermined in numerous ways (Relyea, 2009). The Obama administration's open initiatives influenced the doctrine to represent more than just accountability. Two additional goals, participation and collaboration, have been included in the open government package to bring more citizens and businesses into government inner circles so they can contribute to decision-making. The Obama administration's open government expects citizens to take on new roles with government collectively or individually (Abu-Shanab, 2015). The main frameworks of open government are aligned with the existing laws and regulations, like FOIA, EFOIA, open meeting laws, Privacy Act of 1974, Paperwork Reduction Act of 1980, Information Quality Act of 2000, E-government Act of 2002, etc. On top of that, attached to the open government concept are newly emphasized keywords such as economic opportunity, efficiency, effectiveness, innovation, open data, and quality of life. Table 15.1 summarizes the key aspects of the open government trends categorized into two phases based on the Obama administration.

Table 15.1 Open Government Paths

	1st Generation	*2nd Generation*
Purposes	accountability	transparency participation collaboration
Initiatives	political-centered accountable politics	Internet technology-driven adaptable, useful data
Priorities	disclosure publicity readiness	economic efficiency effectiveness innovation
Retention	confidentiality secrecy	privacy security
Information type	policies government-supplied	service delivery user-centered
Data format	processed data	machine-readable raw data

Open Government Initiatives

Three Dimensions of Open Government

The Open Government Directive in 2009 declared the three principles of transparency, participation, and collaboration as the cornerstone of open government (Orszag, 2009). Transparency literally means availability of government data and documents to the public who can be assisted by open resources for evaluating government actions (Harrison et al., 2012). Producing more and accurate government information results in more transparent governance (Lord, 2006; Reddick & Ganapati, 2011). Prompt information disclosure has been guaranteed in response to any public request, although records could be a case of FOIA's exemptions (Holder, 2009). The directive has indeed pushed federal agencies to improve FOIA request performance through implementing new FIOA guidelines, so government should open not only routine documents but also extensive disclosure requests.

The Department of Justice, which leads in modernizing FOIA, reported a high release rate of over 93% during FY 2013 based on the FOIA statistics site (http://www.foia.gov/data.html). Other major federal agencies also made considerable progress to run effective FOIA systems by improving response times, restructuring operations, and exploring new technologies in FY 2013 (U.S. Department of Justice, 2014). As a result, higher transparency through broad information disclosure can fully claim government accountability and responsiveness. However, ways to present agencies' data on government websites are still not sufficient in making their operations understandable for citizens. USASpending.gov, for example, contains a worthy summary of transactional data for federal spending but less detailed information about the use of the spending (Evans & Campos, 2013).

The second principle of the Open Government Directive, participation, expects broader and profound participation. The rationale behind traditional participation is still valid to support a new participation concept under the directive, which is having well-informed citizens become active participants in government decision-making, because it leads to more positive reactions to government policies. Citizens who are knowledgeable about government tend to perceive their roles as more than consumers, customers, or static voters (Schachter, 1997), so they are willing to communicate with government and provide their opinions on how best to solve public problems. Citizen–government relationships have exceedingly become directive and interactive.

The directive seeks active government actions to solicit expertise from outside government (Executive Office of the President, 2009). The White House's We the People website (https://petitions.whitehouse.gov) is an aggressive case of bringing citizens into government processes. Citizens can petition the Obama administration for action on various issues via this new online platform. If a petition gets sufficient signatures from the public, an official response will be issued. Although the site has challengeable shortcomings to fulfill authentic participation, it attempts to carry out the open government promise that authentic citizen participation is guaranteed by accessibility to government information.

The collaboration pillar operates differently than transparency and participation do in opening government to general citizens. Collaborative efforts expect expert inputs from civic organizations, businesses, or professionals to solve government problems. While collaboration also aims to foster active participation like the participation pillar, collaboration requires high levels of contribution from participants in order to add new values to original government information (Harrison et al., 2012). Participants can be viewed as being co-creators of government outputs or close partners in improving existing service quality (Bovaird, 2007), since they retain their own information or capacities to collaborate with government. Collaboration also occurs between government agencies. Mergel (2015) found that many agencies reused other agencies' codes but made fewer contributions add new values to the existing code.

Table 15.2 Principles of Open Government Directive with Examples

Principle	Objectives	Examples
Transparency	accountability responsiveness data availability	CMS.gov dashboard, data.gov, FederalRegister.gov, FOIA.gov statistics, itdashboard.gov, recovery.gov, USASpending.gov
Participation	democracy data accessibility	regulations.gov comments, petitions.whitehouse.gov, whitehouse.gov/engage
Collaboration	partnership data usability	challenge.gov, data.gov wiki, open source projects

Government wiki or open source projects are good examples of open collaboration. The Obama administration has accelerated the open source and crowdsource approaches by tailoring government-owned data for outside IT professionals. Open source projects are built on the tradition of open source that depends on free access to program source code. Open source, like Linux, allows users great flexibility to work from generic codes for their specific needs and reduces users' dependence on software vendors. In the wiki government case, it intends to maximize crowdsourcing for effective decision-making in various peer-to-peer collaborative settings (Howe, 2006; Nam, 2012). Users of government data are enabled to access raw datasets via data.gov and make government data more linkable and maintainable than the original data.gov datasets. Unlike open source, crowdsourcing invites both nonexperts and tech-savvy groups into a collaboration process. Improving the effectiveness of government by using open data through open source or crowdsourcing is an extended version of collaboration (Chun et al., 2010), but open collaboration practices have mainly occurred between experts and government.

Collaboration seems to be the most debatable dimension of open government. As Veljković, Bodganović-Dinić, and Stoimenov (2014) discussed, a lack of a clear distinction between participation and collaboration exists "where the participation is collaborative or the collaboration is participatory" (p. 279). The idea of open collaboration holds a weak political means, although it still requires active participation of outside government to support accountable government (Noveck, 2009; Wilson & Linders, 2011). Ordinary citizens with limited technical knowledge may have less contribution to the current practices of open collaboration. Its success is also dependent on a technology-enabled collaboration platform that is provided by government (Pyrozhenko, 2015). Table 15.2 presents key objectives and examples of the three open government principles.

Open Government Standards

Open government requires federal agencies to develop their own open government plans, launch direct websites to access data, use various social media computing technologies (e.g., microblogging, activity feeds, social annotations), and solicit feedback from citizens or experts. The open government memorandum requires executive agencies to follow four steps to create a more open government: publish government information online, improve the quality of government information, create and institutionalize an open government culture, and create an enabling policy framework for open government (Orszag, 2009).

Publishing information online requires agencies to disseminate data in a timely and open format via either an agency's own website or a one-stop website. An open format entails platform-independent, machine-readable, and reusable data (McDermott, 2010). Platform independence refers to software compatibility on any operating system without additional modification. Machine readability requires a digital format to be processed by a computer, while reusability means using data assets repetitively. Open format standards stimulate innovation, which provides more economic opportunities for entrepreneurs. Improving the quality of information in the second step is an overarching concept for utility, objectivity, and integrity (Office of Management and Budget [OMB], 2001). Both utility and integrity are straightforward terms, which can be understood as being the usefulness of information and security. Objectivity entails accurate, reliable, and unbiased information (OMB, 2001).

The third step of creating and institutionalizing an open government culture is having sustainable agencies take actions toward openness and accountability (McDermott, 2010). Unlike the previous two steps, the third step is broad and seems to be difficult when it comes to achieving immediate results within a relatively short time frame. Agency cultures have adopted openness practices following the Open Government Directive plans, but cultivating a culture of openness for transparency, participation, and collaboration could be inadvertently limited in terms of organizational and administrative operations. The last step, creating an enabling policy framework for open government, expects agencies to develop feasible plans for improving their existing information and dissemination practices.

Assessment of Open Government

Lee and Kwak (2012) supported the potential of these open government principles by proposing the open government maturity model. The maturity model applied social media communication technologies to advance agencies' open government plans by informing their capabilities, outcomes, and challenges. The model consists of five maturity levels: initial conditions, data transparency, open participation, open collaboration, and ubiquitous engagement. The model proposed that open government status should move from a lower level of transparency to a higher level of collaboration incrementally, which means a previous level should be a precondition for the next level. However, scholars have argued that the Obama administration's openness has misled political, cultural, and administrative practices of government accountability and transparency (e.g., Pyrozhenko, 2015; Yu & Robinson, 2012).

Ironically, the wider boundaries of the recent open government practices tend to dilute the political goals of accountability and democracy. Yu and Robinson (2012) asserted that the recent meaning of open government has been ambiguously used, since technological aspects of open data have been combined into the open conventional government doctrine. In place of political disclosures, open government has weighed the ideas of innovation, attaching to the intensity of the information technology progress, which raises often-observed tensions, particularly between transparency and collaboration in understanding public–private sector relations.

As Pyrozhenko (2015) argued, stimulating collaborative open government seems to take away responsibilities of openness and accountability from public administrators to technology entrepreneurs who tend to become "the real agents of open government" (p. 4). If open collaboration is heavily determined by private entities' interests, it will not be a reciprocal relationship between government and private players. Public values and government functions could be somewhat degraded in response to this radical idea. In general, the perspectives of the three open government dimensions still have limited understanding of their opportunities, prototypes, and roles for inside and outside stakeholders. Therefore, the open government principles should be revisited to align its ultimate goals with accountability, democracy, and participatory governance.

Open Data Practices

Open Data Principles and Requirements

The goal of open data is to make government data freely available to anyone in modifiable forms. The open data concept is a tool of open government directives to promote the three principles via the Internet. The term originated from the open access and open source movements that pursue free distribution of either knowledge or programming code products to the public (Harrison et al., 2012; Yu & Robinson, 2012). Open data focuses more on the growth of data itself rather than on service delivery (Veljković, Bodganović-Dinić, & Stoimenov, 2014).

The memorandum of Open Data Policy in May 2013 institutionalized effective information management to make federal agencies' information more accessible, discoverable, and usable for entrepreneurial opportunities (Burwell et al., 2013). The front slogan of the open data policy, *Managing Information as an Asset*, is advancing interoperability and openness at each stage of the information life cycle. Apparently, this open data movement takes into account a comprehensive approach to managing the impacts of data quality for the public interest. The memorandum designated seven principles of open data and is consistent with the Open Government Directive: public, accessible, described, reusable, complete, timely, and managed post-release (Burwell et al., 2013). The accessible standard requires searchable indexing data formats without user discrimination, while the described rule asks to provide fully explained description of the data elements. The complete option refers to primary data forms when data were originally collected. The timely principle demands immediate release of data to maximize its value, whereas the managed post-release principle requires setting a contact point for responding to all questions after releasing data.

The open data policy requires straightforward actions to improve information resource management for successful implementations of the open data principles. These actions are specified as five requirements: collect or create information in a way that supports downstream information processing and dissemination activities; build information systems to support interoperability and information accessibility; strengthen data management and release practices; strengthen measures to ensure that privacy and confidentiality are fully protected and that data are properly secured; and incorporate new interoperability and openness requirements into core agency processes (Burwell et al., 2013, pp. 6–11). The five requirements aim to build an affordable information resource management system that manages information effectively, so that it can be a valuable resource to the public and comparable to other capital, labor, and infrastructure. While the requirements do not seem to be a comprehensive approach to data resources management, these actions attempt to encompass systematic management of both information and information technologies on open data agenda in a practical way.

These open principles, which focus on the availability and usefulness of machine-readable data, have become the new default for government information (Obama, 2013). With regard to these policies, the Obama administration launched several open data initiatives. For example, federal agencies are mandated to publish a minimum of three high-value datasets at the data.gov portal. This portal has already released 188,151 datasets in 14 topic domains, such as agriculture, business, climate, consumer, ecosystems, education, energy, finance, health, local government, manufacturing, ocean, public safety, and science and research. Most of the agencies' self-evaluations, which determined whether the datasets met the open government principles, reported successful implementations with respect to three levels (meets expectations, progress toward expectations, fails to meet expectations) of a ranking system that the U.S. Office of Management and Budget developed as a formal evaluation system (Evans & Campos, 2013). Executive Office of the President (2011) released 29 agencies' performance scorecards, of which 18, 28, and 22 agencies met expectations for transparency, participation, and collaboration respectively. In addition, 27 out of the 29 agencies reported uploading three high-level datasets at data.gov. Agencies' efforts to institute open data practices seem to follow the open government spirit (Evans & Campos, 2013), so emphasizing a data-driven approach is generally comparable to achieving the purposes of the open government principles of the directive (McDermott, 2010; Napoli & Karaganis, 2010; Peled, 2011).

Sharing government data with unidentified end-users is expected to reproduce new values of the original ideas or products, so the economic value of government data has been significantly emphasized by the new direction of open government. Considering government information as an asset, data has begun to be opened and interoperated on not only by citizens, but also by civic entrepreneurs. Entrepreneurs can add new economic value to the existing markets using government data (Millar, 2011). For example, the highest quality signal of the global positioning system (GPS) originally designed for military use was not available to the public until the government removed the U.S. military advantage to access the accurate positioning data in 2000. Since then, the GPS market has been growing exponentially, and its innovation has continuously created monetary value to the U.S. economy. Government has made significant efforts to upgrade the system in order to meet the growing needs of industry and citizens. This entrepreneurial success shows that the share-the-date approach can efficiently synergize to produce high-value products.

Open Data Projects

One open data project is to launch a government web portal (Kassen, 2013), focusing on continuous improvement of the open data policy and innovative collaboration. Open data government websites do not simply carry static hypertextual data, but operate the standard way of interaction on the web, which is a read/write web in providing data. The idea of open data collaboration between government and users is to allow change in the focus of interaction between government and individual contributors via social computing technologies.

Project Open Data, an online repository developed by the White House in 2013, intended to improve the federal agencies' adoption of the open data policy in an open source base. Ambitiously, the project has shared its resources and plug-and-play tools on the GitHub social coding site, an open source platform of a code-hosting repository. The GitHub infrastructure enables the owner of the code to track other users' actions to the original code, including modification or reuse of the data (Mergel, 2015). The open data project has been effectively and transparently exposed to the large community of developers who can also contribute to enhance the quality of the original coding or provide policy suggestions. The project does not only consist of unidirectional efforts from government to users, but it also involved opposite-directional contributions from users. Beyond sharing open data, social coding interactions offer new possibilities of open collaboration between developers and government.

Open data projects are largely found in education, energy, finance, global development, healthcare, and public safety fields, because many entrepreneurs see numerous potential opportunities in those areas for new startups via a partnership with government, like BrightScope. This case implies that individual inputs or public use of government open data can have positive outcomes to resolve vulnerable government issues. Some resources have also been available on data.gov. A distinctive feature of the exemplary cases in Table 15.3 is adopting an application program interface (API) that allows developers to communicate a set of data from an application for building other applications. An appealing aspect of open data projects is visualizing data. Although it is not a fresh effort, websites have been elaborated to present accurate, immediate reports and customize layouts by the general public for a higher level of transparency. The health system measurement project site (https://healthmeasures.aspe.hhs.gov), for example, has advanced dashboard functions with launch pads that also permit users to access source codes.

Table 15.3 Open Data Initiatives Projects in Federal Agencies

Subject	Portal
Education	college scorecard; learning registry
Energy	EIA's API; energy star APIs
Finance	CFPB's consumer compliant database; FDIC's datasets; U.S. Department of Labor's forms
Global development	USAID's Green Book API; USAID's Development credit authority loan data; USAID's measure demographic health survey; Millennium Challenge Corporation's open data
Health	Medicare provider utilization and payment data; hospital compare; NIH's registry of clinical trials; health indicators warehouse; health system measurement project
Public safety	NHTSA's 5 star safety ratings; U.S. Dept. of Labor's data enforcement; FDA's recalls, market withdrawals, and safety alerts; CPSC's recalls; earthquake hazards program; DOT's developer resources

Lee and Kwak (2012) examined the early efforts of open government data cases in the healthcare area and found that a wide range of users enables the visualization, analysis, and utilization of open data in an easy, prompt, and accurate manner. Federal government has continuously emphasized an aspect of technological innovation of open data projects in order to promote business performance and benefits. However, the reality is that the majority of datasets are duplicated online across agencies, and transparency of the data itself has been unclear. Some agencies are still reluctant to release raw data to broad end-users, which is not an unusual way for agencies to react. It has been happening since e-government was launched. Moreover, a limited scope of datasets has been used by narrow user groups. These changes are not equally available to all citizen groups. Lee and Kwak (2012) concluded that government agencies should focus on matching their open government initiatives with their overall organizational goals and priorities rather than implementing new technologies. These open data projects should tightly comply with e-government to improve the quality of public access to government information, because these projects are apparently considered a part of e-government innovation (Jaeger & Bertot, 2010).

Implementation of Effective Open Data Strategies

Open government data should be accessible to anyone who can redistribute open data, but the public's capacities to innovate and reconstruct open data may be hard to accommodate with the technical sides of open data practices. Open data values may not be equally utilized by the majority of citizens. The original intentions of open data have been rewarded in numerous ways, but the protocols of open data practices are not enough to promote broader citizen participation and richer governmental transparency. The wider range of the open data perspective tends to confuse stakeholders both inside and outside the government about the existing ideas of open government.

In implementing open data initiatives effectively to promote open government principles, administering government data needs to be leveraged by broad users or citizen groups. Most citizens or end-users seem to have less awareness about the usability of open data and the possibilities of open data partnerships. It is not generally the case that if you build virtual platforms, ordinary citizens will come to the sites delivering massive participation (Norris & Curtice, 2006). The presence of open data should be widely distributed and accessible by a broad base of users. The typical discussion, that a well-informed citizenry can actively participate in government, is a baseline for the open data principles of effective data use. A broad outside-in approach via open data services works for achieving the true values of open government for the entire public.

Furthermore, the ordinary public may lack the sophisticated knowledge or skills that are needed to access or use new types of data platforms. Citizens have experienced entry-barriers to open data channels. It may be possible to adopt a choice engine approach like the private sector has already applied, such as Amazon and Netflix. These choice engines will help users decide their selection based on priorities. This application restructures existing datasets to generate new values from that instead of creating new raw datasets. Open data practices should reassess the current approaches to access information for a broad base of ordinary users. Although empowering all citizens seems like a trite formulation in the digital era, it is always a key to reach participative democracy.

To promote open data principles in effective ways, sustainability or robustness of data access or data searches should be guaranteed in unified and user-friendly conditions. A way of presenting government data and information has a significant impact on citizens' acceptance of the open government systems. One of the continuous challenges that citizens are faced with is difficulty navigating or understanding open government information, although the Obama administration announced readily discoverable data by the public (Thaler & Tucker, 2013). The burden of interpreting disclosed data should not be left to citizens who have a limited technological background to contribute to open government projects. Life cycles of electronic data in government are not very stable at holding information seamlessly for sufficient time. The current open data policy lacks clear guidelines for the continued existence of information. Systematic data management should focus on maintaining existing electronic government data sources in order to promote open government in addition to the use of new technologies.

The quality of open data has been inconsistent across federal agencies (Peled, 2011). As an early evaluation study of open datasets, Harper (2010) assessed the release of 41 federal agencies' high-value datasets at data.gov and found that there was little valuable data in the datasets for better understanding government businesses. The quality of the datasets was evaluated by determining the usefulness of information on agency management, deliberation, and results assigning a letter grade of A to F. Only four agencies (Department of Labor, Executive Office of the President, General Services Administration, and Social Security Administration) received a grade of A, whereas nine agencies received F grades. Although the criteria were not sophisticatedly developed to evaluate the quality of the data, it is useful to see the agencies' initial practices in response to the Obama administration's open policies. In line with this study, Peled (2011) observed patterns of dataset uploads and downloads at data.gov to examine interagency information sharing during May 2010 to May 2011. The study noted that the number of uploaded datasets was exponentially increased in the short period of September 2010, and then shortly afterward remained static, with fewer routine updates of datasets. In cases of downloads, the downloading of datasets did not change much during the 52 weeks, which indicated that relatively low-quality datasets were provided by agencies.

Publishing government data on portals with high volume does not secure the quality of open data. The open data initiatives define the status of high-value information as enabling government to "increase agency accountability and responsiveness; improve public knowledge of the agency and its operations; further the core mission of the agency; create economic opportunity; or respond to need and demand as identified through public consultation" (Orszag, 2009, pp. 7–8). However, these definitions do not fully specify sustainable values of data quality in terms of standard procedures and requirements. To improve consistent data quality, assessing data quality with systematic metrics should be necessary. Quality assessment metrics can be developed based on the seven principles of open data, which are public, accessible, described, reusable, complete, timely, and managed post-release.

The open data policy requires privacy and confidentiality of government data to minimize potential harms by releasing data to broader stakeholders, but guidelines to manage these issues are not clear. Considerable conflict has always existed between open government data and privacy. Besides, data protection issues related to copyright and licensing will be complicated when the reuse of data contains restrictions by different users. A reasonable level of openness and a scope of data reuse are not easily identified, but standards should be provided to insure that these challenges are met.

Conclusion

Despite considerable progress of recent open government and open data initiatives, the open government mechanism has faced inherent challenges in working within and outside government. With agencies' limited capacity and lack of motivation to implement open data technologies due to organizational constraints (Dawes, 2010), the processes for creating open government values via open data initiatives have placed both internal and external end-users aside. Since open data tasks are labor intensive, sufficient organizational support should be prioritized to make innovative open data approaches part of daily operations in government.

Studies have noted that high-value datasets have not yielded high value for transparency, citizen participation, and policy decision-making (e.g., Ginsberg, 2011; Peled, 2011). Meeting open government standards by releasing bulk data does not guarantee that data are sufficiently effective in promoting transparency and participation with respect to public demand and expectations. A heavy data-driven approach of open data principles tends to overestimate the public's understanding and perception of government information. To some extent, overly determined endeavors to open government data have rushed initiatives through without either verifying suitability of initiatives or considering the dynamic nature of the open government doctrine in terms of political or social contexts.

The open government movement has offered new growth opportunities to federal agencies by working closely with those outside government, but the openness initiatives need systematic support for holding the origins of open government arguments. Although using data-intensive technologies is a vital part of building innovative partnerships with diverse users, it is not a necessary and sufficient condition making government more transparent and participatory via the Internet. The success of the underlying architecture in open government does not heavily rely on the information technology-driven agenda. Rather, agencies should be authentic in sharing ownership of government data with users, and the open data mechanisms should "be designed to be usable by all" (Jaeger & Bertot, 2010, p. 373). In promoting open data, the government should not exclude the unresponsive and unskilled public. The maintenance of sound open government is essential for government achieving the true legitimacy.

References

Abu-Shanab, Emad A. "Reengineering the open government concept: An empirical support for a proposed model." *Government Information Quarterly* 32, no. 4 (2015): 453–463.

Bovaird, Tony. "Beyond engagement and participation: User and community coproduction of public services." *Public Administration Review* 67, no. 5 (2007): 846–860.

Burwell, Sylvia M., Steven VanRockcl, Todd Park, and Dominic J. Mancini. *Open data policy-managing information as an asset*. Washington, DC: Office of Management and Budget, Executive Office of the President, May 13, 2013. Retrieved from https://www.whitehouse.gov/sites/default/files/omb/memoranda/2013/m-13-13.pdf

Chadwick, Andrew, and Christopher May. "Interaction between states and citizens in the age of the Internet: 'e-Government' in the United States, Britain, and the European Union." *Governance* 16, no. 2 (2003): 271–300.

Chun, Soon Ae, Stuart Shulman, Rodrigo Sandoval, and Eduard Hovy. "Government 2.0: Making connections between citizens, data and government." *Information Polity* 15, no. 1 (2010): 1–9.

Cuillier, David, and Suzanne J. Piotrowski. "Internet information-seeking and its relation to support for access to government records." *Government Information Quarterly* 26, no. 3 (2009): 441–449.

Dawes, Sharon S. "Stewardship and usefulness: Policy principles for information-based transparency." *Government Information Quarterly* 27, no. 4 (2010): 377–383.
Executive Office of the President. *Open government progress report on the American people*. Washington, DC: Executive Office of the President, 2009. Retrieved from https://www.whitehouse.gov/sites/default/files/microsites/ogi-progress-report-american-people.pdf
———. *The open government initiative scorecard*. Washington, DC: Executive Office of the President, 2011.
Evans, Angela M., and Adriana Campos. "Open government initiatives: Challenges of citizen participation." *Journal of Policy Analysis and Management* 32, no. 1 (2013): 172–185.
Ginsberg, Wendy R. *Obama administration's open government initiative: Issues for congress*. Collingdale, PA: DIANE Publishing, 2011.
Harper, Jim. *Grading agencies' high-value data sets*. Washington, DC: CATO Institute, February 5, 2010. Retrieved from http://www.cato.org/blog/grading-agencies-high-value-data-sets
Harrison, Teresa M., Santiago Guerrero, G. Brian Burke, Meghan Cook, Anthony Cresswell, Natalie Helbig, Jana Hrdinová, and Theresa Pardo. "Open government and e-government: Democratic challenges from a public value perspective." *Information Polity* 17, no. 2 (2012): 83–97.
Holder, Eric. "Memorandum for heads of executive departments and agencies: The Freedom of Information Act." *Office of the Attorney General*, March 19, 2009. Retrieved from http://www.justice.gov/sites/default/files/ag/legacy/2009/06/24/foia-memo-march2009.pdf
Howe, Jeff. "The rise of crowd sourcing." *Wired* 14, no. 6 (2006): 176–183.
Jaeger, Paul T., and John Carlo Bertot. "Transparency and technological change: Ensuring equal and sustained public access to government information." *Government Information Quarterly* 27, no. 4 (2010): 371–376.
Janssen, Katleen. "The influence of the PSI directive on open government data: An overview of recent development." *Government Information Quarterly* 28, no. 4 (2011): 446–456.
———. "Open government data and the right to information: Opportunities and obstacles." *Journal of Community Informatics* 8, no. 2 (2012): 1–11.
Janssen, Marijn, Yannis Charalabidis, and Anneke Zuiderwijk. "Benefits, adoption barriers and myths of open data and open government." *Information Systems Management* 29, no. 4 (2012): 258–268.
Kassen, Maxat. "A promising phenomenon of open data: A case study of the Chicago open data project." *Government Information Quarterly* 30, no. 4 (2013): 508–513.
Lee, Gwanhoo, and Young Hoon Kwak. "An open government maturity model for social media-based public engagement." *Government Information Quarterly* 29, no. 4 (2012): 492–503.
Lord, Kristin M. *The perils and promise of global transparency*. New York: State University of New York Press, 2006.
Manyika, James, Michael Chui, Brad Brown, Jacques Bughin, Richard Dobbs, Charles Roxburgh, and Angela H. Byers. *Big data: The next frontier for innovation, competition, and productivity*. McKinsey Global Institute, 2011. Retrieved from http://www.mckinsey.com/insights/business_technology/big_data_the_next_frontier_for_innovation
McDermott, Patrice. "Building open government." *Government Information Quarterly* 27, no. 4 (2010): 401–413.
Mergel, Ines. "Open collaboration in the public sector: The case of social coding on GitHub." *Government Information Quarterly* 32, no. 4 (2015): 464–472.
Millar, L. "Managing open government data," in *Government Information Management in the 21st Century: International Perspective*, ed. Garvin, Peggy. Burlington: Ashgate, 2011, 171–192.
Nam, Taewoo. "Suggesting frameworks of citizen-sourcing via Government 2.0." *Government Information Quarterly* 29, no. 1 (2012): 12–20.
Napoli, Philip M., and Joe Karaganis. "On making public policy with publicly available data: The case of US communications policymaking." *Government Information Quarterly* 27, no. 4 (2010): 384–391.
Norris, Pippa, and John Curtice. "If you build a political web site, will they come?" *International Journal of Electronic Government Research* 2, no. 2 (2006): 1–21.
Noveck, Beth Simone. *Wiki government: How technology can make government better, democracy stronger, and citizens more powerful*. Washington, DC: Brookings Institution Press, 2009.
Obama, B. "Executive Order 13642, Making open and machine readable the new default for government information." *Whitehouse.gov* 9 (2013).
Office of Management and Budget. "Guidelines for ensuring and maximizing the quality, objectivity, utility, and integrity of information disseminated by federal agencies." *67 FR 8452*, October 1, 2001. Retrieved from https://www.whitehouse.gov/omb/fedreg_final_information_quality_guidelines/
Orszag, P. "Open government initiative." *Memorandum for the heads of executive departments and agencies*, 2009. Retrieved from https://www.whitehouse.gov/open/documents/open-government-directive
Parks, Wallace. "Open government principle: Applying the right to know under the constitution." *The George Washington Law Review* 26 (1957): 1–22.

Peled, Alon. "When transparency and collaboration collide: The USA open data program." *Journal of the American Society for Information Science and Technology* 62, no. 11 (2011): 2085–2094.

Pyrozhenko, Vadym. "Open government missing questions." *Administration & Society* (2015): DOI: 10.1177/0095399715581624.

Reddick, Christopher, and Sukumar Ganapati. "Open government achievement and satisfaction in US federal agencies: Survey evidence for the three pillars." *Journal of E-Governance* 34, no. 4 (2011): 193–202.

Relyea, Harold C. "Congress and freedom of information: A retrospective and a look at a current issue." *Government Information Quarterly* 26, no. 3 (2009): 437–440.

Robinson, David G., Harlan Yu, William P. Zeller, and Edward W. Felten. "Government data and the invisible hand." *Yale Journal of Law & Technology* 11 (2012): 160.

Schachter, Hindy Lauer. *Reinventing government or reinventing ourselves: The role of citizen owners in making a better government.* Albany, NY: SUNY Press, 1997.

Thaler, Richard H., and Will Tucker. "Smarter information, smarter consumers." *Harvard Business Review* 91, no. 1 (2013): 44–54.

U.S. Department of Justice. 2013–2014 agency FOIA success stories (August 2014). Retrieved from http://www.justice.gov/oip/2013-2014-agency-foia-success-stories

Veljković, Nataša, Sanja Bodganović-Dinić, and Leonid Stoimenov. "Benchmarking open government: An open data perspective." *Government Information Quarterly* 31, no. 2 (2014): 278–290.

Wilson, Susan Copeland, and Dennis Linders. "The open government directive: A preliminary assessment." In *Proceedings of the 2011 iConference*, pp. 387–394. ACM, 2011.

Yu, Harlan, and David G. Robinson. "The new ambiguity of 'open government'." *UCLA Law Review Discourse* 59 (2012): 178–208.

16
TECHNOLOGY, TRANSPARENCY, AND LOCAL GOVERNMENT
Assessing the Opportunities and Challenges

Gregory A. Porumbescu, Peter Schaak, and Erica Ceka

Rapid advances in the field of information and communication technology (ICT) have served to usher in what many refer to as the "information age" (Keohane and Nye 1998; Fuchs 2007; Castells 2011). Accordingly, through the use of technologies such as computers, mobile devices, and the Internet, citizens today are able to access information on a scale that is without historical precedent. As they relate to government, the implications of such developments are considerable because of the scope with which they stand to affect the way public organizations operate (Weerakkody and Dhillon 2008; Bannister and Connolly 2011). To this end, perhaps one characteristic of public organizations most affected by ICT and the dawning of the information age is their transparency.

Transparency has long been seen as a defining feature of good governance (Meijer 2015). As such, contexts that tend to be more transparent are often found to enjoy a number of benefits, including higher levels of trust in government (Grimmelikhuijsen et al. 2013), to lower levels of public corruption (Park and Blenkinsopp 2011), and improved decision-making in public organizations (Bok 1989). Moreover, through its ability to improve the public's understanding of what their government is doing and why, transparency is also thought of as a key prerequisite of a more responsive public sector. Accordingly, because of its diffuse influence on the way government functions, transparency is reasoned to constitute a "regime value" that dictates the way work is carried out in public organizations (see Piotrowski 2014). Therefore, for public organizations, there is a strong impetus to seek out ways of enhancing transparency. Yet, while the incentives for more transparent public organizations have existed for some time, the means of delivering greater transparency have historically been limited due to technological constraints.

Today, however, due to the rapid proliferation of new ICTs, this long-standing hurdle to greater transparency has been, in large part, overcome in the sense that most governments in the United States now possess the basic technology needed to store and disseminate large quantities of objective information to the public en masse (Porumbescu 2015b). Because of these developments, interest in transparency from practitioners and academics has surged (Piotrowski 2014). In turn, the upshot of this increased interest is a more careful and data-driven assessment of the instrumental benefits commonly said to accompany greater levels of public sector transparency (Welch, Hinnant and Moon 2005; Grimmelikhuijsen et al. 2013). In general, the results of such analyses have helped to foster a growing awareness of a new generation of challenges that accompany attempts to enhance transparency. When taken together, what these new challenges to enhanced transparency serve to highlight is a subtle, yet substantive, shift in terms of the discourse surrounding government transparency (Porumbescu 2015b). Perhaps nowhere is this shift in discourse better illustrated than in the context of local government due to their close proximity to the citizens they serve. The close proximity of local public managers and elected officials to citizens makes them more visible and accountable, which, in turn can motivate local governments to enhance transparency in an attempt to enhance public trust and demonstrate that decisions are responsive to citizens' demands and needs.

To this end, this chapter possesses two primary objectives. The first is, in light of new technologies that are being used to increase transparency, to consider in greater detail the challenges local governments are facing in their attempts to enhance transparency. The second objective of this study is to examine strategies being put into place by local governments in an attempt to overcome such challenges. We focus upon local government in particular in this study because the close proximity between citizens and local government make the linkage between transparency and implications for good governance particularly apparent. Nevertheless, implications for other areas of government may also certainly be inferred, even if they are not addressed explicitly in this study.

This chapter proceeds as follows. First, we outline a definition of transparency and explain how technology is being used to enhance transparency. Second, we review evidence that discusses the various ways enhanced transparency is contributing to "good governance," if at all. Third, we provide an overview of challenges that local governments face when using ICT to enhance transparency. Fourth, we discuss some approaches to overcoming such challenges in an attempt to more fully realize the benefits thought to stem from greater transparency.

1 Government Transparency in the Information Age

Given the great deal of interest the topic of transparency has attracted over the course of the past decade, a variety of definitions of this term has been proffered. Yet, despite this, most definitions tend to hold in common certain key features. Drawing upon these key features, Grimmelikhuijsen et al. (2013: 576) define public sector transparency as "the availability of information about an organization or actor that allows external actors to monitor the internal workings or performance of the organization." Based upon this definition, the extent to which a public organization is transparent can be said to depend upon three factors: the ability to publicly disclose information, the types of information being disclosed to the public, and the scope of public actors able to access and consume the information that is being publicly disclosed. Each of these factors is explained in greater detail below.

The Ability to Publicly Disclose Information

Historically, public organizations have transmitted information to external stakeholders, namely citizens, via direct face-to-face interactions in forums such as town hall meetings. Given the structure of society, the face-to-face transmission of government information to the public was feasible in the sense that communities tended to be smaller and more tightly integrated, thereby facilitating the transmission of this type of information (Meijer 2009). However, as the scale of society has expanded over time, government has been forced to adopt alternative methods of bringing government information to the public, thereby leading to the emergence of various forms of "mediated-transparency" (Hood 2007). While historically, various forms of media, such as print newspapers, television, and radio, have constituted important forms of mediated transparency, today, by far the most prevalent form of mediated transparency is computer-mediated transparency (Grimmelikhuijsen and Welch 2012).

As Meijer (2009: 259) explains, "computer-mediated transparency refers to the ability to look clearly through the windows of an institution through the use of computerized systems." In large part, the increased prevalence of computer-mediated transparency can be attributed to increased diffusion of ICTs, such as the Internet, which has enabled local governments to transmit large volumes of information to the public for very little cost. Moreover, in addition to allowing local governments to publicly disclose large volumes of information, the "always on" nature of the Internet and citizens' easy access to various computing devices mean that the public is imbued with the capacity to access said information whenever they find convenient (Moon and Norris 2005). Therefore, by most accounts the rise of computer-mediated transparency has been seen as a positive development in that it has improved local government's ability to bring relevant information to the public it serves.

The Information Publicly Disclosed

As indicated by the definition of transparency outlined earlier, in order to enhance transparency, the information being publicly disclosed by government must stand to improve the public's understanding of what their government is doing. To this end, it is helpful to assess the contribution information makes to enhancing transparency according along two dimensions. The first dimension relates to types of information disseminated, whereas the second dimension refers to the qualities of the information being disseminated (Grimmelikhuijsen 2012).

With respect to the first dimension, in order for citizens to have a comprehensive understanding of what their government is doing, they must have access to relevant information pertaining to the different activities government engages in. To provide a more systematic understanding of the different types of information that must be publicly disclosed in order to meaningfully enhance citizens' understanding of the activities their government engages in, previous research has offered some helpful frameworks. The first framework attempts to parse out types of information needed to enhance transparency by assuming a process-based perspective (Heald 2003; Grimmelikhuijsen 2012). Accordingly, this framework places information into one of three categories. The first category relates to decision-making and outlines the different factors that were considered in the decision to adopt a particular policy. Following this, the second category of information focuses upon detailing specifics of the policy that has been adopted, such as how said policy intends to address a particular issue, and the implications this policy will have for those in the community. The third category deals with information that explains how a particular policy performed in addressing a particular issue, and therefore focuses upon factors such as outputs and outcomes. *The second framework* attempts to parse out information needed to enhance transparency by focusing upon specific functions government performs (Cucciniello and Nasi 2014). This framework consists of four categories. The first category of information is institutional and offers details on the standard protocols of a particular public institution. The second dimension relates to political information. To this end, this information concerns elected officials and discusses issues such as compensation and participation in various formal and informal events. The third dimension relates to the topic of financial management—how much money various actors and organizations are allotted, and what they are using the money for. The final dimension focuses upon issues related to public service delivery. Specifically, this type of information focuses upon discussing how various public services are performing, as well as how to access particular public services.

When taken together, these two frameworks help to illustrate that, in order to enhance transparency and improve citizens' understanding of their government, citizens must be afforded access to diverse types of information. To this end, attempts to enhance transparency are not simply quantitative in the sense that more information disclosure makes government more transparent, but instead hinge heavily upon ensuring that citizens also have access to all of the different types of information that are needed to accurately observe what their government is doing.

The second dimension that must be considered when evaluating transparency relates to the characteristics of the information being publicly disclosed. To evaluate this dimension, one helpful framework has been put forth by Grimmelikhuijsen (2012), and consists of three characteristics in particular. The first characteristic to be considered is the timeliness of the information. For example, information that is outdated is unlikely to play much of a role in helping citizens to better understand what their government is doing currently. To this end, in order for information to actually contribute to transparency, it must be current. The second characteristic to be considered is the "color" of the information. Oftentimes, there is a tendency for government to avoid disclosing information that is self-critical, or to "spin" information in order to cast government performance in a positive, or less negative, light (Grimmelikhuijsen 2011: 39). Yet, such actions detract from the objective depiction of government performance, and in turn contribute to an inaccurate or biased understanding of government. Thus, in order to enhance transparency, information must be objective. The third characteristic to consider is the comprehensibility of the information being provided to the public. While the details of government performance can be complex, the emphasis here is upon making sure that the general public is capable of processing the information they are afforded access to. In this sense, in order for information to enhance transparency, the general public must be capable of understanding this information.

Public Access to Government Information

A final point to address here is the importance of ensuring citizens' access to government information. While intuitively, emphasis tends to be placed upon the disclosure of information to the public, it is also important to ensure that the information being made public is accessible to the different constituents a particular government serves. The reason for this is that, if transparency is not enhanced to similar extents across different segments of the population, local governments then run the risk of becoming more transparent to some segments of the population and less transparent to others, thereby creating the potential for an erosion of democratic norms.

To date, perhaps the most effective means of ensuring broad access to local government information is to draw upon multiple communication channels, including print media, radio, and various Internet outlets to increase the likelihood that all relevant external stakeholders are able to access information about their local government. By spreading information out over various channels, local governments are better able to reach a broader cross-section of society. The reason for this is that different sociopolitical factors often lead individuals to prefer one information outlet over another, meaning that if a local government pursues a presence on some outlets, but neglects others, there is a risk that some segments of the population will lack access to government information. Thus, in sum, the act of being transparent also necessitates ensuring that all segments of society are able to access government information.

2 The Link between Transparency and Good Governance

For some time, transparency has been seen as a key tool in attempts to improve the quality of governance. In large part, transparency's contribution to good governance relates to the notion that transparency enables the public to better monitor the performance of their government (Porumbescu and Im 2015). In turn, improving the public's ability to monitor the performance of their government is said to contribute to the quality of governance in three broad ways. Below, these three broad benefits are discussed in greater detail.

Improved Interaction between Citizens and Government

The first category of benefits relates to improving the quality of exchanges between citizens and government. As James Madison wrote long ago, "a people who mean to be their own Governors must arm themselves with the power which knowledge gives." (Madison 1999: 790, cited in Piotrowski 2014: 185). To this end, what this popular quote serves to highlight is that any democratic form of government is premised upon the notion of shared decision-making that is centered upon the demands and needs to citizens. If citizens are unaware of what their government does, what it is capable of doing, or why it does things in a certain way, citizen inputs into the decision-making process will be either of limited value, or in the worst case, detrimental to the overall quality of decision-making, as Madison highlights in the quote referenced above.

While there are a number of ways in which citizens may be able to access government information that can help them to better understand what their government is doing, such as mass media outlets, the challenge is always to ensure that citizens are accessing information that is objective. This is important because the intention of democratic processes is to ensure that each citizen is able to assert their own opinion on a particular issue, and this can only be done if citizens are left to make up their own mind on an issue. If citizens are only able to obtain information that adheres to a particular pro- or anti-government slant, their opinion on a particular issue is likely to be heavily biased by the subjective information they are using, which in turn can potentially obstruct the citizen's ability to assert their own opinion. In turn, this can contribute to an erosion of democratic processes. Thus, by providing objective information to citizens, transparency helps citizens to more accurately understand what their government is doing and why, which in turn contributes to their ability to voice their own perspectives regarding various issues in government.

The temporal dimension of transparency also affects the quality of interactions between the citizens and government. If citizens lack access to information before decisions are made and are informed retrospectively about governmental actions, their ability to voice their *own* opinion and participate in the decision-making process is jeopardized. Hence, real-time transparency provides citizens an opportunity to become involved in policy development and enhances that accountability of government at any stage of the policy decision-making process. Therefore, timely information disclosure by government is useful because it serves as a means to build a meaningful two-way interaction between citizens and government.

As such, the quality of interactions between citizens and their local government are heavily contingent upon citizens' understanding of their local government and the timely disclosure of objective government information, as this information stands to improve citizens' understanding of government. Conversely, subjective information or delayed release of government information can detract from citizens' ability to understand what their government is doing, thereby resulting in lower quality interactions between citizens and their government.

More Positive Perceptions of Government

The second category relates to improving citizens' perceptions of government. A wealth of previous literature has indicated that citizens' perceptions of government are often premised upon inaccurate or incomplete information (Orren 1997; Kelly 2002; Im et al. 2014). As a result, citizens are often not aware of how well their government is performing, and the various initiatives that are undertaken to enhance citizens' well-being (Mettler 2011). This vein of argument continues to suggest that citizens' lack of objective information culminates in a situation where information asymmetries said to exist between citizens and their government contributes to more critical evaluations of government.

The comprehensibility of public information plays an important role in citizens' perception of government. When the information disclosed is presented in a simple and clear format to external stakeholders, it does not require an extraordinary effort on the part of citizens to understand it. Thus, citizens, regardless of their age or education level, are not only informed about what their government is doing, but they also are able to comprehend and interpret the information, which may counteract negative evaluations of government performance.

Negative perceptions of government are problematic because citizens' perceptions of government bear heavily upon government efficiency and effectiveness. For example, in contexts where citizens tend to view their government more negatively, costs of implementing policies are generally higher (Scholz and Lubell 1998), recruiting talent to a career in the public service is more challenging (Van de Walle 2004), and levels of citizen participation are often low (Berman 1997). Put differently, when citizens' perceptions of government are more negative, transaction costs for government increase, and it becomes more difficult for government to know just what actions are in the general public's best interests, due to declining levels of citizen participation.

Thus, a common argument is that transparency can serve to improve perceptions of local government because of its role in providing citizens with objective and comprehensible information that outlines in a clear and simple format the different initiatives undertaken by local government that are intended to improve citizens' well-being. In turn, by improving perceptions of local government, local governments are positioned to perform more efficiently and effectively than otherwise.

A More Responsive Government

The third category relates to the important role transparency is said to play in bringing about a more accountable and responsive government. Central to this line of argumentation is that transparency acts as a basis for accountability, in that it enables citizens to document ways in which the performance of government departs from the demands of citizens. Based upon this information, citizens are then able to use various democratic accountability mechanisms to effect changes that lead government to perform in a manner that more closely reflects citizens' demands. All told, what the ideas outlined here serve to suggest is the presence of a causal chain, whereby transparency is said to enhance government accountability, which in turn leads to a more democratic and responsive government. In this sense, transparency can be seen as a method used to reduce bureaucratic autonomy by expanding external oversight (Porumbescu and Im 2015).

However, in addition to the ideas outlined in the preceding paragraph, transparency is also thought to indirectly contribute to more responsive government. In this situation, timely public disclosure of information by government can act as a disincentive for public officials to act in ways that are not consonant with the public's best interests. It is for this reason in part that higher levels of transparency are commonly associated with lower levels of corruption (Bertot, Jaeger, and Grimes 2010).

3   Challenges to Realizing the Link between Transparency and Good Governance

In the previous section, we outlined ways in which transparency is said to contribute to that quality of governance. However, as local government increasingly works to enhance transparency by using different forms of technology, what becomes apparent is that a number of challenges serve to complicate links between transparency and good governance. In this section, we provide an overview of these challenges as discussed in previous empirical research. To structure our discussion of challenges, we draw upon the three broad contributions transparency makes to good governance, as outlined in the previous section.

Improved Interaction between Citizens and Government

The basic argument that underpins the link between transparency and improved quality of interactions between citizens and their local government is that increased information will empower citizens to make decisions that more closely align with their best interests. In this sense, transparency is thought to contribute toward more rational decision-making on the part of citizens (Fox 2007). However, decades worth of empirical research from subdisciplines of psychology, such as consumer psychology or social psychology, suggest that enhancing transparency will have little influence upon the choices citizens make as they relate to local government.

To explain, this body of research typically finds that the way in which we consume and interpret information is subject to a number of cognitive biases. At a very general level, many cognitive biases exist for the purpose of safeguarding existing beliefs and opinions (Festinger 1957; Akerlof and Dickens 1982). This statement is perhaps best illustrated by various applications of cognitive dissonance theory, such as motivated reasoning (Kunda 1990). Research on motivated reasoning typically finds that individuals possess a subconscious motivation to reinforce existing beliefs. As a result of this deep-seated motivation, individuals will avoid information that they believe will challenge their beliefs, and/or selectively interpret information in a way that discredits the veracity of information that calls in to question an extant belief.

The discussion above can be interpreted to suggest that transparency will primarily serve to reinforce citizens' extant opinions and attitudes toward their local government. As a result, transparency would not be expected to alter citizens' decision-making, nor would it be likely to affect their intentions to participate in public affairs. To this end, a first stream of challenges that stand in the way of improving the quality of interactions between citizens and their local government relates to cognitive biases.

More Positive Perceptions of Government

The various cognitive biases outlined above are also likely to detract from transparency's ability to improve citizens' perceptions of their local government. In part, this may be because citizens who tend not to trust their government will also be unlikely to trust information that is disseminated by government, whereas citizens who tend to be dissatisfied with government performance will disregard information that casts the performance of public services in a positive light. Therefore, from this perspective, enhanced transparency may actually serve to contribute to more negative perceptions of local government, especially in contexts where citizens already hold negative opinions of local government.

Another important issue that complicates the relationship between transparency and perceptions of local government is the fact that citizens have been found to perceive various areas of government differently. Specifically, citizens' evaluations may differ according to public services, or according to level of government. In this sense, information needed to improve perceptions in one area of government may differ from the information needed to improve perceptions of other areas of government. In other instances, increasing transparency may positively influence perceptions of some aspects of government, while negatively influencing perceptions of other areas of government. This can relate to particular public services, or different levels of government.

With respect to citizens' evaluations of particular public services, prior research has suggested that evaluations are often contingent upon citizens' level of sympathy for the particular service (Kampen, Van De Walle and Bouckaert 2006). For example, citizens may hold a negative opinion of the Internal Revenue Service, despite that fact that it performs well, whereas the same set of citizens may hold a positive opinion of the police force, despite the fact that the police in their community are performing poorly. Thus, the point illustrated here is that determinants of the way citizens evaluate different areas of government will vary across different facets of government. As a result, improving enhancing citizens' access to objective data on the performance of public services may help to improve perceptions of some public services, while negatively influencing perceptions of others. Conversely, information explicating how a particular service contributes to citizens' well-being may serve to improve citizens' perceptions of some public services, whereas for others this information has no impact at all on perceptions. Thus, in addition to overcoming cognitive biases, the additional challenge highlighted here is knowing how different types of information will relate to citizens' perceptions of different areas of government.

With respect to citizens' evaluations of different levels of government, additional research has found that increasing levels of transparency may actually affect perceptions and evaluations differently across levels of government. To explain, one approach to understanding citizens' perceptions of government is to divide government into three overlapping—micro, meso, and macro—levels (see Bouckaert et al. 2002). The first micro level deals with perceptions of individuals charged with delivering public services, whereas the second level relates to perceptions of public services and public institutions. At the first and second levels of government, evaluations are said to be influenced by citizens' perception that government is "doing things well." The macro level concerns government in a more abstract sense. At this third level of government, evaluations are said to be influenced by citizens' perception that government is "doing the right things." Based upon this framework, research by Porumbescu (2015a) has examined how transparency influences perceptions of different levels of government. What Porumbescu found was that transparency possessed a negative relationship to perceptions of the meso level of government, whereas transparency was found to possess a positive relationship with the macro level of government. Moreover, this study also suggested that part of this relationship might stem from the fact that, while the transparent information citizens were afforded access to occasionally construed public services or institutions in a negative light, citizens appreciated the fact that their government was honest with them and did not attempt to hide this information. In other words, while transparency served to demonstrate to citizens that government did not always do things well, it was doing the right thing, by being honest. Thus, drawing upon the results of this study, the second challenge that is highlighted is that the effects of a single piece of information can differ substantially according to the particular area of government in question. As a result, this can make formulating a comprehensive strategy for enhancing transparency a controversial issue.

A More Responsive Government

The link between transparency and local government responsiveness is premised upon the idea that government will respond to the demands of citizens. What this implies is that initiatives to enhance transparency must be supplemented with the creation of opportunities for citizens to act on the information they have been afforded. In eras where direct or face-to-face transparency was prevalent, citizens' access to government information came from participation in council meetings and direct interactions with government representatives. As a result, eras of direct transparency were marked by a dynamic exchange of information between citizens and government. As such, the creation of such feedback loops were not necessary, due to the direct exchanges of information that occurred between citizens and their government. Today, where computer-mediated transparency is the most prevalent form of transparency, it is no longer possible to take for granted citizens' ability to act on or reply to the information they consume. To this end, a major challenge with respect to linking transparency to government responsiveness relates to affording citizens new forums wherein they can act upon the information afforded to them via computer-mediated transparency.

As many studies have indicated, governments' use of ICT to communicate with citizens typically emphasizes a one-way flow of information from citizens to government (Pina, Torres and Royo 2007; Mergel 2013). This means that governments are generally not using new technologies to afford citizens genuine opportunities to influence existing administrative processes. However, in part, the reluctance to use technology to allow for citizens' inputs may be for good reason. Specifically, as discussions on the digital divide serve to highlight, digital literacy, as well as access to computer-mediated transparency, will differ according to various segments of the population. This means that only small segments of society would be able to act upon the information they were exposed to, whereas many other segments of the population, lacking attributes such as digital literacy or access to high-speed Internet would have no input in such forums of accountability. As a result, the potential would be created for the majority of government decision-making to be driven by a small nonrepresentative segment of the population. To this end, a more discrete challenge in this age of computer-mediated transparency relates to questions of how to create outlets for citizen participation online, while at the same time soliciting input and participation from various segments of the population.

4   Overcoming the Challenges to the Link between Transparency and Good Governance

In the previous section, three broad challenges that complicate the relationship between transparency and good governance were identified. In this section, we detail ways in which local governments are making use of new technologies in hopes of overcoming such barriers. Generally, these initiatives focus upon three strands. The first relates to diversifying methods of online information delivery. The second relates to making local government websites more inclusive. The third relates to developing more personalized methods of information delivery. Each of these initiatives is discussed in greater detail below.

Diversifying Methods of Online Information Delivery

As ICT has matured, the avenues that can be used to disseminate information online have expanded rapidly. In turn, acknowledging that most citizens now use some form of computing device, these developments have enabled local governments to reach out to citizens through the use of a diverse array of technologies, including tablets, smartphone apps, desktop computers, and text messages.

The use of multiple forms of technology to disseminate information by local governments is a positive development, as doing so will help to overcome various challenges posed by an ever-evolving digital divide. The reason for this is that various demographic and political factors can lead an individual to use certain forms of technology to obtain information about government and not others. For example, lower income demographics are typically found to rely heavily upon mobile technology to obtain information about local government, whereas wealthier segments of the population tend to make greater use of laptops and personal computers to search for government information (Van Dijk and Hacker 2003; Wareham, Levy and Shi 2004). For example, a recent analysis by the Pew Research Center (Anderson 2015) has found that African American and Hispanic populations are more likely to use smartphones when searching for information related to education or employment topics.[1] This tendency may be because many members of these groups are only able to access the Internet through their cell phones. Therefore, efforts on the part of local governments to create mobile-friendly web portals and smartphone apps can serve as an effective means of communicating with a broader spectrum of external stakeholders. By expanding citizens' access to government information through the use of different forms of technology, these developments also serve to create the potential for more inclusive online accountability forums.

Making Government Websites More Inclusive

Many in society today may, for various reasons, have difficulty reading information that is posted to local government web portals (Goette, Collier and White 2006). As a result, there is the potential for individuals who, for various reasons, cannot read e-government websites to be left behind. To this end, a second major initiative being undertaken by local governments targets inclusiveness with respect to access to government information by ensuring that government web portals adhere to standards set by the American with Disabilities Act (ADA) and offering multi-language support.

Broadly, these initiatives can be seen as complementary to those outlined in the previous section, in that these changes also focus on inclusiveness, albeit from a slightly different perspective. In this sense, the point of emphasis is upon upgrading the way information is being presented to the public in order to make it more comprehensible. We see a strong tendency for local governments to make great strides in this respect, not only by modifying their portals to make them ADA compliant and providing information in multiple languages, but also by attempting to make information understandable to citizens coming from diverse educational backgrounds. All told, the general trend observed here is one in which local governments are working to capitalize upon the added functionality of ICTs to make government information more accessible to the general public. This is a positive trend, though more must be done.

Developing More Personalized Methods of Information Delivery

A final initiative used by local governments to overcome some of the challenges outlined earlier relates to delivering information to citizens in a more personalized manner. To this end, we see a number of initiatives being undertaken by governments that serve the purpose of decentralizing the flow of information from government to citizens, in order to allow citizens access to information they deem most relevant to them. Moreover, through such efforts at decentralizing the flow of information, citizens are also better able to establish personal connections with those in public office.

One prominent example of this trend is the increased uptake of social media accounts, such as Twitter, by various departments in local governments. Using social media, citizens are able to obtain information that is most relevant to them. Accordingly, by allowing citizens to follow specific aspects of government, they are able to read and see the various ways in which their government is working to contribute to their well-being. As such, by allowing citizens to subscribe to areas of government they are personally interested in, seeds for overcoming various forms of cognitive biases, which detract from citizens' ability to act in their own best interest, are sown (cf. Jost and Andrews 2011). Enabling citizens to better understand just how one area of government is working to advance citizens' best interests could also enable citizens to see just how other areas of government are also working to advance their best interests. In turn, personalized methods of enhancing transparency can initiate gradual and indirect, yet at the same time broad, attitudinal changes with respect to government. A second initiative to note is the use of chat functions on various government websites. The major benefit of these chat functions is that they allow citizens to communicate with government representatives directly and at their own convenience. Through such exchanges, government is able to establish personalized connections with the citizens it serves, which are not possible with other forms of ICTs, with the exception of telephones. Furthermore, these chat functions will also help demonstrate to citizens how, on various levels, their government is working to respond to their needs. A final method that bears mentioning relates to non-emergency 311 call centers. These call centers are rapidly springing up in local governments across the world and, increasingly, occupy a vital function for local governments because they serve to provide citizens with a means of instantaneously obtaining the specific information they are interested in. In this respect, 311 call centers provide citizens with precisely the information they are looking for, while minimizing the transaction costs associated with sifting through mounds of government information.

While the challenges to realizing the transformative benefits of transparency are formidable, it is also apparent that local governments are acquiring the expansive toolset necessary to address such challenges. Moreover, and perhaps most importantly, there is also evidence of a strong desire on the part of local governments to successfully address these challenges in order to establish stronger working relationships with the communities they represent. These are very promising points to bear in mind. Indeed, as is made apparent in this discussion, government already has many of the tools it needs in order to cultivate a broader and richer understanding of what government is doing. Many of the strategies outlined above are in their nascent stages and, despite being at such an early stage in their development, are demonstrating potential to deliver information not only to a broader segment of the population, but also in a way that is easier for various segments of the population to understand and via methods that are easily accessible for them. This is no small feat.

All told, the initiatives outlined here to serve the purpose of delivering government information to citizens in a more personalized manner can play an important role in mitigating the aforementioned challenges. In large part, this is because this method of information delivery allows local governments to craft a more comprehensive and nuanced/tailored transparency policy, which accounts for the possibility that a single piece of information can affect two distinct areas of government in very different ways. By using technologies to deliver information in this way, government is able to instigate a gradual, yet conspicuous, shift in terms of its relationships with multiple segments of the population.

Conclusion and Discussion

Today, transparency is an issue that is receiving a great deal of attention, which partly stems from rapid ICT advances that have enabled local governments to overcome issues that, in the past, have limited its ability to publicly disclose information. As such, through the use of new technologies to disclose greater amounts of information to more citizens, the hope is that local governments will not only be able to enhance their levels of openness and transparency, but also to bring about broad improvements to the quality of governance. However, while many local governments are now pursuing various initiatives to enhance transparency, evidence on how these attempts are affecting the quality of government has been mixed. In light of this uncertainty, the objectives of this study were two-fold. The first was to examine the types of challenges that are quickly coming to the fore as local governments increasingly draw upon ICT as a means of enhancing transparency. The second to examine strategies being used in an attempt to overcome challenges to realizing the benefits of enhanced transparency.

In addressing the first objective, three broad challenges were identified: the first relates to overcoming cognitive biases that influence the way citizens interpret new information; the second relates to difficulties in formulating a comprehensive strategy for enhancing transparency; and the third relates to ensuring broad access to information that is being publicly disseminated. In addressing the second objective, we have identified strategies being put into place by local governments that intend to overcome the aforementioned challenges. These strategies include diversifying methods of information delivery, making local government websites more inclusive, and personalizing the delivery of government information to citizens. Regarding the discussion of challenges and potential solutions, some important implications can be drawn.

Perhaps one of the most important implications stemming from this discussion is that advances in technology have an important influence upon the shape that local governments' efforts to enhance transparency take. In light of local governments' ability to now transmit large volumes of information publicly, we see that governments must also begin to consider more closely how new technologies can be used to render information presented to citizens in a way that is comprehensible to the general public. In part, this will require closer attention to ways in which these new technologies can be used to better structure and present information. While we see some initial progress toward this objective through integrating chat functions into e-government portals and providing access to information in a variety of languages, further work is necessary in this regard.

An additional implication that builds upon the preceding paragraph pertains to the sustainability of initiatives that seek to enhance transparency. Specifically, given that advances in technology are persistently changing the way citizens interact with their governments, the pressure to continually adopt and use new computer-mediated methods of information dissemination is immense. In large part, this is because citizens have demonstrated a tendency to jump from one form of technology to obtain information to another within very short time periods—obsolescence of information dissemination channels is a common occurrence today. Given this situation, sustainability of local governments' attempts to enhance transparency are contingent upon their ability to draw upon *new* and *relevant* technologies to facilitate citizens' access to information that can be used to better understand government, as simply maintaining current information dissemination methods will, over time, result in a reduction in transparency.

Thus, when taking these points together, technology clearly creates the potential for local governments to enhance transparency and, as a result, to improve the quality of governance. However, while local governments have used new technologies to help overcome a long-standing hurdle to transparency, which is ensuring access to government information, they have also pointed to a new generation of challenges that complicate the link between transparency and good governance. This second generation of challenges relate to finding ways of ensuring that the information being disseminated is useful in the sense that the general public is capable of understanding the information they are being afforded.

Note

1. http://www.pewresearch.org/fact-tank/2015/04/30/racial-and-ethnic-differences-in-how-people-use-mobile-technology/

References

Akerlof, George A., and William T. Dickens. "The economic consequences of cognitive dissonance." *The American Economic Review* 72, no. 3 (1982): 307–319.

Anderson, Monica. "Racial and ethnic differences in how people use mobile technology." *Pew Research Center* 30 (2015). Retrieved from http://www.pewresearch.org/fact-tank/2015/04/30/racial-and-ethnic-differences-in-how-people-use-mobile-technology/

Bannister, Frank, and Regina Connolly. "Trust and transformational government: A proposed framework for research." *Government Information Quarterly* 28, no. 2 (2011): 137–147.

Berman, Evan M. "Dealing with cynical citizens." *Public Administration Review* 57, no. 2 (1997): 105–112.

Bertot, John C., Paul T. Jaeger, and Justin M. Grimes. "Using ICTs to create a culture of transparency: E-government and social media as openness and anti-corruption tools for societies." *Government Information Quarterly* 27, no. 3 (2010): 264–271.

Bok, Sissela. *Secrets: On the ethics of concealment and revelation.* New York: Vintage, 1989.

Bouckaert, Geert, Steven Van de Walle, Bart Maddens, and Jarl K. Kampen. "Identity vs Performance: An overview of theories explaining trust in government." *Second Report.* Leuven: Public Management Institute (January 2002).

Castells, Manuel. *The rise of the network society: The information age: Economy, society, and culture.* Vol. 1. West Sussex, UK: John Wiley & Sons, 2011.

Cucciniello, Maria, and Greta Nasi. "Evaluation of the impacts of innovation in the health care sector: A comparative analysis." *Public Management Review* 16, no. 1 (2014): 90–116.

Festinger, Leon. "Cognitive dissonance theory." *1989 Primary Prevention of HIV/AIDS: Psychological Approaches.* Newbury Park, California, Sage Publications, 1989 (originally published 1957).

Fox, Jonathan. "The uncertain relationship between transparency and accountability." *Development in Practice* 17, no. 4–5 (2007): 663–671.

Fuchs, Christian. *Internet and society: Social theory in the information age.* New York: Routledge, 2007.

Goette, Tanya, Caroline Collier, and Jennifer Daniels White. "An exploratory study of the accessibility of state government Web sites." *Universal Access in the Information Society* 5, no. 1 (2006): 41–50.

Grimmelikhuijsen, Stephan G. "Being transparent or spinning the message? An experiment into the effects of varying message content on trust in government." *Information Polity* 16, no. 1 (2011): 35–50.

Grimmelikhuijsen, Stephan G. "Transparency and trust: An experimental study of online disclosure and trust in government." Doctoral Dissertation, Utrecht University, the Netherlands (2012).

Grimmelikhuijsen, Stephan G., Gregory Porumbescu, Boram Hong, and Tobin Im. "The effect of transparency on trust in government: A cross-national comparative experiment." *Public Administration Review* 73, no. 4 (2013): 575–586.

Grimmelikhuijsen, Stephan G., and Eric W. Welch. "Developing and testing a theoretical framework for computer-mediated transparency of local governments." *Public Administration Review* 72, no. 4 (2012): 562–571.

Heald, David. "Fiscal transparency: Concepts, measurement and UK practice." *Public Administration* 81, no. 4 (2003): 723–759.

Hood, Christopher. "What happens when transparency meets blame-avoidance?" *Public Management Review* 9, no. 2 (2007): 191–210.

Im, Tobin, Wonhyuk Cho, Greg Porumbescu, and Jungho Park. "Internet, trust in government, and citizen compliance." *Journal of Public Administration Research and Theory* 24, no. 3 (2014): 741–763.

Jost, John T., and Rick Andrews. "System justification theory." *The Encyclopedia of Peace Psychology* November 13 (2011): 1–5. doi:10.1002/9780470672532.wbepp273.

Kampen, Jarl K., Steven Van De Walle, and Geert Bouckaert. "Assessing the relation between satisfaction with public service delivery and trust in government: The impact of the predisposition of citizens toward government on evalutations of its performance." *Public Performance & Management Review* 29, no. 4 (2006): 387–404.

Kelly, Janet M. "If you only knew how well we are performing, you'd be highly satisfied with the quality of our service." *National Civic Review* 91, no. 3 (2002): 283–292.

Keohane, Robert O., and Joseph S. Nye. "Power and interdependence in the information age." *Foreign Affairs-New York* 77 (1998): 81–94.

Kunda, Ziva. "The case for motivated reasoning." *Psychological Bulletin* 108, no. 3 (1990): 480.

Madison, James. "Letter to William T. Barry, August 4." In *James Madison: Writings 1772–1836*, ed. Jack N. Rakove, 790–93. New York: Library of America, 1999.

Meijer, Albert. "Understanding modern transparency." *International Review of Administrative Sciences* 75, no. 2 (2009): 255–269.

Meijer, Albert. "Government transparency in historical perspective: From the ancient regime to open data in the Netherlands." *International Journal of Public Administration* 38, no. 3 (2015): 189–199.

Mergel, Ines. "A framework for interpreting social media interactions in the public sector." *Government Information Quarterly* 30, no. 4 (2013): 327–334.

Mettler, Suzanne. *The submerged state: How invisible government policies undermine American democracy.* Chicago: University of Chicago Press, 2011.

Moon, M. Jae, and Donald F. Norris. "Does managerial orientation matter? The adoption of reinventing government and e-government at the municipal level*." *Information Systems Journal* 15, no. 1 (2005): 43–60.

Orren, Gary. "Fall from grace: The public's loss of faith in government." In *Why People Don't Trust Government 1997*, eds. Joseph S. Nye Jr., Philip D. Zelikow, and David C. King, 77–107. Cambridge, MA: Harvard University Press, 1997.

Park, Heungsik, and John Blenkinsopp. "The roles of transparency and trust in the relationship between corruption and citizen satisfaction." *International Review of Administrative Sciences* 77, no. 2 (2011): 254–274.

Pina, Vicente, Lourdes Torres, and Sonia Royo. "Are ICTs improving transparency and accountability in the EU regional and local governments? An empirical study." *Public Administration* 85, no. 2 (2007): 449–472.

Piotrowski, Suzanne J. "Transparency: A regime value linked with ethics." *Administration & Society* 46 (2014): 181–189. doi:10.1177/0095399713519098.

Porumbescu, Gregory A. "Does transparency improve citizens' perceptions of government performance? Evidence from Seoul, South Korea." *Administration & Society* July 6 (2015a):1–26. doi:10.1177/0095399715593314.

Porumbescu, Gregory A. "Using transparency to enhance responsiveness and trust in local government can it work?" *State and Local Government Review* 47, no. 3 (2015b): 205–213. doi:10.1177/0160323X15599427.

Porumbescu, Gregory A., and Tobin Im. "Using Transparency to Reinforce Responsibility and Responsiveness." In *The handbook of public administration 3rd edition 2015*, ed. James Perry and Robert Christensen, 120–136. San Francisco: Wiley, 2015.

Scholz, John T., and Mark Lubell. "Trust and taxpaying: Testing the heuristic approach to collective action." *American Journal of Political Science* 42, no. 2 (1998): 398–417.

Van de Walle, Steven. "Perceptions of administrative performance: the key to trust in government?" (2004). Doctoral Dissertation, Instituut voor de Overheid, Leuven, Belgium.

Van Dijk, Jan, and Kenneth Hacker. "The digital divide as a complex and dynamic phenomenon." *The Information Society* 19, no. 4 (2003): 315–326.

Wareham, Jonathan, Armando Levy, and Wei Shi. "Wireless diffusion and mobile computing: Implications for the digital divide." *Telecommunications Policy* 28, no. 5 (2004): 439–457.

Weerakkody, Vishanth, and Gurjit Dhillon. "Moving from e-government to t-government: A study of process reengineering challenges in a UK local authority context." *International Journal of Electronic Government Research* 4, no. 4 (2008): 1–16.

Welch, Eric W., Charles C. Hinnant, and M. Jae Moon. "Linking citizen satisfaction with e-government and trust in government." *Journal of Public Administration Research and Theory* 15, no. 3 (2005): 371–391.

17

PROTECTION OF PERSONALLY IDENTIFIABLE INFORMATION IN GOVERNMENT

A Survey of U.S. Regulatory Framework and Emerging Technological Challenges

Anna Ya Ni

Introduction

Technological innovations have amplified government's dual responsibilities in relation to personal privacy in recent decades. On one hand, as a central user of personal information, government regularly collects detailed information about its citizens and residents, including information on criminal charges, international travels, financial activities, employment status and earnings, medical treatments, personal disabilities, and so on. Such information is necessary for government to maintain law and order, collect revenues, and administer a variety of social welfare programs. Recent strides in technology increase privacy concerns as these upgrades have allowed for faster, easier storage of more data, and aggregation and cross-referencing of that data, even possibly without the owner's knowledge. Government collection of personal data is often perceived as an invasion of privacy. In the past several years, security breaches in government involving personal information have increased steadily (GAO 2008, 2013, 2015). For example, incidents involving breaches of sensitive data, such as government employee records, taxpayer information, public health records, etc., reported by federal agencies have risen from 5,503 in 2006 to 67,168 in 2014 (GAO 2015).

On the other hand, being charged to safeguard privacy, government enacts legislation and implements policies to protect intrusions into personal privacy by agencies, businesses, and other social entities. From its inception onward, the United States has constructed an extensive regulatory framework for the protection of personal information, including the Constitution, the common law of torts, and federal and state legislation, to regulate the right to privacy. In recent years, technological advancements have transformed the realm of privacy, and new sophisticated threats to individual privacy have proliferated. Contrary to the rapid and revolutionary technological changes, in the absence of satisfactory conceptualization of the policy problem, the formulation of policy to protect privacy on the basis of the existing regulatory framework has been slow and incremental, lagging far behind the pace of overall technological advancements.

The U.S. government is facing the challenge of effectively balancing the use of personal information with the requirements to be accountable to the public and protect individual rights to privacy as prescribed by the legislature in an age of accelerated technological and social changes. To help address the challenge, this chapter examines the policy issue in four areas: the U.S. regulatory framework for the protection of personal information, the recent technological innovations and government's technological initiatives as well as their implications to privacy, the problems involving the policy issue, and the European Union's approach to addressing the policy problem.

Privacy, Personal Data, Personal Information, and PII

In the study of information regulation, the terms privacy, personal data, personal information, and PII (personally identifiable information) are sometimes used interchangeably. The term privacy, often taken as "the right to be let alone (Warren and Brandeis 1890)," is relatively vague, ambiguous, and controversial. As a policy issue, "privacy" encompasses a broad range of values, all the way from the right to make personal decisions related to intimate relationships, to the right to be free from government, commercial, or individual intrusions. Bennett (1992) defines privacy as "the exclusiveness of physical space around an individual, to the autonomy of decision making without outside interference, and to the right to control the circulation of personal information" (p. 13). He also notes that the concept holds "much emotive and symbolic appeal" and it is "inadequate to conceptualize and frame" as a policy problem (p. 13).

The terms personal data and personal information share very similar meanings. For example, the European Union (EU) Data Protection Directive defines "personal data" as

> any information relating to a . . . natural person . . . who can be identified, directly or indirectly, in particular by reference . . . to one or more factors specific to his physical, physiological, mental, economic, cultural, or social identity.[1]

The term "personal information" is used in the Privacy Act of 1988 to refer to

> information or an opinion (including information or an opinion forming part of a database), whether true or not, and whether recorded in a material form or not, about an individual whose identity is apparent, or can reasonably be ascertained, from the information or opinion.[2]

Scholars in the field of information studies often differentiate information from data by emphasizing that information is data endowed with relevance and purpose, while data is simply an observation of the state of something. However, such nuance of difference in meaning seems not apparent in the study of privacy policies or information regulations.

The definition of PII, personally identifiable information, is more controversial and lacks consensus (Schwartz and Solove 2011). Generally speaking, PII refers to information that can be used on its own or in combination with other information to identify an individual in a given context (OMB 2007). Such information may include an individual's name, social security number, biometric records, IP address (in certain context), etc., which alone can be used to distinguish or trace the person. It may also be used in combination with other information, such as date and place of birth, name of employer, or mother's maiden name, that is linked or linkable to the individual to identify him/her in a certain context.

Personal data or information, when it cannot be used in any way to uniquely identify a particular person, does not invoke a privacy concern. Therefore, the central privacy concern of personal data or information is directly related to the PII.

Protection of PII only concerns one specific dimension of privacy—the right to have control over the collection, storage, use, transmittal, and disclosure of personal data or information that in any possible way can be used to identify a person. This right involves at least three areas: the control over others' use of one's personal information, the privilege to conceal personal information from others, and the restriction of access by others to one's personal information.

As a policy problem, the protection of PII is not only a legal issue, but also encompasses technical and management dimensions.

The Regulatory Framework of PII Protection

The United States has been using a "sectoral" approach to privacy policy making that relies on a combination of legislation, regulation, and self-regulation, rather than on mere government regulation alone. The resulting framework for the protection of PII constitutes a patchwork of laws, which includes the Constitution, the common law of torts, and federal and state legislation, to regulate the right to privacy.

The U.S. Constitution

The U.S. Constitution does not explicitly guarantee the right to privacy. The Bill of Rights, however, addresses the concern of the founding fathers about government's intrusion into an individual's various aspects of privacy. The First Amendment protects the privacy of speech from government intrusion, warranting the free flow of information. The Third Amendment protects the privacy of one's home against demands to be used for housing soldiers. The Fourth Amendment protects the privacy of a person and his/her possessions against unreasonable searches. The Fifth Amendment warrants the privilege against self-incrimination and prohibits government from taking private property for public use without due process of law and just compensation, thus implying protection for the privacy of personal information. This right was later extended by the Supreme Court to protect stored data in *Ruckelshaus v. Monsanto Co.*[3]

In addition to specific aspects of privacy protection, the Ninth Amendment declares that the "enumeration of certain rights" in the Bill of Rights "shall not be construed to deny or disparage other rights retained by the people," conferring that a right cannot be infringed by government even though it is not explicitly mentioned in the Constitution. The Fourteenth Amendment further extends the right of due process to privacy, as recognized by several Supreme Court Justices in *Griswold v. Connecticut*.[4]

It was not until 1977 in Whalen v. Roe that the Supreme Court first explicitly addressed the issue of the right to information privacy.[5] A lawsuit was brought about by a group of patients, doctors, and two associations of physicians concerning whether a New York statutes' requirement of reporting and storage of prescription information for abused drugs to the state for processing in a centralized computer file constituted an invasion of a patient's right of privacy. Though the statute was upheld, the Court recognized an individual's right to have his personal information remain private.

Common Law Torts

While the Constitution protects one's privacy from governmental invasion, common-law torts extend the protection against intrusions into one's privacy not only from government, but also by private parties. Common-law tort rules against actions that unfairly cause someone to suffer loss or harm. Torts may result from negligent but not intentional or criminal actions. Tort lawsuits generally have a lower burden of proof. According to the American *Restatement (Second) of Torts*,[6] invasion of privacy is a tort, that an aggrieved person can bring a lawsuit against a party who unlawfully intrudes into his/her private affairs (the tort of intrusion of solitude), uses his/her name for personal gain (the tort of appropriation of name or likeness), discloses his/her private information (the tort of public disclosure of private facts), or publicizes him/her in a false light (the tort of false light).

Federal Statutes

A large array of federal statutes govern the use of personal information as a result of the industrial-sectoral approach used by Congress. Instead of prescribing general principles, Congress enacted statutes one at a time to address various specific privacy concerns. Generally speaking, such statutes regulate certain activities, such as the collection of private data, of a specific industry or an economic sector, as well as a government agency. Statutes that govern government agencies generally address the following four aspects of personal information:

1. Protecting individuals from the intrusion or abuse of government

Wiretap Statutes,[7] first enacted in 1934, restrict listening to telephone conversations. The statutes have since been extended to prohibit the use of eavesdropping technology and the interception of electronic mail, radio communications, and data transmission without consent. The Federal Communications Commission statute specifically prohibits the recording of telephone conversations without prior notice or consent. The Administrative Procedure Act,[8] enacted June 11, 1946, governs the way in which federal administrative agencies may propose and establish regulations. The Act establishes detailed procedures for federal agencies to follow during administrative hearings. For example, the Act's provisions prescribe how agencies may collect, present, and evaluate evidence and other data in such hearings.

The Mail Privacy Statute (39 U.S.C. § 3623), enacted in 1971, prohibits the opening of mail without a search warrant or the addressee's consent.

The Privacy Act,[9] enacted December 31, 1974, regulates many aspects, such as the collection, maintenance, use, and dissemination of personal information by federal agencies. The Act mandates that personal data be collected as much as possible directly from the record subject. The Act prohibits collection of information about an individual's exercise of First Amendment rights (e.g., the freedoms of expression, assembly, and religion), as well as the disclosure of information absent the written consent of the subject individual. It also provides an individual the right to access and correct or challenge the content of their records. The Privacy Act was amended in 1988 by the Computer Matching and Privacy Protection Act, which describes the conditions under which computer matching involving the federal government could be performed. The Act is applicable to debt collection or benefit decisions made through computer matching. It requires notice to the beneficiaries and applicants that their records are subject to matching, and an opportunity for them to correct any incorrect information. Additionally, agencies must obtain approval of the matching agreement by, and report their matching activities to, the Data Integrity Boards.

The Right to Financial Privacy Act[10] of 1978 protects the confidentiality of personal financial records. The Act requires federal agencies who seek access to personal financial records to provide individuals with a notice and an opportunity to object before a financial institution can disclose his/her personal financial information to the agencies.

The Privacy Protection Act[11] of 1980 protects journalists and press offices from unannounced searches by government officials. The Act safeguards the security and confidentiality of any work product and documentary materials before they are disseminated to the public.

The Paperwork Reduction Act of 1980[12] was enacted to reduce the total amount of paperwork burden the federal government imposes on individuals and private businesses. The Act prohibits a federal agency from collecting information from the public if another agency has already collected the same information. It established the Office of Information and Regulatory Affairs (OIRA) within the Office of Management and Budget (OMB) to regulate and oversee federal agencies' data collection activities. It also requires each federal data collection form to specify why the information is being collected, how it will be used, and whether the individual's response is mandatory, voluntary, or required to obtain a benefit.

The Tax Reform Act[13] of 1986, a law meant to simplify the income tax code, requires the Internal Revenue Service to issue a notice and provide opportunity-to-challenge procedures, which are similar to those of the Right to Financial Privacy Act, before it seeks access to certain institutional records about an individual in the hands of certain private record keepers. The Act strictly limits disclosure of tax returns and return information. In some cases, it also requires a court order for disclosures to law enforcement agencies for purposes unrelated to tax administration.

The Electronic Communications Privacy Act[14] of 1986 (ECPA) extends government restrictions on wiretaps from telephone calls to include transmissions of electronic data by computer (18 U.S.C. § 2510 et seq.). It also prohibits the intentional disclosure of the contents of a personal electronic communication intercepted by government agencies. The ECPA has been amended by several legislations, such as the Communications Assistance for Law Enforcement Act (CALEA)[15] of 1994, the USA PATRIOT Act[16] of 2001 (and its reauthorization acts), and the FISA (Foreign Intelligence Surveillance Act of 1978) Amendments Act[17] of 2008, which provide legal basis for mass surveillance programs in the United States.

The Computer Security Act[18] of 1987, which was passed to improve the security and privacy of sensitive information maintained in federal information systems, requires each federal agency to provide mandatory training in computer security awareness.

2. Granting individuals the control of personal information collected by government

In addition to the above-mentioned Privacy Act, Right to Financial Privacy Act, and Tax Reform Act, which all require the provision of an opportunity to challenge, the following laws more specifically grant individuals the right to control or correct personal information collected by government.

The Freedom of Information Act[19] (FOIA), enacted July 5, 1967, gives an individual the right to access information from the government. It provides individuals with access to many types of government records that are exempt from access under the Privacy Act, including some categories of personal information. FOIA procedures are also extended to nonresident foreign nationals.

The Family Educational Rights and Privacy Act[20] of 1974 permits a student or the parent of a minor student to inspect and challenge the accuracy and completeness of educational records which concern the student. It also permits some control over the disclosure of information from the records. The law only applies to schools and education agencies receiving public funds that are administered by the U.S. Department of Education, which was vested with the power to terminate federal funds if an institution violates the Act.

The Criminal Justice Information Systems statute,[21] enacted January 7, 2011, requires that federally funded state and local criminal justice information systems must collect, maintain, and disseminate criminal intelligence information in conformance with policy standards that are prescribed by the Office of Justice Programs. The statute specifies that policy standards must be written to assure that such systems shall not violate the privacy and constitutional rights of individuals and to allow individuals to see, copy, and correct information about themselves in the system.

3. Preventing the disclosure of personal information by government to a third party

The Public Health Service Act[22] of 1944 prohibits disclosure of data collected by the National Centers for Health Services Research and for health statistics that could identify an individual in any way.

The Census Confidentiality Statute,[23] enacted August 31, 1954, prohibits the use of census data for any reason other than the original statistical purpose. The Act also prohibits the disclosure of census data that would allow an individual to be identified, except to employees of the Census Bureau and sworn officers.

The Driver's Privacy Protection Act[24] of 1994 is a statute governing the privacy and disclosure of personal information collected by state Departments of Motor Vehicles (DMVs). The Act prohibits state DMVs from releasing personal information from drivers' licenses and motor vehicle registration records. The law does allow the release of information to a third party who may use it for any specific statutory purposes, or any other purposes for which the subject of record was provided with an opportunity to limit the release of information and opted not to do so. It imposes a requirement of record keeping on the resellers of such information as well as a penalty on the procurement of information from motor vehicle records for an unlawful purpose, or false representation to obtain such information. The Act does not restrict a state's ability to enact more stringent laws for greater privacy protection.

4. Granting a government agency the right of surveillance and the access to personal data

The Communications Assistance for Law Enforcement Act,[25] enacted in 1994, preserves law enforcement's ability to engage in lawful electronic surveillance. The Act mandates that telecommunications carriers and manufacturers of telecommunication equipment modify and design their equipment, facilities, and services to ensure built-in surveillance capabilities that allow federal agencies to wiretap any telephone traffic (it has been extended to cover broadband Internet and VoIP traffic). It also requires the government agency obtain a court order before obtaining tracking or location information, but without restricting subscribers' rights to use encryption.

State Policies

State privacy protection laws vary greatly. Some states, such as California, Florida, and Montana, have articulated the right to privacy in their constitutions. For example, the Florida Constitution (Article I, §23) states that

> Every natural person has the right to be let alone and free from governmental intrusion into the person's private life except as otherwise provided herein. This section shall not be construed to limit the public's right of access to public records and meetings as provided by law.[26]

States have also enacted many industry-specific privacy statutes, such as laws that impose restrictions on the collection and use of personal information by health, financial, and educational institutions, as well as by government agencies. Many of the state statutes that govern government agencies' activities mirror their counterparts at the federal level. For example, Criminal Justice Information Statutes generally require law enforcement agencies to permit individuals to review and correct information about themselves maintained in the criminal justice information systems; Fair Information Practices Statutes restrict the type of information that state governments can collect and use about individuals, permit individuals to review and challenge information about them held by the state, and restrict the states' ability to disclose personal data to third parties; Tax Return Statutes prohibit governments from disclosing state tax return information; and so on.

In addressing online privacy issues, state legislatures have enacted various laws to govern activities, such as requiring websites to post privacy policies, barring libraries from disclosing readers' information, and so on. According to the National Conference of State Legislatures (NCSL), as of 2015, at least 17 states require government websites or state portals to establish privacy policies and procedures, or to incorporate machine-readable privacy policies into their websites (NCSL 2015). States such as Arizona, California, and Missouri have passed e-Reader Privacy laws to protect a library patron's use records. For example, the Arizona state legislature (Ariz. Rev. Stat. § 41–151.22) prohibits a library or library system supported by public funds to disclose any record or other information that identifies a user of library services.

Challenges from Recent Technological Advancement and Government's Technological Initiatives

Despite the extensive regulatory framework, the issue of privacy protection has been constantly evolving, demanding new policymaking endeavors. Technological innovations in recent years have dramatically changed the landscape of privacy protection. Perhaps the most striking revolution was bought about by the advent of the Internet and the World Wide Web in the 1990s. Since then, several new waves of technological innovation in a variety of areas have been introduced to the public sector at an unprecedented and accelerated pace, offering new means for data collection and usage, but also undermining the goals established by the existing regulatory framework.

E-Government and M-Government

Starting in the late 1990s, governments at all levels have been deploying e-government strategies, a move which has serious implications for information privacy. Bélanger and Hiller (2006) propose a framework (see Table 17.1) to identify the issue of privacy and illustrate the complex relationships between constituents and the government as various stages of e-government are implemented.

Specifically addressing privacy issues with regard to the FOIA requirements, in 1998, federal agencies were directed to review their systems of records in light of e-government. The review established new guidelines that emphasized the necessity for review of agency records and security features in the burgeoning electronic environment. Several states have also enacted statutes that specifically address publishing information on government websites.

Yet the development of e-government stumbles when it comes to security and privacy threats (Thibodeau 2000; Bledad 2011). Internet users have growing concerns about cyberspace identity theft and privacy violations (Madden et al. 2007). Many citizens are skeptical and mistrust e-government services, perceiving such services as an invasion of their privacy by government (James 2000; Dinev and Hart 2006). Some state and local e-government sites posted citizens' personal information, such as names, social security numbers, property tax records, or other private information on their site without appropriate access control (Myers 2007). Such information has attracted cyber attackers, resulting in nuisance, destructive attacks, and misuse of personal information for financial gain (Symantic 2007). Although most state e-government sites post privacy and security policy statements, many of them do not have active security measures in place (Zhao and Zhao 2010).

In the past decade, the mobile technologies have been significantly expanding government's capacity to deliver public services. The amalgamation of mobile devices and new media applications enable citizens from any place at any time instant access to integrated data and location-based services. M-government, "the adoption of mobile technology to support and enhance government performance and foster a more connected society" (OECD 2012, p. 12), which is a natural extension of e-government, presents new privacy concerns—citizens may fear that their mobile devices can be traced while conducting transactions or expressing opinions. A study by the Global Privacy Enforcement Network indicates that most mobile applications lack an adequate privacy protection mechanism (Walker 2014). Recent GAO research points that existing laws and enforcement actions are incapable to adequately regulate the large amount of personal data generated from online activity and use of mobile phone applications (GAO 2012).

Table 17.1 Mapping of Privacy Issues to E-Government Services

Constraints	Stages of E-Government			
	Information	Two-way communication	Transaction	Integration
Policy	Against "surreptitious use of cookies" memo; policy favors privacy; however, policy must be posted			Focus on creating "customer-centric" websites
Law and regulations	If no record created, Privacy Act does not apply	Record may or may not be necessary; Privacy Act may or may not apply	Record will be created; Privacy Act applies	Sharing information between agencies; Computer Matching Act applies
Technical feasibility	Limiting use of cookies and posting privacy policies easily implemented	Must provide security for identifiable data; more complex technology implementation; can technology allow anonymity in communication?	More complex choices for technology platforms; security is crucial and encryption is required	More difficult implementation; providing access to different platforms may result in privacy and security being more difficult to ensure
User feasibility	Posted privacy policy notice may increase trust	Type of information (such as national ID) may increase privacy concerns	Users are reluctant to conduct transactions; concerned about payment security	Users may not understand how integrated information and customization impacts their privacy

Adapted from Bélanger and Hiller (2006).

Surveillance Technologies

One of the more prominent areas of technological advancement that presents a threat to privacy has been the explosive growth of surveillance capability (especially video surveillance). Government is by far the largest user of such technological innovations. Surveillance involves the continuous observation of a place, person, group, or ongoing activity to gather information for various purposes. While most often used to prevent crimes and terrorist attacks and to ensure traffic safety, surveillance is also very helpful for epidemic disease control, prevention, and other purposes.

Though commonly associated with negative images of espionage on citizens as portrayed in George Orwell's classic novel *1984*, such technologies have gained greater public acceptance as a result of the 9/11 terrorist attacks. Nowadays public spaces, such as parking lots, transportation hubs, construction sites, warehouses, and office buildings, commonly have surveillance technologies installed for the protection of property and public safety. Driven by the smart city initiatives and other e-government policy endeavors, the integration of related video surveillance into a wide range of governmental services is highly likely to be realized in the near future (Mack 2014). The massive utilization of surveillance technologies is without doubt a considerable threat to privacy.

In addition, the recent development of nanotechnology in the form of invisible tags, minute (bio) sensors, intelligent fabrics, smart surfaces, and radio frequency identity chips (RFIDs) has raised a panoply of privacy issues. It transforms the traditional privacy issues that revolve around the ideas of centralization of surveillance, concentration of power, and constraining information flow to one of surveillance at a decentralized level and the information conductivity of designer materials (Van Den Hoven and Vermaas 2007).

Biometrics Technologies

The development of biometrics technologies presents another type of privacy threat. Such technologies collect, process, and analyze human body information, such as DNA, signatures, finger- or palm prints, eye retinas and irises, voice patterns, vascular, facial patterns and hand geometries, and so on, mainly for authentication purposes. Recent biometrics technology advancements have been extended to capture and analyze brain (electroencephalogram) and heart (electrocardiogram) signals (Palaniappan and Krishnan 2004; Palaniappan 2006).

Since biometric identifiers are unique to individuals, they are more reliable in verifying a person's identity than the traditional token and knowledge-based methods. Currently, biometrics (fingerprints) has been used by the federal government to identify foreign visitors and immigrants. Created in March 2013, the Office of Biometric Identity Management (OBIM) in the Department of Homeland Security (DHS) provides biometric identification services to federal, state, and local government decision makers for the purpose of identifying the people they encounter and for determining potential risks. The agency supplies the technology for collecting and storing biometric data, provides data analysis, updates the security watch list, and ensures the integrity of the data.

Despite biometric identifiers' strength in identification, the collection of such information raises concerns about the extensive use of such information. First, for a segment of the population, the use of biometric technology is inherently impossible, offensive, invasive, or embarrassing, owing to personal disabilities as well as a variety of cultural, religious, or personal beliefs. Moreover, fears and worries concerning the perilous impact of the collection, use, maintenance, and disclosure of biometric data are especially hard to address through either system design or legislative requirements. Since such identifiers are essentially biological, personal information from scanned biometric measurements can be extracted and integrated with other data sources to be used for a purpose different than originally stated, for example, to infer health status, physical disability, or other sensitive characteristics. Some biometric collection methods can be inaccurate, leading to the false identification of an individual. In addition, the storage of massive amounts of sensitive personal information can be costly and cumbersome.

In the absence of federal legislation, several states have enacted laws governing the collection, use, or disposal of biometric information by state entities. The substance of these laws varies largely among different states (Ross 2014). For example, both Washington and Oregon have authorized their respective DMVs to use facial recognition technology to prevent persons from obtaining multiple or fraudulent licenses, but only Washington state prohibits their DMV from sharing or disclosing the biometric data it collects. Texas extensively prohibits governmental entities from using an individual's biometric data without obtaining that individual's consent, unless it is required by law or demanded by law enforcement. In addition, Illinois (the Illinois Biometric Information Privacy Act, 740 ILCS 14/1, et seq.) and Texas (Bus. & Com. Code Ann. § 503.001) also regulate a private entity's use, disclosure, and destruction of biometric data.

Geospatial Technologies

Recent developments in geospatial technologies, such as remote sensing, geographic information systems (GIS), and global positioning systems (GPS), along with ancillary technologies including satellite navigation devices, unmanned aerial vehicles (UAV), imaging satellites, mobile phones, web mapping services, and location-based services (LBS) make it easy and fast to collect, process, analyze, visualize, use, and distribute location and other types of geographic information, which provides for a wide range of critical services, including environmental monitoring, land use planning, emergency and disaster management, and military operations. As a result, government entities can gain access to an individual's current and past locations. Technology advancement also enables government agencies to identify individuals with a high degree of certainty based upon their movement patterns and other generally available information. Such collection and use of information on personal location and movement has been seen as threatening privacy, as such information substantively reveals an individual's activities, encounters, and behavioral patterns.

Geospatial technologies transform the traditional conception of location knowledge when location sensors, such as cameras, recording devices, mobile phones, and communication satellites, become ubiquitous. Enormous information on an individual's location can be collected, integrated, and analyzed in real time. Privacy policy design in such a context is facing both theoretical and practical challenges. Giving users control over their location and context data becomes more difficult, as the data gathering often happens invisibly and users generally pay less attention to the information that is gathered about them. This raises a serious concern when data is gathered without a users' knowledge or consent. Geospatial information relies on an interconnected network of services to collect and process data and meet a user's purposes. Interconnected networks increase the chances of privacy violations as a single service point with weak privacy controls may attract a threat to the whole network.

Although this emerging threat to privacy has drawn substantive attention from scientists, media, and policy makers, the existing regulatory framework is incapable of defining a reasonable expectation of privacy from a location standpoint (Pomfret 2012).

Big Data

All the above-described technological changes are contributing to the realm of big data, which refers to any voluminous amount of data that has the potential to be mined for information. Current technologies, such as cookies, sensors, etc., allow easy loading of data on websites or other platforms directly into databases. In the past few years, data collected from commercial firms, medical and financial institutions, governments, social networking, and many other areas has been growing exponentially. For example, Google alone possesses more than 1 million petabytes (1 petabyte = 1 million gigabytes) of data and processes more than 24 petabytes of data daily, which is thousands of times the volume of all printed material in the U.S. Library of Congress.

Meanwhile, the massive advancement in data-mining capacity, along with the constantly dropping cost of data processing, has enabled relationships among separate pieces of data to be discovered in ways that would not have been possible before.

One application of big data by the public sector is the use of microtargeting in digital campaign advertising. Candidates can match voter files with data from a variety of commercial advertising firms that track the online behavior of consumers and registration data from the commercial websites they browsed. Campaign ads thus can be tailored to voters based on their individual characteristics, such as whom they voted for in the last election, what kind of cars they drive, where they visited, what they purchased, and what materials they read. For example, in the 2012 presidential election, two kinds of Republican voters could see two different Romney video ads pop up on the local and national news websites that they visited (Vega 2012). In addition, such matching practices can be extended to reach those "look-a-like" computer users. To achieve this, the browsing histories or other characteristics of verified supporters of a given candidate or political party are analyzed and used to identify other computer users with similar behaviors or characteristics.

Microtargeting is similar to the technique commercial advertisers use to serve up, for example, car ads online to people who recently searched for cars. Much like traditional demographic and geographic targeting, however, microtargeting aims at the individual, or "micro," level. This type of targeting is far more precise and efficient than the other two kinds.

Microtargeting applies a variety of statistical techniques, such as regression analysis, market segmentation, genetic algorithms, and neural network, based on different contexts. The development of computing power in recent years made it possible to undertake large volumes of computations in the limited time frame of a political campaign. For example, computer grids allow multiple computers to work simultaneously to solve a complex problem. Such innovations have made modeling techniques that were once exclusive to big financial institutions available to public sector operations.

Although there are numerous benefits and promising potential from big data, the advancement of big data analytics also presents serious challenges to traditional privacy protection mechanisms. Though government agencies are generally required to report their data collection practices and/or to notify individuals what data are collected and to describe how the data will be used, hidden data collection is still a challenge to privacy. For instance, users often customize their web browsers with personal information, without recognizing that this information can be accessed by websites they are visiting and then stored in the website's databases. This is usually achieved by the use of "cookies." U.S. government agencies are generally advised not to use cookies without prior approval and/or clear and evident notification (OMB 2010), but not all of them take realistic measures to implement it, and some governmental services may be made available on third-party websites that have associated third-party cookies (Gervais 2013/2014). In addition, as the microtargeting technique for campaign advertising indicates, data collected using such means by the private sector may be used for public purposes.

Although cross-referencing of data contained in computer records by government entities is not new, it is the amount of data collected, as well as the capacity and scale of operations, that cause concern. Agencies share information with other agencies for a variety of reasons, including data reconciliation, debt recovery, fraud detection, and verification of eligibility or entitlement to benefits and concessions. Most privacy protection regulations and practices are based on the notion of informed consent for the collection, disclosure, and use of personal data. Yet big data analytics can utilize source data in a variety of ways that were not anticipated at the time it was collected. The connections made by data analytics among individual pieces of information can be used to reveal an individual's identity and infer related sensitive information, and lead to the erosion of anonymity and confidentiality.

Open Data

The notion of big data is also intrinsically intertwined with the idea of open data, which believes that certain data should be made available to the public to republish or to use without copyright, patent, or other forms of control. With the launch of open data government initiatives such as data.gov, there is a growing tendency to release various public data on the Internet. Governments at all levels currently allow individuals and businesses to freely reuse public data for their own purposes. Such data includes, for instance, demographic statistics, crime statistics, energy consumption, addresses in a trade register, and issued construction permits.

Open data initiatives drive the sharing of data, which can potentially make government agencies more transparent and accountable and achieve greater efficiency and economic benefits. Meanwhile, it puts data protection, especially the protection to PII, under increased pressure and will continue to do so as technology progresses and more data becomes publicly available. Technological developments and the increasing amount of publicly available data are blurring the lines between nonpersonal and personal data. For example, a study of the 2000 U.S. census data showed that 63% of the

U.S. population (that was 87% for the 1990 census data) could be identified based on only gender, ZIP code, and date of birth (Golle 2006). As computing power continuously grows and more data becomes publicly available, deanonymization or deaggregation of data will become increasingly easy and present a threat to privacy. Once anonymized or aggregated, open data become personally identifiable, privacy regulation may be extended to the realm of open data, thus obstructing the implementation of open data policies (Kulk and van Loenen 2012).

The Policy Problem of PII Protection

Prior to the passage of the Privacy Act of 1974, there was plainly no comprehensive law protecting personal information in the United States. To address this issue, the country has traditionally depended upon a wide range of actors, including state legislatures, agencies and courts, industry associations, and individual institutions, who are in charge of establishing and executing standards for data protection. The federal government's role to safeguard privacy is restricted to facilitating individual action of self-regulation.

The passage of the Act was partially attributed to the computerization of government record systems, which started in the 1960s. The technological change demanded that Congress, executive agencies, and other interest groups respond in order to address the tensions between individuals' rights for information privacy and governments' new means of personal data collection, usage, and distribution (Regan 1986). The privacy laws, especially those enacted since 1982, are largely responses to technological changes in computers, digitized networks, and the creation of new information products. The laws vary, but a central emphasis is the protection against unauthorized use of collected information and government access to private records.

Ever since the advent of the Internet and World Wide Web, new waves of technological changes have been produced at an unprecedented rate, demanding government's fast and extensive legislative and administrative response to address the resulting privacy threats. However, it is difficult to meet such a demand within the current regulatory framework of PII protection. At least three intrinsic problems exist in the framework that prevent it from effectively and efficiently meeting the demands.

First, the existence of a wide spectrum of policies across various sectors points to the cruel fact that it is difficult to conceptualize, and that there is no agreement about, the policy problem. The conceptualization of privacy is notoriously difficult (Regan 1995). There has been a substantive debate regarding general privacy's status—whether it is a human right or a commodity (Smith et al. 2011). Scholars, such as Posner (1984), suggest that privacy is fundamentally normative and cannot be treated absolutely, as it may conflict with the legal and social frameworks of different cultures. Brenton (1964) points out that privacy is harder to measure than other objects of public concern, for example, environmental pollution. A gap apparently exists between the technical concept of data protection and the legal and moral concept of privacy (Agre and Rotenberg 1997). The definition of PII is more problematic, as the concept is rather fluid and dynamic. Lacking any clear boundary, the interpretation of PII is highly contextually dependent (Smith et al. 2011). The absence of a satisfactory definition has inhibited effective policy debates and has obstructed policy formulation, with clear prescriptions supported by accepted moral premises (Agre and Rotenberg 1997). For example, Regan (1995) argues that the disjuncture between the importance of privacy and the ability to protect it through the U.S. political process is because our emphasis on privacy as an individual interest and right (without acknowledging privacy's social importance) is not a strong base for developing policy.

Second, the current policy framework largely relies on individuals to protect their own interests. Regan (1986) pointed out some of the weaknesses: (1) individuals must be aware of their rights, understand the potential threats, and be willing to take the effort at their own cost to protect their interests; (2) remedies are only provided after the damage has occurred and been proven; and (3) there exists an imbalance of power between the individual and agencies, as the individual is often dependent upon the agency for employment, benefits, and other advantages. These weaknesses are prevalent across the spectrum of privacy policies.

Third, the formulation of policy to protect PII is slow and incremental within the current system. Using a "sectoral approach," privacy policies in the United States tend to be adopted on an ad hoc basis, with legislation arising when certain sectors and circumstances require. The responsive nature of policy formulation makes it difficult to adapt to rapid technological and social changes. There are also intrinsic political interests embedded in the policy problem. In examining the dynamics of congressional policy making in three technological areas (computerized databases, wiretapping, and polygraph testing) of privacy threats, Regan (1995) found that supporters of new technologies triumphed in delaying and ultimately weakening pro-privacy legislation, as they were better organized and had greater financial resources than were their counterpart.

Policy Alternative: The EU Data Protection Directive

Unlike the responsive approach, the European Union (EU) has adopted a proactive policy for data protection, which offers a potential policy alternative for the U.S. problem. Treating privacy as a fundamental right, the European Union implements a consistent set of privacy standards—the EU Data Protection Directive—throughout its member states.

Enacted in 1995, the EU Directive was adopted as a response to the discrepancies of data protection laws among the member states, which hindered economic integration to a single market. The EU directive is intended to advance the development and functionality of an internal market through balancing two competing interests: maintaining strict data privacy protection and facilitating the free flow of information among the member states (Maxeiner 1995).

The Directive specifies the key criteria for the processing of personal data:

Data processing is only lawful if

- the data subject has unambiguously given his consent; or
- processing is necessary for the performance of a contract to which the data subject is party; or
- processing is necessary for compliance with a legal obligation to which the controller is subject; or
- processing is necessary to protect the vital interests of the data subject; or
- processing is necessary for the performance of a task carried out in the public interest or in the exercise of official authority vested in the controller or in a third party; or
- processing is necessary for the purposes of the legitimate interest pursued by the controller or by the third party, except where such interests are overridden by the interests for fundamental rights and freedoms of the data subject which require protection.

(Directive 95/46/EC)

It also lays down the principles of data quality:

- *personal data must be processed fairly and lawfully, and collected for specified, explicit and legitimate purposes. They must also be adequate, relevant and not excessive, accurate and, where necessary, kept up to date, must not be stored for longer than necessary and solely for the purposes for which they were collected;*
- *special categories of processing: it is forbidden to process personal data revealing racial or ethnic origin, political opinions, religious or philosophical beliefs, trade-union membership, and the processing of data*

concerning health or sex life. This provision comes with certain qualifications concerning, for example, cases where processing is necessary to protect the vital interests of the data subject or for the purposes of preventive medicine and medical diagnosis.

(Directive 95/46/EC)

To achieve the free flow of information among member states, the Directive prescribes guidelines and restrictions to ensure that each member state grant an equivalent level of personal data protection. It also specifies that personal data may only be transferred to non-member countries if that country provides an adequate level of protection.

Although the comprehensive Directive was approved by the EU members, the implementation process has never been free from problems. The EU member countries were required to pass their individual implementing legislation before the Directive taking effect; however, only one-third of EU members had achieved so by that time (Fromholz 2000). The remaining countries were mandated to amend their preexisting legal frameworks to conform to the Directive (Newman 2008). The interpretation of some parts of the Directive, such as those concerning transmission of data to third countries, has been controversy. The EU had to mandate a working party to provide further clarification (Fromholz 2000). Even constrained by the shared Directive, EU countries vary tremendously in "decisions about the selection and positioning of privacy regulators, the hard and soft powers they wield, the sources of economic support, the position in the political and policymaking landscape, and their connections to other sources of authority and power" (Bamberger and Mulligan 2013, p. 1637). A review conducted in 2003 found that there was considerable divergence among member states in implementation and policy choices within the margins of the Directive, and subsequent reviews also identified that the Directive did not consider important aspects such as globalization and technological development (Hustinx 2014). Consequently, numerous amendments have been proposed in the European Parliament and the Council of Ministers. In 2009, the European Commission launched a comprehensive review of the legal framework on data protection. With regard to the growing concern about the misuse of sensitive data and the absence of effective legal remedies, on 25 January 2012, the Commission unveiled a draft European General Data Protection Regulation that will supersede the Directive. The new regulation is intended to:

- Modernize the EU legal system for the protection of personal data, in particular to meet the challenges resulting from globalization and the use of new technologies;
- Strengthen individuals' rights, and at the same time reduce administrative formalities to ensure a free flow of personal data within the EU and beyond;
- Improve the clarity and coherence of the EU rules for personal data protection and achieve a consistent and effective implementation and application of the fundamental right to the protection of personal data in all areas of the Union's activities.

(The European Commission 2009)

Despite the proactive approach to data protection, EU policy makers are also facing the challenge of designing policy to keep up with technological development. However, instead of dealing with individual technological instances, the EU policy intends to prescribe principles to address emerging technological threats in general. Their experience may provide valuable insights and lessons to U.S. policy makers.

Suggestions for Seeking Solutions

The complexity and dynamics in regarding to PII protection, in the absence of proved macro policy models, point to the fact that resolving the policy problem will be a long, arduous, and contentious process. In seeking solutions, the following needs shall not be neglected:

The Need of Interdisciplinary Effort for Definition

Traditionally the definition of general privacy has been explored in the disciplines of philosophy, sociology, and law. The Internet's emergence as a medium, which reduces the constraints of space, time, and cost, has highlighted the need to reconsider the character of privacy in the information age. The definition of the policy problem demands concerted effort among researchers not only from the theoretically oriented scholarships of philosophy, sociology, and law, but also from practically aligned disciplines, such as public administration, business administration, communication, and management information systems. Should we consider privacy as a fundamental human right, or a property right, or a commodity that can be controlled through free market approaches (Posner 1984; Smith et al. 2011)? Is it possible to seek a universal policy mechanism governing PII disclosure in the information age, or is the problem absolutely contextual dependent?

The Urge for Transnational Dialogues and Debates

Although it is unlikely that the United States will implement a comprehensive regulatory scheme for privacy protection in the near future, the European experience provides relevant and comparable lessons because of the shared values, such as democracy and human liberty, the historical and cultural connections, as well as the sovereign relationship between the federal government and state governments. For instance, if Congress can adopt similar principles and guidelines established by the EU Directive and unify the state privacy regulations, the costs of compliance with various privacy laws and standards can be largely reduced. Transnational dialogues and debates between the two continents, which are leading the world in various economic, legal, and social policies and practices, will enhance the exchange of lessons of practice and designs of policy instrument and possibly establish global standards for privacy protection (Alo 2013).

The Demand for Reconciliation, Compromise, and Cooperation

Given that privacy is not pursued or defended by public policy makers as a fundamental right, the development of privacy policy is often seen as a struggle between interests in the United States. The protection of PII is of growing concern to multiple stakeholders, such as privacy activists, public policy makers, academic scholars, government regulators, law enforcement officers, information system technicians, business owners, and individual consumers. The large array of players in the policy arenas represents a wide spectrum of political interests. Many view that privacy policies are generally at odds with the prevailing value of economic efficiency, recognizing the imposed costs on actors and agents in ways that cannot be justified in economic terms. Such policies are also often in conflict with homeland security and public safety needs. The policymaking process requires government, institutions, and citizens to reconcile, compromise, and cooperate in order to reach a sustainable balance.

The Call for Empirical Studies and Best Practices

Due to the urgency of PII protection in the information age, the field has accumulated a large body of normative studies of privacy, many of which are either politically engaging or intellectually provoking (Smith et al. 2011). However, normative insertions alone are unlikely to inform further in policy decisions. To fuel effective policy debate, rigorous empirical studies on privacy, especially those that trace the policy processes and evaluate policy impacts, could add substantive value. In addition, carefully delineated policy implementation practices with proved experience are indispensable to guide public administrators.

Conclusion

As technological design, market forces, laws, and public policies continuously construct and shape interactions and relations between people and social institutions, emerging threats to human rights, such as privacy, are inevitable. Significant technological changes in recent years have proliferated new threats to individual privacy, and this trend is unlikely to cease, and likely to accelerate. The existing regulatory framework and the sectoral-based, responsive policy formulation approach of the United States have intrinsic weaknesses in addressing the policy problem. The EU experience, though not free of its own problems, is introduced as a policy alternative for insights and lessons. Although a variety of historical, cultural, political, and social factors have directed the U.S. and the EU to different policy paths and each of them is facing their unique problems, lessons from one another may offer valuable insights for keeping up with similar challenges as a result of accelerating technological changes.

This chapter introduces the policy issue of PII protection by laying out the regulatory framework, enumerating the technological threats, and analyzing the policy problem. Though not intended to explore solutions, it is hoped the knowledge of the problem will encourage and motivate future research for better policies and practices to ensure personal privacy while keeping up with the fast pace of the information age.

Notes

1. "Directive 95/46/EC of the European Parliament and of the Council of 24 October 1995 on the protection of individuals with regard to the processing of personal data and on the free movement of such data." Eur-lex.europa.eu. Retrieved 2015–04–29.
2. Privacy Act 1988 (Cth) s 6(1).
3. Ruckelshaus v. Monsanto Co., 467 U.S. 986 (1984).
4. Griswold v. Connecticut, 381 U.S. 479 (1965).
5. Whalen v. Roe, 429 U.S. 589 (1977).
6. Restatement of the Law, Second, Torts, § 652.
7. 18 U.S.C. § 2510, et seq.; 47 U.S.C. § 605, FCC Rule 47 CFER 164.501.
8. 5 U.S.C. §§ 551, 554–558.
9. 5 U.S.C. § 552a.
10. 12 U.S.C. § 3401, et seq.
11. 42 U.S.C. § 2000aa.
12. 44 U.S.C. § 3501, et seq.
13. 26 U.S.C. §§ 6103, 6108, 7609.
14. 18 U.S.C. § 2510 et seq.
15. 47 U.S.C. 1001–1010.
16. 115 Stat. 272.
17. 50 U.S.C. ch. 36 § 1801 et seq.
18. 40 U.S.C. § 1441.
19. 5 U.S.C. § 552.
20. 20 U.S.C. § 1232g.
21. 42 U.S.C. § 3789g.
22. 42 U.S.C. § 242m.
23. 13 U.S.C. § 9.
24. 18 U.S.C. § 2721.
25. 47 U.S.C. § 1001.
26. "Article I: Declaration of Rights, Section 23: Right of privacy." Constitution of Florida. Florida Legislature. November 5, 1968. URL: http://www.leg.state.fl.us/Statutes/index.cfm?Mode=Constitution&Submenu=3&Tab=statutes&CFID=36371116&CFTOKEN=93270531#A1S23

References

Agre, Philip E. and Marc Rotenberg. *Technology and Privacy: The New Landscape.* Cambridge, MA: MIT Press. 1997.
Alo, Edward R. "EU privacy protection: A step towards global privacy." *The Michigan State International Law Review* 22 (2013): 1095.

Bamberger, Kenneth A. and Deirdre K. Mulligan. "Privacy in Europe: Initial data on governance choices and corporate practices." *The George Washington Law Review* 81 (2013): 1529.

Bélanger, France and Janine S. Hiller. "A framework for e-government: Privacy implications." *Business Process Management Journal* 12: 1 (2006): 48–60.

Bennett, C.J. *Regulating Privacy: Data Protection and Public Policy in Europe and the United States*. Ithaca, NY: Cornell University Press, 1992.

Bledad, A.D. *Trust and Information Privacy Concerns in Electronic Government: Enschede*. The Netherlands: University of Twente, 2011. Accessed January 29, 2016. http://doc.utwente.nl/86135/1/thesis_A_Beldad.pdf.

Brenton, Myron. *The Privacy Invaders*. New York: Coward-McCann, 1964.

Dinev, T. and P. Hart. "An extended privacy calculus model for e-commerce transactions." *Information Systems Research* 17: 1 (2006): 61.

Driscoll K. and S. Walker. "Big data, big questions working within a black box: Transparency in the collection and production of big Twitter data." *International Journal of Communication* 8: 0 (2014): 20.

Fromholz, Julia M. "The European union data privacy directive." *Berkeley Technology Law Journal* 15: 1 (2000): 460–484.

Gervais, Norman. "Governmental Internet information collection: Cookies placing personal privacy at risk." *The ASIS&T Bulletin*, (December 2013–January 2014). Accessed July 16, 2015. https://www.asis.org/Bulletin/Dec-13/DecJan14_Gervais.html.

Golle, P. "Revising the uniqueness of simple demographics in the US population." *WPES'06 Proceedings of the 5th ACM Workshop on Privacy in Electronic Society*. (2006). Accessed July 12, 2015. https://crypto.stanford.edu/~pgolle/papers/census.pdf.

Government Accountability Office (GAO). *Protecting Personally Identifiable Information*. GAO-08–343. (2008). Accessed April 23, 2015. http://www.gao.gov/new.items/do8343.pdf.

———. *Mobile Device Location Data: Additional Federal Actions Could Help Protect Consumer Privacy*. GAO-12–903. (2012). Accessed January 28, 2016. http://www.gao.gov/products/GAO-12–903.

———. *Agency Responses to Breaches of Personally Identifiable Information Need to Be More Consistent*. GAO-14–34. (2013). Accessed January 28, 2016. http://www.gao.gov/assets/660/659572.pdf.

———. *Federal Agencies Need to Better Protect Sensitive Data*. GAO-16–194T. (2015). Accessed January 28, 2016. http://www.gao.gov/assets/680/673678.pdf.

Hustinx, P. "EU data protection law: The review of directive 95/46/EC and the proposed general data protection regulation." *European Data Protection Supervisor*. (September 15, 2014). Accessed July 17, 2015. https://secure.edps.europa.eu/EDPSWEB/webdav/site/mySite/shared/Documents/EDPS/Publications/Speeches/2014/14–09–15_Article_EUI_EN.pdf.

James, G. "Empowering bureaucrats." *MC Technology Marketing Intelligence* 20: 12 (2000): 628.

Kulk, Stefan and Bastiaan van Loenen. "Brave new open data world?" *International Journal of Spatial Data Infrastructures Research* 7 (2012): 196–206.

Mack, Timothy C. "Privacy and the surveillance explosion." *The Futurist* 48: 1 (January–February 2014). Accessed June 3, 2015. http://www.wfs.org/futurist/january-february-2014-vol-48-no-1/privacy-and-surveillance-explosion.

Madden, M., S. Fox, A. Smith, and J. Vitak. *Digital Footprints: Online Identity Management and Search in the Age of Transparency*. Washington, DC: PEW Internet and American Life Project, 2007.

Maxeiner, J.R. Myers, "Freedom of information and the EU data protection directive." *Federal Communications Law Journal* 48: 1 (1995). Accessed July 17, 2015. http://www.repository.law.indiana.edu/fclj/vol48/iss1/4/.

Myers, L. "Online public records facilitate ID theft: Is your local government unwittingly aiding identity thieves?" *MSNBC: Nightly News* (2007). Accessed July 15, 2015. http://www.nbcnews.com/id/16813496/ns/nbc_nightly_news_with_brian_williams-nbc_news_investigates/t/online-public-records-facilitate-id-theft/#.VbBRF7NViko.

National Conference of State Legislatures (NCSL). *State Laws Related to Internet Privacy*. (February 24, 2015). Accessed June 3, 2015. http://www.ncsl.org/research/telecommunications-and-information-technology/state-laws-related-to-Internet-privacy.aspx.

Newman, Abraham. "Building Transnational Civil Liberties: Transgovernmental Entrepreneurs and the European Data Privacy Directive." *International Organization*. 62 (2008): 103–130.

OECD. *Mobile Technologies for Responsive Governments and Connected Societies*. (2012). Accessed January 28, 2016. http://www.oecd.org/gov/public-innovation/m-government.htm.

The Office of Management and Budget (OMB). *Guidance for Online Use of Web Measurement and Customization Technologies*. M-10–22. (June 25, 2010). Accessed July 16, 2015. https://www.whitehouse.gov/sites/default/files/omb/assets/memoranda_2010/m10–22.pdf.

The Office of Management and Budget (OMB). Memorandum for the Heads of Executive Departments and Agencies: Safeguarding Against and Responding to the Breach of Personally Identifiable Information.

M-07-16, (2007). Accessed November 17, 2016. https://www.whitehouse.gov/sites/default/files/omb/memoranda/fy2007/m07-16.pdf ().

Palaniappan, R. "Electroencephalogram signals from imagined activities: A novel biometric identifier for a small population." In E. Corchado, H. Yin, V. Botti, and C. Fyfe, C. (eds.), *Intelligent Data Engineering and Automated Learning—IDEAL 2006*, Lecture Notes in Computer Science, vol. 4224. Berlin, Germany: Springer-Verlag, Berlin Heidelberg, 2006: pp. 604–611.

Palaniappan, R. and S.M. Krishnan, "Identifying individuals using ECG signals." *Proceedings of International Conference on Signal Processing and Communications*, Bangalore, India, (11–14 December 2004): pp. 569–572.

Pomfret, Kevin D. "Summary of location privacy in the United States." In Katleen Janssen & Joep Crompvoets (eds.), *Geographic Data and the Law: Defining New Challenges*. Leuven, Belgium: Leuven University Press, 2012: pp. 77–89.

Posner, R.A. "An economic theory of privacy." In F. Schoeman (ed.), *Philosophical Dimensions of Privacy: An Anthology*. New York: Cambridge University Press, 1984: pp. 333–345.

Regan, Priscilla M. "Privacy, government information, and technology." *Public Administration Review*, 46: 6 (November–December, 1986): 629–634.

———. *Legislating Privacy: Technology, Social Values, and Public Policy*. Chapel Hill, NC: The University of North Carolina Press, 1995.

Ross, Phil. "Biometrics: A developing regulatory landscape for a new era of technology" *Genomics Law Report*. (May 21, 2014). Accessed July 16. http://www.genomicslawreport.com/index.php/2014/05/21/biometrics-a-developing-regulatory-landscape-for-a-new-era-of-technology/.

Schwartz, Paul M. and Daniel J. Solove. "The PII problem: Privacy and a new concept of personally identifiable information." *New York University Law Review* 86 (December 5, 2011): 1814.

Smith, H. Jeff, Tamara Dinev, and Heng Xu. "Information privacy research: An interdisciplinary review." *MIS Quarterly* 35: 4 (2011): 989–1016.

Symantic. "Symantec government Internet security threat report." *Symantec Enterprise Security*, volume 12, (September 2007). Accessed July 15, 2015. http://eval.symantec.com/mktginfo/enterprise/white_papers/ent-whitepaper_Internet_security_threat_report_xii_gov_09_2007.en-us.pdf.

Thibodeau, P. "E-government spending to soar through 2005." *Computerworld* 34: 17 (2000): 12.

Van Den Hoven, Jeroen and Pieter E. Vermaas. "Nano-technology and privacy: On continuous surveillance outside the panopticon." *Journal of Medicine and Philosophy* 32: 3 (2007): 283–297.

Vega, T. "Online data helping campaigns customize ads." *New York Times*, Feb 20. 2012. Accessed November 17, 2016. http://www.nytimes.com/2012/02/21/us/politics/campaigns-use-microtargeting-to-attract-supporters.html?_r=0.

Warren, S.D. and L.D. Brandeis. "The Right to Privacy, 4." *Harvard Law Review* 4: 5 (1890): 193.

Zhao, Jensen J. and Sherry Y. Zhao. "Opportunities and threats: A security assessment of state e-government websites." *Government Information Quarterly* 27: 1 (January 2010): 49–56.

18
AN EXPLORATORY STUDY OF E-PARTICIPATION TECHNOLOGY ADOPTION BY CITIZENS

Jooho Lee

Introduction

Over the past decade, information and communication technologies (ICT) have been widely used to engage citizens in public policy decision-making at different levels of government around the world. The use of ICT in citizen participation—often called electronic participation (e-participation)—has been touted as a means of lowering citizens' psychological and physical barriers to access government and, thus, promoting citizen participation. Recently, a growing number of governments has offered various forms of e-participation technologies, such as email alerts and text messages, and even more interactive e-participation technologies, such as online blogs (hereinafter E-blogs), video sharing sites (hereinafter E-video), and social networking sites (hereinafter SNS) to enhance two-way communications between citizens and policy makers and public managers. Such interactive technologies enable government to hear citizens' voices more effectively, to reach out more to citizens, to improve the quality and quantity of interaction between government and citizens, and to make sound decisions, thus solving policy problems through government–citizen collaboration.

In response to the growing use of e-participation technologies by government, the field of e-participation has progressed significantly. On the one hand, some scholars have discussed and examined the adoption of e-participation technologies by local government (Welch 2012; Mossberger, Wu and Crawford 2013; Feeney and Welch 2014). In a recent study surveying the 75 largest U.S. cities, Mossberger, Wu and Crawford (2013) reported that SNS have been rapidly and widely adopted among these large local governments. The study found that only 13.3 percent of large cities used Facebook in 2009, but that the number dramatically increased to 86.7 percent in 2011. More recent studies (Welch 2012; Feeney and Welch 2014) analyzed the survey results of 902 city managers in the United States and found that many local governments have adopted various e-participation technologies, such as email (93 percent), SNS (54 percent), E-video (20 percent), text messaging (23 percent), and E-blogs (18 percent).

On the other hand, the demand-side research on e-participation has left gaps in our understanding of the barriers and facilitators of e-participation adoption—although recent studies on the adoption of e-government service by citizens (Thomas, Melkers and Streib 2003; Carter and Bélanger 2005; Chen and Dimitrova 2006; Bélanger and Carter 2008; Susha and Grönlund 2012; Hetling, Watson and Horgan 2014; Nam 2014) and business (Lee, Kim and Ahn 2011) have offered relevant insights for e-participation research. For example, some scholars found that citizens' use of e-government services are facilitated by such factors as perceived benefits of e-government (Hetling, Watson and Horgan 2014) and trust in government (Bélanger and Carter 2008).

One distinctive and ongoing challenge facing government leaders and managers is the lack of citizens' participation in offline citizen-participation programs. Likewise, a growing number of e-participation studies have highlighted a similar lack. The full benefits of e-participation technologies will not be realized unless citizens actually use them. On the flipside, the lack of citizen participation has been concerning because it can mislead governments when they are making policy decisions, especially when citizen participants' voices are over- or underrepresentative of community-wide interests. However, with the exception of a few studies (e.g., Macintosh and Whyte 2008; Susanto and Goodwin 2013; Lee and Kim 2014), little information has been presented about the barriers and facilitators of e-participation technology use by citizens. These unresolved issues create the practical challenges facing government leaders and managers who use e-participation technologies to communicate with citizens and make informed decisions—thus, providing quality services to citizens. This research recognizes the issue by asking the question: Who adopts e-participation technologies to interact with government? Drawing on the diffusion and adoption of the innovation model (Rogers 1995) as a guiding framework, I offer an exploratory model of e-participation technology adoption by focusing on the role of citizens' online behaviors with regard to e-government usage and online political participation. The exploratory model was tested using 2009 Government Online survey data collected by the Pew Research Center.

In this research, e-participation is broadly defined as citizens' voluntary participation and involvement in public administration affairs and public decision-making through the use of ICT applications (Kim and Lee 2012). The definition of e-participation involves two key elements: citizen participation and use of ICT, which implies that understanding the use of e-participation technologies by citizens should be informed and framed by at least two streams of research: citizen participation and ICT adoption. One feature of e-participation definition in this research is its connection to conventional citizen participation. The role of citizen participation in public administration has long been discussed and well documented. Some scholars in public administration have considered citizen participation as a means of ensuring public administration to pursue democratic values such as accountability (Pateman 1970; Roberts 2004), while others have argued that citizen participation often inhibits managerial values such as efficiency in public administration (Dahl 1989). Another feature of this definition is characterized as the use of participatory technologies, which include, but are not limited to, E-blogs, E-video (e.g., YouTube), SNS (e.g., Facebook), email alerts, text messages, online discussion forums, and web surveys or polls (Welch 2012). Welch (2012) provides a systematic discussion about technological characteristics of e-participation technologies. For example, SNS enhance different types of two-way communication including rich-data exchange, knowledge sharing, and problem solving (see more details in Welch (2012).

It should be noted that e-participation, by definition, features citizens' involvement in administrative decision-making processes, which should be distinguished from the notion of their political participation (e.g., voting, campaigning, picketing). In this regard, some notions of ICT-enabled participation, such as e-voting (e.g., the use of technology for referendum) and e-campaigning (Brown and Garson 2013), are not considered e-participation technologies in this study.

Literature Review

The use of e-participation technologies can be considered an adoption of innovation, which is defined as an idea, practice, or object that is perceived as new by an individual (Rogers 1995), in that e-participation technologies are relatively new tools designed to communicate with citizens and engage them in public administration decision-making processes. Considering the use of e-participation technology as an innovation adoption, I used the diffusion and adoption of innovation (DOI) model (Rogers 1995)

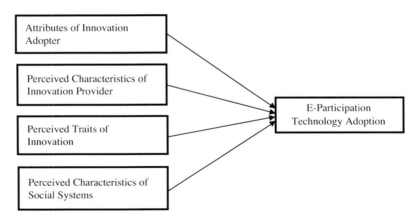

Figure 18.1 Conceptual Model of E-Participation Technology Adoption

as a guiding framework for the literature review on e-participation technology adoption. The DOI model has been widely used to understand various innovations ranging from new public policies to new technologies (Moon 2002; Bélanger and Carter 2008; Kim and Holzer 2007; Jun and Weare 2011). The core idea of the DOI is that innovation diffusion and adoption is shaped by four broader factors: the characteristics of the innovation adopter, the characteristics of the innovation provider, the attributes of innovation, and social systems in which innovation occurs. Drawing on the DOI model (Rogers 1995), Figure 18.1 shows an exploratory model of e-participation technology adoption. Under each factor, I review the demand side of research on e-government and e-participation technology adoption to provide key variables for empirical analysis.

Attributes of Innovation Adopter

As key attributes of innovation adopters (citizens in this study), two types of citizens' online behaviors are highlighted in the model. One is citizens' online behavior with regard to e-government demands, which is relatively unexplored in prior e-participation studies. Early e-government studies offered e-government development stage models (Hiller and Bélanger 2001; Layne and Lee 2001), in which e-participation was explicitly and implicitly considered as an advanced and distinctive stage of e-government development. It is reasonable to argue that e-government does not necessarily develop by following a certain path or stage. In other words, government adopts different e-government stages simultaneously. Nonetheless, the e-government development models imply that it is worthwhile to examine the relationship between e-government and e-participation. I assert that citizens' use of e-government generally reflects their demands for e-government. This means that higher usage of a certain e-government service implies higher demand for that e-government service. In this regard, the use of e-participation technologies can be affected by the extent to which e-participation technologies meet citizens' demands for different types of e-government service. That is, different types of e-government users arguably use different types of e-participation technologies. This argument is consistent with the task-technology fit (TTF) model of technology adoption (Goodhue and Thompson 1995). The key argument of TTF is that new ICT is more likely to be used if the characteristics of that ICT match the features of tasks that the user must perform (Goodhue and Thompson 1995). The TTF model has been applied to predict not only employees' adoption of internal information systems, such as group decision support systems (Zigurs, Buckland, Connolly and Wilson 1999) and accounting information systems

(Benford and Hunton 2000), but also customers' use of electronic commerce systems (Klopping and Earl 2004).

In order to systematically understand the drivers and effects of e-government, e-government scholars have attempted to classify different dimensions of e-government services (Thomas and Streib 2005; Li and Feeney 2014; Nam 2014). For example, Li and Feeney (2014) divided e-government services into e-services and communication technologies, and found that different factors affect the adoption of these two types of e-government service. A recent e-government study (Nam 2014) identified three types of e-government users: government information users, public policy researchers, and transaction-service users. This chapter uses these three types of e-government users (Nam 2014) to explore their relationships with the adoption of different e-participation technologies. As discussed earlier, e-participation technologies are somewhat different from conventional e-government technologies, in that e-participation technologies offer greater communication capabilities through enhanced interactivity. This means that e-participation technologies can be characterized as ongoing interactions between government and citizens, not just one-way traffic from government to citizen. In this regard, e-participation technologies allow citizens not only to act as consumers of government services, but also to serve as constituents who express, deliver, and share their voices with government—as well as coproducers of public services who suggest input or disseminate information about public policy to other peer citizens.

Another dimension of citizens' online behavior is their political participation online. On the one hand, citizen participation literature has emphasized that citizens' participation in public policy decision-making processes is affected by the level of their political participation and their relationship with interest groups (Zukerman and West 1985; Thomas and Melkers 1999). On the other hand, scholars in political science and public administration argue that the use of ICT affects political participation (Norris 2001; Thoma, Melkers and Streib 2003; Oser, Hooghe and Marien 2013). Taking these lines of thought together, it is likely that active political participants adopt e-participation technologies because advanced ICT (e.g., online forums, SNS) provide them another opportunity to reinforce their influence on government and public policy (Verba, Schlozman and Brady 1995; Krueger 2002). Prior empirical research has demonstrated that political participation behaviors, such as lobbying and voting on election days, affect citizens' use of e-government service (Chen and Dimitrova 2006) and the intensity of use of e-participation technologies (Lee and Kim 2014).

Socioeconomic status (SES) has also been studied as key resources that affect citizen participation in general (Verba, Schlozman and Brady 1995; Thomas and Melkers 1999; Norris 2001; Bradbury and Williams 2013) and online participation specifically (Krueger 2002; Best and Krueger 2005; Lee and Kim 2014). Citizen participation scholars have been concerned about the relationship between citizens' socioeconomic background (e.g., race, gender, age, income, education) and their participation in public administration (Thomas and Melkers 1999; Bradbury and Williams 2013). The importance of individual demographics has received attention by early studies on citizen participation in urban planning and governmental budgeting process (Moynihan 1970). Among socioeconomic characteristics, e-government scholars, on the one hand, have found that citizens with such characteristics as younger ages, higher incomes, and higher education tend to adopt e-government services (Chen and Dimitrova 2006). On the other hand, various studies from the e-participation literature have shown mixed findings. Some demonstrated that women tend to use more social media tools (Hampton, Goulet, Rainie and Purcell 2011), while others observed that men tend to use online forums more intensively (Lee and Kim 2014).

Characteristics of Innovation Provider

In relation to innovation provider, which is a government organization in this case, e-government and e-participation research has paid attention to the role of citizens' trust in government as a key characteristic in the adoption of e-government (Carter and Bélanger 2005; Chen and Dimitrova 2006; Bélanger and Carter 2008) and e-participation technologies (Susanto and Goodwin 2013; Lee and Kim 2014). Recently, some e-government studies have found a positive relationship between citizens' trust in government and their use of e-government services (Carter and Bélanger 2005). A more recent study demonstrated that trust in government is positively associated with the use of e-participation technology by citizens (Lee and Kim 2014). For example, Lee and Kim (2014) found that when citizens put greater trust in the government, they tend to post more input on government-run online public forums, which are another type of e-participation technology. Along with this line of research, I expect to find a positive relationship between citizens' trust in government and their adoption of e-participation technology.

Traits of Innovation

The role of the perceived traits of innovation in the adoption of that innovation has been well documented in IT/IS literature (Davis 1989; Moore and Benbasat 1995). In particular, the technology acceptance model (TAM) (Davis 1989) and its extended models (Venkatesh, Morris, Davis and Davis 2003) have been offered and investigated in the context of information systems in both private companies and public organizations (Nedovic-Budic and Godschalk 1996; Berry, Berry and Foster 1998). In addition, e-government and e-participation scholars have applied key variables in TAM—perceived usefulness and ease of use of new technologies—to understand citizens' adoption of e-government (Hetling, Watson and Horgan 2014; Nam 2014) and e-participation technologies (Kim and Holzer 2007). In a similar vein, some traits of innovation, such as relative advantages of new technologies, have been examined and reported as significant factors affecting new technology adoption by end-users, including employees (Nedovic-Budic and Godschalk 1996).

Characteristics of Social Systems

Since an individual citizen is a member of a society, his or her adoption of innovation occurs within a social system. Thus, a social system affects the innovation adoption by individual citizens (Rogers 1995). Rogers (1995) has highlighted the characteristics of social structure and social norms as key social factors influencing innovation adoption, because social structure and norms create opportunities or constraints for individuals to make a decision to adopt (or not adopt) innovation. Social structure refers to the patterned social relationships of an individual citizen in a society, while social norms are broadly defined as "the established behavior patterns for the members of a social system" (Rogers 1995, p. 26). The role of informal social networks and civic norms, in particular, have played positive roles in citizens' engagement in offline and online civic activities (McDonald 2008). However, only a few studies (Lee and Kim 2014) have empirically examined how informal social networks and civic norms affect the adoption of IT innovations such as e-participation technology by individual citizens.

Data and Measurement

To test this study's hypotheses, I used the 2009 Government Online survey data collected by the Pew Internet and American Life Project. A telephone survey was implemented among a nationally representative sample drawn from adults living in continental U.S. households using a random-digit dialing method. The 2009 Government Online dataset includes a total of 2,258 observations. Some of the key demographic statistics of survey participants and adopters of e-participation technologies are summarized in Table 18.1.

Table 18.1 Demographics of Survey Respondents and Adopters of E-Participation Technologies

Variable	Characteristics	Respondents (%)N=2,258	Internet Users (%)N=1,655	E-Blogs Users (%)N=243	E-Video Users (%) N=234	SNS Users (%)N=844	SNS in Government Users (%) N=76	Email Alerts Users (%) N=241	Text Message Users (%) N=45
Gender	Male	993 (56.02)	739 (44.7)	111 (45.7)	125 (53.4)	343 (40.6)	30 (39.5)	110 (45.6)	24 (53.3)
	Female	1,265 (43.98)	916 (55.4)	132 (54.3)	109 (46.6)	501 (59.4)	46 (60.5)	131 (54.4)	21 (46.7)
Race	White	1,806 (79.98)	1,334 (80.6)	196 (80.7)	189 (80.8)	664 (78.7)	62 (81.6)	206 (85.5)	35 (77.8)
	Non-White	452 (20.02)	321 (19.4)	47 (19.3)	45 (19.2)	180 (21.3)	14 (18.4)	35 (14.5)	10 (22.2)
Partisanship	Democratic	862 (38.18)	591 (60.3)	91 (37.5)	104 (44.4)	316 (37.4)	37 (48.7)	103 (42.7)	27 (60.0)
	Other than Democratic	1,396 (61.82)	1,064 (35.7)	152 (62.5)	130 (55.6)	528 (62.6)	39 (51.3)	138 (57.3)	18 (40.0)
Education	Grades 1–8 or less	52 (2.32)	13(.8)	0 (0)	0 (0)	5 (0.6)	0 (0)	1 (0.4)	0 (0)
	High school incomplete	160 (7.14)	66 (4.0)	2 (0.8)	5 (2.2)	38 (4.5)	1 (1.3)	2 (0.8)	0 (0)
	High school graduate	664 (29.63)	378 (23.0)	40 (16.5)	48 (20.6)	188 (22.4)	11 (14.5)	28 (11.7)	9 (20.0)
	Technical, trade, or vocational school	69 (3.08)	47 (2.9)	5 (2.1)	4 (1.7)	13 (1.6)	1 (1.3)	3 (1.3)	0 (0)
	Some college, no 4-year degree	532 (23.74)	435 (26.5)	66 (27.3)	66 (28.3)	234 (27.8)	18 (23.7)	63 (26.3)	6 (13.3)
	College graduate	452 (20.17)	413 (25.1)	66 (27.3)	58 (24.9)	213 (25.3)	19 (25)	71 (29.6)	10 (22.2)
	Postgraduate training/professional school after college	312 (13.92)	291 (17.7)	63 (26.0)	52 (22.3)	150 (17.8)	26 (34.2)	72 (30.0)	20 (44.4)

Measurement

The sample for this study includes five subsamples—1,676 Internet users who adopt or do not adopt E-blogs and E-video in government, 849 SNS users who adopt or do not adopt SNS in government, 1,565 email users who subscribe or do not subscribe to email alerts from government, and 1,113 mobile text users who subscribe or do not subscribe to text messages from government. Thus, the dependent variables are citizens' use of five types of e-participation technologies: E-blogs, E-videos, SNS on government websites, email alerts, and text messages. Citizens' adoption is measured by using five survey items (see survey items in Appendix 1). Each of the dependent variables was coded 1 if the respondent reported that he or she actually viewed E-blogs or E-videos, followed a government agency through SNS, subscribed to email alerts, and used text message services, and 0 otherwise. Separate probit regressions have been employed to assess whether there are differences in the factors affecting the adoption of each type of e-participation technologies.

Independent Variables

As one independent variable capturing the attributes of citizen users as innovation adopters, I constructed citizens' behavior with regard to e-government service use and measured it using 15 survey items about various e-government services. Since those survey questions were designed for the respondent to respond yes or no, each item was coded 1 if the respondent reported yes and 0 otherwise. Following previous literature (Nam 2014), factor analysis of those 15 survey items were conducted to identify distinctive e-government user groups. Due to the discrete nature of each survey item, I computed a tetrachoric correlation matrix as a dataset for the factor analysis of those 15 items. As a result, three types of e-government service were factorized and labeled as information service, policy research, and transaction service. Table 18.2 shows these types of e-government service, survey items corresponding to each type of e-government service, percentage of adoption, and variation explained by each service type. For analytical purposes, I created three summative variables by aggregating the score to capture the overall effect of each type of citizens' e-government usage on their adoption of e-participation technologies.

Citizens' online political participation behaviors were measured through four dummy variables (yes or no) about participation in online town hall meetings, posting comments on online participation platforms about a government policy, uploading photos or videos online about government policy, or joining a group online that attempts to influence government policies (see survey items in Appendix 1).

As to SES, this study included gender, age, race, education, and income in this model. These variables have been identified as important attributes of innovation adopters who adopt e-government and e-participation technologies in previous studies (Krueger 2002; Best and Krueger 2005; Lee and Kim 2014). As a binary variable, gender was coded as 1 if the respondent reported male and 0 otherwise. Age was measured in years. To control for the partisanship effect, partisanship was coded 1 if the respondent reported that he or she leaned more to the Democratic Party and 0 otherwise. Race was coded as 1 if the respondent answered White and 0 otherwise. Education was measured on a seven-point Likert-type scale, with responses ranging from postgraduate (7) to none or grade 1 to 8 (1). Income was measured by using a respondent's household yearly income in 2008, which was scaled from 9 ($150,000 or more) to 1 (less than $10,000).

As one characteristic of an e-participation service provider, the concept of trust in government was used in the analysis. In order to measure trust in government, three survey items in the survey were used (see survey items in Appendix 1). Each question asked about citizens' trust in government

Table 18.2 Types of E-Government Service, Survey Items, Percentage of Adoption, and Variance

Types of E-government Service	Survey Items	Percentage of Yes	Variance explained by each factor
Information service	Advice or information about a health or safety issue	26.5%	2.37
	Downloading government forms	43.9%	
	Information about benefits	21.7%	
	Information about how to apply for a government job	16.4%	
	Looking up what services a government agency provides	47.5%	
Policy research	Recreational or tourism information	33.3%	3.59
	Information about a public policy or issue	50.0%	
	Official government documents or statistics	36.9%	
	Visit a site that provides access to government data (e.g., data.gov, recovery.gov or usaspending.gov)	16.7%	
	Download or read text of any legislation	24.1%	
	Look for information about who contributes to the campaign of your elected officials	14.3%	
	Look to see how money from the recent federal government stimulus package is being spent	23.8%	
Transaction service	Renewing a driver's license or auto registration	32.5%	0.95
	Applying for a fishing, hunting, or other recreational license	11.1%	
	Paying a fine such as a parking ticket	12.0%	

at the federal, state, or local level. The trust variable was measured on a four-point Likert scale, ranging from just about always (4) to never (1), with higher values indicating more trust in government. An aggregate score of the three variables in the model (Cronbach's Alpha = 0.77) was calculated to capture the overall trust effect on the adoption of e-participation technologies.

In order to capture perceived traits of innovation, I used two survey items with a 5-point Likert scale ranging from strongly agree (5) to strongly disagree (1), which reflected the perceived usefulness of e-participation (see Appendix 1). As one key feature of innovation, perceived usefulness has been identified as the strongest predictor of new technology adoption in TAM (Benbasat and Barki 2007). An aggregate score of two items was used in the analysis (Cronbach Alpha = 0.72).

Last, as a characteristic of social systems surrounding citizens, this study explored the effects of social networks among citizens on their use of e-participation technologies. As the 2009 survey data does not include items that directly measure the characteristics of social networks in which citizens are embedded, I used three survey items as proxy (see Appendix 1). These items were chosen to capture the strength of social ties in offline settings. It is assumed that when respondents know most of their neighbors' names, talk face-to-face, and talk over the phone about community issues, it is likely that respondents are strongly tied to their neighbors in the community. Strength of social ties is highly correlated with a dense network, in which information about innovation such as e-participation technology can quickly spread to the members of the network. The aggregated scores were used in the analysis.

Analysis and Findings

As each dependent variable is a binary variable (1 or 0), a probit model was employed. It should be noted that the choice of each e-participation technology is likely to be made only when respondents use other technologies, which implies that selection bias could potentially be an issue. For example, the adoption of E-blogs and E-video by citizens is dependent on their use of the Internet, while the adoption of SNS in government is determined by the use of SNS in general. In order to detect potential selection bias, this research performed a selection bias test to determine the appropriateness of the estimate strategy that controls for selection bias (Green 2007; Vicente and Novo 2014). The results of the selection bias test show that all the estimated *rho* scores are not significantly different from zero and imply that selection bias is not a serious issue across models. Thus, a total of five probit models of participation technology adoption was analyzed and reported in Table 18.3.

Model 1 (E-blog) shows that the adoption of E-blogs was significantly related to more information use ($\beta = 0.16$; $p < 0.01$), policy research ($\beta = 0.12$; $p < 0.01$), and online political participation ($\beta = 0.20$; $p < 0.01$) among the variables capturing attributes of innovation adopter. That is, it is likely that when respondents who have used e-government to gain more government information (e.g., advice about a health or safety issue, government benefits, information about how to apply for a government job) and do more policy research (e.g., official government documents and statistics, and federal government stimulus package) and more actively engage in political participation online (e.g., participate in an online town hall meeting, upload photos or videos online about a government policy and public issues), they would view online blogs in government. Also, greater perception of e-participation value ($\beta = 0.12$; $p < 0.01$) and stronger social ties ($\beta = 0.08$; $p < 0.01$) were significantly associated with the adoption of E-blogs. In other words, respondents who positively assess that the use of e-participation tools such as blogs makes government agencies more accessible are likely to view online blogs in government. And, respondents who have known their neighbors' names and frequently communicated face-to-face with neighbors about community issues are likely to view online blogs in government.

In terms of the role of three types of e-government service use behaviors, Model 2 (E-video) shows a similar pattern to Model 1. That is, more information use ($\beta = 0.23$; $p < 0.01$), policy research ($\beta = 0.20$; $p < 0.01$), and online political participation ($\beta = 0.25$; $p < 0.01$) behaviors were significantly related to the adoption of E-video. Model 2 also demonstrates that democratic partisanship ($\beta = -0.29$; $p < 0.01$) was positively associated with the adoption of E-video, while a higher education level ($\beta = -0.08$; $p < 0.01$) was negatively related to it. In other words, respondents who identified themselves as democrats, compared to republican respondents, are likely to view online video clips in government. It is also likely that respondents with a lower education degree would view video online in government.

In Model 3 (SNS in government), respondents reported that there is no significant association between three types of e-government users and their adoption of SNS in government. However, Model 3 shows that online political participation, age, and household income are significantly related to the use of SNS in government. Specifically, more online political participation ($\beta = 0.28$; $p < 0.01$) and higher household income levels ($\beta = 0.10$; $p < 0.01$) were positively related to the use of SNS in government, while age was negatively related to it ($\beta = -0.02$; $p < 0.01$). That is, it is likely that respondents who have earned more money and are younger would use SNS in government. Model 3 also demonstrates that positive perception of e-participation value was positively related to the use of SNS in government ($\beta = 0.16$; $p < 0.01$). In other words, respondents who positively assess e-participation

Table 18.3 Probit Models of E-Participation Technology Adoption

		Model 1 (E-Blogs=1) Beta (S.E)	Model 2 (E-Video=1) Beta (S.E)	Model 3 (SNS=1) Beta (S.E)	Model 4 (Email=1) Beta (S.E)	Model 5 (Message=1) Beta (S.E)
Attributes of Innovation	Information Use	.16 (.04)**	.23 (.04)**	.02 (.06)	.24 (.04)**	.08 (.07)
Adopter	Policy Research	.12 (.03)**	.20 (.03)**	.04 (.05)	.11 (.03)**	.08 (.05)
	Transaction Service Use	.11 (.06)	.12 (.07)	-.06 (.10)	.10 (.07)	.06 (.12)
	Online Political Participation	.20 (.06)**	.25 (.07)**	.28 (.08)*	.28 (.06)**	.29 (.10)**
	Gender (Male=1)	-.05 (.10)	.19 (.10)	-.02 (.15)	-.06 (.10)	.32 (.18)
	Age	.00 (.00)	-.00 (.00)	-.02 (.00)*	.00 (.00)	.01 (.01)
	Partisanship (Democratic=1)	-.01 (.10)	.29 (.11)**	.18 (.15)	.12 (.10)	.57 (.18)**
	Race (White=1)	-.04 (.13)	.04 (.13)	.25 (.20)	.20 (.14)	-.01 (.22)
	Education	-.04 (.04)	-.08 (.04)*	.05 (.06)	.03 (.04)	.16 (.08)*
	Household Income	.04 (.03)	.04 (.02)	.10 (.04)*	.03 (.03)	-.00 (.05)
Perceived Characteristics of Innovation Provider	Trust in Government	.02 (.02)	-.00 (.03)	.02 (.05)	.05 (.03)	-.01 (.05)
Perceived Traits of Innovation	Perceived Usefulness of E-participation	.12 (.03)**	.04 (.03)	.16 (.06)*	.10 (.03)**	-.02 (.06)
Perceived Characteristics of Social Systems	Strength of Social Ties	.08 (.03)*	.00 (.04)	-.02 (.05)	.02 (.04)	.06 (.06)
Number of observations		1,252	1,251	674	1,186	834
Likelihood ratio		164.56**	252.87**	62.57**	207.52**	63.55**
Percent concordant		77.6	83.3	78.0	80.2	83.8
Percent discordant		22.1	16.4	21.5	19.6	15.4

* $p < .05$; ** $p < .01$

tools (e.g., Facebook, Twitter) as a means of making government agencies more accessible and helping people be more informed about what the government is doing are likely to use SNS in government.

In Model 4 (email alerts), the subscription to email alerts service was significantly associated with more use of government information ($\beta = 0.24$; $p < 0.01$) and policy research ($\beta = 0.11$; $p < 0.01$), and more engagement in online political participation ($\beta = 0.28$; $p < 0.01$). And, the adoption of email alerts was positively related to perception of e-participation value ($\beta = 0.10$; $p < 0.01$). Lastly, Model 5 (text message) showed that active online political participants were positively associated with the sign up of text message services of government ($\beta = 0.29$; $p < 0.01$). Among SES variables, the use of text message was positively associated with respondents who identified themselves as democrats ($\beta = 0.57$; $p < 0.01$) and who belonged to higher education levels ($\beta = 0.16$; $p < 0.05$).

Discussion and Implications

The findings suggest that citizens who mainly use e-government as a means of obtaining government information and of researching public policy show similar patterns with regard to the choice of e-participation technologies. That is, citizens who have already used e-government to find government information and policy-related documents and data would more frequently view E-blogs and E-video in government, and subscribe to email alert/notification service of government. This is probably because that information-oriented and policy research-oriented e-government users seek further information using E-blogs, E-video, and email subscription. Information available at government websites may not be up to date or fully provided; these citizens may need further clarification from government officials or find text-based information too long to conveniently read. In these cases, E-blogs and E-video seem to serve as complementary e-participation technologies that meet citizens' information and policy research demands by offering timely and rich information, providing opportunities to communicate with government officials who post information or video clips (e.g., YouTube video clips of tourism in the State of Nebraska), providing access to peer citizen users' postings or video clips (if any), and/or offering short video clips about public policies. As a result, it appears that E-blogs, E-video, and email alert/notification technologies better fit the needs of information-oriented and policy research-oriented e-government users.

The results also suggest, however, that there is no significant association between three types of e-government users and their adoption of SNS in government and sign up to receive text messages from a government agency. This is probably because SNS in government may not meet the expectations of e-government users. Although information-oriented e-government users, for example, may seek relative advantages of using SNS in government, they might not see fundamental differences between information provided by SNS in government and government websites. This is because SNS in government are often used to deliver similar information to that which is already available or will be available at government websites. Also, government often provides limited information on SNS in government and instead offers links (or government website addresses) for more information. If SNS provide similar information that is (or will be) available at government websites or serves as a gateway to government websites, it is less likely that information-oriented users will choose SNS in government as either complementary or supplementary technology.

The study findings demonstrate that transaction-service users have distinctive behaviors in terms of using e-participation technologies. That is, transaction-oriented e-government users are likely to watch E-video and subscribe to email alert services of government. It appears that E-video services can meet the demands of transaction services (e.g., online vehicle renewal) by posting a short video clip demonstrating how to fill out necessary forms to complete transactions with government (e.g., https://www.youtube.com/user/TexasGov). The subscription to email alert services enables transaction-service users to receive timely information and to make informed decisions about transactions with government, such as email notifications for upcoming deadlines on vehicle renewal or parking ticket payment (e.g., Nebraska Department of Motor Vehicles).

Overall, the results imply that there is no one "best" e-participation technology that meets all types of e-government users. The adoption of e-participation technologies depends on how different e-participation technologies fit the demands of different types of e-government users. Generally speaking, it appears that E-video, E-blogs, and email subscription technologies provide a better fit to two types of e-government user demands (i.e., information and research). It is recommended that e-government leaders and managers expend more effort to understand patterns and behaviors of e-government users in order to facilitate their use of e-participation technologies and engagement in government.

The findings demonstrate that citizens who are actively engaged in political participation online are likely to adopt all types of e-participation technology. It seems that since these active political participants have already used online technologies (e.g., posting comments on online discussion forums, uploading videos), they might choose to utilize E-blogs, E-video, and SNS in government as a complementary means of reinforcing their efforts to influence government policies. It is also likely that active online political participants take advantage of subscription to emails and text messages in order to receive up-to-date information about government activities and services, which can serve as resources for their political interests and actions. A primary lesson learned from this observation is that e-government leaders and managers should be aware that active political participants online are more likely to use various e-participation technologies to engage in public administration.

The findings indicate that some characteristics of SES are related to the adoption of certain e-participation technologies while others (e.g., gender and race) are not. The findings of negative association between age and SNS in government are not surprising, in that younger people tend to adopt new technologies such as SNS earlier. In terms of the relation between partisanship and the adoption of e-participation technologies, the findings imply that respondents with democratic partisanship are likely to watch E-video in government and sign up for text message services from government. According to a recent report from the Huffington Post in 2013 (http://www.huffingtonpost.com/2013/09/06/illiteracy-rate_n_3880355.html), 32 million adults (14 percent) in the U.S. are at a below basic level of reading and writing. Assuming that there is a strong relationship between the level of education achieved and literacy, it is reasonable for citizens with lower level of education to avoid using some e-participation technologies (e.g., text message service) requiring a certain level of literacy and to favor other e-participation technologies (e.g., E-video) minimally requiring that level of literacy. One distinctive feature of E-video in government is that as multimedia, E-video has greater capabilities of making text-only contents in government documents visual and audible. By combining different content forms (e.g., text, audio, video, images), it is likely that viewing E-video as a means of effectively gaining access to information about public services and doing some research on government policies and practices may not require citizens to be equipped with a higher level of education and literacy. However, the subscription of text message services of government may be favored by citizens with a higher level of education and literacy. The relationship between household income and the adoption of e-participation technologies—except for SNS in government—is not supported by the data. The positive relationship between household income and the use of SNS in government means that citizens who enjoy greater financial resources tend to use SNS in government. It can be possibly explained that given the fact that SNS are relatively newer technologies, citizens who have more financial resources are likely to have more time to explore innovative technologies as a means of reinforcing their socioeconomic status by taking relative advantages of SNS, such as strengthening existing social networks and building new social networks.

The roles of perceived characteristics of innovation providers (i.e., trust in government), social systems (e.g., strength of social ties), value of e-participation technologies, and SES in adopting e-participation technology are minimal. For example, previous studies (Lee and Kim 2014) found that trust in government and strength of social ties are significantly related to citizens' intensity of use of government-run online forums. However, this study's data failed to replicate these findings. It is unclear whether this is because of different cultural and social context, technology, or measurement. Future studies are needed to further examine the roles of citizens' perceptions of innovation providers and social systems when they are embedded in the adoption of innovative technologies, such as e-participation technologies. Also, although numerous IT and e-government studies (Kim and Holzer 2007; Hetling, Watson and Horgan 2014; Nam 2014) found a positive role of perceived benefits in the adoption of new technology, perceived value of e-participation technologies is found to be a significant factor affecting the use of email alert services only in this study.

Conclusion

This chapter investigates who uses e-participation technology and attempts to address this question using national e-government survey data from 2009. Considering e-participation technology as an innovation, the DOI model is used as a guiding conceptual framework in which the characteristics of innovation adopters, the characteristics of innovation providers, the attributes of innovation, and particulars of social systems in which innovation occur. Specifically, the focus of this study lies in the roles of innovation adopters' online behaviors, such as the use of different types of e-government services and online political participation in the adoption of five types of e-participation technologies (such as E-blogs, E-video, SNS in government, email alerts, and text message services). By employing the selection model, I found that (1) different groups of e-government users adopt different e-participation technologies, and (2) online political participation behaviors influence the adoption of e-participation technologies.

Certain limitations of this study should also be noted. The adoption of e-participation technologies does not make sense unless government offers such e-participation technologies and services, and citizens are aware of the availability of those technologies and services. However, the study data provide limited information about the availability of e-participation services provided by government and the awareness of e-participation services by citizens. Also, due to the fact that the survey items were originally designed to measure the variables used in this study, it is limited to ensure validity of some measures (e.g., strength of ties).

It is expected that addressing the research question will help local leaders and public managers better understand the major barriers and facilitators of e-participation technology use by citizens. Additionally, considering that e-participation has been an emerging, but underexplored, area of research in citizen participation and public administration literature, I hope to open a dialogue among citizen participation scholars and direct their attention to the role of ICT in citizen participation.

References

Bélanger, France and Lemuria Carter. "Trust and Risk in E-Government Adoption." *Strategic Information Systems*, 17 (2008): 165–176.
Benbasat, Izak and Henri Barki. "Quo vadis, TAM?" *Journal of the Association for Information Systems*, 8, no. 4 (2007): 211–218.
Benford, Tanya and James Hunton. "Incorporating Information Technology Considerations into an Expanded Model of Judgment and Decision Making in Accounting." *International Journal of Accounting Information Systems* 1, no. 1 (2000): 54–65.
Berry, France, William Berry and Stephen Foster. "The Determinants of Success in Implementing an Expert Systems in State Government." *Public Administration Review*, 58, no. 4 (1998): 293–305.
Best, Samuel and Brian Krueger. "Analyzing the Representativeness of Internet Political Participation." *Political Behavior*, 27 (2005): 183–216.

Bradbury, Mark and Marian Williams. "Diversity and Citizen Participation: The Effect of Race on Juror Decision Making." *Administration & Society*, 45, no. 5 (2013): 563–582.

Brown, Mary and David G. Garson. *Public Information Management and E-Government: Policy and Issues*. Hershey, PA: IGI Global, 2013.

Carter, Lemuria and France Bélanger. "The Utilization of E-Government Services: Citizen Trust, Innovation and Acceptance Factors." *Information Systems Journal*, 15 (2005): 5–25.

Chen, Yu-Che and Daiela V. Dimitrova. "Electronic Government and Online Engagement: Citizen Interaction with Government via Web Portals." *International Journal of Electronic Government Research*, 2, no. 1 (2006): 54–76.

Dahl, Robert. *Democracy and its critics*. New Haven, CT: Yale University Press, 1989.

Davis, Fred. "Perceived Usefulness, Perceived Ease of Use, and User Acceptance of Information Technology." *MIS Quarterly*, 13, no. 3 (1989): 319–339.

Feeney, Mary and Eric Welch. "Technology-Tack Coupling: Exploring Social Media Use and Managerial Perceptions of E-Government." *American Review of Public Administration*, 1, no. 1 (2014): 1–18.

Goodhue, Dale and Ronald Thompson. "Task-technology fit and individual performance." *MIS Quarterly*, 19, no. 2 (1995): 213–236.

Green, William. *Econometric Analysis*. New York: Prentice Hall, 2007.

Hampton, Keith, Lauren Goulet, Lee Rainie and Kristen Purcell. *Social Networking Sites and Our Lives*. Washington, DC: Pew Research Center's Internet & American Life Project, 2011.

Hetling, Andrea, Stevie Watson and Meghan Horgan. "We Live in a Technological Era, Whether You Like It or Not: Client Perspectives and Online Welfare Applications." *American Review of Public Administration*, 46, no. 5 (2014): 519–547.

Hiller, Janine and France Bélanger. *Privacy Strategies for Electronic Government*. Washington, DC: IBM Center for the Business of Government, 2001.

Jun, Kyu-Nahm and Christopher Weare. "Institutional Motivations in the Adoption of Innovations: The Case of E-Government." *Journal of Public Administration Research and Theory*, 21 (2011): 495–519.

Kim, Chan-Gon and Mark Holzer. "The Utilization of Online Policy Forums on Government Web Sites and the Practice of Digital Democracy." In *E-Government Research: Policy and Management 20XX*, edited by Donald Norris, 268–295. Hershey, PA: IGI Publishing, 2007.

Kim, Soonhee and Jooho Lee. "E-participation, transparency, and trust in local government." *Public Administration Review*, 72 (2012): 819–828.

Klopping, Inge M. and Earl McKinney. "Extending the Technology Acceptance Model and the Task-Technology Fit Model to Consumer E-Commerce." *Information Technology, Learning, and Performance Journal*, 22, no. 1 (2004): 35–48.

Krueger, Brian. "Assessing the Potential of Internet Political Participation in the United States: A Resource Approach." *American Politics Research*, 30 (2002): 476–498.

Layne, Karen and Jungwoo Lee. "Developing Fully Functional E-Government: A Four Stage Model." *Government Information Quarterly*, 18, no. 2 (2001): 122–136.

Lee, Jooho, Hyun Joon Kim and Michael Ahn. "The Willingness of E-Government Service Adoption by Business Users: The Role of Offline Service Quality and Trust in Technology." *Government Information Quarterly*, 28 (2011): 222–230.

Lee, Jooho and Soonhee Kim. "Active Citizen E-Participation in Local Governance: Do Individual Social Capital and E-Participation Management Matter?" *Proceedings of the Forty-Seven Hawaii International Conference on System Science* (HICSS 2014), 6–9 January, 2014, Waikoloa, Hawaii.

Li, Meng-Hao and Mary K. Feeney. "Adoption of Electronic Technologies in Local U.S. Governments: Distinguishing between E-Service and Communication Technologies." *American Review of Public Administration*, 44, no. 1 (2014): 75–91.

Macintosh, Ann and Angus Whyte. "Toward an Evaluation Framework for E-Participation." *Transforming Government: People, Process and Policy*, 2, no. 1 (2008): 16–30.

McDonald, Jason. "The Benefits of Society Online: Civic Engagement." In *Digital Governance: The Internet, Society, and Participation*, edited by Karen Mossberger, Caroline Tolbert and Ramona McNeal, 47–66. Cambridge, MA: The MIT Press, 2008.

Moon, M. Jae. "The Evolution of E-Government among Municipalities: Rhetoric or Reality?" *Public Administration Review*, 62, no. 4 (2002): 424–433.

Moore, Gary and Izak Benbasat. "Integrating Diffusion of Innovations and Theory of Reasoned Action Models to Predict Utilization of Information Technology by End-Users." *Proceedings of the First IFIP WG 8.6 Conference on the Diffusion and Adoption of Information Technology*, 1995, pp. 132–146, London, UK: Chapman & Hill, 1995.

Mossberger, Karen, Yonghong Wu and Jared Crawford. "Connecting Citizens and Local Governments? Social Media and Interactivity in Major U.S. Cities." *Government Information Quarterly*, 30 (2013): 351–358.

Moynihan, Daniel. *Maximum Feasible Misunderstanding*. Yew York: Free Press, 1970.

Nam, Taewoo. "Determining the Type of E-government Use." *Government Information Quarterly*, 31 (2014): 211–220.

Nedovic-Budic, Zorica and David R. Godschalk. "Human Factors in Adoption of Geographic Information Systems: A Local Government Case Study." *Public Administration Review*, 56, no. 6 (1996): 554–567.

Norris, Pippa. *Digital Divide? Civic Engagement, Information Poverty and the Internet Worldwide*. Cambridge, MA: Cambridge University Press, 2001.

Oser, Jennifer, Marc Hooghe and Sofie Marien. "Is Online Participation Distinct from Offline Participation? A Latent Class Analysis of Participation Types and Their Stratification." *Political Research Quarterly*, 66, no. 1 (2013): 91–101.

Pateman, Carole. *Participation and democratic theory*. Cambridge, MA: Cambridge University Press, 1970.

Roberts, Nancy. "Public deliberation in an age of direct citizen participation." *American Review of Public Administration*, 34 (2004): 315–353.

Rogers, Everett. *Diffusion of Innovations*. New York: The Free Press, 1995.

Susanto, Tony and Robert Goodwin. "User Acceptance of SMS-Based E-Government Services: Differences between Adopters and Non-Adopters." *Government Information Quarterly*, 30 (2013): 486–497.

Susha, Iryna and Åke Grönlund. "E-Participation Research: Systematizing the Field." *Government Information Quarterly*, 29 (2012): 373–382.

Thomas, Clyaton and Julia Melkers. "Explaining Citizen-Initiated Contacts with Municipal Bureaucrats: Lessons from the Atlantic Experience." *Urban Affairs Review*, 34, no. 5 (1999): 667–690.

Thomas, Clayton, Julia Melkers and Greg Streib. "The New Face of Government: Citizen-Initiated Contacts in the Era of E-Government."' *Journal of Public Administration Research and Theory*, 13, no. 1 (2003): 83–102.

Thomas, Clayton and Greg Streib. "E-Democracy, E-Commerce, and E-Research: Examining the Electronic Ties between Citizens and Governments." *Administration & Society* 37, no. 3 (2005): 259–280.

Venkatesh, Viswanath, Michael G. Morris, Gordon B. Davis and Fred D. Davis. "User Acceptance of Information Technology: Toward a Unified View." *MIS Quarterly*, 27, no. 3 (2003): 425–478.

Verba, Sidney, Kay Schlozman and Henry Brady. *Voice and Equality: Civic Voluntarism in American Politics*. Cambridge, MA: Harvard University Press. 1995.

Vicente, Maria Rosalia and Amparo Novo. "An Empirical Analysis of E-Participation: The Role of Social Networks and E-Government Over Citizen's Online Engagement." *Government Information Quarterly*, 31 (2014): 379–387.

Welch, Eric. "The Rise of Participatory Technologies in Government." In *Transformational Government through eGov Practices: Socioeconomic, Cultural, and Technological Issues*, edited by Mahmud Shareef, Norm Archer, Yogesh Dwivedi, Alok Mishar and Sanjay Pandey, 347–367. Bingley, UK: Emerald Publishers, 2012.

Zigurs, Ilze, Bonne Buckland, James Connolly and E. Vance Wilson. "A test of task-technology fit theory for group support systems." *Data Base for Advances in Information Systems*, 30, no. 3,4 (1999): 34–50.

Zukerman, Allen and Darrel West. "The Political Bases of Citizen Contacting: A Cross-National Analysis." *American Political Science Review*, 79, no. 1 (1985): 117–131.

Appendix 1
SURVEY ITEMS USED IN THE ANALYSIS

The Adoption of E-Participation Technologies

For each of the following, please tell me if you have done this in the past 12 months, or not.

	Yes, Have done this	*No, Have not*
Read the blog of government agency or official		
Watched video online on a government website		
Followed or become a fan of a government agency or official through their page on a social networking site		
Signed up to receive email alerts from a government agency or official		
Signed up to receive text messages from a government or official		

Trust in Government

How much of the time do you think you can trust the following government?

	Just about always	*Most of the time*	*Some of the time*	*Never*
The federal government				
Your state government				
Your local government				

Strength of Social Ties

Do you know the names of your neighbors who live close to you or not?

(1) Yes, know all of them
(2) Yes, know most of them
(3) Yes, know only some of them
(4) No, do not know any

Have you talked face-to-face with your neighbors about community issues?

(1) Yes, have done this
(2) No, have not

Have you talked on the phone with your neighbors about community issues?

(1) Yes, have done this
(2) No, have not

Online Political Participation

In the past 12 months, have you used the Internet to . . .

	Yes, Have done this	No, Have not
Participate in an online town hall meeting		
Post comments, queries or information on a blog, online discussion, listserv or other online forum about a government policy or public issue		
Upload photos or videos online about a government policy or public issue		
Join a group online that tries to influence government policies		

Perceived E-Participation Technology Value

As you may know, some government agencies and officials now allow people to get information and submit feedback using NEW tools such as blogs, social networking sites like Facebook, services like Twitter, or text messaging. Please tell me whether you agree or disagree with each of the following statements. Having a way to follow and communicate online with government using these tools . . .

	Strongly agree	Somewhat agree	Somewhat disagree	Strongly disagree	Neither agree nor disagree	Unfamiliar with tools
Makes government agencies and officials more accessible						
Helps people be more informed about what government is doing						

SECTION V

Advancement of Public Service through Technological Innovations

19
PROVIDING CRITICAL EMERGENCY COMMUNICATIONS VIA SOCIAL MEDIA PLATFORMS
Multiple Case Study

DeeDee Bennett

Introduction

Since 2007, social media platforms have become an important channel for information exchange among survivors, volunteer organizations, and nongovernmental organizations during (and after) emergencies and disasters (Fraustino, Liu, and Yan, 2012). Over the last six years, emergency-related government agencies, at the state and local level, have begun to adopt strategies for social media use. At the federal level, the government has begun to standardize social media use specifically for emergencies (Bennett, 2014). In July 2014, the House of Representatives passed the Social Media Emergency Response bill [H.R.4263] to establish standards for social media use (U.S. Congress, 2014). The bill also encourages the federal government to communicate with citizens using emergency support technologies, engage in social media response activity, and apply social media use recommendations (Marcos, 2014).

This chapter highlights the use of social media by emergency management agencies, using multiple case study analysis. Each case represents county-level emergency management agencies that use Twitter to communicate to the public. The benefits and disadvantages emergency managers face using social media are discussed, as well as the technical and organizational issues relevant to the implementation of an emergency management social media presence.

This multiple case study is partially extended from a larger study, which included 13 emergency management agencies and was supported by the Department of Homeland Security (DHS), the Federal Emergency Management Agency (FEMA), and the Integrated Public Alert & Warning System's (IPAWS) program office.[1] The study team conducted semi-structured interviews with representatives from emergency management agencies (EMAs) located in various regions of the United States at the state, county, and local levels. On several interview questions, the study team reached saturation, a point at which no new information was offered from the interviewees (Hesse-Biber and Leavy, 2006; Yin, 2014). Triangulation was used as a validity tool for certain aspects of the findings by incorporating observational analysis of Facebook and/or Twitter pages used by the corresponding emergency management agencies interviewed over a period of 31 days in 2014 (Hesse-Biber and Leavy, 2006; Yin, 2014). In this multiple case study, only Twitter is reviewed. Additionally, archival data from the EMA websites and Internal documents provided by the agencies are included.

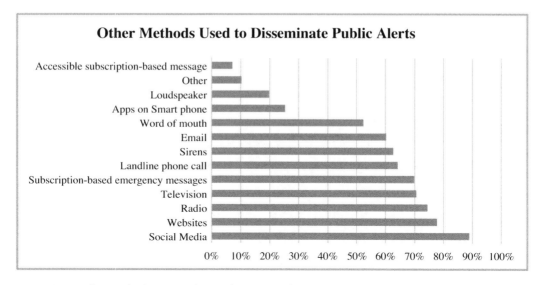

Figure 19.1 Other Methods FEMA Alert Authorities Used to Disseminate Public Alerts

The use of social media platforms by emergency management is important because of their growing adoption among EMAs and the general public. During the same IPAWS research project, 139 FEMA-approved emergency alert authorities were surveyed on their use of different channels for the dissemination of public alerts and warnings. FEMA alert authorities are required to be a recognized alert-capable agency (or organization), complete the online IPAWS course, and sign a memorandum of agreement with FEMA. At the time of the study (in 2014), there were 425 approved alert authorities, and each was contacted to participate in the survey. The survey response rate was 33%. Figure 19.1 shows what channels the respondents used to disseminate emergency alerts. Nearly 90% of the alert authorities surveyed indicated that they use social media to disseminate emergency alerts. Radio and television were their third and fourth most-used methods to communicate emergency alerts, 75% and 70%, respectively. The findings on this question alone should indicate to both emergency managers and government officials the growing reliance of Internet-based platforms, as well as the decrease in the use of traditional-based media for alerts and warnings.

Literature Review

For purposes of this study, the term "social media" will refer to Internet-based platforms created to socially connect users via postings, followings, videos, and/or trending topics. Typically, four distinct features establish an Internet-based platform as social media. For purposes of this multiple case study, we will use an expanded version adapted from Boyd and Ellison's (2008) definition of online social network sites, as used by Bennett (Bennett, 2014). Social media platforms (1) require the identity of all users to be known, usually via a profile; (2) allow users to befriend or follow fellow users; (3) enable users to traverse and review others' profile and postings; and (4) can connect users based on their profile, friends, posts, comments on posts, or their interest in a post (or trending topic).

While some social media platforms can be reconfigured by each user to limit access to their profile or posts, typically users cannot completely opt out of all the features that define social media. However, some hybrids may give visitors to the site the option to join or view without joining. The site may be used as just a source of information from active users (such as blogs and news sites) or as a social media platform where the visitor is required to become an active user if they want to take advantage of all features.

In reality, the definition of social media will constantly change. The market for social media has new additions every year, and all social media platforms have evolved through updates since their initial deployment. Therefore, any definition today may need to be adjusted to include the future developments in social media of tomorrow.

Public Alerts and Warnings

Established research models disaster warning as a three-fold process based on detection, dissemination, and public response (Drabek, 1999; Mileti and Peek, 2000). Detection involves determining the specifics about the potential or occurring threat. Traditionally, several technologies are used, including satellites, Doppler radar, and flood gauges.

In the dissemination phase, information about the threat is given to the public. For decades, the standard channels used for dissemination of information include face-to-face, telephone, sirens, broadcast technology (such as TV and radio), and newspapers (Lindell and Perry, 2004; Sorensen, 2000). New media, such as digital road signs, mobile phones, websites, and social media platforms, are now also being used to disseminate warning messages. The use of new media during the dissemination phase has shifted the way the public receives information. Previously, the long-established model for communicating alerts and warnings began with the mass media, industry, political leaders, and EMAs providing emergency messages to the general public, in a traditional top-down approach (Nigg, 1995; Rodríguez et al., 2007). However, the model is changing, as seen in Figure 19.2. Evidence suggests that mass media, industry, political leaders, EMAs, and the general public are all receiving information at the same time. While mass media, industry, political leaders, and EMAs tend to rely on scientific assessments, the public often bases information on environment assessments. Much of this change is due to the widespread use of social media platforms. In one example, Twitter users in New York were alerted (by the general public) to a 5.8 earthquake in Virginia, prior to feeling the tremors and well before media reports (Indvik, 2015). This is not surprising; since 2006, the U.S. Geological Survey (USGS) has been perfecting an earthquake early warning system, named ShakeAlert, that would perform similarly, by alerting subscribers prior to the tremors reaching their location (USGS, n.d.).

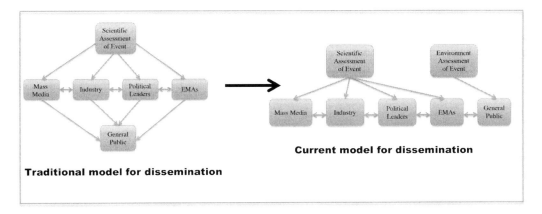

Figure 19.2 Shift in the Model for Disseminating Public Alerts and Warnings. Traditional model adapted from Rodríguez et al. (2007).

The final phase of the warning process, public response, is often influenced by public perceptions about the warning message. It is during this phase that citizens decide whether or not to take protective action (Lindell and Perry, 2004; Mileti, 1999). Sometimes the channel used (or not used) to disseminate warning messages can impact public response. Therefore, multimodal dissemination is most effective, meaning that warnings are disseminated on multiple channels (Mileti, 1999; Rodríguez et al., 2007). Even when providing information on multiple channels, the messages should be clear, concise, and consistent across channels (Mileti, 1999). Furthermore, research has consistently maintained that warning messages be presented in multiple languages to reduce misunderstanding due to potential language barriers (Aguirre, 1998; Lindell and Perry, 2004; Rodríguez et al., 2007). This is most important in the U.S., because the population is a heterogeneous mix of many ethnicities, nationalities, and cultures.

The general public has already embraced social media channels. The most popular platforms used during emergencies, Facebook and Twitter, have over 1.4 billion and 300 million monthly active users, respectively (Facebook, 2015; Twitter, 2015). Numerous state and local safety authorities also have established their presence on some of the most-used social media services, particularly Facebook and Twitter (Mitchell, Bennett, and LaForce, 2011). Unlike other channels used for emergency messaging, social media platforms are able to support two-way communication between alert disseminators and the public. This feature alone may positively influence public response and protective action. Furthermore, social media platforms are able to easily accommodate messages in multiple language formats.

Social Media in Emergency Management

Prior to 2007, many emergency management–related agencies did not use social media. Some of the first studies on the use of social media during emergencies were following the Virginia Tech shooting in 2007 and the Southern California wildfires in 2007. Most emergency management agencies did not use or monitor social media sites prior to 2007, even though the most popular social media platforms, Facebook and Twitter, were popular. Since 2007, researchers have studied how nongovernmental organizations (NGOs) and the general public have been the primary users of social media platforms during emergencies; however, now, emergency management agencies are beginning to use and rely on social media platforms. The majority of emergency managers studied (in these interviews and in the aforementioned survey of 139 alert authorities) began using social media in 2008 or later. This is most likely because NGOs and the public were readily using social media during emergencies, and in 2009, a new FEMA director, Craig Fugate, was appointed, who impressed upon his staff the importance of using as many communication tools as possible to reach everyone in the community. Fugate even joined Twitter, as himself, by August 2009. There is overwhelming evidence to suggest that the public is eager for emergency communications via social media platforms. A study from the American Red Cross (2012) reveals that among those who actively use the Internet, social media platforms (together with mobile apps) rank as the fourth most popular source(s) for emergency-related information. Furthermore, the majority of the public that use social media for public safety emergencies expect that first responders are at least monitoring those sites (American Red Cross, 2012).

Several researchers have studied social media use during emergencies (Bennett, 2014; Prentice and Huffman, 2008; Starbird and Palen, 2011; Sutton, 2010; Sutton, Palen, and Shklovski, 2008). Using survey analysis, Sutton, Palen, and Shklovski (2008) found that social media was used as a form of "back channel communication" among the public following the Southern California wildfires in 2007. A single case study analysis of Broward County, Florida, found that not only does the public use social media during emergencies, but industry and NGOs use them as well (Prentice and Huffman, 2008). Volunteer organizations also use social media during emergencies to organize themselves, reach victims, and gather proper resources (Starbird and Palen, 2011; Sutton, 2010). Specifically, Facebook and Twitter have been used to promote public awareness, disseminate emergency communications, distribute disaster assistance information, and act as a coordination point for volunteers (Bennett, 2014).

Within the last five years, research findings suggest that EMAs are beginning to actively use social media during emergencies, as well (Bennett, 2014; Bird, Ling, and Haynes, 2012; Li, Vishwanath, and Rao, 2014; Sutton, Hansard, and Hewett, 2011). Emergency managers have been found to use social media platforms as a way to directly interact with the public after a tsunami warning had been issued in Hawaii (Sutton, Hansard, and Hewett, 2011) and following a series of tornadoes in Alabama (Bennett, 2014). Social media platforms were used by emergency managers following the Queensland and Victorian floods in Australia as a means to engage in two-way communications with the public (Bird, Ling, and Haynes, 2012). Twitter was proven to be a most useful tool by which Japanese government officials and humanitarian aid organizations shared information with survivors following the Fukushima earthquake, tsunami, and subsequent radiological disaster (Li, Vishwanath, and Rao, 2014). In 2013, the virtual social media working group (VSMG) reported that "more government agencies turned to mobile and online technologies before, during, and after Hurricane Sandy . . . to communicate with response partners and the public in order to share information, maintain awareness of community actions and needs" (DHS, 2013).

Even though use of social media for emergencies has increased in the last several years, concerns surrounding legal issues, rumors, and the spread of misinformation have not been alleviated (Bennett, 2014; Sutton, Hansard, and Hewett, 2011; Wukich, 2015).

Beyond natural disasters, social media platforms have also been used during instances of potential civil unrest and chemical spills (Bennett, 2015a; Sutton, 2010). While there is proof that social media is used by EMAs during emergencies, there is little body of evidence about the challenges or opportunities these new tools provide in terms of dissemination of emergency communications by EMAs. Table 19.1 outlines research on social media sites for emergency communications.

Table 19.1 Select Research on Social Media Sites for Emergency Communications

Year	Event	Social Media Site	Primary user	Type of Use	Citation
2007	Southern California Wildfires	Twitter, Facebook, Flickr	Public	Backchannel communication	(Sutton, Palen, and Shklovski, 2008)
				Finding community	(Shklovski, Palen, and Sutton, 2008)
				Uses of Twitter during response	(Mills et al., 2009)
	Virginia Tech Shooting	Facebook, Wiki	Public	Use of social media during campus shooting	(Palen et al., 2009)
2008	Hurricanes Ike and Gustav	Twitter	Public	Twitter adoption and Mass convergence	(Hughes and Palen, 2009)
	None	Social media	EMAs	Case study on Idaho EMA	(Prentice and Huffman, 2008)

(*Continued*)

Table 19.1 (Continued)

Year	Event	Social Media Site	Primary user	Type of Use	Citation
2009	Red River Valley Floods	Twitter	Public	Geographical locations and public information	(Palen, Starbird, and Vieweg, 2010)
	Oklahoma Grassfires			Information source from people on the ground	(Vieweg et al., 2010)
	Violent Crisis—Seattle, Washington		Public	Examination of Twitter use following civil unrest in Seattle	(Heverin and Zach, 2010)
2010	Haiti Earthquake	Twitter	Public/NGO	Volunteers use of Twitter	(Starbird and Palen, 2011)
		All social media	Public/EMA/NGO	Crowdsourcing	(Gao, Barbier, and Goolsby, 2011)
		MediaWiki, Sharepoint, Intelink	EMA	Emergency knowledge management and social media technologies	(Yates and Paquette, 2011)
	Hawaii Tsunami Warning	Twitter	Public/EMA	Communicating tsunami warning information in Hawaii	(Sutton, Hansard, and Hewett, 2011)
2011	Alabama Tornadoes	Facebook, Twitter	EMAs	Tornado debris characteristics using social media data	(Knox et al., 2013)
				Partnerships, Engaged conversation, and Organization of volunteers	(Bennett, 2012; Bennett, 2014)
	Australian Floods			Use of social media	(Bird, Ling, and Haynes, 2012)
	Japan Tsunami and Nuclear Radiation	Twitter	Public/EMAs	Use of Twitter and power of retweets	(Li, Vishwanath, and Rao, 2014)
2012	Hurricane Sandy	Facebook, Twitter	EMAs, government	Lessons learned	(DHS, 2013)
				Social media as a predictor of PTSD	(Goodwin et al., 2013)
	None	Facebook, Twitter	EMAs	Report on social media use	(Fraustino, Liu, and Yan, 2012)
		All social media	CDC	Use of social media to predict disease outbreaks	(Schmidt, 2012)
			Government	Use of social media from routine to critical	(Kavanaugh et al., 2012)
2013	None	Facebook, Twitter	EMAs	Survey of emergency managers	(San et al., 2013)
2014	None	Twitter		Warning tweets	(Sutton et al., 2014)

Methodology and Background

Originally, the study involved the analysis of 13 interviews of representatives from emergency management agencies. This is important because it gives the context for the initial data collection. The 13 EMAs represented 8 of the 10 FEMA regions and were initially chosen with help from FEMA. The selected agencies were purposefully contacted by email to participate in a telephone interview to discuss their use of social media. The original list from FEMA was augmented with additional emergency management agencies that also used social media, as represented by their websites. The response was low. In each case, study staff interviewed the person most knowledgeable about the use of social media by the EMAs as identified by the EMA director. Since the EMA director selected the persons interviewed, the result was interviews with a variety of individuals with different titles at different levels in the organizations. Due to the timeline of the initial project, the purposely contacted agencies, and the select questions reaching saturation, the study ended with 13 EMAs.

In this multiple case study, the focus is on four EMAs from the original 13 that represent each of the different levels of social media engagement. The four cases were also chosen because they all used Twitter as a social media platform and were all from the same level of government: county, albeit from different regions of the United States. The four EMAs were also chosen because they represented the larger sample in terms of social media engagement.

Each EMA's Twitter feed was observed for the same 31 days in 2014. A detailed coding analysis of each post was not completed for this study. Facebook, YouTube, Instagram, and Tumblr were discussed by the agencies but were not observed. During the 31-day timeline, some emergency management agencies responded to an emergency or disaster (due to their regional location); others did not. Twitter data was reviewed in its entirety online, but not coded unless there was a significant influx in tweets or retweets. Finally, documents on the EMA's website and internal documents provided by the interviewed representatives were also used in this analysis. Due to the unique nature of the study (and how the agencies were chosen), the agencies analyzed and reviewed here are presented anonymously to ensure open and honest conversation. The initial semi-structured interview questions are listed below:

1. When did EMA start using social media?
    a. Why did the EMA start using social media?
2. Which social media platforms are used by your EMA?
    a. Is there a difference in the use for Twitter vs. Facebook vs. YouTube?
    b. Do you follow or like other agencies or organizations and share their information?
3. What types of information are distributed using social media?
    a. Who decides the content? How does the content differ when in the midst of an emergency or disaster?
    b. Have you ever or do you plan on using social media for alerting?
        i. If yes, how/what do you use, Twitter alert/Google alerts/free text?
    c. Are the posts translated into other languages (Spanish, French, ASL)?
4. Have you found a social media platform that is better for reaching people with disabilities or those with access and functional needs?
5. What have been some of your experiences in using social media?
    a. Has information been misinterpreted?
        i. If yes, how did you correct or contain the further spread of the misinterpreted information?

      b. Have there been any legal concerns?
      c. Have there been any examples of misinformation spread via social media? Was it deliberate or incidental?
          i. If so, was the misinformation quickly corrected or contained, or did it become a serious problem?
6. Are there procedures in place for using social media?
      a. Who is (are) responsible for the social media updates?
      b. How often are the sites updated?
      c. How does social media fit within the general structure of the EMA?
          i. In terms of hierarchy?
          ii. In terms of proximity?
      d. Are there any other forms of emergency communication that your EMA uses to connect to people with disabilities or other access and functional needs groups?

In the following case studies, pseudonyms are used for each representative interviewed. Furthermore, any information that may reveal the particular county EMA interviewed is withheld. In the following sections, each case is discussed separately. The summary section provides combined observations on the similarities and differences across the cases.

Case I

Case I is a county-level emergency management agency located in FEMA Region IX. The EMA director, Hillary, was interviewed for this study. Each interviewee was given a pseudonym for reporting purposes to maintain anonymity. In 2009, this EMA began using both Facebook and Twitter to provide preparedness information to the public. In 2011, the EMA also began using YouTube. Hillary stated that their EMA initially began using social media to interact with residents regularly about emergency preparedness and to inform them during times of disaster response. Currently, this EMA has over 67,000 Twitter followers, more than 2,400 likes on their Facebook group page, and 18 subscribers on their YouTube page. Their YouTube page also has more than 4,200 views.

The director of communications is ultimately responsible for social media content in this EMA. Case I did not have a full-time public information officer and instead shares one with other public safety departments in the county. When there is not an active emergency or disaster, the EMA in Case I provides reminders and updates about disaster preparedness, red flag warnings (when there is high fire danger), weather watches, warnings, and advisories. According to Hillary, updates are made on all three social media platforms multiple times a week.

The county has a centralized communications office that employs up to 15 communications specialists. During emergencies, these specialists assist in providing content to their social media sites by independently gathering information from unique software used by the EMA. During an active emergency, the EMA increases the number of updates on social media platforms. They provide shelter information, road closures, and information about where to get assistance, volunteer opportunities, and donations.

There is a difference to the content posted on each of their social media sites. According to Hillary, during a disaster they operate like a newsroom and post "news-style clip video stories" on YouTube. This EMA has access to a full production staff for YouTube videos; they share this capability with the county government. The information produced for YouTube is often expanded upon from topics that appear on their Facebook or Twitter page. While the information is generally the same on both social media platforms, it varies in length, detail, and format. The lists below show the differences in content during an emergency and day-to-day operation.

Day-to-day	Emergency
Preparedness information	Shelter information
Disaster anniversaries	Road closures
Disaster kit tips	Places to get assistance
Potential warnings, advisories	Where to volunteer
	How to donate
	Protective action information

This EMA follows (on Twitter) a number of local first responder organizations, such as fire and police for the cities within the county. By employing Twitter alerts, the EMA can be alerted anytime one of the organizations they follow sends out a tweet. The EMA also follows a local university. During a disaster, Hillary stated that if they needed to scale up their social media monitoring to track trend or rumors, they have a professor at the local university who they enlist.

The director states that while up-to-date information is posted on their social media sites, the social media platforms would not be considered a primary platform for alerts and warnings. The EMA uses a mass notifications system, including Wireless Emergency Alerts during large-scale disasters, as well as reverse 911. They also have a mobile app, available for Apple and Android devices. The content available on the app is the same as that posted on social media. It also provides a map where the public can locate the closest disaster shelter, disaster perimeter information, fire perimeters, areas affected by earthquakes, and disaster kit information. This EMA also uses sign language interpreters who are always present during press conferences in the event of an emergency. According to Hillary, they also employ an accessible alert system, where warning messages are immediately put on a video clip of someone conveying mass notification in American Sign Language (ASL).

Hillary noted one positive aspect of using social media is that they are given the opportunity to counter rumors that develop as a result of misinformation. In her non-emergency management–related example, someone was spreading a rumor on social media about the county withholding ballots during an election. However, during an emergency, she could not remember an instance in which rumors or misinformation was spread via social media.

Hillary feels that the public has an unrealistic expectation of response times when using social media. People assume emergency management services have hundreds of staff members, when they do not. She believes that these unrealistic expectations can cause misconceptions about local government abilities during an emergency. Ironically, in another example, Hillary mentioned that they used Twitter to communicate to the public at a time when electricity was out and TV was not a viable option. By using mobile phones, they were able to send out messages and field questions presented to them by the public who were also using mobile phones. She noted that while it worked during this situation, she thinks it is ineffective because first responders make up less than 1% of her population.

This EMA does not have written procedures in place for how to use social media. Those responsible for posting on social media can do so without a lengthy approval process or bureaucratic red tape. Hillary states that the obstacle in emergency management use of social media is in "having the resources to interact at a level that will gain you the followers to where you actually have an audience when a disaster occurs."

Figure 19.3 shows the frequency of posts observed during a 31-day period. Even though Hillary indicated that the EMA posts to Twitter multiple times a week, the study observation suggests that the EMA may only use Twitter for active emergencies. As shown, the EMA only used social media

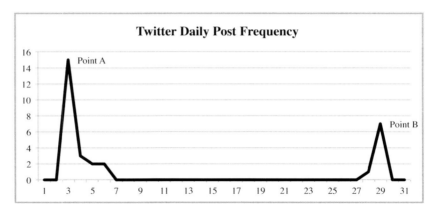

Figure 19.3 Social Media Daily Post Frequency for Case I

during two weeks for the four-week period, but posted over 25 different items. Specific information about the increase in posts is below:

Point A: Twitter post content concerning a large-scale fire in county, traffic delays, and evacuation information.
Point B: Twitter post content concerning wildfire information.

Case II

Case II is a county-level emergency management agency located in FEMA Region X. The EMA program administrator, Lara, was interviewed for this study. Each interviewee was given a pseudonym for reporting purposes to maintain anonymity. In 2012, this EMA began to use both YouTube and Twitter to communicate with the public. Lara explained that the EMA only uses Twitter to communicate to the public and uses YouTube to create public service announcements (PSAs), which are linked back to their website. At the time of this study, the EMA had 600 Twitter followers and no YouTube subscribers. However, their YouTube page has been viewed 62 times.

In this EMA, the police sheriff is also the director, and several people hold positions and have multiple titles. Lara is the program administrator of public relations and crisis communications, comprehensive emergency management planning, and emergency coordination center manager. Their deputy director, however, does not hold multiple titles. The EMA's public information officer (PIO), who reports to Lara, approves (and is responsible for) all social media content.

Case II EMA has incorporated communications in their outreach. According to Lara, they began using social media because it fit in with their preparedness mission. The ability to engage the community is a high priority, and social media is one of the outlets they use to accomplish this goal. They also use social media sites to link with their city fire department and other similar organizations. Typically, the EMA posts more information on Twitter when there is a current active incident. Unlike the EMA in Case I, this EMA actively uses social media for alerting the public.

Table 19.2 Types of Information Distributed on Twitter and YouTube from Case II

	Non—emergencies	*Emergencies*
Twitter	Preparedness information; weather preparedness; and current events.	Evacuation and preparedness information in more detail.
YouTube	*Public service announcements*	*N/A*

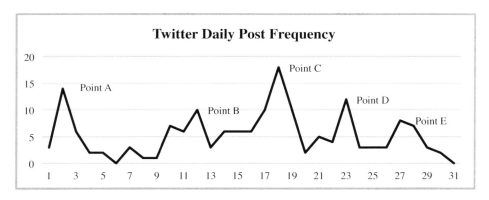

Figure 19.4 Social Media Daily Post Frequency for Case II

Lara indicated that the EMA did not have any legal concerns posting on social media because they consider it a part of their public disclosure. This EMA also did not have any concerns with misinformation or misinterpretation, because they coordinate and facilitate the flow of information carefully. However, Lara mentioned that a neighboring sheriff's office campaign was subject to misinterpretation on Facebook, having received numerous negative comments due to the sheriff's office poor choice of words on an online post. This is one of the reasons why Case II EMA does not use Facebook.

In addition to using social media, this EMA has their own emergency alert system, a Community Emergency Response Team, and a Neighborhood Watch program. Lara also noted that while they have not yet found a way to leverage social media to connect to the whole community, some of their PSAs are dubbed in Russian. When asked if there were other things that emergency management agencies should consider, Lara stated, "social media can be a benefit if you are trying to engage your community."

Figure 19.4 shows the frequency of posts observed during the same 31-day period as the EMA studied in Case I. The content of the posts shows that it is typically during active incidents. As shown, the EMA is more active than the one studied in Case I. Specific information about the increase in posts is as follows:

Point A: Twitter post content about fireworks and road closures.
Point B: Twitter post about a significant wildfire.
Point C: Twitter posts about smoke, donations to victims of the wildfire, and the governor's visit to the area.
Point D: Twitter posts about poor weather conditions, recovery efforts after the wildfire, and debris removal.
Point E: Twitter post that mentions vulnerable populations including elderly, children, and pets.

Case III

Case III is a county-level emergency management agency located in FEMA Region VIII. The EMA director, Sam, was interviewed for this study. Each interviewee was given a pseudonym for reporting purposes to maintain anonymity. In 2009, this EMA began using Twitter. Similar to the other cases, the EMA recognized social media as an additional way to inform and notify the public.

Table 19.3 Types of Information Distributed on Twitter and Facebook from Case III

	Non-emergencies	Emergencies
Twitter	N/A	Emergency response and recovery-related information.
Facebook	Hopes to use for preparedness in the future	N/A

According to Sam, the only information distributed over Twitter is emergency related. It is not used for preparedness information. Their joint information center (JIC) is responsible for content, though as the director of the agency, Sam has administrative rights to the social media pages. The department does not have a public information officer. However, other employees are able to update the Facebook and Twitter accounts. Sam noted that Twitter is not updated on a daily basis and their Facebook is not active. In the future, they would like to use Facebook for day-to-day preparedness information (see Table 19.3).

Even though Case III represents a county-level EMA, they are located within a city's mayoral office. Unlike the other EMAs, evidence of Case III's social media strategy is readily available online. The first strategy for this EMA is to improve information sharing with stakeholders, and the first task under that strategy is to develop and implement a social media strategy, similar to the city's social media strategy. The planning chief and community preparedness coordinator are the task leads.

This agency also has a 12-step social media plan, which is an internal document shared by the director. Their 12-step plan includes researching social media use by other EMAs, creating a daily tweet plan for the year, and running analytics to gauge effectiveness.

Beyond the 12 steps, this EMA has a three-fold objective for social media that includes (1) information resources, (2) monitoring, and (3) emergency coordination. Within the information resources are daily event updates, hazard mitigation techniques, and preparedness guides. With monitoring, they hope to access the "public eye" and see events unfolding through public posts and use that information to inform emergency managers. Finally, through emergency coordination, they hope to create a mobile "net" for people away from home and those without a TV or landline phone. The EMA also hopes that their emergency coordination objective will motivate public action toward overall EMA objectives.

According to Sam, social media is a tool that people can use for conveniences, supposedly as a supplement to other emergency communications channels. Sam stated that it can be time consuming to maintain social media sites, and EMAs do not always have the resources to properly administer information on a consistent basis. Therefore, they also use the Emergency Alerts System (for broadcast TV and radio) and are in the process of gaining access to the Wireless Emergency Alert system.

While Sam did not have any other things to consider about how social media is used by EMAs, he acknowledged, "I think [emergency management agencies are] behind the curve." Figure 19.5 shows the frequency of posts observed during the same 31-day period as the EMAs studied in Cases I and II. As shown, this EMA is more active than the one studied in Case I, but not as active as Case II. Point A highlights where the agency posted on Twitter about a tornado warning.

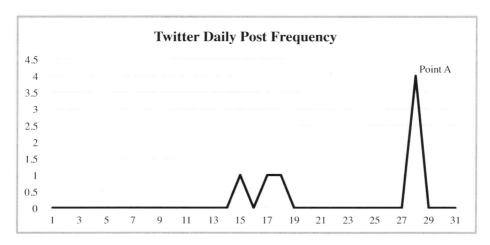

Figure 19.5 Social Media Daily Post Frequency for Case III

Case IV

Case IV is a county-level emergency management agency in FEMA Region VI. Tom, the public information officer, was interviewed for this study. Each interviewee was given a pseudonym for reporting purposes to maintain anonymity. Case IV EMA began using Twitter, Facebook, and YouTube in 2010. According to Tom, the EMA philosophy is that communication is the single most important factor in determining response to disaster. The dissemination of information on social media platforms is just one of the means by which they communicate with the public. At the time of this study, the EMA had 5,184 Twitter followers, over 2,400 likes on their Facebook group page, and 14 YouTube subscribers. However, their YouTube page had over 1,700 views.

The EMA is located under the county judge's office. The county judge is also the director of the emergency management office. The PIO decides what content is posted on social media pages. Typically, four people on the communications staff are responsible for posting the social media content. This EMA has a large staff; therefore, during an emergency the social media staff is augmented with the rest of the PIO office.

Each social media platform is used differently. The content on Facebook is focused solely on preparedness information, while Twitter is focused on response and preparedness. The EMA's YouTube page is used mostly for preparedness messages in video form. During an actual emergency, Twitter becomes the EMAs primary social media outlet, where they send near real-time information. Facebook is updated a couple of times a week and YouTube is used sparingly. Table 19.4 outlines the type of information disseminated on social media.

Table 19.4 Types of Information Distributed on Twitter, Facebook, and YouTube from Case IV

	Non-emergencies	*Emergencies*
Twitter	Preparedness information	Emergency response and preparedness-related information.
Facebook	Preparedness	
YouTube	Preparedness information Videos	Rarely used during emergencies

Tom mentioned the potential negative impacts of social media. He noted,

> The main issue comes with how do we maintain and adequately respond to any potential inquiries [on social media] when we have a major emergency . . . And then secondly, if we do have alerts during a disaster, our concern is how do we sustain that? Can we have somebody dedicated to that 24/7, and to what degree will that responsibility grow during an emergency.

His concern mirrors the concerns from Hillary in Case I and Sam in Case III related to staff and time issues in monitoring social media.

Due to the potential for misinformation spread on social media platforms, this EMA monitors their feeds to be able to correct and provide accurate information. Tom gave an example, "our community is very commuter-centric. In the event that there may be some traffic delays, a post like, 'Oh my God, the freeway is closed,' can be extremely impactful."

Similar to Case III, the EMA in Case IV shared their social media strategy. Their guidelines states that "social media is intended to be an additional channel of emergency public information that directs users to substantive digital content or provides brief, specific directions for immediate life-saving action." The strategies for social media use are separated by platform. For Twitter, the EMA acknowledges that the post must be 140 characters or less, but due to the importance of retweets has set their internal character limit to 120. Each post should also include at least one hashtag (#). During large-scale events, the PIO may determine and set a unique hashtag for the EMA to use. The EMA encourages the use of shortened URLs and will only retweet from recognized partners; most often, retweets from media are prohibited.

For Facebook, the guidelines encourage that all posts should not exceed 300 characters and should include a visual element, such as a picture, graph, or video. The strategy also suggests that Facebook never be the sole method of disseminating urgent information. While the EMA encourages more casual, easy-to-read messaging on Facebook, text/Internet slang (such as st8, b4, and LOL) should be avoided.

On both platforms, the EMA has an open policy, meaning that social media posts and interaction are not deleted. Much like with Case II, the posts on Twitter are considered part of public disclosure. With this EMA, public criticism is not censured. Tom mentioned, "The only thing we delete is if someone leaves racist remarks or if someone uses extremely foul language."

Furthermore, the social media strategy in Case IV encourages engaging the public on social media and states that specific requests should be responded to via private direct message. Upon receipt of a direct message, the EMA should attempt to acknowledge and respond as soon as possible.

According to Tom, the benefits of social media include the ability to engage the public on emergency-related information and to influence the mass media messaging. Tom stated, "The [mass] media is probably not going to follow [a less active or unreliable] organization, but they follow us . . . there's a lot of synergy that comes from that." Social media has helped the EMA to rapidly disseminate information, squash rumors, and inform the public.

Figure 19.6 displays the daily posts of Case IV's Twitter feed over the same 31-day period as the other cases. As Tom mentioned, and reinforced in their social media strategy, majority of their Twitter posts typically reflect the information about active emergencies. The overall content of these posts are detailed below.

Point A: Twitter post about severe thunderstorm and flash flood warnings.
Point B: Twitter post on weather warning information and an Integrated Warning Team information.
Point C: Twitter posts that mention CERT class, tour of Emergency Operations Center, thunderstorm warning, and flash flood warning.

Providing Emergency Communications

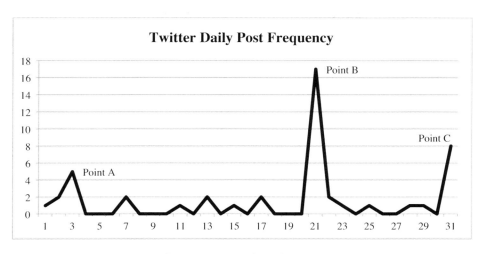

Figure 19.6 Daily Social Media Posts for EMA12 on Both Facebook and Twitter

Findings

The cases presented in this chapter highlighted the use of social media by four emergency management agencies. Each case represents a county-level EMA that uses Twitter to communicate to the public. Among the cases reviewed, there are striking similarities and differences. The similarities may give an indication of how many other EMAs use social media, while the differences may show the limitations of using social media for other agencies with similar conditions. Plenty of information was gained by reviewing these four cases in detail. In the following sections, the similarities and differences are discussed in more detail.

Similarities

Even though the agencies use social media differently, many began using social media for similar reasons: to communicate to and at times engage with the public.

> "To interact with residents around preparedness and also during times of disaster response."
> —*Hillary, Case I*

> "To communicate and engage with our customers."
> —*Lara, Case II*

> "To get the message out to the public and that it's, particularly for some demographics, a more popular, more useful way that people expect to get notified."
> —*Sam, Case III*

> "[Social media] was the place we need to be to have a dialogue, to be able to communicate directly with our constituents."
> —*Tom, Case IV*

The inherent similarities to why each EMA began to use social media are not surprising. FEMA Administrator Craig Fugate has been an avid supporter of social media use during emergencies (Zurer,

2011). In 2011, during a testimony, Mr. Fugate stated, "Rather than trying to convince the public to adjust to the way we at FEMA communicate, we must adapt to the way the public communicates (Fugate, 2011)." It would seem that these particular agencies are aware of just how many of their constituents possibly use social media and that they have decided to add these platforms as an additional method of communication.

Another similarity between the EMAs is that they use social media platforms in the same way when there are no active incidents. Cases I, II, and IV use social media platforms to relay preparedness information, public relations, or information about historical emergencies and disasters. For Case III, Sam indicated that once their Facebook page is running, they intend to use it for day-to-day preparedness information.

The content on social media changes during active emergencies. Each EMA distributes information about locations to get assistance, shelters, road closures, volunteer opportunities, and places to donate. Social media platforms are also monitored during active incidents to gather situational awareness information for the emergency managers. Over the 31-day period, each of the cases had at least one significant weather-related emergency warning message over Twitter.

One platform is used more than the others are during active incidents: Twitter. While Twitter is most popular among these agencies for response information, it is also sometimes used for recovery, mitigation, and preparedness information. Emergency managers typically used YouTube for public service announcements and news-like informational clips.

The public information officer (or a related communications officer) decides the content for the social media platforms for each of the cases studied. However, during times of emergency, most of the agencies expand to include other specialists to assist in posting content to the social media platforms.

Differences

Each EMA was structured slightly different and situated under very different government offices. Case I was a stand-alone agency under the county office; Case II was a stand-alone office, in which the director was also the county sheriff (not uncommon); Case III was a stand-alone office under the mayor's office; and Case IV was a county-connected agency situated under the county judge's office.

There were also differences in the responsibility of social media posts. For example, in Case II and Case IV, the public information officer was responsible for the social media posts for day-to-day posts, as well as during emergencies. However, for Case III, the community preparedness coordinator and the planning chief were responsible (see Table 19.5). Sam, in Case III, indicated that the planning

Table 19.5 The Different Employees Responsible for Sending Out Messages during Emergencies and Non-emergencies

	Responsible for Social Media Content	
	Day-to-day	*Emergencies*
Case I	Director of Communications	Can expand to up to 15 people during emergencies
Case II	Public Information Officer*	Public Information Officer
Case III	Community Preparedness Specialist and Planning Chief	Joint Information Center
Case IV	Public Information Officer + 4 People on communications staff	Public Information Officer + everyone on the team; can vary depending on size of event; typically rotate in 12 hour shifts

* Case II represents the only EMA with a dedicated public information officer.

chief was added only because they were personally an avid user of social media. In the majority of cases studied, the number of people responsible for social media posts increased during an emergency.

While the EMAs mentioned that social media could be useful in terms of "engaging the public," each was not as open to the idea of actively engaging the public, for various reasons. Hillary stated the purpose of using social media was to "interact with residents," however, she cautions:

> There's definitely an unrealistic expectation of response times . . . when people hear office of emergency services, they assume [EMAs] have hundreds of people . . . there's a misconception about local government's ability to keep up and respond during a catastrophic event.

Sam, however, mentioned that "it's just the time . . . not just the staff, but the time required to get involved [in social media], it's not trivial."

The difference in challenges presented by each representative hints to the differences in their prospective EMAs. Smaller EMAs may find it difficult to dedicate the necessary staff to stay active on social media. Larger EMAs may struggle with the aspect of social media being 24 hours a day, seven days a week. Yet, the large agency in Case IV embraced the idea of two-way communication and included strategies for engagement in their social media guidelines. Tom, from Case IV, states:

> The value of social media is that it's a dialogue. We believe that the dialogue part and the interaction between the people that follow us and our organization is part of maintaining credibility. So, we keep the direct message feature on, and we do a pretty good job at responding to direct messages.

The limitations for using social media as an engagement tool have generally included staffing issues, time, and the fear of legal/liability repercussions (Bennett, 2015b). The EMAs that use social media as an engagement tool have used the transparency of platforms as a way of complying with the open records requirement of many government agencies. For example, Lara stated that her EMA did not have any legal issues because the "information is backed up on the county public, and [it is] open to public disclosure anyways." Similarly, Case IV leaves all content online unless it contains foul language.

Table 19.6 identifies how each EMA chose which social media platforms to use during each life cycle of disaster. YouTube is clearly used for public service announcements.

Only one case had access to a full production staff and setup, Case I. Facebook, because of its format, is used for lengthy posts such as detailed preparedness information. Meanwhile, due to the 140-character limit, Twitter is used mostly for response-type information. However, Case I chose to provide more detail of the same information on Facebook.

Table 19.6 The Different Uses of Social Media Platforms per Case across the Life Cycle of Disasters

	Facebook	Twitter	YouTube
Case I	Preparedness, Response, Recovery*	Preparedness, Response, Recovery	PSAs
Case II	N/A	Preparedness, Response, Recovery	PSAs
Case III	Preparedness**	Response	N/A
Case IV	Preparedness	Response	Preparedness videos

* Case I EMA posts the same information on both Facebook and Twitter, but uses Facebook to post in greater detail.

** Case III EMA plans on using Facebook for preparedness once up and running.

Table 19.7 Overview of Each Case

Case		Interview Data			Observational Data				Archival Data
	Region	Start Date	Capacity (# of personnel for posts)	Language other than English	Followers	Following	Average Posts/ Tweets per day	Average Retweets per day (Twitter)	Average Number of Favorites	Social Media Strategy
I	IX	2009	12	no	12,381	2,396	0.97	12	3	No
II	X	2012	2	Russian—PSAs	599	167	5.35	2	0.87	No
III	VIII	2009	2	no	2,130	196	.22	4	0	Yes
IV	VI	2010	5+	no	5,184	166	1.52	4	.83	Yes

Each of the representatives interviewed indicated that social media might provide an avenue for presenting information in different languages. However, each EMA was at different stages of implementing multi-language posts. For Case I, Hillary mentioned that they use an accessible mass notification system that allows for video clips in American Sign Language to be sent to constituents through a subscription service, but due to lack of in-house translation services, they have been unable to post messages in multiple languages. In her location, there are 20–40 different dialects spoken in one community, and she didn't think it would be feasible to have adequate translation services in-house. For Case II, Lara indicated that their EMA has not begun to translate any of their social media posts; however, some of the PSAs on their YouTube page are dubbed in Russian. In Case III, Sam mentioned that they are not currently translating their posts, but that it is something they have identified as a need and want to get started on.

Finally, each case is engaged on Twitter at different levels. Engagement and impact on Twitter is often calculated by number of followers, posts, and retweets. Table 19.7 highlights this information for each of the cases studied. However, according to Twitter, the content of the messages also drive engagement. For example, the use of photos and hashtags can significantly increase the number of retweets for those in government and politics (Twitter, n.d.). In this study, only one EMA had specific references on the use of pictures, hashtags, videos, and links in their social media posts.

According to the National Research Council (NRC) (2013), the use of social media for disaster response should require considerable advance planning. Table 19.7, however, shows that the EMAs with the highest number of followers, average daily posts, and average number of daily retweets did not have a written social media strategy in place. However, the most active social media site, based on average daily retweets, the average number of posts the public "favorited" via Twitter, and number of followers over the 31-day period observed was Case I. Case I also had the most personnel available to post content onto their Twitter site, 12 people. Perhaps, it is more important to have the personnel available to constantly update posts multiple times a day.

Conclusion

Typically, nongovernmental organizations and the general public have been the primary users of social media platforms during emergencies; however, research has indicated that emergency management agencies are beginning to use social media for emergency communications. Increasing evidence suggests that the public is eager for emergency management agencies (EMAs) to use social media platforms as well. In this multiple case study, three EMAs were reviewed to show the differences in use of social media and summarized benefits and disadvantages of using social media relating to the dissemination of emergency communications. There were a few limitations of this study: (1) As with most case studies, the results are not generalizable; however, the details may provide an insight into several factors that influence EMA use of social media platforms. (2) The study revealed that other social media platforms were used differently among the agencies; however, only Twitter was observed over the 31-day period. (3) Only two EMAs were able to provide a clear social media strategy for analysis.

The similarities revealed in this study suggest that Twitter is used overwhelmingly for response information and Facebook typically is used for preparedness information by agencies that use social media platforms, similar to other findings (Bennett, 2014). When YouTube is used for videos, they are most often linked to the EMA website and other social media posts (such as Twitter and Facebook). This is an important finding because Twitter is not the most popular social media site. However, due to the differences in the functionality between Facebook and Twitter, the EMAs studied here find that Twitter is better for alerts, warnings, active emergency information, and situational awareness. In at least one case, the EMA representative mentioned that with Twitter, the EMA was capable of disseminating near real-time emergency messages.

Another interesting finding is that none of these four county-level EMAs was subject to significant misinformation on social media networks. One EMA mentioned that another public safety social media site was subject to public criticism because of the choice of words used in a post, and another EMA mentioned that because the public will exaggerate a situation it is important that EMAs provide accurate, credible information. This was true for the larger study as well, which is important since many EMAs are concerned about misinformation, rumors, and liability (Sutton, Hansard, and Hewett, 2011; Wukich, 2015).

The differences exposed in the case study indicate that the organizational structure might influence the use of social media for EMAs. Staff limitations, clear goals (or strategies), and culture can impact the use of social media among EMAs. Clearly, the inability to expand the number of people who can post on social media platforms during emergencies will hinder the quantity and quality of posts at a most critical time. Additionally, not having clear goals and strategies for use might diminish the importance of social media platforms with regard to emergency communications. If social media is just another communications tool with which EMAs communicate to the public, it should require the same regard as information sent via other mass notification systems, given that multimodal dissemination is the most effective (Mileti, 1999). Furthermore, the organizational culture with regards to new media (often set by the most senior officer) could also influence how the EMA uses social media. The use of social media will be drastically different among agencies that consider social media to be just a trend, an overwhelming burden, or a useful communications tool. However, given that the public is ready and waiting for emergency management–related agencies to engage with them on social media platforms, it may be more effective to consider these platforms as useful tools for communicating with the public (American Red Cross, 2012).

Engaging in two-way communications was another difference found among the EMAs studied. Two of the agencies embraced the idea of direct communication with the public. One agency official even stated that the ability to engage in two-way communication was one of the defining elements of social media. The other two agencies believed that it was unrealistic for them to engage the public on this medium and made it an unwritten policy not to directly communicate with the public. Similarly related, only two EMAs made mention of providing information in multiple languages on social media. One translated videos into American Sign Language and the other dubbed messages in Russian. However, moving forward, emergency managers should consider the use of social media platform's two-way communications feature given the shift in public warnings dissemination (Rodríguez et al., 2007) and the importance of providing messages that are best understood our unique diverse public (Aguirre, 1998; Lindell and Perry, 2004; Rodríguez et al., 2007).

Unlike the study from Sutton, Palen, and Shklovski (2008), these emergency management agencies did not engage in backchannel communications with each other via social media platforms. However, that may be a defining difference in the way first responder agencies and emergency management agencies use social media platforms. Furthermore, there wasn't evidence to support the idea that emergency management agencies use social media platforms to organize themselves, donations, or volunteers using social media platforms in the same way as volunteer agencies (Starbird and Palen, 2011; Sutton, 2010). The only study that found this activity among emergency management agencies was Bennett (2014) during the Alabama tornadoes in 2011. Perhaps the use of social media platforms to organize is only considered during large-scale, multijurisdictional disasters. This would correspond with social media activity highlighted in the DHS report after Hurricane Sandy (DHS, 2013).

This study highlighted the use of social media by four EMAs. One main takeaway from this chapter is that each emergency management agency does not use social media in the same manner. The focus of this study was to showcase the differences in use and gather as much information as to why. The interviews revealed that organizational structure, costs, personnel resources, and leadership may contribute to when, how, and why social media platforms are used in emergency management agencies. Further research may include studying the connection between organizational structure and social media engagement, examining the true costs and benefits to EMAs that decide to engage the public in two-way communications, and analyzing the percentage of misinformation spread via social media platforms during emergencies.

Note

1. The research analyzed in this chapter was collected under a larger contract funded by the Federal Emergency Management Agency, Integrated Public Alert & Warning System (IPAWS), Project Management Office (PMO) under contract # HSFE5–13-R-0031, principal investigator, Helena Mitchell. Contributions to this research were made by Paul Baker, James White, Braeden Benson, and Amelia Williams.

References

Aguirre, Benigno. "The Lack of Warnings Before the Saragosa Tornado." *International Journal for Mass Emergencies and Disasters*, 6 (1998, 1): 65–74.
American Red Cross. "More Americans Using Mobile Apps in Emergencies." *American Red Cross* (2012). Retrieved April 9, 2014 from: http://www.redcross.org/news/press-release/More-Americans-Using-Mobile-Apps-in-Emergencies/
Bennett, DeeDee. "Social media for emergency management." In *Proceedings of the 66th Interdepartmental Hurricane Conference*, Charleston, SC. March 2012.
Bennett, DeeDee. "How Do Emergency Managers Use Social Media?" *Journal of Emergency Management*, 12 (2014, 3): 251–256.
Bennett, DeeDee. "Findings from people with disabilities and emergency managers on the use of websites and social media to deliver accessible emergency alerts." In *National Hurricane Conference*, Austin, TX. May 2015a.
Bennett, DeeDee. "Just Another Communications Tool." *IAEM Bulletin*, 32 (2015b, 6): 26–27.
Bird, D., M. Ling, and K. Haynes. "Flooding Facebook—The Use of Social Media During the Queensland and Victorian Floods." *The Australian Journal of Emergency Management*, 27 (2012, 1): 27–33. Retrieved from http://www.em.gov.au/Publications/Australianjournalofemergencymanagement/Pastissues/Documents/Flooding_Facebook.PDF
Boyd, Danah and Nicole Ellison. "Social Network Sites: Definition, History, and Scholarship." *Journal of Computer-Mediated Communication*, 13 (2008, 1): 210–230.
Drabek, Thomas E. "Understanding Disaster Warning Responses." *The Social Science Journal*, 36 (1999, 3): 515–523.
Facebook. Stats. Retrieved July 12, 2015 from http://newsroom.fb.com/company-info
Fraustino, J.D., B. Liu, and J. Yan. "Social media use during disasters: A review of the knowledge base and gaps." *Final Report to Human Factors/Behavior Sciences Division, Science and Technology Directorate, U.S. Department of Homeland Security*. 2012.
Fugate, Craig. Statement of Craig Fugate, Administrator, Federal Emergency Agency, before the Senate Committee on Homeland Security and Government Affairs, Subcommittee on Disaster Recovery and Intergovernmental Affairs: "Understanding the Power of Social Media as a Communication Tool in the Aftermath of Disasters". Retrieved 2011 from http://www.dhs.gov.ynes/testimony
Gao, Huiji, Geoffrey Barbier, and Rebecca Goolsby. "Harnessing the Crowdsourcing Power of Social Media for Disaster Relief." *IEEE Intelligent Systems*, 3 (2011): 10–14.
Goodwin, Robin, Yuval Palgi, Yaira Hamama-Raz, and Menachem Ben-Ezra. "In the Eye of the Storm or the Bullseye of the Media: Social Media Use During Hurricane Sandy as a Predictor of Post-Traumatic Stress." *Journal of Psychiatric Research*, 8 (2013, 47): 1099–1100.
Hesse-Biber, Sharlene N. and Patricia Leavy. *The Practice of Qualitative Research*. Thousand Oaks, CA: Sage Publications, 2006.
Heverin, Thomas and Lisl Zach. *Microblogging for Crisis Communication: Examination of Twitter Use in Response to a 2009 Violent Crisis in the Seattle-Tacoma, Washington Area*. ISCRAM, 2010.
Hughes, A. and L. Palen. "Twitter adoption and use in mass convergence and emergency events." In *Proceedings of 6th Information Systems for Crisis Response and Management Conference*, Gothenburg, Sweden. 2009.
Indvik, Lauren. "East coasters turn to Twitter during Virginia earthquake." *Mashable*. Retrieved July 12, 2015 from http://mashable.com/2011/08/23/virginia-earthquake/

Kavanaugh, Andrea L., Edward A. Fox, Steven D. Sheetz, Seungwon Yang, Lin Tzy Li, Donald J. Shoemaker, Apostol Natsev, and Lexing Xie. "Social media use by government: From the routine to the critical." *Government Information Quarterly* 29, no. 4 (2012): 480–491.

Knox, J.A., J.A. Rackley, A.W. Black, V.A. Gensini, M. Butler, C. Dunn, and S. Brustad. "Tornado Debris Characteristics and Trajectories During the 27 April 2011 Super Outbreak as Determined Using Social Media Data." *Bulletin of the American Meteorological Society*, 94 (2013, 9): 1371–1380.

Li, J., A. Vishwanath, and H. Rao. "Retweeting the Fukushima Nuclear Radiation Disaster." *Communications of the ACM*, 57 (2014, 1): 78–85.

Lindell, Michael K. and Ronald W. Perry. *Communicating Environmental Risk in Multiethnic Communities*. Thousand Oaks, CA: Sage Publication, 2004.

Marcos, Christina. "House passes bill to boost DHS use of social media in emergencies." *Capitol Hill Publishing Corporation*. Retrieved 2014 from http://thehill.com/blogs/floor-action/house/211643-house-passes-bill-to-boost-dhs-use-of-social-media-in-emergencies

Mileti, Dennis. *Disasters by Design: A Reassessment of Natural Hazards in the United States*. Washington, DC: Joseph Henry Press, 1999.

Mileti, Dennis and Lori Peek. "The Social Psychology of Public Response to Warnings of a Nuclear Power Plant Accident." *Journal of Hazardous Materials*, 75 (2000, 2): 181–194.

Mills, A., C. Rui, L. JinKyu, and H. Rao. "Web 2.0 Emergency Applications: How Useful Can Twitter be for Emergency Response?" *Journal of Information Privacy & Security*, 5 (2009, 3): 3–26.

Mitchell, Helena, DeeDee Bennett, and Salimah LaForce. "Planning for Accessible Emergency Communications: Mobile Technology and Social Media." In *2nd International Accessibility Reaching Everywhere (AEGIS) Conference and Final Workshop Proceedings*, Brussels, Belgium. 2011: 51–58.

National Research Council. *Public Response to Alerts and Warnings Using Social Media*. Washington, DC: National Academies Press, 2013, 21.

Nigg, Joanne M. "Risk Communications and Warning Systems." *Natural Risk and Civil Protection*, 16050 (1995): 369.

Palen, L., K. Starbird, and S. Vieweg. "Twitter-Based Information Distribution During the 2009 Red River Valley Flood Threat." *Bulletin of the American Society for Information Science & Technology*, 36 (2010, 5): 13–17.

Palen, L., S. Vieweg, S. B. Liu, and A. L. Hughes. "Crisis in a Networked World Features of Computer-Mediated Communication in the April 16, 2007, Virginia Tech Event." *Social Science Computer Review*, 27 (2009, 4): 467–480.

Prentice, S. and E. Huffman. "Social media's new role in emergency management." *Idaho National Laboratory*. Retrieved 2008 from http://www.inl.gov/technicalpublications/Documents/3931947.pdf

Rodríguez, Havidán, Walter Diaz, Jenniffer M. Santos, and Benigno E. Aguirre. "Communicating Risk and Uncertainty: Science, Technology, and Disasters at the Crossroads." In *Handbook of Disaster Research*, edited by Havidán Rodríguez, Enrico Quarantelli, and Russell Dynes, 476–488. New York: Springer, 2007.

San Su, Yee, Clarence Wardell III, and Zoë Thorkildsen. "Social media in the emergency management field." (2013).

Schmidt, Charles W. "Trending Now: Using Social Media to Predict and Track Disease Outbreaks." *Environ Health Perspect*, 120 (2012, 1): 30–33.

Shklovski, I., L. Palen, and J. Sutton. "Finding community through information and communication technology during disaster events." In *Proceedings of the ACM Conference on Computer Supported Cooperative Work*, New York: ACM Press. 2008.

Sorensen, J.H., "Hazard Warning Systems: Review of 20 Years of Progress." *Natural Hazards Review*, 1 (2000, 2): 119–125.

Starbird, K. and P. Palen, "'Voluntweeters': Self-organizing by digital volunteers in times of crisis." In *Proceedings of the CHI 2011 Conference*, Vancouver, BC. 2011.

Sutton, J. "Twittering tennessee: Distributed networks and collaboration following a technological disaster." In *Proceedings of the 7th International ISCRAM Conference*, Seattle, USA. May 2010.

Sutton, J., B. Hansard, and P. Hewett, "Changing channels: Communicating Tsunami warning information in Hawaii." *Argonne National Laboratory Center for Integrated Emergency Preparedness*. Retrieved 2011 from http://www.jeannettesutton.com/uploads/Changing_Channels_FINAL_7-5-11.pdf

Sutton, J., L. Palen, and I. Shklovski. "Backchannels on the front lines: Emergent use of social media in the 2007 Southern California Wildfires." In *Proceedings of the 5th International ISCRAM Conference*, Washington, DC, USA. May 2008.

Sutton, J., E. S. Spiro, B. Johnson, S. Fitzhugh, B. Gibson, and C. T. Butts. "Warning Tweets: Serial Transmission of Messages During the Warning Phase of a Disaster Event." *Information, Communication & Society*, 17 (2014, 6): 765–787.

Twitter. "Government & politics: The impact of tweeting with photos, videos, hashtags and links." Retrieved July 13, 2015 from https://media.twitter.com/best-practice/government-politics-what-works-best

Twitter, About. Retrieved July 12, 2015 from. https://about.twitter.com/company

U.S. Congress House. *Social Media Working Group Act of 2014*. HR 4263. 113th Cong. (July 14, 2014) House Report 113–480.

U.S. Department of Homeland Security (DHS). "Lessons learned: Social media and Hurricane Sandy virtual social media working group and DHS first responders group." *U.S. Department of Homeland Security Science and Technology Directorate*. 2013. https://communities.firstresponder.gov/DHS_VSMWG_Lessons_Learned_Social_Media_and_Hurricane_Sandy_Formatted_June_2013_FINAL.pdf

U.S. Geological Survey (USGS). *Earthquake Early Warning*. Retrieved July 12, 2015 from. http://earthquake.usgs.gov/researh/earlywarning/

Vieweg, Sarah, Amanda L. Hughes, Kate Starbird, and Leysia Palen. "Microblogging during two natural hazards events: What Twitter may contribute to situational awareness." In *Proceedings of the SIGCHI Conference on Human Factors in Computing Systems*, ACM. 2010: 1079.

Wukich, Clayton. "Social Media Use in Emergency Management." *Journal of Emergency Management*, 13 (2015, 4): 281–295.

Yates, D. and S. Paquette. "Emergency Knowledge Management and Social Media Technologies: A Case Study of the 2010 Haitian Earthquake." *International Journal of Information Management*, 31 (2011, 1): 6–13.

Yin, Robert K. *Case Study Research: Design and Methods. Fifth Edition*. Sage Publications: London. 2014.

Zurer, Rachel. "Storyboard: FEMA Chief Says Social Media Aid Disaster Response." *Wired Magazine*, January 20, 2011. http://www.wired.com/2011/01/storyboard-fema-craig-fugate/

20
AN ANALYSIS OF MAIN ATTRIBUTES FOR GOVERNANCE IN SMART CITIES

Manuel Pedro Rodríguez Bolívar

1 Introduction

In the early 21st century, the smart cities concept has gained a lot of attention, and cities are actively developing strategies toward the goal of becoming "smart." A smart city is understood as a new concept of partnership and governance in which all tiers of government must increasingly collaborate with one another as well as with nongovernmental organizations of various kinds (private and civic) to pursue their goals (Scott 1999). In accordance with this understanding, a smart city initiative needs to create a community where all citizens can engage more easily and effectively (Paskaleva 2009). From this point of view, the coproduction model has become an important reality for public services in this framework, a framework that implies greater involvement of service users and communities in the public service chain, both in extent and in intensity of engagement (Löffler 2009).

To achieve this aim, governments in smart cities are called on to play a key role in developing capacities (Rodríguez Bolívar 2015b), and they are increasingly using ICTs in creating interactive, participatory, and information-based urban environments (Bătăgan 2011; Batty et al. 2012), as well as in improving public services and the functioning of the administration (Deakin 2012). Coproduction is defined by the mix of activities that both public service agents and citizens contribute to the provision of public services (Parks et al. 1981; Ostrom 1996). It describes processes through which diverse inputs are contributed by individuals and organizations that are not part of an official government agency primarily responsible for producing a particular public good or service (Ostrom 2013). With this new diversity in input contribution, traditional institutions and classical processes of governing become inappropriate to manage the cities (Cosgrave and Doody 2015), and therefore new and innovative forms of governance are needed to meet the need for governance decentralization in the information age (Innes and Booher 2010). Indeed, it seems clear that transformation of urban processes will only be achieved with better urban governance (Puppim et al. 2013).

This new governance model is based on the concept of network governance. Although all networks comprise a range of interactions among participants, a focus on governance involves the use of institutions and structures of authority and collaboration to allocate resources and to coordinate and control joint action across the network as a whole (Provan and Kenis 2008). Under this approach, the role of management is critical for effective network governance, especially in the handling of tensions inherent in each governance form (Provan and Kenis 2008). Essentially, the focus is not on networks as a means of governance, but on the governance and management of networks themselves.

This new smart city model of governance fits well within a public management perspective that emphasizes that solving societal problems is not merely a question of developing good policies but much more a managerial question of organizing strong collaborations between government and other stakeholders (Torfing 2012). These collaborative relations are strong in a smart city (Rodríguez Bolívar 2015b). In this regard, the application of this new model of governance for smart cities has been called "smart governance" (Giffinger et al. 2007). Although smart governance has only been rudimentarily developed (Scholl and Scholl 2014), it incorporates the integration of within-city and across-city governance, including services and interactions that link and (where relevant) integrate public, private, and civil organizations so the city can function efficiently and effectively as one organism (Manville et al. 2014). In any case, smart governance includes transparent governance, as well as participation in decision-making and public services (Albino, Berardi and Dangelico 2015).

However, governance within smart city contexts is often complex, and governments are not always familiar with the options that this new position offers. Governments are expected to work more with networks in which they have less authority, while at the same time they are increasingly held accountable for performance and improved outcomes (Span et al. 2012a). Because of this, the role of management is critical for effective network governance, especially regarding the handling of tensions inherent in each governance form (Provan and Kenis 2008). To date, studies on smart governance have lacked consensus on approach to governance in smart cities. Therefore, additional research is needed to advance public management research and knowledge about the various manners in which local governments can best manage their network (Van Slyke 2007).

Based on the network governance (Kooiman 2003, 2008) and coproduction literature (Span et al. 2012b), governance models in public administrations can be categorized through the identification and analysis of some primary dimensions of managing the city. Specifically, steering (Peters and Pier 1998), alignment (Span et al. 2012b), dependency (Span et al. 2012b), role of government (Span et al. 2012b), and governance model (Fazekas and Burns 2012) are advocated to be key dimensions in the urban governance of smart cities. The adoption of different alternatives in these governance dimensions could lead to different patterns in governing smart cities (European Parliament 2014).

Nonetheless, despite the increasing number of studies on smart cities recently published in leading international journals and books, little research has been undertaken to examine the dimensions of governance to promoting smart cities. Therefore, this chapter analyzes the relevance of the main dimensions of governance models and their presence in both prior theoretical and empirical research; this analysis is critical for understanding these dimensions and their alternatives for governance models in smart cities. To achieve this aim, the chapter performs a literature review to overview prior research and answer the following research questions:

RQ1: What relevance do these dimensions of governance models have in the prior literature regarding smart cities?
RQ2: Into what categories do the dimensions analyzed in prior research fall?

In addition, with the aim of establishing grounded foundations for the dimensions of governance in smart cities, empirical research is undertaken to measure the perception of local European governments with an interest in smart cities regarding the key dimension categories analyzed in this chapter of smart governance. Therefore, the third research question of this study is

RQ3: How do smart city practitioners perceive these dimensions of smart governance?

2 The Governing of Smart Cities and the Dimensions of Governance

The smart city concept has been defined from three main positions: the techno-centered approach (Walravens 2012; Lee, Hancock and Hu 2014), the human-centered approach (Shapiro 2006; Winters 2011), and the integrated approach (Hollands 2008; Sauer 2012; Nijkamp and Kourtit 2013). These distinct positions on the concept of smart city have introduced different approaches to smart city governance in prior research, ranging from institutional conservation (traditional governance of a smart city) to institutional transformation (smart urban governance) (Meijer and Rodríguez 2013). However, none of these positions is acknowledged as the best way to govern smart cities.

In any case, the integrated approach to smart city highlights governance shared among stakeholders and institutional factors (Nam and Pardo 2011; Chourabi et al. 2012). This relationship among stakeholders in urban transformation is considered the cornerstone of smart cities (Giffinger and Gudrun 2010; Belissent 2011). Thus, the central spirit of governance under the smart cities' framework supports building structures based on the negotiated involvement of multiple public and private stakeholders operating at different scales (Preissl and Mueller 2006; Pinnegar, Marceau and Randolph 2008). It involves a transformation in the role, compass, power, and activities of the state in economy and society (Kitthananan 2006). The different institutional models of urban governance describe diverse systems of values, norms, beliefs, and practices (Pierre 1999). Therefore, it has become paramount to better understand such concepts to draw boundaries and single out the components of smart cities (Misuraca, Reid and Deakin 2011). Based on the network governance literature (Kooiman 2003, 2008; Provan and Kenis 2008; Fazekas and Burns 2012) and the coproduction literature (Span et al. 2012b), Table 20.1 details the key dimensions in the urban governance of smart cities.

Table 20.1 Dimensions, Codes, and Categories of Governance Models

Dimensions of governance (codes) and categories		
Steering	Steering should be understood about setting priorities and defining goals (Peters and Pier 1998).	(1) Local government; (2) Joint steering; (3) Self-steering
Boundary conditions	Conditions that determine the goals, mission, resources, capacity, responsibility, and accountability of the task to be performed (Kettl 2006).	(1) Fixed boundaries by local governments; (2) Jointly set boundaries; (3) Boundaries set by the parties
Alignment dimension	Alignment refers to which party coordinates the smart city development (Span et al. 2012b).	(1) Strategic planning of local governments; (2) Joint alignment; (3) Alignment by the parties
Dependency dimension	Dependency is understood as being dependent on the power wielded by local governments based on rules and procedures (Span et al. 2012b).	(1) Formal dependency; (2) Informal dependency
Role of local governments	This could be arrayed along a spectrum, as a continuum of top-down to bottom-up processes (Span et al. 2012b), ranging from the role of "executor (commissioner)", to the role of "initiator (facilitator)."	(1) Commissioner or Executer; (2) Coproducer; (3) Facilitator
Governance model	It refers to the model of governing societies in a situation where no single actor can claim absolute dominance (Fazekas and Burns 2012).	(1) Bureaucratic model; (2) Collaborative model; (3) Participative model; (4) Self-Governance model

Source: Own elaboration based on Kooiman (1993), Peters and Pierre (1998), Denhardt and Denhardt (2000), Kettl (2006), Fazekas and Burns (2012) and Span et al. (2012b).

The steering mechanism, which involves setting priorities and defining goals (Peters and Pier 1998), is often mentioned as a main dimension of governance (Provan and Milward 2001). In a smart city, steering can be performed directly by the local government, be performed jointly with others actors involved in the smart city, or incorporate self-steering by parties outside the local government. On the other hand, boundaries typically occur in complex combinations (Dawes, Cresswell and Pardo 2009) and are central to the administrative process. They define which organizations are responsible for doing what, as well as what powers and functions lie elsewhere (Kettl 2006), especially under networking environments where the identification of boundaries is sometimes permeable (Nalbandian et al. 2013). In a smart city, the vertical boundaries to horizontal arrangements are not always a viable solution (Kettl 2006; Nalbandian et al. 2013), and boundary development calls for the creation of an "extended governance," whereby the intelligence and the attention of actors residing outside governmental boundaries are harnessed in the management of public resources, making it possible to "organize without organizations" (Ferro et al. 2013).

The alignment dimension seeks to identify the role that local government administration must play in the coordination of smart city development. Evolution of smart cities in Europe has demonstrated the need to adopt a strategic, planned approach (Schaffers, Komninos and Pallot 2012). This strategic approach assumes a dialogue with traders, a reduction of authoritative attitudes in favor of negotiation with stakeholders (Belissent 2011), and the identification of participative instruments so that the evolutionary process can be real and not just a program (Testoni and Boeri 2014).

In addition, governance systems need to identify the power dependencies involved in the relationships between institutions engaged in collective action (Kitthananan 2006). Networks are often characterized by informal relationships between essentially equal agents or social agencies; in contrast to market or hierarchy relationships, networks coordinate through less formal, more egalitarian and cooperative means (Thompson 1991). This dimension of governance is also linked to the role that local government must play in the development of smart cities. This role is essential for an understanding of urban governance (Pierre 1999), but its specifics remain unclear because the distinction between top-down and bottom-up approaches appears blurry (Nijman 2014). The top-down approach is mainly represented by the role of commissioner or broker of services and suggests that the networks are coordinated primarily through authoritarian procedural mechanisms, rather than relying on social mechanisms (Herranz 2008; Ryan et al. 2008).

In contrast, other smart initiatives are promoted through bottom-up processes, which make governments play the role of "facilitators," mainly in complex processes of cooperation with economic operators to attract private capital (Bussi 2014). Finally, other smart projects are difficult to characterize as either top-down or bottom-up and seem to take a more "hybrid" approach, including collaborations between public and civic actors (Nijman 2014). In this last context, the role of local government is to coproduce the smart initiatives with the public and, therefore, plays the role of "coproducer." The role of "coproducer" is embedded in market relationships in which the local government is primarily accountable for production but organizes coproduction through contracts with other producers (Rodríguez Bolívar 2015a).

Finally, according to Kooiman (1993), a governance model is seen as the pattern or structure that emerges in a sociopolitical system as a "common" result or outcome of the interacting intervention efforts of all involved actors. Urban development and planning has long been dominated by top-down "blueprint" approaches (Schaffers et al. 2012), and local governments have acted as administrative leaders that remain largely grounded in the bureaucratic model of governance (Uhl-Bien, Marion and McKelvey 2007). Nonetheless, this model is not able to effectively reflect the degree of civil society development, because it does not respond to information technology advances more focused on democratic participation (Kim 2004). The interdependence of the constituent parts of the contemporary social system fosters a way of governing that is necessarily less hierarchical and more shared with citizens, through a smart public administration (Dragoman 2013). In the smart city era, there is a need for other new governance models, ranging from participative to collaborative and, finally, self-governing models, depending on the degree of participation of the networking actors and the governance independence of governments (see Table 20.1).

3   Data and Method

3.1   Data Collection

The data collection for this chapter was performed using two different data collection methods. The first one is based on a literature review to analyze the dimensions of governance models for smart cities. This first data collection method is useful to answer RQ1 and RQ2. The second method is based on a questionnaire (about dimensions of smart governance) designed to capture perceptions of city practitioners with an interest in smart cities (See Table 20.2). This second data collection method is relevant to answer RQ3.

The literature review was carried out in two stages. In the first stage, the literature review consisted of three open searches that sifted through titles, author-supplied keywords, and abstracts for the following phrases: "smart cities" and "governance," "smart governance," and "smart administration." First, the search was conducted in the three library databases suggested by Webster and Watson

Table 20.2 Questionnaire Design

1.	*Who should steer the smart city?*
	Local government
	Local government jointly with a group of stakeholders
	Self-governance by various societal actors (private firms, stakeholders, citizens)
2.	*Who sets the goals for smart city development?*
	Local government sets the common goals
	Local government and a group of interested stakeholders set common goals
	There are no common goals for smart city development
3.	*The strategic planning for the smart city development is performed by . . .*
	Exclusively the municipality
	Equally by the municipality and stakeholders
	Exclusively by stakeholders
4.	*The level of dependency between all actors involved in smart city development is:*
	The other actors are dependent on the municipality
	There are no dependency links among actors
5.	*The model of participation in developing the smart city in your municipality is . . .*
	Exclusively the municipality. No participation of other actors.
	Municipality and selected stakeholder participation
	Open participation
6.	*Who is responsible for smart city development?*
	Local government
	Local government with the consultation process to a broad and open group of stakeholders
	Local government jointly with the participation of a small group of selected stakeholders
	A group of stakeholders

(2002): ABI/Inform (ProQuest), ISI Web of Science, and Scopus EBSCO Host. Next, the search was conducted in the full contents of seven academic journals that were found to be the core outlets for e-government publications suggested by Scholl (2009): *Electronic Government, An International Journal (EGaIJ)*, *Electronic Journal of E-Government (EJEG)*, *Government Information Quarterly (GIQ)*, *Information Polity (IP)*, *International Journal of Electronic Government Research (IJEGR)*, *Journal of Information Technology and Politics*, and *Transforming Government: Process, People, and Policy (TGPPP)*. Finally, the search was conducted in the proceedings of International IFIP EGOV Conference which, according to Scholl (2009), is one of the three core conferences for e-government research. The search method, combining an open search with a strategic selection of journals and conferences, has generated a reasonably representative set of articles (a total of 315 papers: 52, 104, and 76 papers in the case of the databases, respectively; 76 papers published in the selected journals; and 7 papers in the selected conference proceedings).

The second stage of literature review consisted of a selection of relevant papers based on their abstracts and objectives. The abstracts and the introduction sections, especially the objectives of the papers, were read, and an overview of the structure for each paper was checked. Those papers of a specific technical nature that did not examine any of the domains analyzed in this paper were eliminated from the sample. In addition, literature reviews were removed from the sample since they don't make new contributions to the domains. Finally, double counting of papers was avoided by counting only the papers that were different across the databases and the searches performed in the specialized journals and conference proceedings. These processes resulted in a final sample of 40 papers (both theoretical and empirical studies).

The second data collection method is based on a questionnaire about attributes and dimensions of smart governance that was sent to all representatives of local governments labeled as "smart cities" that are members of the EUROCITIES network. This network is composed of the elected local and municipal governments of major European cities. It brings together the local governments of over 130 of Europe's largest cities and 40 partner cities, which between them govern 130 million citizens across 35 countries; the network's objective is to reinforce the important role that local governments should play in a multilevel governance structure. The EUROCITIES network acts as either coordinator or partner in a range of EU-funded projects that touch upon the policy areas that it focuses on or that involve its members. In this regard, the most significant current challenge for the EUROCITIES network is the translation of smart cities into the broad political area (EUROCITIES 2011). Also, the EUROCITIES network is currently promoting the translation of smart cities into the broad political area to city members (EUROCITIES 2011), and 70 members of this network are actually involved in two EU-funded projects focused on smart cities, as well as in a forum and a working group that have been created in the network.[1]

3.2 Methods

For the literature review analysis, the overall analytical approach adopted largely followed the conventions of template analysis, in which the researcher produces a list of codes (template) representing themes identified in the textual data (King 2004). In this study, the dimensions of governance were coded into broad categories (see Table 20.2) based on prior research discussed on section 2 of this chapter, as well as on prior research on network governance and coproduction literature. These codes and categories were refined during the analysis process with the aim at creating a template. All selected papers were analyzed with the template analysis technique in order to answer the research questions previously mentioned and to map the governance models in smart cities, which are shown in the next section of this chapter.

Regarding the empirical research, the survey instrument was administered through a follow-up online questionnaire. The questions were expressly constructed for the purposes of this study. Each one of these questions was designed to determine the position of respondents on each of the dimensions of the governance models previously identified by prior research (steering: Q1, boundary conditions: Q2, alignment dimension: Q3, dependency dimension: Q4, role of local governments: Q5, and governance models: Q6). In this regard, the responses provided for each one of the questions were identified with each one of the categories included in each dimension of governance (see Table 20.1). Finally, for each question included in the questionnaire, only one response was allowed.

In order to validate analysis of the questionnaire responses, as an experimental approach, the text of the initial version of the questionnaire was sent to two researchers on smart cities and two city practitioners who participated in the study. The purpose of this communication was not to obtain answers to the questionnaire, but rather to ascertain the opinions of these persons on the following: (a) the understandability of the questionnaire text and (b) the clarity of and possible ambiguities in the questions posed. The received suggestions were analyzed and, when considered appropriate, incorporated into the text of the questionnaire. In addition, the questionnaire was translated into different languages, and a list of definitions was provided to facilitate the clear understanding of its questions.

The second version of the questionnaire, after including received suggestions, was sent to the 70 leading smart cities in Europe mentioned previously, and 64 responses were received (91.42% of sample smart cities). The introductory letter to the practitioner in each sample local government stressed the need for him/her, before answering the questions, to have clearly understood the meaning of each questionnaire item and the ultimate goals of this study. Moreover, these practitioners were offered the opportunity to clarify possible doubts before completing the questionnaire. For this purpose, an email address was provided to direct questions about the questionnaire. Some emails were received concerning the exact meaning of some of the items; these questions were answered, and thus we may be reasonably sure that the questions measured the intended constructs. Therefore, the results of this part of the questionnaire could help to characterize the smart governance function in a smart city.

4 Analysis of Results

RQ1: What relevance do these dimensions of governance models have in the prior literature regarding smart cities?

Figure 20.1 shows the main dimensions of governance models that prior research has indicated as essential in both empirical and theoretical studies, dimensions related to the governance

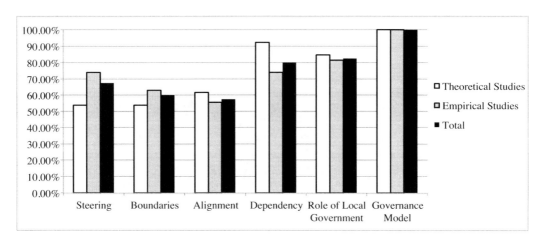

Figure 20.1 Relevance of Dimensions According to Their Presence into Prior Research (Theoretical Studies, Empirical Studies, and Total Prior Research)

model, the role of local government in smart cities, and the dependency dimension. In any case, all the dimensions identified in this chapter are relevant for defining governance models in smart cities; further, prior research supports the positioning of local governments into each of the above categories, as doing so could be relevant to characterize the governance model in smart cities.

When looking at the main dimensions of governance in empirical studies alone, the relevant dimensions are those related to the governance model and to the role of local governments in smart cities, the dependency dimension, and the steering dimension. Therefore, practices seem to point out the need to set priorities and define goals for the development of smart cities, perhaps because of bad experiences from a lack of coordination in smart initiatives in some cities (Smart Cities Portugal 2014).

The alignment dimension is also relevant for both theoretical and empirical studies. However, the steering and boundaries dimensions are only used in half of the theoretical studies; in empirical studies, these dimensions are present in more than 50% of the studies.

Therefore, results seem to indicate that the relevance for governing smart cities is mainly focused on the role of local government and the governance model chosen for governing the city this is the style of government. Therefore, policy makers and public managers should analyze and debate this question before planning steps to transform a city into a smart city. To achieve this aim, the strategic planning of smart initiatives, as well as the methods for how these initiatives are later debated and put into practice, is critical for success. Indeed, theoretical studies advocate the responsibility of local authorities to undertake strategic planning of smart cities, although these studies also point out the need for joint steering in the development of smart initiatives.

RQ2: What categories into these dimensions are those analyzed in prior research?

Results indicate that prior research promotes collaborative and participatory models of governance over corporate or even self-governance models (see Figure 20.2 for a graphic of percentage for dependency, role of government, and governance models in total prior research). Indeed, theoretical and empirical studies emphasize the role of coproducer for the local government, which should be implemented under collaborative and participatory models of governance (either lead organization-governed network or the interactive governance model). In this context, informal dependency seems to be the best method of relationship with governments.

Nonetheless, the literature review seems to indicate that this collaboration and participation for developing smart cities is previously planned by the local governments. Therefore, according to our results, local governments have the responsibility to design the strategic planning for the development of the smart city and then seek the involvement of stakeholders to collaborate and participate in the smart projects designed previously by the local authorities.

Furthermore, local governments could either consult on and/or fix the boundaries jointly with the stakeholders. Some prior research points out that the local government should manage the steering of smart projects alone; other research indicates these projects should be steered jointly with stakeholders. Indeed, differences between theoretical and empirical studies exist. Although theoretical studies are not clear, it appears that authors advocate fixing the boundaries jointly with stakeholders, whereas empirical practices seem to indicate that boundaries should be fixed by the local government. In addition, theoretical studies advise that the priorities and goals for smart cities development should be settled jointly by local governments and stakeholders. In contrast, empirical studies propose that the steering function is solely the responsibility of the local government.

Therefore, results appear to indicate that the involvement of stakeholders in developing smart cities should be mainly focused on the collection of knowledge and ideas about the smart projects that

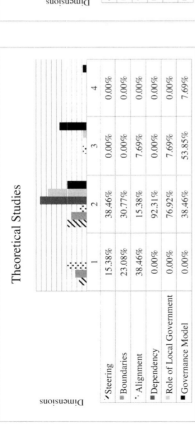
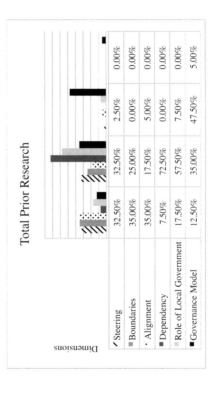

Figure 20.2 Relevance of Categories in Each Analyzed Dimensions in Prior Research

should be undertaken to advance the smart city. Nonetheless, the local government is the lead organization for undertaking the strategic planning of the city, and only in a very few cases do they promote the involvement of the stakeholders in this task (see Figure 20.2 for the percentage of category 3 in the alignment dimension). This current state of government-stakeholder roles may explain why authors indicate that, up to now, informal dependency has reported been the best way power should be wielded. That is, no rules or procedures are introduced to regulate the relationship between governments and stakeholders (see Figure 20.2 for the value of category 2 in the dependency dimension).

In brief, the literature review seems to introduce the need to transform local governments in processes of cities becoming smart; prior research advocates the need for local governments to retain the key role in the accountability and in the monitoring activities in these cities.

RQ3: How do smart city practitioners perceive these dimensions of smart governance?

As for the perceptions of smart city practitioners, results indicate that all dimensions receive high scores (see Figure 20.3). This means that the surveyed practitioners think that these dimensions are essential to take into account in managing the smart city. Regarding the style of governing the city, results indicate that respondents are clearly in favor of local governments monitoring the strategic planning of smart cities. Indeed, it seems clear that the strategic planning, the fixing of the boundaries, and the steering tasks must be performed by local authorities. Nonetheless, results are not clear regarding the role of governments.

Indeed, practitioners mainly advocate for collaborative models of governance, but results are not conclusive in this matter. In this regard, different from prior research, practitioners point out that the local government should play the role of coproducer or only the "facilitator" role (this last result has not been found in prior research). However, those surveyed indicate the collaborative model of governance is preferred; the participatory model of governance and the self-governance model are less frequently mentioned in responses to the questionnaire. In addition, practitioners advocate informal dependency links between stakeholders and local governments but, at the same time, they highly recommend the bureaucratic model of governance (nearly 30% of responses), which is built on formal dependency links. Therefore, future research should analyze this issue further.

In any case, it seems clear that practitioners think that local government must maintain some control over the management of smart cities, because they indicate that local governments must bear the responsibility for the strategic planning of the smart cities. Additionally, practitioners' responses suggest that they believe these governments must be leaders in the management model implemented in these cities, because they think that local governments must implement bureaucratic or collaborative models of governance. In both of these governance models, the local government must be the lead organization of the management systems.

5 Conclusion and Discussion

Prior research has been mainly focused on the implementation of ICTs as a key tool to improve smart systems (i.e., sustainable environment and smart mobility), but new urban structures need new forms of governance for an online world. Network governance literature (Kooiman 2003, 2008; Provan and Kenis 2008; Fazekas and Burns 2012) and coproduction literature (Span et al. 2012b) highlight the need for analyzing dimensions of governance in order to identify governing patterns and styles, especially in the information society. Therefore, this chapter has focused its interest on determining the governing styles in smart cities according to the smart cities literature and the perception of practitioners in smart cities.

This study's findings indicate that the dimensions of governance have been mainly drawn from empirical experiences rather than from theoretical studies (see Figure 20.1). Indeed, smart governance is

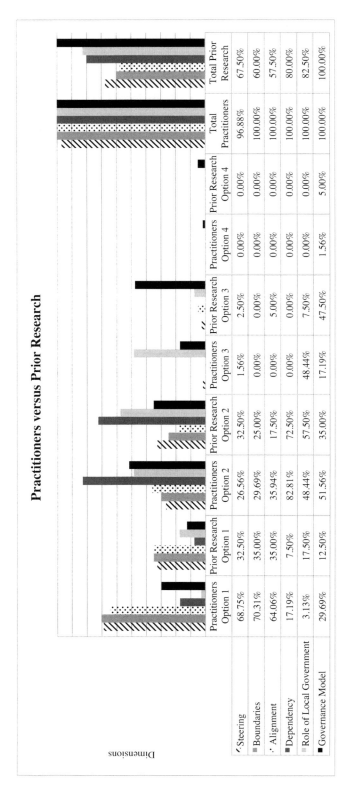

Figure 20.3 Relevance of Categories in Each Analyzed Dimensions in Practitioners' Perceptions versus Prior Research

understood to be an essential need for governing smart cities. This issue has also been confirmed by the empirical research undertaken, because practitioners demonstrate an awareness of the need to analyze dimensions of governance to successfully undertake smart city projects (see Figure 20.3). Therefore, there is a current need to develop new theories based on network management, interactive decision-making, and coproduction theories to model new links and interactions among governments and other stakeholders.

Another finding is the leading role of local governments in the strategic planning, boundary setting, and steering and monitoring of smart initiatives. This finding has been emphasized in the perceptions of practitioners and is present in the empirical experiences of smart cities. In this regard, empirical studies could be catalogued as government-centric forms of public management in smart cities. Nonetheless, this finding could be explained by the fact that the smart city experience is a new phenomenon. Perhaps, in the future, smart cities could assign these functions to a joint structure with stakeholders (collaboration model/participatory model of strategic planning) or even on self-steering and self-alignment by the parties. Therefore, future research could compare and analyze differences in strategic planning between early adopters and later adopters of smart initiatives to explore the evolution of a city once it is labeled as "smart city."

In any case, findings indicate that the role of "coproducer" is the most mentioned role of governments in prior research and is also a relevant role according to practitioners in smart cities. This new perspective on governance highlights the importance of new approaches to enhance governing capacity, in which governments reach outward and downward to localities, engage with markets, and expand out into civil society (Pierre and Peters 2000). Nonetheless, theoretical studies seem to indicate the need for the coproduction of smart initiatives in a participatory framework more than in a collaborative one, whereas this meaning is inverted in empirical studies and in practitioners' perceptions.

Thus, theoretical studies seem to indicate that, in smart cities, the classic hierarchical model of public administration does not work, and that a number of forms of "horizontal arrangements" and interrelationship with stakeholders have arisen in its place. By contrast, empirical experiences and practitioners in smart cities advocate a model in which stakeholders are involved in providing knowledge and ideas regarding smart city development, but the local government remains the leading organization in the management of these cities (collaborative models or even the bureaucratic model of governance). In any case, future research should undertake studies regarding strategies involved in the role of governments in smart cities. This analysis could lead to new theories about smart governance and could strengthen our knowledge about the reasons for local governments to play roles in smart cities.

In conclusion, the empirical implementation of new governance models under smart city frameworks will require better understanding and analysis of their relevance in the current networking environment produced by the development of these cities. First, government needs to utilize Internet-based technologies to understand "smart society" more fully. Second, government needs to develop a more relational style of contracting and learn from the sharp variations in contracting regimes across the world. Third, leaders of governmental organizations need to accept that digital technologies are now at the core of a wide range of their activities and adopt policymaking processes according to this innovation (Margetts 2005). Their knowledge of and commitment to smart cities are recognized as key factors in the successful implementation of smart governance initiatives. A key question arises from our study as a last reflection for future research: Are there efficient or inefficient patterns of governance for smart cities?

Acknowledgments

This research was carried out with financial support from the Regional Government of Andalusia (Spain), Department of Innovation, Science and Enterprise (Research project number P11-SEJ-7700).

Note

1. See http://www.eurocities.eu/eurocities/activities/working_groups/Smart-Cities&tpl=home

References

Albino, Vito, Umberto Berardi, and Rosa Maria Dangelico. 2015. "Smart cities: Definitions, dimensions, performance, and initiatives." *Journal of Urban Technology* 22.1: 3–21.

Bătăgan, L. 2011. "Smart cities and sustainability models." *Informatica Economică* 15.3: 80–87.

Batty, Michael, Kay Axhausen, Giannotti Fosca, Alexei Pozdnoukhov, Armando Bazzani, Monica Wachowicz, Georgios Ouzounis, and Yuval Portugali. 2012. "Smart cities of the future." *The European Physical Journal Special Topics* 214.1: 481–518.

Belissent, Jennifer. 2011. *The Core of a Smart City Must Be Smart Governance*. Cambridge: Forrester Research, Inc.

Bussi, Federico. 2001. *Formazione, partecipazione e cambiamento: il ruolo del facilitatore*. http://db.formez.it/storicoarchivionews.nsf/ForpaPubblicheNotiziePerTipo/f462f8c915e7d793c1256c77003d7d46?OpenDocument, (accessed September 2014).

Chourabi, Hafedh, Taewoo Nam, Shawn Walker, J. Ramon Gil-Garcia, Sehl Mellouli, Karine Nahon, Theresa Pardo, H. Jochen Scholl. 2012. "Understanding smart cities: An integrative framework". Paper presented at the 45th Hawaii International Conference on System Sciences, Maui, HI, USA, January, 4–7.

Cosgrave, Ellie, and Léan Doody. 2015. *Delivering the Smart City–Governing Cities in the Digital Age*. London: Arup.

Dawes, Sharon S., Anthony M. Cresswell, and Theresa A. Pardo. 2009. "From 'need to know' to 'need to share': Tangled problems, information boundaries, and the building of public sector knowledge networks." *Public Administration Review* 69.3: 392–402.

Deakin, Mark. 2012. "Intelligent cities as smart providers: CoPs as organizations for developing integrated models of e-government services." *Innovation: The European Journal of Social Science Research* 25.2: 115–135.

Denhardt, Robert B., and Janet Vinzant Denhardt. 2000. "The new public service: Serving rather than steering." *Public Administration Review* 60.6: 549–559.

Dragoman, Ion. 2013. "Smart public administration." *Academic Journal of Law and Governance* 1.summer: 30–43.

EUROCITIES. 2011. *Developing Europe Urban's Model. 25 Years of EUROCITIES*. December. http://nws.eurocities.eu/MediaShell/media/Developing_Europe_s_urban_model_-_25_years_of_EUROCITIES-NVAT_12212.pdf (accessed December 2011).

European Parliament. 2014. *Mapping Smart Cities in the EU*. Brussels: European Parliament, Directorate General for internal policies.

Fazekas, Mihaly, and Tracey Burns. 2012. *Exploring the Complex Interaction between Governance and Knowledge in Education*. OECD Education Working Papers, No. 67, OECD Publishing. http://dx.doi.org/10.1787/5k9flcx2l340-en (accessed November 2012).

Ferro, E., B. Caroleo, M. Leo, M. Osella, and E. Pautasso. 2013. "The role of ICT in smart cities governance." Paper presented at the International Conference for E-Democracy and Open Government, Krems, Austria, May, 22–24.

Giffinger, Rudolf, Christian Fertner, Hans Kramar, Robert Kalasek, Nataša Pichler-Milanović, and Evert Meijers. 2007. *Smart Cities: Ranking of European Medium-Sized Cities*. Vienna. http://www.smart-cities.eu/download/smart_cities_final_report.pdf (accessed December 2007).

Giffinger, Rudolf, and Haindlmaier Gudrun. 2010. "Smart cities ranking: An effective instrument for the positioning of the cities?." *ACE: Architecture, City and Environment* 4.12: 7–26.

Herranz, Joaquín. 2008. "The multisectoral trilemma of network management." *Journal of Public Administration Research and Theory* 18: 1–31.

Hollands, Robert G. 2008. "Will the real smart city please stand up? Intelligent, progressive or entrepreneurial?." *City* 12.3: 303–320.

Innes, Judith E., and David E. Booher. 2010. *Planning with Complexity: An Introduction to Collaborative Rationality for Public Policy*. Oxon: Routledge.

Kettl, Donald F. 2006. "Managing boundaries in American administration: The collaboration imperative." *Public Administration Review* 66.s1: 10–19.

Kim, S.T. 2004. "Toward a new paradigm of e-government: From bureaucracy model to governance model." Paper presented at the 26th Congress of Administrative Sciences, Seoul, Korea, July, 14–15.

King, Nigel. 2004. "Using templates in the thematic analysis of text." In *Essential Guide to Qualitative Methods in Organizational Research*, edited by C. Cassell and G. Symon, 256–270. London: Sage.

Kitthananan, Amornsak. 2006. "Conceptualizing governance: A review." *Journal of Societal & Social Policy* 5.3: 1–19.

Kooiman, Jan. 1993. "Findings, speculations and recommendations." In *Modern Governance: New Government Society Interactions*, edited by Jan Kooiman, 249–262. London: Sage.

Kooiman, Jan. 2003. *Governing as Governance*. London: Sage.

Kooiman, Jan, Maarten Bavinck, Ratana Chuenpagdee, Robin Mahon, and Roger Pullin. 2008. "Interactive governance and governability: An introduction." *Journal of Transdisciplinary Environmental Studies* 7.1: 1–11.

Lee, Jung Hoon, Marguerite Gong Hancock, and Mei-Chih Hu. 2014. *Towards an Effective Framework for Building Smart Cities: Lessons from Seoul and San Francisco*. Technological Forecasting and Social Change. In press, corrected proof. http://www.sciencedirect.com/science/article/pii/S0040162513002187 (accessed October 2013).

Löffler, Elke. 2009. "Why co-production is an important topic for local government." *Governance International*. http://www.govint.org/fileadmin/user_upload/publications/coproduction_why_it_is_important.pdf

Manville, Catriona, Gavin Cochrane, Jonathan Cave, Jeremy Millard, Jimmy Kevin Pederson, Kåre Thaarup, Andrea Liebe, Matthias Wissner, Roel Massink, and Bas Kotterink. 2014. *Mapping Smart Cities in the EU*. Brussels: European Union.

Margetts, Helen. 2005. "Smartening up to risk in electronic government." *Information Polity* 10.1–2: 81–94.

Meijer, Albert J., and Manuel Pedro Rodríguez Bolívar. 2013. "Governing the smart city: Scaling-up the search for socio-techno synergy". Paper presented at the EGPA Conference 2013, Edinburgh, Scotland, September, 11–13.

Misuraca, Gianluca, Alasdair Reid, and Mark Deakin. 2011. *Exploring Emerging ICT-Enabled Governance Models in European Cities*. Seville: JRC-IPTS Technical Note.

Nalbandian, John, Robert O'Neill Jr., Michael Wilkes, and Amanda Kaufman. 2013. "Contemporary challenges in local government: Evolving roles and responsibilities, structures, and processes." *Public Administration Review* 73.4: 567–574.

Nam, Taewoo, and Theresa A. Pardo. 2011. "Conceptualizing smart city with dimensions of technology, people, and institutions." Paper presented at the 12th Annual International Digital Government Research Conference: Digital Government Innovation in Challenging Times, Maryland, USA, June, 12–15.

Nijkamp, Peter, and Karima Kourtit. 2013. "The 'new urban Europe': Global challenges and local responses in the urban century." *European Planning Studies* 21.3: 291–315.

Nijman, Hanke. 2014. *Dynamic Roles in Smart City Development: Blurring Boundaries in Smart City Pilots Projects*. The Netherlands: Master Thesis, University of Twente.

Ostrom, Elinor. 1996. "Crossing the great divide: Coproduction, synergy, and development." *World Development* 24.6: 1073–1087.

Ostrom, Elinor. 2013. "Foreword." In *New Public Governance, the Third Sector, and Co-Production*, edited by Victor Pestoff, Taco Brandsen and Bram Verschuere, Vol. 7., xv–xvii. NewYork: Routledge.

Parks, Roger B., Paula C. Baker, Larry L. Kiser, Ronald J. Oakerson, Elinor Ostrom, Vincent Ostrom, Gordon P. Whitaker, and Rick K. Wilson. 1981. "Consumers as coproducers of public services: Some economic and institutional considerations." *Policy Studies Journal* 9.7: 1001–1011.

Paskaleva, Krassimira A. 2009. "Enabling the smart city: The progress of city e-governance in Europe." *International Journal of Innovation and Regional Development* 1.4: 405–22.

Peters, B. Guy, and John Pierre. 1998. "Governance without government? Rethinking public administration." *Journal of Public Administration Research and Theory* 8.2: 223–243.

Pierre, Jon. 1999. "Models of urban governance the institutional dimension of urban politics." *Urban Affairs Review* 34.3: 372–396.

Pierre, Jon, and B. Guy Peters. 2000. *Governance, Politics and the State*. London: Macmillan.

Pinnegar, Simon, Jane Marceau, and Bill Randolph. 2008. "Innovation for a carbon constrained city: Challenges for the built environment industry." *Innovation* 10.2–3: 303–315.

Preissl, Brigitte, and Jürgen Mueller (Eds.). 2006. *Governance of Communication Networks: Connecting Societies and Markets with IT*. Heidelberg, Germany: Physica-Verlag.

Provan, Keith G., and Patrick Kenis. 2008. "Modes of network governance: Structure, management, and effectiveness." *Journal of Public Administration Research and Theory* 18.2: 229–252.

Provan, Keith G., and H. Brinton Milward. 2001. "Do networks really work? A framework for evaluating public-sector organizational networks." *Public Administration Review* 61.4: 414–423.

Puppim de Oliveira, Jose A., Christopher N. H. Doll, Osman Balaban, Ping Jiang, and Magali Dreyfus. 2013. "Green economy and governance in cities: Assessing good governance in key urban economic processes." *Journal of Cleaner Production* 58: 138–152.

Rodríguez Bolívar, Manuel Pedro. 2015a. "Governance models for the delivery of public services through the Web 2.0 technologies a political view in large Spanish municipalities." *Social Science Computer Review*. 0894439315609919.

Rodríguez Bolívar, Manuel Pedro. 2015b. "Smart cities: Big cities, complex governance?." In *Transforming City Governments for Successful Smart Cities*, edited by Manuel Pedro Rodríguez Bolívar, 1–7. Switzerland: Springer International Publishing.

Ryan, Neal, Trevor Williams, Michael Charles, and Jennifer Waterhouse. 2008. "Top-down organizational change in an Australian government agency." *International Journal of Public Sector Management* 21.1: 26–44.

Sauer, Sabrina. 2012. "Do smart cities produce smart entrepreneurs?." *Journal of Theoretical and Applied Electronic Commerce Research* 7.3: 63–73.

Schaffers, Hans, Nicos Komninos, and Marc Pallot (Eds.). 2012. *Smart Cities as Innovation Ecosystems Sustained by the Future Internet*. Fireball White Paper. http://www.urenio.org/wp-content/uploads/2012/04/2012-FIREBALL-White-Paper-Final.pdf (accessed December 2012).

Scholl, Hans J. 2009. "Profiling the EG research community and its core". Paper presented at the 8th international conference on electronic government, EGOV 2009, Linz, Austria, from August 31 to September 3.

Scholl, Hans J., and Margit C. Scholl. 2014. "Smart governance: A roadmap for research and practice." Paper presented at the iConference 2014 Proceedings, Berlin, March 4–7.

Scott, Allen J., J. Agnew, E. W. Soja, and M. Storper. 1999. "Global city regions: Conference theme paper." Paper presented at the Global City-Regions Conference, Los Angeles, UCLA School of Public Policy and Social Research.

Shapiro, Jesse M. 2006. "Smart cities: Quality of life, productivity, and the growth effects of human capital." *The Review of Economics and Statistics* 88.2: 324–335.

smart cities Portugal. 2014. *smart cities Portugal: Roadmap*. Lisboa: INTELI—Inteligência em Inovação, Centro de Inovação.

Span, Kees C. L., Katrien G. Luijkx, René Schalk, and Jos M.G.A. Schols. 2012a. "What governance roles do municipalities use in Dutch local social support networks?" *Public Management Review* 14.8: 1175–1194.

Span, Kees C. L., Katrien G. Luijkx, Jos M. G. A. Schols, and René Schalk. 2012b."The relationship between governance roles and performance in local public interorganizational networks: A conceptual analysis." *The American Review of Public Administration* 42.2: 186–201.

Testoni, Chiara, and Andrea Boeri. 2014. "Smart governance: Strategic planning and urban regeneration: Manchester and Turin case studies." *Architectoni.ca* 4: 21–28.

Thompson, G., Jennifer Frances, Rosalind Levacic, and Jeremy C. Mitchell. 1991. *Markets, Hierarchies and Networks: The Coordination of Social Life*. London: Sage.

Torfing, Jacob. 2012. *Interactive Governance: Advancing the Paradigm*. Oxford: Oxford University Press.

Uhl-Bien, Mary, Russ Marion, and Bill McKelvey. 2007. "Complexity leadership theory: Shifting leadership from the industrial age to the knowledge era." *The Leadership Quarterly* 18.4: 298–318.

Van Slyke, David M. 2007. "Agents or stewards: Using theory to understand the government-nonprofit social service contracting relationship." *Journal of Public Administration Research and Theory* 17.2: 157–187.

Walravens, Nils. 2012. "Mobile business and the smart city: Developing a business model framework to include public design parameters for mobile city services." *Journal of Theoretical and Applied Electronic Commerce Research* 7.3: 121–135.

Webster, Jane, and Richard T. Watson. 2002. "Analyzing the past to prepare for the future: Writing a." *MIS Quarterly* 26.2: 13–23.

Winters, John V. 2011. "Why are smart cities growing? Who moves and who stays." *Journal of Regional Science* 51.2: 253–270.

21
CYBERINFRASTRUCTURE FOR COLLABORATIVE SCIENTIFIC NETWORKS

Institutional Design and Management Strategies

Yu-Che Chen and Rich Knepper

Introduction

Advancing technological and scientific innovation is a key component of national competitiveness strategies. The United States has a long and rich tradition in supporting scientific innovations via its National Science Foundation (NSF) grants and partnership with universities. Recent growth in both scientific and government data and computational technologies (National Science Foundation 2012) has made the provision of computational power a new engine to enable and accelerate scientific discovery. Recognizing the enabling potential, the U.S. NSF and the scientific community have been exploring the development of a cyberinfrastructure to aid in the depth and reach of scientific research since early 2000 (NSF TeraGrid Program 2011).

The focus of this study is on NSF-funded programs to develop and operate a distributed large-scale research cyberinfrastructure to spur scientific innovations. The first program is the TeraGrid, initiated in 2003 and subsequently funded in 2005 for five years. The second program, succeeding and expanding on the first one, is the Extreme Science and Engineering Discovery Environment (XSEDE), created in 2011 and also funded for five years (The Program Office of the Extreme Science and Engineering Discovery Environment (XSEDE) 2012a). The primary goal of both TeraGrid and XSEDE programs is to leverage the combination of supercomputing power and distributed networks to provide high-performance computing capabilities to researchers around the country, and even around the globe, to promote collaboration and innovation across organizational boundaries, disciplines, distance, and time (The Program Office of the Extreme Science and Engineering Discovery Environment (XSEDE) 2011).

The study of the development and implementation of distributed computing cyberinfrastructure for scientific research can contribute to public management and administration scholarship in the following ways. First, the evolution from TeraGrid to XSEDE constitutes a natural experiment that helps shed light on the effect of institutional design and management strategies on the effectiveness of a collaborative network. Studies of networks have called for more attention on the evolution and the role of institutional design and management strategies (Isett et al. 2011; Milward et al. 2010). Second, the extensive utilization of information and communication technologies (ICTs) by these cyberinfrastructure programs provides a unique opportunity to understand the role of ICTs in governance, management, and performance. Last, this study adds to the existing literature by pursuing a less-studied type of collaborative networks—namely large-scale distributed networks for scientists—and by integrating insights from the studies of cyberinfrastructure and virtual organizations.

The practical significance of a cyberinfrastructure for computational disciplines lies in the size and duration of investment, geographical scope, and salience in national competitiveness. Both the TeraGrid and XSEDE programs constitute over 100 million U.S. dollars of government investment, spanning from 2005 to 2010 for TeraGrid with 150 million invested and from 2011 to 2016 for XSEDE with 121 million invested. The programs' geographic scope is primarily national, with national labs and universities located across the country. In addition, scientists around the globe are utilizing the computing resources via research collaboration with U.S. researchers to solve complex, sometimes global problems (i.e., global climate modeling). Moreover, cyberinfrastructure is central to advances in science and technology in the United States for national competitiveness. This cyberinfrastructure provides the computing and collaborative infrastructure to accelerate and enable new discoveries for increasingly computing-intensive scientific research.

The overarching research question is: What institutional design and management strategies, coupled with the use of information and communication technologies, can help improve the effectiveness of collaborative networks? The next section develops a conceptual framework drawing from institutionalism, as well as network management and governance. Research design, data, and methods follow. Next is the analysis of the cyberinfrastructure's evolution based on the framework to link institutional design and management strategies to network performance. Then, this chapter discusses findings and their implications. It concludes with a summary of the main points as well as opportunities for future research.

Governance Structure and Interaction: An Institutional Analysis and Development (IAD) Perspective

Institutional analysis and development, as developed by Ostrom and her colleagues (Ostrom 2010, 1998, 1990), offer a grounded categorization of rules for the analytical components of governance structures. Such categorization allows for operationalization of governance structure and facilitates understanding of the structure facing actors, either individuals or organizations. Position rules specify what positions each participating individual and organization can take. For a public management network, an example of a position rule can be about whether a participating organization can take the position of dictating the information system used for the entire network. Boundary rules delineate who participates in the governance structure. For instance, boundary rules outline the eligibility criteria for members to participate in a public management network and/or the criteria to serve on its board.

Payoff rules dictate the costs and benefits associated with an action taken by individuals or organizations in an institution. The payoff for a network member can be access to resources that are otherwise not available, while the cost could be some loss of autonomy in making resource allocation decisions. Information rules govern who has access to what information and when. Information rules are likely to shape interactions and outcomes, as documented in the prisoner's dilemma, which demonstrates that a lack of information sharing leads to suboptimal outcomes. Aggregation rules determine how individual decisions can be aggregated to a higher level, such as group and/or system level. For a public management network, an example of an aggregation rule is whether consensus rule or majority rule is followed in aggregating individual decisions. This type of rule has implications for the extent of influence a member organization can exert on an outcome.

Authority rules specify the set of decisions that can be made by participants. These rules delineate the section of decisions that participants have authority to make. For instance, a network participating organization may have the authority to make personnel decisions on their network representatives or decisions about the time and resources it will invest. However, this organization may not have the authority to make personnel decisions for the administrative unit for the entire network. Scope rules stipulate the outcomes that can be affected by the decision. This is to provide the specifics for linking decisions to outcomes. For instance, a decision by a participating organization to use its own information system rather than the one prescribed by the network could result in penalty.

The influence of rules on outcome is not uniform across various categories of rules. Payoff rules are critical for governance structures that rely heavily on incentives to shape the behavior of participants. For instance, in the case of an irrigation system management, payoff rules are critical in determining its effectiveness (Tang 1994). A boundary rule about who can or cannot participate has been shown to be critical in inducing all important actors to respond to a crisis effectively (Kapucu 2006). For a public management network, such as those managing the cyberinfrastructure we discuss, it is conceivable that scope rules specifying the scope of outcomes that result from resource-sharing decisions can make a difference in the effectiveness of the network. Moreover, it is the configuration of rules, rather than the individual category of rules, that makes a difference in outcomes. The interplay of various rules, rather than a single category of rules, is key to understanding the desirable outcomes (Ostrom, Gardner, and Walker 1994). For instance, both a boundary rule allowing for citizen participation and a payoff rule providing relevant incentives for citizen participation are needed for coproduction of e-government applications between governments and citizens.

Moreover, initial conditions are critical for understanding the impact of rules on institutional effectiveness. The evolution and impact of institutions are rather path-dependent (North 1990). The underlying calculation is the cost involved in moving from one state of the institution to another. For a public management network for the production and delivery of social services, the existence of a robust network of providers is likely to render payoff rules more relevant, as opposed to boundary rules, in shaping the outcome. Moreover, the extent of change possible also depends on the initial conditions. A well-functioning public management network is likely to benefit from the utilization of innovative technologies for better communication. In contrast, a dysfunctional network with the basic problems of politics and misalignment of goals is unlikely to have the flexibility to take advantage of innovative technologies.

The IAD framework explicitly recognizes the role of the strategic actions of participants and their interactions in shaping outcomes (Ostrom 2010). The strategic actions of, and interactions between, participants should be articulated in understanding the impact of governance structure. An analogy from the public network management literature is the specific network management strategies and techniques to address institutional constraints. These could be changes made on the constitutional, collective, and operational levels.

Network Form of Public Service Production and Delivery: Perspectives of Public Management and Administration

The public administration and public management literature provides several perspectives for enhancing our understanding of the networked form of public service production and delivery. First, the resource dependency perspective helps explain the motivation, payoff, and interactions between organizations within a network (Pfeffer and Salancik 2003). Organizations are motivated to participate in a network arrangement by access to resources otherwise unavailable to them individually. In the context of receiving government grants, governments can make membership in a network a requirement for individual institutions to get funding. The majority of the activities taking place in a network are about bargaining, exchange, and allocation of resources. Rethemeyer and Hatmaker (2008) further developed a typology of resources to include material resources as well as social ones. The relevant salience of the type of resource for a particular network depends on the nature of the network in terms of service provided and incentives for participation.

A second perspective highlights the notion of politics, which challenges the assumption that network organizational participants are pursuing a common good rather than self-interest (Park and Rethemeyer 2014; O'Toole and Meier 2004). One of the insights of interorganizational collaboration and network studies is the tension created by dual loyalty (Milward, Kenis, and Raab 2006; Bardach 1996). Such tension could be a simple matter of time allocation between working for the network and working for the home organization. A more complicated matter is the strategic move of participating organizations in advancing their own interests at the expense of other organizations' (or even network) priorities. As a result, conflicts are common in the management of public management networks (O'Leary and Bingham 2009; Bryson, Crosby, and Stone 2006). Moreover, politics in way of bargaining for network resource allocations is a reality in public management/service networks (O'Toole and Meier 2004).

A third perspective integrates various studies of network management to identify the conditions for effective design and implementation of a collaborative arrangement. Several conditions are considered most prominent in driving success. First is to have a shared goal that is in alignment with the goals of participating organizations (Gray et al. 2003; Gray 1985). Second is the practice of following the norm of reciprocity and building trust among participants. A stream of studies of interorganizational collaboration has highlighted the importance of reciprocity (Chen and Thurmaier 2009; Chen 2008). Trust is also critical for successful interorganizational arrangements (Gil-Garcia et al. 2010; Chen 2008). A third condition is the existence of a governing structure to resolve conflicts for adaptation to the changing environment. The ability for a network governance structure to resolve conflicts is important, as conflicts are an unavoidable part of network life (Bryson, Crosby, and Stone 2006).

Another perspective is the focus on management activities that aid in the success of public management networks. Most of prescribed management activities are research propositions but grounded in practice. One way of grouping these activities is put them into four categories: activating, framing, mobilizing, and synthesizing (McGuire 2002). Another is to classify these activities in terms of their purposes. For instance, trust building is considered as one of such management activities (Bryson, Crosby, and Stone 2006). Resource planning and resource commitment are other important activities (Bryson, Crosby, and Stone 2006; Thomson and Perry 2006). What is unique in the context of network management is resource sharing (pooling) for joint production and delivery of public services. As a result, resource sharing is another main area of activity and has empirical support for its relevance in producing desirable network outcomes (Chen 2008).

One relevant insight from the network management and governance literature is the conceptualization of effectiveness. The effectiveness of a public management network is mostly formulated as outcomes. These outcome measures can be client satisfaction, efficiency in service production, cost of services, etc. Provan and Milward (2001) advance the discussion by articulating the need to differentiate between organization/participant level and two higher levels of aggregation, namely network-level and community-level effectiveness. Being explicit about the level of aggregation and the criteria for effectiveness evaluation is important for a rigorous empirical investigation. The outcome measures typically extend beyond those for a single organization (i.e., Provan, Huang, and Milward 2009; Chen 2008; Bryson, Crosby, and Stone 2006; Provan and Milward 1995). Process-based outcomes are relevant for public management networks because, sometimes, the sole purpose of a network is to build social capital for coordination and information sharing.

A Conceptual Framework for the Scientific Collaborative Network

The literature reviewed above provides the basis for the development of the framework outlined below. The organizing perspective is the one of governance infrastructure that includes technologies, systems, people, relationships, and their interactions in support of governance (Johnston

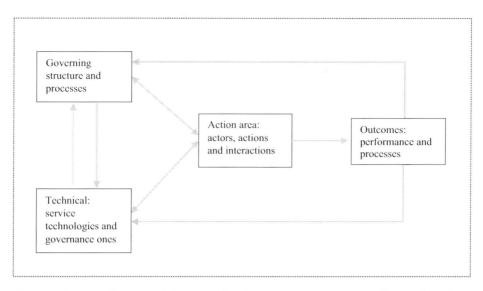

Figure 21.1 A Conceptual Framework for a Distributed Public Management Network for Cyberinfrastructure

2010). The main components of the system are governance, technical, and actors/interactions, as depicted in Figure 21.1.

Governance Structure

The governance structure and mechanism are composed of the rules as articulated by Ostrom and her colleagues (Ostrom, Gardner, and Walker 1994). These rules can be put into two broad categories for adapting them to the analysis of a public management network. One category is for the overall structure, including position rules determining the legitimate positions in a governance structure and boundary rules identifying legitimate participants and what positions they can assume. The other category of rules is related to decision-making. Information rules govern who has access to what information, which is a major consideration in collective decision-making, as illustrated by game theory. Payoff rules shape the incentive structure for governance. Since politics involve resource allocation, payoff rules are essential in understanding structural incentives. Choice rules specify the choice sets available for making a decision (choice) and are usually tied to positions. Aggregation rules are about how these choices can be aggregated to a higher level (i.e., from individuals to board using majority or consensus rule). Scope rules link decisions to outcomes by specifying the scope in which outcomes can be shaped by decisions. Such differentiation of rules allows a higher level of specificity in modeling and understanding the implications of changing one kind of rules for outcomes. It is important to note that configuration of rules, rather than rules separately, would affect the outcome (Ostrom 2010).

For a collaborative scientific network, specific rules are germane to the two broad categories. Boundary rules are critical ones for understanding the governance structure, as the evolution from the TeraGrid to XSEDE has expanded the boundary rules to be more inclusive. A more expansive boundary rule is likely to spur the inclusion of previously nonparticipating organizations. However, at the same time, it creates resource competition for staff time and energy to support other activities. For decision-making, the most prominent rules are about payoffs and information. Payoffs are likely to be on two levels. On the organizational level, payoff rules determine how each participating organization allocates resources across its home organization and the collaborative network. A more generous payoff for getting involved in the collaborative is likely to allow participating organizations to allocate more resources toward the collaborative. A similar dynamic exists for individuals to allocate their time between home organizations and the collaborative.

Overall, these rules affect resource allocations that are the source of politics. The configuration of rules defines the winners and losers in the cyberinfrastructure network. Such configuration is linked to outcomes, as the individual payoffs can be seen in various stakeholder groups or the entire network as a whole. Moreover, these governance and management structures can have both short-term and long-term consequences.

Role of Information and Communication Technologies

The technical component of the framework is a major modification to the standard perspective of public management networks. Such modification is essential, as changing technology is a major driving force in a governance system that relies heavily on technology for service production and delivery. The adoption of information and communication technologies can shape governance structure, interactions, and outcomes (Fountain 2001). The technical component has two parts.

The first part identifies the infrastructure in terms of telecommunication infrastructure, data standards, and technical service capability. Telecommunication infrastructures, such as a fiber optic backbone and connectivity of various devices, provide connectivity across a large geographic region for service delivery and information sharing. Therefore, telecommunication infrastructure is a critical element for public management service networks that cover a large geographic area and for which there is a need for bandwidth for data transmission. For instance, for the National Health Service of the United Kingdom, a telecommunication infrastructure is the backbone for the transmission of electronic health data for the provision of health services (Department of Health 2002).

Data standards also constitute a critical part of the infrastructure. A common data standard is needed for a public management network whose primary function is informational. The ease of sense making of the information gathered is a function of how easily data can be interpreted. Within a single organization, a common data standard is less likely to be a concern. However, it has become more of an issue across organizational boundaries when participating organizations have disparate data standards and definitions. Such heterogeneity can impede information interoperability. Such a problem is particularly pronounced in a crisis management situation when information interoperability is a requirement for establishing a common operating picture (Comfort and Haase 2006). A common data standard can also enable machine-readable information processing to increase efficiency and effectiveness of data exchange across organizational boundaries.

Technical service capability is the last element of the technical infrastructure. This element is about providing user-centered technical support for the information and communication technology employed by a public management network. This element should be viewed as a continuum. For a public management network with a low technical service requirement, this element could be as simple as video conference call services. For a network whose primary goal is to provide technical service, this could require a whole division providing technical service.

The other main aspect of the technical component concerns technology and applications used in the governance of service production and delivery. Collaborative technologies can aid in the generation of relevant service information such as use, demand, and effectiveness in service delivery for decision-making purposes. Moreover, collaborative technologies can help with communication, coordination, and project management. Such use of technology can make communication and coordination more effective. For instance, the use of video conference call options could create a media-rich experience for enhancing shared understanding and trust building. The cost of coordination can also be reduced if facilitated by proper use of information and communication technologies. A more advanced use of information and communication technology involves the use of a decision support system for making data-driven decisions on the allocation of network resources for improving performance.

Actors, Actions, and Interactions: Linking to Outcomes

Both the governance structure and technical aspect of the framework feed into the component encompassing actors and interactions as seen in Figure 21.1. The network and collaborative public management literature, along with the IAD framework, is informative in articulating the actors and interactions. Actors here are defined as organizations (and/or individuals) participating in the governance system. The list of actors is typically defined by boundary rules, and the legitimate actions that can be taken by these actors are delineated by choice rules. The collaborative public management literature also emphasizes the importance of identification of the participating organizations. One of the first steps in understanding any network is to identify all the actors. Such practice has been used in the study of the network of organizations in emergency response (Kapucu, Augustin, and Garayev 2009; Comfort and Haase 2006; Kapucu 2006).

Ostrom and her colleagues have emphasized the strategic actions of actors in a governance system. Actors inside an action area will engage in strategic actions to maximize their payoffs (Ostrom 2010). Actors are not merely passive recipients of governance rules. They also engage in actions to modify rules to advance their utility as captured by the two-way arrow in Figure 21.1. The same dynamic is observed between actors and the technical component. The kind of actions that actors can take is constrained by the technical capacity of the system when technology is an integral part of service production and delivery. At the same time, actors can decide which technology to enact to support the institutional and managerial arrangements that are in favor of their interests (Fountain 2001). For production and delivery of service, the managers of public service networks can deploy various management strategies, such as activation and mobilization (McGuire and Silvia 2010; McGuire 2006).

These actions and interactions lead to specific outcomes and can be classified into two levels. One is the collective level, which makes the policy decisions on institutional design and adoption of major technical infrastructure and applications. Another level is operational, which covers day-to-day operational decisions on the production and delivery of services. The actions and interactions on both levels can affect the outcomes.

Outcomes are measured as relevant to the goals of the network. The proposed framework recognizes the perspectives of various stakeholders and the three levels on which effectiveness can be measured: the levels of participants, program, and community (Provan and Milward 2001). Moreover, this framework differentiates between outputs and outcomes as made in performance measurement and the use of logic models (Frechtling 2007). These outcomes will become part of the feedback loops, as indicated in Figure 21.1, that various stakeholders can utilize to determine their actions.

Research Design, Data, and Methods

This chapter's emphasis on the evolution of the cyberinfrastructure programs and the interplay between governance structure, technology, and outcomes calls for a combination of research designs. The main research design for this study is the embedded case study design (Yin 2003), which includes program-level cases, cases for specific service areas, and even cases focused on a specific area of scientific research. The case study design has been chosen for its exploratory and holistic approach, which also enables identification of the key forces of changes (Yin 2003). This epistemological orientation is consistent with key features of these two cyberinfrastructure programs in terms of evolution, rule configuration, and interactions in affecting outcomes. The other main research design followed by this study is longitudinal in nature and uses time-series information as opposed to cross-sectional design with one or two time points (Eller, Gerber, and Roberson 2013). Time-series information is used to understand changes over time and the lagged effect in seeing the desirable impact after policy change. For this study, time-series information, especially about changes in processes and structure as well as program performance, is incorporated in understanding dynamics.

The primary data sources are internal documents and publicly available reports for both TeraGrid and XSEDE supplemented by field observations. More specifically for TeraGrid, some documents were gathered from its resource website. Some of the documents were obtained from an online workspace for the TeraGrid staff and members. The documents for XSEDE are mostly available on its main website. Annual reports on XSEDE and other information on XSEDE activities are available on its resource website. For the data analysis of XSEDE, we have relied mainly on two annual program reports covering the first two years of program activities (July 2011 to June 2013), as well as the evaluation report for the first three program years. There are numerous announcements, updates, news items, technical documentation, and management plans as related to both TeraGrid and XSEDE. The relevance and validity of the statements, as well as some additional insights on structure, strategies, and impact, are further assessed by field observations and informal conversations.

The data collection and analysis method is a mixed-method one with qualitative method as the dominant factor (Creswell and Clark 2011). The data collection effort focuses on gathering major program documents that have information on the key components and dynamics identified in Figure 21.1. This data collection effort is guided by the conceptual framework while allowing for interactions between the research question and data/methods, among others (Maxwell 2013). Key components from the documents include governance rules, technical infrastructure and applications, and, more importantly, interactions and strategic moves. For outcomes, both qualitative and quantitative information is utilized for understanding and measuring outcomes. Moreover, the dynamics demonstrate how these components collectively determine program outcomes. The identification of relevant documents is assisted by consultation with responsible program managers. Document review as a data collection method is supplemented by direct observation by and insights from program managers and participants. Some of the data used in the analysis come from the observations of program managers, especially in regards to the change from the TeraGrid to XSEDE and how such change affects program outcomes.

Data analysis follows the basic principles and techniques of case study methods with the focus on qualitative data. Given the number of documents involved, we first established a hierarchy of the documents utilized in terms of both salience and authority. For instance, the statements made in the annual reports are weighed more heavily than similar statements made in other program publications, because annual reports represent the most authoritative source of information for the programs. We then began by establishing the history and context for the cyberinfrastructure for collaborative scientific networks by identifying the barometric events and major changes (Miles, Huberman, and Saldana 2014). Then, we identified relevant statements in these key documents to determine the extent to which these statements shed light on the governance and management structure, technical components, actors and interactions, and links to outcomes. These can be seen as the main organizing structure to understand the key variables for the case. We also utilized the techniques of causal maps to link components to outcomes (Miles, Huberman, and Saldana 2014).

Description and Analysis of the Cyberinfrastructure Public Management Network

Program History and Description

The initial development of a national cyberinfrastructure for distributed computing began in early 2000. It was first formalized as the TeraGrid project (Catlett 2002). This project was funded by a Major Research Equipment (MRE) award given by the U.S. National Science Foundation. The goal was to establish a national cyberinfrastructure and complete its first phase of development by the end of 2003 (Catlett 2002). This project is a combination of three programs within NSF's TeraScale initiative. The objectives were to deliver increasing computational capability commensurate to the advances in technology to enable scientific research via a distributed system (Catlett 2002).

The official launch of the TeraGrid program in 2005, at the level of 150 million dollars for five years, marked a major effort to integrate various programs into one. Funding was provided by the National Science Foundation's Office of Cyberinfrastructure (OCI). The primary goal of the TeraGrid program has been scientific and engineering discovery, while including education and outreach as secondary goals. This program meets these goals by providing supercomputing capability, massive storage, visualization services, and science gateways through the integration of resources from participating laboratories and universities. All are connected by a high-bandwidth grid with integrated services. On the operational level, the service is mostly about the application, approval, and delivery and support of allocation of computational services. Evolving into the later part of the program period, the TeraGrid program consists of Grid Infrastructure Groups (GIG), 11 resource providers, and 6 software integration partners (TeraGrid Office 2009). Grid Infrastructure Groups are responsible for TeraGrid's program and service areas such as "User Services and Support" and "Science Gateways." Resource providers are national laboratories and universities. Services are supported by computational science and technology experts.

Beginning in 2011, XSEDE represents a new chapter in the development and implementation of the cyberinfrastructure for providing computational capability for scientific and engineering discovery. It was funded by the National Science Foundation for 121 million U.S. dollars (The Program Office of the Extreme Science and Engineering Discovery Environment (XSEDE) 2012a) to support a dozen supercomputers and high-end visualization and data analysis resources. In terms of services, XSEDE provides a suite of resources similar to those of TeraGrid, including computing, storage, visualization, and data analysis. The name XSEDE implies that it "exceeds" TeraGrid in various areas such as usability, performance, productivity, and science impact. The XSEDE is led by a single institution, the University of Illinois' National Center for Supercomputing Applications, with 19 partners including supercomputing labs, universities, and even professional research associations and education institutions.[1] Most of the partners in TeraGrid continued as partners in XSEDE. Operationally, the XSEDE program has strengthened its extended collaborative support services and increased focus on areas such as project management, cybersecurity, education, and outreach (The Program Office of the Extreme Science and Engineering Discovery Environment (XSEDE) 2012b).

Institutional Environment and Governance Structure of the Collaborative Cyberinfrastructure

The ecosystem of the collaborative cyberinfrastructure for providing supercomputing service includes a wide collection of stakeholders, such as the National Science Foundation, who fund a similar computing infrastructure program: the Open Science Grid, a grid organized by volunteers to provide similar, as well as other, services. Both the TeraGrid and XSEDE programs, serving as a framework for a distributed service network, can encompass a large group of local and regional players, such as Research & Education Networks (RENs), the ACI-REF program, and the Track II program or Major Research Instrumentation (MRI) programs. The focus of the discussion below is on the central governance and management system as defined by the TeraGrid program and the XSEDE program for the purpose of empirical investigation.

The governance structure for TeraGrid is composed of major resource providers (RPs) with a coordination and integration body (Zimmerman and Finholt 2008, 18). The list of resource providers has grown since the inception of the TeraGrid projects. The initial eight resource providers were Indiana

University (IU), Oak Ridge National Laboratory (ORNL), the National Center for Supercomputing Applications (NCSA), the Pittsburgh Supercomputing Center (PSC), Purdue University (PU), the San Diego Supercomputer Center (SDSC), the Texas Advanced Computing Center (TACC), and the University of Chicago/Argonne National Laboratory (UC/ANL). By the end of 2007, three more resource providers—namely the National Center for Atmospheric Research (NCAR), the Louisiana Optical Network, and the National Institute for Computational Sciences—were added to the list to make 11. Each RP acts as an autonomous institution and receives a separate but cross-referenced NSF award to operate and support resources (Catlett, Goasguen, and Cobb 2006, 2). These resource providers are tied together via a Grid Infrastructure Group that was funded by a separate NSF award to UC/ANL, a distributed body that provides integration and coordination across the project (Catlett et al. 2008). The GIG supports common services (i.e., user support and authentication services, education, outreach, software coordination, backbone, etc.) and common processes (i.e., accounting, authorizations, and allocations peer review).[2]

The main governance body of TeraGrid is the TeraGrid Forum, including one representative from each resource provider as well as the GIG (TeraGrid Office 2009). Working groups, with representations from all sites, serve the function of service coordination, including accounting, allocation, data, user services, and security. Typically, working groups last for a year or more. For finding problems and appropriate solutions, the TeraGrid Forum relies on a "Requirement Analysis Team" that is staffed by a small number of experts working for 6–10 weeks on a specific topic. In addition, TeraGrid has a user advisory group formally known as the Cyberinfrastructure User Advisory Committee (CUAC), comprised of users of cyberinfrastructure (Zimmerman and Finholt 2008, 15–16). Such governance structure has been characterized as a virtual organization that is distributed across space and time with dynamic processes as well as computationally enabled and enhanced collaboration and interfacing with users (Cummings et al. 2008, 18). Virtual organizations are characterized by a geographically distributed range of actors, with members of the organization in multiple locations, with responsibilities spread across these units. Frequently arrangements between members of virtual organizations have their basis in contractual agreements, and the organizational structure is reconfigurable to meet task needs (Desanctis and Monge 1998). While initial conceptions of the virtual organization strictly divided management and decision-making tasks from service delivery (Mowshowitz 1994), some virtual organizations align function with location, but others may distribute tasks and members equally. Virtual organizations are also characterized by the ability to change service delivery mechanisms as well as the services delivered. For the rise of "grid" services, particularly grid computing, virtual organizations are central to the development of a distributed governance model which manages resources which are likewise distributed (Foster, Kesselman, and Tuecke 2001). These distributed sets of actors, with individual membership often having distinct needs as well as responsibilities, is sometimes characterized as a "collaboratory" (Finholt and Olson 1997). The trust that forms the basis of these one-to-many relationships between members of the virtual organization is facilitated with reliable ICT implementation; understanding of the tasks, environment, and stakeholders of the organization; and shared ethics (Kasper-Fuehrera and Ashkanasy 2001).

XSEDE's organizational structure has a central project management office with managers responsible for various functional areas. XSEDE is defined as a project managed by the University of Illinois with other partner institutions. The governance body is essentially the XSEDE Senior Management Team (SMT) that integrates both operational and advisory roles into a single decision-making body by the function of membership on the team (XSEDE 2013, 1). The Senior Management Team is chaired by the program director. On the operational side, the SMT includes directors of Operations, Users Services, Extended Collaborative Support Services-Projects,

Extended Collaborative Support Services-Communities, Education and Outreach, and Technology Integration Service. In addition to the specific operational areas, the Project Office also has the senior project manager, the senior systems engineer, the architecture and design coordinator, and the software development and integration lead (XSEDE 2013, 81). This Senior Project Management Team meets every two weeks.

The Senior Project Management Team, as the main management operation, also receives advice from three main groups of stakeholders: users, service providers, and the scientific community. Each group of stakeholders has a distinct advisory body. Users are represented by the XSEDE User Advisory Committee. The XSEDE Service Providers Forum solicits inputs from service providers. The XSEDE Advisory Board represents the broadest spectrum of the scientific community that XSEDE serves (XSEDE 2013, 87–88).

In terms of boundary rules, TeraGrid's composition of governance and management teams are more decentralized in comparison with the XSEDE. This decentralization was a function of the governance structure: each resource provider represented in the Grid Infrastructure Group does not have direct oversight over their operation. Each resource provider can, however, decide on their commitments as discussed and negotiated. Such decentralization can also be seen in the choice rule that specifies the amount of enforcement power of the Grid Infrastructure Group, as well as the aggregation rules that govern how individual service providers' decisions get aggregated to the group level. In contrast, the governance structure for XSEDE is much more centralized in its operation. There is a clear division of labor that covers various functional areas as indicated above. The project management office has both the service capability and accountability mechanisms in place to ensure that participating institutions carry out their commitments. It is no longer up to the resource provider to make the ultimate decisions.

The governance and management structure of TeraGrid is more in flux compared with that of XSEDE. The addition of resource providers over the first three years of the TeraGrid program by the NSF makes the boundary rules of participation more dynamic. Adding to the dynamic is the role of the NSF in determining the boundary rules, as opposed to having these rules determined by the main governance body, the GIG. In contrast, the boundary rule for the participating institutions for XSEDE was set at the creation of XSEDE, and further determined by the Service Provider Forum, which developed a charter and guidelines for levels of service. The main partner institutions have been relatively stable ever since XSEDE's inception in 2011, but lower-level service providers can join XSEDE by submitting an application to the Service Provider Forum and demonstrating a set level of interoperability with XSEDE's services. Moreover, it is mainly the choice of the Senior Project Management Team to select the partner institutions.

The payoff rules need to be understood at both the institutional and individual levels. The general payoff structures have not seen major change from TeraGrid to XSEDE. The payoff for participating institutions is to secure NSF funding as one of the main funding sources for their supercomputing facilities and staff. In addition, the payoff to be part of the cyberinfrastructure is to gain capability that is not otherwise directly available. For individuals, payoff is about the tangible future career opportunities in the large network of organizations providing supercomputing capabilities and services.[3] The intangible benefit is the recognition that comes with being part of a larger network and assuming greater responsibility otherwise not available in an individual home institution.[4] For institutions that join the Service Provider Forum, participation is a way of demonstrating to grant funding agencies the level of participation, technical ability, and commitment to the ecosystem, hopefully inspiring the acceptance of larger grant proposals. It should be noted that there is a significant variation in the payoff for a specific institution because of the different percentages of the funding provided by the collaborative network across institutions.

Role of Information and Communication Technologies: Service Production and Management

The cyberinfrastructure for a collaborative scientific network is likely to be at the high end for telecommunication infrastructure and service, and about medium for data standards. For the telecommunication infrastructure, the need for distributing supercomputing power across the grid requires a reliable and high-bandwidth telecommunication network. The quality and speed of such infrastructure can have a direct influence on outcome and performance. The demand for technical service capability is also likely to be on the high end. All that supercomputing power requires a large technical service team to make it useful for researchers, because a majority of the researchers may not be trained to utilize the supercomputing power available via the grid. There are additional issues (such as data storage and access) that are integral parts of scientific discovery utilizing supercomputing power. Data standards are less vital as compared with the other two aspects, because the primary function of this cyberinfrastructure involves computing power service rather than information exchange. Therefore, the discussion below will focus on technical service capability and technology for governance and management.

Technical Service Capability

The role of information and communication technologies in providing user services has seen an evolution from TeraGrid to XSEDE. TeraGrid offered an array of services. For the telecommunication and supercomputing service network, TeraGrid had a dedicated area for network, operation, and security. For user services, TeraGrid offered software integration, user and user support, as well as data and visualization. Science Gateways was a specific strategy that targeted major scientific research areas to offer more integrated technical services. The third area of the technical services was to support education, outreach, training, and external relations (TeraGrid Office 2009).

In the user-service area, one of the major changes from TeraGrid to XSEDE has been the improvement of the "Extended Collaborative Support Service." Originally intended to help code run more efficiently on TeraGrid systems, this group has been extended to include the construction of workflows, parallelization of serial codes, and coding science gateways. This Extended Collaborative Support Service focuses on providing an integrated service model with the focus on specific scientific research areas as identified in science gateways (XSEDE 2013). This moves beyond the advanced user support available in TeraGrid to provide in-depth integrated support ranging from performance analysis and petascale-optimization techniques to building Science Gateways and workflow systems (The Program Office of the Extreme Science and Engineering Discovery Environment (XSEDE) 2011). Examples of Science Gateways include seismic research and genomic sequencing. Moreover, the technical service of XSEDE has also developed new capabilities. These new capabilities include architecture and design, software integration services, new technology investigation service, etc., (XSEDE 2014, 46–59).

Information Technologies for Communication and Governance

For TeraGrid, there were a number of communication and coordination mechanisms in place. These mechanisms include communication among the working group members as well as utilization by requirements analysis team members of various communication technologies, such as video conference calls. Moreover, TeraGrid management met regularly using telephone conferencing and the access grid. In addition, there were quarterly face-to-face meetings and gatherings at the annual TeraGrid conference. The specific technologies used include numerous electronic mail lists, a TeraGrid central database, and a TeraGrid Wiki. Email lists were utilized by the specific groups to meet their own needs. The TeraGrid central database helped document the use of TeraGrid resources. The TeraGrid Wiki provided a depository of program documents, such as annual reports, site reports, and evaluation studies (Zimmerman and Finholt 2008, 26–30).

The technology use for governance and management in XSEDE has evolved and expanded along with the new governance, project management, and goals of XSEDE. With a tighter project management structure, there was a move to a project management tool for communication and project management (XSEDE 2013, 89–90). The use of technology is also supplemented by tighter and more structured quarterly meetings. The more advanced use of technology expanded to the functional lines: for example, the use of "Use Cases" and "Digital Object Repository" for the software and system engineering (XSEDE 2013, 90–91). In addition, the auditing software program allows for service auditing, even for a particular facility and a risk registry, and project planning systems improve XSEDE's ability to conduct planning activities for each program year (XSEDE 2013, 92–93).

XSEDE has also utilized an extensive centralized database (XDCDB) for service outputs (XSEDE 2013, 95–96). This database covers three areas of information that are essential for the operation and performance evaluation of XSEDE. The first area is "jobs" and provides metrics for jobs run on XSEDE resources, including information on job sizes, resource utilization, wait times, etc. With the analytics, data can be aggregated by user, PI (principal investigator), institution, resource, service provider, field of science, gateway, queue, and allocation. The second area is "allocations" and encompasses the allocations of computing resources to users. This area has both current and historical data on active and expired allocations across the entire XSEDE. Information is also available on burn rate, usage rate, and total SUs allocated and used. Again, data can be aggregated to a high level or unit such as PI, resource, field of science, and allocation type. The last area is "accounts" and includes information on the number of accounts created, opened, and closed aggregated to a certain period. Information from the XDCDB is provided to service providers in order to ensure that accounts and allocations information is current across the system, and is also used in the XSEDE User Portal to inform users what resource allocations are available to them. Finally, XDCDB and other information feeds into the XSEDE Metrics on Demand service (XDMoD), which allows for real-time queries on PI, allocation, and system usage, and provides application profiling services to improve performance across XSEDE.

Strategic Actions and Interactions: Big Forces and Links to Outcomes

Fundamental Challenges for a Distributed Public Management Network

The strategic actions and interactions can be organized around the two main tensions for a distributed public management network that has evolved from TeraGrid to XSEDE. This approach addresses the major forces affecting the public management network. The first tension requires managing usually competing commitments to a home organization and to the distributed network. This tension is documented in policy implementation and network literature as well as the literature of virtual organization (i.e., Cummings et al. 2008). Such tension is also documented in the TeraGrid 2008 evaluation, as articulated as cultural differences across participating organizations in a network (Zimmerman and Finholt 2008). This tension is also mentioned in some of the responses of the XSEDE staff members about the challenges to balance the demand from the network and the demand from the home organization.

The other tension of this distributed cyberinfrastructure is from the multitude of goals and objectives. The existence of multiple goals and objectives, and the potential tradeoffs between them, has been cited as a source of problems for information technology use by government as opposed to the same use by corporations (Rocheleau 2006; Bretschneider 1990). The need for shared understanding is one of the main conditions for successful interorganizational collaboration. The multitude of goals impedes the development of such understanding to a certain extent (Gray et al. 2003). Such diversity in goals, and the stakeholders who are defined by it, can be one source of management challenges.

TeraGrid has a three-part mission. One goal is to support the most advanced computational science for various science domains. The second goal is to reach out, serve, and empower new communities of users. The third goal is to offer resources to the broader cyberinfrastructure (Zimmerman and Finholt 2008). Each goal has its advocates and stakeholders. The core stakeholders for advanced computational science are the teams of scientists who rely heavily on advanced supercomputing power for their research (i.e., climate change and earthquake modeling). This group of stakeholders is different from that of social scientists, who may have never heard of or used any supercomputing power in their research. Moreover, there is competition for time and resources between goals. For instance, the second goal demands resources for outreach and educational activities that compete for time and attention from the staff, who are also responsible for providing computing resources to advanced users of computational resources.

Such tensions also exist in the XSEDE project. There is competition for XSEDE resources between serving existing advanced users and new novel users. The kind of support needed for advanced users is different from that for novel users. Novel users need to have basic training in the rudimentary use of computational resources, such as how to submit a "computational" job, as opposed to advanced users needing help on accessing, processing, and storing terabytes of data in a short period. The significant resource demand for supporting advanced users is seen in the 40% of the XSEDE budget allocated for the Extended Collaboration and Support Services.[5] Moreover, tension also exists among the stakeholders benefiting from the advancement of computational science and those of the broad community of public, private, and nonprofit organizations sustaining the ecosystem of supercomputing capabilities.

Linking Strategies to Outcomes

Several governance and management actions may be taken to alleviate the tension between individuals' commitment to home organizations and to the distributed network of organizations providing supercomputing infrastructure. Moving from TeraGrid to XSEDE, the creation of a centralized project management structure with accountability measures articulates the boundary and expectations of individuals' roles and responsibilities as related to the network. The formalization of full-time employee (FTE) status for people working with XSEDE is also an important progress in formalizing such relationships in XSEDE. The results of a climate survey suggest that such tension is less so for directors who are employed by XSEDE as 100% FTE than for those who are employed by XSEDE 50% of their time.[6] Overall, such tension has been reduced over time.[7]

Another mechanism for understanding and addressing possible tension is the staff climate survey to understand attitudes and concerns. This survey began in the second program year of XSEDE. The relatively high response rate for the first and second staff climate surveys, with 48% and 62% response rate respectively, provides quality and representative information on the staff climate (XSEDE 2014, Section F). This process mechanism is further strengthened by the expediency of the survey analysis as well as the use of staff climate survey data for process improvement (XSEDE 2014, Section F).

The evolution from TeraGrid to XSEDE has spurred efforts to address the potential competition between multiple goals. One of the main mechanisms is a clear identification and resource allocation for each goal. For instance, 40% of the XSEDE budget is allocated for the Extended Collaboration and Support Services. These teams take existing code and optimize or create workflows that get data from instrument to analysis to results, or build web gateways for communities of researchers. There are specific activities and resources allocated for reaching out to minority institutions and researchers as "underrepresented community engagement programs" and "campus bridging programs."[8] The XSEDE has also budgeted significant resources for the development of the STEM workforce and MSI development (NSF Broader Impacts activities) in order to achieve the goal of serving the broader community and minority institutions. Moreover, each of the main areas is headed by a director who oversees the operation, as evident in the organizational chart of XSEDE. These operations are also captured in the Work Breakdown Structure (WBS).

Another mechanism is the explicit performance management system that keeps track of the key performance indicators for various areas. For instance, there is specific matrix for the Extended Collaborative Support Service (ECSS) (XSEDE 2014, Section B, p. 17). Detailed information on various services in the first three program years has been provided by the ECSS. For instance, in the area of extended science gateways support, there is accounting of how many projects have been initiated and completed. In addition, information is being tracked on the diversity of users in terms of demographics such as gender and ethnicity (XSEDE 2014, Table G.1). Moreover, such a performance management system integrates performance information into process improvement as mentioned earlier (XSEDE 2014, Section F).

Findings and Discussions

The findings presented below are based on the investigation of various components and the dynamics suggested in the conceptual framework. We will organize information around the main findings as well as their implications. The centralized governance structure and management is one of the factors that has helped with program accountability and effectiveness (NSF TeraGrid Program 2011). The move from a federated system of project management in TeraGrid to a centralized project management system in XSEDE, as previously discussed, is a major shift to centralized operation. It was one of the main lessons learned as indicated in the final report of TeraGrid (NSF TeraGrid Program 2011). Such centralization has improved accountability by providing a clear line of accountability and responsibilities that were not evident in the TeraGrid program. Moreover, effectiveness has been improved in terms of both knowledge and outcomes. The new centralized database for XSEDE has detailed information on output and outcomes that can be aggregated to various units and levels. The improvement in effectiveness is also seen in the number of service units rendered and the number of users (XSEDE 2014; TeraGrid Office 2009).

This finding underscores the need for a network management organization, as the operation and management of a public management network has become more complex (Provan and Kenis 2008). The complexity of gaining knowledge about operation and effectiveness requires a more centralized mechanism for tracking and accountability. A practical implication of organizational design for a large, distributed public management network is the need to establish a central management unit to facilitate decision-making and program implementation. The cost of having two or more centers to provide the same level of distributed computing services is significantly higher than having only one centralized administrative office to do so (XSEDE 2014).

Taking a learning approach and focusing on process improvement help address the two main sources of tensions identified, including the competing commitments to home organization and networks as well as the multitude of program goals. The history of TeraGrid and XSEDE has demonstrated various mechanisms and openness for organizational learning. Quarterly meetings and annual meetings, plus numerous working groups, are forums for management to learn the challenges and issues as well as the effectiveness of proposed solutions. In addition, formal evaluations and studies have been conducted on the effectiveness of the TeraGrid program in achieving its goals. TeraGrid had both a rigorous mid-term review and end-of-the-program evaluation. More importantly, these lessons learned from TeraGrid have informed the organizational design of XSEDE. The most significant change, as guided by the TeraGrid experience, is having a central project management office. Such creation has created both knowledge about the extent of goal attainment and the respective resource inputs required (XSEDE 2014). Consequently, with a central office, adjustments can be made accordingly. In addition, the creation of a central accounting structure (FTE equivalent) and employment of high-level managers by the network at the 100% level mitigate the tension for individuals between network and home organization.

The other supporting strategy is to implement a formal process improvement mechanism with a staff climate survey. The formal process improvement mechanism was introduced into XSEDE as a broad-based one with rigorous validation methodologies for tracking improvement. Such improvement includes areas such as leadership, customer focus, measurement, analysis, knowledge management, workforce focus, and results. Moreover, XSEDE has seen specific improvements being implemented, including areas such as organizational analysis and innovation, as well as learning and strategic improvement (XSEDE 2014). With the staff climate survey, the project management office has timely information on the key issues facing staff and the program and is able to address these issues quickly. One-time funding awards to address resource needs, as well as provision of training and career opportunities to the staff, induce them to stay motivated and contribute to the program. As a result, the tension between home organization and the network (program) has been trending consistently downward for the last five years.

The combination of these strategies has theoretical implications for the public management network and collaborative management network literature. The most significant one is the need to establish a process improvement mechanism that is rarely mentioned in this literature. Moreover, the literature needs to advance beyond the general areas of network management, such as mobilization and activation, to focus on continuous improvement and adaptation.

The development of technical capabilities and new technology uses has increased the ability of the cyberinfrastructure programs to be more effective in providing services. This part is particularly critical, as the main service provided by this public management network is technical support. The advancements are accomplished by focusing on user needs and user support. The enhanced capability to provide extended collaborative support service is an example of such advancements. It is one of the main forces that bring in an increased number of computing resource utilizations and scientific breakthroughs.

Moreover, the experiences of TeraGrid and XSEDE show that appropriate use of technologies can support governance, management, and organizational learning. The use of information and communication technology, such as a centralized database and communication platform, has reduced the cost of information gathering and coordination. One of the biggest challenges associated with a network is to gather information from disparate entities that potentially have various standards and practices. Both governance and management can be data-driven when the appropriate technologies are utilized. The detailed nature of the reporting on the key performance indicators in the XSEDE evaluation report is the evidence supporting data-driven practices for accountability and performance.

The main theoretical implication is the importance of integrated technologies for service production and delivery, as well as management and governance. The existing literature on public management networks has not provided adequate attention to and analysis of the ways in which technology can improve service delivery capability and governance effectiveness. The experience of TeraGrid and XSEDE serves as a case for the relevance of appropriate use of information and communication technologies. One practical implication for a broad range of public management networks is the need for focusing on technology that can reduce information gathering, increase data analytics, and provide performance information for continuous improvement.

One main lesson of institutional design and management from TeraGrid to XSEDE is the importance of open collaboration for the sustainability of the ecosystem to support the goals of a supercomputing cyberinfrastructure. The general approach of TeraGrid and XSEDE is not to fully replace various initiatives or programs that have similar goals. Rather, the focus has been on developing an ecosystem that is healthy enough for long-term sustainability and adaptation. This focus is seen particularly in the XSEDE program, such as in the collaboration with Open Science Grid, an alternative for providing supercomputing power in a distributed environment. Moreover, XSEDE has specific programs that support and advance the entire ecosystem of cyberinfrastructure.[9] Another example is the XSEDE's partnership with the popular LIGO project, representing collaboration in individual domain-specific projects. The comparison between XSEDE and PRACE-RI, a similar European project with a relatively closed model of collaboration, further highlights the benefit of open collaboration.[10]

The next main lesson for institutional design and management is to focus on the program level, rather than the centers at the lower levels, for better adaptation. The TeraGrid and XSEDE programs provide a framework that sustains and grows the capabilities of the network as a whole, even with changes at the lower (center) level. For instance, if the funding for a particular supercomputing center ended, and the talents exited that particular center, it could be a major setback for a single organization. However, the experience of XSEDE shows that these talents can seek employment in other supercomputing centers as well as facilities either within the XSEDE or in the larger ecosystem.

Another lesson is the value of focusing on clustering and synergistic research communities with a strong core. TeraGrid grew out of the need and vision of the supercomputing community to provide this power as an enabler to advance scientific discovery. Science Gateways have been a way to focus on these innovative research communities clustering around a particular research area (TeraGrid Office 2009). Such a program enables domain scientists to make good use of sophisticated cyberinfrastructure without being computational science experts themselves, as in the South California Earthquake Consortium (TeraGrid Office 2009, 39). The tremendous growth in 2008 in the research performance of Science Gateways is evidence of the benefit of this approach. The effectiveness of the Science Gateways approach is supported by the way in which scientists work with one another. The most significant clustering in the network is still in a specific research knowledge domain (Knepper 2011). XSEDE further strengthened the support for Science Gateways by providing more tools and services with well-defined project plans and means for their execution (The Program Office of the Extreme Science and Engineering Discovery Environment (XSEDE) 2013; 2011). Accomplishments can be seen in the science and engineering highlights in the areas of economics, bioscience, seismology, aeronautics, etc., as well as in the growth of the number of publications in various science and engineering domains.

These lessons inform the theory and practice of institutional and organizational design. The open collaboration model suggests the effectiveness of a more flexible institutional framework in terms of gaining partnership and support from organizations in the large supercomputing ecosystem beyond specific programs such as TeraGrid and XSEDE. A large-scale distributed public management network can take note of such an open approach for sustainability and effectiveness. This lesson also raises an interesting distinction between operational service provisions that need to be more structured and broad-based partnerships that can be more open and flexible. Moreover, enabling domain communities with supercomputing power has proven productive. This productivity suggests the utility of understanding how people affiliate and work with each other in scientific discovery. Such a finding highlights the value of understanding social networks and their shared needs in ensuring results.

Conclusion

This study is one of the first investigations into the evolution in the governance and management of a large distributed public management service network that extends beyond state borders and is truly national in scope. Another unique contribution of this study is its examination of the role of information and communication technologies in service production and delivery, as well as the governance and management of the network. Moreover, it is one of the few articles extending beyond standard public services area to the scientific community for national competitiveness and innovation.

This study integrates insights from various bodies of literature to inform the analysis of such a large distributed public management service network. These main bodies of literature include institutional analysis and development framework, public management network management, and collaborative public management. Although useful in its own right, each body of literature has only partially explained the evolution in governance and management structures as well as their effectiveness. This integrated framework provides a more comprehensive understanding of these relationships.

Moreover, this study offers theoretical and practical implications for the study of public management service networks. The results support the need for a centralized project management structure and office for a large distributed network. It provides additional support to the argument that a network management organization for complex networks is necessary. The importance of organizational (network) learning provides a new factor for effectiveness of public management networks, which has been rarely studied or established as one of the main factors. Such learning and various mechanisms to support learning make this cyberinfrastructure for supercomputing particularly adaptive and effective.

The study also shows the salience in using enabling information and communication technologies for both service production and delivery, and governance and management. Even for public management networks that use little technology for service production, the use of information technology for governance and management is still instructive and typically not sufficiently studied. This chapter offers insights into the ways in which technology use can be an enabler. The last set of findings is about institutional design and management. Open collaboration with partners in the ecosystem, focus on network-level design allowing for flexibility at the sublevel, and focus on sublevel communities to create more impact are all instructive for theory and practice of designing and managing such large distributed networks.

This study also faces some limitations that could also serve as opportunities for future research. First, the sheer amount of information and documentation makes distilling the main mechanisms, forces, and findings challenging. Annual reports are typically 300 to 500 pages long with detailed information. As a coping mechanism, the authors rely on field observations, review of key evaluation documents, and annual reports, as well as a focus on high-level analysis with key variables identified in the framework. To address this limitation, the authors will conduct interviews of key managers to leverage their insights and triangulate the findings. Moreover, more process tracing will be done at the sublevel of the cyberinfrastructure network as a way to isolate the potential causal links of the major governance and management strategies to outcomes. Second, this case of cyberinfrastructure could be a theoretical case rather than a typical case in the world of public management service networks. Therefore, caution is needed for generalization because of the size and scope of the TeraGrid and XSEDE programs. To address this limitation, it would be productive to study a more regional public management network (i.e., multi-state one) to understand the relevance of the findings. Another front for increasing generalizability is to study a network in which information technology is used for management and governance but less in the production and delivery of services. This would offer further insights into the role of information technology for a typical distributed network.

Notes

1. https://www.xsede.org/leaders
2. More detailed information about TeraGrid's organizational structure, governance, and operations is available in Catlett et al. (2008) and Catlett, Goasguen, and Cobb (2006).
3. This is based on the discussion with the evaluation team and evaluation results.
4. This is based on the discussion with the evaluation team and the evaluation results of staff climate survey for XSEDE.

5. This is based on the information gathered from internal project discussions.
6. Results from the XSEDE evaluation office.
7. It is based on the results from the XSEDE evaluation office.
8. For details, see https://www.xsede.org/home
9. New push to assemble "volunteer" cluster capacity and assist with integration: local staff gets training/knowledge boost and local institution gets benefit of being "XSEDE-certified." It leverages existing training and relationships in order to produce more capacity in aggregate (per Rich Knepper).
10. This is based on a note on the interview with Towns in August 2014.

References

Bardach, Eugene. 1996. "Turf Barriers to Interagency Collaboration." In *The State of Public Management*, edited by Donald Kettl and Brinton Milward, 168–192. Baltimore, MD: Johns Hopkins University Press.

Bretschneider, Stuart. 1990. "Managing Information Systems in Public and Private Organizations: An Empirical Test." *Public Administration Review,* 50(5):536–545.

Bryson, John, Barbara Crosby, and Melissa Middleton Stone. 2006. "The Design and Implementation of Cross-Sector Collaborations: Propositions from the Literature." *Public Administration Review,* 66 (Supplement to Issue 6 (Special Issue)):44–55.

Catlett, Charlie. 2002. *The TeraGrid: A Primer*. Lemont, IL: Argonne National Lab.

Catlett, Charlie, and et al. 2008. "TeraGrid: Analysis of Organization, System Architecture, and Middleware Enabling New Types of Applications." In *High Performance Computing (HPC) and Grids in Action*, edited by L. Grandinetti, 225–249. Amsterdam, the Netherlands: IOS Press.

Catlett, Charlie, Sebastien Goasguen, and John Cobb. 2006. TeraGrid Policy Management Framework (TG-1: Policy).

Chen, Bin. 2008. "Assessing Interorganizational Networks for Public Service Delivery: A Process-Perceived Effectiveness Framework." *Public Performance & Management Review,* 31(3):348–363.

Chen, Yu-Che, and Kurt Thurmaier. 2009. "Interlocal Agreements as Collaborations: An Empirical Investigation of Impetuses, Norms, and Success." *American Review of Public Administration,* 39(5):536–552.

Comfort, Louise, and Thomas Haase. 2006. "Communication, Coherence, and Collective Action: The Impact of Hurricane Katrina on Communications Infrastructure." *Public Works Management and Policy,* 10(4):328–343.

Creswell, John, and Vicki L. Plano Clark. 2011. *Designing and Conducting Mixed Methods Research*. Second ed. Los Angeles, CA: Sage.

Cummings, Jonathon, Thomas Finholt, Ian Foster, Carl Kesselman, and Katherine A. Lawrence. 2008. Beyond Being There: A Blueprint for Advancing the Design, Development, and Evaluation of Virtual Organizations. NSF.

Department of Health. 2002. *Delivering 21st Century IT Support for the NHS*. London: Department of Health.

Desanctis, Gerardine, and Peter Monge. 1998. "Communication Processes for Virtual Organizations." *Journal of Computer-Mediated Communication,* 3(4). doi:10.1111/j.1083-6101.1998.tb00083.x

Eller, Warren S., Brian J. Gerber, and Scott E. Roberson. 2013. *Public Administration Research Methods: Tools for Evaluation and Evidence-Based Practice*. New York: Routledge.

Finholt, Thomas A., and Gary M. Olson. (1997). "From Laboratories to Collaboratories: A New Organizational Form for Scientific Collaboration," *Psychological Science,* 8(1): 28–36.

Foster, Ian, Carl Kesselman, and Steven Tuecke. 2001. "The Anatomy of the Grid: Enabling Scalable Virtual Organizations." *International Journal of High Performance Computing Applications,* 15(3):200–222.

Fountain, Jane. 2001. *Building the Virtual State: Information Technology and Institutional Change*. Washington, DC: Brookings Institution Press.

Frechtling, Joy. 2007. *Logic Modeling Methods in Program Evaluation*. San Francisco: Jossey-Bass.

Gil-Garcia, J. Ramon, Ahmet Guler, Theresa A. Pardo, and G. Brian Burke. 2010. Trust in Government Cross-Boundary Information Sharing Initiatives: Identifying the Determinants. Paper read at 43rd Hawaii International Conference on System Sciences (HICSS-43), 5–8 January 2010, at Koloa, Kauai, HI.

Gray, Andrew, Bill Jenkins, Frans Leeuw, and John Mayne. 2003. *Collaboration in Public Services*. New Brunswick, NJ and London: Transaction Publishers.

Gray, Barbara. 1985. "Conditions Facilitating Interorganizational Collaboration." *Human Relations,* 38(10):911–936.

Isett, Kimberley R., Ines A. Mergel, Kelly LeRoux, Pamela A. Mischen, and R. Karl Rethemeyer. 2011. "Networks in Public Administration Scholarship: Understanding Where We Are and Where We Need to Go." *Journal of Public Administration Research and Theory,* 21 (Supplement 1):i157–i173.

Johnston, Erik. 2010. "Governance Infrastructures in 2020." *Public Administration Review,* 70 (Special Issue):S122–128.

Kapucu, Naim. 2006. "Interagency Communication Networks During Emergencies: Boundary Spanners in Multiagency Coordination." *American Review of Public Administration, 36*(2):207–225.

Kapucu, Naim, Maria-Elena Augustin, and Vener Garayev. 2009. "Interstate Partnerships in Emergency Management: Emergency Management Assistance Compact in Response to Catastrophic Disasters." *Public Administration Review, 69*(2):297–313.

Kasper-Fuehrera, Eva C., and Neal M. Ashkanasy. 2001. "Communicating Trustworthiness and Building Trust in Interorganizational Virtual Organizations." *Journal of Management, 27*(3):235–254.

Knepper, Richard. 2011. The Shape of the TeraGrid: Analysis of TeraGrid Users and Projects as an Affiliation Network. Paper read at TeraGrid '11, July 18–21, at Salt Lake City, Utah.

Maxwell, Joseph. 2013. *Qualitative Research Design: An Interactive Approach.* Third ed., Applied Social Research Methods. Thousand Oak, CA: Sage.

McGuire, Michael. 2002. "Managing Networks: Propositions on What Managers Do and Why They Do It." *Public Administration Review, 62*(5):599–609.

McGuire, Michael. 2006. "Collaborative Public Management: Assessing What We Know and How We Know It." *Public Administration Review,*Supplement to *66*(6):33–43.

McGuire, Michael, and Chris Silvia. 2010. "The Effect of Problem Severity, Managerial and Organizational Capacity, and Agency Structure on Intergovernmental Collaboration: Evidence from Local Emergency Management." *Public Administration* Review, 70(2):279–288.

Miles, Matthew B., A. Michael Huberman, and Johnny Saldana. 2014. *Qualitative Data Analysis: A Methods Sourcebook.* Third ed. Los Angeles: Sage.

Milward, H. Brinton, Patrick Kenis, and Jorg Raab. 2006. "Introduction: Towards the Study of Network Control." *International Public Management Journal, 9*(3):203–208.

Milward, H. Brinton, Keith G. Provan, Amy Fish, Kimberley R. Isett, and Kun Huang. 2010. "Governance and Collaboration: An Evolutionary Study of Two Mental Health Networks." *Journal of Public Administration Research and Theory, 20* (Supplement 1):i125–i141. doi: 10.1093/jopart/mup038.

Mowshowitz, Abbe. 1994. "Virtual Organization: A Vision of Management in the Information Age." *The Information Society, 10*(4):267–288. doi: 10.1080/01972243.1994.9960172.

National Science Foundation. 2012. *NSF Leads Federal Efforts in Big Data.* Washington, DC.

North, Douglass C. 1990. *Institutions, Institutional Change, and Economic Performance.* Cambridge, MA: Cambridge University Press.

NSF TeraGrid Program. 2011. *NSF Extensible Terascale Facility—TeraGrid: Final Report.* Washington, DC: National Science Foundation.

O'Leary, Rosemary, and Lisa Blomgren Bingham, eds. 2009. *The Collaborative Public Manager: New Ideas for the Twenty-First Century.* Washington, DC: Georgetown University Press.

O'Toole, Laurence, and Kenneth J. Meier. 2004. "Desperately Seeking Selznick: Cooptation and the Dark Side of Public Management in Networks." *Public Administration Review, 64*(6):681–693.

Ostrom, Elinor. 1990. *Governing the Commons: The Evolution of Institutions for Collective Action.* Cambridge: Cambridge University Press.

Ostrom, Elinor. 1998. "A Behavioral Approach to the Rational Choice Theory of Collective Action." *American Political Science Review, 92*(1):1–22.

Ostrom, Elinor. 2010. "Institutional Analysis and Development: Elements of the Framework in Historical Perspective." In *Historical Developments and Theoretical Approaches in Sociology,* edited by C Crothers, 261–288. UK: EOLSS (Encyclopedia of Life Support Systems).

Ostrom, Elinor, Roy Gardner, and James Walker. 1994. *Rules, Games and Common-Pool Resources.* Ann Arbor, MI: The University of Michigan Press.

Park, Hyun Hee, and Karl Rethemeyer. 2014. "The Politics of Connections: Assessing the Determinants of Social Structure in Policy Networks." *Journal of Public Administration Research and Theory, 24*(2):349–379.

Pfeffer, Jeffrey, and Gerald Salancik. 2003. *The External Control of Organizations: A Resource Dependence Perspective.* Stanford, CA (originally) and New York: Stanford University Press (Originally) Harper and Row in 1978.

The Program Office of the Extreme Science and Engineering Discovery Environment (XSEDE). 2011. The Transition from TeraGrid to XSEDE.

The Program Office of the Extreme Science and Engineering Discovery Environment (XSEDE). 2012a. What is XSEDE?: National Science Foundation.

The Program Office of the Extreme Science and Engineering Discovery Environment (XSEDE). 2012b. XSEDE (eXtreme Science and Engineering Discovery Environment): Program Plan for Program Year 2. Illinois: National Center for Supercomputing Applications.

Provan, Keith G., Kun Huang, and H. Brinton Milward. 2009. "The Evolution of Structural Embeddedness and Organizational Social Outcomes in a Centrally Governed Health and Human Services Network." *Journal of Public Administration Research and Theory, 19*(4):873–893. doi: 10.1093/jopart/mun036.

Provan, Keith, and Patrick Kenis. 2008. "Modes of Network Governance: Structure, Management, and Effectiveness." *Journal of Public Administration Research and Theory* no. 18 (2):229–252.
Provan, Keith, and Brinton Milward. 1995. "A Preliminary Theory of Interorganizational Network Effectiveness: A Comparative Study of Four Community Mental Health Systems." *Administrative Science Quarterly* no. 40:1–33.
Provan, Keith G., and Brinton Milward. 2001. "Do Networks Really Work? A Framework for Evaluating Public-Sector Organizational Networks." *Public Administration Review*, 61(4):414–423.
Rethemeyer, Karl, and Deneen Hatmaker. 2008. "Network Management Reconsidered: An Inquiry into Management of Network Structures in Public Sector Service Provision." *Journal of Public Administration Research and Theory*, 18(4):617–646.
Rocheleau, Bruce. 2006. *Public Management Information Systems*. Hershey, PA: Idea Group Publishing.
Tang, Shui Yan. 1994. "Institutions and Performance in Irrigation Systems." In *Rules, Games, and Common-Pool Resources*, edited by Elinor Ostrom, Roy Gardner and James Walker, 225–246. Ann Arbor: The University of Michigan Press.
TeraGrid Office. 2009. NSF Extensible Terascale Facility (TeraGrid): Report for January 1, 2008 through December 31, 2008 & Program Plan for August 1, 2009 through July 31, 2010.
Thomson, Ann Marie, and James Perry. 2006. "Collaboration Processes: Inside the Black Box." *Public Administration Review, 66* (Supplement to Issue 6):20–32.
XSEDE. 2013. XSEDE Program Year 2 Annual Report (July 1, 2012— June 30, 2013). XSEDE Office.
XSEDE. 2014. XSEDE: PY1–3 Comprehensive Report (July 1, 2011 through June 30, 2014). Illinois: XSEDE Office.
Yin, Robert. 2003. *Case Study Research: Design and Methods*. Third ed. Thousand Oaks, CA: SAGE Publications, Inc.
Zimmerman, Ann, and Thomas A. Finholt. 2008. Report from the TeraGrid Evaluation Study, Part 1: Project Findings. Ann Arbor, Michigan: Collaboratory for Research on Electronic Work, School of Information, University of Michigan.

22
E-GOVERNMENT IN CHINA[1]

Nan Zhang and Xuejiao Zhao

Introduction

According to a United Nations (2004) report, e-government is "the use of information and communication technology (ICT) and its application by the government for the provision of information and public services to the people." The potential benefits of e-government are manifold: improved transparency, accountability, and access and increased trust in government. In the first decade of the 21st century, many countries launched e-government initiatives, which not only facilitate government reform, but also promote economic development and social progress. Chinese governmental organizations—in the most critical stage of industrialized, informationized, and modernized development—are also depending on information technology to better perform their functions in economic growth, market development, social advancements, and public service. However, in the current post-informationization era, when the first upsurge of theoretical exploration and construction practice of e-government has receded, we are still unable to present satisfactory answers to questions raised in the process of e-government development. During the Tenth Five-Year Plan period (2001–2005), the objective of promoting e-government was to enhance administrative efficiency. After 2008, however, the objective was redefined as strengthening social management and public service in the Annual Report of the Work of the Government (Zhang and Guo 2014).[2]

E-government has played a strong supporting role in China's economic development, improving the Chinese government's performance in macro control, market supervision, social management, and public service (Hong and Du 2013). The rise of the Internet of Things, cloud computing, and big data will provide new opportunities and challenges to China's e-government development. This chapter examines the current status of China's e-government by detailing its international and domestic rankings, stages of development, key issues, and practical cases. The rest of this chapter is organized as follows: First, we will present China's rankings in the United Nations Global E-Government Development Reports; domestic rankings of Chinese government websites will also be introduced. The second part describes the stages of e-government development in China. In the third part, we will provide an overview for the results of the "China E-Government Key Issues Survey" conducted in 2012. The fourth part provides examples of e-government initiatives in China from both the central and local governments. Finally, we will close this chapter by discussing China's e-government development from the perspectives of culture, institution, and network information technologies.

China's E-Government Rankings

Most researchers and practitioners from other countries obtain their information on China's e-government from the United Nations' reports and rankings. Although these rankings are very important, a more complete understanding can be acquired from national portals such as www.gov.cn. Since China now has more than 80,000 government websites, we need a more comprehensive perspective to discuss them.

United Nations Global E-Government Development Reports and Other International Rankings

The United Nations Global E-Government Development Reports and Survey present a systematic assessment of how governments use information and communications technology to provide public services. The survey's E-Government Development Index (EGDI) "has gained wide acceptance as a global authoritative measure of how public administrations provide electronic and mobile public services" (United Nations 2014, 13). In 2014, China's EGDI score was 0.5450, and the nation ranked seventieth among 193 member states. Figure 22.1 compares China with other countries, including its East Asian neighbors (Japan and South Korea), other BRICS countries (Brazil, Russia, India, and South Africa), and the United States. Although China's EGDI score increased from 0.4160 in 2003 to 0.5450 in 2014, its rankings remain comparatively low (see Figure 22.2). China's best ranking was fifty-seventh in 2005.

Structurally, the EGDI is a composite measure of three important dimensions of e-government: provision of online services, telecommunication connectivity, and human capacity. The EGDI is calculated as a weighted average of three normalized scores on the three dimensions: (1) scope and quality of online services, (2) development status of telecommunication infrastructure, and (3) inherent human capital. In 2014, China's scores for online service, human capital, and telecommunication

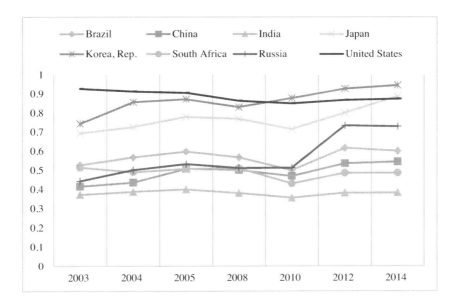

Figure 22.1   E-Government Development Index (EGDI), 2003–2014

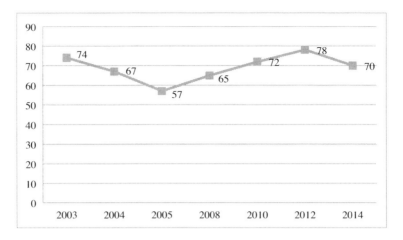

Figure 22.2 China's Rankings on E-Government Development Index (EGDI), 2003–2014

Source: United Nations

Table 22.1 The Three Components of the E-Government Development Index (EGDI), China, 2003–2014

Year	Country	Online Service Index	Human Capital Index	Telecommunication Infrastructure Index	E-Government Development Index (EGDI)
2003	China	0.33187	0.8	0.11599	0.41595
2004	China	0.4054	0.79	0.11132	0.43557
2005	China	0.56923	0.83	0.12411	0.50778
2008	China	0.50836	0.83657	0.15999	0.5017
2010	China	0.36825	0.85353	0.19125	0.46998
2012	China	0.52941	0.77446	0.30385	0.5359
2014	China	0.60629	0.6734	0.3554	0.54501

Source: United Nations

infrastructure were respectively 0.60629, 0.6734, and 0.3554. Compared with its scores for online service and human capital, China's score for telecommunication infrastructure was relatively low (see Table 22.1).

Besides the United Nations, the Organization for Economic Cooperation and Development (OECD), Waseda University, and the International Academy of CIOs (IAC) also conducted international e-government rankings.[3] These assessments have evaluated China's e-government readiness, focusing on central government websites. To provide a full picture, it is necessary to examine the e-government development of local governments in China.

Evaluation Reports of Chinese Government Websites

To assess the e-government development level in China, the China Software Testing Center (CSTC) published the Evaluation Report of Chinese Government Websites since 2002. CSTC evaluated government websites according to seven aspects: accessibility, transparency, online

Table 22.2 Leading Indicators of 2015 Evaluation Report of Chinese Government Websites

Indicators	Weight
Accessibility: Homepage update frequency, link availability, and column maintenance.	30
Transparency: The disclosure of information about government agencies, leadership, statistics, regulations, and budget; the availability of information disclosure catalogue; the update frequency of the information mentioned above.	18–22
Online Services: The scope and quality of online services.	12–24
Electronic Participation: The availability of columns such as Inquiry and Answer; the availability of online channels for collecting public opinions regarding a current/future policy to promote the public to take part in policymaking process.	10–12
Responsiveness: Regarding key policies and popular issues, if the government website holds online interviews or press conferences to interpret the policies; the frequency and the effect of the interviews and the press conferences.	8–14
Other Functions: The availability of social media access, search function, security policies, and a mobile version.	10–12
Pioneering Practices: If a government website is regarded by the public and experts as one of the best websites in terms of transparency, services, interaction, policy interpretation, management, and technology.	10

services, electronic participation, responsiveness, other functions, and pioneering practices (see Table 22.2). Different levels of government websites are assigned different weights. In terms of online services, compared with central government agencies, local governments are closer to the public and provide more services on their websites; therefore, the weight of online services for local government websites (at the level of cities and counties) is twice that of central government departments.[4] Taking provincial government websites as an example, the top 10 provinces with the highest scores in 2015 include Beijing, Shanghai, Sichuan, Guangdong, Zhejiang, Fujian, Hainan, Hubei, Hunan, Anhui, Jiangsu, and Jiangxi (see Table 22.3). For government websites at the city level, the top 10 cities include Foshan (Guangdong), Suzhou (Jiangsu), Suqian (Jiangsu), Liuzhou (Guangxi), Liangshanzhou (Sichuan), Weifang (Shandong), Wuxi (Jiangsu), Zhongshan (Guangdong), Wenzhou (Zhejiang), Zhenjiang (Jiangsu), and Ordos (Neimenggu) (see Table 22.4). In addition, provinces and cities from different regions vary enormously in their e-government performance. In accordance with the National Bureau of Statistics of China, China is divided into four areas: the eastern areas, the central areas, the western areas, and the northeast areas.[5] In 2015, the eastern areas led with the highest score, followed by the northeast areas, the central areas, and, finally, the western areas. Based on the performance of government websites, e-government development in China is unbalanced.

E-Government Development Stages in China

Although it has not achieved elite status in the e-government rankings of the United Nations, China's e-government in the last 15 years has still made important progress. To depict such progress, we have used a diffusion statuses framework, dividing it into three stages. The significance of the distinction among the different stages not only lies in the longitudinal discussions, but also is beneficial for different regions to identify their current development stages in uneven development China.

Table 22.3 2015 Rankings of Provincial Government Websites in China

Rankings	Provinces	Accessibility	Transparency	Online Services	Electronic Participation	Responsiveness	Other Functions	Pioneering Practices	Score
1	Beijing	0.89	0.85	0.73	0.83	0.63	0.78	0.9	89.4
2	Shanghai	0.88	0.83	0.7	0.82	0.65	0.76	0.9	88.3
3	Sichuan	0.82	0.86	0.71	0.81	0.65	0.78	0.9	87.3
4	Guangdong	0.85	0.81	0.76	0.78	0.6	0.72	0.9	86.4
5	Zhejiang	0.83	0.78	0.79	0.75	0.54	0.72	0.9	84.8
6	Fujian	0.75	0.78	0.76	0.76	0.63	0.71	0.85	82.5
6	Hainan	0.77	0.74	0.76	0.75	0.64	0.72	0.85	82.5
7	Hubei	0.83	0.71	0.68	0.75	0.6	0.72	0.85	81.7
8	Hunan	0.86	0.74	0.58	0.75	0.63	0.66	0.75	80.5
8	Anhui	0.8	0.72	0.67	0.76	0.64	0.73	0.75	80.5
9	Jiangsu	0.86	0.63	0.68	0.71	0.63	0.65	0.7	78.7
10	Jiangxi	0.84	0.62	0.66	0.68	0.58	0.67	0.75	77.5
11	Guizhou	0.81	0.66	0.64	0.62	0.58	0.62	0.85	76.9
12	Guangxi	0.85	0.61	0.61	0.58	0.43	0.72	0.85	75.2
13	Neimenggu	0.83	0.62	0.59	0.63	0.63	0.64	0.65	74.9
14	Shaanxi	0.8	0.63	0.61	0.7	0.6	0.63	0.55	73.7
15	Hebei	0.79	0.59	0.55	0.66	0.58	0.58	0.65	71.2
16	Yunnan	0.77	0.58	0.53	0.53	0.52	0.58	0.7	68.5
17	Shandong	0.75	0.58	0.46	0.62	0.39	0.56	0.75	66.7
18	Gansu	0.77	0.55	0.48	0.6	0.49	0.55	0.5	65.1
19	Liaoning	0.77	0.55	0.46	0.61	0.43	0.51	0.55	64.4
20	Tianjin	0.76	0.51	0.45	0.56	0.48	0.52	0.6	63.6

Source: China Software Testing Center (http://www.cstc.org.cn/wzpg2015/zbg/zbglist.html)

Table 22.4 2015 Rankings of Government Websites at the City Level in China

Rankings	Cities	Accessibility	Transparency	Online Services	Electronic Participation	Responsiveness	Other Functions	Pioneering Practices	Score
1	Foshan	0.85	0.72	0.64	0.71	0.64	0.67	0.9	81.7
2	Suzhou	0.83	0.71	0.63	0.68	0.7	0.66	0.9	80.8
3	Suqian	0.83	0.71	0.63	0.62	0.71	0.64	0.85	79.3
4	Liuzhou	0.82	0.71	0.59	0.69	0.73	0.67	0.8	78.9
5	Liangshanzhou	0.81	0.71	0.6	0.7	0.68	0.69	0.75	78.2
6	Weifang	0.81	0.71	0.55	0.68	0.68	0.73	0.75	77.2
6	Wuxi	0.85	0.68	0.62	0.66	0.69	0.66	0.6	77.2
7	Zhongshan	0.81	0.73	0.6	0.65	0.74	0.64	0.6	76.7
8	Wenzhou	0.84	0.7	0.57	0.64	0.7	0.65	0.65	76.5
9	Zhenjiang	0.81	0.67	0.58	0.73	0.7	0.62	0.7	76.2
10	Erdos	0.8	0.7	0.55	0.63	0.66	0.59	0.85	76
11	Nanping	0.82	0.68	0.58	0.66	0.65	0.69	0.6	75.5

Rankings	Cities	Accessibility	Transparency	Online Services	Electronic Participation	Responsiveness	Other Functions	Pioneering Practices	Score
12	Liu'an	0.82	0.71	0.58	0.58	0.66	0.65	0.65	75.3
13	Longyan	0.82	0.71	0.59	0.57	0.64	0.61	0.65	74.9
14	Panzhihua	0.81	0.73	0.55	0.69	0.61	0.57	0.65	74.6
15	Chenzhou	0.83	0.69	0.52	0.61	0.56	0.61	0.75	74
16	Ningde	0.81	0.71	0.53	0.67	0.56	0.49	0.75	73.4
17	Weihai	0.81	0.71	0.53	0.65	0.6	0.61	0.55	72.8
18	Yichang	0.83	0.71	0.54	0.58	0.59	0.45	0.65	72.1
19	Shantou	0.81	0.68	0.53	0.65	0.55	0.55	0.6	71.8
20	Jiangmen	0.82	0.6	0.51	0.68	0.54	0.62	0.65	71.4

Source: China Software Testing Center (http://www.cstc.org.cn/wzpg2015/zbg/zbglist.html)

Diffusion Statuses Framework

Working within a framework of IT/IS maturity in the corporate context, the IT/IS application status in enterprises can be examined along the flexibility and visibility dimensions (Evgeniou 2002). According to an even earlier model, e-government application was projected to progress in four consequent stages toward maturity (Layne and Lee 2001), a projection that can be traced back to classical theories that tend to describe the development process of IT/IS application in organizations as connected phases consisting of evolution and revolution (Greiner 1972; Nolan, Croson, and Seger 1993). In Layne and Lee's model, e-government development is divided into four stages: cataloging information, business information, longitudinal integration, and horizontal integration. The model is considered a good description of e-government development progress and of tasks and characteristics in every stage (Andersen and Henriksen 2006). Both of the frameworks mentioned above provide valuable clues for understanding e-government development statuses.

Since the innovation diffusion theory (IDT) was established by Rogers in 1962, the process of technology diffusion has been described as a phenomenon like the spread of waves through water (Rogers 1995). While studying the diffusion of software engineering technology, Bayer and Melone (1989) noticed that different users and organizations may adopt and utilize new technologies in different depths. Later, Chen and Reimers (2002) defined the two dimensions for judging the states of IT/IS diffusion in enterprises. One dimension in the model is Diffusion Width, or the degree of expansion, representing the extent to which IT/IS has reached in the organization. The other is Diffusion Depth, or the degree of penetration, representing the extent to which an organization depends on IT/IS (Chen and Reimers 2002). Ideally, the IT/IS diffusion in governmental organizations should progress in both directions. In practice, however, expanding is often easier than penetrating. In order to examine the statuses of IT/IS diffusion in our focus government, we inherited the two dimensions in this research; the diffusion status framework we used is illustrated in Figure 22.3.

As shown in Figure 22.3, Status I can be regarded as the initial stage of diffusion, when both degrees of expansion and penetration are low. As the diffusion process progresses, the e-government application in the organization may evolve to Status II, when only some crucial tasks heavily rely on IT/IS. Finally, Status III can, to some extent, be regarded as the maturity stage, when the diffusion of e-government fully permeates the organization.

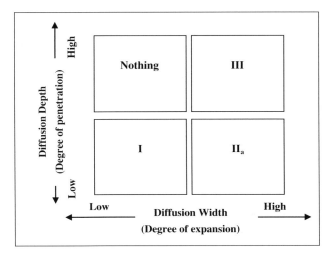

Figure 22.3 Diffusion Status Framework

Three Stages in China: From Expanding to Penetrating

According to the framework, e-government development in China can be correspondingly divided into three basic stages as follows.

The initiation stage (from the early 1980s to the late 1990s): Office automation (OA) projects were launched in the central and local governments, and governments established internal informational internets in longitudinal and horizontal directions. In 1993, the information work leading group of the State Council laid down the Ninth Five-Year Plan for National Informationization and the 2010 Prospect (Outline), in which the State Council claimed the former Ministry of Electronics had vigorously coordinated with related ministries. The startup projects for national economy informationization were the Three Golden Projects: the Golden Bridge Project, the Golden Gate Project, and the Golden Card Project. These systematic projects, as the foundation for Chinese e-government development, featured informationized government management and services that were led by the Chinese central government.

The propulsion and development stage (from 1999 to 2006): In January 1999, chief information officers from more than 40 ministries jointly launched the Government Online Project through which governmental information resources and application projects were provided, government sites were equipped with office automation, and department functions were closely connected. Thus, the government sites became windows offering service to the public. Government functions were utilized to initiate industrial user online projects, such as the Enterprise Online Project and the Family Online Project, enabling Internet penetration into all walks of life and every household. As a result, the Cyber Society was formed to share information and realize various social functions through Internet.

In 2002, Chinese president Jiang Zemin's Report at the 16th Party Congress pinpointed clearly that it was imperative to deepen administrative regime reform, further transform government functions, improve managerial methods, promote e-government, enhance administrative efficiency, and reduce costs in order to form a public administration system that featured standardized behaviors, coordinated operation, fairness and transparency, honesty, and high efficiency. In response, China's informationized government management and service has made periodical achievements over the past two decades. A majority of government functional departments—such as the Tax Administration, the Bureau of Industry and Commerce, and Customs and Public Security—have established private networks covering the integrated system. Currently, over 70 percent of the prefectural-level cities have opened service windows on the Internet, and more than 3,000 government websites have been established.[6]

The post-informationization stage (from 2006 to present): From a macroscopic perspective, the first two stages of e-government development can be regarded as an informationization age, in which informationization infrastructure and application of technological approaches constitute the core of all practices. As e-government becomes increasingly mature and diversified, application problems are revealed; authorities start to transform their thinking from construction to application. At the end of 2005, the General Office of the CPC Central Committee and the General Office of the State Council issued the 2006–2020 National Informationization Developmental Strategy, in which an application-oriented development goal was proposed. Hu Jintao's report at the 17th Party Congress emphasized that China should promote e-government and strengthen social management and public service. The report explained the objective and content of e-government and linked e-government development with service-oriented government construction. The post-informationization phase corresponds to the third and fourth stages of Layne and Lee's model; therefore, integration is the emphasis. Since 2010, Chinese governments have used a variety of e-government applications based on Web 2.0 and social media. However, horizontal and vertical barriers among different levels or different sectors of government still exist.

E-Government Key Issues in China

Besides descriptions of stages, the e-government key issues survey is one of the most effective tools for describing the characteristics of e-government. In 2007 and 2012, the Chinese government conducted two rounds of e-government key issues surveys. The results of the later one have been reported in Zhang et al. (2015).

Key Issues Research

Key issues in information technologies and information systems (IT/IS) management are generally defined as the primary set of challenges facing IT/IS managers over the forthcoming three to five years that deserve the most resources, time, and attention (Gottschalk 2000). Because today's government IT/IS departments are confronted with various challenges in a fast-changing environment, the current key issues of e-government construction involve the government's main requirements, the primary focus, and the challenges of e-government construction now and in the future. The research on the key issues aims to explore the government's cognition and attitude toward related problems and discusses the government's focus on the construction process to identify valuable e-government experiences by analyzing the rankings of those key issues (Niederman, Brancheau, and Wetherbe 1991).

Early study of key IT/IS management issues in the public sector was conducted in the early 1990s, when some researchers attempted to survey and discuss the diversity of key issues between governments and corporations (Sharon, Gorr, and Newcomer 1991). Since that time, empirical research on this topic has not continued. However, with the development of e-government, lessons have been learned from e-government practices, including the planning and implementation of numerous e-government initiatives worldwide. Scholars and practitioners have collected lessons about key issues from case studies, surveys, and post-implementation audits that, if applied to future e-government initiatives, may increase the potential for success. Based on these studies and practical experience, some researchers have examined key or critical issues for e-government application through literature reviews (Gil-García and Pardo 2005, Rose and Grant 2010). In this way, critical issues have been identified that have significant impacts on the success of e-government programs. These studies have used program management and aspects of marketing theory as frameworks to classify and analyze key issues (Rose and Grant 2010). Based on the insights of these efforts into e-government application and management, the time is ripe to probe the key issues in e-government management. However, it is also reasonable to expect that key issues in e-government management may significantly differ from those of companies due to the special characteristics of government organizations.

Survey and Results

The first key issues survey was distributed to 150 local government branches in 2007. In total, 101 responses were received. With uncompleted questionnaires omitted, 76 responses were used in our statistical analysis. Most of the respondents were the directors, associate directors, or chief engineers for IT/IS offices in local governments, who can be regarded as playing the same roles as CIOs in the corporate context. The second survey (2012) sampled government employees who had participated in the training series "Information Technology and Government" at Tsinghua University during the last five years. We chose 185 candidates and delivered questionnaires via email, online survey sites, and face-to-face interviews. In total, we received 128 responses. Excluding incomplete responses, we had 108 usable responses for our final analysis.

We must admit that the results of the two surveys are limited. First, most participants in the 2007 survey came from Beijing, while the respondents of the 2012 survey came from 21 provinces based on alumni networking. Although we believe the results could still reflect the characteristics of the development of e-government in China, the differences between the two samples might influence the results. Second, according to the progress of e-government-related technologies, we expanded some items and deleted others from the 26 items in the 2007 survey via several rounds of the Delphi method before the 2012 survey was administered. In the questionnaires of both surveys, we asked respondents to rate candidate items on a five-point scale. The analysis mentioned above provided us with the top 10 e-government key issues in China. Those key issues and their rankings in the two surveys are shown in Table 22.5.

Table 22.5 Top Ten E-Government Issues in China

Key Issues	2012 Rankings	2007 Rankings
Acquisition, organization, and utilization of high-quality data	1	4
System integration among departments for one-stop service center usability	2	10
Ensuring the timeliness and validity of information provided	3	N/A
Long-term and consistent ICT development planning	4	6
Aligning ICT in strategic planning	5	5
Workflow redesigning and organizational restructuring	6	14
Connecting governments, enterprises, and citizens through ICT	7	17
Testing, obtaining feedback, and modifying technical projects before system running	8	N/A
Ensuring citizens' ability to use the technologies	9	11
Internal managerial and organizational levels of IT/IS departments	10	20

Discussion of Top Key Issues

Two key issues—"acquisition, organization, and utilization of high-quality data" and "system integration between departments for one-stop service center usability"—rank in the top two spots of the 2012 rankings, higher than their positions in the 2007 survey results. This phenomenon means that interaction and compatibility constitute the principal focus of the current government with respect to technology. The fundamental software and hardware facility essentially has been built. On the basis of that facility, to better realize the function of e-government in protecting people's livelihoods and innovating social management, the government must employ technical means of e-government construction that have greater interaction and compatibility. For example, in terms of protecting people's livelihoods, some functions, such as interdepartmental information sharing in the field of social security and multifunctional business cooperation in administrative services, require realization. With respect to social management, some roles in the field of safety supervision include overall cover, dynamic track, natural calamities and forecasts, early warning, and analysis and evaluation of public emergency events. The current government is willing to promote online work and strengthen its interaction with citizens, who are the voice of the society. The achievement of all of these functions requires technical means with stronger interaction capabilities. In the meantime, the availability of compatibility also lays the foundation for further overall technological integration of e-government systems.

The new key issue in 2012—"ensuring the timeliness, validity of information provided"—ranks in the third position. The government is relatively backward in its service philosophy of e-government. Developing e-government activity is a strategic measure to build a service-oriented government with which people are satisfied. In recent years, although the development of e-government has played an important role in improving public service, the government has paid less attention to service philosophy and capability in e-government than it has to organization and technology. The process of offering related applications and services through e-government systems raises numerous issues, such as low integration of administrative and technological applications, large gaps between application effects and the requirements of service-oriented government construction, and difficulty in implementing information-sharing and related business. Moreover, it is particularly common that some leaders' mailboxes remain unresponsive over a long period. In spite of the government's rigorous efforts to offer high-quality and efficient information services, even with a background of relatively mature technology, the government's attitude toward and understanding of service are comparatively backward in regard to the strategic goal of an overall improvement in public service quality and the construction of service-oriented government. The reasons for this are dual. On one hand, the government is short on propaganda, education, and the supervision of service awareness among public servants; is behind in the development of service functions; and lacks effective evaluation of service quality. On the other hand, compared with the advancement of strategic significance at the organizational level and adoption of new technology in the system, enhancing public servants' awareness and encouraging them to accept and use information comprehensively will take a longer time.

Three key issues—"long-term and consistent ICT development planning," "aligning ICT in strategic planning," and "workflow redesigning and organizational restructuring"—rank from fourth to sixth in the top 10. These results not only show the value of ICT integration in achieving the goal of organizational restructuring, but also demonstrate that in today's China, macro planning is one of the most important means of fulfilling the goal of integration, as far as CIOs are concerned. As an area of great concern for governments at all levels, e-government construction occupies a high strategic position. In its Eleventh Five-Year Plan (2006–2010), China proposed e-government to enhance administrative efficiency and reduce costs. Afterward, a large number of provinces and cities, one after another, introduced local Eleventh Five-Year Plans related to e-government, in which the significance of top design and overall planning were emphasized. China's Twelfth Five-Year Plan (2011–2015) demonstrated that central and local governments at all levels have been paying close attention to the development of e-government and regard e-government construction as assisting in strategic restructuring of the economy, protection and improvement of people's livelihoods, enhancement and innovation of social management, and promotion of service-oriented government. The central government's focus on the development of e-government made its local counterparts at all levels pay more attention to the integration and overall planning of information construction, further rely on e-government to enhance internal innovation, plan initiatively inside their organizations, and implement recombination of workflow and organizational reform. It is equally noteworthy that the potential change to authority structure involved the process of governmental workflow adjustment, which was the vital determinant of the implantation effects following that round of planning.

E-Government Development in China

The development of e-government in China has achieved noticeable gains. On the national level, the Golden Projects played a significant role in improving governance and the delivery of public services; government websites have also increasingly become windows for government departments to serve the public. The issuance of the *Regulations on Open Government Information* promoted the opening and sharing of government and social information, and the development of the "Internet Plus" Action Plan demonstrated China's ambition to improve its e-government level utilizing new technologies, such as mobile Internet, cloud computing, big data, and the Internet of Things. On the local level, e-government projects improved administrative efficiency and enhanced public service. This section first examines the national projects previously mentioned, and then introduces two e-government cases in local government: the Official Document Exchange via Microblog program in Haining and the Smart Urban Governance project in Beijing.

National Level

The Golden Projects

The Golden Projects (*jinzi gongcheng*) are regarded as the Chinese government's first move in the direction of building e-government (Ma, Chung, and Thorson 2005). Besides the above-mentioned three Golden Projects (the Golden Bridge, the Golden Gate, and the Golden Card), there are eight other projects: the Golden Macro (*jinhong*), the Golden Tax (*jinshui*), the Golden Wealth (*jincai*), the Golden Agriculture (*jinnong*), the Golden Audit (*jinshen*), the Golden Quality (*jinzhi*), the Golden Social Security (*jinbao*), the Golden Shield (*jindun*), and the Golden Water (*jinshui*). The projects had three goals: (1) to build a national information highway as a path to modernization and economic development; (2) to drive development of information technology in China; and (3) to serve as a tool of unification for the country (from the center to the provinces) and of the government (across ministerial and industrial demarcation lines) (Lovelock, Clark, and Petrazzini 1996). The Golden Projects have produced impressive results. For instance, the e-customs system of the Golden Gate (*jinguan*) project enables private enterprises to electronically declare customs information, track export permits and vouchers, and provide inspections data. The system also facilitates the customs administration's ability to share and exchange data with enterprises and conduct online inspections. According to the Guangdong Customs, the e-customs system can save 0.5 billion yuan per year in terms of customs clearance (Hong and Du 2013). As to the Golden Shield (*jindun*) project, its applications—such as the household registration management system, the crime case management system, and the110 police alarm system—are now used by all government departments.

Government Online Project

On January 22, 1999, the Government Online Project (GOP, *Zhengfu Shangwang Gongcheng*) was formally launched by China Telecom and the State Economic and Trade Commission along with more than 40 central government departments. The Government Online Project is scheduled to take place in three phases: Phase One focuses on connecting 800–1,000 government offices and agencies to the Internet; Phase Two mainly involves having government offices and agencies move their information systems into compatible electronic form; and Phase Three works toward the goal of becoming a "paperless government" (Lovelock and Ure 2002). The project was expected, on one hand, to create a centrally accessible administrative system; on the other hand, it was designed to make government information available to the public. Within a few months (from the end of 2000 to March 2001), 10 provincial governments announced their own plans for government digitalization, such as "Digital Beijing," "Digital Shanghai," and "Digital Fujian" (Zheng 2008). According to the 2012 Report of China's E-Government Development, by the end of 2012, all central government departments and provincial governments had their own websites, as did 99.1 percent of city governments and about 85 percent of county governments. As of December 2014, China had 57,024 domain names under gov.cn (China Internet Network Information Centre (CNNIC) 2015).

The Issuance of Regulations on Open Government Information

On April 5, 2007, *Regulations on Open Government Information* was adopted by the State Council and became effective on May 1, 2008. According to Article 2, "government information" referred to information made or obtained by administrative agencies in the course of exercising their responsibilities, and recorded and stored in a given form. The purposes of the *Regulations on Open Government Information* are:

> To ensure that citizens, legal persons and other organizations obtain government information in accordance with the law, enhance transparency of the work of government, promote administration in accordance with the law, and bring into full play the role of government information in serving the people's production and livelihood and their economic and social activities.

Articles 10, 11, and 12 of Chapter 2 of the regulations give an expanded list of disclosure information. Governments at the county level and above and their departments should disclose the following government information: (1) administrative regulations, rules, and regulatory documents; (2) plans for national economic and social development, plans for specific projects, plans for regional development, and related policies; (3) statistical information on national economic and social development; (4) reports on financial budgets and final accounts; (5) items subject to an administrative fee and the legal basis and standards thereof; (6) catalogs of the government's centralized procurement projects, their standards, and their implementation; (7) matters subject to administrative licensing and their legal bases, conditions, quantities, procedures, and deadlines and catalogs of all the materials that need to be submitted when applying for the administrative licensing, and the handling thereof; (8) information on the approval and implementation of major construction projects; (9) policies and measures on such matters as poverty assistance, education, medical care, social security and job creation, and their actual implementation; (10) emergency plans for, early warning information concerning, and counter measures against sudden public events; and (11) information on the supervision and inspection of environmental protection, public health, safe production, food and drugs, and product quality. *Regulations on Open Government Information* "mark a significant shift from the culture of government secrecy to transparency in China" (Rana 2015, 131). The regulations have also "inspired the public to request government-held information and willfully use their right to know" (Piotrowski et al. 2009, 131).

Government Websites Supervision and the First National Government Websites Survey

Since the 1990s, the government has started establishing websites at various levels. Government websites played an important role in publishing government information and providing public services. However, many government websites, especially at local levels, have become inactive and are never updated. In December 2014, the State Council issued a document (the No. 57 document) ordering all government departments to make their websites more interactive and efficient. Government agencies were urged to speed up response to opinions, complaints, and proposals submitted by the public, and to do so within 7 to 15 days, depending on the importance of the complaint. In March 2015, the State Council launched a national survey to monitor the efficiency of government websites. This was the first national government websites survey organized by the central government in history. All government bodies above county level and affiliated institutions, and all ministries and commissions under the State Council and their affiliated institutions, were covered in the survey. There were four major concerns of the public about official government websites: a website is not responsive; information is not delivered in a timely manner; information is inaccurate; or information is not useful. Conducted from March to December 2015, the survey found that a total of 84,094 government portals had been in operation by the end of November, of which 16,049 were shut down for serious problems (for example, failing to open, publishing fraudulent content, or failing to respond to public inquiries within three months), and 1,592 remain to be restructured. Through the survey, a database of government websites was also established, recording their names, addresses, managing departments, and operation status. Moreover, government websites now are being updated in a more timely and accurate manner. Many have also improved interaction with the public.

The "Internet Plus" Action and the Use of Big Data in Government

The "Internet Plus" Action Plan was first proposed by Premier Li Keqiang in March 2015 when delivering the government work report:

> We will develop the "Internet Plus" action plan to integrate the mobile Internet, cloud computing, big data, and the Internet of Things with modern manufacturing, to encourage the healthy development of e-commerce, industrial networks, and Internet banking, and to guide Internet-based companies to increase their presence in the international market.

The action plan has been introduced as China enters a crucial period for deepening reform and restructuring. On July 4, 2015, the State Council issued the guidelines on the "Internet Plus" Action. In the section of "Internet Plus" public services, governments are encouraged to take advantage of the Internet to innovate serving modes in healthcare, education, tourism, and social security. Moreover, the State Council on July 1 issued an opinion on using big data technology to improve the government's supervisory responsibilities and services for market entities. The document represented the government's latest effort to improve work efficiency and promote the transformation of its functions amid the challenges and opportunities brought by big data. To improve the government's ability to use big data technology, the State Council suggested strengthening the building of e-government and encouraging local governments to purchase big data resources and technology services from the private sector.

Local Level

Government Microblogs in Chinese Local Governments

In April 2011, the Justice Bureau of Haining City in Zhejiang Province started its Official Documents Exchange via Microblog (ODEM) program: all nonconfidential official document exchanges were to be conducted on Sina Weibo, a Chinese microblogging service that is similar to Twitter. The bureau's first notice was about the management of community service work during the Tomb-Sweeping Festival. According to *China Daily*, the bureau's 14 judicial offices, one legal aid center, and one notary office created accounts on Sina Weibo to publish new government notices and links to government regulations. In addition, 18 officials within the bureau also created personal microblog accounts (Yu 2011). The Justice Bureau of Haining became among the first nationwide to publish notices and regulations via microblog (Fu 2011).

The adoption of the government microblog in the Haining Justice Bureau is attributable to three factors: technological, organizational, and environmental (Tornatzky, Fleischer, and Chakrabarti 1990; Zhang, Zhang, and Meng 2011). The ODEM was built on the basis of the wide application of information technology in the city of Haining. Individual access to microblogging services also facilitated the launch of the ODEM project. The director of the Bureau of Justice in Haining, Zhongyi Jin, opened his personal microblog in 2009, which had 100,000 followers in 2011 (1.3 million followers in 2015). With respect to organizational factors, the functions of microblogging services were in accordance with the objectives of the Bureau of Justice. With the help of Weibo, government agencies were given more channels and opportunities to interact with the public. Moreover, the leadership's support was also very important. Director Jin has been a total supporter of the ODEM program. He regarded the beginning of the ODEM as an ideal opportunity to take advantage of the Internet to make the bureau's work more transparent and efficient by inviting experts and netizens to take part in online interaction (Yu 2011). Additionally, because of the word limit of a microblog post (140 characters), Director Jin argued that government agencies would be inclined to publish posts that are clearer and easier for the public to read. In terms of the environmental factor, the city of Haining is located in Zhejiang province, one of the most developed provinces in China. Haining's GDP per capita is much higher than the average level in China, and people here are more likely to accept new things. The microblog of the Bureau of Justice of Haining now has 125,936 followers. For netizens in Haining, the microblog has turned into an essential tool for news updates and government information.

Besides Haining's ODEM program, many Chinese local governments have created government microblog accounts on Weibo, the most popular microblogging platform in China. For example, "Vibrant Shifang" is the official microblog of the city of Shifang, Sichuan province. Operated by the information office of the Shifang government, Vibrant Shifang served as an important interaction platform between the public and the Shifang government during the Shifang Incident, which was a large-scale environmental protest that occurred in 2012. The protest was against a proposed molybdenum-copper plant that residents feared posed environmental and public health risks. Publishing 24 posts through the duration of the Shifang Incident, the Shifang government implemented five governance strategies in different periods: introducing, appealing, explaining, rumor-refuting, and decision-making. Vibrant Shifang played a critical role in the Shifang Incident. According to the 2014 Report on Government Microblogs, which was edited by the People's Daily Public Opinion Monitoring Office (PDPOMO), there are 130,103 Chinese government microblogs on Weibo (PDPOMO 2015). Government microblogs currently extend throughout China.

The Smart Urban Governance Project in Beijing

Since 2005, Beijing has implemented the Smart Urban Governance (SUG) project aimed at enhancing the urban governance level by incorporating elements of Living Lab and Fab Lab. Living Lab is a new model of innovation, which focuses on experimentation and co-creation with real users in real-life environments where users—together with researchers, firms, and public institutions—gather to search for new solutions, new products, new services, or new business models (Almirall and Wareham 2011; De Moor et al. 2010; Edwards-Schachter, Matti, and Alcántara 2012; Liedtke et al. 2012; Wareham, Busquets, and Austin 2009). Fab Lab is generally equipped with tools for every aspect of the technology development process: design, fabrication, testing and debugging, monitoring and analysis, and documentation. The core idea of the concept is personal fabrication. The SUG project includes three key phases.

The initial aim of SUG originated from the effort to satisfy the social demands arising from city management utilizing information technology. The Beijing Municipal Administration Commission made an attempt to construct a virtual park called "Application Innovation Park (AIP)" for city management: an open and nonprofit technology platform through which government could better understand users' needs and improve public services. The construction of the AIP adopted elements of the Living Lab practices after AIP managers met European Living Labs promoters during the 2007 China–Finland Seminar on Living Labs held in Beijing. The API innovation process is very similar to Living Lab practices, in which user involvement plays a key role. First, user needs are collected through the API platform; then, the user needs are analyzed and tested by research institutions. The collection, analysis, and testing of user needs is an iterative interaction process between institutions and users. Finally, a third party is invited to check the designed products to determine if they measure up to the initial objectives. Using this approach, a series of innovation technologies have been proposed and improved, such as the Informational City Management System and a mobile terminal called "Chengguantong" (Guo and Zhang 2010).

In 2010, two reform initiatives brought new opportunities and challenges for the SUG project. On one hand, Beijing's restructuring of the public sector gradually shifted the project under the management of the Beijing Municipal Bureau of City Administration and Law Enforcement (MBCALE), requiring that the SUG pay more attention to people's participation because of the management focus of MBCALE.[7] On the other hand, the issuance of the Action Plan of Smarter Beijing showed that building a smarter city was increasingly being emphasized in Beijing, which provided the SUG project team the opportunity to build a new framework for a smarter city based on prior experience. The overall plan for a brand new smarter city management system was based on the Internet of Things, and it was composed of four levels: the sensing layer, the transport layer, the supporting layer, and the application layer. The sensing layer identifies locations and images through multiple sensing equipment—such as radio frequency identification, satellite positioning, video surveillance, noise monitoring, and condition monitoring. The transport layer, based on the wired and wireless broadband co-built by the entire city, connects government agencies with the objects of city management; it also connects government workers with the general public. The supporting layer provides IT infrastructure for the platform of the Internet of Things to construct a city management cloud, which enables smooth interaction between the "Chengguantong" for government and the "Chengguantong" for citizens. The application layer, led by a public service system based on the city management map service platform, constructs a new model of public service through the Internet of Things and cloud computing. Applications such as the government Wikipedia and government microblogs strengthen flat command and reaction capacity. Furthermore, guided by a comprehensive integrated approach from qualitative to quantitative method (based on patrol inspection, comprehensive law enforcement, and public service) the application layer builds a synthetic platform according to the idea of a smarter city; forms an application integrating intelligence; and strengthens scientific decision-making, intelligent command, and humanized service ability.

The "I Love Beijing" City Administration Public Service Map and Mobile App is an online crowdsourcing and information-provision platform (including both website and mobile app platforms) of SUG. It developed out of a pilot project commissioning middle-aged unemployed workers using PDAs to report on city management issues such as potholes, broken street lights, fly-tipping, etc. The Beijing Municipal Bureau of City Administration and Law Enforcement felt that engaging citizens to provide this kind of data input into city administration would be more effective and leverage existing data in government departments to be of use to city residents. A multi-stakeholder working group—including representatives from multiple departments, academics, business partners, and citizens—was set up to develop the online platform.

Concluding Remarks

As discussed in this chapter, China's e-government development is faced with a complicated situation: in international rankings, China seems to have encountered a bottleneck after its explosion stage and stagnated for the past decade; however, this stagnation has not prevented various e-government innovations combined with the latest technology trends of e-government to emerge in a multitude of local governments. E-government has changed into new brands such as the "Internet of Things" or "big data," but remains a focus for the important growth point of China's ICT industry. At present, while we are impressed by the Web 2.0 era of new public participation, a review of the Chinese e-government's stage of development and the key issues is also necessary.

This chapter introduces the present situation of Chinese e-government as well as our evaluation and comments from the international rankings, stage of development, key issues, and cases from the central and local levels of government. Faced with the transforming process from expansion to penetration, the change in key issues shows that service-oriented data integration, future-oriented development planning, and participation-oriented mechanism design are the most important trends in Chinese e-government development. From the institutional perspective, there is an urgent demand for open government data policies and institution settings (such as "action compendium for promoting the development of the big data") just issued by the State Council of China. From the perspective of network information technology, this demand is the inevitable result of Web 2.0 and social media technology development. Under the comprehensive influence of multiple perspectives, Chinese e-government affairs in the future will most likely no longer be led by the government, but will involve more public participation and public innovation.

Notes

1. This work was partly supported by the National Natural Science Foundation of China (71473143), and the Tsinghua University Initiative Scientific Research Program (20131089260).
2. The term "electronic government" has been mentioned five times in the Annual Report of the Work of the Government since 2002. While the 2002, 2003, and 2005 annual reports categorized e-government development as a topic of government development, e-government was a topic of social development in the 2008 and 2012 annual reports.
3. Waseda University, Tokyo, in cooperation with the International Academy of CIOs (IAC), has released their newest results of the annual international e-government rankings survey for 2015. http://www.waseda.jp/top/en-news/28775
4. In 2015, the online services weight for central government agencies and governments at the city and country level is respectively 12 and 24.
5. According to the National Bureau of Statistics of China, the eastern areas include 10 provinces and municipalities: Beijing, Tianjin, Hebei, Shanghai, Jiangsu, Zhejiang, Fujian, Shandong, Guangdong, and Hainan; the

central areas cover 6 provinces: Shanxi, Anhui, Jiangxi, Henan, Hubei, and Hunan; the western areas include 12 provinces, autonomous regions, and municipalities: Inner Mongolia, Guangxi, Chongqing, Sichuan, Guizhou, Yunnan, Tibet, Shaanxi, Gansu, Qinghai, Ningxia, and Xinjiang; and the northeastern areas include 3 provinces: Liaoning, Jilin, and Heilongjiang.
6. According to the first National Government Websites Survey, there were 84,094 government websites in China in November 2015.
7. The SUG project was under the management of both the Beijing Municipal Commission of City Administration and Environment (MCCAE) and the Beijing Municipal Bureau of City Administration and Law Enforcement (MBCALE).

References

Almirall, Esteve, and Jonathan Wareham. 2011. "Living Labs: Arbiters of Mid-and Ground-Level Innovation." *Technology Analysis & Strategic Management* no. 23 (1):87–102.

Andersen, Kim Viborg, and Helle Zinner Henriksen. 2006. "E-Government Maturity Models: Extension of the Layne and Lee Model." *Government Information Quarterly* no. 23 (2):236–248. doi: http://dx.doi.org/10.1016/j.giq.2005.11.008.

Bayer, Judy, and Nancy Melone. 1989. "Comparative Software Methods: A Critique of Diffusion Theory as a Managerial Framework for Understanding Adoption of Software Engineering Innovations." *Journal of Systems and Software* no. 9 (2):161–166. doi: http://dx.doi.org/10.1016/0164-1212(89)90018-6.

Chen, Guoqing, and Kai Reimers. 2002. *Information Systems: Organization, Management, and Modeling*. Beijing: Tsinghua University Press.

China Internet Network Information Centre (CNNIC). 2015. The 35th Report of China's Internet Development (in Chinese). http://www.cac.gov.cn/2015-02/03/c_1114222357.htm

De Moor, Katrien, Katrien Berte, Lieven De Marez, Wout Joseph, Tom Deryckere, and Luc Martens. 2010. "User-Driven Innovation? Challenges of User Involvement in Future Technology Analysis." *Science and Public Policy* no. 37 (1):51–61.

Edwards-Schachter, Mónica E., Cristian E. Matti, and Enrique Alcántara. 2012. "Fostering Quality of Life through Social Innovation: A Living Lab Methodology Study Case." *Review of Policy Research* no. 29 (6):672–692.

Evgeniou, Theodoros. 2002. "Information Integration and Information Strategies for Adaptive Enterprises." *European Management Journal* no. 20 (5):486–494. doi: http://dx.doi.org/10.1016/S0263-2373(02)00092-0.

Fu, Wen. 2011. "East China City Justice Bureau Pioneers Microblogging Notices, Regulations." *Global Times*, 04/07/2011. http://www.globaltimes.cn/content/641991.shtml

Gil-Garcia, J. Ramon, and Theresa A. Pardo. 2005. "E-Government Success Factors: Mapping Practical Tools to Theoretical Foundations." *Government Information Quarterly* no. 22 (2):187–216. doi: http://dx.doi.org/10.1016/j.giq.2005.02.001.

Gottschalk, Petter. 2000. "Studies of Key Issues in IS Management Around the World." *International Journal of Information Management* no. 20 (3):169–180. doi: http://dx.doi.org/10.1016/S0268-4012(00)00003-7.

Greiner, Larry E. 1972. "Evolution and Revolution as Organizations Grow." *Harvard Business Review* no. 50:37–46.

Guo, Xunhua, and Nan Zhang. 2010. "User Attitude towards Mandatory Use of Information Systems: A Chinese Cultural Perspective." *Journal of Global Information Management (JGIM)* no. 18 (4):1–18.

Hong, Yi, and Ping Du. 2013. *Annual Report on China's E-Government Development (2012)*. Beijing: Social Sciences Academic Press.

Layne, Karen, and Jungwoo Lee. 2001. "Developing Fully Functional E-Government: A Four Stage Model." *Government Information Quarterly* no. 18 (2):122–136. doi: http://dx.doi.org/10.1016/S0740-624X(01)00066-1.

Liedtke, Christa, Maria Jolanta Welfens, Holger Rohn, and Julia Nordmann. 2012. "LIVING LAB: User-Driven Innovation for Sustainability." *International Journal of Sustainability in Higher Education* no. 13 (2):106–118.

Lovelock, Peter, Theodore C. Clark, and Ben A. Petrazzini. 1996. "The 'Golden Projects': China's National Networking Initiative." *Information Infrastructure and Policy* no. 5 (4):265–277.

Lovelock, Peter, and John Ure. 2002. "Assessing China's efforts in constructing an e-government." In *China's Digital Dream: The Impact of the Internet on the Chinese Society*, edited by Junhua Zhang and Martin Woesler, 187–211. Bochum, Germany: The University Press Bochum.

Ma, Lianjie, Jongpil Chung, and Stuart Thorson. 2005. "E-Government in China: Bringing Economic Development through Administrative Reform." *Government Information Quarterly* no. 22 (1):20–37. doi: http://dx.doi.org/10.1016/j.giq.2004.10.001.

Niederman, Fred, James C. Brancheau, and James C. Wetherbe. 1991. "Information Systems Management Issues for the 1990s." *MIS Quarterly* no. 15 (4):475–500. doi: 10.2307/249452.

Nolan, Richard L., David C. Croson, and Katherine N. Seger. 1993. "The stages theory: A framework for IT adoption and organizational learning." In *Harvard Business School Note*. Boston: HBS Publishing.

PDPOMO. (2015). 2014 Report on Government Microblogs. http://yuqing.people.com.cn/GB/392071/392730/index.html

Piotrowski, Suzanne J., Yahong Zhang, Weiwei Lin, and Wenxuan Yu. 2009. "Key Issues for Implementation of Chinese Open Government Information Regulations." *Public Administration Review* no. 69:S129–S135. doi: 10.1111/j.1540-6210.2009.02100.x.

Rana, Renu. 2015. "China's Information Disclosure Initiative: Assessing the Reforms." *China Report* no. 51 (2):129–143. doi: 10.1177/0009445515570443.

Rogers, E.M. 1995. *Diffusion of Innovations*. New York: The Free Press.

Rose, Wade R., and Gerald G. Grant. 2010. "Critical Issues Pertaining to the Planning and Implementation of E-Government Initiatives." *Government Information Quarterly* no. 27 (1):26–33. doi: http://dx.doi.org/10.1016/j.giq.2009.06.002.

Sharon, L. Caudle, Wilpen L. Gorr, and Kathryn E. Newcomer. 1991. "Key Information Systems Management Issues for the Public Sector." *MIS Quarterly* no. 15 (2):171–188. doi: 10.2307/249378.

Tornatzky, L.G., M. Fleischer, and A.K. Chakrabarti. 1990. *The Processes of Technological Innovation*. Lexington, MA: Lexington Books.

United Nations. 2004. Global E-Government Readiness Report: Towards Access for Opportunity. New York.

United Nations. 2014. United Nations E-Government Survey 2014: E-Government for the Future We Want. New York.

Wareham, Jonathan D, Xavier Busquets, and Robert D Austin. 2009. "Creative, Convergent, and Social: Prospects for Mobile Computing." *Journal of Information Technology* no. 24 (2):139–143.

Yu, Ran. 2011. "Justice Takes Steps onto Blogs." *China Daily*, 04/07/2011.

Zhang, Nan, and Xunhua Guo. 2014. *Electronic Government Adoption in China: Multiple Research Perspectives in the Post-Informationization Age*. Beijing: Tsinghua University Press.

Zhang, Nan, Q. Meng, X. Guo, C. Yin, H. Luo. 2015. "Key E-Government Issues in China: An Empirical Study Based on the Orientation-Maturity Framework." *Electronic Commerce Research* no. 15 (3): 407–425.

Zhang, Nan, Zhongwen Zhang, and Qingguo Meng. 2011. Government Information Open in Microblog—Reality or Utopia? A Case Study on Local Government Practices in China. Paper read at the Third International Conference on Public Policy and Management at Beijing.

Zheng, Yongnian. 2008. *Technological Empowerment: The Internet, State, and Society in China*. Stanford, CA: Stanford University Press.

23

CRITICAL FACTORS BEHIND KOREAN E-GOVERNMENT SUCCESS

A Conversation with the Chairman of Korea's Presidential Special Committee of E-Government

Michael J. Ahn

Introduction

For many researchers, South Korea has been an important case worthy of close examination from academics and practitioners alike, as the country has been regarded as one of the leaders in the field of e-government. Korea has firmly maintained top ranking at many highly recognized e-government evaluation studies,[1] and since the development and launch of e-government in early 2000, Korea has provided some of the most advanced online government services and e-democracy-type applications that allow citizens to perform various online transactions with the government and view and participate in government affairs. Korean e-government has been a frequent subject of e-government research, and it has been taught at public administration programs in Korea, for domestic as well as international students and government officials, as the model has been heavily benchmarked and exported to countries developing their own e-government systems. From a development point of view, Korean e-government is interesting in that it was developed in a top-down fashion as a top policy agenda for Korea's eighth President Kim Dae-jung and had a relatively short development period of two years. In other words, it had a clear beginning, and there were distinctive development steps that created what is Korean e-government today.

This chapter examines this process of e-government development from an interview with the chairman (Prof. Ahn Moon-Suk) of the Presidential Special Committee of E-Government, who developed Korea's first national e-government system. In light of its remarkable success, this chapter will explore questions such as: How did the Korean e-government project start and why? What was the strategy behind its development process? What contributed to its enormous success? What were the challenges during the development process and how did the committee overcome them? This chapter will explore these questions as recognized by the committee's chairman and conclude with his vision of e-government's future with the emergence of new technologies, which continue to expand the technological boundary of e-government.

Background

As a scholarly field, e-government has become a relatively well-researched topic that has gained much attention from the scholars of public administration, as the role of information technology in public administration has greatly expanded over time. Much research has been devoted to the subject of e-government, and many researchers focus on identifying key factors that lead to the adoption of e-government applications and successful e-government outcomes (Ahn 2011; Ahn and Bretschneider 2011; Dawes 2008; Fountain 2004; Lee, Kim and Ahn 2011; Moon 2002; Norris and Moon 2005; Schwester 2009; West 2005). This stream of research effectively uses various quantitative data drawn from government documents or professional associations (such as the International City/County Management Association—ICMA) or research institutions that evaluate e-government quality. The basic premise in many of these studies is that e-government is an outcome of organizational capacities of the government (Ahn and Bretschneider 2011; Chen and Thurmaier 2008; Ho and Ni 2004; Moon 2002; Norris 1999; Norris and Moon 2005; Reddick 2005; Tolbert, Mossberger and McNeal 2008), characteristics of the users (Bélanger, France, and Carter 2008; Jun and Weare 2011; Weare, Musso and Hale 1999), and the various environmental characteristics under which e-government operates (Rufin et al. 2014). In many cases, e-government research is approached with statistical analysis measuring several aspects of e-government quality and adoption as dependent variables and the attributes of the government organizations (measuring various organizational capacities) and the surrounding environment (including the characteristics of the citizens and political and economic attributes) as explanatory variables. This approach has resulted in useful insights in identifying factors that correlate with high-quality e-government. The common findings from this stream of research show that financial capacity, technical expertise, and leadership support of the adopting government and high demand for online services from the citizens are correlated with high-quality e-government.

While these findings are helpful in identifying the necessary conditions for successful e-government, it is difficult to understand how these factors are coordinated or integrated together to effect successful e-government. That is, we know which factors are necessary for high-quality e-government, but we know little about the process through which such outcomes are produced. Does having all the necessary factors spontaneously translate into high-quality e-government, or does it require skillful and strategic maneuvering and facilitation in order to maximize its potential? This chapter examines this development aspect of e-government from an interview with the chairman of the Presidential Special Committee of E-Government (termed "the e-government committee" hereafter), who built what is now Korea's e-government. The interview explored how the first Korean e-government came into existence; how the e-government committee developed the initial government projects; how challenges were overcome; and what factors helped the committee's successful completion; and the chapter ends with speculation on the future direction for e-government.

The Chairman of the E-Government Committee

Dr. Ahn Moon-Suk was the chairman of the e-government committee in 2001, and he is regarded as the founding father of the Korean e-government by most government officials and scholars in Korea. As a professor of public administration, he has been involved in numerous government works, such as acting as the co-chairman (with the prime minister of South Korea) of the Government Regulatory Reform Committee which revised, eliminated, or streamlined all government regulations that have turned into varying forms of government red tape. He also worked as the chairman of the Convergence Committee of Broadcasting and Telecommunication for the prime minister. He helped the mayor of the Seoul Special City as an advisor in designing Seoul City Government's OPEN System—an online anti-corruption e-government application developed by the city government to combat corruption—which was recognized by the UN as a case example of using technology to reduce corruption. Academically, Professor Ahn has served as the professor of public administration at Korea University for 29 years, four years of which he had worked as the provost and executive vice president. In professional associations, he served as the president of the Korean Association for Policy Studies. Currently, he is professor emeritus at Korea University and continues to give advice in government committees and forums. He is currently serving as the chairman of the e-government for the Park Geun-hae administration.

The interview took place over the phone and via electronic means, such as email, in late 2015. An online messenger was also used to clarify some content previously discussed in the interview. In the following section, the conversation with Dr. Ahn is organized by the questions explored, and the findings from the interviews are organized as answers to these interview questions. These are, however, not the direct transcription of the conversation but a streamlined summary of his responses in a first-person narrative.

Questions Explored

Can you give a brief history of Korea and its experience with information and communication technologies prior to its development of e-government?

In the 1950s, 60s, and well into the 70s, Korea was one of the poorest nations in the world. There was nothing left in Korea after the long exhaustive Japanese occupation and ensuing Korean War that left the country devastated. However, Korea managed to leap to becoming the world's tenth largest economy and became a member of OECD countries in just 50 years. What is interesting in this short but remarkable history of national development is that Korea has a relatively long history with computers and information technology. The country began experimenting with computers starting in the late 60s despite its poor economic standing, and it was just starting its "5-Year Economic Development Plan" to move the country out of poverty.

Korea Institute of Science and Technology (KIST) was founded in 1966 by President Park Chung-hee, and it invited foreign-educated Korean scholars to work in the institute in the fields of science and technology. Many prominent scientists joined KIST at the time: I joined the KIST computer center as a research team leader in 1968. At that time, there was a shared vision and dedication among the prominent scholars and elite government officials to work together to move Korea out of its poverty and into prosperity. We had all agreed that an era of Information Society will come sooner or later to Korea and other nations in the world and we had an ambition of preparing the country to be a leader in the coming age. There was a slogan we shared that read "We [Korea] were late in industrialization of the 19th century, let us be the forerunner in the coming Information Society!" The group at KIST worked very hard to accomplish this vision. KIST installed the CDC 3300 computer in the early 1970s, which was one of the largest computers in the Asian continent at that time. The KIST computer team introduced high-level languages like FORTRAN and COBOL to Korean people who began to use computers in their work. It marked the introduction of the computer to the Korean society.

President Kim Dae-jung established the e-government committee, and e-government was launched in year 2002. Do you know how the idea of building a national e-government came to him?

I heard it was Bill Gates. I heard this from President Kim Dae-jung at the e-government launching ceremony in 2001 at the Blue House (Korea's presidential residence). President Kim said, "Bill Gates visited Korea in 2000. I met him. And there he said, 'since Korea successfully built the Information Super Highway, it would be useful for the Korean government to build an e-government.'" Actually in 2000, prior to the e-government special committee of 2001, the Minister of Government Administration and Home Affairs reported an "e-government plan" to President Kim Dae-jung at a ministry's yearly briefing ceremony. I attended the briefing and explained about the potential of an e-government at the request of President Kim at that time. After the briefing, President Kim endorsed the e-government plan and instructed the minister to develop the plan. I had an impression that President Kim Dae-jung had already good knowledge of e-government.

However, Bill Gates wasn't the only inciting factor. At the end of 1997, Korea fell into a severe financial crisis (the Asian Financial Crisis) that started with the collapse of Thai Baht, suffering devalued stock markets and asset prices that led to a precarious rise in private debt and bankruptcies. President Kim Dae-jung had to find a way to revitalize the economy. He selected the Information Super Highway project (which began in the previous Kim Young-sam administration) as one of his major policy instruments to stimulate the economy, which helped many domestic IT firms survive through the crisis. Kim Dae-jung's government pushed the Information Super Highway project to be completed earlier than planned. During this period, President Kim Dae-jung forced establishing a special fund from mandatory reduction in government official's salaries. And the government used it to hire young, unemployed individuals who then worked on digitizing public sector documents to build various government databases. President Kim wanted to stimulate the economy and help domestic information industry to survive through this difficult time while providing employment opportunities for young job seekers. Early completion of the Information Super Highway and building of the various government databases are believed to have increased the chances of starting the Korean e-government project, together with Bill Gates's advice.

Can you tell me a little more about this Information Super Highway project? So this is something that was built before the e-government project got started?

Yes. But prior to this, in 1980, the Korean government started the Five National Computer Network Initiative that connected all computing powers in the public sector into one of the five national computer networks. These networks are: (1) Government Security Network, (2) National Security Network, (3) National Defense Network, (4) National Education and Research Network, and (5) Banking and Finance Network. This project required joint development of common software, sharing of computing powers located at different agencies, and building of government databases and operation of the five national computer networks. To accelerate the project development, special laws were passed to enable the policy of "invest first, pay later through government budget." And the National Computerization Agency (NCA) was founded during this period for technical support and the evaluation of these projects. In order to reduce the barriers among different agencies and ministries, a coordinating committee for national computer networks was built under the president's office and was directed by the president's top secretary directly.

Before the 90s, computer networks were connected only within the same government entity and were not open to outside users. However, the emergence of the Internet in the early 90s changed this, opening a new potential of interactivity between citizens and the government. After establishing the Five National Networks, Korea focused its effort on constructing the Information Super Highway as its next national priority. The construction of the information highway required huge expenses, and government alone could not bear the cost. So the government provided incentives for private companies to take part in the long-term national plan to build the information highway.

The Information Super Highway project was completed during President Kim Dae-jung's administration earlier than planned. By this time, the Internet was widely used by the general public in

Korea. The direct and open nature of the Internet and its increasing use by citizens began to put pressure on government to use the Internet to provide services and government information. President Kim was someone who was keenly aware of the importance of information technology and, with the completion of the Information Super Highway project, he immediately put e-government as his top policy priority and established the e-government committee.

Can you tell me more about the e-government committee?

When the Presidential Special E-government Committee was established in 2001, no one earnestly believed the committee would succeed. I had no office to work in. The committee's first meeting was held in a hotel. No official fund was allocated and I had to start from nothing at first. In order to secure strong support from the government, I personally promised the president, through his top secretary, that my committee would build the e-government within two years and that the projects would become the most valued asset to his administration. From then on, the president and the government supported my committee fully and this helped me keep my promise. When I was appointed as the chairman of the e-government committee by President Kim, I was a professor of public administration at Korea University. Nine vice ministers were appointed as committee members from the government side[2] and from the private sector, six nongovernmental committee members.[3] The working-level committee was co-chaired by President Kim Dae-jung's planning secretary and the president of NCA. The president of NCA helped the committee with technical issues and the presidential planning secretary worked to facilitate cooperation from government agencies in building the e-government. I operated the committee as a matrix organization where a committee member was assigned to a specific function and target project. And they monitored the progress of the projects and reported problems back to the committee. Any problems and obstacles were discussed and addressed at the committee meetings. During the development process, President Kim received a weekly progress report through the presidential planning secretary and the regular committee meetings were held at the Blue House. President Kim often stressed the importance of building e-government during the cabinet meetings, and this endorsement from the top gave a considerable amount of power to the committee. Without the president's strong support, the Korean e-government projects would not have succeeded.

In the beginning phase of the project, I was worried about possible power drain coming from the short time left in President Kim's term. We only had a total of two years to complete the project, so I declared that we should finish the initial e-government projects in 18 months. Once the election cycle began, no one in the government would pay attention to the e-government projects, so I had to complete the tasks months earlier. I thought if we could not finish them within 18 months, the e-government projects might fail. As a result, I limited the scope of the e-government committee to the 11 key projects.

My committee had three visions and objectives in the initial e-government projects. First, e-government should provide top-quality administrative services to citizens; second, e-government should help create the most supportive environment for business; and third, e-government should advance transparency and democracy in government administration. Based on these visions, the committee gathered proposals from government ministries and more than 20 projects were proposed to the committee. Eleven projects were selected that are thought to have great future potential. The initial 11 projects were as follows:

1. Government for Citizens project for the Ministry of Interior
2. Social Insurance Information Sharing System for the Ministry of Health and Welfare
3. Integrated Electronic Procurement System for the Procurement Office

4. Home Tax Service through the Internet for the National Tax Office
5. National Financial Information System for the Ministry of Finance and Economy
6. Local Government Information Network System for Local Government
7. National Education Information System for the Ministry of Education
8. Personnel Administration Support System for the Civil Service Commission
9. E-approval System
10. Government PKI System
11. Government-wide Integrated Computer Center

The committee did complete these 11 projects in the 18-month period by October 2002; there was a large ceremony at the Blue House where the committee members were decorated by the president. At the ceremony, President Kim Dae-Jung highly praised the successful outcome of the e-government project. He said, "I (as democracy advocator and politician) have few good days in my life. Today is apparently one of the few good days." He was very satisfied with the result of the e-government project. The initial 11 projects were expanded into 32 projects in the following Roh Moo-hyun administration, and the basic foundation of the Korean e-government was completed with the successful installation of the first e-government project.

What were the most significant challenges that the committee faced during the development period?

There were many challenges, but two stick out as most significant. First, I realized that the building of the e-government project required significant revisions in the existing laws and regulations. I found that nearly 250 individual laws had to be revised in order for the 11 e-government projects to operate properly. Instead of revising individual 250 laws, the committee drafted the Basic Law of E-Government and passed it in the national assembly, which overrode the individual laws that got in the way of e-government operations. The Basic Law of E-Government laid out the principles of realizing e-government projects and obliges government organizations to collaborate on the process of the e-government project. For instance, the basic law obliges government entities to share data and communication networks and collaborate on government process reengineering necessary for e-government applications to function. It laid out the principles of an open data policy by subjecting government entities to publish government information and data that may advance citizens' well-being (with exception of data labeled as confidential). It instructed the government not to require citizens to submit paper documents when they can be searched and verified online by the government, and allowed government officials to access government systems remotely (however, it asks to implement the necessary security measures to ensure data security). The law also allowed electronic notifications of public notices when requested by citizens, and recommended using private sector vendors for e-government system development and management, unless in-house development is deemed superior in terms of effectiveness, efficiency, and security. At the same time, the basic law forbid using citizen's personal information against their will and allowed government entities to choose not to share data relating to national security. The basic law helped the committee enormously, as we did not have to revise all relevant individual laws that got in the way of the e-government project. The basic law grew in size and scope to become what is now e-government law in Korea.[4]

The second challenge was the difficulty in sharing data and facilitating cooperation from relevant government ministries. I had to "summon" bureau directors to the committee's breakfast meetings (which we held every week to check on the progress) to persuade them to cooperate with the committee's project effort. We had 56 breakfast meetings during the 18-month period. The presidential planning secretary played an important role in securing cooperation from the ministries.

Do you think the best practice model of e-government could be copied by other developing countries to build their e-government? What do you consider to be factors that matter in creating successful and sustainable e-government?

E-government is not a simple transfer of government functions to the cyberspace. E-government is more than a mirror reflection of the brick and mortar government. In my experience as an advisor for the Korean government, I saw how e-government is closely linked to government reform. Without proper reform, an effective and fully functioning e-government is difficult. To enable this, the e-government committee needed to have substantial administrative authority, and this is reflected in the administrative position of the special committee as a subcommittee of the Government Reform Committee. As the title shows, it was the "Presidential Special Committee" that carried some weight in facilitating collaboration from various government ministries. So, I view e-government as an effective instrument of government reform rather than a simple provision of government services online.

On your second question about the best practice, I don't think there is one best practice of e-government that can be applied to all other nations. Each country comes with unique environments and conditions. And there may be varying kinds of "good e-government" reflecting these characteristics. However, you may say there are certain conditions that matter in e-government development such as the technological, economic, political, and cultural attributes of a nation.

First, as an essential condition, there should be sufficient penetration of computers and the Internet, as it provides the fundamental medium of e-government operations. Second, the government should have the necessary financial capacity to bear the large costs in building and maintaining e-government. In addition, there should be an economic cost–benefit projection of e-government, where the ratio between the costs and benefit should be above 1 to justify the large investment. However, the benefit does not only include savings of budget from e-government systems, such as fees and revenues generated through e-government service, but it should also include the opportunity costs saved for citizens as they receive government services online instead of having to visit government offices. From this standpoint, developed nations would have greater incentives for investing in e-government as their citizens have higher opportunity costs for visiting government offices.

Next, in order for a nation to evolve to a more advanced stage of e-government like C4G in a true sense (Citizen for Government or more commonly known as Collaborative Governance), the nation should be politically democratic and have a strong civil society. This is not a necessary condition for e-government, as non-democratic government can develop highly performing e-government, but to fully achieve the next step in e-government, this democratic condition would play an important role. E-government in democratic nations tends to increase government transparency and facilitate citizen participation in government affairs.

Lastly, the nation should be culturally or religiously open to the use of the Internet. If a country's culture is not compatible with the Internet e-government, it is unlikely to flourish. These are general conditions that can be labeled as the necessary conditions of e-government: However, they don't necessarily ensure the development of successful e-government—that is, they are not the sufficient conditions of successful e-government.

If you could identify specific factors that contributed to Korea's e-government success, what would they be? That is, if the general conditions you just mentioned were necessary conditions, what were the factors in Korea that drove these conditions into a successful e-government outcome?

From my experience, I would say that it was the strong support of President Kim as well as previous presidents and their interests in information technology; the availability of the technologies in the country that enabled e-government; the champions (in this case the e-government committee) who would aggressively and strategically push to build and maintain high-quality e-government; the citizens' acceptance of e-government and technology in general; the presence of active civil society and NGOs in Korea; the establishment of KIST which provided technological assistance to government; the establishment of the Ministry of Information and Communication that functions as a control tower of IT projects in Korea; the Asian economic crisis and its pressure on government to reform; and the existence of elite government officials with a futuristic vision for Korea and their commitment to accomplish it. I would also add that the scientific nature of Korean language, Hangul, and Korea's excellent national ID system helped facilitate building strong e-government.

If I have to further reduce the list and just pick four factors, I would say that they are the existence of committed government officials and scholars with a vision of e-government, the strong support from the president, the availability of the information technology in Korea, and the robust and active civil society. However, it is important that there should be an effective champion (such as our e-government committee) who can strategically coordinate and integrate these elements into a successful e-government outcome.

How did you facilitate citizens' acceptance of e-government?

To increase citizens' acceptance of e-government, I let relevant ministers of e-government projects appear on national TV, on radio, and in newspapers to talk about e-government to explain what it is (as the concept was new when it was launched to many) and what it does to their policy clients. I also actively connected with foreign academic and professional associations, such as the American Society for Public Administration, to introduce the Korean e-government project. It was fortunate that the UN adopted the OPEN system of the Seoul Metropolitan Government as a case model to reduce corruption through technology, which positively affected the image of Korean e-government.

After its initial launch at the end of President Kim Dae-Jung's term, the 11 e-government projects were expanded into 32 projects during President Roh Moo-hyun's administration, as President Roh was also enthusiastic about e-government and its potentials. President Roh is known to have designed and patented an electronic reporting system himself. The Korean e-government won first place in UN e-government evaluation three consecutive times in six years. I was very proud of it.

Do you have any future vision for the next generation of Korean e-government in light of the recent rise of new information technologies, such as the Internet of Things, big data, cloud computing, and the smartphone?

Information technology continues to advance and new technologies create new demands and expectations from citizens. Such new citizen demands and expectations keep pushing the frontiers of e-government as they are reflected in the next generation of e-government. It is my belief that every e-government should be remodeled to accommodate the new technologies and the corresponding (new) demands from citizens. Emerging technologies such as smartphones, apps, social network services, big data, and cloud computing have all begun to reshape e-government. The next generation of e-government is characterized by the multiplicity in its names, as well as its distinctively different approach in creating and providing services to citizens. It comes in the names such as d-government (data government), p-government (platform government), C4G government (Citizens for Government), and s-government (smart government). The availability of a large amount of real-time data will have significant impact in shaping the future of e-government.

For me, the future vision of e-government is a collaborative government that freely works across government boundaries. E-government will be designed to allow effective collaboration between citizens (including businesses and NGOs) and the government in solving and providing smart solutions. This will enable the government to provide individually customized services to citizens to meet their particular and special needs. This will be a significant break from the traditional bureaucratic model of government (as it is reflected in traditional e-government) which provides standardized public services to address the majority of the citizens' needs, while the rest of the population must fit into the standardized services, at times, with heavy transaction cost. So, the next generation of e-government should enable the government to provide customized solutions to individual citizens in a timely manner. Furthermore, it should not only be more responsive, timely, and effective in response to emerging public problems and needs, but also be able to monitor and predict any possible national disasters that loom over the horizon. Smart early warning systems should be incorporated into the next generation of e-government so that it can predict and address large-scale disasters (economic, social, and natural in nature) effectively. Prevention is the best way to remedy disasters, and with increasingly available data and the rise of big data analysis, "predictive government" will be possible at some point in the future.

Conclusion

This chapter aimed to take a glimpse into the black box of e-government development to understand the process of developing a successful e-government with an interview with the chairman of South Korea's Presidential Special Committee of E-Government, which built the country's first national e-government system. We found that the general factors of e-government, such as technological, economic, political, and cultural conditions, do matter as necessary conditions of building and maintaining highly effective e-government. However, we also learned the importance of an effective champion of e-government with full support from the top leadership, who can skillfully guide and persuade involved government entities to collaborate on e-government projects and effect the legal and regulatory changes necessary for full e-government operation.

Korea has experimented with information technology from the 1960s on as national strategic initiatives by a number of farsighted past presidents, and dedicated scholars and top government officials pursued a vision of Korea as a leader in the information age that provided for a fertile ground for successful adoption and development of information technology in the country. Such an early introduction familiarized the country—its citizens, government, and private sector entities—with information technology, facilitating the country's wide acceptance to technology, which eventually contributed to the country's successes in the IT field—in the private as well as the public sectors. This fertile ground was then sown skillfully by a champion of e-government who had a well-defined and futuristic vision of e-government as a new paradigm of government operation and governance. His vision could take root in Korean e-government and bore much fruit as the top leadership, such as President Kim Dae-jung and his successor President Roh Moo-hyun, shared the same vision and fully supported and maintained the effort.

This chapter revealed that while what is known in e-government literature about the important factors of successful e-government are true, if we go back further in the history of Korean e-government, it was the vision of national leaders and their strategic investment in information technology and the vision and dedicated effort of scholars and elite government administrators to develop the country to be a leader in information technology that eventually enriched the conditions of successful e-government. This fertile ground of information technology then must be sown by an effective champion with full support from the top leadership in the country to result in highly effective and advanced e-government.

Korea's e-government wasn't built in a day, as the country has had decades-long experimentation and trials and errors with information technology before developing its first national e-government system. As Prof. Ahn mentioned, e-government is a process rather than an outcome, one that continues to evolve with changing technology. Pushing the boundary of e-government toward more effective and smart government and more effective collaboration with citizens requires constant attention and reinvention of the existing system. If the vision of Korea in the information society that started in the 60s eventually led to what is Korean e-government today, another vision will be necessary now to pave the way for the next generation of e-government.

Notes

1. These include e-government evaluation studies from United Nation's E-Government Surveys, Brown University's Taubman Center for Public Policy, Rutgers University's School of Public Affairs and Administration, and Brookings Institution's Governance Studies.
2. They were vice ministers from the departments of Finance and Economy, Education and Human Resources, Government Administration and Home Affairs, Information and Communication, Health and Welfare, Labor, and Planning and Budget; vice mayor for Administrative Affairs of the Seoul Metropolitan Government; and assistant minister for Public Policy Coordination of the Presidential Secretariat.
3. These are the president of National Computerization Agency (NCA), senior researcher of Korea Information Society Development Institute, and three university professors.
4. The details of the law can be found at http://www.law.go.kr/[INSERT SYMBOL HERE] or http://goo.gl/eIOCjz (short URL)

References

Ahn, Michael J. "Adoption of e-communication applications in US municipalities: The role of political environment, bureaucratic structure, and the nature of applications." *The American Review of Public Administration* (2011): 428–452. doi:10.1177/0275074010377654.

Ahn, Michael J., and Stuart Bretschneider. "Politics of e-government: E-government and the political control of bureaucracy." *Public Administration Review* 71, no. 3 (2011): 414–424.

Bélanger, France, and Lemuria Carter. "Trust and risk in e-government adoption." *The Journal of Strategic Information Systems* 17, no. 2 (2008): 165–176.

Chen, Yu-Che, and Kurt Thurmaier. "Advancing e-government: Financing challenges and opportunities." *Public Administration Review* 68, no. 3 (2008): 537–548.

Dawes, Sharon S. "The evolution and continuing challenges of e-governance." *Public Administration Review* 68, no. s1 (2008): S86–S102.

Fountain, Jane E. *Building the virtual state: Information technology and institutional change*. Washington, DC: Brookings Institution Press, 2004.

Ho, Alfred Tat-Kei, and Anna Ya Ni. "Explaining the adoption of e-government features a case study of Iowa county treasurers' offices." *The American Review of Public Administration* 34, no. 2 (2004): 164–180.

Jun, Kyu-Nahm, and Christopher Weare. "Institutional motivations in the adoption of innovations: The case of e-government." *Journal of Public Administration Research and Theory* 21, no. 3 (2011): 495–519.

Lee, Jooho, Hyun Joon Kim, and Michael J. Ahn. "The willingness of e-government service adoption by business users: The role of offline service quality and trust in technology." *Government Information Quarterly* 28, no. 2 (2011): 222–230.

Moon, M. Jae. "The evolution of e-government among municipalities: Rhetoric or reality?" *Public Administration Review* 62, no. 4 (2002): 424–433.

Norris, Donald F. "Leading edge information technologies and their adoption: Lessons from US cities." *Information Technology and Computer Applications in Public Administration: Issues and Trends* (1999): 137–156. In *Information Technology and Computer Applications in Public Administration: Issues and Trends* edited by David Garson, 137–156. IGI Global, 1999. DOI: 10.4018/978-1-87828-952-0.ch008

Norris, Donald F., and M. Jae Moon. "Advancing e-government at the grassroots: Tortoise or hare?" *Public Administration Review* 65, no. 1 (2005): 64–75.

Reddick, Christopher G. "Empirical models of e-government growth in local governments." *E-Service Journal* 3, no. 2 (2005): 59–84.

Rufín, Ramón, France Bélanger, Cayetano Medina Molina, Lemuria Carter, and Juan Carlos Sánchez Figueroa. "A cross-cultural comparison of electronic government adoption in Spain and the USA." *International Journal of Electronic Government Research (IJEGR)* 10, no. 2 (2014): 43–59.

Schwester, Richard. "Examining the barriers to e-government adoption." *Electronic Journal of E-Government* 7, no. 1 (2009): 113–122.

Tolbert, Caroline J., Karen Mossberger, and Ramona McNeal. "Institutions, policy innovation, and e-government in the American states." *Public Administration Review* 68, no. 3 (2008): 549–563.

Weare, Christopher, Juliet A. Musso, and Matthew L. Hale. "Electronic democracy and the diffusion of municipal web pages in California." *Administration & Society* 31, no. 1 (1999): 3–27.

West, Darrell M. *Digital government: Technology and public sector performance*. Princeton, NJ: Princeton University Press, 2005.

24
CONCLUSION
The Future of Information Technology in Government

Michael J. Ahn and Yu-Che Chen

This concluding chapter assesses the contributions of the chapters to the five main themes of this Handbook, namely, (i) theories of IT innovations in government, (ii) emerging technologies and their applications in government, (iii) technology-driven collaboration between citizens and government, (iv) advancement of democratic accountability and public values through technology, and (v) advancement of public service through technological innovations. Following this assessment, the chapter provides concluding thoughts and recommendations on the opportunities and future of information technology innovations in government.

First, on the theories of IT innovation in government, our chapters featured various theories and methods that provide useful insights in improving our understanding of information technology in government. Data-driven decision-making will likely spur the rise of big data in government, and the development of theory and methods will be necessary to improve our understanding of the new approach in data analysis. Explicit modeling of the changing role of ICTs in service production and delivery is an important focus and requires careful integration of theories from various bodies of literature. The analytical frameworks and tools featured in this book will help manage increasing complexity and implementation challenges of major ICT initiatives. Future endeavors would benefit from studying the role of increasingly abundant and available data and information from the public as well as private sectors as effective and strategic resources for government policy and decision-making.

As discussed in some chapters of the Handbook, emerging technologies present new opportunities as well as challenges. For instance, the growth of big data creates significant challenges associated with privacy and security, as well as responding to FOIA requests; the location and personal behavioral information of individual citizens can undermine privacy, and the emergence of new technologies leads to a new type of digital divide among people with varying degrees of access. From the management perspective, the emerging big data analytics create new challenges in combining traditional data sources with emerging data sources (such as social media, sensor feeds, and location and behavioral data) to assist public policy and service decision-making. Obtaining, analyzing, and making sense of an enormous amount of data coming from a variety of new and old sources in order to make informed and effective policy decisions is likely to be the most significant opportunity, as well as challenge, for public administrators of the 21st century.

The chapters in the section on technology-driven collaboration between citizens and the government highlight the importance of understanding the collaborators (citizens, businesses, and NGOs) in the emerging practice of coproduction of government services and information. The opportunities for trust building lie in the government's ability to deploy various platforms of communication (such as social media) to foster not only effective information dissemination, but also meaningful discourse with citizens. This section highlights the tremendous opportunities for collaboration between citizens and the government that signal a new approach to addressing public problems: they could be data collection and sharing for local government services, development of new websites and apps, or provision of data analytics to help identify public challenges and illuminate effective solutions.

The section on advancing democratic accountability and public values examines various ways in which ICTs can help foster and protect public values. Topics such as government transparency, citizen participation, government openness, and privacy are explored to show how emerging technologies can be harnessed to advance and ensure government accountability. The importance of resource investment, management strategies, and institutional and political attributes in government are highlighted as key determinants behind democratic accountability. Some chapters underscore how the increasing customization and tailoring of government services enabled by the new technologies can facilitate more effective interactions between citizens and government; such customization produces valuable information that can, in turn, be incorporated in government services. Future studies should continue to explore this aspect of citizen–government interaction and investigate key challenges to online citizen participation, open data, and online privacy.

The section on advancing public service through technological innovations raises the importance of understanding supportive political and institutional environments. The chapters on the use of social media in emergency management and smart city illustrate the need for effective organizational and institutional design. The cases of China and South Korea in developing their e-government systems underscore both the importance of political support as well as the synergistic relationship between e-government and administrative reform. In addition, the Chinese and South Korean experiences demonstrate the importance of leadership in realizing the potential of information technology in advancing public service.

Sphere of Possibilities: Technology, Government, and Public Service Transformation

As many of our chapters show, against the backdrop of ever-expanding possibilities enabled by emerging new technologies, the government continues to hold the key position in determining how much change it will allow in government administration. That is, the new technologies present new possibilities for government, expanding its "sphere of possibilities," increasing the range of what the government can do and doing it more effectively and efficiently. However, it is the government that eventually determines how many of the new possibilities it will take advantage of. For instance, as we have witnessed, the emergence of the World Wide Web presented enormous new potential in government, which prompted some scholars to predict this would cause a significant transformation in the way government operates. Years later, however, the eventual outcome depended largely on the part of the adopter of the new technology, the government, resulting in a wide variation in the quality of e-government around the world: some e-government leaders expanded the government's capability into the new sphere of possibilities with dramatic improvement in the quality of public service, while others merely stayed at the periphery of the new possibility.

What makes the present moment remarkable is the kind of unprecedented possibilities offered by new technologies. The growth in technology has exploded in recent years, expanding the sphere of possibilities for government such that, if fully enabled, it could signal a new chapter not only in the e-government field, but also in public administration and management in general. Big data, smartphones and connected devices, open government, social media, smart government, technology-enabled government call centers, the Internet of Things, and artificial intelligence offer extraordinary opportunities for government—a giant leap forward from what "traditional e-government" could offer previously. These new technologies provide a new vision of the future of e-government in a multiplicity of terms like (as suggested in chapter 23) d-government, p-government, predictive governance, C4G, and fully customizable government. These do not merely present a vision of the distant future, as some of these visions have already materialized or are at early stages of experimentation as many of our chapters illustrate. However, the authors of these chapters also emphasize that in order to materialize these new possibilities, the government must be willing to and capable of undergoing a significant process of reengineering and reform. As elaborated in some chapters, such willingness and capability are then influenced by a complex web of factors inside and outside the government that determine the extent to which the new technologies will eventually impact government administration.

This is an exciting time for public administration scholars and practitioners in the field of e-government, as the explosion in technological advancement has presented unparalleled opportunities in public administration. The interaction between the technology push and the corresponding government reaction to this push will likely continue in this new exciting chapter of e-government. Some governments will emerge as leaders while others will lag behind, just as we have seen with traditional e-government. However, the gap between the leading e-governments and those that fall behind is expected to be far greater than it was in the traditional e-government setting, taking into account the much greater possibilities offered by new technologies. The concept of digital divide may become applicable not only to individuals, but also to government organizations, as the differences between government organizations that actively and strategically employ new technologies and those that do not will be clearly visible in the way they operate: the way they identify critical problems, the way they design and develop policy solutions, the way they implement these solutions, and the way they refine the solutions over time. As this Handbook has illustrated, the role of technology is no longer a useful option for a government to complement and aid its operation, but an inevitable necessity in order for that government to function effectively in our complex and rapidly changing environment. The old and new ways of running government will become apparent with increasing adoption of new technologies. At this important juncture, where new technology-enabled public administration is beginning to emerge from traditional public administration, it is our hope that this Handbook has provided a useful overview of key emerging technological trends in the field, their potential impact in government administration, and critical factors that facilitate successful adoption and integration of new technologies in government.

INDEX

311: case study of Jacksonville, FL 180–95; as a citizen service information system 58–60; generation of performance data 99; for non-emergency service 115–16; open 115–16

Ahn, Moon-Suk xx, 381–2

big data: analysis of public opinions 139–40; case study of Kansas City, MO 99–103; defining characteristics 96, 138; impact on privacy 275; methodologies 138; use in local management 97
Bretschneider, Stuart 49, 61, 168, 353, 381

civic engagement: for collaborative community actions 96; definition 219; mobile platforms 116; online 219; research results 232–5
civic hacking: definition 202; future 209; history 197–202; works 203–6
cross-boundary collaboration: use of ICTs for public service 52–65
Code for America 116, 117, 197, 199, 201, 211
cyberinfrastructure: NSF programs 347–8; for scientific innovations 341

digital governance: features 3; issues 106

e-government: case of South Korea 380–90; development in China 365–9, 372–6; early stages 6; impact 15; key issues in China 369–71; maturity models 13
e-participation: analysis of 2009 Government Online data set 288–92; change in municipality between 2009 and 2011 223–8; conceptual model of adoption 285–8; interactivity in municipal government 220–1; research review 284–5

FOIA (Freedom of Information Act): legal implications 31–2, 40; for open government 240–1; statistics 242; right and procedures 270; response to requests 391
Fountain, Jane XIX, 13, 16, 135, 381

government service transformation: applications 14; concept overview 23; theory 12–14

Holzer, Marc 158, 182–3, 220

information policy: conceptual frameworks 33–8; history of U.S. 29–33; purpose-driven framework 38–42
institutional analysis and development (IAD) 342; types of rules 342–3
internet of things (IoT): Chinese cases for public service 129–34; connections to public values 127–9; definition 125–6

location-based services: applications for the public sector 113–18; challenges 118–19; enabling technologies 109–11; evolution 111–13

m-government: examples 20; impact and implications 20
microblog: adoption by local governments in China 375; number of Chinese government microblogs 375

NASA (The National Aeronautics and Space Administration): social media strategy 176–7
network governance: role of management 326–7; for scientific discovery 345–8; *see also* public management networks
Norris, Donald 220, 230, 254, 381

open data: impact on privacy 276; implementation strategies 247–9; principles and requirements 245–6; projects 246–7

Index

open government: Chinese information regulation 373; history in the U.S. 240–1; three dimensions of 242–3; *see also* FOIA; Open Data

personally identifiable information (PII): definition of personal information 267; governing policies 278–9; impact of big data on 275–6; impact of open data on 276–7; regulatory framework for protection of 268–72; *see also* privacy
Pew Internet and American Life Project 288
privacy: basic principles 41; mapping issues to e-government services 273
public management networks: management 344; roles of ICTs 352–3; *see also* public service networks

public service networks: integrative framework utilizing ICTs 52–65

smart city: definition 326; governance models 328; literature review on governance 331–4; smart urban governance in China 376
social media: barriers to use 170; communication modes 173–5; definition 168; drivers for use 171; in emergency management 306–8, 169
social networking site/service (SNS) 165, 284, 294–6
system dynamics: applications in policy domains 79; definition 72; modeling 73; simulation 82–5

transparency: and good governance 255–62; in the information age 253–5
trust: definition 154; impact of e-government on 155